GIRLHOOD IN AMERICA

An Encyclopedia

THE AMERICAN FAMILY

The six titles that make up **The American Family** offer a revitalizing new take on U.S. history, surveying current culture from the perspective of the family and incorporating insights from psychology, sociology, and medicine. Each two-volume, A-to-Z encyclopedia features its own advisory board, editorial slant, and apparatus, including illustrations, bibliography, and index.

Adolescence in America

EDITED BY Jacqueline V. Lerner, Boston College,
and Richard M. Lerner, Tufts University;
Jordan W. Finkelstein, Pennsylvania State University,
Advisory Editor

Boyhood in America

EDITED BY Priscilla Ferguson Clement, Pennsylvania State
University, Delaware County, and Jacqueline S. Reinier,
California State University, Sacramento

The Family in America

EDITED BY Joseph M. Hawes, University of Memphis,
and Elizabeth F. Shores, Little Rock, Arkansas

Girlhood in America

EDITED BY Miriam Forman-Brunell,
University of Missouri, Kansas City

Infancy in America

EDITED BY Alice Sterling Honig, Emerita, Syracuse University;
Hiram E. Fitzgerald, Michigan State University;
and Holly Brophy-Herb, Michigan State University

Parenthood in America

EDITED BY Lawrence Balter, New York University

GIRLHOOD IN AMERICA

An Encyclopedia

Volume 1
A–I

Miriam Forman-Brunell, EDITOR
Associate Professor of History
University of Missouri
Kansas City, Missouri

FOREWORD BY **Susan J. Douglas**
Professor of Communication Studies
University of Michigan — Ann Arbor
Ann Arbor, Michigan

A B C 🟰 C L I O

Santa Barbara, California
Denver, Colorado
Oxford, England

Library of Congress Cataloging-in-Publication Data
Girlhood in America : an encyclopedia / Miriam Forman-Brunell, editor;
foreword by Susan Douglas.
    p. cm. — (The American family)
Includes bibliographical references and index.
    ISBN 1-57607-206-1 (set : alk. paper) — 1-57607-550-8 (e-book)
    1. Girls—United States—Encyclopedias.   I. Forman-Brunell, Miriam.
II. American family (Santa Barbara, Calif.)
HQ777.G5745   2001
305.23'0973'03—dc21

                                                                2001001346

07 06 05 04 03 02 01   10 9 8 7 6 5 4 3 2 1 (cloth)

ABC-CLIO, Inc.
130 Cremona Drive, P.O. Box 1911
Santa Barbara, California 93116-1911

This book is also available on the World Wide Web as an e-book. Visit
www.abc-clio.com for details.

This book is printed on acid-free paper ∞
Manufactured in the United States of America

For my own
Zoë Gabriella Brunell

ADVISORY BOARD

CONTENTS

A-to-Z List of Entries

Contributors and Their Entries

Susan R. Applebaum
Independent Scholar
Overland Park, Kansas
  Daughters and Mothers

Cecilia J. Aragón
Arizona State University
Tempe, Arizona
  La Quinceañera

Lori Askeland
Wittenberg University
Springfield, Ohio
  Adoption
  Orphans and Orphanages

Joe Austin
Bowling Green State University
Bowling Green, Ohio
  Graffiti

Elizabeth R. Baer
Gustavus Adolphus College
St. Peter, Minnesota
  Fairy Tales

Dale Baker
Arizona State University
Tempe, Arizona
  Mathematics and Science

Amy L. Best
San Jose State University
San Jose, California
  Prom

Carla Bittel
Cornell University
Ithaca, New York
  Arts and Crafts

Kay J. Blalock
Saint Louis Community College–
  Meramec
Saint Louis, Missouri
  Catholic Girls

Stephan F. Brumberg
Brooklyn College
Brooklyn, New York
and The Graduate Center
The City University of New York
New York, New York
  Jewish Education of Girls

Susan K. Cahn
State University of New York–Buffalo
Buffalo, New York
  Sports

Cordelia Candelaria
Arizona State University
Tempe, Arizona
  Chicana Girls

Silvia Sara Canetto
Colorado State University
Fort Collins, Colorado
  Suicidal Behavior in Girls

Marsha Propst Carothers
University of Missouri–Kansas City
Kansas City, Missouri
  Handbags

Barbara J. Coleman
University of Colorado–Boulder
Boulder, Colorado
  Barbie
  Hair

Krista Comer
Rice University
Houston, Texas
  Surfer Girls

Delia Crutchfield Cook
University of Missouri–Kansas City
Kansas City, Missouri
  African American Girls in the
    Twentieth Century

Rebecca Daugherty
Independent Scholar
Atlanta, Georgia
  Punk Rock

Rachel Devlin
Tulane University
New York, New York
  Daughters and Fathers

Hasia R. Diner
New York University
New York, New York
  Immigration

Gary L. Ebersole
University of Missouri–Kansas City
Kansas City, Missouri
  Captivity

Mary Elliott
Sonoma State University
Rohnert Park, California
  Tomboys

Miriam Forman-Brunell
University of Missouri–Kansas City
Kansas City, Missouri
  Babysitting
  Diaries
  Dolls
  Domesticity
  Girls' Culture
  Girls' Rooms
  Indentured Servants
  Play
  Pocahontas
  Puritan Girls
  Slumber Parties
  Southern Belles
  Tea Parties
  Witchcraft
  Work

Ruth Formanek, Emeritus
Hofstra University
Hempstead, New York
  Sexual Harassment

Samantha Yates Francois
University of California–Davis
Davis, California
  Cosmetics

Susan K. Freeman
Ohio State University
Columbus, Ohio
  Female Sexuality

Donna Gaffney
Pace University Women's Justice Center
White Plains, New York
  Acquaintance Rape

Jane Greer
University of Missouri–Kansas City
Kansas City, Missouri
  Diaries
  Literacy
  Mill Girls

Katherine C. Grier
University of South Carolina
Columbia, South Carolina
  Pets

Anita Gurian
New York University School of
  Medicine
New York, New York
  Depression and Girls
  Gifted Girls
  Learning Disabilities, Reading
    Disorders, and Girls

Mary Ellen Hanson
University of New Mexico
Albuquerque, New Mexico
  Cheerleaders

Gina Hausknecht
Coe College
Cedar Rapids, Iowa
  American Girls Collection

Kathleen C. Hilton
The University of North Carolina–
  Pembroke
Pembroke, North Carolina
  4-H
  Rural Girls

Kristi Holsinger
University of Missouri–
  Kansas City
Kansas City, Missouri
  Girl Gangs
  Juvenile Delinquents

Lisa Jacobson
University of California–
  Santa Barbara
Santa Barbara, California
  Allowances and Spending Money
  Consumer Culture

Kathleen W. Jones
Virginia Polytechnic Institute and
  State University
Blacksburg, Virginia
  Child Guidance

Judith V. Jordan
Wellesley College
Wellesley, Massachusetts
  Relational Theory

Mary Celeste Kearney
University of Texas–Austin
Austin, Texas
  Television
  Zines

Cherie Kelly
Independent Scholar
Kansas City, Missouri
  Comic Books

Kathryn R. Kent
Williams College
Williamstown, Massachusetts
  Lesbians

Kristen Kidder
Bowling Green State University
Bowling Green, Ohio
  Teenybopper

Wilma King
University of Missouri–Columbia
Columbia, Missouri
  Enslaved Girls of African Descent
  Free Girls of African Descent

Kelly E. Kinnison
University of Missouri–Kansas City
Kansas City, Missouri
　Child Abuse

Melissa Klapper
Rutgers University
Highland Park, New Jersey
　Bat Mitzvah

Greta Grace Kroeker
University of California–Berkeley
Berkeley, California
　Mennonite Girls

Kate Clifford Larson
University of New Hampshire
Durham, New Hampshire
　Saturday Evening Girls

Nina E. Lerman
Whitman College
Walla Walla, Washington
　Technology

Alejandra Marchevsky
California State University–Los Angeles
Los Angeles, California
　Latina Girls

Randy D. McBee
Texas Tech University
Lubbock, Texas
　Dances and Dancing

Carole McCann
University of Maryland at
　Baltimore County
Baltimore, Maryland
　Birth Control

Michelle L. McClellan
University of Georgia
Athens, Georgia
　Substance Abuse

Kristine M. McCusker
Middle Tennessee State University
Murfreesboro, Tennessee
　Communication

Erin McMurray
New York University
New York, New York
　Camp Fire Girls

Julia Mickenberg
University of Texas–Austin
Austin, Texas
　Red Diaper Girls

Tara Mitchell Mielnik
Tennessee Historical Commission
Nashville, Tennessee
　College Girls

Mary Miles
Cornell University
Ithaca, New York
　Sororities

Natalia Molina
University of California–San Diego
San Diego, California
　Latina Girls

John Morrow
Independent Scholar
Overland Park, Kansas
　Cars

Ilana Nash
Bowling Green State University
Bowling Green, Ohio
　Nancy Drew Mysteries

Sharon H. Nathan
Menninger Clinic
Topeka, Kansas
　Eating Disorders
　Psychotherapy

Claudia Nelson
Southwest Texas State University
San Marcos, Texas
  Girls' Fiction

Rebecca R. Noel
Harvard University
Cambridge, Massachusetts
  Hygiene

Fran O'Connor
Nassau Community College
Garden City, New York
  Disabilities

Jo B. Paoletti
University of Maryland at College Park
College Park, Maryland
  Clothing

Rita Papini
University of Missouri–Kansas City
Kansas City, Missouri
  Dating and Courtship
  Temple, Shirley

Leslie Paris
University of British Columbia
Vancouver, British Columbia, Canada
  Dollhouses
  Summer Camps for Girls

Jennifer Phegley
University of Missouri–Kansas City
Kansas City, Missouri
  Reading

Elizabeth Pleck
University of Illinois–
  Urbana Champaign
Champaign, Illinois
  Kinaaldá

Sharon G. Portwood
University of Missouri–Kansas City
Kansas City, Missouri
  Child Abuse

Heather Munro Prescott
Central Connecticut State University
New Britain, Connecticut
  Adolescent Health
  Menstruation

Anita Reznicek
St. Teresa's Academy and
University of Missouri–Kansas City
Kansas City, Missouri
  Education of Girls

Joel P. Rhodes
Johnson County Museums
Shawnee, Kansas
  Radical Feminism

Melisa Rivière
University of Minnesota
Minneapolis, Minnesota
  Graffiti

Kimberley Roberts
University of Virginia
Charlottesville, Virginia
  Girl Power
  Girls' Culture
  Riot Grrrls

Elizabeth Rose
Trinity College
Hartford, Connecticut
  Little Mothers

Mary Rothschild
Arizona State University
Tempe, Arizona
  Girl Scouts

Barbara Ryan
University of Missouri–Kansas City
Kansas City, Missouri
    Domestic Service

Georganne Scheiner
Arizona State University
Tempe, Arizona
    Fan Clubs
    Girl Scouts
    Movies, Adolescent Girls in

Kelly Schrum
George Mason University
Fairfax, Virginia
    Girls' Magazines

Deborah B. Smith
University of Missouri–Kansas City
Kansas City, Missouri
    Home Economics Education

Rickie Solinger
Independent Scholar
Boulder, Colorado
    Teen Pregnancy

Peter N. Stearns
George Mason University
Fairfax, Virginia
    Emotions

Rabbi Bonnie Steinberg
Temple Beth El
Huntington, New York
    Bat Mitzvah

Kathleen Thompson
Independent Scholar
Chicago, Illinois
    African American Girls in the
        Twentieth Century

Linda J. Tomko
University of California–Riverside
Riverside, California
    Dance Classes

Benson Tong
Wichita State University
Wichita, Kansas
    Asian American Girls
    Native American Girls

Lynne Vallone
Texas A&M University
College Station, Texas
    Advice Books

Luise van Keuren
Green Mountain College
Poultney, Vermont
    Samplers

Shirley Teresa Wajda
Kent State University
Kent, Ohio
    Collecting
    Domesticity

Elliott West
University of Arkansas
Fayetteville, Arkansas
    Frontier Girls

Wendy A. Woloson
The Library Company of Philadelphia
Philadelphia, Pennsylvania
    Girls and Sweets

Anne Burri Wolverton
University of Chicago
Chicago, Illinois
    Pickford, Mary

Kathryn J. Zerbe
Menninger Clinic
Topeka, Kansas
    Body Image

FOREWORD

Already it seems like a tintype: pre-teen girls, dancing around in the den, singing "I'll tell ya what I want, what I really, really want." Now disbanded, another piece of 1990s ephemera, the Spice Girls were, in 1997, a mammoth international media phenomenon. They sold ten million albums worldwide; their single "Wannabe" topped the charts in thirty-five countries across four continents. Dismissed by most critics as flash-in-the-pan, no-talent, crassly commercial opportunists, the Spice Girls nonetheless evoked enormous passion and loyalty among their largely preteen female fans.

More than just another pop group, the Spice Girls enjoyed the success that they did because they were promoting "girl power," their "freshened up" version of feminism in which, as they said, "you have a brain, a voice, and an opinion," and get respect even though you're wearing a wonder bra and fuchsia platform boots. Girls wanted to believe the group's liner notes, which promised that the "Future Is Female." They wanted to believe that their pop culture, and their cultural practices, mattered as much as boys'. Marketers for all sorts of products co-opted that desire and sold it back to girls through tee shirts, eye shadow, and athletic gear. Feminist scholars and critics, some of whom had already paved the way for "girl power" by warning parents

and educators about the crash in self-esteem among adolescent girls, asked what this new confluence of quasi-feminism and girl-centered marketing might mean for the future of feminism and for the lived experiences of these future women.

Indeed, in the early and mid-1990s, feminist scholars charted out two large areas in the study of girlhood in America. Carol Gilligan and Lyn Mikel Brown in *Meeting at the Crossroads*, Mary Pipher in *Reviving Ophelia*, and others focused on how girls navigated the shoals of female adolescence in what Pipher called a "hostile media environment." Millions of parents became aware of the way girls learned to silence themselves and their ambitions once they hit their teenage years, and thus many were happy (at least grudgingly) to have their daughters belt out pop lyrics that affirmed female friendships and that told boys who refused to respect them to buzz off. The other area of research, as exemplified by Joan Jacobs Brumberg's *The Body Project* and Miriam Formanek-Brunell's *Made to Play House: Dolls and the Commercialization of Girlhood*, began to explore the cultural history of growing up female in America, and how commercial forces powerfully shaped that experience.

Some of this research informed government initiatives, like the one promoted by U.S. Department of Health and Human Services Secretary Donna Shalala titled, you guessed it, "girl power." Apparently marketers had also been reading Mary Pipher: suddenly, in shops like The Limited 2, targeted to preteen girls, one could find tee shirts that proclaimed "Girls Rule" or "Stand Back Boys—Soccer Is a Girls' Job." So what we witnessed in the mid- and late 1990s was an important new confluence of academic interest in girlhood, of new cultural expressions of girls' feistiness, and of the discovery of the financial potency of the girl, preteen, and teenage market. The Spice Girls' mega-hit CD both drew from and enhanced these trends, and signaled that girls had indeed become very important, to very different people, for very different, often contradictory reasons.

This encyclopedia on *Girlhood in America* engages many of these interests and concerns, and does so with enormous compassion and rigorous critical acuity. It gives expression and shape to a crucially important yet consistently neglected—if not dismissed—foundation of our society: the study of what it means, and what it has meant, to be a girl in America. For much too long, the history and sociology of children and of youth cultures, when they have been done at all, have focused primarily on boys. What girls did for the first fifteen or twenty years of their lives—baby-sitting, cheerleading, going to slumber parties, working, writing in their diaries—wasn't on most academic radar screens as mattering at all in furthering our understanding of the anthropology and sociology of everyday life. But if we don't understand how girls grow up, we cannot possibly appreciate how their everyday practices during their formative years shape so much in our society, from workplace dynamics to family life to the struggle for social justice.

What you will also find especially striking and welcome in this collection is its refusal to consider only white, middle class, heterosexual girls. Entries on slavery; on Latinas, Asian American, Native American, and African American girls; and on lesbians emphasize how the lives of girls have differed powerfully depending on race, locale, class, and/or sexuality. And yet, we are also reminded of what can still unite girls in their experiences of marginality—and of bonding because of that marginality—in a society where, still, more than three decades after the women's liberation movement, women make seventy-five cents to a man's dollar, are still the primary caregivers to children and aging parents, and suffer ongoing violence at the hands of men.

But this collection also insists on reclaiming the exuberance of girlhood, and on reclaiming what girls have done and still do as culturally significant. You will be sobered by what we yet have to accomplish for our daughters—all of them. But you will also be buoyed by how far we have come, by girls' refusal to turn back the clock, and by their ingenious, inventive, joyful, and defiant games, rituals, and strategies that help them survive and advance the struggle for equality in what someday may not be primarily a man's world.

Susan J. Douglas

PREFACE AND ACKNOWLEDGMENTS

Girlhood in America: An Encyclopedia examines American girls' histories and cultures over more than 400 years of our nation's past. Written by nearly 100 established scholars and rising stars in the academy, the 120 comprehensive historical entries in these two volumes consider many aspects of a diverse population of girls of different races, classes, genders, religions, regions, ethnicities, ages, abilities, and sexual orientations. The variety of girls considered here—African American, Native American, Asian American, Latinas, Chicanas, Caucasian girls—those of privilege and those with challenges, make it clear that American girlhood has been far more heterogeneous than the dominant white, middleclass model that has shaped our popular imagination. The differences and the similarities in girlhoods across race and class lines can be attributed to such profound historical transformations as industrialization, immigration, and urbanization in addition to other forces and factors critical in framing girls' lives: dominant race and gender ideologies; socioeconomic contexts; religious and ethnic traditions; family life, schools, and other institutions; consumer and popular culture; *and* girls themselves.

All of these factors along with standard historical markers are included here, but the sustained focus is on girls. In this A-to-Z reference work, students, scholars, researchers, and writers can expect to find the prevalent and the particular in the everyday lives of American girls, beyond the scope of what one might expect to find in a work that is part of a larger series on the American family. This work aims to provide a solid basis for understanding American girls who have been an unrecognized part of the national past by examining their families, organizations, methods of socialization, education and vocation, their forms of work, and their types of play. This preface serves to highlight only some of the many prominent topics in the history of American girlhood that follows.

A variety of institutions have assumed a salient role in shaping girlhood in America. We examine many of the most influential, beginning with the family and the culturally constructed role of daughters. "No matter what the individual differences may be, the mother-daughter relationship plays a central role in the lives of both daughters and their mothers." In her entry, Rachel Devlin explains how historically a girl's relationships to men, family, society, and to herself have been shaped by the defining relationship of daughters and fathers. According to Katherine C. Grier, "When Sarah Josepha Hale, author and editor of *Godey's Lady's Book*, published 'Mary's

Lamb' in 1830 [better known as 'Mary Had a Little Lamb'] she offered her young readers a concise story that connected little girls, kindness to animals, and keeping pets in a manner that reflected changing attitudes toward all three subjects." In entries like these that privilege the role authoritative ideologies about gender and race have played in shaping families, we consider the vast differences in girls' childhood experiences.

We also explore the shifting boundaries between the socialization and vocation of girls within the context of family life. For example, entries such as Carla Bittel's on girls' arts and crafts activities demonstrate how "the meaning of craft production for girls has changed over time, evolving from work that was part of the family economy in early America to a leisured activity rooted in peer culture in the late nineteenth and twentieth centuries." The entry on the history of girls' work; others on enslaved, indentured, and domestic servants; and an entry on babysitters reveal that girls have assumed, expected, and accepted domestic roles and feminized employment whether raised on a farm or plantation, in the city or in suburbia. Such was often the case among Asian American girls and those of other ethnic groups who helped support family economies by doing housework and providing child care.

Entries on Puritan, Catholic, Jewish, Mennonite, and other girls shed light on the distinctive ways in which families' religious beliefs and faith-based institutions have generated both obstacles and opportunities for girls. For example, while Catholic education has served to contain girls within traditional patriarchal roles, it has also provided girls (especially inner-city African American and Latina girls) with significant educational advantages. The gender differences in religious rituals, beliefs, customs, curricula—as well as access to them—are addressed in entries on Catholic and Jewish education. Such sacred and secular markers of the passage from girlhood to adolescence include communion, the Navajo puberty rite of *Kinaaldá*, cosmetics, and proms. The *quinceañera*, a Mexican-American girl's coming-of-age ceremony, also "celebrates the transition to womanhood, with [an] emphasis on her conventional feminine qualities and potential value as a wife."

The context and content of girls' formal education is the focus of entries on schools, colleges, and curricula (e.g., math, science, and sex education). Entries on literacy, gifted girls, and learning disabilities address the pleasures as well as the problems that many female students have faced in their intellectual development. Other institutional agents of socialization include the Girl Scouts, 4-H, the Saturday Evening Girls, and summer camps. Like many others, the Camp Fire Girls combined traditional notions of hearth and home with more modern values about girls. Though many clubs excluded African American girls or provided segregated facilities before integration, clubs, organizations, and sororities are nevertheless noteworthy for engendering community support and racial pride among the African American girls they did serve.

Hornbooks, handbooks, and "texts" of all sorts have served to socialize girls. Lynn Vallone's entry on advice books, which have been prominent since the early 1800s, demonstrates how recent Internet sites still provide proscriptions and prescriptions about acceptable feminine behavior. Samplers (a common feature of girlhood education in early America) can also be read as texts that promoted gendered ideals (e.g., industry, femininity, virtue, piety, and friendship), and taught literacy and mastery of domestic skills. The extensive history of girls' domestic education is also addressed elsewhere in entries on domesticity, arts and crafts, home economics, and tea parties.

Whether learning how to sip tea or sew textiles, girls' bodies have served as powerful sites of socialization, sexuality, sickness, and stress. These themes are explored in Heather Prescott Munro's entry on the role of medical and psychological experts for whom the sexuality and reproduction of adolescent girls were at the forefront of their thinking and their treatment. The historical and psychological dimensions of girls' bodies are also considered in entries on the Barbie doll, body image, eating disorders, hygiene, menstruation. Scholars also consider the cultural meanings and social uses of clothing, cosmetics, and hair. Struggles between social services (e.g., clinics, courts, and prisons) and girls over the control of the female adolescent body are the focus of entries that examine discourses about abortion, lesbians, sexuality, and teen pregnancy. As for birth control, Carol McCann explains that "throughout U.S. history, anxiety about the sexual activity of adolescent girls has played a central role in public debates about contraception." Violence against girls has also harmed their bodies, influenced their identities, and shaped their behavior. Thus, we examine sexual harassment, acquaintance rape, and child abuse as well as girls in colonial and Victorian captivity narratives, sermons, and sentimental literature. Also examined are the age- and gender-specific dimensions of girls' psychological lives in entries on child guidance, depression, psychotherapy, substance abuse, and suicide.

Other entries focus on the commodification of girls, especially since the burgeoning of the consumer culture in the early 1900s. The role of consumption and financial autonomy in the lives of girls and female adolescents is explored in regard to allowances and spending money, girls' magazines, shopping, and teenyboppers. Entries on consumer goods—and over 100 archival and artifactual illustrations— shed light on the seemingly antithetical values marketed to girl consumers. "Through shopping," writes Lisa Jacobson about consumer culture, "many girls have discovered a new brand of independence that comes from making their own consumer choices. At the same time, however, consumer culture has also steered girls toward prescribed gender roles and culturally acceptable aspirations." This is readily apparent in the Pleasant Company's American Girls collection encoded with positive messages about females as well as more traditional notions about domesticity, maternity, and consumption. Though geared toward older adolescents, car advertisements similarly emphasize how girls behind the wheel can achieve independence, identity, self-expression, control, equality, *and* romance.

The changing context of ideals about girlhood and female adolescence in American social and cultural history is clarified in numerous entries. The eroticization of girls—and the exoticization of Asian American females—have led scholars to examine the ethos and ideology that have informed a variety of tropes about girls in the popular culture. Scholars demonstrate how representations of cheerleaders and babysitters among others in movies reveal larger anxieties about adolescent female autonomy. The fashioning of girls' imaginations, fantasies, and desires is further explored in entries on dating, emotions, and teeny-bopper culture. Essays on fairy tales, girls' fiction, and girls' magazines similarly deconstruct misogynist, racist, and stereotyped representations of girls in the print culture. Comics produced by the Walt Disney Company and Warner Brothers Studios, for example, "encouraged girls to be nurturers and represented female characters in typical domestic situations" in postwar America. Other writers analyze the music, cartoons, and sitcoms that have also played a role in establishing, reflecting, and maintaining ideals. Entries on the performative nature of cheerleaders, prom queens, and southern belles also provide insight into these prominent patriarchal cultural constructions. Barbie, Nancy Drew, Mary Pickford, and Shirley Temple are the focus of entries on pop culture icons of girls.

What has all of this meant to girls? What role have they played in shaping their own girlhoods? In the many socializing sources and sites they encounter over the course of their upbringing, girls have often read oppositional meanings. Making meanings other than the preferred ones has enabled girls to negotiate, resist, and contest dominant cultural values that trivialize girls and render them powerless. For example, although their mothers often read the diaries that charted the path of their daughters' self-discipline and moral development, "Victorian girls nevertheless used diaries in order to nurture an identity separate from family." In other venues, girls have transformed cultural products like clothing and dolls for purposes other than what they were originally intended. Although dollhouses encouraged girls to learn consumer habits and homemaking, they were also symbols of girls' power and control over their miniature domain.

Other studies of girls' play (especially among enslaved girls), sports, and reading shed light on some of the many ways in which girls have subverted the ideals of normative female identity embedded in American culture. Movies, too, have been reappropriated for girls' use as fantasies of agency.

Scholars who study American girls' history agree that, to one degree or another, girls have played a role in shaping their *own* girlhoods. Across cultures and classes, races, regions, and religions, girls of all ages have challenged the restrictions that have contained them. Although commercialized girls' cultures have aimed to instill socially acceptable notions of gender, girls have forged more rebellious versions by transforming commodities and contexts. The research shows that even such cultural practices as slumber parties can be transformative, at least for a night. "Through their fan activities" as well, explains Georganne Scheiner, "girls have found cultural authority, agency, and a uniquely creative voice." The underground communications culture of note passing, phone calls, and talking has nurtured girls and provided them with feelings of sorority and protection.

Adolescent feminists, female juvenile delinquents, girl gang members, girl surfers, lesbians, and tomboys are some of the many girls who have used more public spaces and more radical cultures to explore alternatives to feminine ideals. Defiant African American girls like Linda Brown challenged racial segregation in the streets, at schools, and in the courts of postwar America. Entries that consider girls' explorations of other masculine methods and arenas include those on graffiti and punk rock, which opened up new spaces for successive generations of young women in popular music. Other girl cultural producers are included in the history of girl bands, the riot grrrl movement, zines, and the multivalent girl power ethos. Grrrls' comix have also addressed feminist issues rather than offering advice on boy-catching and husband-getting. Entries such as these elucidate girls' most recent efforts at reconstructing girlhood along explicitly feminist lines.

There are still many girls about which we know very little. "Not enough is known about the experience of black girls in this society," writes feminist scholar bell hooks in her autobiography, *Bone Black: Memories of Girlhood*. According to Hasia Diner in her entry, "To understand what it meant to be an immigrant girl must be cobbled together from studies of other aspects of immigration." "Few, if any, scholars have analyzed the complex role disabilities have played, either in fictional or cinematic representations of girls with disabilities or in the lives of real American girls," writes Fran O'Connor. Like others, "It remains an area ripe for historical and literary study." It is our hope that this work will serve as a useful reference to researchers as they continue to trace the paths of more girls and chart the history of other girlhoods in America.

Acknowledgments

I am deeply grateful to Marie Ellen Larcada of ABC-CLIO, the best acquisitions editor I have known. Marie Ellen offered me this project and I cannot thank her enough for the opportunities it has provided me. First, I have been privileged to work with a wonderful team of editors: Jennifer Loehr organized the encyclopedia's massive databases, sent out contracts, and sent gentle reminders to contributors about approaching deadlines. Karna Hughes's good cheer, enthusiasm, faultless organization, and tireless prod-

ding kept me and this project on schedule. This project would not have become a book without Beth Partin, the copy editor, who edited more than 320,000 words. Melanie Stafford—a fellow feminist traveller—skillfully shepherded this work through copyediting, typesetting, proofreading, indexing, and assembling the volumes you now hold in your hands.

Editing is an opportunity to learn, and I have learned about the history of girls from reading and rereading the excellent essays written by the nearly 100 contributors chosen for their expertise. I deeply appreciate the bevy of scholars—such as Anita Gurian and Sharon Nathan—who took time out from their hectic careers and personal lives to research, write, and rewrite the outstanding entries that have made this work possible. I owe special thanks to my good friends Jane Greer, Barbara Ryan, and Leslie Paris, who wrote entries drawn from their own pathbreaking research. Youth studies scholars Joe Austin and Michael Willard put me in touch with other talented contributors like Ilana Nash whose e-mails I still relish. My thanks to Kitty Sklar, who led me to dance historian Linda Tomko and to Eileen Boris for Kimberley Roberts whose own wonderful work on girl power has enabled me to better understand the recent history of babysitters in my current research. Advisory Board members—especially Joan Jacobs Brumberg, Wilma King, Steven Mintz, and Lynne Vallone—provided useful assistance and fruitful leads. My thanks to Darlene Clark Hine for Kathleen Thompson, a goddess-send. And if someone ever coins a feminist equivalent to "Mensch" or "the Dude," Susan J. Douglas deserves such a title.

This work would have taken much longer if not for the support of other colleagues, administrators, and students.

Some of my colleagues—especially Gary Ebersole, Jennifer Phegley, and Kristi Holsinger—wrote fascinating entries on varied aspects of girls' issues. Pat Peebles, chair of the history department at the University of Missouri–Kansas City (UMKC), calmly tolerated the dwindling of office supplies (e.g., reams of paper and boxes of ink cartridges) that enabled me to print and reprint entry after entry until they were perfect enough to send off to ABC-CLIO. Undergraduate and graduate students (especially Anita Reznicek, Rita Papini, Greta Kroeker, and Joel Rhodes) and those in my Girlhood and Boyhood in America course provided me with the opportunity both to learn from them and to teach what I love. I received a generous faculty leave from James Durig, dean of the College of Arts and Sciences, before the corporatization of academic life threatened the integrity of the humanities.

My deepest thanks are to my family. As always, my mother's copyediting expertise enriched my writing and clarified my thinking. Claude, Perry, and Zoë Brunell made room for this project at home, on vacations, and in their lives in general. My husband, Claude, edited my prose and did more than his share of washing dirty dishes and scrubbing grubby faces. He also provided me with much needed encouragement when I felt overwhelmed by the enormity of my tasks: editing a two-volume encyclopedia while raising two children, tending five pets, teaching full-time, and directing UMKC's Women's and Gender Studies Program. My seven-year-old daughter, Zoë, to whom this work is dedicated, listened to rough drafts of entries about the history of girls' dolls, tea parties, slumber parties, and play with some interest and enormous patience. Still, it is from *her* that I have learned the most about girls and their girlhoods and I thank her for that.

Miriam Forman-Brunell
Associate Professor of History
University of Missouri–Kansas City
Kansas City, Missouri

INTRODUCTION

Until recently, the history of girls and their cultures had been largely subsumed within fields that categorized girls more generally as children, adolescents, daughters, or young women. But this undifferentiated lumping neglected not only knowledge of girls, but also the processes by which womanhood developed out of girlhood. Building on the work of Angela McRobbie in the 1970s and Joan Jacobs Brumberg in the 1980s, girls' culture emerged as a field of scholarly inquiry in the 1990s with such outstanding works as Susan Douglas's *Where the Girls Are: Growing Up Female with the Mass Media* (1994).[1] Scholarly anthologies such as *The Girl's Own: Cultural Histories of the Anglo-American Girl, 1830–1915* (1994) and *Delinquents and Debutantes: Twentieth Century American Girls' Cultures* (1998) highlighted the new scholarship on girls' cultures, but unfortunately could do no more than provide an introduction to the subject.[2]

Picking up where collections on "girls' culture" have left off, this two-volume encyclopedia includes 120 topics that examine the everyday lives of girls of different ages, races, classes, sexualities, religions, ethnicities, and abilities as well as discourses about them. What has made it possible to chart the terrain of America's girls, adolescents, and young women—the portion of the female life span this work broadly encompasses—has been the outpouring of the conceptually creative and methodologically rigorous scholarship based on the information about girls that is everywhere woven into the tapestry of our nation's past. One only need look for girls to find them.

Whether working, writing, playing, or protesting, girls have shaped American history and culture in indelible ways, though only some achieved the status of national myths. Pocahontas, the teenage daughter of a powerful Native American chief, is still very much at the center of one of our nation's most cherished—and regularly reinvented—historical legends. Girl accusers of witchcraft in seventeenth-century Salem, Massachusetts, provoked one of our country's deepest cultural crises. But immigrant and migrant girls also played a crucial part in the life and labor of the American frontier where Native American girls had been thriving for millennia.[3] Enslaved girls were important to the economy and culture of the plantation South, and free girls in the industrializing Northeast. For centuries, girls have contributed to agricultural, domestic, industrial, service, informal, and underground economies and made history by laboring in fields and factories. In the twentieth century, our popular culture has been shaped by adolescent girls who have played a formative role in the history of American movies just as teenyboppers, "with more economic capital at their disposal," have influenced trends in pop music since the 1960s.[4] What music, movies, legends, and letters reveal is that girls served the needs and enriched the cultures of families, communities, and the country while also carving out their *own* history and shaping their own distinct cultures.

Although girls from Pocahontas to punk rockers have been integral to American culture, most have been overlooked, their lives undervalued. Perceived as insipid and insignificant, and essentialized as passive and pretty, girls have been judged as undeserving of serious scrutiny, critical analysis, and hence scholarship. Fortunately for those of us who study girlhood, fathers like Thomas Jefferson had a lot to say about their daughters. In fact, references to "good girls" and "bad girls" appear often in letters and other primary sources written by the little known and the reknowned. Colonial historian Mary Beth Norton recently observed in *Founding Mothers and Fathers* (1996) that "daughters . . . appeared in Locke's and Filmer's political writings solely as disruptive influences."[5] Nevertheless, perceptions of girls as pliant left them embedded within broader historical fields of study. As a result, retrieval of information about them has been one of the central challenges facing researchers. Arthur W. Calhoun's *A Social History of the American Family, vol. 1 Colonial Period* (1917) was the first scholarly book that privileged girls' historical experiences with an index listing, but most works did not, and do not still.[6]

A less practical matter than indexing, however, has been teasing out girls' experiences from those of others. In part, this has been due to the scholarship on the history of childhood that emerged from Progressive-era reform, which centered on child study and child welfare. Over one hundred years ago, Alice Morse Earl was surprised by "how little is told of child life in history."[7] Using letters and diaries, portraits, and other primary sources, Earle documented the ordinary lives of Euro-American children in *Child Life Colonial Days* (1899), though from a largely Eurocentric and ungendered perspective. Native American girls, for example, are conspicuous by their absence.

The republication of Arthur Calhoun's *A Social History of the American Family* in the 1960s, along with Edmund S. Morgan's revised 1944 classic on New England family life, led to a wave of outstanding studies on families, childhood, and adolescence.[8] But the "new" social histories generated by postwar permissiveness and the rise of 1960s youth culture perpetuated the use of age as the only tool of analysis. Though the new scholarly approach to studying the past "from the bottom up" opened up opportunities for the study of nations' youngest populations, most works overlooked the gendered dimensions of children and adolescents: girlhood was subsumed within childhood, childhood within family life. Many insightful works provided little more than a glimpse into what experiences could clearly be discerned as particularly girls'.[9] Although more recent works on the history of children have tended to incorporate girls into narratives, analyses of how gender has worked and how girls destabilized gender systems still remain largely undeveloped.

One might have expected information about girls to be abundant within the "new" women's history scholarship.[10] But the influence of second-wave feminism on women's history scholarship, which shaped the field's research agenda for decades, posed surprising challenges for those interested in younger females. Adult women remained very much at the center of most studies despite the focus on the "private side" of women's lives. Girls and adolescents were integrated into Mary Beth Norton's *Liberty's Daughters* (1980) and Christine Stansell's *City of Women* (1987), but these early works remained notable exceptions and did not initiate a new scholarly direction as far as girls were concerned.[11] In general, the vast number of women's history monographs that focused on womanhood yielded little about girlhood. Instead, women and "women's culture" obscured the existence of girls, an analysis of "girls' cultures," and the acknowledgment of the decisive role that girlhood as an ideological construct played in shaping women's roles in particular and American society in general.

Fortunately, the more recent scholarship on women has proven to be more fertile, especially for the study of female adolescents. Pathbreaking works by historians such as Barbara Sicherman and Jane Hunter have drawn upon reader response and other postmodern theories to examine girls' reading and writing.[12] Studies such as Joan Jacobs Brumberg's and Heather Prescott Munro's on the diseases and treatment of girlhood and female adolescents have led to a revision of girls as an age category within the literature on the social history of medicine.[13] The pioneering studies of historians such as Kathy Peiss, Mary Odem, Regina Kunzel, Ruth Alexander, Rickie Solinger, and others have led to the development of a viable narrative about how notions about female adolescent sexualities ebbed and changed along with definitions of delinquency and deviance.[14]

Though "youth studies" has generally favored boys' experiences over girls', studies of "girls' culture" have leveled the playing field.[15] By placing girls at the center of historical inquiry, scholars of U.S. history and culture have now broken new ground by examining girls' agency as well as their accommodation.[16] Scholars who study girls and female adolescents have drawn upon the theoretical insights of feminist theory and cultural studies and made use of a wide variety of methodologies. They "read" or interpret popular culture[17] as well as girls' bodies as texts.[18] Some researchers have used interdisciplinary approaches including ethnographic methods.[19] They synthesize prescriptive sources such as advice manuals with subjective ones like diaries and letters. They problematize girlhood activities, athletics, and events, and privilege primary sources previously regarded as historically insignificant.[20] Many are reexamining the ways in which girls of all kinds have been educated.[21] They utilize "material culture" sources as legitimate historical methodologies and bodies of evidence.[22]

These two volumes aim to summarize and synthesize the scholarly literature and to analyze and contextualize numerous primary sources. New books, movies, and magazines about girls and by girls are *everywhere* in movie theaters and bookstores today.[23] Because not everyone burned the letters "filled with the chat of young girls" as suggested by the author of *The Young Lady's Friend* (1837), there is also no shortage of extant sources that document girls' subjectivities. Sermons, advice books, magazines, and other cultural scripts that proscribed and prescribed gender roles are everywhere in archives and attics.

It is my hope that the research on girls and female adolescents presented in 120 different historical contexts will prove useful to those currently mapping the material worlds and cultural terrain of girls. In schools across the country, a wide variety of child-centered classes and gender-focused courses are taught in departments of history, sociology, psychology, English, education, women's studies, family studies, and media studies. What we uncover about girls, I hope, will lead to the reconceptualizations of the history of childhood, adolescence, women, and the family upon which this work draws and to which it aims to make its biggest contribution. Already museums and historical societies are revising standard historical narratives as they reorganize their toy collections and mount interpretive exhibits. The goal of this work is to make the information gathered here about American girls accessible to everyone: from researchers to writers, students to scholars, teachers to curators, and girls to women.

Notes

1. Joan Jacobs Brumberg, *Fasting Girls* (Cambridge, MA: Harvard University Press, 1988); Susan J. Douglas, *Where the Girls Are: Growing Up Female with the Mass Media* (New York: Times Books, 1994); Angela McRobbie, *Feminism and Youth Culture*, 2d ed. (New York: Routledge, 2000).

2. Sherrie A. Inness, *Delinquents and Debutantes: Twentieth-Century American Girls' Cultures* (New York: New York University Press, 1998), p. 5; Claudia Nelson and Lynne Vallone, eds., *The Girls' Own: Cultural Histories of the Anglo-American Girl, 1830–1915* (Athens: University of Georgia Press, 1994).

3. Elliott West, "Frontier Girls" entry.

4. Kristen Kidder, "Teenybopper" entry; Georganne Scheiner, "Movies" entry.

5. Mary Beth Norton, *Founding Mothers and Fathers: Gendered Power and the Forming of American Society* (New York: Alfred A. Knopf, 1997), p. 99.

6. Arthur W. Calhoun, *A Social History of the American Family, vol. 1 Colonial Period* (New York: Barnes & Noble, 1960), first printed in 1917.

7. Alice Morse Earle, *Child Life in Colonial Days* (New York: Macmillan, 1899), p. vii.

8. Robert A. Bremner et al., *Children and Youth in America: A Documentary History*, 3 vols. (Cambridge: Harvard University Press, 1970–1974); Arthur W. Calhoun, *A Social History of the American Family, vol. 1 Colonial Period* (New York: Barnes & Noble, 1960); John Demos, *A Little Commonwealth: Family Life in Plymouth Colony* (New York: Oxford University Press, 1970); Glen H. Elder, *Children and the Great Depression: Social Change in Life Experience* (Chicago: University of Chicago Press, 1974); Philip J. Greven, *The Protestant Temperament* (New York: Meridian, 1979); Joseph Kett, *Rites of Passage: Adolescence in America 1790 to the Present* (New York: Basic Books, 1977); Edmund S. Morgan, *The Puritan Family: Religion and Domestic Relations in Seventeenth-Century New England* (New York: Harper and Row, 1944); Danill Blake Smith, *Inside the Great House: Planter Life in Eighteenth-Century Chesapeake Society* (Ithaca, NY: Cornell University Press, 1980), chap. 2; Bernard Wishy, *The Child and the Republic: The Dawn of Modern American Child Nurture* (Philadelphia: University of Pennsylvania Press, 1968, reprinted in 1972). See also Paula Fass, *The Damned and the Beautiful: American Youth in the 1920s* (New York: Oxford University Press, 1977) and Steven Novak, *The Rights of Youth: American Colleges and Student Revolt* (Cambridge, MA: Harvard University Press, 1977).

9. Essays in N. Ray Hiner and Joseph M. Hawes, *Growing Up in America: Children in*

Historical Perspective (Urbana: University of Illinois Press, 1985). Anthologies continued to be organized around the concept of childhood. See Elliott West and Paula Petrik, eds., *Small Worlds: Children and Adolescents in America, 1850–1950* (Lawrence: University of Kansas Press, 1992).

10. Jacqueline Jones, *Labor of Love/Labor of Sorrow: Black Women, Work and the Family from Slavery to the Present* (New York: Vintage, 1986); Mary P. Ryan, *Cradle of the Middle Class: The Family in Oneida County, New York, 1790–1865* (New York: Cambridge University Press, 1981).

11. Mary Beth Norton, *Liberty's Daughters: The Revolutionary Experience of American Women, 1750–1800* (Ithaca, NY: Cornell University Press, 1980); Christine Stansell, *City of Women: Sex and Class in New York, 1789–1860* (New York: Alfred A. Knopf, 1986).

12. Carolyn Stewart Dyer and Nancy Tillman Romalov, *Rediscovering Nancy Drew* (Iowa City: University of Iowa Press, 1995); Shirley Foster and Judy Simons, *What Katy Read: Feminist Re-Readings of "Classic" Stories for Girls* (Iowa City: University of Iowa Press, 1995); Jane Hunter, "Inscribing the Self in the Heart of the Family: Diaries and Girlhood in Late Victorian America," *American Quarterly* 44, no. 1 (March 1992): 51–58; Sherrie A. Inness, ed., *Nancy Drew and Company: Culture, Gender, and Girls' Series* (Bowling Green, OH: Bowling Green State University Popular Press, 1997); Shirley Marchalonis, *College Girls: A Century of Fiction* (New Brunswick, NJ: Rutgers University Press, 1995); Barbara Sicherman, "Reading *Little Women*: The Many Lives of a Text," pp. 245–266 in *U.S. History as Women's History: New Feminist Essays*, edited by Linda Kerber et al. (Chapel Hill: University of North Carolina Press, 1995).

13. Joan Jacobs Brumberg, *Fasting Girls: The Emergence of Anorexia Nervosa as a Modern Disease* (Cambridge, MA: Harvard University Press, 1988); Heather Munro Prescott, *"A Doctor of Their Own": The History of Adolescent Medicine* (Cambridge, MA: Harvard University Press, 1998).

14. Ruth M. Alexander, *The "Girl Problem": Female Delinquency in New York, 1900–1930* (Ithaca, NY: Cornell University Press, 1995); Beth Bailey, *From Front Porch to Back Seat: Courtship in Twentieth-Century America* (Baltimore: Johns Hopkins University Press, 1988); Carole McCann, *Birth Control Politics in the United States, 1916–1945* (Ithaca, NY: Cornell University Press, 1994); Mary E. Odem, *Delinquent Daughters: Protecting and Policing Adolescent Female Sexuality in the United States, 1885–1920* (Chapel Hill: University of North Carolina Press, 1995); Kathy Peiss, *Cheap Amusements: Working Women and Leisure in Turn-of-the Century New York* (Philadelphia: Temple University Press, 1986); Rickie Solinger, *Wake Up Little Susie: Single Pregnancy and Race before Roe v. Wade* (New York: Routledge, 1992).

15. Joe Austin, *Taking the Train: Youth, Urban Crisis, and Graffiti* (New York: Columbia University Press, 2001); Joe Austin and Michael Willard, eds., *Generations of Youth: Youth Cultures and History in 20th Century America* (New York: New York University Press, 1998).

16. Miriam Formanek-Brunell, *Made to Play House: Dolls and the Commercialization of American Girlhood, 1830–1930* (Baltimore: Johns Hopkins University Press, 1998); Sherrie A. Inness, *Delinquents and Debutantes: Twentieth Century Girls' Culture* (New York: New York University Press, 1998); Sally Mitchell, *The New Girl: Girls' Culture in England, 1880–1915* (New York: Columbia University Press, 1995); Claudia Nelson and Lynne Vallone, eds., *The Girls' Own: Cultural Histories of the Anglo-American Girl, 1830–1915* (Athens: University of Georgia Press, 1994); Lynne Vallone, *Disciplines of Virtue: Girls' Cul-*

ture in the Eighteenth and Nineteenth Centuries (New Haven, CT: Yale University Press, 1995).

17. Beverly Lyon Clark and Margaret R. Higonnet, Girls, Boys, Books, Toys: Gender in Children's Literature and Culture (Baltimore: Johns Hopkins University Press, 1999); Susan J. Douglas, Where the Girls Are: Growing Up Female with the Mass Media (New York: Times Books, 1994); Sherrie A. Inness, Tough Girls (Philadelphia: University of Pennsylvania Press, 2000).

18. Joan Jacobs Brumberg, The Body Project: An Intimate History of American Girls (New York: Random House, 1997).

19. In addition to Angela McRobbie, see Amira Porweller, Constructing Female Identities: Meaning-Making in an Upper Middle Class Youth Culture (Albany: State University of New York Press, 1998) and Valerie Walkerdine, Daddy's Girl: Young Girls and Popular Culture (Cambridge, MA: Harvard University Press, 1997).

20. Amy L. Best, Prom Night: Youth, Schools, and Popular Culture (New York: Routledge, 2000); Susan Cahn, Coming On Strong: Gender and Sexuality in 20th Century Women's Sport (Cambridge, MA: Harvard University Press, 1995).

21. Dale Baker and Michael Piburn, Constructing Science in Middle and Secondary School Classrooms (Needham Heights, MA: Allyn and Bacon, 1997); Stephan F. Brumberg, Going to America, Going to School: The Jewish Immigrant Public School Encounter in Turn-of-the-Century New York City (New York: Praeger, 1986); Sherrie A. Inness, Intimate Communities: Representation and Social Transformation in Women's College Fiction, 1895–1910 (Bowling Green, OH: Bowling Green State University Popular Press, 1995).

22. Karin Calvert, Children in the House: The Material Culture of Early Childhood, 1600–1900 (Boston: Northeastern University Press, 1992); Miriam Formanek-Brunell, Made to Play House: Dolls and the Commercialization of American Girlhood, 1830–1930 (Baltimore: Johns Hopkins University Press, 1998).

23. Jennifer Baumgardner and Amy Richards, Manifesta: Young Women, Feminism, and the Future (New York: Farrar, Straus and Giroux); Chelsea Cain, Wild Child: Girlhoods in the Counterculture (Seattle: Seal Press, 1999); Carol Cassidy, Girls in America: Their Stories, Their Words (New York: TV Books, 1999); Ophira Edut, ed., Adios, Barbie: Young Women Write about Body Image and Identity (Seattle: Seal Press, 1998); Andrew Garrod, Janie Victoria Ward, Tracy L. Robinson, and Robert Kilkenny, Souls Looking Back: Life Stories of Growing Up Black (New York: Routledge, 1999); Lori Gottlieb, Stick Figure: A Diary of My Former Self (New York: Simon and Schuster, 2000); Pamela Haag, Voices of a Generation: Teenage Girls Report about Their Lives Today (New York: Marlowe, 2000); Kathryn Harrison, The Kiss (New York: Random House, 1997); Sherrie A. Inness, ed., Millennium Girls: Today's Girls around the World (Lanham, MD: Rowman and Littlefield, 1998); Susanna Kaysen, Girl, Interrupted (New York: Turtle Bay, 1993); Caroline Kettlewell, Skin Game (New York: St. Martin's Press, 1999); Mimi Nichter, Fat Talk: What Girls and Their Parents Say about Dieting (Cambridge, MA: Harvard University Press, 2000); Mary Pipher, Reviving Ophelia: Saving the Selves of Adolescent Girls (New York: Ballantine, 1994); Sara Shandler, Ophelia Speaks: Adolescent Girls Write about Their Search for Self (New York: HarperPerennial, 1999); Katherine Tarbox, Katie.com: My Story (New York: Dutton, 2000); Niobe Way, Everyday Courage: The Lives and Stories of Urban Teenagers (New York: New York University Press, 1998).

A

Acquaintance Rape

The statistics are numbing. The number of females sexually assaulted at a young age is shocking and almost too frightening to believe. Yet the figures are supported by study after study: 54 percent of completed or attempted rapes were experienced by women age seventeen and younger (Tjaden and Thoennes 1998); 96 percent of women forced to do something sexual were forced by a nonstranger (Laumann 1996); 77 percent of completed rapes are committed by nonstrangers (Bureau of Justice Statistics 1994); and in sexual assaults of older girls who are between the ages of twelve and seventeen, the assault is more likely to be perpetrated by twelve- to twenty-four-year-old acquaintances (Snyder and Sickmund 1999). The Centers for Disease Control and the National Institute of Justice define rape as forced oral, vaginal, or anal sex (Tjaden and Thoennes, 1998). However, it is crucial to remember that this is not consensual "sex" but an assault resulting from coercion, physical force, or any number of related maneuvers that can include verbal and nonverbal threats, pressure, deception, and harassment (Byers and O'Sullivan 1996). Often the term *sexual assault* is used interchangeably with the word *rape*; in fact, some jurisdictions no longer use the word *rape* in their statutes. Rape can be further classified as stranger or nonstranger or acquaintance rape. Acquaintance rape is a broad category that can include any type of relationship in which the victim knows the perpetrator. Date rape is very specific to social or dating situations, that is, it is sexual assault occurring within the confines of a social or date situation. Many adolescent girls do not report the assault because they believe, on some level, that they are responsible for the occurrence. However, it is impossible to comprehend the nature of acquaintance rape and understand its impact on the lives of adolescent girls without exploring the history of sexual assault in Western civilization, the evolution of dating and courtship customs, and the revolution of the women's movement. Although this brief entry cannot do justice to the importance of the topic, it will serve as a launching point for those who wish to study further.

A Convergence of Historical Events

More than twenty-five years ago Susan Brownmiller wrote her landmark book, *Against Our Will: Men, Women and Rape* (1975). The journalist concluded from her historical research that cultural acceptance of sexual force gives rise to a pervasive process of intimidation that affects all women. Her book was published a mere five years after the first "speak out" against rape in New York City. Just when

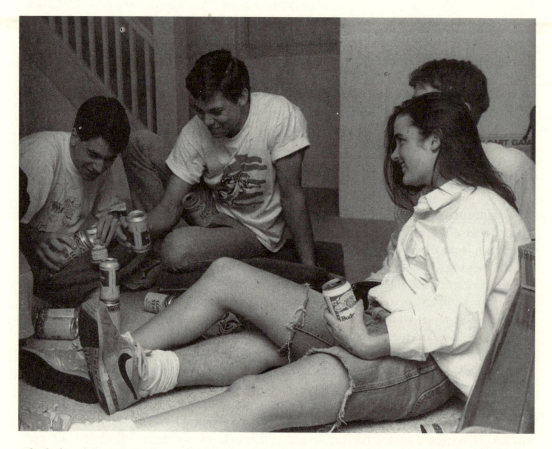

Alcohol and drugs have been identified as a factor in some acquaintance rape situations, especially with the advent of "date-rape drugs" added to girls' drinks, which are sometimes lethal. (Shirley Zeiberg, 1996)

women were achieving sexual independence and control over their own bodies with the advent of the birth control pill in 1960 and the Supreme Court decision legalizing abortion in 1973, women also stood up and asserted that rape, the unspeakable secret filled with shame and guilt, would no longer be silenced (Brownmiller 1975).

The year Brownmiller's book was published was also the year the Vietnam War was coming to a close. Veterans returned home and raised the public's consciousness regarding the psychological effects of war. Their grassroots efforts resulted in

the first wide-range research on the effects of trauma among combat veterans. Simultaneously, women's groups began to address the effects of another kind of trauma, that caused by sexual assault. In 1974, Ann Burgess and Lynda Holmstrom published their research on the psychological effects of rape, or "rape trauma syndrome." The women's movement served as the thread joining these significant sociopolitical events of the 1970s. Not only did the movement raise public awareness, but it initiated new social responses to survivors of sexual assault: the rape crisis center and the rape crisis advocate.

However, it was not until 1980 that the issue of acquaintance rape moved onto the national agenda. Although Brownmiller was the first to introduce the term *date rape,* it was not addressed in the popular literature until *Mademoiselle* ran an article nearly five years later. In 1985 *Ms.* magazine ran an extensive story based on Mary Koss's (1985) research on young adults. The author suggested there was a date rape "epidemic" on college campuses (Sweet 1985). This story also marked the beginning of a deluge of articles focusing on the topic of date rape that continued into the twenty-first century.

The question remains, is this a new "epidemic" or an old problem unearthed? Rape, sex crimes, and sexual assault were not addressed in the professional or the public press until the last half of the twentieth century. In 1955, the first articles began to appear, although they were infrequent and primarily written from a legal perspective. Two decades later, the first research studies on the psychological consequences of rape were published (Burgess and Holmstrom 1974). By 1985, nearly three dozen scholarly publications appeared each year on the effects and causes of rape. In the popular literature, the word *rape* first appeared in 1956. Articles on rape were far outnumbered by the dozens on "sexual ethics," which advised young women on how to protect their reputations and self-respect, the evils of the sexual revolution, the double standard, and how to stay "out of trouble." From those first magazine articles, the citations in the popular press multiplied each year; in 1985, nearly forty-eight articles appeared, and in 1999, almost 100 articles. The publishing trends moved from the effects of rape to the causes of sexual assault and finally to prevention. In 1996 a new topic emerged: date rape

drugs. This new subject outnumbered nearly all other articles on sexual assault by the beginning of the twenty-first century.

The media introduced the threat of acquaintance rape to all young women. They were warned to watch out for the "boy next door" and to be wary of going places and doing things that would put them at risk. The first public service campaign to highlight this issue was initiated by the Santa Monica Rape Treatment Center. Posters flooded college campuses. The goal was to educate students on the dangers of sexual assault, especially among their friends and acquaintances (Abarbanel 2000). But surely, since girls and boys had been in intimate contact for as long as time itself, how is it that acquaintance rape was finally "revealed" at the end of the twentieth century? Perhaps Emily Post can best answer this question.

The Disappearance of Courtship
In a 1965 issue of *PTA* magazine, the noted sex educator Mary Calderone wrote: "We have done away with chaperones, supervision, rules, close family relations and privacy from the intrusion of communication media" (Fishman 1966). Although she addressed the need for sex education, Calderone's statement on the changing landscape of adolescent sexual relationships is central to the issue of acquaintance rape.

The chaperone was alive and well in 1922 when Emily Post first published her book, *Etiquette in Society, in Business, in Politics and at Home.* Her chapter on "Chaperons and Other Conventions" stressed that "a young girl who is unprotected by a chaperon is in the position precisely of an unarmed traveler walking among the wolves—his only defense is in not attracting their notice" (Post 1922, chap. 29). The purpose of the chaperone was to preserve the young girl's honor and reputation by protecting her from situations that would bring her censure by the community: namely, the suspicion that girls who were alone with boys were behaving improperly. Although a boy was involved, it was the girl who was censured or judged by society. The chapter on chaperones disappeared by 1937, but the belief that women are responsible and that their reputation suffers for any unacceptable behavior continues to this day. The fact that a woman might be unable to protect herself or that force was used to gain sex was not even considered.

The concern for girls was not that they were assaulted but that they might get pregnant because they could not help themselves. An inflammatory article in a 1966 *New York Times Magazine* headline announced that every sixth adolescent girl in Connecticut would get pregnant out of wedlock. Even the pioneer of sex education, Mary Calderone, offered the explanation that "neither fear nor external restraints such as curfews keep teenagers chaste any longer" (Brecher and Brecher 1966, 18).

At the outset of the women's movement and the sexual revolution, as young women were establishing their sexual freedom, critics called a woman's newfound liberation a moral dilemma. Although engaging in sexual intimacy was "morally wrong," forcible sex was not addressed at all. In January 1967 Joyce Brothers told the readers of her column, "On Being a Woman," that girls did not have to say more than "no" to a boy's pressure to have sex. Yet she also remarked that the sexual revolution had

given women conflicting messages about intimacy and that girls should not tease boys because they were the more excitable ones in the relationship. Although it was acceptable for "growing" boys to get their sexual experience on the other side of town or with "loose" girls, it was not acceptable for girls. It was the ultimate double standard.

The proponents of sexual ethics placed the responsibility for and the cause of premarital sex and all its consequences on the female. They did not consider the possibility that a girl could be coerced, intimidated, or forced to do something she was not ready or did not want to do. What was it about Western culture that propagated such an idea?

Characteristics of a Rape Culture
Although there have been many descriptions of a rape culture, the definition remains consistent: it is a system of beliefs in which sexual assault is condoned, excused, and even perpetuated. Emilie Buchwald, Pamela Fletcher, and Martha Roth further describe a rape culture as one "that encourages male sexual aggression and supports violence against women" (1993, preamble). It is a society in which violence and sex are inextricably linked, and the causes are rooted in the basic premises of power, sexuality, and ultimately gender relationships. Perhaps the place to begin is in the earliest centuries of Western civilization, when women were the property of either their fathers or their husbands. They did not have rights to rule or hold any significant possessions of their own. Likewise, a woman's body was the property of her owner. A violated woman was worthless to her father, so to make amends for the dowry that could never be paid, the rapist

offered to marry the woman, a custom known as bride capture (Brownmiller 1975).

The socialization of male and female behaviors begins at an early age. Girls and boys learn they have distinct ways of dressing, playing, and interacting with each other. Women are instructed to be polite and considerate, whereas men are aggressors and competitors. Paradoxically, men are also instructed to protect women. A quotation from an 1876 book of virtues, *The Royal Path of Life*, exemplifies the attitudes about male dominance in life and in relationships prevalent at the time. The chapter on "Men and Women" contained this statement: "Man has his strength and the exercise of his power, he goes about, thinks, looks forward to the future and finds consolation in it. But woman stays at home, remains face to face with her sorrow, from which nothing distracts her" (Haines and Yaggy 1876). Similar messages continue to this day. The more traditional the attitudes held by men regarding sex roles and relationships, the more likely these individuals are to accept rape myths and be sexually aggressive than are men who do not have such traditional values (Muehlenhard and Linton 1987).

The messages of sex, violence, and seduction are on the airwaves nearly every day. Although the nightly news may provide young audiences with stories of sex crimes, the regular programming and advertising seduce the youngest viewer with subtle messages about men, women, and sex. Not only is it suggested that having sex at an early age is the norm, but the way sexual behaviors are negotiated is portrayed as well. Helen Benedict describes the portrayal of women on television as "sex

object and glamour girl" (1992). She points out that there is a blending of images of women and the traditional rape myths: "The Vamp version: The Woman by her looks, behavior or generally loose morality, drove the man to such extremes of lust that he was compelled to commit the crime. The Virgin version: The Man, a depraved and perverted monster, sullied the innocent victim, who is now a martyr to the flaws of society" (Benedict 1992, 23). The media messages extend beyond television and film. Magazines, advertisements, and even greeting cards characterize women as less able members of the human race.

The Theories of Acquaintance Rape
Although changing social customs and cultural implications of sexual aggression may contribute to an environment that facilitates sexual assault, the etiology of date rape is much more complex and requires further analysis. For years researchers believed that rape was simply a matter of miscommunication: a boy overestimated a girl's interest and underestimated her refusals, and the girl was reluctant to refuse unwanted sex. The miscommunication theories also promote the idea that women are gatekeepers, that they are responsible for ensuring their partners' understanding of what they do or do not want. Only recently have prevention programs emphasized the need for men to be clear about their own communication and their responsibility to listen to the messages of others. However, Jodee McCaw and Charlene Senn (1998) found that relatively few men engaged in sex without knowing what they were doing. They understood the cues and behaviors of their partners but proceeded regardless of whether

Girls are now taught to be cautious about placing themselves in dangerous situations with acquaintances as well as strangers. (Skjold Photographs)

behavioral cues were consistent with their partners' verbal communication.

Eugene Kanin (1957) was the first to explore male aggression in dating and courtship relationships. He later identified the male social support theory (1967). He proposed that boys who already have a tendency toward sexual aggression seek out others who share their attitudes. Once away from the home, these individuals find other young men who reinforce and support each other's beliefs, verbally or nonverbally. It is not the assault of women per se that motivates these men but a high erotic goal, the need to "score." When they are

frustrated in achieving this goal, aggression and violence result, and sex is gained through power and control.

Walter DeKeseredy (1988) proposed the male peer support theory as an explanation for acquaintance rape. He contends dating involves stress, both internal and external to the relationship, for which males seek out support. Under certain conditions, this support may reinforce or encourage sexual assault. A more current model put forth by DeKeseredy and Martin Schwartz (1993) expands the contributing factors to include familial and courtship patriarchy, alcohol consumption, membership in formal social groups (fraternities or sports teams), and absence of deterrence. In most social groups there are factors that encourage or support behaviors of members. Social groups also adhere to specific sanctions. These communications make clear to the membership that certain behaviors are not acceptable and thus deter such actions on the part of group members. The patriarchal environment was addressed earlier in this entry, which now turns to the effects of alcohol.

Alcohol and drugs have long been at the center of the acquaintance rape debate. Although some researchers believe that the physiological effects of alcohol increase the probability of rape, most authors suggest that alcohol is not causative but may play a part in the student's lifestyle and that unwanted sex is a product of that lifestyle (Ward et al. 1991). In one study alcohol was a permissive cue. For those men who were sexually aggressive, alcohol served to delay their decision to stop their sexual advances (Bernat, Calhoun, and Stolp 1998).

All the mechanisms mentioned herein perpetuate rape mythology. Acquaintance rape in particular is a complex situation with a multitude of variables that can influence the outcome of sexual aggression. But how does the young survivor respond to all of this?

The Effects of Acquaintance Rape
Burgess and Holmstrom (1974) identified rape trauma syndrome as the survivor's reaction to the traumatic experience of being raped. They described two distinct phases, a phase of disorganization that occurred immediately after the event and a second phase that involves a longer-term reorganization process. Other responses to the trauma of rape include acute stress disorder and posttraumatic stress disorder. The survivor's experience in the days, weeks, months, and even years after the rape can include anxiety, somatic complaints, lifestyle disruption, and the inability to establish new intimate relationships. Koss and her colleagues (1988) found that survivors of both stranger and acquaintance rape experienced anxiety, depression, and sexual and relationship dissatisfaction. Non-stranger rape experiences often lead the victim to believe she is responsible for what happened. This can cause her to suffer lower self-esteem and higher psychological distress and to take longer to recover than survivors of stranger rape. Compared to students who had not been raped, survivors of acquaintance rape indicated significantly more trauma symptoms and lower self-esteem (Shapiro and Schwarz 1997). The age of the survivor is crucial: at what age do the symptoms of trauma become more significant, creating lifelong consequences? One might expect that younger adolescents would be more traumatized. In light of the fact that many young girls do not report their date rape, it is nearly impossible to determine the magnitude of the psychological consequences of this traumatic event.

Special Considerations for Adolescent Girls in the Twenty-first Century
Much of the research in the field of sexual assault and, particularly, acquaintance rape focuses on the college-age population. It is often more convenient to study a group of college students rather than younger teens in communities and public schools. This has put scholars and clinicians at a serious disadvantage. There is not enough information about ten- to seventeen-year-old survivors of rape. Serious efforts must be made to access this population.

The discussion in this entry has centered on heterosexual relationships, but rape can happen in gay and lesbian relationships as well. Using language that assumes heterosexuality or making assumptions that the perpetrator was a member of the opposite sex can alienate the survivor, resulting in inadequate care or losing contact with the survivor altogether.

It is important to evaluate cultural differences when working with young people who may have been sexually assaulted. Assuming that disclosure to family and friends will be beneficial can lead to conflict between the survivor and the family. There are numerous organizations that can guide scholars and clinicians in culturally sensitive ways to meet the needs of young survivors.

Prevention
If young adolescents are not informed about the risks of acquaintance rape, they will be less likely to acknowledge that they are victims or recognize the risks. In

1991 the Sex Information and Education Council of the United States (SIECUS) published sex education guidelines for elementary, middle, and high school students. Sexual coercion, including date rape and stranger rape, was among the topics. Twenty-one junior and senior high school sex education programs were evaluated for content on sexual coercion (Beyers and Ogletree 1998). The topic covered most consistently in any of the curricula was "sexual pressure"; sexual harassment was not addressed at all. Two-thirds of the programs covered date rape, and one-third dealt with stranger rape. Most curricula focused on a narrow view of sexual coercion. Some schools have developed programs that focus on gender relations in addition to sex education. The gender relations curriculum builds on the concepts of respect and communication as well as concentrates on the influences of culture and society. It is apparent that educators and researchers still have a great deal to learn about acquaintance rape and coercive sex, especially among younger adolescents. It will continue to be challenging to design appropriate educational programs to meet the needs of middle school students if educators are not aware of their concerns and questions regarding their intimate experiences.

Donna Gaffney

See also Birth Control; Child Abuse; Dating and Courtship; Depression and Girls; Female Sexuality; Psychotherapy; Sexual Harassment; Substance Abuse; Suicidal Behavior in Girls; Teen Pregnancy

References and Further Reading

Abarbanel, Gail. 2000. Personal communication, March 25.

Benedict, Helen. 1992. *Virgin or Vamp.* New York: Oxford University Press.

Bernat, Jeffrey, Karen Calhoun, and Stephanie Stolp. 1998. "Sexually Aggressive Men's Response to a Date Rape Analogue: Alcohol as a Disinhibiting Cue." *The Journal of Sex Research* 35, no. 4: 341–348.

Beyers, Christine, and Roberta Ogletree. 1998. "Sexual Coercion Content in 21 Sexuality Educational Curricula." *The Journal of School Health* 68, no. 9: 370–375.

Brecher, Ruth, and Edward Brecher. 1966. "Every Sixth Teen-Age Girl in Connecticut." *New York Times Magazine* (May 29).

Brothers, Joyce. 1967. "On Becoming a Woman." *Good Housekeeping* (January).

Brownmiller, Susan. 1975. *Against Our Will: Men, Women and Rape.* New York: Simon and Schuster.

Buchwald, Emilie, Pamela Fletcher, and Martha Roth, eds. 1993. *Transforming a Rape Culture.* Minneapolis, MN: Milkweed Publications.

Bureau of Justice Statistics. 1994. *Criminal Victimization in the United States.* Washington, DC: Bureau of Justice Statistics, U.S. Department of Justice.

Burgess, Ann, and Lynda Holmstrom. 1974. "Rape Trauma Syndrome." *American Journal of Psychiatry* 131, no. 9: 981–986.

Byers, E. Sandra, and Lucia F. O'Sullivan, eds. 1996. *Sexual Coercion in Dating Relationships.* New York: Haworth Press.

Davis, Terry C., Gary Q. Peck, and John M. Storment. 1993. "Acquaintance Rape and the High School Student." *Journal of Adolescent Health* 14, no. 3 (May): 220–224.

DeKeseredy, Walter. 1988. "Woman Abuse in Dating Relationships: The Relevance of Social Support Theory." *Journal of Family Violence* 3: 1–13.

DeKeseredy, Walter, and Martin Schwartz. 1993. "Male Peer Support and Woman Abuse: An Expansion of DeKeseredy's Model." *Sociological Spectrum* 13: 393–413.

Fishman, Katherine. 1966. "Sex Becomes a Brand New Problem." *New York Times Magazine* (March 13).

Haines, T. L., and L. W. Yaggy. 1876. *The Royal Path of Life.* Chicago: Western Publishing House.

Kanin, Eugene. 1957. "Male Aggression in Dating-Courtship Relationships." *American Journal of Sociology* 63: 197–204.

———. 1967. "An Examination of Sexual Aggression as a Response to Sexual Frustration." *Journal of Marriage and the Family* 29: 428–433.

Koss, Mary. 1985. "The Hidden Rape Victim Personality, Attitudinal and Situational Characteristics." *Psychology of Women Quarterly* 9: 193–212.

———. 1989. "Hidden Rape: Sexual Aggression and Victimization in a National Sample of Students in Higher Education." Pp. 145–168 in *Violence in Dating Relationships: Emerging Social Issues.* Edited by M. A. Pirog-Good and J. Stets. New York: Praeger.

Koss, Mary, T. Dinero, C. Seibel, and S. Cox. 1988. "Stranger and Acquaintance Rape: Are There Differences in the Victim's Experiences?" *Psychology of Women Quarterly* 12: 1–24.

Laumann, Edward. 1996. "Early Sexual Experiences: How Voluntary? How Violent?" P. 40 in *Sexuality and American Social Policy: A Seminar Series.* Edited by M. D. Smith, et al. Menlo Park, CA: Henry J. Kaiser Family Foundation.

McCaw, Jodee, and Charlene Senn. 1998. "Perception of Cues in Conflictual Dating Situations." *Violence against Women* 4, no. 5: 609–624.

Muehlenhard, C., and M. Linton. 1987. "Date Rape and Sexual Aggression in Dating Situations: Incidence and Risk Factors." *Journal of Counseling Psychology* 34: 186–196.

Page, Randy M. 1997. "Helping Adolescents Avoid Date Rape: The Role of Secondary Education." *High School Journal* 80, no. 2 (December–January): 75–80.

Parrot, Andrea, and Laurie Bechhofer, eds. 1991. *Acquaintance Rape: The Hidden Crime.* New York: Wiley.

Post, Emily. 1922. *Etiquette in Society, in Business, in Politics and at Home.* New York: Funk and Wagnalls.

Schwartz, Martin, and Walter DeKeseredy. 1997. *Sexual Assault on the College Campus: The Role of Male Peer Support.* Thousand Oaks, CA: Sage Publications.

Shapiro, Brenda, and J. Conrad Schwarz. 1997. "Date Rape: Its Relationship to Trauma Symptoms and Sexual Self-esteem." *Journal of Interpersonal Violence* 12, no. 3: 407–419.

Snyder, Howard, and Melissa Sickmund. 1999. *Juvenile Offenders and Victims: 1999 National Report.* Washington, DC: Bureau of Justice Statistics and Office of Community Oriented Policing Services, U.S. Department of Justice, 29–30.

Sweet, Ellen. 1985. "Date Rape: The Story of an Epidemic and Those Who Deny It." *Ms.* 14, no. 4 (October).

Tjaden, Patricia, and Nancy Thoennes. 1998. *Prevalence, Incidence and Consequences of Violence against Women: Findings from the National Violence against Women Survey.* Washington, DC: National Institute of Justice, U.S. Department of Justice.

Ward, S., K. Chapman, E. Cohen, S. White, and K. Williams. 1991. "Acquaintance Rape and the College Social Scene." *Family Relations* 40: 65–71.

Adolescent Health

Adolescent health is more than the absence of disease: it is also the objective and subjective state of well-being that is present when the physical, psychological, and social development of a girl are in harmony with her own possibilities, goals, and prevailing living conditions. Throughout its history, the field of adolescent medicine has striven to address the needs of the whole person from a variety of psychological, sociological, and physiological perspectives, not simply diseases or disorders that affect adolescents. Currently, the trend in adolescent health care has been to go even further beyond the disease paradigm and examine not only health risks but also assets in the environment that contribute to a

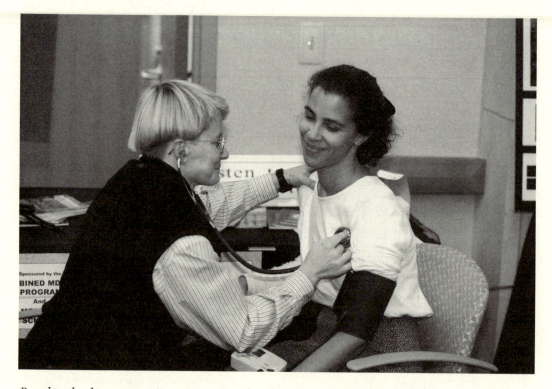

Regular checkups are an important part of maintaining health after a girl reaches puberty. (Skjold Photographs)

young woman's physical and emotional well-being.

From the colonial period until the early twentieth century, the most prevalent disease affecting adolescent girls was tuberculosis. The leading cause of death for all age groups, tuberculosis took an especially heavy toll on young women because of the biological and social features of female adolescence. Rapid growth during puberty encouraged the disease to flourish. Close contact between girls in homes, schools, and workplaces allowed the disease to spread rapidly from individual to individual. Finally, poor nutrition among the working classes and racial minorities increased the likelihood that these girls would develop the disease (Rothman 1994). Girls were also vulnerable to other

childhood diseases such as diphtheria, measles, mumps, and rubella and nutritional deficiency diseases such as rickets and pellagra that affected adolescent growth and development (Halpern 1988).

In addition to the physical diseases mentioned above, the ways in which American society regards girls and their proper social roles have helped frame female adolescent health issues. In the case of adolescent girls, concerns about sexuality and reproduction have been at the forefront of both medical and lay thinking. During the nineteenth century, anxieties about precocious sexuality in girls were closely linked to fears about the impact of immigration and the emancipation of African Americans. Many scientists at this time endorsed racist ideas about human difference and looked for physical traits that would demonstrate that white, upper-class individuals of northern European descent were superior to other racial categories (Gould 1981). One of the physical signs that was used to "prove" the inferiority of African Americans, Asians, and other racial and ethnic minorities was early age of menstruation since this trait seemed to place these groups closer to animals. Scientists claimed that these groups experienced an early onset of menstruation because they had "looser" morals than white, upper-class girls and noted that bodily maturation in girls could be accelerated by indulging in conversations with men, kissing, or other sorts of sexual encounters.

As a result of the views described above, white middle-class and upper-class parents in the United States became alarmed if a daughter entered puberty before the age of fifteen, which was the average age of menarche during the nineteenth century. Medical advice literature during this time advised mothers to prevent their daughters from masturbating, reading romantic novels, and indulging in any activity that might excite the sexual passions. Many physicians also believed that too much consumption of meat contributed to precocious sexual longings and development in young girls and could even cause insanity and nymphomania. Doctors therefore advised mothers to restrict their daughters' intake of meat in order to prevent such disasters from occurring.

Concerns about protecting female virtue also affected the kind of health care young women received. For example, until the mid-twentieth century, it was extremely unusual for adolescent girls to receive a pelvic exam from a physician.

This practice was based on Victorian views about young women, which stated that girls should remain chaste and pure until marriage. Many physicians believed that a vaginal exam would not only damage the hymen, the physical proof of a young woman's virginity, but could also arouse sexual passions in the patient by drawing unnecessary attention to this area of the anatomy. As a substitute for the pelvic exam, medical textbooks advised that physicians could receive all the information they needed from a rectal examination, which they claimed would be far less upsetting to the patient and had the added benefit of preserving the young patient's hymen. In the rare case when a vaginal exam needed to be performed for accurate diagnosis, textbooks recommended performing the exam under anesthesia to avoid traumatizing the young patient.

Advances in American medicine since 1900 have eliminated many of the health problems that affected adolescent girls in the past. Improved public health practices and environmental reforms in the late nineteenth and early twentieth centuries dramatically reduced both the incidence of and mortality from infectious diseases such as typhoid fever, diphtheria, and cholera. Research in nutrition and the discovery of vitamins in the 1910s allowed physicians to prevent and control deficiency diseases and improve adolescent growth and development. The discovery of the sulfonamides during the 1930s and of penicillin during the 1940s gave doctors the ability to treat life-threatening infections such as tuberculosis, sexually transmitted diseases, and pneumonia. The development of vaccines in the early twentieth century greatly reduced the incidence and severity of many diseases that had affected girls, including measles, mumps, rubella, and polio. Improved medical technology has also reduced mortality from noninfectious diseases, such as cancer, diabetes, and cystic fibrosis (Halpern 1988).

The discovery of hormones affecting growth and development during the 1920s and 1930s made hormonal therapy an increasingly popular option for treating girls with developmental abnormalities. Physicians were especially apt to use hormone treatment for sex-inappropriate developmental characteristics that they believed originated from hormonal imbalances. For example, girls who were considered tall for their age would often be given estrogen therapy to prevent further growth. Similarly, girls who failed to menstruate or grow breasts by their midteens were given estrogen to encourage development (Oudshoorn 1994).

Declines in the incidence of physical illness allowed physicians to focus on emotional problems common to adolescents. Although physicians since the mid-nineteenth century had been aware of the fact that adolescence was frequently accompanied by emotional stress, interest in adolescent psychological problems intensified in the early 1900s as a result of the mental hygiene movement. Founded in 1909 by Clifford Beers, a former mental patient, the mental hygiene movement was based on a "dynamic" approach to mental illness that emphasized the role of childhood experiences and family and social environment in psychological development. Since many mental problems were believed to have their roots in childhood and adolescence, the mental hygiene movement focused much of its preventive efforts on these age groups. Adolescent psychologists drew upon the ideas of the Viennese psychoanalyst Alfred Adler, who is best known for developing the concept of the inferiority complex. Mental hygienists observed that adolescents as a group were especially prone to feelings of inferiority. Although all girls were vulnerable to this problem, those who were different from their peers because of illness, disability, or some other physical or emotional disorder were particularly likely to suffer from inferiority complexes. Some girls reacted to their distress by becoming passive and withdrawn, whereas others overcompensated for their perceived inadequacies by acting out in socially unacceptable ways.

Victorian attitudes toward adolescent girls and their bodies also began to change in the 1920s as a result of new behaviors adopted by girls and young women during the late 1910s and 1920s. This period constituted the first "sexual revolution" in American society, during which young women abandoned Victorian reticence and became more frank and open in their sexual behavior. Although intercourse before marriage was still considered inappropriate during this period, petting and necking became so acceptable, even among girls from "respectable" families, that Victorian notions of female sexual purity were seriously called into question.

These changes in female adolescent behavior prompted new views about the psychological development of adolescent girls. Before the 1920s, most writers on adolescent female psychology argued that healthy female development involved protecting the young girl from premature awakening of sexual longings. Under this view, only delinquent girls succumbed to their sexual instincts. By the 1920s, it became increasingly obvious that this view had to be revised as growing numbers of "respectable" girls engaged in what had previously been regarded as delinquent behavior. Rather than label these girls delinquents, experts in adolescent mental hygiene revised their views of female adolescent psychology and made sexual curiosity and a certain degree of sexual experimentation a normal part of healthy female development. In fact, mental hygiene experts worried more about girls who did not adopt an avid interest in the opposite sex by the middle years of adolescence and argued that such girls might become lesbians or otherwise fail to attain the normative adult feminine role of marriage and motherhood.

This new view of adolescent female psychology had a profound impact on adolescent health care. By the mid-twentieth century, doctors became much more willing to perform pelvic examinations on girls. Physicians also became concerned about how illness might affect a young woman's sexual identity. Physicians recognized that some diseases such as tuberculosis and diabetes could inhibit menstruation and the development of secondary sexual characteristics. Medical experts warned that underdeveloped girls might become so discouraged by their lack of "feminine" features that they would fail to marry or would become lesbians.

After World War II, the concept of the inferiority complex prompted a number of medical experts to begin focusing more attention on the health needs of teenage girls. Dermatology benefited from adolescent anxiety about pimples and the psychological consequences of having a flawed complexion. Before World War II, treatment of acne was considered a luxury, since it was seldom life threatening. By the 1950s, concerns about the impact of a bad complexion on peer acceptance and self-esteem led to increased medical interest in acne and other skin disorders. Likewise, fields such as plastic surgery, orthodontics, endocrinology, and orthopedics drew on new ideas about the relationship between physical appearance and adolescent peer adjustment. Even experts in serious chronic and acute diseases in adolescents became concerned not just with the physical effects of illness but with the psychological consequences of diseases that made a girl different from her peers.

This new interest in the health problems of teenagers led to the development of a new medical field known as adolescent medicine. Throughout its history, adolescent medicine has emphasized looking at the "whole patient" from a variety of psychological, sociological, and physiological perspectives. The first medical unit in the United States devoted exclusively to adolescents was founded at Boston Children's Hospital in 1951. The Boston Adolescent Unit served as a model for other hospitals in North America. By the mid-1960s, there were fifty-five adolescent clinics in hospitals in the United States and Canada, and by the 1970s nearly half of all hospitals in the United States had units dedicated to the health care of teenagers. The expansion of adolescent health services led to the creation of a professional organization for adolescent health experts, the Society for Adolescent Medicine, established in 1968 (Prescott 1998).

During the 1960s and 1970s, girls began to engage in behaviors that placed them at risk for new health problems. Changing social norms during this period exposed girls to sexually transmitted diseases, drug addiction, violence, and pregnancy. Although these problems have affected the population as a whole, they appear to affect teenagers disproportionately and may be responsible for the fact that adolescent mortality has risen since 1960, while mortality for other age groups has declined (Schulenberg, Maggs, and Hurrelmann 1997).

Since the 1960s, changes in female adolescent behavior and gender role expectations for women have prompted a revision of medical theory on female adolescent health problems. The second "sexual revolution" of the twentieth century led to higher rates of premarital sexual activity among American teenagers. Feminist health care publications promoted self-determination in women's health care and challenged traditional ideas about femininity that mandated marriage and motherhood as the only acceptable roles for women. In the area of adolescent medicine, feminist practitioners claimed that girls deserved the same access to health care as adult women and helped eliminate laws that required parental consent for medical procedures, particularly those related to contraception and abortion.

Adolescent health care has improved considerably since 1900, but girls still face major risks to their health. Teenagers are the only age group in the United States whose mortality rate has actually increased since 1970. Parents and physicians are more likely to gear preventive health care toward young children. Adolescents are also less likely than other age groups to have health insurance. Unlike diseases of the past, such as measles and polio, many problems affecting modern teenagers cannot be treated with a drug or vaccine. Instead, many of today's adolescent health risks grow out of a combination of biological, psychological, and social factors, including poverty, peer pressure, street culture,

and conflicts with parents. Even diseases such as juvenile diabetes or cystic fibrosis, which are caused by a specific biomedical factor, can be complicated by the psychological and social pressures of adolescence (Schulenberg, Maggs, and Hurrelmann 1997).

Adolescence as a social category also appears to be both disappearing and expanding. Children are exposed to violence, sexuality, and other "adult" themes at ever earlier ages (Elkind 1998). There is even evidence that children are literally "growing up" faster than ever before, since improved health care and nutrition have caused a steady decline in the age of puberty (Brumberg 1997). At the same time, growing numbers of young adults are living with parents for longer periods of time because of unemployment, divorce, graduate education, loneliness, or the high cost of housing. Since the late 1960s, the number of adult children living with parents has more than doubled from 2 million to 5 million, and it is estimated that nearly 40 percent of all young adults have returned to their parents' home at least once. Therefore, it appears that the period of economic dependency usually associated with adolescence is expanding into the twenties and, for some individuals, the thirties and forties. The Society for Adolescent Medicine responded to these changes in both the biological and social features of adolescence by recently adopting a position statement that declared that adolescent medicine covered the ages of ten to twenty-five, with some members even arguing that the field should be extended to cover the late twenties and early thirties (Prescott 1998).

Experts in adolescent medicine have also attempted to deal with the complex issues that continue to plague adolescents by reconceptualizing health as more than the absence of disease or risk. Rather, the current trend in adolescent health involves bringing together families, schools, youth-serving organizations, congregations, and other institutions that can provide teenagers with the foundations for healthy lifestyles.

Heather Munro Prescott

See also Body Image; Child Abuse; Child Guidance; Eating Disorders; Female Sexuality; Hygiene; Menstruation; Psychotherapy; Substance Abuse; Suicidal Behavior in Girls; Teen Pregnancy

References and Further Reading
Alexander, Ruth M. 1995. *The "Girl Problem": Female Delinquency in New York, 1900–1930*. Ithaca, NY: Cornell University Press.
Bailey, Beth L. 1988. *From Front Porch to Back Seat: Courtship in Twentieth-Century America*. Baltimore: Johns Hopkins University Press.
Benson, Peter L. 1998. *Healthy Communities, Healthy Youth*. Minneapolis: Search Institute.
Brumberg, Joan Jacobs. 1988. *Fasting Girls: The Emergence of Anorexia Nervosa as a Modern Disease*. Cambridge: Harvard University Press.
———. 1997. *The Body Project: An Intimate History of American Girls*. New York: Random House.
Elkind, David. 1998. *All Grown Up and No Place to Go*. Reading, MA: Addison-Wesley.
Gould, Stephen Jay. 1981. *The Mismeasure of Man*. New York: W. W. Norton.
Haiken, Elizabeth. 1997. *Venus Envy: A History of Cosmetic Surgery*. Baltimore: Johns Hopkins University Press.
Halpern, Sydney. 1988. *American Pediatrics: The Social Dynamics of Professionalism 1880–1980*. Berkeley: University of California Press.
Oudshoorn, Nelly. 1994. *Beyond the Natural Body: An Archaeology of Sex Hormones*. London: Routledge.
Prescott, Heather Munro. 1998. *"A Doctor of Their Own": The History of Adolescent Medicine*. Cambridge, MA: Harvard University Press.
Rothman, Sheila. 1994. *Living in the Shadow of Death: Tuberculosis and the Social Experience of Illness in American History*. New York: Basic Books.
Schulenberg, John, Jennifer L. Maggs, and Klaus Hurrelmann. 1997. *Health Risks and Developmental Transitions during Adolescence*. New York: Cambridge University Press.
Tanner, James Mourilyan. 1981. *A History of the Study of Human Growth*. New York: Cambridge University Press.

Adoption

Adoption is the procedure by which a parent-child relationship is established by law, usually fully transferring parental care and authority from a girl's biological parents to other adults, whether "strangers" or relatives. Although historical and anthropological evidence suggests that adoptive relationships have long been established across human cultures, full legal adoption was not accepted by the English common law tradition that was adapted by most of the United States from colonial days. This legal barrier was gradually eroded over the latter half of the nineteenth century and the entire course of the twentieth century by streamlined adoption statutes—a process that represents a dramatic change in domestic family law and is largely due to the increased demand of U.S. adults for adopted children. At the same time, infant girls have moved from being the least readily adopted to potentially the most attractive option for adopting parents, as all babies and girls in particular have come to embody innocence and fragility, characteristics central to the Western notion of childhood that arose during this period. Embroiled in complex and unresolved legal, social, and economic debates—involving critical issues both within the United States and on the international scene—the adoption of girls remains a controversial subject that deeply affects the lives of young females in the United States today.

English fears about jeopardizing the inheritance rights of the adopting parents' legitimate "heirs of the body," which were of course primarily males under traditional inheritance laws, long predominated in England and its colonies. The common law tradition was thus always more skeptical of adoption than were other Western traditions, particularly Roman civil law, which dominated in France and Spain and their colonies. The latter tradition was, however, eventually undermined by the efforts of the Roman Catholic Church and by Protestant reformers because it was frequently used by wealthy European males to legitimize their "natural sons," primarily to continue the male line of succession and inheritance. Illegitimate girls, however, seem to have had little value for such purposes. Traditionally in Western culture, impoverished girls, but particularly those deemed "bastards," have been the least valuable of all children in need of care and have therefore suffered most from the severe legal, social, and economic penalties long associated with illegitimacy. Because of this emphasis on male inheritance rights, by the seventeenth century full legal adoption was nearly nonexistent in Europe, although quasi-adoptive measures such as apprenticeships and other voluntary or involuntary transfers of child custody were widely practiced.

In both England and the United States, parents in most social and economic classes, along with the church and town authorities responsible for orphaned and bastard children, placed virtually all boys and many working-class girls into other families for labor and education, sometimes in circumstances that today might be formalized by legal adoption. Wealthier girls living with both parents were, however, the least likely to leave home before marriage. Early American citizens could, moreover, otherwise informally adopt children or use their wills to provide for younger relations, goddaughters, or others placed in their care in a procedure known as "testamentary adoption." But more easily than their English counterparts, American adults could also ultimately appeal to state legislatures to pass private adoption acts that would fully surmount the legal barrier that the English-based legal system prescribed.

This long, expensive process eventually became too cumbersome for the states, not to mention for the families involved, as a variety of cultural forces at work during the middle of the nineteenth century increased the demand for adoption. The demise of the traditional apprenticeship system, the increasingly wage-based industrializing economy, and the waves of European immigrants arriving in the United States and then generally forced into appalling living conditions created a substantial population of children struggling for existence outside the structures that traditionally would have provided adult supervision or care. Girls outside the family system and without a well-established kinship network were particularly vulnerable to such an existence, since urban life in particular provided few life-sustaining jobs for young women beyond prostitution. The public, moreover, typically viewed these impoverished girls as at best a drain on resources, particularly during their earliest years, or at worst a potential threat to the virtues of home and family, rather than as victims of the social and economic system or as holding any inherent or symbolic value in themselves.

Yet, as the nineteenth century passed, children, and girls especially, were increasingly seen as innocents needing adult protection and—ideally—maternal nurturing, rather than paternal guidance and labor under the supervision of a "master." This view of girls was promoted by individual women writers like Catharine Beecher, Lydia Maria Child, and popular journalists like Fanny Fern, and also by conservative and liberal women's organizations. Using the popular media, women successfully spread the idea that motherhood was not only a virtuous state that inherently created a higher, spiritual relationship to children but also a profession that required training and complex skills. Various private responses to these children, rather than federalized or even coordinated state-level solutions, thus arose in the mid-nineteenth century, many of them arguing that institutionalizing these girls was cruel and inhumane because it separated them from a mother's loving care. The forerunners of the adoption and foster care movements were among these private responses.

Under the pressure of this private response, states one by one began passing laws to move the adoption process out of the legislative system and into the judicial system, which served to streamline and democratize the process. By 1929, all the existing states had enacted some form of adoption law. Although a few states, notably Texas and Louisiana, based their law on the civil law tradition mentioned earlier, which viewed adoption primarily as a transfer of property rights, most U.S. adoption laws were based on the groundbreaking law passed by Massachusetts in 1851. That law created a means of establishing familial relations between adults and children that would ideally honor the needs and interests of all the members of the new family. Beyond immigration and the industrializing economy, republican sentiments seem to have balked at the binding nature of indentures, which often gave even older girls and boys little or no say in their placements and few rights or avenues of redress if they were neglected or maltreated by their masters. Many scholars, in fact, argue that such a feeling was at least in part a manifestation of the strong antipatriarchal sentiment that undergirded American notions of revolutionary nationhood. The rhetoric of the era often portrayed America as a child growing away from and ultimately rejecting the rule of king and "fatherland."

Perhaps not surprisingly, then, a notion of the rights of children also seems to have emerged in real families to challenge the father's exclusive right to the care and custody of even his legitimate children. Legal codes governing custody disputes began to emphasize "the best interests of the child" by the mid-nineteenth century. These laws then explicitly charged the courts with ensuring both that the custodial parent was truly "fit" to nurture the girl and that the relationship would promote her welfare. These new notions about childhood also served to emphasize adoption and family-based foster care programs, all but replacing the Jacksonian era's orphanages over the course of the twentieth century.

Yet at the same time, what was perhaps most radical about the new adoption laws was that they ultimately had the effect of valuing this new legal relationship over any and all preexisting blood connections. Despite recent moves toward open adoptions—which are not fully encouraged, enforced, or even recognized by all states—most adoption laws continue even today to terminate, and often even seek to erase, all relations between the child and her birth parents. Of course, adoptions by relatives probably account for about half of all U.S. adoptions and are generally treated with less scrutiny and secrecy than adoptions by nonrelatives, or "strangers," as the law typically calls them. But the state still recognizes only two parents. Even in cases in which a parent retains her children but remarries after a divorce and then seeks to have her second spouse or partner adopt her children, the original spouse must agree to the termination of his or her legal relationship to the child. In the case of infant adoptions by strangers, original birth certificates are typically sealed by the state, with strict rules about the disclosure of any information on them, and replaced by a new certificate with the adopting parents' names and the new name of the child. Although a significant percentage of the U.S. population has had a direct connection with adoption, particularly since the baby boom generation, the federal government ceased collecting statistics on adoption in 1975, so the actual number of girls adopted per year is not verifiable.

In a culture that still stigmatizes and distrusts adoptive relationships, all this secrecy both creates and feeds numerous tensions and fears, fostering insecurity and shame for the parties involved. In the late twentieth century, regular reports erupted in the media surrounding the contested "ownership" of children. In some cases, biological parents have reported that they felt coerced into giving up their child, which may be particularly true for unwed, adolescent mothers. One particularly notorious case involved a girl known in the national media as "Baby Jessica," who was returned to her biological parents after living with adoptive parents for over two years. In this case, the father was misidentified by the birth mother, so the male partner did not give up his parental rights. Paperwork was mishandled, and all the adults involved claimed a powerful attachment to the young girl, whose life was presented as hanging in the balance. As a result of such cases, various movements have emerged to support the rights of the children and all the adults involved in adoption.

Although typically the adopted infants and girls in question and the birth parents are poorer and less powerful than the adopting adults, the would-be parents still often feel shame. Infertility is still stigmatized in American culture. Having to "prove" one's value as a parent for a social welfare agency can feel invasive, especially to persons who are used to relative autonomy in their private relations. Unmarried people and same-sex couples are not allowed to adopt in every state, and even where they are, residual social stigmas surrounding homosexuality and nonmarital relations often make adoptions difficult and painful, even those of young relatives or the children of one of the partners. Birth mothers, moreover, are often left with conflicting fears that the child will show up on their doorstep years later or, on the contrary, that the child will disappear from them forever. After a divorce, noncustodial parents may feel anger and resentment at the legal termination of their parental relationship. And an adopted girl may begin to feel like a transportable commodity, an item of exchange between adults who may at times seem more concerned with their own "best interests" than with hers. Such children often report feeling strong and conflicting desires both to love and honor their adoptive parents and to find and possibly meet their biological parents, who are so frequently shrouded in secrecy and who may sincerely desire to remain unknown to their children.

All of these shifts have, thus, created an atmosphere in which the valuation of the child has changed radically, particularly for girls. In what has been called the "sacralization" of the child (Zelizer 1985, 11), the child most easily "placed" into another family has changed from being a male child, old enough to provide real work to a farm or business, to a white, blue-eyed baby, often ideally a dimpled girl, holding primarily sentimental value to the adoptive parents. During the nineteenth and early twentieth centuries, children changed from being viewed primarily as a form of economic aid to the family and insurance against old age to being an expensive, luxury item with largely indefinite returns—to be indulged in only according to one's means. Girls, in particular, have been viewed in this light: incapable of carrying on "the family name," they are still under pressure to accept the burden of remaining innocent, which for girls is still frequently tied to notions of sexual "purity" and filling the desires and dreams of their parents.

Meanwhile, abortion and a host of other cultural forces have made that "healthy white infant girl" quite rare on the adoption "market," even as most adults seeking stranger adoption are middle- to upper-class white, heterosexual couples. Transracial adoption has, moreover, been viewed with great skepticism by many parties. Beyond the potential racial prejudices and desires of adopting couples themselves, who frequently would prefer a child who "looks like" themselves, fears of interracial sex and racial prejudice generally can lead to hostility against the child within her new "community" and against the family as a whole. Some people question the ability of parents who do not share their child's ethnicity to create an environment that nurtures her self-esteem. Moreover, transracial adoption suggests a form of cultural genocide to some critics. The Multiethnic Placement Act of 1994 forbids adoption agencies from creating separate waiting lists for girls and boys based on race or ethnicity but allows ethnicity as a consideration in questions of parental "fitness" to provide for the best interests of the child. All too frequently, the voices of the girls involved in these cases are not heard, lost in adult noise and almost assuredly in the unavoidable confusion created by such complex and competing interests.

Despite all these difficulties, even persons of somewhat moderate aims will pay large sums of money to adopt a child. Although the idea of actually buying children outright remains repugnant to most Americans, childless couples will spend tens of thousands of dollars on prenatal care and other birth-related expenses, as well as legal fees for the adoptive process, often including legal counsel for the biological mother to ensure that she cannot legally claim to have been coerced into giving up her child. Fees can be particularly high for international adoptions, which typically involve travel and use of various intermediaries in both countries because of linguistic, legal, and cultural differences that require translation.

China, in particular, has figured prominently in this debate, especially since it established the "one family, one child" rule in 1979. Since Chinese culture has traditionally valued boys over girls, thousands of girls are being abandoned each

A mother and her two-year-old adopted Asian American daughter visit the Vietnam Wall on Memorial Day. (Skjold Photographs)

year in China and sent to orphanages (U.S. Department of State 2000). It should be noted, however, that Chinese leaders instigated this rule in order to combat serious threats of famine and overpopulation, although they took measures that appear severe by Western standards. Indeed, the "one-child" rule itself applies only in urban areas, where it was softened in the 1990s to allow more people to try for second children, and contains exceptions for Han-Chinese and other ethnic minorities. Thousands of American adults now adopt girls from developing nations and particularly from China each year, which has led to new international legislation to protect the interests of adoptees. The Hague Convention on Intercountry Adoption, for instance, was signed by the United States in 1993 and ratified in September 2000. However, questions still arise from many corners surrounding the ethics of such adoptions: do these adoptions ultimately serve to support repressive regimes? Do they finally serve the needs and interests of American adults more than the Chinese girls while doing nothing to challenge the inequities inherent in the larger social and economic forces that create such a huge population of unwanted girls?

New technological options for people seeking children, moreover, have recently included the employment of surrogate mothers and the use of egg or sperm donors, thus creating an entirely new and complex set of laws related to adoption. Critics point out that young women in their late teens and twenties are at the peak of their fertility during the period of their life when the current social and economic system virtually requires them to be pursuing education and careers. These young females are thus the most likely candidates for donating "unwant-ed" children, reproductive labor, or ova. Yet there are grave concerns about their access to free choice in their role in the process, the effects on their health and their own fertility later in life, and fears that young women will be induced to "sell" their reproductive abilities to the highest bidder.

Probably the saddest issue related to cost, however, is the continued cultural devaluation of children who are "difficult to place" because of mental, physical, or emotional health conditions or, more simply, age. Girls over six years of age do not have the labor value of their nineteenth-century counterparts, who would at least have been employed in domestic service from a young age. Nor, however, do these girls retain the emotional, symbolic value of the infant girl who does not retain memories of her biological family. Such children cannot fulfill the fantasy of a clean slate for adopting parents to fill up, a fantasy that also has its roots in eighteenth- and nineteenth-century European American culture. Older girls may retain memories, emotional attachments, and the scars of early psychological, physical, or sexual trauma that may continue to haunt the new relationship. Without comprehensive mental and physical health coverage in the United States, girls of any age who are born with illnesses or suffer from acquired disorders and who then are orphaned, abandoned, or otherwise given up represent a financial and emotional burden that many Americans—not just adopting parents—simply feel unable or unwilling to accept.

Lori Askeland

See also Birth Control; Child Abuse; Orphans and Orphanages; Teen Pregnancy

References and Further Reading

Carp, E. Wayne. 1998. *Family Matters: Secrecy and Disclosure in the History of Adoption.* Cambridge, MA: Harvard University Press.

Grossberg, Michael. 1985. *Governing the Hearth: Law and the Family in Nineteenth-Century America.* Chapel Hill: University of North Carolina Press.

Hollinger, Joan A., et al., eds. 1989. *Adoption Law and Practice.* New York: Matthew Bender Press.

May, Elaine Tyler. 1997. *Barren in the Promised Land: Childless Americans and the Pursuit of Happiness.* Cambridge, MA: Harvard University Press.

Modell, Judith S. 1994. *Kinship with Strangers: Adoption and Interpretation of Kinship in American Culture.* Berkeley: University of California Press.

UNICEF (United Nations Children's Fund). 2000. "Intercountry Adoption Information Portfolio." http://old. unicef-icdc.org/information/portfolios/ intercountry-adoption/.

U.S. Department of State. 2000. "1999 Country Reports on Human Rights Practices: China." http://www.state. gov/global/human_rights/1999_hrp_ report/china.html.

Zelizer, Viviana A. 1985. *Pricing the Priceless Child: The Changing Social Value of Children.* New York: Basic Books.

Advice Books

From the nineteenth century onward, American advice literature—especially books, columns, and now Internet sites—has communicated messages of normative femininity to adolescent girls. Although the content of these messages has changed dramatically from the nineteenth century, as social texts—examples of strongly held views of female behavior—advice books stand as a significant subgenre within young adult nonfiction. Undergirding this literature is the belief that girls are lacking in guidance and that the advice given in manual, column, or Internet form will provide the warnings, information, or encouragement that they need on their way to becoming "normal" women. In its earliest incarnation, advice literature was essentially domestic in scope, educating readers (often from the middle class) in "modern" methods of housekeeping, childrearing, and cooking as preparation for running a household. Etiquette and social conduct were other pervasive topics of early advice manuals. This literature filled a void that the relatively fluid class structure of the nineteenth-century United States had opened: middle-class and upper-class girls whose families relied upon servants for domestic service were in need of practical instruction in basic homemaking skills in case their fortunes fell, and lower-class girls with intentions to rise in status required hints in etiquette and social conduct as a means to shed any behavioral or sartorial "markers" of poverty. In general, the audience for advice books was white (heterosexual) girls of either the middle or lower class. Immigrant and African American girls were largely ignored in early advice literature. By the mid-twentieth century, advice literature for girls began to focus on beauty, fashion, and relationships. This shift maintained the pressure on girls to please men—but in this case, the emphasis was on sexual attractiveness rather than housekeeping or mothering skills. Although training the girl both in the "rules" of physical beauty through makeup and fashion advice and in the ways of generating male attention continues to dominate advice literature for girls in the late twentieth and early twenty-first centuries (particularly through mass media teen magazines), there is also a significant second-

Girl learning her lesson.

"Girl Learning Her Lesson," John Frost, Easy Exercises, *1839, p. 21.*

ary strain of advice literature that is feminist in nature and focuses on developing self-esteem, health, and independence within girls of all backgrounds, races, and ethnicities. Much of this literature is not mediated by an adult, "parental" voice but is advice given to girls by girls.

Although nineteenth-century advice literature for middle-class girls was primarily domestic in nature, it also included information on the body and mind. Catharine Beecher's housekeeping compendium, *Treatise on Domestic Economy for Use of Young Ladies at Home and at School* (1841), read by girls as preparation for marriage and household management, was highly successful and reprinted almost annually through 1856. The expansion of this volume, *The American*

Woman's Home, appeared in 1869 as the work of Beecher and her sister, Harriet Beecher Stowe. *Miss Leslie's Behaviour Book: A Guide and Manual for Ladies* by Eliza Leslie (1859) instructed girls in the niceties of decorum in the home (hosting "tea visiters" [sic] or engaging in polite conversation, for example) and outside it: "in the street," at a hotel, church, or even on shipboard. Early in 1868, just before she tried her hand at writing the "girls' story," *Little Women,* that would make her famous, Louisa May Alcott was pleased to accept $100 from the *New York Ledger* to write an advice column for young women. Alcott titled her sketches of contented "old maids" "Happy Women" and in it advocated an active life of intellectual pursuits such as medicine and literature, social work, and self-sacrifice for girls. Physical fitness was another favorite topic of advice book authors of the nineteenth century. As a means to preserve health and to promote a vigorous work ethic, homeopathic physician Dio Lewis encouraged his readers in *Our Girls* (1871) to reject corsets and become physically fit through calisthenics and outdoor exercise. To improve posture, he suggested that the iron "gymnastic crown" (his own invention) be worn for fifteen minutes morning and night. Factory girls working in the Lowell, Massachusetts, textile mills, whose work ethic needed no prompting, received inspiration and encouragement from their fellow workers in the *Lowell Offering*, edited by Harriet Farley from 1842 to 1845 (it became *The New England Offering* in 1847–1850). For frank discussions of sexuality, reproduction, and health, girls had few options in the nineteenth century. Edward H. Clarke's book *Sex in Education, or a Fair Chance for the Girls* (1873) has been called "the great uterine manifesto of the nineteenth century" for its theory that educating girls would cause uterine atrophy (Ehrenreich and English 1978, 127–128). For a sex education manual written by a sympathetic female physician, girls could consult Mary Wood-Allen's *What a Young Girl Ought to Know* (1897). Founded on the belief that too much information about sexuality could be dangerous to a girl, *What a Young Girl Ought to Know* proceeds cautiously, relating the fictional dialogues of a girl and her mother after the birth of a baby brother. Their conversation begins with plant reproduction and fish fertilization and culminates in this delicate description of sexual intercourse: "'The germ of life ... would never wake up unless it

were touched by the power that only the father could give'" (Campbell 1979, 20). The book also discusses masturbation, morality, and mental and physical hygiene and ends where Beecher's manual begins, with woman's natural role as wife and mother and as caretaker for the home and its occupants.

The importance of periodical literature in contemporary advice literature for girls, now as well as in its past, cannot be underestimated. *The Juvenile Miscellany: For the Instruction and Amusement of Youth* (1826–1836), founded by Lydia Maria Child, was the first American children's magazine to include entertaining (as well as didactic) features. *The Juvenile Miscellany* was directed toward both boys and girls, but most of its writers were female, some of them prominent authors such as Lydia Sigourney and Sarah Josepha Hale. The magazine included fiction informed by the British "rationalist" school (found in the work of Maria Edgeworth and Thomas Day, for example), poetry, biographical sketches of notable figures, dialogues about natural history or proper behavior, and puzzles, as well as guidance in the form of essays about virtues such as "Filial Obedience" and "Self-knowledge." Under the able tutelage of Mary Mapes Dodge (who edited the magazine for thirty-two years), *St. Nicholas* (1873–1940) became perhaps the best-known periodical for children of the nineteenth century. Scribner, publishers of the *Scribner's Monthly* and *The Century*, was also the parent company of *St. Nicholas*. Their popular literary magazine was directed toward the children of Scribner's upper-middle-class readers. Dodge's editorial page and advice column, "Jack-in-the-Pulpit" (1873–1896), discussed morals and manners. Targeting the Christian market, *The Girls' Com-*

panion (1902–1949) was a Sunday school periodical emphasizing morality and Christian duty in girls aged eight to twenty. In its advice column, "Light Hearted School Girls," the true Christian girl was encouraged to attend to her role as junior homemaker. *The Brownies' Book* (1920–1921) was a short-lived periodical for African American children in which the overarching "advice" was to promote racial pride and unity. Each number included a column called "The Judge," written as a conversation with readers about conduct, education, family life, and so on, and "The Jury," which consisted of readers' letters.

Today, a girl (of any economic background) is likely to find advice about sexuality, health, fashion, beauty, relationships, and personal problems most easily in the many readily available and inexpensive monthly magazines targeted at teens such as *Seventeen, Young and Modern (YM)*, and *Teen*. The topics most often covered in magazine advice are physical appearance (the search for beauty and the perfect body) and romantic attachments with young men (Currie 1999, 171–202). Research on readers' responses to advice pages within "teenzines" shows that these columns are the favorite feature of an overwhelming majority of girls from thirteen to sixteen years of age (Currie 1999, 162). As in the past with other forms of advice literature, the pleasure that comes from reading "agony columns" in teenzines stems from both the satisfaction felt after gleaning useful information from such columns and the creation of a social community among "real-life" girls who share common concerns.

The messages contained in the typical fashion and beauty teenzine represent a kind of advice literature that many (adults) find misleading and unwelcome.

In response to the myriad accounts of the problems of the lack of self-esteem within female adolescents (published in research by Carol Gilligan, Peggy Orenstein, Mary Pipher, and others), and as a backlash against the overwhelming emphasis in teenzines on physical appearance, consumer goods, and romance, periodicals and books for girls with a feminist approach began proliferating in the 1990s. The sourcebook *The Girls' Guide to Life: How to Take Charge of the Issues That Affect You* by Catherine Dee offers guidance on diverse subjects such as sexual harassment, pay equity, the arts, media, government, and education. *New Moon: The Magazine for Girls and Their Dreams* combines youth participation (through the all-girl editorial board) with positive messages of female empowerment, intelligence, health, and body image for girls aged eight to fourteen. The *New Moon* format supports reader participation through its many write-in columns, including an advice column, "Ask a Girl," which prints readers' responses to problems sent in by troubled readers. The desire to foster girls' autonomy similarly informs the book *Girls Know Best: Advice for Girls from Girls on Just about Everything*, which resulted from a "Girl Writer Contest" designed to encourage girls to be creative and confident in their own ideas about the most effective ways to survive adolescence, sibling rivalry, divorce, boredom, and boyfriend anxiety, among other topics. Girls with access to the Internet can visit websites such as gURL.com (for older teens), a lively and highly interactive website with pages on sports, pets, music, reader artwork, shopping links, and "Help Me Heather," an advice page by an adult who consults with experts to answer readers' e-mailed questions. Readers can also visit the community chat room for girls only. Whether the advice literature originates from an adult or peer source and is accessed through books, newspapers, magazines, or websites, contemporary advice literature continues in the tradition of the nineteenth century—albeit communicating a substantially different message—in helping to create and reinforce the boundaries of conventional girlhood.

Lynne Vallone

See also Child Guidance; Girls' Culture; Girls' Fiction; Girls' Magazines; Hygiene; Reading

References and Further Reading
Campbell, Patricia J. 1979. *Sex Education Books for Young Adults, 1892–1979.* New York: R. R. Bowker.
Currie, Dawn H. 1999. *Girl Talk: Adolescent Readers and Their Magazines.* Toronto: University of Toronto Press.
Dee, Catherine. 1997. *The Girls' Guide to Life: How to Take Charge of the Issues That Affect You.* Boston: Little, Brown.
Ehrenreich, Barbara, and Deirdre English. 1978. *For Her Own Good: 150 Years of the Experts' Advice to Women.* New York: Doubleday.
Roehm, Michelle, comp. 1997. *Girls Know Best: Advice for Girls from Girls on Just about Everything.* Hillsboro, OR: Beyond Words Publishing.

African American Girls in the Twentieth Century

The average black girl born in the United States during the twentieth century faced obstacles few Americans can imagine. The barriers between her and a happy, fulfilling life varied from prodigious to insurmountable during three major historical periods. From the turn of the century through the Great Depression, the lives of African American girls, like those of their parents, were largely defined by

the brutal oppression called Jim Crow—struggling to live under it, resisting it, and moving to the North to try to escape it. Beginning with World War II, the movement for civil rights built momentum, and the lives of African American girls were actively rooted in the civil protest activities of their communities. From the passage of the Civil Rights Act in 1964 until the end of the twentieth century, African American girls were far less separate from the mainstream culture, which brought both advantages and severe problems.

1900 to World War II

As the twentieth century dawned, the American South was under the thrall of Jim Crow. A quarter of a century had passed since the end of Reconstruction and the removal of federal troops from the former Confederate states. In that quarter century, African American freedom had been attacked on all fronts—political, legal, and social. Political rights had ceased to exist entirely as soon as the federal presence exited southern states. The guiding legal principle was "separate but equal," as endorsed by the U.S. Supreme Court. Finally, southern society had reverted to a state as near to that prevailing under slavery as it was possible to achieve, enforced by economic restrictions and by violence. And northern society, as it had since the antebellum years, reflected the racism of the South in its own ways. Those ways, although usually more subtle, were often just as oppressive.

Black girls sought to create strong identities in a world that saw them in blatantly stereotyped terms. Foremost in the dominant culture were images of the mammy, the maid, the temptress, and, for young girls, the pickaninny. Black women in films, on the stage, in books,

A group of students from the National Training School for Women and Girls in Washington, DC. (Library of Congress)

and on the radio were either asexual servants or hypersexual women of loose morals. Against these images, black girls had the weapons of family, community, and education. For all too many, these were not enough. Education, for one thing, was hard to come by.

At the turn of the twentieth century, almost half of African Americans—boys, girls, and adults—were unable to read. At that time, 90 percent of the black population lived in the South, and southern states were simply not willing to provide a decent education to black children. This situation continued throughout this first historical period. According to scholar Valinda Littlefield (1997), "A 1930 survey revealed that eleven Southern states spent an average of $12.57 per black child [per year], as opposed to

$44.31 to educate a white child. At the time, the average expenditure for the nation was $99.00 per child" (17). In other words, Americans were spending $1.20 to educate a black girl in the South for every $10 they spent to educate a white girl in the North. Littlefield goes on to state: "As late as 1937, 64 percent of schools for Southern African Americans were one-teacher schools, and 19 percent were two-teacher schools" (17). She also quotes a description of a typical black school from Pauli Murray's *Proud Shoes: The Story of an American Family:*

West End looked more like a warehouse than a school. It was a dilapidated, rickety, two-story wooden building which creaked and swayed in the wind as if it might collapse. . . .

Outside it was scarred with peeling paint from many winters of rain and snow. At recess we [were] herded into a yard of cracked clay, barren of tree or bush, and played what games we could improvise like hopscotch or spring-board, which we contrived by pulling rotten palings off the wooden fence and placing them on brickbats. . . .

The floors were bare and splintery, the plumbing was leaky, the drinking fountains broken and the toilets in the basement smelly and constantly out of order. We'd have to wade through pools of foul water to get to them. (Cited in Littlefield 1974, 16)

Outside school, life for black girls was even more difficult. The largest proportion of black families were agricultural workers. Some owned their own farms. Far more were sharecroppers or tenant farmers, working land that belonged to white men in exchange for rent and a share of the crop. Every child in a share-cropper family was needed as a "hand." Indeed, white owners often threatened to throw families off their farms if children and women were kept out of the fields. The memoirs of black women are filled with stories from girlhood of picking cotton until their hands bled and coming home from school to pick up a cotton sack and head out to the field.

Like the majority of their mothers, black girls also worked outside the home. In the early decades of the twentieth century, as many as 54.7 percent of black girls ten and older were employed, in contrast to white girls, of whom only 17.9 percent had to work outside their homes during childhood. Black girls found work as domestics, washerwomen, and child care providers. Elizabeth Clark-Lewis described this work life in her book

Living In, Living Out (1996). For the book, she interviewed ninety-seven women who were born in the South and came to the North during the Great Migration, which took place in the early years of the twentieth century. After several months of working with their mothers and other adult women in their families, most of these girls were sent out to work by themselves for at least three months a year. By the time they were nine years old, "all of the women had worked in the house of a white family near their homes as servants." One of them described how it felt to go live with a strange family and work in their house:

On the first job you was scared. Oh, I cried and even ran back home. But they always took you back. Most started at summer—you'd help the white missus all summer and then when school started, you'd go home. You'd get to go home on Sunday during the summer. . . . All summer you worked like a dog! They didn't care you were a child. They saw you as a worker. And they worked you hard. (46)

Working in white homes increased the risk of sexual assault for young black girls. This was true for all girls and young women who worked as domestic servants at that time, but the problem was even worse for African American girls in the South. Enslaved women and girls had been considered the sexual property of their owners and were often forced into terrible acts of resistance. The attitudes of white men in the South changed little when slavery ended. A 1904 article appearing in *The Independent* claimed that "few colored girls reached the age of sixteen without receiving advances from [southern white men] (Lerner et al. 1992,

158). One of the women interviewed by Clark-Lewis explained: "You couldn't be out working 'til you know how people was raped. You'd know how to run, or always not to be in the house with the white man or big sons. Just everyone told you something to keep you from being raped, 'cause it happened, and they told you" (48).

To escape the increasingly severe and violent oppression of the South, African Americans migrated to the North in the 1910s by the tens of thousands. Black men often found jobs in factories in Chicago, Detroit, and a handful of other northern cities. The number of African Americans in Detroit increased from 5,741 in 1910 to 120,066 in 1930. Chicago, meatpacking center of the country, had a black population in 1910 of 44,103 (Hine 1998, 214). By 1930, it was 233,903. Black women and girls, however, did not find work in the automobile plants or the meatpacking houses. For the most part, they continued to do domestic work. Black girls as young as seven or eight years old found themselves caring for siblings while their mothers cleaned whites' houses. Girls of twelve or thirteen were sent by their families in the South to care for the children of brothers and cousins.

Despite the conditions in which they often lived, African American girls were not merely victims of race and gender roles. They were members of a community that was deeply committed to their welfare. One highly visible sign of this commitment came from the black women's club movement. Growing out of the mutual benefit societies and literary groups of the eighteenth and early nineteenth centuries, women's clubs grew in number and force in the 1880s and 1890s. By the early years of the twentieth century, they were providing most of the social services available in black communities. The club women ranged from the daughters and wives of wealthy businessmen to female entrepreneurs to educated domestic workers. They founded homes for the aged and infirm, schools, orphanages, and homes for girls.

Mary Church Terrell, the first president of the National Association of Colored Women (NACW), argued that "the real solution of the race problem lies in the children" (Giddings 1996, 100). The NACW focused on the establishment of day care centers and nurseries to support working women and to educate and provide play activities for their children. The Virginia Federation of Colored Women's Clubs founded a rehabilitation center for troubled girls and the Virginia Industrial School for Colored Girls, which trained black girls in work skills. Victoria Earle Matthews, president of the Brooklyn Women's Club and Woman's Loyal Union, worked with other club women to found the White Rose Home for young working girls. Fredericka Douglass Sprague Perry (granddaughter of abolitionist Frederick Douglass) established the Colored Big Sister Association in 1934 in Kansas City, Missouri. Perry concentrated her efforts on delinquent girls who were unable to obtain state-supported foster home care. These were only a few of the institutions black women created to help black girls.

Educators such as Mary McLeod Bethune, Charlotte Hawkins Brown, and Nannie Helen Burroughs devoted their lives to the uplift of the race and the development of young black girls. Bethune founded the Daytona Normal and Industrial Institute for Negro Girls in Daytona Beach, Florida, in 1904. Her students, all girls, helped Bethune make the sweet potato pies and ice cream she sold to make a down payment on land for the school. At the age of twelve, Charlotte Hawkins Brown organized a kindergarten in the Sunday school of the Union Baptist Church. At nineteen she established the Palmer Institute in 1902 in North Carolina as "a finishing school for young black girls." In 1909, twenty-one-year-old Burroughs established the National Training School for Women and Girls in Washington, D.C. Often called "the School of the 3 B's," it emphasized the Bible, the bath, and the broom. Black girls also benefited throughout the twentieth century from organizations such as the Phyllis Wheatley Clubs and Homes; Jack and Jill Clubs; the Links; and the sororities Alpha Kappa Alpha, Delta Sigma Theta, Sigma Gamma Rho, and Zeta Phi Beta. These organizations enforced communal support of African American girls.

Many black girls also took control over their own lives in adventurous ways. Black entertainers such as Ethel Waters, Aida Overton Walker, Bessie Smith, Gertrude "Ma" Rainey, and Billie Holiday were among thousands of black girls who sang and danced on street corners for tips or appeared in third-rate vaudeville shows. The stereotyping of African Americans as "amusing" and "natural entertainers" allowed them to scrape livings for themselves in these ways while they were still children. Florence Mills was an important source of income for her family by the time she was five or six. At eight, she was traveling as a "pickaninny" in a white vaudeville act. At fourteen, she and two of her sisters formed their own act, and she was on her way to being the first black superstar. The childhood lives of these entertainers illustrate two sides of oppression for poor black girls. Far too often, they were forced to adopt adult roles and responsibilities, but sometimes those roles

offered them a measure of freedom that white and middle-class black girls could not begin to enjoy.

Toward the end of this historical period, the United States faced the Great Depression. The already difficult lives of black girls were further disrupted by this economic crisis. Thousands of tenant farmers were evicted when crop prices fell. Black girls and their families found themselves homeless. Relief efforts, usually administered on a local level, were rife with discrimination. When World War II was declared, jobless fathers and brothers volunteered by the thousands for economic as well as patriotic reasons.

Postwar to 1964

After World War II, African Americans confronted as never before the persistent racism and inequality in American society. Black girls were full participants in the civil rights struggle. In her autobiography, *Soldier: A Poet's Childhood*, June Jordan eloquently says, "there was a war against colored people and I had to become a soldier." Her words are echoed in the lives of countless African American girls. The majority of the ground troops in the civil rights army were black women, and they started very early.

Black girls passed out flyers, stood in the front lines of peaceful demonstrations, and ran mimeograph machines. They cooked for bake sales that kept the Montgomery bus boycott going, and they were arrested for praying at segregated lunch counters and bowling alleys. They were beaten by white police and sprayed with fire hoses. When "separate but equal" was tested in the courts, seven-year-old Linda Brown of Topeka, Kansas, was at the center of the case. Before the final ruling, Linda walked past several schools for whites and even through a railway yard to reach an all-black school. She and her family agreed to become a test case for the National Association for the Advancement of Colored People (NAACP) legal team. The landmark 1954 *Brown v. Board of Education of Topeka, Kansas,* decision found separate schools to be "inherently unequal," overturning the 1896 *Plessy v. Ferguson* decision. A decisive part of the NAACP's strategy involved testimony from psychologists Kenneth and Mamie Clark that black children preferred white dolls to black dolls, confirmation that racism was embedded even in leisure activity, began early, and afflicted children negatively.

Black girls were members of the "Little Rock nine," a group of teenagers who were instrumental in desegregating Central High School in Little Rock, Arkansas, in 1957. Arkansas NAACP president Daisy Bates gathered these students, who were screened and tested for their ability to stand up under pressure, and every move of the group was carefully planned. Then, at the last minute, it was decided that white protest had made the momentous entry through the doors of the school on September 23, 1957, too dangerous. It was postponed. But Bates failed to get the message to one student, Elizabeth Eckford. When Elizabeth arrived alone at the campus, violence broke out. She was surrounded by white segregationists who jeered at her and threatened her. Two sympathetic white people may very well have saved her from being lynched. A photograph of Eckford walking with head high and books clutched to her chest was printed in newspapers across the country, and she became a symbol of the character of black youth.

All of the girls in the Little Rock nine, which included Minnijean Brown, Thelma Mothershed, Melba Patillo, Gloria

Ray, and Carlotta Walls, were kicked, called names, and harassed unmercifully for the entire school year. In her 1995 book, *Warriors Don't Cry,* Melba Patillo Beals recounts her fears not only about mob violence but about her clothes, friends, and dating.

When Ruby Bridges and three other girls desegregated schools in New Orleans in 1961, the city rioted for days. Ruby prayed twice a day for the people crowded around Frantz Elementary school when she entered. Anne Moody disclosed the radicalizing effect segregation had on her in *Coming of Age in Mississippi* (1976). Her poverty, her blackness, and her girlhood were handicaps in rural Mississippi, but Anne turned them in her favor as a young civil rights worker for the NAACP and the Congress on Racial Equality (CORE). In *Pushed Backed to Strength: A Black Woman's Journey Home* (1995), Gloria Wade-Gayles stated that her civil rights activism was born out of a girlhood in Memphis, Tennessee, filled with love, family, a segregated community, and true faith to tackle racism and sexism.

One of the most infamous events during the civil rights movement involved Addie Mae Collins, Denise McNair, Carole Robertson, and Cynthia Wesley. The Alabama Ku Klux Klan bombed their Birmingham church on September 15, 1963, ending their young lives. Three of the girls were fourteen, and one was eleven, and they had gathered in the church basement for choir practice. Joan Baez's song "Birmingham Sunday" and director Spike Lee's 1997 documentary *4 Little Girls* emphasize the loss caused by the bombing and the contributions these girls could have made. The four little girls are best remembered for making

Americans look segregationist hatred squarely in the face.

1964 to the Present
The passage of the Civil Rights Act of 1964 changed life for all American girls. It took a few years for the legal changes to begin to have an impact, but educational, economic, and social conditions were forever altered. Black girls and boys found themselves bussed into white schools. Their college applications began to be accepted. By the 1970s, African American girls had opportunities to become more full-fledged American citizens. In addition to being race workers or civil rights activists, black girls could finally dream of becoming successful businesswomen or even elected officials as their mothers and aunts broke into all realms of American life. Shirley Chisholm ran for president in 1972. The Supremes became the most successful American rock and roll group of the 1960s. Fashion model Naomi Sims became the first black woman to appear on the cover of *Ladies' Home Journal* (1968) and *Life* (1969).

Black girls redefined their images along with their lives and ambitions. Some African American girls have fond memories of straightening their hair and wearing ponytails in the 1950s, but during the late 1960s and 1970s the "natural" Afro won favor. Both hairstyles symbolized beauty and the revolutionary politics of the civil rights and Black Power movements. By the 1990s, African American girls opted for intricately braided hairstyles like those worn by the talented athletes Serena and Venus Williams. They often spent more time beading their hair than it took them to win a tennis match at Wimbledon.

Since the 1970s, black women have begun to talk about black girlhood in important ways. They have revealed in literature and film the suffering of black girls at the hands of both white and black men. Maya Angelou's paternal grandmother, Annie Henderson, helped her recover from sexual assault at the hands of her mother's boyfriend. Similarly, talk show host Oprah Winfrey suffered sexual molestation by an uncle and recovered at her grandmother's home. Both women spoke out about this abuse, as did many others. African Americans were not generally receptive to having their secrets exposed to the entire American public, but "lifting a veil of silence" about sexual molestations was important in legitimizing the experiences of black girls.

Gains made during the civil rights movement dissipated with the Republican presidential administrations in the 1980s. Economically, African Americans fared worse in the late twentieth century than they had in the 1950s. The fallout of this instability is reflected in the lives of black girls. The 1990 census revealed that almost half of all black families were headed by single mothers, and 46.1 percent of families headed by black women were under the federal poverty line. The same is true of only 24.8 percent of single white mothers (Hine 1998, 311).

For young black girls in the United States race is so persistent and pervasive an issue that it masks many other social ills. Black girls face poverty, gangs, teen pregnancy, acquired immunodeficiency syndrome (AIDS), and serious unemployment rates. Instead of fortifying family structures, grandmothers and extended families are now too often the primary caregivers as black men and women succumb to drugs and the penal-industrial

African American girls play at St. Ambrose Day Camp, a camp for inner-city children. (Shirley Zeiberg)

complex (Smith and Horten 1997, 355–358). Yet black girls defy these struggles and stereotypes on a daily basis with grace, pride, femininity, the undaunted faith of their ancestors, vision, and hope. That too is African American girlhood in twentieth-century America.

Delia Crutchfield Cook
and Kathleen Thompson

See also Enslaved Girls of African Descent; Free Girls of African Descent; Work

References and Further Reading

Angelou, Maya. 1996. *I Know Why the Caged Bird Sings*. Reprint, New York: Random House.
Beals, Melba Patillo. 1995. *Warriors Don't Cry*. New York: Pocket Books.
Boyd, Barbara. 1993. *In the Company of My Sisters: Black Women and Self-Esteem*. New York: Penguin Books.
Carroll, Rebecca. 1997. *Sugar in the Raw: Voices of Young Black Girls in America*. New York: Crown Press.
Clark-Lewis, Elizabeth. 1996. *Living In, Living Out: African American Domestics and the Great Migration*. New York: Kodansha International.
Collins, Patricia Hill. 2000. *Black Feminist Thought*. Reprint, New York: Routledge.
Comer, James P., and Alvin F. Poussaint. 1992. *Raising Black Children*. New York: Penguin Books.
Gibbs, Jewelle Taylor. 1985. "City Girls: Psychological Adjustment of Urban Black Adolescent Females." *Sage: A Scholarly Journal on Black Women* 2, no. 2: 28–36.

Giddings, Paula. 1996. *When and Where I Enter.* New York: William Morrow.

Grant, Linda. 1984. "Black Females' 'Place' in Desegregated Classrooms." *Sociology of Education* 57 (April): 98–111.

Greenfield, Eloise. 1993. *Childtimes: A Three-Generation Memoir.* New York: Harper.

Hine, Darlene Clark, ed. 1997. *Facts on File Encyclopedia of Black Women in America.* New York: Facts on File.

Hine, Darlene Clark, and Kathleen Thompson. 1998. *A Shining Thread of Hope: The History of Black Women in America.* New York: Broadway Books.

Hine, Darlene Clark, Elsa Barkley-Brown, and Rosalyn Terborg-Penn, eds. 1992. *Black Women in America: An Historical Encyclopedia.* Brooklyn: Carlson Publishing.

hooks, bell. 1996. *Bone Black: Memories of Girlhood.* New York: Henry Holt.

Jones, Jacqueline. 1986. *Labor of Love, Labor of Sorrow: Black Women, Work and the Family from Slavery to the Present.* New York: Vintage.

Jordan, June. 2000. *Soldier: A Poet's Childhood.* New York: Basic Books.

Leadbetter, Bonnie, and Niobe Way, eds. 1996. *Urban Girls: Resisting Stereo-types, Creating Identities.* New York: New York University Press.

Lerner, Gerda, et al. 1992. *Black Women in White America: A Documentary History.* New York: Random House.

Lewis, Mary C. 1988. *Herstory: Black Female Rites of Passage.* Chicago: African American Images.

Littlefield, Valinda. 1997. "Introduction." In *Facts on File Encyclopedia of Black Women in America.* Edited by Darlene Clark Hine. New York: Facts on File.

Moody, Anne. 1976. *Coming of Age in Mississippi.* Reprint, New York: Dell.

Roberts, T., et al. 1997. *Am I the Last Virgin? Ten African American Reflections on Sex and Love.* New York: Aladdin Paperbacks.

Rooks, Noliwe M. 1996. *Hair Raising: Beauty, Culture, and African American Women.* New Brunswick, NJ: Rutgers University Press.

Shaw, Stephanie J. 1996. *What a Woman Ought to Be and to Do: Black Professional Women Workers during the Jim Crow Era.* Chicago: University of Chicago Press.

Smith, Dianne. 2000. *Womanish Black Girls: Dancing Contradictions of Resistance.* New York: Peter Lang.

Smith, Jessie Carney, and Carrell P. Horten. 1997. *Statistical Record of Black America.* 4th ed. Detroit: Gale.

Snyder, Thomas. 1993. *120 Years of American Education: A Statistical Portrait.* Washington, DC: Government Printing Office.

Wade-Gayles, Gloria Jean. 1995. *Pushed Back to Strength: A Black Woman's Journey Home.* New York: Avon Books.

———. 1998. *Father Songs: Testimonies by African-American Sons and Daughters.* Boston: Beacon Press.

Way, Niobe. 1998. *Everyday Courage: The Lives and Stories of Urban Teenagers.* New York: New York University Press.

Wharton, Linda F. 1983. "The Significance of Black American Children's Singing Games in an Educational Setting." *The Journal of Negro Education* 52, no. 1 (Winter): 46–56.

White, Renee T. 1999. *Putting Risk in Perspective: Black Teenage Lives in the Era of AIDS.* Lanham, MD: Rowman and Littlefield.

Allowances and Spending Money

The practice of giving girls allowances developed in the early twentieth century, when children's spending habits became a subject of concern and an object of reform. Girls' increasing participation in the burgeoning culture of consumption as purchasers of movie tickets, clothing, candy, and toys not only provoked inter-generational tensions over the proper use of spending money but also raised broad-er concerns about how to tame children's seemingly boundless impulse to buy. Parents, child experts, and educators conceived various strategies to regulate children's use of spending money, includ-ing allowances and mandatory savings bank programs in the public schools. Allowances, however, were a decidedly middle-class phenomenon during the first half of the twentieth century. As a result, middle-class girls who did not work but received allowances often enjoyed more financial autonomy than wage-earning, working-class girls who gave their families most, if not all, of their incomes.

Predating the introduction of allowances, concern with children's spending initially led to the formation of school savings banks in the late nineteenth century. Many believed that children were driven by powerful acquisitive instincts that made them incapable of postponing gratification. To stifle these spendthrift impulses, the school savings bank movement sought to make lessons in thrift a regular feature of public education. Beginning modestly in the mid-1880s and gradually becoming a national phenomenon in the early twentieth century, school banks required girls and boys to deposit money on a weekly basis in hopes that regular practice in saving would eventually become habit. Although student bankers enjoyed some adult banking privileges such as receiving interest on their accounts, schools strictly regulated withdrawals in order to discourage "foolish" purchases. Progressive reformers advocated such compulsory saving as a way to Americanize immigrant children and stem the growth of pauperism, welfare dependency, intemperance, and crime.

For many immigrant families, the morality of family obligation imposed its own form of discipline on the spending of adolescent daughters—perhaps even more effectively than the institutional restraints of school banking. During the late nineteenth and early twentieth centuries, limited family resources and the pull of family duty circumscribed the spending of adolescent immigrant daughters who had left school to join the work-

force. Though wage earners, immigrant daughters were expected to relinquish their unopened pay envelopes to their mothers in deference to family needs. Although immigrant parents often permitted wage-earning sons to pay half their wages for board and retain the rest for themselves, no such allowances were made for adolescent daughters. Immigrant daughters encountered resistance and family displeasure when they attempted to extend their financial independence by withholding some of their paychecks or sneaking money from their envelopes to spend on themselves.

During the buoyant 1920s, enthusiasm for thrift education reached beyond those who sought to control the lower classes. School savings banks adopted a new mission as bulwarks against the reckless pleasure-seeking that allegedly typified middle-class youth. But the spendthrift habits of the flapper generation also highlighted the irrelevance of compulsory saving to an increasingly affluent population of middle-class children—a group well enough supplied with nickels and dimes not to miss the few they ritually deposited on school bank day.

By the 1920s, child experts had come to view allowances as the solution to the money training problems and needs of middle-class children. Proponents of children's allowances rejected the school banking movement's exclusive focus on saving, arguing that teaching children the value of money also required teaching them to be wise consumers. Though sharing the school banking movement's eagerness to discourage foolish child spending, allowance advocates sought to do so by teaching children to spend within a budget. Critical of sentimental parents who haphazardly doled out spending money on demand, allowance boosters believed that lack of a system in children's money experiences accounted for their lack of money sense. By contrast, a weekly allowance—a regular but fixed supply of spending money—would help systematize both children's learning and their spending. Reflecting the progressive penchant for order and scientific management, allowance advocates sought to instill economic responsibility by rationalizing children's money training.

Popularizing their ideas in parenting guidebooks and women's magazines such as *Good Housekeeping* and *Parents' Magazine,* child experts regarded allowances as strictly educational money set aside for children's consumer training. They criticized using allowance money as a payment for household chores, a reward for good grades or good behavior, or a punishment for delinquencies. Doing so, they argued, confounded principles of duty and family obligation with the principles of the marketplace. As experimental money, allowances entrusted girls and boys with responsibility not only for their own spending choices but for their spending mistakes. Child experts believed such experiential learning was more effective than parental admonitions or interventions in helping children improve their taste; enhance their fiscal awareness; and gain a better sense of their favorite colors, flavors, and toys. Experts also believed allowances helped children develop habits of saving and restraint because children came to value saving as a means to obtain goods whose value exceeded their weekly allowance.

The introduction of allowances was an important measure of the democratization of middle-class family life in the early twentieth century. Allowances both acknowledged and elevated the economic status of dependent children. Child experts stressed the importance of allowances to children's sense of power and independence and recommended that parents expand them as children grew into adolescence in order to combat resentment of economic dependence. Allowance money thus entitled middle-class children to spend long before having to earn. Such economic entitlements, however, did not necessarily require the dissolution of parental control. Though allowance money gave girls and boys greater spending freedom, it also promised parents an end to children's incessant begging and a means to mold children's taste to adult standards.

Though child experts recommended allowances as important consumer training for both boys and girls, gender neutrality did not always inform their assessments of the spending needs and problems of girls. Some viewed adolescent girls as more susceptible to the fashion of their peers and powerless against the sway of shop windows, echoing long-standing stereotypes of women's alleged vulnerability to consumer excess. By their lights, adolescent girls threatened to strain the family's pocketbook and goodwill with their perpetual demands for new clothes. Faced with fewer opportunities to earn spending money than boys, middle-class girls relied much more on gifts, allowances, or parental largesse for their source of disposable income. Within some middle-class families, expanded clothing allowances for girls became a way to reduce family friction, keep adolescent resentment at bay, and gain some control over girls' stepped-up requests for clothes. More commonly, however, gifts and parental indulgence rather than allowances boosted the spending-money supply of middle-class girls. As sociologists Robert and Helen Lynd reported in *Middletown*, their mid-1920s study of Muncie, Indiana, a mere 47 percent of girls received spending money through earnings and allowances compared to 85 percent of boys. Deprived of the opportunity to earn and manage a part of their money, Muncie girls not only lacked boys' habits of financial independence but readily manipulated parents in their quest for greater funds. For some girls, economic dependence brought unintended rewards. As one Muncie high school senior insisted, "Some of us don't want an allowance; you can get more without one."

Within working-class families during the interwar years, adolescent girls often earned money but enjoyed far less financial autonomy than their middle-class counterparts. Coming from economically disadvantaged families in which children's earnings were essential to the family economy, wage-earning daughters continued to turn over most, if not all, of their paychecks to their families. By contrast, sons typically retained a portion of their earnings, owing partly to their higher wages but also to gendered expectations that honored male autonomy in the marketplace. Although some wage-earning daughters negotiated a greater degree of economic autonomy for themselves than previous generations—paying board, for example, in exchange for control over their earnings—expectations of filial duty still limited the economic autonomy of most.

Working-class girls nevertheless made demands on the family budget for clothing and recreation, and family conflicts over such expenditures were often animated by long-standing gendered assumptions about women's vanity, their propensity for self-indulgence, and their use of earnings as "pin money." A harsh economic reality, however, lay at the root of these family conflicts over girls' spending. Because of their low wages and higher clothing expenses, girls often spent more of the family's resources than was offset by their meager wages.

The Great Depression had a varied impact on attitudes toward girls' spending. It intensified expectations within both working-class and middle-class families that girls should adopt a cooperative attitude and not place too many demands on the family budget. In keeping with traditional ideals of feminine self-sacrifice, girls' economic obligations were to their families before themselves. Depression-era advice columnists also urged adolescent girls to be more respectful of their dates' wallet by offering to pay their own way, shunning taxis for cheaper public transportation, and opting for less expensive entertainment and items on the restaurant menu. At the same time, however, the Depression also liberalized attitudes toward spending and reinforced the efficacy of allowances as a form of consumer training. During the 1920s, allowance boosters had discouraged borrowing as a violation of the basic principle of an allowance—learning to live within a budget. By the 1930s, however, the modern world of installment buying and easy credit had persuaded allowance advocates of the need to give girls experience in borrowing as well as earning and spending. As the New Deal linked consumption to economic recovery, children's spending impulses also underwent a dramatic reassessment. Once seen as dangerous and insatiable, children's consumer desires were now evidence of a well-adjusted personality, and excessive thriftiness signaled a lackluster imagination. Even cases of consumer excess found sympathetic treatment, being understood as signs of unmet psychological needs rather than moral failure.

Although the ideological rationale for children's allowances had been firmly established in earlier eras, the heyday of children's allowances did not arrive until the 1950s. Children were among the primary beneficiaries of the rising standard of living in the postwar United States. According to a 1960 survey by *Seventeen*, the average teenage girl had a weekly income of $9.53. Receiving allowances in greater numbers than ever before, girls developed a strong sense of their economic and cultural clout as consumers, a sense advertisers all too eagerly reinforced as they aggressively sought the brand loyalty and disposable incomes of teens. As allowances became increasingly commonplace during the last four decades of the twentieth century, parents and children also came to see them more as an economic entitlement than a consumer training tool. Since the 1960s, allowance rates have climbed along with the cost of living and children's sense of economic entitlement. According to a 1999 Rand youth poll, the typical weekly allowance for high school students ranged from $30 to $46, with girls receiving on average $5 more than boys. In the face of aggressive mass marketing aimed at children, child experts and financial advisers have continued to press for the educational value of allowances, reviving older discourses that speak in new ways to wider concerns about the potential perils of permissive parents and gullible child consumers.

Lisa Jacobson

See also Consumer Culture; Girls and Sweets; Girls' Culture; Work

References and Further Reading
Benson, Susan Porter. 1998. "Gender, Generation, and Consumption in the United States: Working-Class Families in the Interwar Period." Pp. 223–240 in *Getting and Spending: European and American Consumer Societies in the Twentieth Century.* Edited by Susan Strasser, Charles McGovern, and Matthias Judt. Cambridge: Cambridge University Press.
Jacobson, Lisa. Forthcoming. *Raising Consumers: Children, Childrearing, and the American Mass Market, 1890–1940.* New York: Columbia University Press.
Lynd, Robert S., and Helen Merrell Lynd. 1929. *Middletown: A Study in American Culture.* New York: Harcourt, Brace and World.
Peiss, Kathy. 1986. *Cheap Amusements: Working Women and Leisure in Turn-of-the-Century New York.* Philadelphia: Temple University Press.
Rand Youth Poll. 1999. Cited in Kathy Kristof, "Do Your Kids Know That Money Doesn't Grow on Christmas Trees?" *Los Angeles Times* (December 3, 2000): A1.
Zelizer, Viviana A. 1985. *Pricing the Priceless Child: The Changing Social Value of Children.* New York: Basic Books.

American Girls Collection

Extremely popular among eight- to twelve-year-old girls, the American Girls Collection is a set of seven dolls with accompanying books and accessories representing seven different phases in American history. Pleasant Company, which manufactures American Girl dolls, claims as its mission the enriching of girls' play through educational toys that impart positive messages and a sense of the history of girlhood in the United States. Although the company now produces a wide array of consumer goods for girls, the flagship product remains the historical American Girl dolls, 18-inch cloth and vinyl dolls, each associated with a given year: Felicity (1774), Josefina (1824), Kirsten (1854), Addy (1864), Samantha (1904), Kit (1934), and Molly (1944). At the heart of the very successful appeal to parents is the interweaving of readership into the marketing of the fairly expensive dolls and accessories. Each doll is the protagonist of seven books that offer a window onto the time period to which she is linked, and every doll must be bought with at least one of these books. Although the dolls are not available in retail stores, the books can be found in any bookstore and in public and school libraries and have made their way into many school curricula. The books play a further marketing function: the clothing, furniture, and objects featured in the stories (and on display in the books' illustrations) are also for sale.

Pleasant Company was founded in Middleton, Wisconsin, in 1986 by Pleasant Rowland, a former elementary school teacher, television reporter and anchor, and writer and publisher of educational materials. Kirsten, Samantha, and Molly were the first dolls in the series, with Felicity following in 1991, Addy in 1993, Josefina in 1997, and Kit in 2000. Matching historical fashions for girls were introduced in 1987 so that girl and doll could dress alike. In 1991 the company began to sponsor American Girl activities at living history museums, beginning with "Felicity's Elegant Tea Party" in Colonial Williamsburg. Programs are now featured at several sites, including Greenfield Village in Dearborn, Michigan, and Heurich House Museum in Washington, D.C. Activities like "Samantha's Ice Cream Social," "Josefina's Fiesta," and an American Girl fashion show travel around the country. A school curriculum based on the American Girls Collection was introduced in 1993. Company offerings

expanded further in 1995 to include contemporary dolls and books and girls' clothing. Products now include several different lines of dolls, a magazine, *American Girl*, games, crafts, an array of books and CD-ROMs, an extensive line of girls' clothing and accessories, a television show, and a stage revue and restaurant at American Girl Place, a theme store in Chicago.

Pleasant Company has been remarkably successful in staking a claim to a niche market and steadily expanding it. Many elements of the American Girls Collection have been copied by other toy companies, including creating historical dolls, making dolls the same approximate size (and the strategy of sizing one's dolls differently from industry standards so outfits are not interchangeable), and pairing dolls with books. Girls' enthusiastic response to American Girl dolls includes a lively Internet subculture. Many girls maintain and many more write into American Girl fan websites, which include discussions about American Girl dolls, pictures of girls and their dolls, and often polls that allow visitors to vote for their favorite American Girl dolls.

The books, billed in the American Girl catalogue as "historical fiction," underscore Pleasant Company's emphasis on education and learning and are widely praised by parents, teachers, and the press for making history appealing to girls. The books locate each of the seven dolls in a different American landscape and historical context, using larger cultural events as the backdrop for girls' stories that center around personal problem-solving and conflict-resolution skills. Felicity Merriman is a shopkeeper's daughter in Colonial Williamsburg, Virginia, where her stories play out against the events of the American Revolution. Josefina Montoya, the only doll whose books are available in Spanish, lives on a ranch in New Mexico ninety years before statehood, and her family's struggles include change within a traditional community (Josefina and her sisters, unlike their mother before them, learn to read) and the effects of contact with Caucasian America. Pioneer girl Kirsten Larson has immigrated with her family from Sweden to Minnesota, where Kirsten learns English and, disregarding parental opposition, befriends a Native American girl. The Josefina and Kirsten books attend to the American experience of difference, assimilation, and accommodation. Discrimination and racism are addressed more directly in the books about Addy Walker, a North Carolina slave girl who, with her mother, escapes to freedom in Philadelphia. Although Addy is separated from her father and siblings in the first book, the family reunites by the series' conclusion and, despite experiencing racism in Philadelphia, is hopeful about the future after emancipation. Samantha Parkington, the most romantic figure among the seven and the most popular doll, is a beautiful orphan whose series begins with her living with a cold but kind wealthy grandmother in New Bedford, New York, and ends with her adoption by her dashing young uncle and his glamorous suffragist wife in New York City. Kit Kittredge, who grows up in Cincinnati during the Great Depression, learns about thrift and selflessness as her family struggles to cope with their reversal of fortune. Molly McIntire lives in Illinois during World War II; her mother works for the Red Cross, while her father, a doctor, is serving in England; his safe return is the climax of the final book.

At the end of each book, after the conclusion of the story, a section called "A Peek into the Past" offers several pages of historical information and archival photographs corresponding in a general way to issues raised in the story. For example, the book in which Addy escapes from slavery features a "Peek into the Past" about the slave trade and plantation system; educational and career options for girls at the turn of the century are discussed in the book in which Samantha's Aunt Cornelia gives a rousing suffragist speech in a park. Although the stories themselves are illustrated with colorful paintings of scenes and objects, the historical images are, by contrast, photographs, mostly black and white, and much more somber in their realism. These images, drawn from museums, libraries, galleries, archives, historical societies, and private collections, testify to the thorough research invested in each of the historical sketches. The sketches, which are more explicit about social and economic difficulties than the stories, nonetheless do tend to stress progress and improvement, usually ending on an upbeat note. American Girl history is noticeably positive: thus Addy, for example, despite her recent escape from slavery and the near-poverty in which her family labors, enjoys lots of nice toys, furniture, and clothing, and her possessions are exactly parallel to those "owned" by the other dolls, including the affluent Samantha.

Although the books particularize the experience of seven different periods and regions in the American past, the overarching emphasis, frequently mentioned in the catalogue, is that American girls across time and space are fundamentally the same. The structure of each book series and the layouts of the catalogue serve to underscore this message. The books have identical titles and follow the same cyclical pattern: the first book in each set (*Meet Felicity, Meet Josefina, Meet Kirsten,* and so on) takes place during the summer of the protagonist's ninth year, the second during that autumn, followed by a Christmas story, a springtime birthday story, a summer story, and a final winter story (*Changes for Felicity, Changes for Josefina, Changes for Kirsten*). The lessons each girl learns in her books are much the same, and the ways in which she learns them are quite similar: in one recurrent story line, by befriending another girl despite differences between them, and in another, by risking the consequences of disobeying an adult. All the stories focus on thoughtful decisionmaking, and the girls' choices are rewarded with treats: special foods, fancy dresses, and toys. Each girl has a cherished pet and an even more cherished doll. Although the meticulously detailed accessories and clothing reflect specific historical periods, the exacting parallelism of the catalogue offerings and the books produces remarkable visual conformity: the girls' poses on the covers of the corresponding books are identical, as are the catalogue layouts, with the dolls always standing or sitting in exactly the same relation to an array of toys, clothes, and home furnishings.

Although the stories all focus on the hardship of each historical situation, the catalogue clearly conveys that being an American girl means to like entertaining, home furnishings, and clothes. Critics note the materialism of the American Girl product line. The focus on acquisition is emphasized by the way in which the books themselves function as catalogues by providing illustrations for those outfits and objects in the stories that are for sale as toys. History and commerce make some conflicting demands. The insistent consumerism of the prod-

uct line calls into question aspects of its historical authenticity, imagining as it does that American girls have always owned extensive wardrobes and lots of toys; certainly the eighteenth- and nineteenth-century dolls have more manufactured consumer goods than real girls in those periods and places. In addition, the company is lauded for its sensitivity to multiculturalism, although marketing considerations undoubtedly place some limits on inclusiveness. Even as the line has become more racially and ethnically representative with the additions of Addy and Josefina, Muslim and Jewish girls have not been introduced, presumably because Christmas is not only the subject of the third book but the real lifeblood of the company, the primary selling season for toy makers.

Pleasant Company prides itself on providing positive images and messages for girls and is widely praised for depicting girls as active, independent, and capable. American Girl products, from the books to the Chicago stage show, are celebrated for offering girls an alternative to mass-market girls' culture, with its sexualization of even very young girls and preoccupation with appearances, body image, and the conventional trappings of femininity. The books consistently represent their protagonists as lively and strong-minded, and the dolls have sturdy, even chunky bodies, of realistic and healthy proportions. The constant point of comparison is the Barbie doll with its much-criticized body shape and its play context of clothes and glamour. Pleasant Company deliberately positions itself against cheap, disposable toys; the line's genesis, according to a corporate history published on the company website and occasionally in catalogues, was in Pleasant Rowland's frustrated search for a high-quality Christmas gift for a niece. Among the salient differences between a Barbie and a Molly is the cost. At $82 for a doll with a paperback book ($88 for hardcover), $20 outfits, and furniture costing up to $155, American Girl dolls are priced for an upscale market and are not, presumably, available for the kind of casual and irreverent treatment Barbies receive at the hands of their young owners. American Girl products are also commended for encouraging girls to develop their imaginations through reading and interactive media play: a CD-ROM lets girls script their own dramas using the American Girl characters. However, the books present girls in highly normative domestic settings and as interested and involved in homemaking chores, nurturing of others, and very well-mannered. When the press covers American Girl events at local venues—tea parties and ice cream socials, often packed—abundant appreciative attention is showered on girls clamoring to learn "old-fashioned" social graces. Skeptical observers question whether in looking to the past the company does, in fact, help liberate girls from the pressures and constraints of modern American culture, or whether the focus on etiquette, clothes, home decor, and ardent consumerism reinforces traditional and sexist social roles.

Gina Hausknecht

See also Dolls; Girls' Fiction; Nancy Drew Mysteries; Play; Reading

References and Further Reading
Acosta-Alzuru, Maria Carolina. 1999. "The American Girl Dolls: Constructing American Girlhood through Representation, Identity, and Consumption." Ph.D. dissertation, University of Georgia.
Cross, Gary. 1997. *Kids' Stuff: Toys and the Changing World of American Childhood.* Cambridge, MA: Harvard University Press.
Inness, Sherrie A. 1998. "'Anti-Barbies': The American Girls Collection and Political Ideologies." Pp. 164–183 in *Delinquents and Debutantes: Twentieth-Century American Girls' Cultures.* Edited by Sherrie A. Inness. New York: New York University Press.

Arts and Crafts

Arts and crafts is an activity practiced by American girls from colonial times to the present that involved the production of material items for both functional and decorative purposes. Throughout American history, girls from diverse backgrounds have learned such skills as sewing, weaving, spinning, painting, and pottery making from elder members of their families and communities. The meaning of craft production for girls has changed over time, evolving from work that was part of the family economy in early America to a leisure activity rooted in peer culture in the late nineteenth and twentieth centuries. Although there is a vast literature on the decorative and folk arts in America, more attention should be paid to the history of arts and crafts as a social and cultural practice of American girls.

In the eighteenth century, most young white women in America lived on farms with their families. A gendered division of labor governed their households: fathers oversaw financial, agricultural, and public functions, and mothers managed domestic duties. Mothers taught their daughters domestic skills and assigned them a variety of tasks, such as washing, ironing, cooking, and cleaning. Daughters learned the crafts of soap and candle making, spinning, weaving, and sewing as part of their sex-role socialization. Girls learned to sew and mend as preparation for their domestic roles as housewives. Clothwork was the primary duty of young women in the early American farm household. Many girls spent the majority of their time spinning wool or weaving flax into cloth. Diaries reveal the monotony of this work. However, the drudgery was overcome at social gatherings like quilting bees, where young women worked side by side at sewing or exchanged tasks to help one another. Young women were so tied to cloth production that the spinning wheel came to symbolize femininity and proper domestic character in early America.

Although the spinning wheel stood for feminine work, the loom was equally important to women's household production by the late eighteenth century. Once the craft of male artisans, weaving became a feminized skill after 1750 as more households owned looms, and more men found opportunities to earn wages for their skilled labor in the expanding consumer market. Weaving allowed young women to significantly contribute to the household economy, giving them a sense of personal satisfaction and material gain. They produced cloth items for their families and came to dominate weaving in some New England communities where friends and neighbors sought their skills. Surviving rugs and coverlets show that clothwork was also a medium for creativity. But in the "age of homespun," the practice of spinning, weaving, and sewing constituted the work of domestic life and had genuine economic value in the early American family.

Privileged families in the eighteenth and early nineteenth centuries sent their girls to private schools and special academies, where girls received instruction in painting and needlework in addition to reading and writing. Girls learned embroidery through the making of samplers, one of the most important art forms in early America. On linen or silk, girls stitched domestic or outdoor scenes with images of people, animals, or flowers. They also stitched poetic or biblical verses, numbers, the alphabet, their own names, and the dates of their work. Samplers served as pedagogical tools, and their designs conveyed religious and domestic values. The long and intricate process of making samplers taught girls discipline and sewing skills they could use as adult women in married life. Many young women also learned to paint with stencils, a process known as theorem painting. By the early nineteenth century, both painting and embroidery had become signs of status and represented proper feminine accomplishments.

Work dominated the lives of enslaved African American girls prior to the Civil War. Historians believe that childhood was brief for slave children because most began to labor like adults at age four or five. Girls worked in the fields, cared for other children, and did household chores. But free black women and slaves who served as house servants were able to develop special skills, such as soap and candle making, cooking, and basket weaving. Textile work, above all, was a valued craft for African American women. Free young women learned sewing, dressmaking, spinning, and weaving from their elders and then either sold or used their finished products. This strong tradition of textile work carried over into the post–Civil War period, when black women made quilts that expressed their creativity and their resistance to oppression. For example, historians believe the Bible quilts of Harriet

Powers, a former slave, exemplify the craft skills and values of African American women during this period. Textiles, once the labor of both slave and free black women, were also art forms and sources of tradition learned by girls and passed on from generation to generation.

In the mid-nineteenth century, the rise and expansion of the middle class enabled more families to release their daughters from duties associated with the family economy. Industrialization transformed the household, changing it from a place of production to a site of consumption. The new market economy employed middle-class fathers outside the home on behalf of the entire family. Mothers hired domestic help and purchased goods from the market. No longer needed for baking bread and spinning wool, girls lost their economic function in the home, and consequently the craft traditions that were so central to household production shifted from being a form of work to a source of leisure.

In the late nineteenth century, girls began to attend public high schools at an unprecedented rate, and as a consequence, their role in the home became unclear, especially because of their newfound leisure time. Filling the leisure time of girls became a major concern among members of the middle class, who feared that new commercialized forms of entertainment would corrupt the morals of the nation's youth. As immigrant working girls flooded dance halls, vaudeville shows, and amusement parks seeking pleasure and freedom as a reward for their labors, middle-class parents worried that their own daughters, freed from housework, would explore these new forms of recreation. Department stores, also new centers of entertainment, were very attractive to middle-class girls.

These attractions and the increasing consumer orientation of American youth stimulated several women writers to promote arts and crafts as a healthy and productive alternative activity for girls.

Between 1880 and 1915, Lina and Adelia Beard, Helen Campbell, Lilla Elizabeth Kelley, A. Neely Hall, and Dorothy Perkins presented girls with "new ideas for work and play" in a series of "activity books" geared to adolescent girls (Beard and Beard 1902). The Beards encouraged girls to learn spinning and weaving, the traditional crafts of the preindustrial household. Kelley gave advice on knitting and crocheting, and Campbell offered guidelines for making dollhouses, wax flowers, and wood carvings. These authors also directed girls on furniture making and included instructions for building bookshelves, stools, and dressers. Woodworking required strong physical activity, as did hiking and camping, just two of the many outdoor activities that were also promoted by these authors.

By advocating arts and crafts, the writers of activity books sought to reconstitute girls' productive roles in the home by giving them new forms of useful work. They tried to draw them away from the lures of the commercial market by promoting the value of homemade items over mass-produced items. These books also promoted a new model of American girlhood, one that was active, healthy, and useful, to combat the image of the idle Victorian girl who spent her days quietly and passively in the parlor. In this way, the Beards and other writers who promoted arts and crafts were part of a feminist revision of American girlhood.

At the same time that activity books encouraged girls to take up craftwork, adult men and women began to participate in the American arts and crafts movement. Based on the ideas of the English craftsmen John Ruskin and William Morris, the movement responded to industrialization, urbanization, and modernization in the United States by calling for a return to manual production, craftsmanship, and the functionality and simplicity of material goods. Middle-class Americans who felt disillusioned with mechanization or idle from a lack of physical work could reinvigorate their creative skills and manual talents through glassmaking, pottery making, furniture making, bookbinding, and ironwork.

Leaders of the arts and crafts movement tried to disseminate and institutionalize their craft ideals in school training programs. Gustav Stickley, the founder of *The Craftsman*, believed that crafts could save children from the negative impact of modern industrial life by providing occupation for the idle rich and uplifting poor and immigrant children. In Chicago schools, for example, privileged students had courses in aesthetic culture and built furniture and household items that reflected the tastes of the larger arts and crafts movement. Manual training programs for working-class children prepared pupils for work in adult life. Chicago's Jewish Manual Training School instructed children in drawing, painting, and design and taught girls lessons in sewing and cutting for future garment work. In schools, girls learned craft skills deemed appropriate for their gender.

Efforts to revive and instill craft traditions in American girls carried over into the twentieth century with the formation of girls' outdoor organizations, such as the Girl Pioneers, the Girl Scouts, and the Camp Fire Girls. As middle-class Americans tried to get "back to nature" and escape the problems and stress of urban, industrial life, scouting movements, like activity books, encouraged girls to experience nature and pursue handicrafts in the outdoors. Girls would knit and sew in the outdoors, but more often they were encouraged to imitate Native American craft traditions and make pottery, Navajo blankets, and Indian dolls. Nature offered girls inspiration for art designs and a way to re-create the domestic sphere in the context of the outdoors. Scouting movements provided middle-class girls with new leisure activities and work roles with the goal of reestablishing a productive role for girls in the family and society. At the end of the twentieth century, the Girl Scouts still remain one of the strongest sources of arts and crafts instruction for American girls.

While middle-class girls made faux "Indian" crafts, Native American women worked hard to maintain indigenous craft traditions in their communities. The crafts of many native cultures have survived because women remained dedicated to teaching girls specialized skills. For example, women on the plateau of the northwestern United States cultivated craft talents in girls by encouraging them to go on spiritual quests to discover their talents. Grandmothers were important teachers who, through example, showed young women how to do beadwork and basketry. Plateau women specialized in weaving twined and coiled baskets, working and tanning hides, and doing beadwork. Traditionally, items such as baskets were functional and used for gathering and preparing food, but such items were also decorated with beautiful geometric designs and often served as gifts or items for trade. Today, families and friends in these Native American communities still exchange craft items

Three girls weave baskets, Hopi Reservation, Arizona, 1903. (Edward Curtis/Library of Congress)

as gifts, and grandmothers often watch with great pride as young girls wear their beaded regalia for traditional dancing.

Mexican American mothers and grandmothers have also been key figures in the preservation of arts and crafts traditions in the twentieth century. In Mexican communities in Texas, many women inherited the art of quilting from their mothers and grandmothers when they were girls. Today, older women quilt as a source of enjoyment rather than out of a need to produce warm blankets for the family. Mexican women in Texas also have a tradition of making paper flowers for weddings, *quinceañeras* (fifteenth-birthday celebrations), and funerals. This tradition is still practiced by women and girls at the end of the twentieth century.

Despite efforts to maintain and revive cultural practices and formalize the teaching of arts and crafts, the practice of arts and crafts has declined steadily in the twentieth century. Commercialized leisure offers girls forms of entertainment and pleasure that focus on what they can purchase instead of what they can make. Rather than paint or weave, adolescent and teenage girls more often use their bodies as a canvas to express themselves. Girls also have fewer day-to-day ties to adult women in their families and communities who could teach them craft traditions. But little girls, between the ages of four and ten, do remain enthusiastic about arts and crafts. Beadwork, latch hooks, and lanyards are among the many handicrafts that are popular for

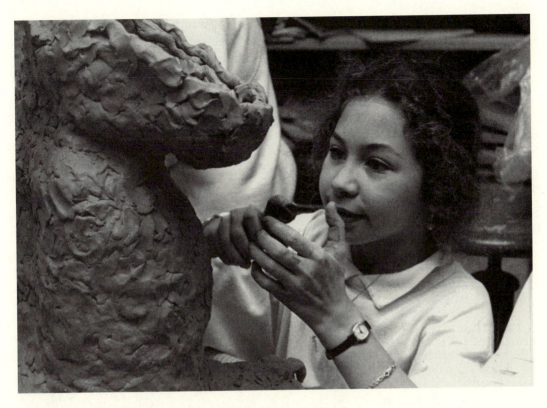

A young girl models a monster out of clay. (Shirley Zeiberg)

girls who turn to booklets, magazines, and ready-made kits as guides. Craft production no longer serves a functional purpose and is no longer the main medium for socializing girls into feminine roles. Yet it survives as one source of leisure and play for young girls today.

Carla Bittel

See also Clothing; Consumer Culture; Dollhouses; Girls' Culture; Handbags; Play; Samplers; Saturday Evening Girls

References and Further Reading

Ackerman, Lillian A. 1996. *A Song to the Creator: Traditional Arts of the Native American Women of the Plateau.* Norman: University of Oklahoma Press.

Beard, Lina, and Adelia Beard. 1887. *The American Girls' Handy Book: How to Amuse Yourself and Others.* Foreword by Anne M. Boulard. Reprint, Boston: David R. Godine.

————. 1902. *New Ideas for Work and Play: What a Girl Can Make and Do.* New York: Charles Scribner's Sons.

Bishop, Robert, and Jacqueline Marx Atkins. 1995. *Folk Art in American Life.* New York: Viking Studio Books.

Boris, Eileen. 1986. *Art and Labor: Ruskin, Morris, and the Craftsman Ideal in America.* Philadelphia: Temple University Press.

Brumberg, Joan Jacobs. 1997. *The Body Project: An Intimate History of American Girls.* New York: Random House.

Ferris, William, ed. 1983. *Afro-American Folk Art and Crafts.* Boston: G. K. Hall.

Graham, Joe S., ed. 1991. *Hecho en Tejas: Texas-Mexican Folk Arts and Crafts.* Denton: University of North Texas Press.

Hine, Darlene Clark, and Kathleen Thompson. 1998. *A Shining Thread of Hope: The History of Black Women in America*. New York: Broadway Books.

Macdonald, Anne L. 1988. *No Idle Hands: The Social History of American Knitting*. New York: Ballantine Books.

Norton, Mary Beth. 1980. *Liberty's Daughters: The Revolutionary Experience of American Women, 1750–1800*. Ithaca, NY: Cornell University Press.

Oak, Jacquelyn. 1994. *Sotheby's Guide to American Folk Art*. New York: Simon and Schuster.

Peiss, Kathy. 1986. *Cheap Amusements: Working Women and Leisure in Turn-of-the-Century New York*. Philadelphia: Temple University Press.

Swan, Susan Burrows. 1977. *Plain and Fancy: American Women and Their Needlework, 1700–1850*. New York: Routledge.

Ulrich, Laurel Thatcher. 1998. "Wheels, Looms, and the Gender Division of Labor in Eighteenth-Century New England." *William and Mary Quarterly* 55: 3–38.

Asian American Girls

Across more than a century of migration, labor, family life, acculturation, and identity formation, Asian American girls have been unacknowledged actors in the larger transpacific story of mobility and circumscribed opportunity. Since the second half of the nineteenth century, Asian immigrant and second-generation girls have played a necessary role in supporting the family wage economy in a context of race, gender, class, and sexual boundaries that were essentially transnational as families became divided by racialized, gendered, and orientalist U.S. immigration policies. Regardless of their occupations and the low value placed on their waged labor that resulted from the distorted passive image of Asian women, they more than simply augmented the wages of male breadwinners. To study

Asian American girlhood is also to reveal the ambivalent impact of popular culture and socializing agents (schools, churches, and social agencies) on representations, family socialization, and community life—overlapping experiences that have framed as well as limited Asian American girls' efforts to develop their multifaceted womanhood.

Few Asian American girls (or boys) were visible in cities, towns, or the countryside of the late nineteenth-century United States. A recent study suggests that the percentage of native-born Chinese children in late nineteenth-century San Francisco did increase over time, suggesting the possibility that more and more such immigrants in that city regarded the United States as their home community. Few Chinese parents, however, brought infants or children to the United States. The relatively small number of children had little to do with the "sojourner" mentality or the desire to maintain temporary residency in the United States and more with externally imposed constraints (Chen 2000, 56–57). The minuscule number of girls (and boys) stemmed from anti-Asian immigration laws. Following the passage of the race- and class-based Chinese Exclusion Act in 1882 and other related legislation, Chinese arrivals were turned back unless they qualified as one of the exempt classes (officials, teachers, students, merchants, and travelers). Gradually, versions of such legislation were extended to other Asian arrivals. Strictly enforced until their repeal in 1943, these laws stymied family immigration to the United States (Hing 1993, 44–48).

Until the 1940s, Asian immigrant communities showed a skewed sex ratio, which thwarted reproduction, perpetuated divided family units, and engendered a male-dominated community life. Asian immigrant women not only were barred by the same laws that kept men out but were also excluded by officials' belief that many were prostitutes or "immoral" (Peffer 1999, 8–9). Cultural traditions that proscribed the movement of women away from their extended family unit also limited the female inflow into the United States. Fear of racially motivated violence and the itinerant nature of labor also discouraged their immigration. Left behind in Asia, these women missed the opportunity, through education and labor in the United States, to possibly transform androcentric Asian immigrant cultures. The few Chinese and Japanese girls of the late nineteenth-century United States grew up in communities that privileged male offspring over female ones, as suggested in this Chinese proverb: "a boy is born facing in; a girl is born facing out."

Within the Chinese American community, patriarchy and a skewed sex ratio engendered the phenomenon known as *mui-tsai* (in Cantonese dialect, "little sister"). Sold by poverty-stricken parents in China into domestic service, these *mui-tsai* were brought to the United States to serve in affluent Chinese homes or brothels. Such girls typically received no wages for their labor, although they often were freed through marriage in their late teens. Unable to leave of their own free will, many suffered from economic and sexual exploitation at the hands of their employers. Upon attaining womanhood, some were resold into prostitution, considered a lucrative venture in the predominately male Asian communities. Bereft of any legal recourse, some girls ran away to so-called rescue homes established by maternalist Protestant missionary women. Though pressured to

adopt gender roles that emphasized female purity, piety, and domesticity, many ignored such ideals, and few converted to Christianity (Yung 1996, 37–41; Tong 1994, 176–191).

By the 1920s the *mui-tsai* system, due to the efforts of missionary women and Chinese social reformers, had almost entirely disappeared. Yet the participation of girls in supporting the family livelihood continued on. Japanese American immigrant and second-generation girls played several roles in supporting the family economy. Some of the immigrant young women came as "picture brides," a phenomenon that occurred during the first few decades of the twentieth century. Usually in their late teens or early twenties, they moved to the United States to join their typically much older husbands in these arranged marriages. Issei (immigrants, or first-generation) picture brides often toiled in rural areas, laboring in sugar beet fields, lumbering camps, and horticulture. In addition to working alongside their husbands in these endeavors, these Issei young women shouldered the burden of domesticity in a frontierlike environment (Glenn 1986, 42–48).

Other Asian rural girls recalled that their childhoods were arduous. After the 1913 Alien Land Act was passed in California and other states followed suit, Asian immigrants—Chinese, Japanese, Korean, and Asian Indian—could not own land or lease it for longer than three years. To compensate for that, Asian farmers resorted to labor-intensive farming, which demanded the effort of all family members. Daughters labored as fruit pickers, did cannery work, helped with housework and child care, and sometimes were hired out as domestics. Such responsibilities often delayed or interrupted their education. This lot was shared by countless Chinese, Japanese, Korean, and Asian Indian girls. Mary Paik Lee, born in Korea in 1905, not only cared for her siblings and foraged for food but also washed other people's laundry, cleaned a schoolhouse, and worked as a servant girl in various California localities (Lee 1990, lix). Punjabi Mexican girls in California of nonfarming families became part of the labor migratory circuit, earning the same wages as their parents as they labored in vineyards, fields, and orchards. Such Asian girls had little time for a social life; isolated from the larger society, their Americanization was retarded.

Most rural second-generation Asian girls (and boys) played the important function of landholders. As U.S. citizens by birth, they could own the agricultural land that their parents coveted. In the interwar years, Punjabi farmers in the Imperial Valley bought land in the names of their children and then managed it as guardians through probate (Leonard 1992, 135).

Compared to their rural peers, urban Asian girls led more comfortable, though not affluent, childhoods. Unlike their rural counterparts, they typically worked shorter hours and avoided heavy manual labor. Monica Sone, a Nisei (children of immigrants, or second-generation Japanese) who grew up in Seattle, fondly recalled the "games"—one of which was "climbing the laundry"—she and her brother devised whenever they assisted their parents with the housekeeping of their family-owned residential hotel (Sone 1953, 13). Mrs. Watanabe (first name is unavailable) and her siblings were sent to Japan—a not unusual occurrence—to be raised by relatives so that both parents could run their laundry (Glenn and Parreñas 1996, 135). In early twentieth-century San Francisco, Chinese American working-class girls were groomed to become virtuous wives and mothers. Since their mothers led sheltered but still work-oriented lives, their daughters helped with the shopping and housework, sometimes even holding part-time service-oriented jobs. In spite of the limited time for play, these girls enjoyed Chinese celebrations, Chinese opera, and church meetings. Chinese American girls who hailed from educated, middle-class, and often Christian-influenced families led far more leisurely lives than their working-class sisters; growing up in the 1910s, Florence Chinn Kwan taught English to Chinese immigrants but contributed her earnings to a missionary society (Yung 1996, 110–114).

Regardless of subregion or locale, most Asian American girls received socialization through the Christian church, paid labor, and most important, public schooling. In these schools both boys and girls came into contact with non-Asian Americans and learned American culture. Most Asian American children were motivated to learn the English language and Euro-American mannerisms to fit in with their peers. Among some middle-class Asian American children, the drive to excel in their studies was also encouraged partly by parental stress on securing a good education for upward mobility.

Through their interactions with teachers, employers, and peers, girls realized that being American meant having certain freedoms. As a teenager Jade Snow Wong, later a well-known writer, worked as a domestic for Euro-American families. During her service, she formed the impression that American social relations were warm and affectionate, whereas Chinese culture seemed rigid and restrictive. Since Asian boys enjoyed relatively more freedom than girls, the issue of personal freedom became paramount for the latter. Constrained by gender boundaries, some hoped to leave traditions behind, step into the public sphere, and receive recognition for individual accomplishments (Chan 1998, 135, 144). In a time when assimilation reigned supreme and cultural pluralism was not a choice, Asian American youth showed a strong preference for the American part of their legacy.

One such girl was Sone, who recalled that during her childhood days before World War II, she "found herself switching [her] ... personality back and forth daily like a chameleon" (Sone 1953, 22). Shuttling back and forth between her American public school and the Japanese-language institution, she developed a dual personality. Robust and active in the public school, she turned demure and self-effacing in the Japanese one. Encouraged to step into the model of the larger society's "new woman" of the early twentieth century, she was also nudged to conform to the ethnic community's image of motherhood. For most of her childhood, she could not envision herself being a "Yankee and Japanese at the same time" and found herself strongly drawn to the former (Sone 1953, 19).

But often deep-seated racial prejudices thwarted such aspirations. Fellow students frequently taunted Asian girls, and teachers were either condescending or blatantly racist. Mary Paik Lee, a Korean American born outside the United States who immigrated before the end of high school, recalled that when she protested about receiving lower grades than white students, the teacher retorted, "If you don't like it, get the hell out of here. We don't want you here anyway" (Lee 1990, 56). Esther Wong of San Francisco remembered that her French teacher, in response to her reading aloud in class, said: "Well, you read all right, but I don't like you. You belong to a dirty race that spits at missionaries" (Yung 1996, 129). Social science studies of Japanese American students in the 1920s and 1930s showed that their Americanization foundered because of racism (Yoo 2000, 23). Perhaps such tensions in the schools discouraged Asian American girls from choosing professional careers or a college education. A 1937 study of Chinese high school students in San Francisco concluded that Chinese females were more accepting of the idea of marriage than career (Yung 1996, 130). Racial discrimination only served to make these girls more self-conscious—even ashamed—of their ethnic cultures.

Young Asian American women also ran headlong into demeaning popular images that eroticized as well as exoticized the female body. Asians in literature and early Hollywood films were portrayed as being either "good" or "bad," with the former taking the forms of helpless heathens, loyal allies, or sidekicks and servants, and the latter sinister villains and brute hordes. Stock figures such as Fu Manchu, the diabolical paragon of Chinese evil, and Charlie Chan, the model of the benign Chinese, underscore the white as superior in all aspects. Young female adolescents grew up knowing or watching films that featured Asian American actresses playing roles in the image of the "Lotus Blossom" (subservient and passive) or "Dragon Lady" (promiscuous and untrustworthy). Anna May Wong, the pioneer Chinese American actress of the interwar years, played only "exotic doll" roles available for white male dominance. Since Chinese deemed female artists to be "loose" women, Wong, who made her acting debut at twelve years old, both defied her parents and ignored public perceptions. And yet racial discrimination throttled her full potential because she never played complex characters (Tong 2000, 154, 156).

Scientific studies of the interwar period also deemed the Asian body to be strange, peculiar, and weak. Scientists were interested in establishing a classification for the physical racial type of the Asian. Japanese American students in California in the 1920s underwent intelligence testing—which often did not take into account differing language skills and socialization—that produced results seemingly confirming the belief that whites were more intelligent than Asians (Chun 2000, 21–22; Yoo 1994, 57–65).

By the eve of World War II, Asian American girls found themselves torn between two worlds: treated at times like ethnographic spectacle but always deemed alien, they were also ambivalent about their parents' culture. That ambivalence was heightened by tensions over the question of dating, standards of beauty, and female autonomy. Most Asian American youngsters did not cross the color line; interracial dating was taboo in a time when antimiscegenation laws held sway. Filipino parents, recalling the customs of the Islands, expected their daughters to accept chaperonage and strict hours, and Punjabi fathers, in deference to the custom of arranged marriages, often rebuffed potential beaus who were vying for their daughters' attention. Many Nisei girls were not allowed to "go out," except for club or group activities. Some girls accommodated their parents' demands, but others resisted (Leonard 1992, 153; Matsumoto 1993, 77; Posadas 1989, 281). Mary Paik

Lee asked her father for permission before she went out with her future husband (Lee 1990, 62). Yoshiko Uchida, however, expressed her exasperation aloud whenever her father demanded that she, even during her college days, return from her dates before nine in the evening (Uchida 1982, 43). Flora Belle Jan, perhaps a Chinese flapper and more interested in postwar consumerism and romance, simply ignored her tradition-bound parents' disapproval of her active social life and sometimes disappeared for days on end (Yung 1996, 123–124).

World War II marked a turning point for some Asian American girls. Nisei young women found themselves incarcerated during the duration along with other people of Japanese descent. Families were divided, and community life broke down. Confusion colored Japanese American lives; at the age of seven Jeanne Wakatsuki puzzled over the disappearance of her father, who was taken away by agents in the Federal Bureau of Investigation. Like so many other young Nisei girls, Wakatsuki was also perturbed by her family's uprooting from a social milieu consisting of peer relatives, schoolmates, and teachers (Houston and Houston 1973, 8–14). The education she and others received in the concentration camps—which emphasized the message of Americanization—was incongruous with their imprisoned status. These girls joined the boys in staging mass walkouts, some of which led to vandalism. But because the incarceration years threw them together with other coethnics in confined spaces, their ethnic consciousness became heightened and would survive in the postwar years even as racial-ethnic enclaves declined (Yoo 2000, 106–110, 174). For other Asian American girls (and boys), the war years marked change in a positive direction. Exclusion was gradually chipped away following the repeal of the Chinese Exclusion Act in 1943. Women—often along with their foreign-born children—could now enter the United States as part of the family reunification process, eventually producing a new generation of native-born offspring. Legislation initiated in 1965 eventually pried open the door for even more family reunifications and some admissions based on occupational skills, with the latter initiating the migration of educated, middle-class Asians.

During the 1950s and early 1960s rebelling against their parents' family-centered values and worldview was a way for many native-born Asian girls to assert their own selfhood in a climate in which the mainstream youth culture extolled consumerism and rebellion against conformist family life. Foreign-born Asian youth could not escape intergenerational tension either, since the emotional reunification was tempered by the harsh reality of poverty and reassertion of parental supervision. Juvenile delinquency partly stemmed from a breakdown in family life. Sue Jean Lee Suettinger, raised in New York's Chinatown of the 1960s and involved with a Chinese American youth gang that was often embroiled in scuffles with Italian gangs, explained her generation as simply wanting to "be independent, grow up, and have an identity" (Suettinger 1992, 39).

Contemporary Asian American girls live in a world that seems much smaller but also more complex. Most refugees and recent immigrant children, along with their families, have fled countries haunted by a legacy of U.S. imperialism that resulted in distorted Western influences, political and economic chaos, and even war. Those uprooted forcibly from

their native lands—Southeast Asian immigrants being an obvious example—often, at least for the first generation, maintain an emotional attachment to their country of birth (and families left behind) long after their settlement in the United States (Kibria 1993, 161–162; Rutledge 1992, 62).

The fortunes of Asian girls in the United States have also been shaped by economic forces. Global restructuring—rapid global economic integration—has led to a contraction in United States of high-paying manufacturing jobs and an expansion of low-wage assembly and service-sector jobs that rely heavily on female labor. Among Vietnamese and Hmong refugees, the increasing involvement of women in paid work has given them an opportunity to gain qualified personal freedom and contest the traditional hierarchies of family life. Household tension, spousal abuse, and even divorce have ensued from this partial reconfiguration of gender relations, though radical change in traditional male roles and behaviors rarely occurred (Espiritu 1997, 75–76; Muzny 1989, 134).

Not only do some female immigrant youngsters confront a conflict-ridden household, but many more face the burden of poverty, in part a by-product of conditions in their country of origin. For children caught in the throes of these conflicts, confusion reigns. "As a child, I did not understand why we had to work so hard and live so poorly," Maijue Xiong, who grew up in Laos, recalled (Chan 1994, 121). To overcome poverty in the United States, recent working-class immigrant children have had to help with family-run businesses or hold part-time jobs.

The adjustment to life in the United States has been somewhat eased by the

Having diverse role models is important for the self-development of girls. (Courtesy Girl Scouts of the USA)

continuance of family ties and traditions. Yet some of the continuities placed these girls on a collision course with their parents. Xiong, for example, resented the inordinate attention paid to her brothers and the overbearing protection of her parents. She felt ashamed of her native language and longed to change her identity or risk rejection from her peers (Muzny 1989, 133–139; Chan 1994, 128).

The development of transnational ties for certain Asian American families—a by-product of the flow of capital from Asia to the United States and also the reverse—in recent decades has reshaped the socialization process of some girls. Asian American entrepreneurs and working-class parents often left their children in the care of relatives in their countries of birth so that they could pursue their occupations in the United States. They

might bring older progeny over to the United States to take advantage of schooling, but then sometimes fathers would spend time away from the United States, taking care of business in Asia. Without close parental supervision and possessing an evolving mind-set, children often develop their own conceptions of personal, ethnic, and national identities (Leonard 1997, 152; Chen 1992, 56–57).

Further, the flow of information and the filtering of Western influences to Asian countries—particularly those that have had political ties to the United States—have also determined the pace of their Americanization. Catherine Tagudin grew up in the Philippines in the 1960s on a staple of Disney movies and tales from letters written by relatives in the United States, but upon her arrival in the United

Three nineteen-year-old friends attend an Asian American festival. (Skjold Photographs)

States, she discovered a world quite unlike the idyllic paradise she had come to believe in (Tagudin 1996, 194–196).

Contemporary Asian American girls face challenges not unlike those encountered by their peers of the past. Race and gender remain markers of difference. Language acquisition and the social pressure to discard "foreign accents" are also continuities from the era of exclusion. Many bemoaned the "culture shock" they endured (Kim and Yu 1996, 131–132; Dublin 1996, 176, 209). As in the past, migration to the United States also enhanced intergenerational tensions, which stemmed from cultural clashes between generations and the concomitant decline in the power and authority of family elders. Parents with little English-language fluency and familiarity with the U.S. bureaucracies have had to rely on the mediation of their children, which in turn has given them more leverage in shaping family dynamics. Cultural clashes with elders have tended to differentiate along the axis of age: older girls tend to define their struggle against their Asianness (and against their parents) in terms of interpersonal roles and relations, but younger girls, being cognitively immature, see Asianness as simply material manifestations of ethnicity. Compared to young girls, older ones experienced a duality that is more psychologically driven.

Benson Tong

See also Immigration; Work

References and Further Reading
Bacon, Jean. 1996. *Life Lines: Community, Family, and Assimilation Among Asian Indian Immigrants.* New York: Oxford University Press.

Chan, Sucheng. 1998. "Race, Ethnic Culture, and Gender in the Construction of Identities among Second-Generation Chinese Americans." Pp. 127–164 in *Claiming America: Constructing Chinese American Identities during the Exclusion Era.* Edited by K. Scott Wong and Sucheng Chan. Philadelphia: Temple University Press.

Chan, Sucheng, ed. 1994. *Hmong Means Free: Life in Laos and America.* Philadelphia: Temple University Press.

Chen, Hsiang-shui. 1992. *Chinatown No More: Taiwan Immigrants in Contemporary New York.* Ithaca, NY: Cornell University Press.

Chen, Yong. 2000. *Chinese San Francisco, 1850–1943: A Trans-Pacific Community.* Palo Alto, CA: Stanford University Press.

Chun, Gloria Heyung. 2000. *Of Orphans and Warriors: Inventing Chinese American Culture and Identity.* New Brunswick, NJ: Rutgers University Press.

Dublin, Thomas, ed. 1996. *Becoming American, Becoming Ethnic: College Students Explore Their Roots.* Philadelphia: Temple University Press.

Espiritu, Yen Le. 1997. *Asian American Women and Men: Labor, Laws, and Love.* Thousand Oaks, CA: Sage.

Glenn, Evelyn Nakano. 1986. *Issei, Nisei, and War Bride: Three Generations of Japanese American Women in Domestic Service.* Philadelphia: Temple University Press.

Glenn, Evelyn Nakano, and Rachel Salazar Parreñas. 1996. "The Other Issei: Japanese Immigrant Women in the Pre–World War II Period." Pp. 110–124 in *Origins and Destinies: Immigration, Race, and Ethnicity in America.* Edited by Silvia Pedraza and Rubén G. Rumbaut. Belmont, CA: Wadsworth Publishing.

Hing, Bill Ong. 1993. *Making and Remaking Asian America through Immigration Policy, 1850–1990.* Stanford, CA: Stanford University Press.

Houston, Jeanne Wakatsuki, and James D. Houston. 1973. *Farewell to Manzanar.* Boston: Houghton Mifflin.

Kibria, Nazli. 1993. *Family Tightrope: The Changing Lives of Vietnamese Americans.* Princeton, NJ: Princeton University Press.

Kim, Elaine H., and Eui-Young Yu. 1996. *East to America: Korean American Life Stories.* New York: New Press.

Lee, Mary Paik. 1990. *Quiet Odyssey: A Pioneer Korean Woman in America.* Edited by Sucheng Chan. Seattle: University of Washington Press.

Lee, Robert G. 1999. *Orientals: Asian Americans in Popular Culture.* Philadelphia: Temple University Press.

Leonard, Karen Isaksen. 1992. *Making Ethnic Choices: California's Punjabi Mexican Americans.* Philadelphia: Temple University Press.

———. 1997. *The South Asian Americans.* Westport, CT: Greenwood Publishing.

Matsumoto, Valerie. 1993. *Farming the Home Place: A Japanese American Community in California.* Ithaca, NY: Cornell University Press.

Muzny, Charles C. 1989. *The Vietnamese in Oklahoma City: A Study of Ethnic Change.* New York: AMS Press.

Peffer, George Anthony. 1999. *If They Don't Bring Their Women Here: Chinese Female Immigration before Exclusion.* Urbana: University of Illinois Press.

Posadas, Barbara M. 1989. "Mestiza Girlhood: Interracial Families in Chicago's Filipino American Community since 1925." Pp. 273–282 in *Making Waves: An Anthology of Writings by and about Asian American Women.* Edited by Asian Women United of California. Boston: Beacon Press.

Rutledge, Paul James. 1992. *The Vietnamese Experience in America.* Bloomington: Indiana University Press.

Sone, Monica. 1953. *Nisei Daughter.* Boston: Little, Brown.

Suettinger, Sue Jean Lee. 1992. "West Side Story." Pp. 38–44 in *Asian Americans: Oral Histories of First to Fourth Generation Americans from China, the Philippines, Japan, India, the Pacific Islands, Vietnam, and Cambodia.* Edited by Joann Faung Jean Lee. New York: New Press.

Tagudin, Catherine. 1996. "My Experience with Immigration/ Assimilation in America." Pp. 193–197 in *Becoming American, Becoming Ethnic: College Students Explore Their Roots.* Edited by Thomas Dublin. Philadelphia: Temple University Press.

Tong, Benson. 1994. *Unsubmissive Women: Chinese Prostitutes in Nineteenth-Century San Francisco.* Norman: University of Oklahoma Press.

———. 2000. *The Chinese Americans.* Westport, CT: Greenwood Press.

Uchida, Yoshiko. 1982. *Desert Exile: The Uprooting of a Japanese-American Family.* Seattle: University of Washington Press.

Wong, Jade Snow. 1945. *Fifth Chinese Daughter.* New York: Harper and Row.

Yoo, David K. 1994. "Growing Up Nisei: Second-Generation Japanese Americans of California, 1924–1945." Ph.D. dissertation, Yale University.

———. 2000. *Growing Up Nisei: Race, Generation, and Culture among Japanese Americans of California, 1924–1949.* Urbana: University of Illinois Press.

Yung, Judy. 1996. *Unbound Feet: A Social History of Chinese Women in San Francisco.* Berkeley: University of California Press.

B

Babysitting

Babysitting, most typically associated with adolescent girls who receive payment for part-time child care in the home of employers, is a relatively modern form of labor. Since World War II, babysitting has remained the nearly universal introduction of girls into the labor force. The word *babysitting*, first coined shortly before World War II, did not emerge as a significant service industry until the postwar period because of the baby boom, suburbanization, prosperity, permissive childrearing, and other forces. Feeling exploited by employers, in 1947 babysitters attempted to organize unions and issue manifestoes that delineated mutual responsibilities. Drawing upon notions set forth by sitters, educators, experts, and others established a code of conduct meant to contain teenage girls seen as irritatingly irresponsible. It also spelled out for parents the importance of providing appropriate sources and resources for babysitters. In the 1960s, fears about the decline of community cohesion and other influences led to the widespread circulation of urban myths. The "man upstairs" who was incorporated into popular movie plots in the late 1970s sheds light on the fears of children, sitters, and employers. In the 1980s, representations of insane sitters more clearly revealed the anxieties of employers about female adolescents.

The decline in the number of teenagers by the mid-1980s was one among a number of factors that led to the idealization of preadolescent girls as babysitters. Glorified in girls' culture, babysitting became the province of increasingly younger girls. Graduates of babysitting courses are today seen as especially competent caretakers.

Before babysitting there was "minding the children," the paid activity of girls and boys, women and men, kin, and neighbors. During the Depression, some boys who cared for youngsters even established their own informal babysitting clubs. Despite government attempts to conscript high school students to serve as an army of babysitters to guard the home front during World War II, it was often grade school children who answered the call. One 1943 study reported in the *Journal of Home Economics* revealed that as many as two-thirds of fourth, fifth, and sixth graders in Elmira, New York (a small city with a booming war industry), regularly cared for children (between two months and nine years old) from the late afternoon until early morning (Pollock 1943, 31). The exigencies of World War II also led male college students at the City College of New York, Columbia, and Harvard to seek jobs as babysitters. Though the war generated a demand for child care, female adolescents and others were more

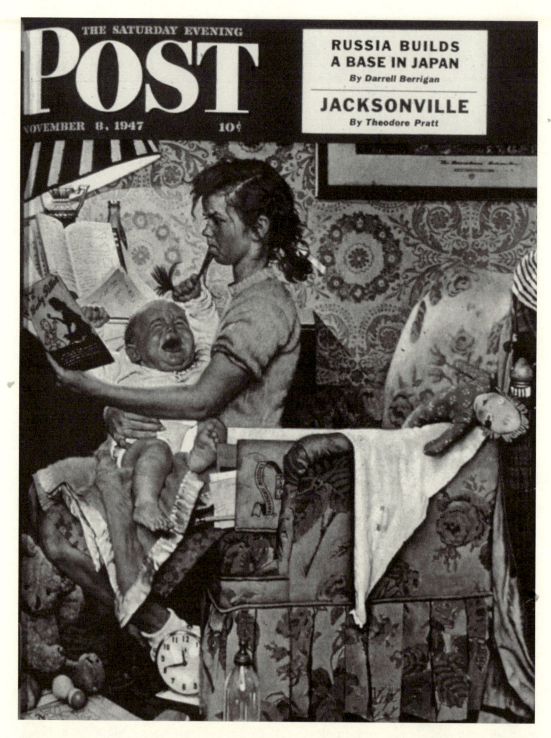

This 1947 Saturday Evening Post *cover depicts Norman Rockwell's notion of babysitting. (Library of Congress)*

PROTEST - Excessive housework and insufficient briefing head the list of sitters' complaints.

*In postwar periodicals, babysitters were represented as militant radicals. (*Christian Science Monitor *April 10, 1948: 5)*

likely to take advantage of wartime job opportunities instead of babysitting.

That babysitting was not as yet professionalized led employers to pay sitters low wages (25 to 50 cents per hour) to watch the children and clean the house. Poor working conditions led teenage girls in three suburban communities in the Northeast and Midwest to draw upon the notion of class conflict in an effort to eliminate "exploitation," assert their "sitters' rights," and reshape the "industry." Through contracts, codes, and manifestoes, girls articulated their grievances over low wages, inadequate heat, and housework.

Although boys mowed lawns at three times the babysitter's hourly rate, teenage girls had few socially acceptable options for earning money other than

babysitting, which became a $750 million industry by 1948. In the 1950s, babysitting mushroomed because of new employment opportunities for women, rising affluence, the baby boom, suburbanization, a child-centered family life, the popularization of teen culture, and the expansion of consumer culture. But many parents who hired adolescent girls for 50 cents per hour did so with the expectation that girls—by virtue of their sex—were motivated more by maternity than by money. This discrepancy in expectations perpetuated labor conflict. In *Parents' Magazine* and *Family Home Guide* as elsewhere, mothers and fathers routinely complained about unruly, unreliable, and irresponsible babysitters who ran up phone bills and left the refrigerator bare. Fed-up fathers motivated less by profit than by the promise of a free evening out participated in babysitter co-operatives typically organized by their wives, who were eager for time off. In movies such as *Sitting Pretty* and on TV, men who babysat (as did comedian Sid Caesar) were widely represented in the popular culture. Parents who felt frustrated with the self-absorbed teenage girls in their suburban neighborhoods followed the advice of experts who promoted boy sitters in popular magazines such as *Life* (1945), educational journals, and etiquette manuals. Many boys attended courses on babysitting offered by local nursing associations, where they practiced on life-size dolls. Despite wider concerns over male juvenile delinquency, boy sitters were said to possess an androgynous combination of "gentle determination." By the early 1960s, the relationship between a teen and a toddler was even celebrated in the rock and roll hit "Baby Sittin' Boogie."

By the 1960s, however, the publication of articles about babysitting in popular magazines significantly diminished. Instead, employers—along with babysitters and children—expressed their frustrations and fears in a new medium: the urban legend. Circulated as "true stories," these legends shed light on the anxieties of everyone involved: the parent anxious about leaving a stranger in charge; the anxious child worried about abandonment; and the babysitter, often alone and isolated in a dark house at night. In "the man upstairs," the most common babysitter legend, a persistent caller (a murderer who is actually inside the house!) makes threatening phone calls to a self-absorbed female babysitter. The raspy male voice (actually calling from an upstairs extension) asks the question on the lips of every parent: "Have you checked the children?" She has not. In the end, the babysitter's negligence (she is watching television) makes her nearly as dangerous as the maniac who, as it turns out, is more vigilant than she.

Beginning in the 1970s, a frightened as well as frightening babysitter became a pop culture icon in horror films of the period. *When a Stranger Calls* (1979), about a teenage girl who unwittingly attracts the maniac who threatens her life and the safety of the children she has been hired to protect, is closely based on the urban legend. In *Halloween* (1978) the sexually active babysitters are victimized by a homicidal maniac. In both the popular and pornographic movies and fiction that followed, the iconic babysitter is represented as a vixen or villain who threatens marital fidelity and family stability. This characterization has continued to dominate the news media.

In the 1980s, simultaneous changes in demographics (e.g., fewer teens) and increased job opportunities (e.g., the fast food industry) contributed to the search for alternative child care providers. Some parents hired young men, mature women (especially through babysitter agencies), and friendly neighbors (organized into parent cooperatives) as they had in the 1950s. But they also turned with increasing frequency to preadolescent girls, a source of labor untapped since World War II. Though girls had been "minding the children" during World War II, child experts in the 1950s advised mothers *not* to hire a babysitter who was younger than her mid-teens. But thirty years later the idealized preadolescent "super sitter" was everywhere in American popular culture. A commercial girls' culture that emerged in the mid-1980s aimed to shape the preadolescent girl into a responsible professional.

The enormously popular Baby-Sitters Club book series, movies, and fan club, which glorified babysitting and idealized the preadolescent sitter in the mid-1990s, became a site of postfeminist socialization that aimed to prepare preadolescent girls for both motherhood and the marketplace. The negotiation of new social realities along with changing expectations and ideals about gender, girlhood, and female adolescence can be gleaned from the hundreds of books in the book series, the movies, and from girls' fan letters to Ann M. Martin, the series' author. The Baby-Sitters Club girls were shaped by the fledgling "girl power" ethos soon to flourish in the popular culture of the 1990s. This commercial form of postfeminism that empowered the fictionalized babysitters as well as contained them satisfied the needs of real girls, the families that hired them, the communities they served, and the consumer culture that absorbed their wages. Unlike previous depictions of babysitting as an isolated activity, however, members of the club make the job seem like a far more social experience than it usually is. Certified training courses (e.g., Safe Sitters) have similarly aimed to educate, acculturate, and elevate.

Among those who babysit are some who appreciate the opportunity to keep the money they earn. Iselda, a migrant farmworker, is happy not to have to work in the fields on weekends. Unlike the wages she earns as a migrant worker, which she is obligated to turn over to her parents, the money she earns babysitting is her own to keep ("Migrant Workers' Children"). But for others perhaps less desperate, babysitting still leaves much to be desired. The chief complaints of babysitters in this undervalued, feminized field are low pay, last-minute calls,

cancellations, parents who come back late (sometimes drunk), sexual harassment, and having to care for the "brat pack." For their part, parents continue to complain either about inaccessible girls who prefer to flip hamburgers or about incompetent ones who charge too much and give too little.

Miriam Forman-Brunell

See also Domesticity; Work

References and Further Reading
The Babysitter (motion pictures, 1964, 1965, 1969, 1975, 1981, 1992, 1995).
Forman-Brunell, Miriam. *Sitting Pretty: Fears and Fantasies about Adolescent Girls.* New York: Routledge, forthcoming.
"Graduate Course in Baby-Sitting." 1945. *Life* (April 12): 107–108.
Kourany, Ronald F., et al. 1980. "Adolescent Babysitting: A 30-Year-Old Phenomenon." *Adolescence* 13, no. 60 (Winter): 939–945.
Margolin, Leslie. 1990. "Child Abuse by Baby-Sitters: An Ecological-Interactional Interpretation." *Journal of Family Violence* 5, no. 2 (June): 95–105.
"Migrant Workers' Children." http://www.users.owt.com/rpeto/migrant/html.
Neus, Margaret. 1990. *The Insider's Guide to Babysitting: Anecdotes and Advice from Babysitters for Babysitters.* Master's thesis, Emerson College, Boston.
Pollock, Kathryn M. 1943. "Helping the Mother-Aides." *Journal of Home Economics* 35, no. 1 (June): 31.

Barbie

Much has been written on the Barbie doll. Revered and vilified in the print media since her introduction, Barbie is still one of the most popular toys in the world. Despite common criticism that she is a materialistic, appearance-oriented, blonde bimbo, millions of these dolls have been sold since 1960. Mattel has estimated that two Barbie dolls are purchased every second somewhere on the planet. and if they were put end to end, they would encircle the globe three-and-a-half times. Although critics differ as to her social significance, most would still agree that her longevity and popular appeal have entitled her to claim a piece of the American zeitgeist.

A doll that becomes whatever a girl wants her to be, Barbie is alternatively a bitch, conformist, airhead, and plucky little blonde. No single interpretation seems to define her. Critics claim that her figure, hair, and accouterments suggest a life saturated with consumer goods and sexist dating rituals, but the doll's social significance is really created by the girls who play with her. In all her manifestations, Barbie reveals American cultural ideals of femininity, beauty, and gender roles. Because Barbie exists as a reflection of the hopes and dreams of the girls who play with her, she is a perfect vehicle for exploring attitudes toward women in American society. In her incarnations throughout the latter half of the twentieth century, she has managed to change consistently with the times. In the late 1950s, Barbie's shape and fictive life resonated with postwar Americans. As a teenage fashion model, she represented the glamorous world of postwar haute couture. With her car and fashionable apartment, she spoke to ebullient consumption, affluent teen culture, and captivating sexuality. In the 1970s, she had *Saturday Night Fever* and went disco dancing with Ken. In the career-oriented 1980s, she left the world of fashion modeling for life as a doctor, astronaut, and business executive. She was and is a perfect picture of her time.

Before her entrance into the marketplace, Barbie's prototype was a notoriously acquisitive sex symbol. According to fashion designer and Barbie collector Billy Boy, Barbie was modeled after Lili, a doll purchased by young German bachelors to flaunt their playboy status. She had evolved, in turn, from a popular gold-digging cartoon character of the same name drawn by Reinhard Beuthien. Lili's talent was her ability to wrest money from wealthy men. She debuted as a doll on August 12, 1955, four years earlier than Barbie, but was not commercially successful. Despite the charming tale of Mattel's then executive vice president and president, Ruth and Elliot Handler, Barbie was probably *not* the exclusive idea of their young daughter— also named Barbie—who wanted a teenage doll with beautiful clothes. Barbie and Lili's characteristics seem too similar for coincidence. Some writers, including Jane and Michael Stern and M. G. Lord, have concluded that Barbie was copied directly from Lili. The dolls' exaggerated eyebrows, blonde hair pulled back from their faces in the popular 1950s ponytail, sly side glances, pursed lips, and seductive hourglass figures seem almost identical.

Despite her phenomenal popularity, Barbie was not well received when she first debuted in 1959. Although little girls seemed intrigued by her, parents were not sure what to make of such a sexy little toy. Before Barbie, most dolls resembled infants, and little girls played at mothering them. With Barbie, the object of the game changed. In Barbie's universe, the focus was on youth, consumption, sexiness, and exciting careers. The toy was not designed to teach the motherly, caretaking functions usually associated with baby dolls. Rather, Barbie encouraged girls to project themselves into her world as an exciting and glamorous teenage fashion model. To the horror of many, she did not have parents for disciplinary guidelines or even a boyfriend for emotional support. Her single status did not hinder her; she had everything she wanted, including an elegant apartment, a snazzy convertible, an extensive wardrobe, and an enviable figure.

And it was Barbie's voluptuous figure that caused such consternation for the general public. What would little girls do with Barbie in the privacy of their own bedrooms? Would her sexy shape and provocative clothes give children inappropriate ideas about proper sexual behavior? Would Barbie be a bad role model? Utilizing the advice of advertising executive Ernest Dicter, Mattel's marketing plan countered this bad girl image by insisting that children would identify with Barbie, projecting their dreams and aspirations into her play world. One of Barbie's inventors, Ruth Handler, said that the original Barbie concept was based upon the idea that little girls wanted to identify with teenagers. Handler stated, "These dolls became an extension of the girls. Through the doll, each child dream[ed] of what she would like to be" (Zinsser 1964, 73). Mattel promised that as girls played with Barbie, they would practice the arts of accessorizing, hairstyling, and appropriate grooming habits, all important skills for their lives as suburban teens and—in the age of 1950s hyperdomesticity—eventual suburban wives.

Barbie epitomized the social world of postwar abundance with her cars, elaborate wardrobe, and fancy apartment. The toy was marketed as a training vehicle for practicing the rules of etiquette, as well as for learning to fit into David Riesman's "outer-directed" world of the American consumer. She was promoted as instructive and good clean fun, in spite of her tantalizing appearance. Her fictive life revolved around shopping and boys, and her image epitomized the exciting world of teen culture. Mattel championed Barbie as a symbol of 1950s euphoria. For millions of Americans, she was the ideal teenage image of the period, with her perky sexuality, innocence, and enthusiasm for postwar consumption. As one writer gushed in 1964, Barbie was "long-legged and full-bosomed [and] . . . beautiful in the button-nosed tradition that America reveres in its drum majorettes" (Zinsser 1964, 72).

For many consumers, however, Barbie still remained problematic. Despite Mattel's protestations that Barbie was not about sex, seeing was still believing. Her figure was that of a seductively mature woman and with her blonde hair, large breasts, and fetching Dior gowns, Barbie connoted sexiness. Barbie *looked* too aggressive and too controlling to be appropriately deferential, as was demanded of women and girls in the 1950s. For many parents who grew up in the scarcity of the Depression, Barbie's world seemed narcissistic and extravagant. Her life revolved around obtaining material comforts and flaunting her arrogant sexuality. Barbie was supposed to be a teenager, but she looked thirty-five with her heavily made-up eyes and womanly shape.

In 1960, Mattel responded to this criticism. After her public relations makeover, Barbie went under the knife for some minor reconstructive surgery. Mattel modified her face in just a few subtle ways, but her overall appearance changed dramatically. Mattel's designers relaxed Barbie's eyebrows, gave her more flesh-toned skin, and less angular eyeliner. The most important difference, however, was in her eyes. Her blue irises were enlarged like a toddler's. As a result, Barbie's face became more childlike. She had soft, baby blue eyes to accompany her seductive shape. With a few subtle manipulations on the part of Mattel, Barbie now fit the paradoxical image of a perfect 1950s girl, who was, as fashion historian Doreen Caldwell notes, "a curious mixture of innocence and . . . primitive physical allure" (Caldwell 1981, 89).

The saucy blonde teenager with innocent eyes and sexual magnetism became the feminine aesthetic ideal of the late decade. Noting Barbie's shapely hourglass figure, the *New York Times* stated that Barbie "arrived as a fully developed nymphet" (Kahn 1991, 24). Describing a young girl who is sexually desirable, the word *nymphet* became a popular addition to everyday vocabulary after the 1955 publication of Vladimir Nabokov's novel *Lolita*, the story of a middle-aged man's passion for a nubile twelve-year-old girl.

This interest in teenage sexuality reflected the fact that the first wave of baby boomers born in 1946 and 1947 was reaching puberty. By 1959, the Little Miss America Pageant was instigated, *Teenbeat* magazine premiered, and Pepsi reminded the listening audience of the importance of "thinking young." But this fascination went beyond a mere appreciation of youth. Television and cinema promoted the blossoming prepubescent woman. Training bras in such unlikely sizes as 28AAA became the rage, as girls prepared for an adult life of elasticized undergarments.

Despite or because of this sexual innuendo, Barbie was a great success for Mattel. By 1961, one-half of the company's sales were in dolls, and its total sales volume tripled. Because of Barbie, Mattel claimed to have gone from ninth place in the toy market to first place in just a few short years. With Barbie's success came Ken, her boyfriend (1961); Midge, her best girlfriend (1963); Skipper, Barbie's sister (1964); and Allan, Midge's boyfriend (1963–1964). In 1961–1962, a board game titled "Barbie, Queen of the Prom" was marketed: to win, you had to be like Barbie and have a steady boyfriend, a prom dress, and be elected president of a school club. Barbie even cut a record called the "Busy Buzz" in 1961 in which she proclaimed, "I never bothered with romance or gave any boy a second chance and then I met Ken." By 1964, more than 25 press agents, 45 advertising executives, 5,000 workers in Japan who made the actual dolls and costumes, and 800 employees of Mattel worked to produce enough Barbies to meet the increasing demand. Barbie's success surpassed the Handlers' wildest dreams. By 1963, *Life* reported that Barbie was receiving more than 500 letters a week and had a national fan club and a bimonthly fan magazine ("Most Popular Doll in Town" 1963, 73). *The Nation* claimed that by 1964, Barbie's fan mail had increased to 10,000 letters a week. She had a personal secretary and 15 assistants, and her fan club consisted of 8,500 chapters with 500,000 members ("Barbie Doll Set" 1964, 407).

Mattel capitalized on the Barbie craze in every possible way. In 1964, the company actually diversified into girls' apparel and featured such items as sportswear, lingerie, sweaters, and hosiery. The theme of the ads was "Barbie's Designer Designs for You," and the line consisted of color-coordinated outfits in sizes 5–12 for—as the ad stated—"shopworn mothers who have scoured the market to match colors and sizes to their growing-up girls' needs." The Barbie phenomenon was remarkable. From clothes to records to comic books, she permeated every available preteen market. Mattel's marketing savvy and ability to capitalize on an ebullient postwar culture contributed to making Barbie one of the most sought-after toys of the decade.

If Barbie had remained in her original 1950s form, she would probably have become obsolete, but part of Barbie's enduring popularity is that she changes with the times. Although interest in her waned with the resurgence of the women's movement in the late 1960s, she bounced back as a polyester disco queen in the late 1970s; sales of the doll have not lagged since, partially because Mattel has worked tirelessly to keep Barbie current. For example, to reflect the changing position of women in the workforce in the 1980s, Barbie became a career girl and sported a blue power suit. Recognizing changing demographic data, Mattel introduced African American and Hispanic Barbies in the 1980s. All these measures have added to her popularity among girls. Today, many girls own multiple Barbies. Buyers scramble to purchase limited editions of the doll, only to keep it in its original box as a hedge on its future value as a collectible. Barbie conventions attract the faithful by the thousands.

As the decades come and go, Barbie's reincarnations continue to reflect Americans' complex attitudes toward gender, race, and class as well as changing demographics in the late twentieth century. But it is gender attitudes that matter most in the debate over Barbie. As M. G. Lord stated, "Femininity is the toxin; Barbie is [merely] the scapegoat" (Lord 1994, viii). Because she has become such

a potent symbol of femininity, Barbie is often the butt of jokes and the object of countless performance pieces. In a well-publicized prank, the Barbie Liberation Organization switched the voices of GI Joe and Barbie in December 1993. Children pulled the chords on their new dolls and were surprised to find that the burly Joe whined "Let's go shopping," and Barbie screamed "Eat lead, Cobra! Vengeance is mine!" One the most poignant uses of Barbie was in the video *Superstar* (1987) by Todd Haynes and Cynthia Schneider. It chronicled the tragic death of Karen Carpenter from anorexia and starred a plastic Barbie doll as the heroine.

Despite the fact that Barbie has reinvented her personality again and again since 1959, her perfect figure and affluent lifestyle continue to reflect cultural ambiguity regarding the role women play in American culture. Ann duCille suggested that "deconstructing Barbie may be the only release from the doll's impenetrable plastic jaws" (duCille 1999, 141). In other words, Barbie will cease to be contentious when Americans finally understand themselves.

Barbara J. Coleman

See also Body Image; Consumer Culture; Dollhouses; Dolls; Girls' Culture

References and Further Reading
"Barbie Doll Set." 1964. *The Nation* (April 27): 407.
Boy, Billy. 1987. *Barbie: Her Life and Times.* New York: Crown.
Caldwell, Doreen. 1981. *And All Was Revealed: Ladies Underwear 1907–1980.* New York: St. Martin's Press.
DuCille, Ann. 1999. "Barbie in Black and White." Pp. 127–142 in *The Barbie Chronicles: A Living Doll Turns Forty.* Edited by Yona Zeldis McDonough. New York: Touchstone.

Kahn, Alice. 1991. "A Onetime Bimbo Becomes a Muse." *New York Times* (September 29): H24–25.

Lord, M. G. 1994. *Forever Barbie: The Unauthorized Biography of a Real Doll.* New York: William Morrow.

McDonough, Yona Zeldis, ed. 1999. *The Barbie Chronicles: A Living Doll Turns Forty.* New York: Touchstone.

"Most Popular Doll in Town." 1963. *Life* (August 21): 73–75.

Riesman, David. 1950. *The Lonely Crowd.* New Haven, CT: Yale University Press.

Stern, Jane, and Michael Stern. 1990. *The Encyclopedia of Bad Taste.* New York: HarperCollins.

Zinsser, William K. 1964. "Barbie Is a Million-Dollar Doll." *Saturday Evening Post* (December 12): 72–73.

Bat Mitzvah

According to halakah, or Jewish law, girls and boys reach legal maturity at ages twelve and thirteen, respectively. From that time forward they are personally responsible for fulfilling the commandments and adhering to traditional laws, rituals, and customs. Rabbinic sources assumed that girls would reach both social maturity and puberty earlier than boys and thus assigned them an earlier age for becoming bat mitzvah, or "daughter of the commandment," than when boys became bar mitzvah, or "son of the commandment." This original meaning of the phrases *bat mitzvah* and *bar mitzvah* referred to legal and social categories based on age and accountability within the Jewish tradition rather than a particular event. In practice, however, Jewish boys have for centuries enjoyed a public demonstration of their religious adulthood that followed naturally from their religious education and preparation for participation in the full complement of ritual activities. Jewish girls, with generally limited access to extensive formal religious education, received no such training and no such inclusion in the public aspects of Jewish religious life. Until the twentieth century, their arrival at the age of bat mitzvah remained a private, often unremarked event.

The emergence of liberal forms of Judaism during the nineteenth century included gradual changes in ideas about women that eventually led to the development of the bat mitzvah at both the conceptual and ritual levels. The growth of Jewish educational systems that attempted to reach girls as well as boys raised questions about some of the traditional gender divisions in Jewish religious life. As Reform Judaism in the United States introduced mixed seating in family pews at synagogue services, and traditional ritual observance decreased, a small but growing number of American Jewish families began to enroll their daughters as well as their sons in some form of Jewish education. Girls' and boys' religious instruction resembled each other more than ever before. Communal confirmation ceremonies offered largely to Reform groups of adolescents who had attained a certain level of religious training further eroded gender differences in childhood and adolescent religious experiences among liberal Jews. At the same time, however, the pattern of bar mitzvah rituals became more standardized among traditional Jews. On or near their thirteenth birthdays, boys celebrated their coming of age by participating in the public rituals of synagogue ceremonies. They recited the blessings over the Torah, read a portion of the Torah directly from the scroll, and chanted the complementary section from the Book of the Prophets, the Haftarah. They often conducted parts of the service and delivered speeches interpreting the Torah portion. No such

A girl reading the Torah at her Bat Mitzvah. (Richard T. Nowitz/Corbis)

public ritual option was available either to Reform girls, whose denomination initially de-emphasized individual coming-of-age ceremonies, or to traditional girls, whose participation in public ritual was inconceivable according to established interpretations of Jewish law.

Not until 1922 did an American girl participate in a bat mitzvah ceremony analogous, though still not identical, to the bar mitzvah ceremonies that had become common. On March 18, 1922, in New York City, Judith Kaplan recited the blessings over the Torah, read a selection from a printed Torah, and chanted the Haftarah. Her father, Rabbi Mordecai Kaplan, developed this ceremony as part of his evolving approach to modern Judaism, which took him on a personal journey from traditional religious life to

his founding of Reconstructionist Judaism. Perhaps influenced by the suffrage movement, his ideas about Jewish ethics and individuals, or his close relationship to his mother, sister, and daughters, Kaplan was committed to the idea of women's religious equality. Yet even this pioneer retained some aspects of traditional religious practice. During services at his new synagogue, the Society for the Advancement of Judaism, men and women sat separately. Judith did not read from the Torah scroll itself. Her mother and grandmother were ambivalent about the ceremony and sat in the back with the other women, while Judith carried out her part in front of the synagogue.

Judith Kaplan's bat mitzvah did not spark an immediate or widespread interest in bat mitzvah ceremonies. As liberal Judaism became increasingly committed to the religious education of girls, however, such ceremonies became more common. The increasing popularity of Jewish summer camping also played a role because the leaders of these camps supported a variety of religious innovations as well as traditions. Kinereth Dushkin, for example, celebrated her bat mitzvah in 1934 at Camp Modin in Maine, one of the earliest Jewish summer camps. The daughter of leading Jewish educator Alexander Dushkin, who also helped found Camp Modin, Kinereth learned to chant the Haftarah in a week, although she, too, did not read directly from a Torah scroll.

Because Reform Judaism continued to stress confirmation ceremonies and Orthodox Judaism continued to uphold gender divisions within ritual practice, bat mitzvah ceremonies first became common within Conservative Judaism, the most popular denomination in the United States by the 1950s. These bat mitzvahs, an event in themselves instead of a descriptive phrase, resembled but did not equal bar mitzvahs. Girls generally celebrated their bat mitzvahs on Friday nights by participating in the service and reading the Haftarah. Not until the late 1970s did bat mitzvah ceremonies become nearly universal among Reconstructionist, Reform, and Conservative Jews, and even then the format of bat mitzvah celebrations continued to vary widely.

Orthodox Judaism has also recognized the positive value of celebrating twelve-year-old girls' coming of age as responsible Jewish adults. Although maintaining tradition, Orthodox Jews have developed many approaches to bat mitzvahs. Celebrations often include festive meals, speeches, and blessings. Some synagogues invite bat mitzvah girls to deliver talks

about the Torah portion. Many announce girls' bat mitzvahs from the pulpit. Some modern Orthodox girls celebrate their bat mitzvahs in the context of women's prayer groups, where they may participate in rituals inaccessible to them in more traditional synagogue settings. Even when not directly linked to communal synagogue worship, the widespread celebration of bat mitzvahs among Orthodox girls demonstrates the nearly universal acceptance of bat mitzvahs as life cycle events with spiritual significance beyond the boundaries of denominations.

The influence of bat mitzvah ceremonies extends beyond girls' coming-of-age rituals. The prevalence of such ceremonies requires equitable religious education for girls and boys. It also raises questions about women's role in the synagogue more generally because it seems problematic to many that after participating in public synagogue rituals as twelve- or thirteen-year-old girls, women might be relegated to apparently second-class status. The gradual acceptance of women's full integration into the synagogue owes much to the evolution of bat mitzvah ceremonies. The contemporary idea of a bar mitzvah or bat mitzvah is clearly associated with adolescence rather than adulthood, which requires further thought about age as well as gender within Judaism. Many older women, denied the opportunity of a ceremonial bat mitzvah as adolescents, embark on Jewish study and celebrate adult bat mitzvah ceremonies individually or in groups.

By the end of the twentieth century, the bat mitzvah ceremony encompassed social and religious importance as both an individual rite of passage and a family milestone. Twelve- or thirteen-year-old girls typically spend a year or more joining their peers in a variety of bat mitzvah and bar mitzvah observances. The rounds of celebratory services and parties are often supplemented by charitable activities that illustrate bat mitzvah girls' dedication to principles of Jewish social justice as well as religious education and ritual participation. Celebrating their bat mitzvahs gives girls access to values-oriented guidance and Jewish leadership and encourages them to take charge of the Jewish and spiritual dimensions of their lives.

Bonnie Steinberg and Melissa Klapper

See also Jewish Education of Girls;
    Kinaaldá; La Quinceañera

References and Further Reading
Berman, Donna. 1996. "Bat Mitzvah." In
    The Dictionary of Feminist Theologies.
    Edited by Letty M. Russel and J.
    Shannon Clarkson. Louisville, KY:
    Westminster John Knox Press.
Blocker, Hadassah. 1999. Personal
    communication to Bonnie Epstein.
Gensler, Kinereth Dushkin. 1999.
    Personal communication to Bonnie
    Epstein.
Goldin, Barbara Diamond. 1995. *Bat
    Mitzvah: A Jewish Girl's Coming of
    Age.* New York: Viking Press.
Hyman, Paula E. 1990. "The Introduction
    of Bat Mitzvah in Conservative Judaism
    in Postwar America." *YIVO Annual* 19:
    133–146.
Koller-Fox, Cherie. 1976. "Women and
    Jewish Education: A New Look at Bat
    Mitzvah." In *The Jewish Woman: New
    Perspectives.* Edited by Elizabeth
    Koltun. New York: Schocken Books.
Metter, Bert. 1984. *Bar Mitzvah, Bat
    Mitzvah: How Jewish Boys and Girls
    Come of Age.* New York: Clarion
    Books.
Meyer, Michael A. 1988. *Response to
    Modernity: A History of the Reform
    Movement in Judaism.* New York:
    Oxford University Press.
Mushr, Hadassah Kaplan. 1999. Personal
    communication to Bonnie Epstein.
Scult, Mel. 1993. *Judaism Faces the
    Twentieth Century: A Biography of
    Mordecai M. Kaplan.* Detroit: Wayne
    State University Press.

Birth Control

First used by Margaret Sanger in 1914 to spark a social movement to repeal laws banning contraception, the phrase *birth control* refers to various methods for preventing conception. Although women in the United States may take contraception for granted today, it has not always been legally available. Over the course of the nineteenth century, demand by married couples for effective means of preventing pregnancies spurred a booming patent medicine industry. But by the 1870s, contraception was banned as a threat to the moral well-being of American youth. The twentieth-century birth control movement, spurred by the activism of Sanger, secured the legalization of contraceptives. It also molded social acceptance of a woman's right to choose whether and when she will become a mother. Throughout U.S. history, anxiety about the sexual activity of adolescent girls has played a central role in public debates about contraception. The unproven belief that access to contraceptives would encourage girls to engage in premarital sex justified laws prohibiting contraceptives and posed a significant barrier to legalization until the 1960s. Concerns about contraception's influence on girls' sexual morality have been tied to fears about illegitimacy, the decline of the family, and the moral decay of society; and they have led to policies regulating sexuality and fertility, especially among young women, poor women, and women of color.

Historical evidence about contraceptives is scarce because they are usually employed in intimate moments of life and because frank public discussion of sexual matters is taboo. Historians have found some evidence in sources ranging from women's diaries and letters to recipe books and patent medicine ads. Prolonged breast-feeding, withdrawal, and marital abstinence were some of the earliest methods mentioned in eighteenth- and nineteenth-century sources. Prolonged breast-feeding was widely discussed by women as a means to space their pregnancies. Withdrawal was also common enough to be referred to by colloquialisms such as "minding his pullbacks" (Brodie 1994). Marital abstinence may have been used, but as the ideal of romantic marriage took hold in the nineteenth century, forgoing intimacy became increasingly unacceptable. Abstinence was an uncertain technique, anyway. The monthly cycle of human fertility was not well understood, so each woman had to figure it out on her own by trial and error, if she wanted to avoid sex when conception was most likely. Douches, vaginal herbal suppositories, condoms, and other barrier methods became increasingly available as a contraceptive market emerged in the mid-1800s. The water cure, which was very popular with women, recommended several cold water douches per day as well as before and after intercourse. Instructions for homemade herbal concoctions to use for douches or as vaginal suppositories were published in recipe books, and commercial preparations were also available by mail order. The cost of condoms declined after the development of rubber manufacturing, and they became a common method among married couples by the 1870s.

Direct evidence about the birth control practices of immigrant women and African American women in slavery and freedom is even more scarce. They probably had far fewer resources for controlling their fertility, however. Physicians cost money, as did the commercial prod-

ucts that were often marketed under euphemistic names, requiring both cash and knowledge of English idioms to acquire them. Slave women had no rights to their persons and were expected to produce many children, especially after the end of the slave trade in 1808 when birth became the only source of new slaves. Planters often complained that slave women knew secrets to prevent pregnancies and induce miscarriages. It is quite possible that the folk methods for homemade contraceptives and abortifacients were shared by oral tradition among African American women and women in immigrant communities.

Women's diaries and letters also convey their doubts about and frustrations with contraception. Even with a wide variety of techniques available, women did not often succeed in controlling their fertility as well as they might have wished. Yet women also worried about the morality of separating sex from procreation. This ambivalence was expressed in their practices. Typically, women did not try to control their fertility until after the birth of their first child. Their efforts (and frustrations) increased over their married lives as they had more children, with women trying particularly to limit the number of births they had after age thirty. In the eighteenth century, women seemed resigned to failure. But over the course of the nineteenth century, women's frustration grew, and they expressed the desire for more effective methods. When contraceptives failed, women often relied on abortion, which was legal until the 1860s.

The main argument advanced to support fertility control in this period was the necessity of protecting women's health. This argument was a persuasive counterbalance to moral concerns about contraception because the risk of death in childbirth was very real. In fact, maternal mortality rates did not decline dramatically until the 1940s. Beyond death, which deprived children of their mothers' love, chronic illness and disability were also associated with childbirth. The ability to control when and if they became pregnant promised to give women greater control over their own lives in a very literal way. However they managed it, the birthrate among white, native-born women fell dramatically. In 1800 they could expect to have seven children in their lifetime, but by 1860 this number fell to five, and by 1900 it fell to three and a half (Coale and Zelnik 1963). Fertility rates among African Americans and immigrants were higher and declined more slowly than those of native-born white women. As discussed below, these differences raised concerns about what kind of people were having the most children.

Most of what is known about historical birth control practices concerns married women, not girls. However, it is important to recall that the average age of marriage for girls has shifted throughout U.S. history; many women married at ages that would be considered too young at the beginning of the twenty-first century. Before universal birth registration and compulsory education through high school became the law in the twentieth century, the age dividing childhood and adulthood was not precise. More than their age, what made people adults was their assumption of adult roles, and throughout most of U.S. history, legally and culturally, marriage marked the transition from girlhood to womanhood. Age-of-consent laws, which indicate the age at which society thinks girls are too young to marry, were very

low (ten to twelve) in colonial and nineteenth-century America. Although few girls married as young as age twelve, teen marriages were not uncommon. In these circumstances, girls' sense of a need for birth control may not have been great. "A hastily arranged marriage" was the time-honored method for resolving the problem of a premarital pregnancy (Luker 1996). In the 1850s, 10 percent of brides were pregnant. Between 1880 and 1910, when both contraceptives and abortions were newly illegal, that figure rose to 23 percent (Odem 1995). Although frowned upon, the pregnant bride was accepted into society. The greater concern centered on those girls who were seduced and abandoned by married men. There was no socially approved remedy for that situation, and the resulting illegitimacy "ruined" the girl's life.

By the end of the century, profound social changes raised growing concerns about the perilous transition from girlhood to womanhood. Between 1870 and 1910, girls entered into the labor force in great numbers. They also moved away from domestic work and entered the factories and stores of growing urban centers. These jobs drew them away from the strictures of family life and exposed them to emerging commercial entertainments. In the eyes of many social leaders, this new urban landscape contained great dangers. According to Anthony Comstock, president of the New York Society for the Suppression of Vice, sexually explicit materials, including contraception, along with gambling, prostitution, and alcohol, posed a grave danger to the morality of American youth. He believed that exposure to such material would irreparably harm young people and that knowledge about contraception would undermine premarital chastity. What else would keep daughters chaste, if not the fear of pregnancy? In 1872, following Comstock's logic, Congress prohibited distribution of all sexually related images and texts as obscene. The exhaustive list of obscenities included all contraceptive information and devices. By 1885 twenty-four states had enacted similar legislation, but only Connecticut prohibited the actual use of contraceptives. Books that were widely distributed earlier in the century were rewritten, and devices that had been available through the patent contraceptive market were suppressed.

Comstock himself was very hostile to changes in women's roles. He opposed contraception because of his distaste for the independence it promised to give women. However, the law he championed was part of a larger movement to promote social purity that also drew support from women's organizations. For instance, the Woman's Christian Temperance Union (WCTU), known mostly for its anti-alcohol campaign, actively campaigned for laws that would raise the age of consent. The WCTU worried about innocent working-class girls who, adrift from family, overworked, and drawn to the new social pleasures of dance halls and amusement parks, were vulnerable to the advances of unscrupulous older men. Any girl who was seduced would be ostracized. The seducer, however, faced no penalty. The goal of raising the age of consent was to challenge this double sexual standard by imposing punishment on men. Other organizations, like the Young Women's Christian Association (YWCA), provided safe alternative entertainments for working girls.

The representation of girls as victims of male lust ran up against the reality of young women who eagerly explored the new freedoms of work and city life. An older age of consent, justified as protection, also defined adolescent girls as incapable of making their own sexual choices. Girls who challenged sexual conventions and resisted efforts to save them thus confounded their elders. By the early twentieth century, the new field of psychology provided an explanation for the rebelliousness of "modern" girls: adolescence. Defined as a specific developmental stage of life, adolescence was characterized by dramatic bodily changes and immature judgment. Thus characterized as beings who had strong desires but who lacked mature restraints, adolescents were beginning to be seen as too young to assume adult responsibilities. Compulsory education laws, child labor laws, and stricter age-of-consent laws passed by state legislatures in this period reflect this growing concern with activities appropriate for teenagers. Since the adult roles defining womanhood involved marriage and motherhood, social concerns about adolescent girls fastened onto nonmarital sex and pregnancy. Adolescent sexual activity became a signal of dangerous precociousness, an abnormal desire to assume adult roles too quickly. By the 1910s, reformers labeled this "the girl problem" and enlisted the state in imposing controls, especially on working-class girls and girls of color. During World War I, girls could be arrested for public flirting and sent to reformatories. The concern about the sexual rebelliousness of modern girls intertwined with concerns about legalizing contraceptives. If adolescence was characterized by high emotions and bad judgment, then open access to birth control would only undermine the fear of illegitimacy that kept most girls from

The July 1919 cover of the Birth Control Review, *Margaret Sanger's magazine that was taken to court by Anthony Comstock for promoting "obscenity." (General Research Division, The New York Public Library, Astor, Lenox, and Tilden Foundations)*

engaging in premarital sex. In legislative debates about contraception, legislators often justified restrictions as necessary for this reason.

Although debate about the morality of legalized birth control increased, religious organizations, except the Catholic Church, had little to say about the issue. In the 1900s, mainstream Protestants and Jews were silent or supported legalized birth control, although not enthusiastically. Fundamentalist Protestants condemned it as secular and worldly but did not actively oppose it before the 1970s. The Catholic Church's opposition emerged early, with condemnation of all artificial means of preventing conception. This opposition stemmed from the view that sex should only be indulged in for the purpose of procreation and contraception frustrated that purpose. Only natural methods such as abstinence during fertile times were acceptable. Throughout twentieth-century efforts to legitimate contraception, the Catholic Church has actively opposed it.

The first sustained challenge to the Comstock laws came in the wake of Margaret Sanger's activism. In 1914, Sanger was arrested for writing about abortion and contraception in her magazine, the *Woman Rebel*. She also wrote and distributed "Family Limitation," a pamphlet that provided detailed descriptions of various contraceptive methods. In 1916, she and two other women opened the first U.S. birth control clinic, in Brooklyn. The police shut it down after ten days, and Sanger and her compatriots spent thirty days in jail. After her release, Sanger traveled across the nation encouraging others to open clinics and challenge laws. She opened her second clinic in New York City in 1923 (it remained open until 1974) and helped establish a nation-

al network of clinics that joined together as Planned Parenthood in 1942. These clinics contributed to the development of accurate pregnancy tests and supported the initial development of spermicides, diaphragms, intrauterine devices (IUDs), and the birth control pill. Sanger also continued to lobby for changes in the Comstock law. However, Congress refused, often citing the danger that open access to contraception would encourage promiscuity among single young women. In 1936, a federal court ruled that it was permissible for physicians to prescribe contraceptives in the interests of the health of their married patients. By that time, there were more than 300 birth control clinics nationwide.

Planned Parenthood's goal was to make legal, safe, and effective contraceptives accessible to all (married) women. From its earliest days, clinics were hesitant to provide contraceptives to single women for fear of being charged with corrupting their morals. Thus before the 1970s, their services were in practice available only to married women in cities that had clinics, like New York, Chicago, Philadelphia, Los Angeles, Little Rock, and Baltimore. Young women, single women, and women without access to clinics still had to rely on the commercial contraceptive market, which grew quickly in the 1930s. Massengill and Lysol both advertised their products as douching agents. Condom manufacturers expanded their reach to gas stations and restaurant bathrooms. A wide variety of foams, tablets, and suppositories that purportedly contained spermicides were also available. These patent medicines were semilegal, unregulated, and of uncertain effectiveness. Thus, whether a women succeeded in controlling her fertility in this period was often still a matter of luck, age, marital status, and financial resources. Even though illegal, abortions were widely used as a backup for contraceptive failure.

A twentieth-century woman might have had more luck in limiting her fertility, but young women, poor women, and women of color faced another threat: efforts by government and social bigots to control their contraceptive options. Alongside the birth control movement grew a national movement to legalize sterilization. Grounded in eugenics, which claimed to apply scientific principles of heredity to human reproduction, this movement helped pass laws in twenty-eight states between 1907 and 1931 that required sterilization of institutionalized mentally retarded and mentally ill people. Thus, the first birth control technique that was legalized in the twentieth century was actually surgical sterilization performed by court order.

The standards by which people were labeled unfit to bear children were influenced by social prejudices. The majority of people sterilized under these laws before the 1960s were adolescent girls who were committed to institutions for the feebleminded because they were deemed to be promiscuous. Many were committed specifically so that they could be sterilized. In fact, the 1927 Supreme Court decision upholding compulsory sterilization involved the case of a seventeen-year-old girl, Carrie Buck, who had been committed to Virginia's Colony for the Epileptic and Feeble-Minded because she was pregnant out of wedlock. Because she was the daughter of an unwed mother and social workers said her newborn daughter looked odd, the state declared that Carrie was feebleminded and ordered that she be sterilized before being released. The Supreme

Court agreed. Saying "three generations of imbeciles is enough" (Roberts 1997), it enshrined eugenics logic about the relationship among age, poverty, social problems, and illegitimacy in the law. According to this logic, sex outside marriage as a teenager was the main symptom of feeblemindedness in girls because no responsible, intelligent girl would risk the social shame and ruin of an out-of-wedlock birth. Those who were sexually active were automatically deemed irresponsible, incompetent, and likely to pass these traits on to their children, either in their genes or through inadequate parenting. The Court reasoned that although society might not be able to control the sexual conduct of these problem girls, it could at least protect itself from their irresponsible fertility.

In the 1950s and 1960s the focus of sterilizations shifted to poor black, Hispanic, and Native American women. These women were often coerced into consenting to the operation through tactics such as threatening to revoke their welfare benefits and refusing to give medical care during labor or provide abortions until women agreed to the operation. Many of these women were quite young, such that when the federal government issued guidelines for Medicaid reimbursement of sterilization costs in 1978, it specifically prohibited the use of federal funds to sterilize women under age twenty-one. Although abuses may have been curtailed, the eugenics idea that excess fertility causes poverty and that birth control is the solution informs much of the current debate about teen pregnancy and welfare mothers. Also behind that debate are concerns about the new reproductive choices women gained in the 1960s.

That decade witnessed a great deal of social change involving birth control.

A sixteen-year-old couple waits outside a family planning clinic. (Skjold Photographs)

Contraception was legalized in a 1965 Supreme Court decision, *Griswold v. Connecticut*, which ruled that married couples had a right to privacy in the matter of fertility control. This right to privacy was extended to single women in *Eisenstadt v. Baird* (1972). The right of teenagers to have access to contraceptives was not clearly established until 1977, in *Carey v. Population Services*, which struck down a New York state law that prohibited the sale of nonprescription contraceptives to anyone under sixteen. Even before the 1977 case, however, federal funds for contraceptive services for poor, sexually active teens were initiated in 1971 and reauthorized in 1977. A

renewed feminist movement also reinvigorated birth control debates by championing the principle of a woman's right to choose. Feminists argued that as owners of their bodies, women had a basic civil right to control their sexuality and reproduction without interference from the government. Also, with increased focus on the well-being of children, the idea that an unwanted child was just punishment for the moral lapse of premarital sex was seen as cruel to the child.

These social changes coincided with dramatic changes in contraceptive technologies. In 1960, the birth control pill was introduced. For the first time in U.S. history, women had legal and practical access to a contraceptive method that was almost 100 percent effective. The safety of the Pill has been debated since its introduction, however. The side effects and long-term health risks posed by synthetic hormones have led many women to stop using it. Thus, although the Pill is often credited with causing the great decline in fertility since the 1960s, sterilization is the leading form of birth control in the United States and is the contraceptive choice of older women. The contraceptive choices of young women are still fraught with conflicts.

The prospect of a foolproof birth control method reinvigorated moral concerns, which once again focused on the sexual activity of young women. The Pill (and feminism) are often blamed for the sexual revolution of the 1960s and the moral decline of the 1970s. In turn, sexual permissiveness and moral decline are blamed for the crisis of teen pregnancy, and that crisis is blamed for poverty and related social problems. The crisis of teen pregnancy is greatly overstated, however. In the 1970s, the rates at which teenage girls engaged in premarital sex did increase (40 percent of urban, unmarried teens). At the same time, older women's fertility rates began to drop precipitously. Thus it appeared that there was a sudden dramatic increase in teen pregnancy. In fact, there was an increase in the proportion of nonmarital and teen pregnancies among all pregnancies. Rates of teen contraceptive use have lagged behind those of older women, as has teenagers' access to birth control, and thus their fertility has declined more slowly. But rates of birth control use among teens have increased in recent years. Just under one-half of teens used contraceptives the first time they had sex in 1982; by 1995 that proportion increased to 76 percent. Moreover, the teen birthrate is actually lower at the turn of the twenty-first century than in the 1950s (Moore and Sugland 1999).

The main difference between the 1950s and today is that in the 1950s, more teen mothers were married when they gave birth. Although nonmarital births have increased as a proportion of all births, two-thirds of nonmarital births are to women who are *not* teenagers. Moreover, the overwhelming majority of teenage mothers are eighteen- and nineteen-year-olds, who are legally adults and whose age was quite typical of teenage mothers in the 1950s. Also during the 1960s, as a result of court challenges, the proportion of unwed (although not teen) mothers increased among welfare recipients. This increase raised renewed concerns about who was having children. However, the complex demographic and legal reasons for these social changes were obscure. Instead, the weight of anxiety about changing sexual mores settled on teen mothers in debates about birth control and welfare reform.

In 1994, the newest contraceptive, Norplant, brought the historical strains of birth control debates to the surface again. Norplant uses the same hormonal control as the Pill but is implanted under the skin of the upper arm. Once implanted, a women's fertility is fully regulated for five years. Norplant was immediately hailed by some as a means to control the fertility of poor women of color and thereby solve inner-city social problems. Although state governments denied public funding to sex education, they quickly moved to subsidize the distribution of Norplant to poor women through Medicaid. Young, poor women of color rapidly became the primary users of this expensive method (Roberts 1997). The public provision of Norplant has been widely criticized as reminiscent of the 1960s rush to sterilize poor women of color. Many women have complained of being pressured into using it, not being fully informed of its side effects, and having their requests for its removal ignored.

The Norplant episode demonstrates the extent to which birth control policy still hinges on two misconceptions. Public provision of birth control continues to be based in the belief that teen pregnancy causes poverty and related social problems. In fact, the reverse is true: poverty is a major cause of teen pregnancy. The poorest girls in the United States have the highest teen pregnancy rates, but poverty precedes pregnancy. These girls have bleak prospects for employment and education, which might otherwise give them a reason to avoid pregnancy. They are also least likely to have access to health care clinics, which in a society that often still does not offer comprehensive sex education, is where so many girls learn about and obtain contraceptives. The lack of comprehensive sex education reflects the second misconception embedded in public policy. Policy continues to assume that contraceptive information and access will encourage more teen sex, but research shows it increases the amount of protected sex (Luker 1996). In 1996 this misconception was incorporated into federal sex education programs. Abstinence-only programs suggest that teen sex is dangerous to teens and to society. According to these programs, the only appropriate sex is adult sex, which it continues to confuse with marital sex.

Birth control will continue to be both widely accepted for married couples and controversial for teens as long as our society confuses marital sex and adult sex. Because it gives girls autonomy over their sexual and reproductive lives, birth control will continue to frustrate efforts to control their sexuality. Yet since the average age of marriage for U.S. women reached twenty-five in 1998, unmarried girls' and young women's real need for accessible birth control information and devices will also continue.

Carole McCann

See also Adoption; Female Sexuality; Teen Pregnancy

References and Further Reading

Brodie, Janet Farrell. 1994. *Contraception and Abortion in Nineteenth Century America*. Ithaca: Cornell University Press.

Coale, Ansley, and Melvin Zelnik. 1963. *New Estimates of Fertility and Population in the United States*. Princeton: Princeton University Press.

Luker, Kristin. 1996. *Dubious Conceptions: The Politics of Teenage Pregnancy*. Cambridge: Harvard University Press.

McCann, Carole. 1994. *Birth Control Politics in the United States, 1916–1945*. Ithaca: Cornell University Press.

Moore, Kristin, and Barbara Sugland. 1999. "Piecing Together the Puzzle of Teenage Childbearing." *Policy and Practice of Public Human Services* 57, no. 2: 36–42.

Odem, Mary E. 1995. *Delinquent Daughters: Protecting and Policing Adolescent Female Sexuality in the United States, 1885–1920*. Chapel Hill: University of North Carolina Press.

Roberts, Dorothy. 1997. *Killing the Black Body: Race, Reproduction, and the Meaning of Liberty*. New York: Pantheon Books.

Body Image

Body image refers to the mental picture a girl or boy has of his or her body. When a girl looks into a mirror and likes what she sees or closes her eyes and has a generally affirming attitude about her body, she is said to have a positive body image. Body image changes over the course of the life cycle but should ideally be a source of affirmation and positive self-worth. One girl explained that her dance teacher said she could not be a cheerleader or a dancer until she lost five pounds. This made the girl believe that she needed to go on a diet quickly to look the way her teacher thought she should. Today it is argued that from adolescence to adulthood, both girls and boys are so preoccupied with their physical appearance that they tend to downplay other virtues or abilities as signs of self-worth. Fashion and media images are viewed as a driving force, but achieving a perfect body or body image may reflect a deeper personal and societal preoccupation with narcissism. For example, one boy was feeling puny and insecure, so he decided to begin weightlifting in order to "be a man and make friends." Few individuals

The Large Bathers *by Auguste Renoir. (Philadelphia Museum of Art: The Mr. and Mrs. Carroll S. Tyson, Jr. Collection)*

ever achieve the perfect body image of a fashion model or Olympic athlete, but most are affected by the pressures of Western society to conform to an ideal standard of attractiveness. For example, one ten-year-old girl told her mother she "felt fat" because her friends teased her. In fact, she was not fat at all, but she still thought so. Girls who are especially vulnerable to society's emphasis on attaining a "perfect" body and measure their self-regard primarily by their appearance and body image are at high risk for developing an eating disorder (e.g., anorexia nervosa or bulimia nervosa).

Body image is formed over the course of a girl's early life from many different kinds of sensations, including visual images, touch, and even smell. Girls tend to compare the mental image of their bodies with an ideal human form. Ever since antiquity, painters and sculptors have rendered these ideal masculine and feminine images, and a brief trip through any art museum will supply numerous examples of these "ideal" bodies. Clearly, what is considered beautiful has shifted over the centuries; in earlier centuries beautiful women were considerably heavier than contemporary supermodels. Since the creation of the Gibson Girl model in the 1890s and the flapper after World War I, thinness has become an integral part of female attractiveness.

Usually, focusing on outward appearance is not problematic for a girl because she can shift quickly to other life-enhancing activities, like study, play, or work. When a girl becomes exclusively preoccupied with chasing an illusive ideal of a perfect body image or bases her self-esteem primarily on her shape and weight, she has developed one of the cardinal features of an eating disorder and is at risk for numerous associated medical and psychological problems. Today body image problems affect all cultures and socioeconomic groups—girls, boys, Caucasians, African Americans, Hispanics, heterosexuals, homosexuals, and rich and poor.

Cultural attitudes are believed to play a major role in the large number of body image disturbances affecting American society. As the feminine ideal has become thinner since the 1960s, both boys and girls, but particularly young women, have come under extreme pressure to become slender and stay thin. For example, in one study 60 percent of girls had placed themselves on diets to lose weight; in another study of high school students, 80 percent of senior year women wanted to lose weight, and 30 percent were actively on a diet. By contrast, only 20 percent of boys wanted to lose weight, and only 6 percent were actively dieting (Piran, Levine, and Steiner-Adair). In one poll of 33,000 women, 85 percent were dissatisfied with their bodies, and those that had negative body images were more likely to have had mothers who were critical of their appearance (Wooley and Kearney-Cooke 1986, 476–502).

Family and friends also unwittingly emphasize maintaining a slender, fit physique. Girls tend to be preoccupied with feeling too fat and strive to lose weight. In contrast, boys are more preoccupied with increasing their body mass and tend to engage in physical activity such as bodybuilding, running, or gymnastics as a means of controlling weight and building up lean body mass. Sometimes, girls and boys can feel so compelled to maintain a certain weight that they will exercise relentlessly, restrain their eating continually, and even attempt self-induced purging.

Evidence has accumulated that cultures exposed to Western values quickly and radically assimilate the ideal-body stereotype of the West. For example, in 1983 A. Furnham and N. Alibhai explored how body image concerns developed in women who immigrated from Africa to Great Britain. In general, these traditional Kenyan women greatly enjoyed their fuller figures and lovingly adorned themselves in bright robes and headdresses when living in their homeland. Within four years of moving to Britain, these women adopted the British viewpoint with respect to size and shape. Just like the British women interviewed in the same study, these Kenyan immigrants desired to have a smaller physique. The investigators speculate that media images and societal beliefs about attractiveness played an important role in the shift in the Kenyan women's attitudes about their bodies.

In another example, in 1995 television was introduced to the South Pacific island of Fiji. Before 1995, women and girls were actually encouraged to put on weight—in essence, the bigger, the more beautiful. After introducing television to Fiji, girls in the rural coastal villages watched television shows like *Friends*, *Melrose Place*, and *Beverly Hills 90210*. Within thirty-eight months, 74 percent of the Fiji teens studied said they felt "too big or fat" at least some of the time, 62 percent said they had dieted in the past month, and a significant number had begun to go to excessive means (i.e., vomiting) to lose weight. Although media images and cultural changes are not the only factors responsible for how teens and adults experience their bodies, the acute and constant bombardment of certain images in the media appears to be quite influential. Parents and educators are encouraged to help adolescents question their acceptance of these images, and high school and youth groups are employing discussions and educational panels to critique these media messages.

Medical science has also studied how changes in the brain influence body image. For example, research carried out during World War II showed that starvation can affect how people feel about their bodies. Ansel Keys took a group of fit volunteers and placed them on a low-calorie diet until they lost a great deal of weight. He observed the same psychological changes and unusual food behaviors other writers described in their experiences in concentration camps. Both the volunteers and the people starved in the camps became depressed, irritable, lacked energy, and were preoccupied with food. They also described changes in how they felt about their bodies and appearance, and sometimes these poor feelings about their bodies lasted after they regained enough pounds to be in a normal weight range.

Recently, psychiatrists have begun to describe a different kind of profound disturbance in body image called body dysmorphic disorder. Girls with this syndrome are preoccupied with an imagined defect in their physical appearance, even though there is no physical anomaly present. The girl's reaction to the misperceived flaw is always intense (i.e., focus on a mole, prominent nose, large feet, or breasts) and leads her to consult plastic surgeons. It is usually quite difficult to persuade these individuals that they have an actual psychiatric disorder that can be treated successfully with medication and psychotherapy.

Clearly, concerns about body image in American society fall on a continuum from a normal, everyday concern of wanting to be attractive to a pathological concern with physical defects and an obsession with measuring up to an ideal weight or standard of attractiveness. Because concern with physical appearance in American culture is nearly universal, most girls also want to know what to do so as not to become overly preoccupied with body image concerns.

Individuals and families must face down the problem by having discussions about the inordinate emphasis society places on attractiveness, especially thinness. They should encourage girls to recognize that how they feel about their bodies is determined by individual, familial, and societal factors and help them to remember that the prejudice American society tolerates toward the obese person would never be tolerated toward other religions or races.

Girls should be encouraged to explore their thoughts and feelings about weight and shape, especially the degree to which they affect their self-evaluation. Emphasizing positive aspects of a girl's character (such as her ability to make friends or her artistic and academic interests) other than appearance can also be helpful in placing body image in perspective. In addition, when families get together for meals, inadvertent comments about weight, diet, or other emotionally charged subjects should be curtailed. Instead, mealtime should be an experience where all family members, girls included, get psychological as well as physical nourishment.

As girls age, their bodies will change; thus their body image must also change. For example, as people age, their metabolic rate naturally slows. To some extent, genetic heritage plays a significant role in the propensity to gain weight. Although the role of the environment is also significant (in times of famine, very few people are obese), few men or women maintain the same weight in adulthood as they did in adolescence. Trying to control weight and have a perfect body image proves extremely difficult—if not futile—because it leads to an increased preoccupation with body size and food. Girls are thus encouraged to try to moderate the inordinate emphasis American society places on physical appearance and body image. A helpful maxim publicized by the National Eating Disorders Organization addresses the issue of finding a balanced self-image and body image succinctly: "Don't weigh your self esteem. It's what's inside that counts."

Kathryn J. Zerbe

See also Consumer Culture; Cosmetics; Depression and Girls; Eating Disorders; Female Sexuality; Girls' Culture; Hair; Psychotherapy; Suicidal Behavior in Girls

References and Further Reading

Becker, A. E. 1999. "Acculturation and Disordered Eating in Fiji." Paper presented at the Annual Meeting of the American Psychiatric Association, Washington, DC.

Furnham, A., and N. Alibhai. 1983. "Cross-cultural Differences in the Perception of Female Body Shapes." *Psychological Medicine* 13: 829–837.

Phillips, K. A. 1996. *The Broken Mirror: Understanding and Treating Body Dysmorphic Disorder.* New York: Oxford University Press.

———. 1998. "Body Dysmorphic Disorder: Clinical Aspects and Treatment Strategies." *Bulletin of the Menninger Clinic* 62, no. 4: A33–A48.

Piran, N., M. P. Levine, and C. Steiner-Adair, eds. *Preventing Eating Disorders: A Handbook of Intervention and Special Challenges.* Philadelphia: Brunner-Routledge.

Werne, J., ed. 1996. *Treating Eating Disorders.* San Francisco: Jossey-Bass.

Wooley, S. C., and A. Kearney-Cooke. 1986. "Intensive Treatment of Bulimia and Body Image Disturbance." In *Handbook of Eating Disorders: Physiology, Psychology, and Treatment of Obesity, Anorexia, and Bulimia.* Edited by K. D. Brownell and J. P. Foreyt. New York: Basic Books.

Zerbe, K. J. 1993. *The Body Betrayed: Women, Eating Disorders and Treatment.* Washington, DC: American Psychiatric Press.

———. 1999. *Women's Mental Health and Primary Care.* Philadelphia: W. B. Saunders.

C

Camp Fire Girls

In 1910, Luther Halsey Gulick and his wife Charlotte Vetter Gulick hosted a small group of girls at their camp on Lake Sebago, near South Casco, Maine. Clad in bloomers, middies, long black stockings, and white tennis shoes, these seventeen campers were the inaugural members of the Camp Fire Girls, the first nonsectarian girls' organization in the United States. Although the Gulicks were the official founders of the Camp Fire Girls, their organization shared philosophies and leadership with the Boy Scouts, Young Men's and Young Women's Christian Associations (YMCA and YWCA), and Boy Pioneers of America. By 1913, there were 60,000 active members of local groups, called "Camp Fires," in every state as well as the Alaskan and Hawaiian territories.

The organization's motto was "Wo-He-Lo," the first two letters each of work, health, and love, and reflected the founders' goal of bringing the "qualities and spirit of the home into the community." Luther and Charlotte Gulick posited the Camp Fire Girls as devoted to preparing girls for the "new and splendid social world" by elevating the virtues of hearth and home while emphasizing the importance of proper female citizenship. The early twentieth century witnessed the proliferation of the "new woman" who was more interested in the professions and votes than in motherhood. Although the Gulicks welcomed women's suffrage and expanded public roles, they decried what they perceived as the erosion of women's unique contributions to civic life. They viewed the combination of work, health, and love as indispensable to training girls to combine their public and private lives.

In many ways, the Gulicks' roles within the Camp Fire Girls reflected their ideal and revealed the paradoxes of a combined public and private life. Luther Gulick held several distinguished administrative posts in his career leading to the Camp Fire Girls and had wide-ranging professional affiliations. He was head of the Department of Child Hygiene at the Russell Sage Foundation, close friends with famed child psychologist G. Stanley Hall, and the director of physical education for all of the public schools in greater New York. In addition, he designed the triangle symbol for the YMCA, formed the American School Hygiene Association, served twice on the U.S. Olympic Committee, and was instrumental in establishing the Playground Association of America. Gulick was a national figure, frequently asked to speak publicly concerning childrearing and appropriate play for children. His close ties to luminaries within children's organizations fueled the Camp Fire Girls' success.

Camp Fire Girls raise the American flag at Camp Paxson in Montana, 1941. (Corbis)

Charlotte Vetter Gulick was a less nationally recognized figure, yet her contributions to the Camp Fire Girls have continued to reverberate. Gulick was close friends with Ernest Thompson (Seton), the famed nature writer and founder of the Woodcraft Indians in 1902, and consulted with him to formulate the organization's Wo-He-Lo philosophy. Seton's Woodcraft Indians was a boys' organization devoted to "playing Indian" through writing and memorizing Indian lore and dressing up as "braves." Seton believed that encouraging boys to behave as "savages" built character and brought them into closer communion with nature. Using designs created by Seton, Gulick taught girls how to sew their own

"squaw" [sic: *squaw* is a pejorative term that means "vagina"] dresses and beaded headbands. Gulick chose an Indian name for herself (Hiiteni, meaning "life, more abundant and desire for attainment") and for her husband (Timanous, meaning "guiding spirit"). Each Camp Fire Girl chose her own Indian name that best reflected her aspirations and personality. Likewise, the girls decorated their dresses with symbols that represented their self-perception—indeed, Charlotte Gulick claimed to express herself more precisely through symbols than through words.

Charlotte Gulick's encouragement of girls to express themselves through symbolism and "playing Indian" reveals her personal idiosyncrasies as well as the boundaries of the organization's democratic philosophy. The Gulicks strove to collapse racial, class, ethnic, and religious barriers among girls by encouraging them to dress as Indian women. Whether or not they achieved their goal remains in question—a glance through photographs of the earliest Camp Fire Girls reveals that white girls appeared most frequently in organizational literature. Dressing like Indians also reinforced gender roles for Camp Fire Girls—girls were expected to sew their dresses themselves and choose colors, patterns, and skirt lengths that flattered their coloring and figures.

As for reducing class barriers, though the Camp Fire Girls' founders sought to elevate and glorify work, the work for which girls were rewarded was largely unpaid labor such as learning to care for an infant, walking 2 miles a day, or memorizing an "authentic" Indian poem. Membership in the Camp Fire Girls required free time and resources that many poor and working-class girls did not have. Camp Fire Girls were required to attend meetings, sometimes twice weekly, and many longed to travel to overnight camps in the summertime. As the organization's popularity grew, commodities associated with the Camp Fire Girls flooded the marketplace. By 1913, the availability of Camp Fire Girl fiction, songbooks, "outing" clothing manufactured by the Camp Fire Outfitting Company, and the Camp Fire Girls monthly magazine *Wo-He-Lo*, later *Everygirls' Magazine*, demarcated girls who could and could not afford to enjoy every aspect of Camp Fire membership.

Despite such limitations, the Camp Fire Girls was undoubtedly the first and most popular girls' organization of its kind in the years leading to World War I.

By 1912, the organization created Blue Bird Nests, local groups of six- to twelve-year-old girls who wished to join their older sisters and friends in Camp Fire. In the same year, the Camp Fire Girls headquarters in New York City was receiving 500 letters per day and sending out nearly 10,000 pieces per week. Luther Gulick had the Camp Fire Girl handbook translated into Braille to include blind girls, and by 1914 the New York Public Library included several Braille handbooks in its collection. As the organization's membership steadily increased, the Gulicks formalized the training for Camp Fire leaders, or Guardians. They conducted training programs for Guardians across the nation, boasting that 42 percent of the guardianship were college graduates and that 73 percent had training beyond high school. The expanding administrative staff required girls to begin to pay annual dues for membership in the Camp Fire Girls, despite internal opposition from several Guardians.

The Camp Fire Girls' efforts during World War I reflected the Gulicks' belief in women's and girls' unique citizenship. Upon the war's commencement, Luther Gulick implemented the Minute Girl Program within the Camp Fire Girls to support the nation by keeping girls fit and healthy as well as advocating food and resource conservation. In a letter to President Woodrow Wilson, Gulick proposed the Minute Girl uniform for *all* women and girls in the United States. The uniform consisted of a red tie, white blouse, blue skirt, and white navy cap, and Gulick recommended that it be worn at work and school and that the money women and girls saved on clothing be donated to the American Red Cross. Although Wilson did not adopt the Minute Girl Program for the nation, he praised the Camp Fire Girls' patriotism and devotion to the war effort. The program was a partial success; 58,558 Camp Fire Girls joined the Minute Girl Program, but it was not nearly as popular as the organization's Red Cross program, in which 83,356 girls participated.

Gulick's missive to President Wilson revealed both his commitment to the Camp Fire Girls and his boundless energy. His death in 1918 left thousands of Camp Fire Girls bereft, yet the organization persisted despite countless financial setbacks ushered in by the Depression. *Everygirl's Magazine* folded in 1933, and membership dropped in the 1920s and 1930s. By 1943, the organization had no investments or endowments, and links between local Camp Fires and national headquarters were feeble. The 1943 appointment of Martha F. Allen as the first female national director of Camp Fire Girls revitalized the ailing organization. Under Allen's tutelage, local Camp Fires donated nearly $54,000 in war bonds to bolster the national organization's financial resources and enable it to employ a field and public relations staff. In 1960, the Camp Fire Girls celebrated its Golden Jubilee with the help of $100,000 in contributions from individual members. With the help of child psychologists and social workers, Allen and her administration modified the Gulicks' unique vision to ensure the Camp Fire Girls' vitality and relevance. Committed to improving local-national ties, encouraging a larger and more diverse membership, immersing the organization in community service, and training volunteers professionally, Allen nearly doubled the number of local Camp Fires by 1960.

The national transformations of the 1960s reverberated within Camp Fire Girls as well. In September 1962 the organization presented a dramatically transfigured national program. Camp Fire Girls were divided into three age groups rather than two, ascending from Blue Birds to Junior Hi Girls and then to Camp Fire Girls. The program's traditional emphasis on interpersonal relationships and socializing was replaced with an emphasis on community service. In 1965, Camp Fire undertook the "Widen Your World" project during the United Nations International Year of Cooperation. Camp Fire Girls "widened their worlds" by befriending children and adults from diverse backgrounds. In 1964, August 4 was set aside as Camp Fire Day at the New York World's Fair; a new era in Camp Fire was afoot.

In 1963, after receiving a generous grant from the Department of Health, Education, and Welfare, Camp Fire established local groups in underrepresented neighborhoods in Boston, Detroit, and Washington, D.C., under the auspices of the Metropolitan Critical Areas Project. Camp Fire instituted troops in rural areas, in migrant worker camps, and on Native American reservations as well. In 1966, Camp Fire continued to expand its visibility through the Horizon Club Conference, during which more than 1,000 Camp Fire Girls traveled to Puerto Rico, Colombia, and Jamaica as "good ambassadors" to the world.

In the same year, Martha Allen resigned her post as national director to Hester Turner, a former dean of students at Lewis and Clark College. She inherited Allen's expansive organization and instituted additional changes in the Camp Fire Girls, apparent in the "psychedelic" version of "America the Beautiful" sung at the Quadrennial Conference in 1967 and the dissemination of pamphlets concerning the dangers of lysergic acid diethylamide (LSD). Also in 1967, Turner appointed Camp Fire Girls themselves as members of the board in order to ensure that girls' voices were heard amid the cacophony of adult voices. In the tradition of their activities during World Wars I and II, Camp Fire Girls participated in war relief for the Vietnam War, sending toys to young refugees in Vietnam and cookies to American soldiers overseas.

The changes within the organization were visible to all—indeed, Turner stipulated that Camp Fire uniforms be made from permanent-press, stain-resistant fabrics to relieve parents of excessive ironing. The "Take a Stand" National Council Meeting of 1970 revealed that still more changes would follow. Articles in *The Camp Fire Girl* magazine (later called *Today's Girl*) reflected contemporary concerns of adolescents; articles entitled "Youth and Drugs: A Language Gap" and "Unwed Motherhood" earned the magazine top honors in a contest hosted by the Community Agencies Public Relations Associations. In 1970, high school boys were permitted to join Camp Fire and men were allowed to become group leaders, perhaps the most significant decision in Camp Fire's history. One local leader wrote that Camp Fire choosing to remain single-sex would perpetuate destructive role stereotyping. Camp Fire's new magazine, *Today's Girl*, was evidence of the organization's new self-perception as well as broader national transformations. For example, in the October 1971 issue, Cesar Chavez wrote an article for the magazine concerning racial discrimination. Though the magazine could not be sustained beyond 1972, it testified to the organization's commitment to encompassing a broader constituency. Camp Fire established projects specifically addressing the needs of Catholic, Jewish, eastern Orthodox, Lutheran, and Buddhist youth in order to avoid excluding local church organizations.

Despite Camp Fire's attempts at inclusiveness and augmented membership, by 1972 the program was losing nearly 40,000 members per year. The Membership Growth Campaign of 1970 fell short of its 1-million-member goal. By 1975, there were 453,000 Camp Fire Girls, evidence of a 10 percent drop in membership annually. Declining birthrates after the baby boom generation along with a range of choices beyond Camp Fire for boys and girls called the organization's survival into question. In May 1973, the organization's planning committee, called "New Day," reaffirmed Camp Fire's commitment to remaining unaffiliated with other youth groups. Changes from within were dramatic—the planning committee replaced the National Council with a congress of delegates elected locally. This decision increased local councils' autonomy and rendered dues paying a local, rather than national, decision. In addition, in response to local councils' votes, Camp Fire relocated from its Worth Street, New York City, address to Kansas City, Missouri. A massive flood in Kansas City flooded the local Camp Fire office, yet the national headquarters' move was finalized in 1979. New Day also extended membership to boys in all age groups with some slight changes in name: for example, Blue Birds became Blue Jays. In admitting boys, Camp Fire perceived itself as expanding rather than severing its commitment to enhancing girls' lives. Organizational leaders interpreted boys' presence as meeting a feminist goal by allowing them to explore the importance of learning how to do housework, express emotions, and perform other activities typically unavailable to boys without embarrassment.

The Camp Fire Girls changed their name to the Camp Fire Boys and Girls and have retained that title. The organization has persisted predominantly in the western United States, and its membership remains lower than that of the Boy Scouts and Girl Scouts, yet it leaves an innovative legacy as the nation's first character-building organization for girls.

Erin McMurray

See also Girl Scouts; Saturday Evening Girls; Summer Camps for Girls

References and Further Reading
Buckler, Helen, May F. Fielder, and Martha F. Allen. 1961. *Wo-He-Lo: The Story of the Camp Fire Girls 1910–1960*. New York: Holt, Rinehart, and Winston.
Deloria, Philip Joseph. 1998. *Playing Indian*. New Haven: Yale University Press.
www.campfire.org

Captivity

Captivity has been an important theme in American literature and the arts from the seventeenth century to the present. As such, it has served as a vehicle in popular culture for reflecting upon critical social and existential issues, ranging from divine providence to the family and gender roles and from the dichotomy between the civilized and the primitive to the frailty of individual and collective identity. No short essay can do justice to the diversity and complexity of the representations of captivity over the centuries. My focus here will be limited to Indian captivity and, more narrowly, to the representation of female captives, especially girls.

Indian captivity has occupied the Western popular imagination ever since the European "discovery" of the New World at the end of the fifteenth century. In narrative tales, sermons, poetry, drama, painting, sculpture, and more recently the cinema, Indian captivity has proven to be symbolic of a fundamental boundary situation. A captive loses her freedom, of course, but more importantly she also faces the prospect of having her individual, social, and communal identity stripped away. In critical ways, the idea of captivity raised troubling questions concerning human nature, the precarious state of personal and social identity, gender roles, interpersonal power relationships, and morality. These and other issues were raised in narrative accounts and visual representations of actual abductions by Indians, but they are also found in fictional accounts, as well as in pictorial clichés and stereotypes.

It is important to note from the start that no narrative or visual representation of captivity is ever a purely "objective" depiction. All representations of captivity are value-laden interpretations. To be sure, some seek to re-create accurately the events and experiences of actual captives, but even these are informed and shaped by the author's or artist's cultural-historical milieu. For social and cultural historians, however, fictional or imaginary representations of captivity—especially stereotypical ones—are also important. This is so because they encode cultural values in a condensed form capable of evoking a shared response in readers or viewers. Thus, even though such representations may not provide much "hard" information about an actual captivity, they provide invaluable insight into the cultural values and the prevailing ideology of people in a given time and place.

The earliest stories of captivity in North America come from the Puritans of New England in the late seventeenth century. They are markedly different from captivity narratives of later centuries. The taking of captives by Native Americans began only after the Puritans attempted to displace the natives from their land and burned their fields and stores of food in 1675–1676. Most Puritans, however, did not recognize their own culpability here. Rather, they saw God's hand in these events and ascribed all power and sovereignty to God. The self-image of the New England Puritans, who had emigrated to the New World seeking freedom of religion, was shaped in part by their identification with the Israelites in the biblical story of their captivity. Thus, the official seal of the Massachusetts Bay colony depicts the Puritan colony as a female captive in the wilderness. In this case, then, the biblical theme of captivity was crucial for the Puritans *even before* the first captive was taken in King Philip's War in the late seventeenth century.

Perhaps the most famous captivity narrative of all time, *A True History of the Captivity and Restoration of Mrs. Mary Rowlandson* (1682), written by the wife of a well-known minister, is typical of Puritan works in that it correlates events of the time with similar events in the Bible. Rowlandson interpreted the tragic events swirling around her through selected tales from the Bible. Rowlandson's children figure in her narrative largely as victims of Indian brutality, although one son is portrayed as a faithful Christian, reading his Bible and praying regularly even in captivity.

Historians argue that there was no concept of "childhood" in Puritan culture. As a result, there were few forms of juvenile literature. Instead, Puritan children largely read the same texts (e.g., the Bible, *Pilgrim's Progress* by John Bunyan) and heard the same tales and sermons that adults did. Although some children in outlying farms and settlements may have known Indian captivity firsthand, most would have known of it through oral accounts, sermons, and written works. One frequently conveyed message was that Indian captivity and the depravations suffered by settlers were due to their having affronted God in some way. Children, like adults, were taught that human nature was inherently sinful. After the Fall, all persons, including children, were sinful by nature; all were "captives of the devil." This sinful nature was sometimes referred to as an "inner captivity," whereas actual abduction by Indians was called "outward captivity."

Accounts of the horrors of captivity were sometimes used to frighten children and adults into "being good." For instance, after recounting the torture and death suffered by some boys and girls at the hands of the Indians, Cotton Mather, a famous Puritan minister, warned all children: "Oh! See that you become Serious, Pious, Orderly Children, Obedient unto your Parents, Conscientious to keep the Lord[']s Day, and afraid of committing any Wickedness." The clear threat was that if they did not behave properly, God might punish them by causing the Indians to swoop down on their homes and carry them off into the wilderness. Girls learned that women and girls were the special objects of the horrible violence of "brutish" and "ravenous" Indians. As a form of moral didacticism, Puritan ministers invited readers and auditors to imagine themselves in the position of captives. "Read, therefore, peruse, ponder, and from hence lay up something from the experience of another, against thine own turn come," Increase Mather wrote in the preface to Rowlandson's narrative.

The following depiction of the horrors of captivity from the pen of Cotton Mather is typical of Puritan texts:

> How many Women have been made a prey to those Bruitish men, that are Skillful to Destroy! How many a Fearful Thing has been suffered by the Fearful Sex, from those men! Let the Daughters of our Zion think with themselves, what it would be, for fierce Indians to break into their houses, and brain their Husbands and their Children before their Eyes, and Lead them away a Long Journey into the Woods; and if they began to fail and faint in the Journey, then for a Tawny Salvage [savage] to come with Hell fire in his Eyes, and cut 'em down with his Hatchet; or, if they could miraculously hold out, then for some Filthy and ugly Squaws to become their insolent Mistresses, and insolently to abuse 'em at their pleasure a thousand inexpressible ways; and, if they had any of their Sucking Infants with them, then to see those Tender Infants handled at such a rate, that they should beg of the Tygres [tigers, or the Indians], to dispatch 'em out of hand.

An equally frightening prospect for Puritan girls was that a girl would be carried off and "go native," becoming an Indian herself. In 1704, John Williams, a Puritan minister, his wife, and their five children were abducted from their home in Deerfield, Massachusetts. Most eventually were safely returned, but Eunice Williams, seven years old when she was taken, was adopted by a Mohawk family in New France (present-day Canada) and never returned. With the passage of time, she forgot the English language, married a Mohawk man, and refused to return to Massachusetts. Eunice's story was told in many different ways and in many different genres in New England and beyond, but most accounts sent shivers down the spines of readers and auditors who contemplated the real possibility that they might revert to a savage state of being. Girls and women shuddered at the idea of being sexually possessed by "savages."

Even more frightening, however, was the prospect of a girl being carried off to New France, put in a convent, and forced to convert to Roman Catholicism. It is hard for people today to appreciate the deep fear Puritans had, in the wake of religious wars in England and on the European continent, of being forced to convert to Catholicism. From their perspective, the child's eternal soul was at risk if she were carried away by "Papists." Even "going native" was preferable to this form of religious conversion.

In the eighteenth and nineteenth centuries, the Puritan providential narratives of Indian captivity were largely replaced by sentimental tales. The latter share some elements with the earlier genre but also are markedly different. Sentimental literature was consumed utilizing reading practices similar to those assumed in Puritan texts, most especially the expectation that the reader would imagine herself into the existential situation of the main characters. The "feeling" reader would learn moral lessons by vicariously experiencing the vicissitudes of life through the travails of the protagonists. The understanding of human nature and relationship between the human and the divine found in sentimental literature, however, is notably different. Sentimental literature expresses a radical change in the understanding of human nature and in the image of children.

Sentimental works frequently represent the nuclear family—a father, mother, and young children—as enjoying "heaven on earth." They live an idyllic pastoral life amid the bounty of nature, yet this Edenic state is always threatened by evil forces from outside, such as crude, greedy, and dishonest men or menacing "savages." Gender relations are critically important in sentimental works, as are familial relations.

One of the most important cultural developments found in sentimental tales is the image of the pure, innocent, and perfect child. Shedding the theological view of human nature as inherently sinful, sentimental authors presented a new middle- and upper-class view, which suggested that persons of the "better sort" were naturally good moral beings. Sentimental authors represented the domestic sphere as the primary site of moral education for children. Ann Eliza Bleeker's novel, *The History of Maria Kittle* (1790), is typical in its description of the main protagonist as a child and, later, her daughter Anna as well-behaved, obedient, industrious, caring, and considerate toward others and as having "every special grace." Such characters were ideals for girls and women to emulate. Yet it was precisely the purity, innocence, and goodness of such female characters that heightened the tragedy of the misfortune and suffering that inevitably befell them. The very idea of being ripped from the "bosom of family" and carried off into the wilderness by Indians led generations of readers to more highly value the warmth and security of the family home.

In sentimental works of literature, pure boys and girls had the power to change the world by melting the hard hearts of grownups. Little Eva in *Uncle Tom's Cabin* is perhaps the best-known character of this sort, though many are found in Indian captivity tales as well. The following passage from Sarah Larimer's *The Capture and Escape* (1870) is typical in reimagining the death of a young girl as a blessing in disguise, for suffering innocents and children were immediately transported to heaven:

> The body of little Mary had been found pierced by three arrows, and she had been scalped by the ruthless knife. . . . But it was only the passage from death into life, from darkness into daylight, from doubt and fear into love and endless joy. Those little ones, whose spirits float upward from their downy pillows, amid the tears and prayers of broken-hearted friends, are blest to enter into heaven's shining gate, which lies as near little Mary's rocky, blood-stained pillow in the desolate waste as the palace of a king, and when she had once gained the great and unspeakable bliss of heaven, it must have blotted out the remembrance of the pain that won it, and made no price too great for such delight.

Indian captivity allowed writers, poets, painters, and filmmakers to explore diverse issues over the years. In the nineteenth century, female captives were one of the most common subjects of American sculpture and figured in the lively cultural discourse on gender. The meaning of captivity was never set, however. Young and adult female captives provided the opportunity for authors and artists to proffer the public everything from racist diatribes against the Indians to

Rousseau-like paeans on the "noble savage." A few used the theme of captivity to offer sexually titillating scenarios of girls and women at the mercy of semi-naked men. Such works presaged a subgenre of the romance novel in the twentieth century, frequently featuring a cover depicting an unconscious female being carried off in the arms of a brawny, dark-skinned male. A few women even used their experience of captivity to mount in an indirect way a feminist critique of their own patriarchal society. In *Dakota War Whoop* (1863), Harriet M'Conkey Bishop, writing about her experience among the Indians, argued for the existence of a universal female nature—caring, peaceful, and moral—that had been repressed, to the detriment of society as a whole, by men.

> We are glad that we have comparatively small record to make of [Indian] women being the aiders and abettors of the transactions which brought such dismay to our frontier. As a general thing, they have "fed the hungry and clothed the naked" when in their power to do so. True, they have been subject to their liege lords, obliged to do their bidding, but whenever left to themselves, we are convinced that the fundamental elements of true womanhood live in the hearts which beat beneath their dirty short gowns and rusty old blankets. Remove the shackles which the men inflict upon them, and they would soon arrive to the dignity of white women.

Many girls read not only captivity narratives but also stories about Indian maidens like Pocahontas. What they almost never found, however, was any story of children born of a mixed marriage. This certainly is true in the classic Hollywood westerns produced down through the 1950s, but it even continues in late-twentieth-century films with a captivity plot element, such as *A Man Called Horse* (1970) and *Dances with Wolves* (1990). Both films romanticize Plains Indian culture in some ways while portraying the brutality of whites. In *A Man Called Horse*, the male protagonist marries an Indian maiden, and they have a child. In a reversal of the typical captivity tale, though, both the mother and child are killed in an attack on their home by white cavalry men. In *Dances with Wolves*, Kevin Costner's character voluntarily lives among the Indians and marries a woman who had been captured by the Indians as a small girl.

This brief and partial survey has demonstrated that captivity has fascinated people for centuries. It has captured the imagination of boys and girls, not to speak of adults, leading them to imagine a different life and even a different identity in an alien world. The captivity theme has allowed people to imaginatively enjoy forbidden pleasures as well as to confront their deepest fears. The idea of captivity has captivated people for different reasons throughout American history, speaking no doubt to escapist fantasies, utopian reveries, and deep-seated fears and anxieties.

Gary L. Ebersole

See also Enslaved Girls of African Descent; Frontier Girls; Pocahontas

References and Further Reading
Breitwieser, Mitchell. 1990. *American Puritanism and the Defense of Mourning: Religion, Grief and Ethnology in Mary White Rowlandson's Captivity Narrative.* Madison: University of Wisconsin Press.

Burnham, Michelle. 1997. *Captivity and Sentiment: Cultural Exchange in American Literature, 1682–1861.* Hanover, NH: University Press of New England.

Castiglia, Christopher. 1996. *Bound and Determined: Captivity, Culture-Crossing, and White Womanhood from Mary Rowlandson to Patty Hearst.* Chicago: University of Chicago Press.

Demos, John. 1994. *The Unredeemed Captive: A Family Story from Early America.* New York: Alfred A. Knopf.

Derounian-Stodola, Kathryn Zabelle, and James Arthur Levernier. 1993. *The Indian Captivity Narrative, 1550–1900.* New York: Twayne.

Drinnon, Richard. 1972. *White Savage: The Case of John Dunn Hunter.* New York: Schocken.

Ebersole, Gary L. 1995. *Captured by Texts: Puritan to Post-Modern Images of Indian Captivity.* Charlottesville: University Press of Virginia.

Kasson, Joy. 1990. *Marble Queens and Captives: Women in Nineteenth-Century American Sculpture.* New Haven: Yale University Press.

Namias, June. 1993. *White Captives: Gender and Ethnicity on the American Frontier.* Chapel Hill: University of North Carolina Press.

Vaughan, Alden T., and Edward W. Clark. 1981. *Puritans among the Indians: Accounts of Captivity and Redemption, 1620–1675.* Cambridge: Belknap Press of Harvard University Press.

Cars

The changing role of cars over the course of the twentieth century has surprising significance to the lives of girls. As early as 1910, girls' serial novels described teenage girls taking thrilling automobile trips to distant places. During the 1920s, cars replaced the parlor as the site for teenage courtship. By the late 1930s, drive-ins had supplanted the local "lovers' lane" as the preferred location for dating. With the 1950s came the not-so-surprising discovery that nearly half of all girls who engaged in premarital intercourse did so in a car. Later on, after the novelty of auto technology wore off, cars offered opportunities for girls to experience independence, gender equality, and self-expression and consumption. Throughout the century the car has never lost its prominent place in the history of girlhood.

Mass market publishers capitalized on the country's fascination with automobiles by offering serial novels about the adventures of girls who traveled around the country in automobiles of their own. Artemus first began publishing *The Automotive Girls* in 1910, along with Stratemeyer Literary Syndicate and Cupples and Leon, which published *The Motor Girls*. Soon after, Hearst Publishing introduced *The Motor Maids*. All described teenage girls' travel exploits with similar messages about technology that publishers probably hoped girls would adopt. Although the novels appeared to challenge conventional notions about women's relationship to machines, they reaffirmed women's roles as consumers, not creators of technology. The novels encouraged a girlhood fling with cars, but the expectation was that they would return to more traditional roles after reaching maturity.

In the 1920s the car became the focal point of conflict between female adolescents and their parents. Robert and Helen Lynd concluded that "the fact that 348 boys and 382 girls in the upper three years of high school placed 'use of the automobile' fifth and fourth respectively in a list of twelve possible sources of disagreement between them and their parents suggests that this may be an increasing decentralizing agent" (Lynd and Merrell 1929, 257). No longer able to monitor their daughters during courtship, parents grew fearful of sexual promiscuity. With the car's backseat, gone were the days of dating safely confined to the parlor or to the swing on the front porch.

Schools, also concerned by the new freedoms cars offered girls, took a hard line on students' use of automobiles. Paula Fass noted that "more and more schools were banning automobiles on campus in the twenties. By 1927, 17 of the 35 leading institutions had such a ban" (Fass 1977, 432). Students circumvented the rules and replaced them with their own form of self-regulation, however. Although the car offered the opportunity for premarital intimacy, it was the mores of the peer group that drew the line. According to the diary of nineteen-year-old Yvonne Blue, "[She] was not ready for intercourse, although she was primed for more restrained forms of sexual negotiation and interaction such as necking and petting" (Brumberg 1997, 154). Necking and petting were the two automobile activities sanctioned by teens in the 1920s.

The secluded "lovers' lanes" of the 1920s came out into the open as cars filled the landscape of American life. The auto's role as a place of passion was enhanced as more drive-in movies sprang up. Young people had "an excuse for being out late at night in a car with a person of the opposite sex" (Marsh and Collett 1987, 16).

In 1950s movies, the car became an icon of the teenage search for identity in addition to its association with dating and sex. In *Rebel without a Cause* (1955), James Dean, the newcomer in school, is spurned by Natalie Wood. Her peer identity is secured through her relationship to her boyfriend Allen, who drives a hot rod and dons a leather jacket. By accepting Allen's masculine challenge to a "chickie run," a contest between two drivers to determine who could drive their cars closest to the edge of a cliff before jumping to safety, Dean seeks acceptance by the group as well as the attention of Wood. A guy with a car was more attractive to a girl. Writing several decades later about her high school years in Kansas, Anemona Hartocollis noted in a similar vein: "I don't remember the guy who took me to the Kansas State Fair, but I do remember his car, a two-seat Corvette Stingray, nosing the ground like a giant bottom-feeding fish" (Hartocollis 1996, 28).

Since the 1950s, the car and more recently the van have retained their association with masculinity, sexuality, and dating. In the 1960s, the Volkswagen (VW) bus (subsequently renamed a van) became associated with the counterculture and, later, feminism. Hippies adopted the VW bus as their own, more readily available version of the 1939 International Harvester school bus that Ken Kesey and the Merry Pranksters used on their 1964 "trip" across the country. The statement "You're either on the bus, or off the bus" became the central metaphor for the trip and was repeated endlessly by all participants and documented by Tom Wolfe in his book *The Electric Kool-Aid Acid Test*. Images of hand-painted peace symbols and flowers on VW buses became a staple of late 1960s iconography.

During the 1980s and 1990s, girls had their own cars to drive, although they usually did not own them. Recently, television ads have portrayed high school girls receiving new cars from their parents as graduation gifts and as expressions of gender equality and independence. In one commercial, the father's handing over the keys to his daughter symbolizes his acceptance and even support of her independence.

A mother teaches her fifteen-year-old daughter safe driving skills. (Skjold Photographs)

When Sue Zesiger bought her new 1995 Porsche, she discovered more than just an attractive, high-performance car. Sue got the feeling that "nothing could touch me—a feeling that surpasses the thrill of a new job, a new suit, a new love . . . you can hit the gas, play with those alluring new boundaries, and enjoy your position: in the lead" (Zesiger 1995, 288). Others have described their cars as parts of their psyche. Just as boys were attracted to the sexy, feminine design of cars in the 1950s and 1960s, girls and women today, according to Jerry Palmer, director of design for General Motors North American Design Center, "would really rather have a vehicle that is more masculine" (Meredith 1999, sec. 4). The popular sports utility vehicles reflect this prefer- ence for more "muscular" cars by girls and their mothers.

Girls have progressed from the early days reflected in serial novels, when their relationship to the technology was super- ficial and transient. In the present, they recognize mastery of technology as a way to gain equal footing in their relationships. How comfortable girls are at taking con- trol, however, remains to be seen. Writing in *Seventeen Magazine*, Amy Lumet asked her readers: "Do you notice how we girls hand over our keys whenever a guy is around? I think it's symbolic of the way we give up power in a relationship." Her remedy for girls' temptation to let boyfriends drive is to "know your car. You'd be surprised at how your confidence and skills increase as you learn how things work" (Lumet 1994, 132). Since

1950, girls' place has moved from the backseat to the driver's seat, as they have gained a significant measure of independence, identity, self-expression, and equality through their cars.

John Morrow

See also Consumer Culture; Dating and Courtship; Technology

References and Further Reading
Brumberg, Joan Jacobs. 1997. *The Body Project: An Intimate History of American Girls.* New York: Random House.
Fass, Paula S. 1977. *The Damned and the Beautiful: American Youth in the 1920s.* New York: Oxford University Press.
Hartocollis, Anemona. 1996. "She Drives Like a Man." *Life* (Winter).
Lumet, Amy. 1994. "Sex Drive." *Seventeen* (March).
Lynd, Robert S., and Helen Merrell Lynd. 1929. *Middletown: A Study in American Culture.* New York: Harcourt Brace.
Marsh, Peter, and Peter Collett. 1987. "Driving Passion: There Seems to Be No Slowing Down Our Ongoing Love Affair with the Car." *Psychology Today* (June).
Meredith, Robyn. 1999. "Hey, Nice Headlights: In Detroit, a Sex Change." *New York Times* (May 16).
Romalov, Nancy Tillman. 1995. "Mobile Heroines: Early Twentieth Century Girls' Automobile Series." *Journal of Popular Culture* (Spring).
Scharff, Virginia. 1991. *Taking the Wheel: Women and the Coming of the Motor Age.* Albuquerque: University of New Mexico Press.
Zesiger, Sue. 1995. "Velocity Girl: In Tomorrow's High-Performance Automobiles, Speed Becomes Sexier—and Safer." *Harper's Bazaar* (September).

Catholic Girls

Catholic girls' education served to condition females to fit within their traditional role as defined by the church and patriarchal society. In a predominantly Protestant country, the church pushed an educational platform that taught Catholic children to keep the Catholic faith and to maintain Catholic culture and tradition. Until the advent of World War I, ethnic consciousness, both language and culture, served as another educative goal. As a role model for women, the church offered Mary, the Virgin Mother, or the wife-mother. Because mothers in the home and nuns in the schools served as primary educators, the church supported the education of Catholic girls who would one day fill these positions.

During the colonial period, few Catholics migrated to the American colonies. Those who did followed the general custom of the age; they prepared their daughters for societal roles through informal education. Daughters learned from their mothers and other adult women in the home what would be expected from them, and they learned to carry out traditional domestic tasks. Trained for gender-appropriate roles, girls received a practical though informal education.

Girls' education outside the home began in earnest with the arrival of nuns who established academies beginning in the eighteenth century. The Order of Saint Ursuline (OSU), or the Ursulines, arrived in New Orleans in French colonial Louisiana in 1727. The sisters became renowned for educating girls in academies and eventually in parochial schools. In the early years, lessons served to prepare young girls for motherhood. Girls who attended the Ursuline academy in New Orleans received lessons in reading, writing, arithmetic, catechism, and industrial training. Daily prayers, mass, and examination of conscience were a part of the curriculum as well. Students hailed from the upper levels of the socioeconomic hierarchy, whose parents could best afford academy fees. Later academies concentrated on the introduction of social skills or ornamental studies, such as dancing and music, that augmented girls' attractiveness in the marriage market. In rare instances, girls gained access to the so-called masculine branches of learning. Study in the masculine fields of knowledge (Latin, mathematics, and science), some believed, more adequately prepared a future mother to guide her sons in their role as American citizens. At the same time, the conventlike atmosphere of the academies provided a safe learning environment for Catholic daughters.

The academies existed where support by a religious community could be found. In addition to educating young women, the academies provided financial support for the growing number of religious communities and served as recruiting bases for new vocations. The nuns taught the importance of marriage and motherhood while providing evidence of the value of women outside the traditional role of the wife-mother—as woman religious, reformer, and teacher. Whether intentionally or not, the church offered Catholic girls an acceptable and appropriate alternative: a religious vocation.

Unlike so many other areas of American life, a religious vocation helped to negate class differences, though it did not resolve ethnic ones. During the late nineteenth and early twentieth centuries, a religious vocation provided young girls from working-class and rural backgrounds an education and other opportunities their families could ill afford. In the immediate post–World War II

decades, the prototypical Catholic family hoped that at least one daughter would choose a religious vocation. Bright, creative, and ambitious girls found an outlet for their talents and energy. Disciplined, competitive, and sex-segregated Catholic schools offered girls an advantage in a world that reportedly cheated young women in their acquisition for knowledge and recognition.

Italian families seemed to prefer public schools and believed that educating daughters wasted money because girls did not need an education to marry or to raise children; evidently a religious vocation would not serve familial plans. In general, Italian families' lack of concern for female education continued into the 1960s. For Latinas, as well, a religious vocation seemed to go against the cultural values attached to family and children. Today, Latinas continue to fight family and peers in their pursuit of higher education. Ethnicity remained a determinant in the education of Catholic girls and their futures throughout the twentieth century.

During most of the nineteenth century, the church hierarchy strongly believed in, and perhaps rightly so in some instances, the danger of a public school education. The Third Plenary Council, meeting in Baltimore in 1884, commanded that all parishes establish, within two years, a parochial school. Not all parishes could afford the luxury of a parochial school, however, and parents continued to send their children to public schools. Local governments allowed public funds to be used for parochial schools, and in many ethnic neighborhoods public school boards allowed nuns to teach in public schools. In some locations, a large percentage of lay teachers were themselves products of a Catholic education or upbringing. Whether they attended the academies and parochial schools or public schools, Catholic girls received the benefit of highly trained teachers who also served as competent and strong female role models.

The council's directive led to the establishment of teacher preparation programs. Catholic female academies and seminaries provided the much-needed teacher training. Although females would not be admitted to Catholic colleges until 1911, by 1925, they were able to choose from fifty-one liberal arts Catholic colleges. Higher education for Catholic girls, however, would continue to emphasize religion and motherhood alongside teaching. If she married, a teacher had to leave the public stage for the more private one in the home.

Church-supported education also provided vocational opportunities other than the religious or teaching. Working girls received the benefit of practical training when religious women in growing urban centers began to establish trade schools to help unskilled females. Working girls and wives, whose need for wages necessitated moving beyond the domestic realm, found companionship and enlightenment in the summer and evening schools as well as the reading circles established by the nuns.

The trade schools often had a distinct ethnic quality. Not only did girls seek those who shared similar backgrounds, but also different immigrant groups often responded to one trade over another. Parochial schools in the parishes served national interests as well. German Catholics called for church schools to preserve their language and culture during the nineteenth century. In the early twentieth century, Poles in particular ensured their daughters received knowledge of Polish language, literature, and history, alongside the standard American subjects such as math, science, and English. Czechs, Lithuanians, and French Canadians followed the Poles' example to some extent. With the Americanization movement heralded by World War I, national or ethnic interests gave way to American patriotism, and the parochial schools became American institutions, teaching Catholic girls how to be Catholic and American. Irish Americans realized this from the beginning; their daughters, seemingly more than others, took advantage of what the academies, convent schools, and parochial schools offered. Irish Catholic girls were the first to enter the teaching profession, and they outnumbered other ethnics in entering a religious vocation as well.

Catholic girls' academies remained as educational institutions for adolescent daughters of the growing Catholic middle class. They offered the only secondary education for girls until the early twentieth century. The boarding schools, such as those sponsored by the Society of the Sacred Heart, catered to the elite and provided instruction for the daughters of wealthy and powerful Catholics. From the establishment of the society's first school in the 1820s and continuing into the early twentieth century, daughters of the Catholic elite could attend one of the society's boarding schools in urban centers throughout the country. The academies trained young ladies to be gentlewomen and proper wives and mothers, not teachers or nurses. Whether elite or common, religion formed the core of Catholic girls' education.

Before the 1920s, parochial schools probably offered a better education than could be found in the public school system. Catholic girls received a more strenuous academic background than would have been possible in the public system. Training in Catholic faith, culture, and tradition shaped the lives of girls who attended these schools, regardless of their future plans. The emphasis on female orientation, supported by the nuns through examples and use of "she" in the educative process, resulted in more Catholic girls attending secondary schools in the late nineteenth and early twentieth centuries than their male counterparts. Many would give back, in various ways, to the Catholic community that nurtured them. For example, the church supported the training of young women during World War I to serve at home and abroad in the war effort by establishing the National School of Social Service at the Catholic University of America in Washington, D.C. Whether convent-trained, a product of the academies, or graduates of the parochial school system, Catholic girls became nuns, teachers, social settlement workers, nurses, and mothers.

After World War II, the parochial school curriculum paralleled that offered in public institutions. The church added religious instruction to reading, arithmetic, grammar, history, geography, nature study (science), and writing. A major difference between parochial and public schools, however, was the content of textbooks. Religious rather than secular themes and interpretations became the norm. The postwar years brought a renewed emphasis on motherhood and family rather than professional training in Catholic girls' education. But by the

1960s and throughout the rest of the twentieth century, the emphasis would shift toward offering girls opportunities to gain a preparatory education for careers or higher education. However, studies have shown that sex-segregated classes that offer girls an equal and competitive playing field in the learning process contribute to high self-esteem. A list of renowned and often powerful women in today's world claim their Catholic girlhood education as a contributor to their success. Today, there exists no social or denominational need for Catholic parents to send their daughters to a convent or parochial school. Yet, they continue to do so, as do many non-Catholics who feel that the educational challenges offered by such an education can only benefit their daughters. For many late-twentieth-century Catholic girls, parochial education parallels an experience in a private sorority. Attendees learn a certain "codified language" that allows them to speak with and understand other graduates of the system, whether they attended the same school or not.

The largest ethnic group within the church is Latinos, few of whom choose religious vocations for their daughters. The connections to family and the importance of motherhood combine with cultural values to make such a choice less desirable for them than for other Catholic girls. The importance of the Virgin Mary, particularly her role as mother, plays a significant role in the lives of Latinas. Direct offerings to her in coming-of-age ceremonies, or *quinceañeras*, and weddings symbolize the importance of motherhood in the future lives of young Latinas. Like Italians of an earlier age, many Latino families today see little value in

Uniformed students walk to Mass at the all-girls' Academy of the Sacred Heart in Grand Coteau, Louisiana. (Philip Gould/Corbis)

education for girls whose primary function in lives is to become mothers. This continued focus on the home, within a world in which girls' choices for their futures are many, feeds what scholar Ana María Díaz-Stevens refers to as the "matriarchal core." For Latinas, their role in the home constitutes more than the duties normally associated with the wife-mother. The importance and authority that are a part of this matriarchal core are historically grounded and important as stabilizing factors for a culture in transition in the United States. For Latinos, unlike other ethnic Catholics, religion and culture, including language maintenance, remain home-based, suggesting that parochial schools that serve to instill the faith and a more general Catholic culture would not serve the needs of Latinas. Less than 10 percent of the entire Latino population in the United States send their daughters to parochial schools, though the parochial schools in inner cities are largely composed of Latinos and African Americans, who desire education in a secure environment (Díaz-Stevens 1994). And those girls who do attend parochial schools are more likely to seek education beyond the secondary level, a threat to the traditional values imposed by their culture. Despite these restrictions, more and more Latinas are taking advantage of the educational opportunities offered them; their biggest supporters, in many cases, are their mothers.

Catholic girls come from diverse backgrounds. Their goals differ as well. The education offered perhaps remains more a personal matter than the institutions and the church that sponsors them would care to admit. Sister Antonia McHugh, dean of the College of St. Catherine, offers this advice to Catholic girls: "Fill your minds with great things and there will be no room for trivialities. . . . She who would be woman must avoid mediocrity!" (Coburn and Smith 1999, 159).

Kay J. Blalock

See also Education of Girls; Jewish Education of Girls; Mennonite Girls

References and Further Reading

Coburn, Carol K., and Martha Smith. 1999. *Spirited Lives: How Nuns Shaped Catholic Culture and American Life, 1836–1920.* Chapel Hill: University of North Carolina Press.

Díaz-Stevens, Ana María. 1994. "Latinas in the Church" and "Latino Youth and the Church." Pp. 240–277 and 278–307 in *Hispanic Catholic Culture in the U.S.* Edited by Jay P. Dolan and Allan Figueroa Deck, S.J. Notre Dame: University of Notre Dame Press.

Kenneally, James. 1990. *The History of American Catholic Women.* New York: Crossroad.

Whitney, Catherine. 1999. *The Calling: A Year in the Life of an Order of Nuns.* New York: Crown Publishers.

Cheerleaders

A cheerleader is one who uses verbal commands and body motions to direct a crowd to cheer in unison. The word *cheerleader* signifies two American icons: the wholesome, popular high school goddess and the gorgeous dancer on the sidelines at professional football games. Whether envied school leader or marginalized starlet, the cheerleader is perceived as a feminized role reflecting positive and negative cultural values ascribed to girls and women. This gendered identification is ironic because cheerleading was invented by nineteenth-century American college boys as an entirely masculine enterprise. The evolution of cheerleading from a male collegiate experience to one shared by girls in venues as diverse as secondary schools, national competitions, and professional sport franchises reflects profound changes in the opportunities and expectations of American girls.

The cheerleader's original function, to lead yells in support of an athletic team during competition, endures and has expanded to include entertaining the crowd with spectacular tumbling and acrobatic stunts. Spirit groups—pep squads, song girls, and drill teams—evolved from the early yell leaders and marching bands to increase the pageantry of sport contests. Educators and entrepreneurs have assigned cheerleaders additional roles as school leaders, consumers, and marketing devices. The spontaneous yelling of the first cheerleaders evolved into stylized, physically demanding routines performed by trained specialists. Elite practitioners now participate in competitive cheerleading as a sport in its own right. The development of cheering from a student lark to a formalized, extracurricular activity and sport is the result of adult intervention at college, school, and community levels prompted by pedagogical rationales and the emergence of a profitable industry to equip and train cheerleaders.

The institutionalization and commercialization of cheerleading determined who participated, defined cheerleader roles off the field, shaped performance style, and entrenched it as a pervasive symbol in mass media and popular culture. Cheerleading as an activity can provide girls with expanded opportunities or reinforce the constraints of peer and adult expectations. The cheerleader as a symbol presents girls with contradictory images that reflect cultural ambivalence about female roles.

American intercollegiate athletics developed during the mid-1800s at private colleges that were restricted to male students. The first intercollegiate football game took place in 1869 between Rutgers and Princeton. The earliest cheerleader was probably a student who stood up and urged fellow spectators to yell encouragement during a game. By the 1890s some colleges had a designated yell leader to direct cheering at games. These students, also known as "rooter kings," "yell kings," "yell captains," or "yell marshals," were chosen for their enthusiasm and charisma. Alumni, community, and media interest in college games grew rapidly, and the trappings of big-time athletics—paid coaches, marching bands, mass rallies—were established by the early 1900s. Grandstands and stadiums were built to hold thousands of spectators. Colleges added multiple yell leaders who did synchronized acrobatics and cheers to focus the attention of ever larger crowds.

As college athletics grew in the late 1800s, state-supported and land-grant institutions began to admit female students. They participated in pep clubs, which formed organized cheering sections in the stands at games. By the 1920s coeducational pep clubs gave women the opportunity to serve as yell leaders. With the development of college fraternities and, later, sororities, affiliated women students became involved in social and extracurricular activities centered around sports. In the 1920s, beauty pageants and movies promoted female display in mass

entertainment. The collegiate sport spectacle, with performing cheerleaders, also incorporated feminine allure. By the 1930s some women made the transition to coeducational cheering squads, but they were excluded from Gamma Sigma, the national cheerleaders' fraternity, and were not eligible for all-America status with the men. Through the 1940s, college cheerleading continued to be viewed as an athletic, masculine role. After World War II, women students entered college cheering in greater numbers. Today, both men and women cheer at the college level.

As college cheerleading expanded from emotional support of the team to entertainment of the crowd, two types of feminized spirit groups emerged: song girls and drill teams. Incorporating music and choreography, each contained elements that would form the prototype for today's professional cheerleader dance troupes. In 1929 the University of California at Los Angeles featured song girls in addition to its male yell leaders. During games a small group of girls led crowds in singing school songs played by the band. Dance routines were incorporated and replaced singing by the 1950s. Drill teams, larger groups of girls performing precision marching and dance elements, may have grown out of the traditions of marching bands and elaborate, musical comedy revues. Gussie Nell Davis, who in 1940 organized the Kilgore College Rangerettes of Kilgore, Texas, is credited with establishing this genre, which features complex, synchronized formations set to music. Drill teams became popular at the college level and were widely adopted by secondary schools as an activity in which many girls could participate. Song girls, dance teams, and drill teams require space and time for their musical routines, limiting their performances to breaks during games. Compared with the emotional support role of cheerleaders, the entertainment function of dance and drill teams is more removed from the action of a game.

Organized athletics, cheerleading, and pep clubs spread from colleges to high schools in the early 1900s and to middle and elementary schools by the 1950s. Public school educators stressed school spirit and leadership as part of a broader curriculum of socialization and citizenship. They established cheerleaders as student role models, adding scholarship and character criteria to a formal selection process. When girls participated in cheerleading, they gained opportunities to serve as school leaders as long as they conformed to behavioral and academic standards set by school authorities. Throughout the 1920s and 1930s educators debated the appropriateness of girls as cheerleaders, voicing concerns about their ability to do athletic stunts and the erosion of ladylike behavior; others acknowledged girls' success as cheerleaders and argued that since most sports were restricted to boys, cheerleading (emotionally supportive and attractively presented) was a valid activity for girls. By the 1950s, cheerleading in middle and secondary schools was feminized to the extent that boys became the exception.

Cheerleading, like athletics and other extracurricular activities, became institutionalized and professionalized under adult control. Educators added adult sponsors or coaches to train and supervise cheerleaders. In 1927, an instruction manual was published to promote the skills and principles of cheerleading. A national compilation of cheers, George M. York's *Just Yells*, was published the same year. In the 1940s high schools offered brief clinics led by college cheerleaders to advise and critique school cheerleaders. Lawrence Herkimer, head cheerleader at Southern Methodist University in 1947–1948, was one of the first entrepreneurs to offer cheer clinics and camps as a full-time business. Cheer entrepreneurs formed companies to teach clinics, publish manuals, and supply uniforms, businesses that today earn millions of dollars serving hundreds of thousands of cheerleaders. To increase demand for their services, cheer entrepreneurs began to sponsor competitions among squads who could qualify at their camps and advance through regional to national contests. These competitions played a major role in establishing cheerleading as an athletic sport in its own right.

In 1983 the Entertainment and Sports Programming Network (ESPN) televised a high school competition sponsored by the Universal Cheerleading Association, followed in 1984 by the Universal Cheerleading Association (UCA) contest for college squads. Such events are now regular fare on cable television. Today, hundreds of private cheerleading clubs train and compete solely in events sponsored by cheerleading companies, providing girls an athletic outlet beyond interscholastic competition.

Cheerleading, first institutionalized as a student activity, is now also recognized as a competitive sport. Interscholastic cheer meets sponsored by public schools took place in the 1940s, and by the 1960s local Catholic Youth Organizations sponsored contests among parochial schools. Today, school activity associations field statewide championship cheerleading and drill team competitions. Where cheering is designated as a sport, schools provide coaches, athletic trainers, insurance, transportation, and uniforms. If

A group of high school cheerleaders in Minnesota. (Skjold Photographs)

cheering is designated as an activity, cheerleaders may have to provide their own funding. As college and high school girls joined early squads, they continued in the athletic tradition established by male cheerleaders and promoted by cheer entrepreneurs. Today, many all-girl and coeducational squads perform physically demanding lifts, tosses, catches, and pyramids. They participate in year-round conditioning and weight training and take formal gymnastics training to prepare for cheerleading. Like all athletes, cheerleaders incur injuries, ranging from sprains to permanent vocal damage to spinal cord trauma. Safety and liability issues face participants and school, conference, and cheer industry officials.

Title IX, federal legislation enacted in 1972 prohibiting sex discrimination in educational programs and activities receiving federal financial support, had paradoxical implications for cheerleading. In mandating equal opportunities for girls and boys, Title IX enabled girls to participate in sports previously closed to them. Title IX required that girls' and boys' teams receive comparable support; thus if cheerleading squads appeared at boys' games, they must also appear at girls' games. Girls previously limited to cheerleading could now compete in other sports, which created more teams needing cheerleaders.

Cheerleading provides various options to participants. Some colleges offer athletic scholarships to cheerleaders. After their own cheerleading stints, girls can continue as cheer coaches, instructors, competition judges, and entrepreneurs.

Cheerleaders with dance training can try out for professional cheerleading squads. Girls have different reasons to get involved in cheerleading. They may seek development of leadership, dance, or athletic skills; the enjoyment of extracurricular activity; the camaraderie of training, performing, and competing in a squad; or the recognition, even celebrity, attached to cheerleaders. For some, cheerleading is an incidental activity in their lives; for others, cheering is significant enough to be mentioned in their obituaries.

Positive and negative images of cheerleaders are pervasive in American media and culture. The cheerleader who appears in advertisements, television, movies, visual art, cartoons, tabloids, and fiction for adults and children is almost always female. Cheerleaders are portrayed as wholesome "good girls" and promiscuous "bad girls," as straight-A students and mindless bimbos, as social leaders and sexual trophies, as the pinnacle of adolescent success and the poor unfortunate who peaked too soon. These images convey mixed messages about cultural expectations for girls. Should girls be supportive and ornamental or independent leaders and athletes? Are they valued for their appearance or their accomplishments? Do they belong on the field or on the sidelines? Are they victims or heroes? Girls see the as victim in slasher horror movies and a warrior in the movie *Buffy, the Vampire Slayer* (1992) and its spin-off television series.

Cheerleading is sold to girls in general via merchandise such as Barbie and Madame Alexander dolls. It is sold directly to cheerleaders via the services, products, and publications offered by cheer entrepreneurs. At its best, cheerleading gives young women the benefit of adult coaching and mentorship. At its worst, cheerleading is a vehicle for fanatical adult ambition harmful to child participants. A notorious example is Wanda Webb Holloway, the so-called cheerleader hit mom, who was tried in 1991 for plotting to murder the mother of a thirteen-year-old girl who was competing with Holloway's daughter for a spot on their junior-high cheerleading squad. Although cheerleading reflects negative cultural values and stereotypes that can limit girls' potential, it also offers beneficial opportunities. As a school activity, sport, competitive challenge, or means to a college scholarship, cheerleading gives girls many options to develop their physical, social, and mental skills.

Mary Ellen Hanson

See also Sports

References and Further Reading

Chappell, Linda Rae. 1997. *Coaching Cheerleading Successfully.* Champaign, IL: Human Kinetics.

Gradler, Frank A. 1927. *Psychology and Technique of Cheer-leading: A Handbook for Cheer-leaders.* Menomonie, WI: Menomonie Athletic Book Supply.

Hanson, Mary Ellen. 1995. *Go! Fight! Win! Cheerleading in American Culture.* Bowling Green, OH: Bowling Green State University Popular Press.

Hawkins, John. 1991. *Texas Cheerleaders: The Spirit of America.* New York: St. Martin's Press.

Neil, Randy. 1983. *The Official Pompon Girl's Handbook.* New York: St. Martin's Press/Marek.

Villarreal, Cindy. 1994. *The Cheerleader's Guide to Life.* New York: Harper Perennial.

Chicana Girls

Information about Mexican American girlhood comes from a variety of formal

A five-year-old Mexican American girl at a Cinco de Mayo Festival. (Skjold Photographs)

Chicana girls in Texas jump rope in front of a large mural commemorating the Battle of Puebla and Cinco de Mayo. (Philip Gould/Corbis, 1988)

and informal sources, including diaries, letters, and other personal *testimonios* (i.e., autobiographical accounts, especially of individuals in extremely oppressed conditions), literary texts, oral history accounts, personal observation, and scholarly studies. It is important to emphasize that formal scholarship on the subject is sparse and "until the Chicano Renaissance of the 1960s Mexican-American women in their totality were unrecognized" (Rebolledo and Rivera 1993, 1). Chicana girlhood is part of the subset of Mexican Americans in the United States known as Latinos (or Hispanics), the fastest-growing ethnic population in the United States, numbering approximately 20 million in 1990 and expected to exceed that in the 2000 census (Gutiérrez 1995,

179ff.) About 60 percent of Latinos are Mexican Americans, also known as Chicanas and Chicanos, a gender-inclusive self-description for Mexican-origin people whose continuous North American culture is older than that of any other European immigrants. Along with their large population and continuous presence, Chicanas/os are important to any study of American history because of the crucial role in the Western Hemisphere played by Mexico, Spain, and *mestizaje*, the racial and cultural hybrid resulting from Native American and Spanish exchange.

Like other U.S. females, girls of Mexican descent traditionally have been socialized in a largely uncontested patriarchal world with defined gender boundaries separating feminine and masculine roles and ignoring or ostracizing androgynous, lesbian, homosexual, and other expressions of gender (Dietrich 1998, 3–9; Mirandé and Enríquez 1979, 96–117). Unlike the vast majority of other American girls, however, young Chicanas (a term used interchangeably with *Mexican American* in this entry for convenience) share a complex range of sociohistorical and bilingual/bicultural features that—depending on upbringing, socioeconomic class, and identification with Mexico—provide many developmental opportunities and challenges that are different from the majority (Baca-Zinn 1993, 161–166; Chavira-Prado 1994, 247–253). The most important of these cultural differences include language, immigration, and ethnic and racial discrimination, but it must be underscored that these features vary within the population itself. There is a diversity of in-group variations, from monolingual English speakers with U.S. roots dating before 1848 (the date of the signing of the Treaty of Guadalupe Hidalgo), to bilingual girls whose parents are monolingual Spanish speakers of recent immigration into the United States, to a wide range of bilingual bicultural forms in between.

Traditionally (i.e., pre-1960s), Mexican American girlhood was seen as training for becoming a *mujer* (woman) and, her parents hoped, a *dama* (lady) and *doña* (an especially respected lady). The formal rites of passage designed to ensure the success of this socialization for Roman Catholics, who constitute more than 80 percent of the total Mexican American population (Weaver 1994, 24), consist primarily of baptism in infancy, first communion between ages six and nine, confirmation occurring after first communion to the early teens, and membership in Catholic Youth Organizations (CYOs) during adolescence usually until marriage (Morales 1994, 194–196). Another formal, albeit secular, tradition that affects the gendering of many Mexican American girls is the *quinceañera*, a fifteen-year-old's "coming-out" event that celebrates the girl's transition to womanhood, with emphasis on her conventional feminine qualities and potential value as a wife. Standard garb for both the first communion and *quinceañera* are "virginal white" dresses and veils, although veils are disappearing from contemporary coming-out celebrations. Finally, formal education is generally highly prized among Mexican Americans, and the vast majority of girls attend public schools, although a significant number of parents will endure great sacrifices to pay for private, usually Catholic education for their children.

The institution of *compadrazgo*, or "coparenthood" (an elaborate social structure of kinship through godparenting), is deeply integrated into traditional Mexican American cultures and has a strong influence on female socialization. It is a complex set of interlocking relationships between parents, godparents, and child, starting with baptism and expanded at confirmation by godmothers for girls and godfathers for boys and also at marriage by godparents (see discussion of matron of honor and best man customs) for the couple. Many variations of *compadrazgo* naturally occur, but it is a recognized tradition for extending the kinship structure to provide a social and spiritual network upon which the individual can depend in times of need.

Cumulatively, these customs promote a gendering process that places the Virgin Mary and the biological mother at the center. That is, the adoration of the Virgin Mary, known as "Mariolatry" or "Marianism," produces a feminine ideal based on the Madonna that traditional Mexican American mothers (*madres*), grandmothers (*abuelas*), and godmothers (*madrinas*) put forward as a role model of virtue, love, compassion, and strength through suffering, as in the famous pietà images. In Mexican American history and culture, the most important Madonna icon is the Virgin of Guadalupe, known as the patron saint of Mexico for her combined religious, political, and historical meaning (Wolf 1976, 55). Her importance to girls and women traditionally has been as an image of purity, goodness, and nurturance intended to reinforce societal notions of proper feminine conduct. Many of the numerous sources of information about Chicana girlhood chronicle this religious socialization experience favorably (e.g., Helen Hunt Jackson's *Ramona*, Fabiola Cabeza de Baca Gilbert's *We Fed Them Cactus*, and Jovita Mireles Gonzalez and Eve Raleigh's *Caballero: A Historical Novel*), but others give a much different and more complex account (e.g., Estela Portillo Trambley's *Day of the Swallows, Rain of Scorpions*, and *Sor Juana*; Cherrie Moraga's *Loving in the War Years*; Ana Castillo's *Sapogonia* and *Massacre of the Dreamers*).

The formal traditions are supplemented by informal practices that, depending on upbringing and other individual socioeconomic variables, include learning traditional domestic work like cooking, proper housecleaning, sewing, shopping, babysitting, and related responsibilities. Along with the formal religious rites, these informal activities combine to teach girls proper feminine behavior and social decorum. These traditions coexist with the values and practices of the majority American culture, but they often give way to assimilation to mass popular culture forms of Americanization (see José Antonio Villareal's *Pocho* and Denise Chávez's *Face of an Angel*, two fictional treatments of this transnational, cross-cultural exchange).

One of the central challenges facing Chicanas in the late twentieth century and into the new millennium has been to recover, rewrite, and re/vision the full complexity of their humanness *and* humanity *as females* to correct and expand the record. The *feminista* recuperation and re/presentation of girls fittingly begins with Malinalli Tenepal, also known as Doña Marina, also known as La Malinche (ca. 1502–1527), for she enters the human record at the dawn of European-Mesoamerican contact. As the teenage interpreter, guide, and mistress of the conqueror Hernán Cortés, La Malinche is the only female associated with the Conquest (1519–1521) whose name survived the start of Spanish colonial occupation in the Americas (Candelaria 1980). A native Nahua (or "Aztec"), she served the Spaniard dutifully, bore him two sons, and because of her remarkable role at this singular crossroads in history, was perhaps the first "American" to confront publicly what we recognize in the twenty-first century as the gender, ethnicity, race, and class issues of mestizo cultural identity, bilingual consciousness, and transnational discourse. Nevertheless, her role was discounted or scorned by history, and La Malinche eventually was reconstructed as a traitor and scapegoat. Fortunately, feminists in the late twentieth century have recuperated her biography as a woman *and* girl and reclaimed her place as an important actor in the landmark events of her lifetime (Candelaria 1995).

Another historical figure significant to the history of Mexican American girls was Juana de Asbaje (1651–1695), a Roman Catholic nun known as Sor Juana, the preeminent Spanish poet of the colonial era, even acclaimed as the "New World Muse." Other than her extensive poetry, her most famous writings are the essays *Athenagoric Letter* (1690) and *Response to Sor Filotea* (1691), which argue forcefully for the right of girls to be educated formally to better prepare them for their roles as women (Peden 1982). Known facts of her girlhood include that she learned to read her grandfather's books when she was only three years old, that she began writing verse soon thereafter, and that she composed her first lyric play when she was eight. Because of her amazing intellectual and creative gifts, unrelenting curiosity, and courage in challenging the status quo even at the cost of personal freedom, contemporary Latina and other writers look to her example as a brilliant beacon of possibilities in a male-dominated world.

Although not a historical personage, another female who has had extraordinary influence on Chicana girls is La Llorona, the weeping woman, a Mexican folk legend that teaches that immoral behavior produces bad results for women. Sometimes seen as a mythic version of La Malinche, the kernel plot of La Llorona's life involves a poor peasant who abandons or kills her children in retaliation for their father's unfaithfulness and who is punished by being eternally condemned to wander in grief-stricken search of her children. Many variants describe her as sexually promiscuous because of her husband's infidelities. Frequently used as a *bruja*, or witch, tale "to coerce obedience from children" whom she might kidnap "to replace her babies" and from adolescent girls who are reminded of her punish-

ment "if they emulate her sexual misconduct," La Llorona has been compared to Medea, Lilith, Pandora, and other madwomen in the patriarchal attic of received traditions (Candelaria 1995). In the late twentieth century, however, several writers and scholars have reexamined her persistence in folklore and have emphasized her attributes as a resister of unjust power, like Antigone, Joan of Arc, Sor Juana, and 1930s Chicana labor activist Emma Tenayuca. In this rereading, she is a woman who refuses to subject her children to life as victims of classist and sexist conventions and decides their destiny by instead choosing eternal suffering for herself and merciful death for them.

Whether traditional, modern, or hybridized versions, La Malinche, the Virgen de Guadalupe, Sor Juana, and the Llorona stories persist as cultural images of powerful female complexity. From these crucial historical and mythic seeds (as well as from such later portraits of Chicana/Latina girlhood as María Amparo Ruiz de Burton's 1885 novel *The Squatter and the Don*; Jackson's 1888 romance *Ramona*; Katharine Anne Porter's 1939 Miranda stories; Frida Kahlo's self-portraits of the artist as a girl; González and Raleigh's 1930s *Caballero, A Historical Novel* and others) emerge many of the Chicana representations of girls and girlhood in the late twentieth and early twenty-first centuries.

A brief entry of this sort can only survey key examples of the actual changes and impact of *feminista* images of girlhood in Mexican American culture, one being the short fiction of Estela Portillo Trambley. Her story "The Paris Gown" offers a classic rendering of a Chicana adolescent's agency toward self-determination, and her story "If It Weren't for the Honeysuckle" depicts active sisterhood in the defense of a teenage girl from physical abuse. The frequently anthologized poetry of Lorna Dee Cervantes exhibits similar cultural thickness in the construction of girl narrators negotiating their place in adult, mostly urban worlds (e.g., "Beneath the Shadow of the Freeway," "Uncle's First Rabbit," and her *pachuca* poems). Another view of urban life appears in poet and playwright Cherrie Moraga's *Loving in the War Years: Lo que nunca pasó por sus labios*, a poignant, mixed-media memoir of growing up lesbian. One of the most popular treatments of *muchacha* experience is Sandra Cisneros's *The House on Mango Street*, a Chicago-based fiction told by and about a Chicana adolescent. In a later collection of short stories, *Woman Hollering Creek*, Cisneros adds several other well-rounded characters to the roster of girlhood that for over a century has been dominated by such familiar types as Alice in Wonderland, Nancy Drew, Laura Ingalls Wilder of The Little House on the Prairie series, Shirley Temple, Holden Caulfield's little sister Phoeby, and Heloise.

A very noteworthy contributor to an expanded roster of girlhood that includes *doncellas* (maidens), *chicas* (little girls), and *muchachas* is Tiffany Ann Lopez's short fiction collection *Growing Up Chicana/o* containing ten rite-of-passage stories by Chicanas, including three especially remarkable titles: "The Ruins" by Patricia Preciado Martin, author of *Songs My Mother Sang to Me*; "The Moths" by Helena Maria Viramontes, author of the girl-narrated novel *Under the Feet of Jesus*; and "The McCoy Hotel" by Denise Chávez, author of *The Last of the Menu Girls*, also narrated by a Chicana adoles-

cent. Other powerful inscriptions include Alicia Gaspar de Alba's *The Mystery of Survival and Other Stories* set on the Texas-Mexico border; Norma Cantú's postmodernistic *Canícula: Snapshots of a Girlhood en la Frontera*; Elva Treviño Hart's autobiographical novel, *Barefoot Heart*, about growing up in a migrant farmworker family; as well as the important visual artwork of Carmen Lomas Garza, which includes vibrant images of girls, women, families; and others. Another indispensable domain of Chicana definition and identity is formal academic research, including such cultural studies titles relating to girls as Dietrich's book, *Chicana Adolescents: Bitches, "Ho"s, and Schoolgirls*; Dicochea's master's thesis, "Salsera Heterosexualities: Chicana/Latina Agency and the Feminist Politics of Mestizaje"; and Aragon's work on "Coming of Age Themes in Drama by Kennicott, Moraga, and Lopez."

Cordelia Candelaria

See also Catholic Girls; Latina Girls; *La Quinceañera*

References and Further Reading

Baca-Zinn, Maxine. 1993. "Mexican-Heritage Families in the United States." Pp. 161–172 in *Handbook of Hispanic Cultures in the United States: Sociology*. Edited by Felix Padilla. Houston and Madrid: Arte Público Press and Instituto de Cooperación Iberoamericana.

Candelaria, Cordelia. 1980. "La Malinche: Feminist Prototype." *Frontiers: Journal of Women Studies* 5, no. 2 (Summer): 1–6.

———. 1993. "Latina Women Writers: Chicana, Cuban American, and Puerto Rican Voices." Pp. 134–162 in *Handbook of Hispanic Cultures in the United States: Literature and Art*. Edited by Francisco Lomeli et al. Houston, TX, and Madrid, Spain: Arte Público Press and Instituto de Cooperación Iberoamericana.

———. 1995. "La Malinche." P. 468 in *The Oxford Companion to Women's Writing in the United States*. Edited by Cathy N. Davidson and Linda Wagner-Martin. New York: Oxford University Press.

Cantú, Norma Elia. 1995. *Canícula: Snapshots of a Girlhood en la Frontera*. Albuquerque: University of New Mexico Press.

Cervantes, Lorna Dee. 1980. "Beneath the Shadow of the Freeway" and "Uncle's First Rabbit." In *Emplumada*. By Lorna Dee Cervantes. Pittsburgh: University of Pittsburgh Press.

Chavira-Prado, Alicia. 1994. "Latina Experience and Latina Identity." Pp. 244–269 in *Handbook of Hispanic Cultures of the United States: Anthropology*. Edited by Thomas Weaver. Houston and Madrid: Arte Público Press and Instituto de Cooperación Iberoamericana.

Dietrich, Lisa C. 1998. *Chicana Adolescents: Bitches, 'Ho's, and Schoolgirls*. Westport, CT: Praeger.

Gaspar de Alba, Alicia. 1993. *The Mystery of Survival and Other Stories*. Tempe, AZ: Bilingual Review/Press.

Gutíerrez, David G. 1995. *Walls and Mirrors: Mexican Americans, Mexican Immigrants, and the Politics of Ethnicity*. Berkeley: University of California Press.

Lopez, Tiffany Ann, ed. 1993. *Growing Up Chicana/o*. Tucson: University of Arizona Press. (See stories by Patricia Preciado Martin, Denise Chávez, and Helena Maria Viramontes.)

Mirandé, Alfredo, and Evangelina Enríquez. 1979. *La Chicana: The Mexican-American Woman*. Chicago: University of Chicago Press.

Morales, Beatriz. 1994. "Latino Religion, Ritual, and Culture." Pp. 91–207 in *Handbook of Hispanic Cultures of the United States: Anthropology*. Edited by Thomas Weaver. Houston and Madrid: Arte Público Press and Instituto de Cooperación Iberoamericana.

Peden, Margaret Sayers. 1982. *A Woman of Genius: The Intellectual Autobiography of Sor Juana Inés de la Cruz*. Translation of *La Respuesta* (i.e., *Response to Sor Filotea*). Salisbury, CT: Lime Rock Press.

Rebolledo, Tey Diana, and Eliana Rivero, eds. 1993. *Infinite Divisions: An Anthology of Chicana Literature*. Tucson: University of Arizona Press, 1.

Trambley, Estela Portillo. 1975. "The Paris Gown" and "If It Weren't for the Honeysuckle." In *Rain of Scorpions and Other Writings*. Berkeley, CA: Tonatiuh International.

Weaver, Thomas. 1994. *Handbook of Hispanic Cultures of the United States: Anthropology*. Houston and Madrid: Arte Público Press and Instituto de Cooperación Iberoamericana.

Wolf, Eric, ed. 1976. *The Valley of Mexico: Studies in Pre-Hispanic Ecology and Society*. Albuquerque: University of New Mexico Press.

Child Abuse

Each day, girls of all ethnicities, incomes, and family backgrounds become the victims of child maltreatment. In the vast majority of cases, this abuse occurs at the hands of an adult who is known to the child—often a family member. Although much of the research and commentary on the maltreatment of girls has focused on sexual abuse, child maltreatment also includes physical abuse, psychological or emotional abuse, and neglect. Relatively little is known about its precise causes and consequences. Likewise, there is no consensus regarding the scope of acts that should be identified as maltreatment. For example, while accepted as an appropriate form of discipline by many, spanking is considered by others to be a form of maltreatment.

The historical roots of child maltreatment are intertwined with early views of children, and female children in particular, as being the property of the father. At various points throughout history, infanticide (e.g., the killing of young children) has been a common practice across Western and a variety of other cultures, many of which have devalued female offspring. In the United States, public attention to

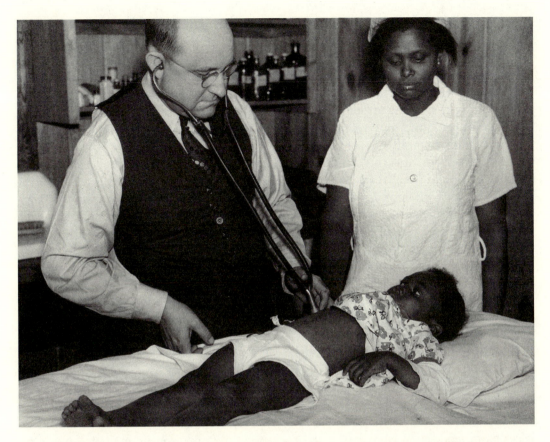

Medical examinations of children did not include looking for symptoms of child abuse until the late twentieth century; now, by law, a doctor must report suspected child abuse to the authorities. Child abuse occurs across all classes and races. (Library of Congress, 1939)

the issue of child abuse and neglect began with the 1874 case of Mary Ellen Wilson, an eight-year-old victim of severe physical abuse and neglect. At the time Mary Ellen's plight came to the attention of a local church worker, Etta Wheeler, there were no social services in place for abused children; accordingly, Wheeler directed Mary Ellen's case through the only available alternative—the Society for the Prevention of Cruelty to Animals (SPCA). In 1875, in response to the case of Mary Ellen, the Society for the Prevention of Cruelty to Children (SPCC) began an organized child protection movement.

However, not until 1935 did child protection receive attention in federal legislation with the passage of the Social Security Act, which mandated child welfare services for neglected children.

Today, all fifty states have laws that provide for both criminal and civil prosecution of child abuse and neglect. Likewise, since 1974, legislation in all states has mandated reporting of suspected cases of maltreatment of girls and boys. Although individual state laws vary as to who is required to report as well as the procedures for reporting, all states identify physicians, nurses, emergency room personnel, coroners, medical examiners, dentists, mental health professionals, social workers, day care personnel, and law enforcement officers as mandated reporters. Nonetheless, many commentators believe that many, if not a majority, of cases of child maltreatment go unreported for a multitude of reasons, not the least of which is the lack of clear definitions of child maltreatment in the law as well as in the minds of reporters. Along with perceived socioeconomic status of the family, the age, race, and gender of the child, the offender, and the reporter appear to factor into a decision to report. These same factors may also affect whether a report of suspected abuse or neglect is substantiated by social services or law enforcement. Only if a case is deemed meritorious by one of these agencies will it move forward for possible prosecution in a court of law. As an end result of this series of evaluations, through which an increasing number of cases go unreported, unsubstantiated, or unprosecuted, many believe that only a fraction of actual incidents ever reach a courtroom.

The failure to reach a uniform definition of what constitutes maltreatment of girls as well as boys has not only frustrated attempts to identify and respond to cases of abuse and neglect but has also complicated efforts at research and reform. Even maltreatment statistics are affected by a lack of uniform definition. For example, prevalence rates, although commonly believed to reflect very severe acts, may include more culturally accepted forms of violence toward children, such as spanking. Another factor that has complicated efforts to reach a unified definition of child maltreatment is the issue of consent. For example, some have contended that an act cannot be considered abusive if the girl has given her "consent," which raises additional questions regarding the voluntary nature of that consent given the power differentials that often characterize abusive relationships and, arguably, male-female relationships more generally. Despite the potential for including or excluding individual acts within the umbrella of child maltreatment, a majority of experts believe that most statistics, which in any event typically encompass only reported cases, seriously underestimate the actual number of incidents of maltreatment.

Boys may be abused as frequently as girls; however, the majority of reported cases of sexual abuse involve females. Victims of child prostitution are often female, and girls may more often be tricked or forced into participating in child pornography. Again, definitional dilemmas, such as whether noncontact abuse (e.g., exposure of genitals, solicitation) as well as contact abuse (e.g., fondling, intercourse, oral sex) should be included, have made attempts to determine the number of female victims of sexual abuse extremely difficult. For example, according to statistics from the National Committee to Prevent Child Abuse, the percentage of females estimated to have experienced some form of sexual abuse before age eighteen currently ranges from as high as 75 percent to well below 15 percent (National Committee to Prevent Child Abuse 1994).

National Committee to Prevent Child Abuse statistics also document that the average age of sexual abuse victims differs by gender. Female victims tend to be older, eleven to fourteen years old on average, than male victims, who are between four and six years old on average. Several factors that have been identified as placing a child at risk for sexual victimization may also differ by gender. Among these risk factors are social isolation, a mother who is often absent or unavailable, the presence of a stepfather in the home, and marital problems between parents in the home. Incest offenders claim that the seductiveness or promiscuity of the victim serves as a contributing factor. However, links between the physical attractiveness of the daughter and incest have not been established. Data related to daughters' promiscuity indicate that such behavior may itself be related to problems within families, as are other vulnerability factors, such as restrictions on a girl's ability to say "no." Despite this growing body of research on risk factors, it is important to note that there is no reliable profile for the "typical" victim of sexual abuse.

In the short term, at least some victims of sexual abuse may suffer from fear, anxiety, depression, anger, and inappropriate sexual behavior. The data on the long-term effects of sexual victimization are more clear. Women who were sexually abused as girls appear to be at increased risk for depression, sleep disturbances, poor self-esteem, difficulties in relating interpersonally, sexual behavior labeled as deviant, substance abuse, and victimization in intimate partnerships. However, long-term outcomes may be mediated by a number of factors, including the frequency and duration of the abuse, the relationship between the victim and the perpetrator, the presence of force, and the availability of family support.

Physical and emotional abuse can be defined as nonaccidental physical or psychological injury to a child, respectively. Although gender has frequently been examined as a variable in studies on these types of abuse, there has been little discussion of its impact beyond the find-

ing that boys are more often the victims of physical abuse than are girls. The implication is that boys and girls experience these forms of abuse in the same way, even though such a conclusion seems counterintuitive.

In contrast to the other forms of abuse previously discussed, neglect typically involves omissions rather than acts that cause or threaten injury to a child. Neglect covers a range of behaviors, including educational, supervisory, medical, physical, and emotional neglect, as well as abandonment. Particularly within the category of neglect, which comprises the majority of cases of child maltreatment, there is a general consensus that socioeconomic considerations have resulted in African American children being overrepresented as victims of abuse, whereas white children have been underrepresented. Statistics further indicate that children under age six are at higher risk for neglect as well as for physical abuse (Crosson-Tower 1999).

Less is known about the short- and long-term consequences of physical and psychological abuse and neglect than sexual abuse. Nonetheless, available data point to effects on the physical, psychological, cognitive, and behavioral development of children and adolescents. Negative consequences may include brain dysfunction, mental retardation, language deficits, poor academic performance, attention deficits, poor social skills, and reduced emotional stability. Although girl victims of abuse and neglect are at increased risk for delinquent behaviors in adolescence, it is important to note that the majority do not exhibit such behavior. Not only delinquency but other problem behaviors, including teenage pregnancy and alcohol and drug use, may be affected by a number of factors that are often confounded with maltreatment, such as separation from one's family and socioeconomic status. Other factors, such as high intelligence and certain temperaments, may serve a protective function and provide at least a partial explanation for why a large number of victims of abuse and neglect grow up to function successfully as adults.

Researchers and advocates have begun to point to the coexistence of child abuse and domestic violence. Feminists point to the pattern of men abusing girls in part as a means of hurting their partner. Girls are also at risk for a wide range of behavioral and emotional problems simply by virtue of their exposure to marital violence. Girls who witness violence in their homes may experience anxiety, internalization of problems, and less empathy in comparison to their male counterparts.

Although there is a consensus as to the many potentially detrimental effects of abuse and neglect, the majority of treatment programs continue to focus on family-based services rather than providing direct programmatic attention to the psychosocial problems of the girl victim. Feminists are among those who have favored adopting a rape crisis model with an emphasis on victim advocacy. Those direct treatment services that do exist tend to borrow extensively from approaches designed for treating other disorders in childhood and adolescence with a similar symptom profile. Even within the medical community, which is often the first point of contact for girls and their families in cases of physical injury, there is little knowledge regarding recommended treatment. In fact, many experts agree that a great deal of work remains to be done in regard to the identification and detection of

potential maltreatment across a wide range of professional disciplines that confront these cases, including law, medicine, education, and social services, as well as the general public.

Many modern commentators have begun to focus on the need for prevention over intervention and treatment of child abuse and neglect in their various forms and stress the importance of strengthening potential victims. However, such methods place undue responsibility on the girl victim and may, in fact, lead to the mistaken inference that the girl is to blame when abuse does occur since she failed to "prevent" it. Other prevention efforts have concentrated on parent training. Although there is a continued need for evaluation of prevention services and programs, a number of features appear to be linked to the success of programs directed at parents, including initiating services as close to the birth of the first child as possible, providing training relevant to the developmental stage of the child, creating links to other parents, and recognizing cultural differences in family functioning and parent-child interactions. To date, efforts at effecting public policy and other system-level reforms, which many believe to be crucial to prevention, have been relatively limited. For example, arguments that the high incidence of child neglect should be addressed through policies designed to provide relief from the severe poverty that often accompanies such cases have yet to inspire significant policy changes. Resources and support for the social service system, which is charged with investigating, monitoring, and addressing the overwhelming number of cases of child abuse and neglect, also remain limited.

There is still a great deal to be learned about how girls experience abuse and neglect. Although feminists have long pointed to the unique nature of girlhood, research on boys is still the norm, except in the case of sexual abuse. The result is an implication that boys and girls experience and respond to abuse in the same way and that child maltreatment can be adequately addressed without attention to the gender of the victim. Future efforts are needed to develop better intervention and prevention efforts tailored specifically to girls and young women. In addition, more careful consideration of the links between girlhood abuse, spousal violence, and the sexual abuse of women is needed to clarify the nature of the interconnectedness of systems of oppression.

Sharon G. Portwood
and Kelly E. Kinnison

See also Acquaintance Rape; Body Image; Depression and Girls; Orphans and Orphanages; Psychotherapy; Sexual Harassment; Suicidal Behavior in Girls

References and Further Reading
Briere, John, Lucy Berliner, Josephine A. Bulkley, Carole Jenny, and Theresa Reid, eds. 1996. *The APSAC Handbook on Child Maltreatment*. Thousand Oaks, CA: Sage.
Crosson-Tower, Cynthia. 1999. *Understanding Child Abuse and Neglect*. 4th ed. Needham Heights, MA: Allyn and Bacon.
Finkelhor, David. 1986. *A Sourcebook on Child Sexual Abuse*. Newbury Park, CA: Sage.
Haugaard, Jeffrey J., and N. Dickon Reppucci. 1988. *The Sexual Abuse of Children*. San Francisco: Jossey-Bass.
Holden, George W., Robert Geffner, and Ernest N. Jouriles. 1998. *Children Exposed to Marital Violence*. Washington, DC: American Psychological Association.
Lutzker, John R. 1998. *Handbook of Child Abuse Research and Treatment*. New York: Plenum Press.
National Committee to Prevent Child Abuse. 1994. *Current Trend in Child Abuse Reporting and Fatalities: The Results of the 1993 Annual Fifty State Survey*. Chicago: National Committee to Prevent Child Abuse.
National Research Council. 1993. *Understanding Child Abuse and Neglect*. Washington, DC: National Academy Press.

Child Guidance

Child guidance is a twentieth-century concept that refers to the principles of psychodynamic psychology and particularly to psychoanalytic constructs of child development as they were applied to prescriptions for everyday childrearing and to diagnoses and treatment of child and adolescent behavioral problems and juvenile delinquency. These ideas flourished as part of the early-twentieth-century mental hygiene movement committed to promoting mental health through preventive programs and early intervention. The institutional base of child guidance was the child guidance clinic, staffed by a multidisciplinary team of psychiatrist, psychologist, and social workers. The idea for a specialized clinic originated during the Progressive era as an adjunct of the juvenile court and was expanded during the 1920s to handle both delinquency and nondelinquent behavioral problems.

Professional proponents of child guidance held that the early years of life were the "golden age" of mental hygiene, the formative period for behavioral habits and patterns of thought that would mark the adult man or woman as either emotionally balanced or psychologically damaged, or (un)happy and (in)efficient, to use the language of child guidance. For infancy and early childhood, child guiders promoted habit training to teach patterns of obedience and regularity to both girls and boys. For the adolescent years, child guidance held that acceptable and unacceptable expressions of sexuality, intellectuality, and sociability were determined by a girl's need for security and understanding as she developed an identity independent of her parents. These needs applied to both boys and girls, although the precise meaning differed for each gender. For a girl, independence meant emotional distancing from the family of origin so that she would be psychologically ready for marriage and motherhood. As found in both popular advice and clinical practice, the tenets of child guidance usually located the source of emotional and behavioral problems in flawed family relationships and in particular in what came to be termed the "pathological" mother. During the mid-twentieth century, the child guidance view of behavioral problems dominated childrearing literature and shaped public policy debates about children and adolescents. The child guidance framework for child nurture was clearly evident in the most popular mid-century childrearing manual, Benjamin Spock's *Baby and Child Care* (1945). Although the term *child guidance* is no longer fashionable (having been replaced by child development, child psychiatry, child psychology, and other disciplinary specialties), the concepts and the clinical practices associated with child guidance remained evident in late-twentieth-century approaches to the emotional and behavioral problems of young people.

Child guidance emerged from the efforts of Progressive reformers to curb what appeared to be a rising tide of juvenile delinquency sweeping over urban working-class neighborhoods. The first child guidance clinics were created to assist juvenile court judges and they provided medical and psychological assessments of delinquents and social work evaluations of their families. In 1899 Illinois became the first state to enact legislation setting up a juvenile court system to handle youthful offenders through a separate judicial system. Passage of the Illinois law was the result of years of lobbying efforts by local "child savers," women and men committed to salvaging the lives of children from impoverished, immigrant families. Other states followed the Illinois example, creating a nationwide juvenile justice system during the first decade of the twentieth century. Although most of the young people brought before juvenile court judges were boys charged with theft or truancy, girls were seen most often because of shoplifting or "sex delinquency," a term that covered a broad range of behavior from aggressive flirting to intercourse.

The juvenile court—and by extension child guidance work—reflected middle-class ideals of girlhood and boyhood as a time of innocence to be spent either in school or at play. Like compulsory education laws, the juvenile court statutes sought to extend those values to a class of children who from an early age were expected to contribute to the family income, who left school early with only a rudimentary knowledge, and whose innocence was called into question by the frequent charges of inappropriate sexual behavior filed against teenage girls. In hopes of intervening during the formative years, juvenile court judges applied an individualistic kind of justice that was more akin to therapy than to punishment. They used probation liberally and frequently sent "wayward" girls to charitable homes or institutions for the "feebleminded" rather than to reformatories.

As they monitored the court's work, the Chicago child savers responsible for the original legislation found that a significant portion of the young people who passed through their juvenile court were "recidivists," or repeat offenders. In an effort to make the court more efficient, these child savers turned for help to the new fields of psychiatry and applied psychology. With the financial support of Ethel Sturges Dummer, a wealthy patron of child saving, the Chicago reformers established a clinic and a research program headed by local physician William Healy. Named the Juvenile Psychopathic Institute when it opened in 1909, this agency is regarded as the first child guidance clinic.

Healy's work at the clinic, published in 1915 as *The Individual Delinquent*, became a major text of American criminology and ultimately a cornerstone of the child guidance movement. Healy was an eclectic practitioner; his approach to delinquency blended the individualized therapeutic approach of psychiatry and psychology with the environmental perspective of his Progressive patrons. Much of his system was built around the ideas of the psychiatrist Adolf Meyer. Meyer viewed mental illness as a problem of adjustment between the individual and the environment. Healy was also indebted to the child study expert G. Stanley Hall, whose ideas represented adolescence as a unique developmental stage, a time of angst as girls and boys made the transition to independent adulthood. Moreover, Healy appropriated concepts from the writings of Sigmund Freud. Although Freudian psychology was in its infancy in the United States when Healy was constructing *The Individual Delinquent*, psychoanalysis appealed to Healy and his child guidance colleagues. Hidden motives for misconduct, particularly emotional conflicts occasioned by guilt over sexual thoughts or behavior, motives that could only be uncovered through a talking relationship with a therapist, enabled him to explain the recidivism rates in the juvenile courts. Unless judges were made aware of the underlying cause of the behavior, their efforts to turn a delinquent around would be unsuccessful. The ideas of Meyer, Hall, and Freud shaped the child guidance movement of the early twentieth century. But the eclecticism of child guidance can be seen in the frequent use of behaviorist methods in clinic recommendations for changing child behavior.

At the Juvenile Psychopathic Institute (and the network of court-affiliated child guidance clinics that followed the Chicago model), the psychiatrist supplied only a part of the diagnosis. Psychological testing, particularly the Stanford-Binet intelligence quotient (IQ) test, was a required part of the evaluation, as was an assessment of the delinquent's home and neighborhood environment. Moreover, Healy, like the child savers before him, argued that only by looking at the specific circumstances, the life history and the intellectual and emotional background of the individual delinquent as collected by a trained social worker, could the problem of juvenile delinquency be solved. Child guidance clinics always relied on a multidisciplinary team of professionals that included a psychologist to administer the tests and a social worker for family assessments. But even though it represented the work of several professionals, the child guidance evaluation privileged the voice of the psychiatrist, for only someone with medical-psychiatric training was deemed capable of uncovering the hidden causes of delinquency.

Healy's studies and the evaluations made by other child guiders directly affected juvenile delinquent girls in two ways. First in acknowledging child and adolescent sexuality, Healy's work merged with a nascent sex education movement, one that urged parents to teach young people the "facts of life" before they were guilt-stricken by misinformation learned on the streets. As Healy and later child guidance professionals defined the sex delinquencies of girls, these behaviors were to be treated not as evidence of immorality and certainly not as marks of psychopathology but as signs of emotional troubles, symptoms of problems, and expressions of hidden conflicts in otherwise "normal" adolescent females, problems better subjected to treatment by the psychiatrist than prosecution by the judge. As child guiders reinterpreted the causes of juvenile delinquency, they helped to decriminalize female adolescent sexuality.

Second, Healy's conclusions represented a challenge to the then popular view that delinquent behavior and adolescent sex delinquency in particular were evidence of mental retardation or "feeble-mindedness," an idea identified at the time with the psychologist Henry H. Goddard. According to this perspective, an adolescent female who consorted with young men must be doing so because she lacked the mental capacity to conform to higher moral standards. Moreover, any adolescent found to show evidence of mental retardation had to be assumed to be at risk for sexual delinquency. Because of this identification with mental retardation, institutionalization was a favored sentence for the "sex delinquent" and for girls deemed mentally "unfit." As he examined the unique combinations of factors found in individual delinquents,

Healy undercut such one-dimensional explanations of behavior; although mental retardation continued to represent a risk factor for delinquency, a child guidance examination was expected to look beyond the surface expression of mental capacity to the personality of the delinquent and the environment in which she lived. With a good personality and a regulated home environment, the "feeble-minded" girl would not necessarily become a threat to sexual order. The tendency to relate promiscuity to mental retardation (and to worry that mental retardation would lead to sex delinquency) did not disappear in the wake of child guidance challenges, but the child guiders certainly made the simple equation far more complex.

The term *child guidance* was coined in 1922 at the Commonwealth Fund, a wealthy private agency that, along with the Laura Spelman Rockefeller Memorial, financed many of the early-twentieth-century parent education programs as well as clinical services and research studies of childhood and adolescence. During the 1920s the Commonwealth Fund sponsored eight pilot projects modeled on the Juvenile Psychopathic Institute (and on Healy's second clinic, the Judge Baker Foundation of Boston, opened in 1917). Initially, *child guidance* referred only to the diagnostic work of these court-affiliated programs. The clients, like those that filled juvenile court dockets, were working-class adolescents, often from families that had recently immigrated to the large urban centers capable of supporting both court and clinic.

By the 1930s child guidance practitioners had modified, augmented, and publicized their ideas to attract a new clientele of families with troubled and troublesome but nondelinquent youths from all socioeconomic classes. The decade of the 1920s was a turbulent decade for young people, as all age groups responded to a rapidly developing consumer culture and a culture of new leisure activities. Rebellious daughters, particularly daughters of middle-class families with disposable income to spend on professional advice, attracted the attention of child guidance experts looking to secure the professional legitimacy of their discipline by expanding the range of clinic services. The behavior of these girls was more troubling than it was delinquent because they termed the values of the older generation puritanical or straitlaced and sought peer group acceptance instead. They demanded the right to create and participate in sexualized dating rituals, activities that seemed outrageous and scandalous to their mothers and fathers. Wearing makeup, frequenting movie theaters, going "automobiling," going on unchaperoned dates, staying out late, choosing friends parents did not approve of—the behaviors brought to the child guidance clinics of the 1920s and 1930s seem tame and inconsequential in the wake of late-twentieth-century epidemics of teen pregnancies and schoolyard shootings. But during these years of transition to a modern, consumer, leisure culture, they symbolized changes that many parents were unwilling to accept in girls. As they looked for ways to control their daughters and their sons, middle-class parents turned for help to the child guiders.

Through therapeutic sessions at a child guidance clinic (in 1936 more than 600 clinics were available for parents who were particularly vexed) or in the form of childrearing advice published in popular magazines, in parent-training manuals, and by the federal Children's Bureau and state extension programs, child guiders popularized their message. Although it is impossible to know for sure the impact this information had on parent practices, it is known that when parents looked for advice after the 1920s, they were quite likely to encounter something written from within the broad field of child guidance.

The child guidance message to parents was one of reassurance. Girls needed a sense of emotional security (child guiders disapproved of divorce, but they were far less concerned with evidence of economic security) and understanding (in place of physical punishment). Most important, once they reached the teen years, young people needed the freedom to develop emotional independence. Parents with rebellious adolescent daughters, therefore, were advised to lighten up and to recognize that often a youth's contemporaries had a firmer grasp of requirements for social success than did the girl's more traditional parents. For the very young, "habit clinics" introduced parents to deliberate methods of behavior modification (reward systems and star charts), but the principles of security, understanding, and a gradual releasing of parental control framed child guidance advice about children of all ages.

By midcentury, the eclecticism of the early child guidance practitioners gave way to a more thorough identification with the constructs of psychoanalysis. This intellectual shift was evident throughout the post–World War II mental health professions. The Freudian stages of childhood—oral, anal, and genital—dominated advice on child development and shaped therapeutic services. Helene Deutsch's views on femininity—motherhood as female destiny—shaped child guidance literature much more so than the iconoclastic ideas of Karen Horney. For girls, this thoroughgoing shift to psychoanalysis only strengthened already strong cultural pressures to pursue behavior that would lead to heterosexual relationships during adolescence and to see maternity as the ideal female career goal.

Although the writers of child guidance advice manuals were stressing gender differences and emphasizing female independence during adolescence as the necessary prelude to marriage, child guidance practitioners were, at the same time, creating a powerful critique of mothers as the source of juvenile emotional and behavioral problems and the emotional unhappiness of their adult sons and daughters. Indeed, mothers were seen as so entirely to blame for everything from personal neuroses to social problems such as inner-city youth drug use and violence that some child guidance experts began to speak of the need for "family guidance" or "parent guidance" as a more appropriate goal of their practice.

During the 1920s and 1930s, child guidance psychiatrists and social workers conducted studies and reported anecdotal accounts of emotionally detrimental mothering. The child guiders thought they had discovered a class of mothers whose personal emotional needs led them to smother their children with inappropriate care and concern and prevent the emergence of a healthy psychological independence. "Maternal overprotection" was the clinical diagnosis for what the popular press called "smother love." The behaviorist John B. Watson was certainly a believer in the evils of motherhood, dedicating his childrearing book, *The Psychological Care of Infant and Child*, to the first mother to raise a

happy child, and some of the psychoanalysts focused on relationships with mothers as well as fathers in their efforts to uncover the roots of adult neuroses. However, it was the New York City psychiatrist David Levy who named the disease and observed that motherhood could be downright psychopathological. Levy's work at the Institute for Child Guidance was consolidated in the book *Maternal Overprotection*, first published in 1942.

In clinical practice and in Levy's studies, most of the sufferers of maternal overprotection were boys; Levy, however, applied the diagnosis to girls as well. Overprotection of girls led to rebellion during adolescence, but more importantly, it disturbed a girl's ability to transfer allegiance from her mother to her husband; thus maternal overprotection had to be regarded as a primary cause of marriage failure. By the 1940s child guiders were equally, if not more, concerned about the consequences of "maternal rejection," or a mother's emotional distancing from her child. Indeed, like Levy, many believed that overprotection was only a mask for rejection of motherhood, a rejection caused by emotional needs that had gone unmet during the mother's girlhood. It was a conundrum for mothers—how to provide security, understanding, and independence while at the same time avoiding the pitfalls of overprotection and rejection. In an effort to alleviate some of the guilt, advice books, most importantly the best-selling *Baby and Child Care*, told mothers to trust themselves, but at the same time, these guides cautioned mothers to turn to the experts, such as those from child guidance, whenever signs of trouble appeared.

The post–World War II years, the years of the baby boom and the glorification of suburban family culture, were the heyday

Youth centers are the modern-day version of child guidance clinics; here, a social worker counsels a group of teens. (Shirley Zeiberg)

of child guidance. With support from the federal government, community mental health clinics were established across the nation; programs for children and adolescents formed an important component of the national agenda. Throughout the last decades of the twentieth century, the institutions and ideas of child guidance retained a powerful hold on both parents and professionals, despite challenges from the 1960s liberal faith in environmental explanations of behavior, from an emerging feminist movement, from the youth rebellion of the Vietnam era, and from a psychiatric community newly attuned to the possibilities of drug therapy for children. The fundamentals of child guidance—misbehavior as a consequence of emotional problems and unmet emotional needs often traceable to flawed family dynamics—remain a guiding paradigm for contemporary psychotherapeutic work with young people.

Kathleen W. Jones

See also Adolescent Health; Advice Books; Female Sexuality; Hygiene; Juvenile Delinquents; Menstruation

References and Further Reading
Hawes, Joseph M. 1997. *Children between the Wars: American Childhood 1920–1940*. New York: Twayne Publishers.
Horn, Margo. 1989. *Before It's Too Late: The Child Guidance Movement in the United States, 1922–1945*. Philadelphia: Temple University Press.
Jones, Kathleen W. 1999. *Taming the Troublesome Child: American Families, Child Guidance and the*

Limits of Psychiatric Authority. Cambridge: Harvard University Press.

Odem, Mary E. 1995. *Delinquent Daughters: Protecting and Policing Adolescent Female Sexuality in the United States, 1885–1920.* Chapel Hill: University of North Carolina Press.

Richardson, Theresa. 1989. *The Century of the Child: The Mental Hygiene Movement and Social Policy in the United States and Canada.* Albany: State University of New York Press.

Schneider, Eric C. 1992. *In the Web of Class: Delinquents and Reformers in Boston, 1810 to the 1930s.* New York: New York University Press.

Clothing

The history of American girls' clothing reflects all the changes that have occurred in the education and social position of girls and women in American society. In less than 400 years, girls' clothing has gone from being miniature versions of women's clothing, with all of its trappings and restrictions, to offering a huge array of choices. In part, this transformation has occurred in synchrony with the emergence of modern women's fashions; part is owed to changes in children's clothing in general. In most cases, major stylistic changes accompanied alterations in girls' education, leisure activities, and eventual roles as adult women.

Fashionable girls of the colonial era wore three styles of dress as they grew from babies to women: the genderless clothing of infancy, the simplified women's styles worn by young children, and the elaborate gowns of womanhood. Babies up to four months of age were wrapped in layers of cloth that immobilized their arms and legs. Once out of these swaddling clothes, babies wore long wool or silk dresses that were based on women's fashions over long linen or cotton shifts. The outer dresses were very colorful—dark red, yellow, blue, and other fashionable colors—and the underclothing was generally white.

As the baby girl became a toddler, she exchanged her plain dresses for clothing that was much more similar to adult clothing. A "pudding" (a padded hat that tied under the child's chin) protected her from bumps on the head as she learned to walk and run. Toddlers' clothing also featured leading strings, long strips of fabric that hung from the shoulders of their dresses. Leading strings were used to restrain the child's movements, for example, to tie her to a table leg to keep her away from the fire in the hearth. Twentieth-century conventions of gender distinction for little children would have seemed quite inappropriate to eighteenth-century adults. Although men and women were believed to be quite different—in fact, opposites—infants were perceived as having undeveloped sexuality. More gendered clothing would be introduced as the child matured and began to exhibit masculine or feminine traits. For that reason, other than the pudding and leading strings, clothing for both boys and girls from one to six years of age was quite similar. One exception to this pattern was that girls began to wear stays (corsets) when they were about four years old, while boys rarely wore stays. Stays helped mold the growing girl's body into the ideal posture and were part of a larger process of training her in adult ways.

By the time a girl was seven, she was well on the way to entering the adult world and already dressed in scaled-down versions of women's clothes. At a time when girls married in their teens, no one looked askance at an eight-year-old girl who was a precise replica of her mother, down to her high-heeled brocade shoes. She was destined to be hostess, mistress of a household, wife, and matriarch, and dressing the part was a significant part of her training.

By the end of the eighteenth century, the educational philosophies of John Locke and Jean-Jacques Rousseau gained new acceptance, to the point of transforming children's clothing. For the first time, dress for infants and children was designed for comfort and freedom. Swaddling fell from favor, and the use of stays for little girls drew a great deal of criticism. In general, girls' clothing became more simple and unrestrictive. Simple white cotton muslin or gauze frocks that hung from the shoulders, bound only by a simple ribbon at the waist, were the ideal garments for babies, toddlers, and girls as old as twelve or thirteen. During the period from 1780 to 1820, women's clothing came to resemble girls' clothing rather than vice versa. Partly this occurred because adolescent girls and young women declined to adopt the restrictive styles of their mothers, having been raised with relatively more freedom of movement. But the romantic notion of the childlike woman was also reinforced by fashions that made so many women look like girls.

Eventually, the vogue for simple, flowing styles faded and was replaced by more structure and elaborate trim. Infants' dresses were the exception; from 1820 to 1890 baby dresses were both scanty and plain. Though their hemlines ended just above the floor, most had low necklines and short sleeves, exposing much more of the child's body than had once been acceptable. Most were quite plain, although it was not uncommon to see frocks with a touch of embroidery around the hem. Only in the 1860s and

1870s, as sewing machines became more popular, did baby and toddler clothing begin to be more elaborately trimmed. Because of its extreme plainness, it is sometimes hard to distinguish baby clothing from the 1820s from that worn a generation later.

Slightly more fashionable dresses were adopted for girls from the age of three through early puberty (from thirteen to fifteen years). School-age girls wore simple cotton frocks with no boning. White was associated with little girls and special occasions, and daintily printed cottons were also popular for everyday wear. The narrower skirts and slightly shorter hems of the early 1800s revealed more of girls' legs, which led to the introduction of cotton underdrawers, or pantalettes. These were two separate legs gathered into a waistband but with a completely open crotch from front to back. "Closed drawers," with a completely sewn crotch seam, were not commonly used until the 1880s. Parents who found the idea of any form of trousers for women to be abhorrent could substitute cotton tubes that looked like pantalettes but went only to the knee or just above.

From 1820 through the 1840s, fashions for little girls were miniature versions of women's clothing, with the main distinctions found in the fit of the bodice, length of the skirt, and choice of fabric. The waistline for young children conformed to the natural waistline or fell just slightly above it, even as women's fashionable styles shifted to deeply pointed waistlines. Light stays were once more used for little girls, reversing the gains of the late 1700s. In the 1820s, girls' dresses became even shorter, usually reaching to a point between the calf and the knee, revealing more of the pantalettes, which became longer and more elaborate than they had been, filling the gap between hem and boot-top.

By midcentury, fashionable dress for women was becoming more complex and elaborate, and styles for girls followed suit. Clothing became more elaborately trimmed, primarily due to the availability of sewing machines and inexpensive trimmings. Colors were deep and vivid, and textured fabrics such as velvet were favored for clothing and trimmings. The 1870s and 1880s marked the high point of elaborate dress for girls. Reflecting trends in women's fashions, a single outfit might be made up in three fabrics and trimmed in several different trims. The dominant reason for this complexity was the technological advances in textile manufacturing, which had resulted in an enormous increase in the varieties of fabric available at lower and lower costs. Designers and dressmakers responded to this abundance by using as many different materials as possible in a single outfit.

Multipiece costumes were much more popular than one-piece dresses, to the point that dresses for two- to four-year-olds were designed to look like suits, with bodices, vests, overskirts, and underskirts all sewn into one garment. Waistlines dropped to the hip or lower in the late 1870s, freeing the child's torso but sometimes hobbling the upper legs instead. For older girls, dress bodices became more fitted, and corseting became more rigid.

Little children's skirts had become short in the 1820s, but women wore floor-length dresses; some way had to be devised to lower girls' hems as they grew older. This was usually done by making dresses with lower-calf-length skirts when the girl was about ten and putting her in floor-length skirts at fourteen or fifteen. Fashions for adolescent girls

began to appear in the women's magazines during the 1860s. For the most part, these featured a semifitted bodice to accommodate the girl's changing body without drawing attention to it. White and pastel shades were considered most appropriate for older girls who were not yet part of adult society. Still, to the modern eye, late-nineteenth-century girls in their late teens often look much more adult than their counterparts today.

The period from 1890 to 1919 was one of great change for girls' fashions. The fitted bodice and matching skirt were replaced by separates: shirtwaists and other loose-fitting tops worn with a plain skirt. Beginning in the 1890s, one-piece lingerie dresses (ready-to-wear, lace-trimmed cotton dresses) offered girls comfort in hot weather. Sports were popular, especially bicycling; active sportswear such as knickers and pullover sweaters found wide acceptance. Girls benefited from this trend much more than adult women, since physical education was an increasingly familiar part of schooling, but there were fewer opportunities for adult women who wished to participate in sports.

Dresses lost most of the upholstered look found in the clothing of the late 1870s and 1880s. For little girls, dresses with deep yokes were favored, the dress falling in gathers or pleats from the yoke to the hem. Dresses for very little girls (one or two years old) usually had no waistline at all; girls from three to thirteen or fourteen years wore dresses with loose belts or sashes at about hip level. Sailor-style dresses were very popular, as were middy blouses worn with baggy "bloomers." Rompers and overalls were introduced in the 1890s and became overwhelmingly popular for preschoolers' play clothes. In many ways, the clothing of the early twentieth century was reminiscent of the soft, loose styles of the neoclassical period a century earlier.

The same innovations can be seen in styles for schoolgirls. Even though some adult trends were reflected in girls' fashions, the silhouettes were different. The lowered waistline was used extensively, rather than the hourglass shape favored for women. Both women's and girls' clothing featured shorter hemlines: skirts for children under the age of five were usually just above knee-length, with short socks leaving an expanse of bare leg. School-age girls wore their skirts at or just below the knee, and girls approaching their teens wore calf-length skirts. These were the girls who grew up to wear knee-length skirts during the 1920s.

Public schooling was becoming more common, and the demands of school activities resulted in some changes to girls' wardrobes. "School dresses"—sturdy, modestly trimmed, and easy to wash and iron—became much more important. As more schools added physical education to the curriculum, middy blouses and bloomers became the standard uniform. Another new item of clothing was the graduation dress. Prior to the turn of the century, girls had just worn their best clothes to graduation. As grammar school and high school graduation became significant rites of passage, white dresses became the expected costume for girls. Sometimes, the graduation dress was made by the girl herself, as the final project in home economics class.

Girls of this period from 1920 to 1946 enjoyed new freedom in dress. Unstructured, slender, lightweight dresses; short, uncomplicated hairstyles; and simple underwear were popular throughout the 1920s. Sleeveless and short-sleeved dresses worn with long-sleeved sweaters in colder weather were the most common school costume. Sometimes adults wrote disapproving editorials or attempted to regulate girls' dress with dress codes and even local ordinances, but it was also adults who created, marketed, and sold these new teenage styles.

For all the bleakness of the Depression years, girls' clothing contained increasing elements of fun and whimsy, thanks in large part to the styles made popular by Shirley Temple. The red-and-white polka-dot dress she wore in Stand Up and Cheer (1934) was sold by the millions and was the first of many children's fashions she inspired.

Although girls wore dresses most of the time, all kinds of pants and trousers— from dresses with matching panties to overalls and dungarees—were worn for play. In the 1940s, playsuits consisting of a one-piece romper with a separate skirt were popular for school-age and adolescent girls. The practicalities of girls' active lives were gradually eroding the taboo against women in trousers.

The war in Europe influenced girls' clothing from the late 1930s on. Dirndl skirts, inspired by the folk costumes of occupied countries, were immensely popular. The emergence of a strong teenage market during World War II provided an important new source of fashion influence for younger girls. Where once little girls had dressed like their mothers, more and more of the trends for grade-school girls were set by high school and college students. What eventually emerged as a dominant and powerful youth culture in the 1960s had its origins in the girls' and teens' clothing markets of the 1930s and 1940s.

School-age children's clothing of the first half of the postwar period was not very different from that worn in the late

This elaborate dress shows off actress Anna Held's "hourglass figure." (Library of Congress, 1900)

Girls learn at an early age to enhance their appearance with clothing and accessories.
(Genevieve Naylor/Corbis)

1930s. Plaid, full-skirted, cotton dresses with white collars and cuffs were the staples of the schoolgirl's wardrobe through the early 1960s. Jumpers were a popular alternative. Western styling was a strong influence, with cowboy shirts and "squaw" [sic—this term is actually a pejorative reference meaning vagina] dresses (cotton dresses with tiered skirts trimmed with rick-rack). Dress styles inspired by Alice in Wonderland or Heidi appeared in girls' departments, and Walt Disney characters adorned slippers, pajamas, and T-shirts.

Teen clothing in the 1950s and the early 1960s continued to diverge more sharply from children's wear and from adult fashions. Girls rejected school dresses in favor of separates, usually a tailored blouse or sweater and a full skirt. Slacks, pedal-pushers, and shorts were also popular for casual wear for high school–age girls. Few schools permitted trousers in any form for school activities other than sports.

During the social and cultural upheaval of the 1960s, the differences between little girls and teenagers became even more dramatic. For girls not yet in their teens, fashions mingled an old-fashioned look with modern easy care and durability. The classic styles worn by the many Kennedy children also won widespread acceptance. The loose silhouette and short skirts of the miniskirt era were translated very successfully into clothing for toddlers and younger girls.

Clothing for teenagers became increasingly troublesome for parents and educators. For many adults, the confusing smorgasbord of youth fashion offered few acceptable choices. Popular styles, included mod British styles (including the miniskirt), West Coast surfing styles and, in the late 1960s, the exotic hippie style, which mixed ethnic clothing with thrift- and surplus-store chic (especially Navy-issue bell-bottom jeans). In the face of the miniskirt, many schools dictated that hemlines could be no shorter than 1 inch above the knee and forbade girls to wear trousers; by 1969, skirts had become so short that pants were a welcome alternative, so school systems changed their dress codes to permit girls to wear trousers.

Another major issue in girls' clothing was gender stereotyping. The women's liberation movement and arguments over pants for women and long hair for men had heightened awareness of how costume reflects the roles we play. In the early 1970s, the idea of nonsexist child-rearing encouraged many parents to dress their children more androgynously. Girls wore jeans, overalls, and knitted shirts, even to school.

Since then, the clothing available to girls has continued to include a wide range of styles, from frilly to preppy to Goth. Dresses came back, and trouser styles now include leggings and shorts as well as jeans. This presents a different set of challenges to girls and their parents than girls' clothing of the late nineteenth century or earlier, when female clothing reflected a much more restricted notion of acceptable gender roles.

Jo B. Paoletti

See also Arts and Crafts; Body Image; Consumer Culture; Domesticity; Eating Disorders; Girls' Culture; Hair

References and Further Reading

Calvert, Karin. 1992. *Children in the House: The Material Culture of Early Childhood, 1600–1900.* Boston: Northeastern University Press.
Ewing, Elizabeth. 1977. *History of Children's Costume.* New York: Charles Scribner's Sons.
Worrell, Estelle Ansley. 1980. *Children's Costume in America 1607–1910.* New York: Charles Scribner's Sons.

Collecting

The accumulation of objects gathered for study, comparison, and exhibition generally defines collecting, past and present. Collecting by girls and boys, however, has at times been vaguely and variously defined by adults as play and work, as innate and learned. Some scholars view girls' collecting as an instinctive drive, a gathering through play of what adults may consider incongruent objects, resulting in a perceived hoard of trash or junk. At other times girls' collecting has been studied as a learned habit of diligent and serious attention to a single genre of objects as a means of knowledge acquisition. It is in the very process of collecting, however, that the girl learns the myriad physical features of the world in which she lives and, especially in the modern era, creates through the processes of consuming and collecting a self. A *collected* person, after all, is one who is *self-possessed*. In the United States, girls' and boys' collecting in the nineteenth and twentieth centuries mirrored both the childrearing concepts of parents, teachers, advice writers, and social reformers and the increasing intrusion of the market into children's collecting habits. In both respects gender differentiation and attendant cultural and economic value may be discerned in the means and types of material culture collection.

The Enlightenment belief in the child as a tabula rasa explains in part advice writers' admonitions to parents to encourage their offspring's "natural" curiosity. Born innocent and with an innate sense of wonder, girls as well as boys were considered most susceptible to the lessons of God's creation. Europeans had early recognized that children learned through direct sensory experience. Johann Amos Comenius's *Orbis Sensualium Pictus* revolutionized children's education in Europe in the seventeenth and eighteenth centuries. Comenius, a Czech Brethren minister faced with teaching unlettered children, sought an instrument for universal education to convey his belief in the unity of all knowledge—what Comenius called "pansophic" wisdom. He created for his young charges a picture book, which used both German and Latin to teach language skills and incorporated the knowledge of the entire world. Printed first in 1658 in Nuremberg and a year later in London, the *Orbis Pictus* (as it was commonly called) featured pictures of "a world of things" ordered by categories derived by both biblical precept and Western social and political organization. The first American edition of the *Orbis Pictus* was published in 1810, although copies of the volume had been earlier carried to the United States through the settlements of the Moravian Brethren in Pennsylvania and North Carolina.

In the years after the American Revolution, advice writers and parents considered the gathering, assembling, and study of natural history specimens as a primary means of acquiring worldly knowledge *and* a Protestant Christian identity. This activity mirrored Americans' faith in Enlightenment natural theology and adults' interests in the new nation's natural wonders and wealth, in scientific investigation, and in the creation of cabinets of curiosities or museums in which such investigation and display of national power took place. The employment of scientific methods and the exploration of scientific principles thus did not necessarily lessen the widespread belief in God's creation of the world. In the first years of the nineteenth century, Charles Willson Peale's museum, for example, offered visitors a tour of the nation's natural history and wealth through habitat groups of stuffed animals and the use of Linnaean nomenclature to order that "world in miniature." At the same time, visitors could pause to read biblical quotations appearing on the walls. A circa 1820 floor plan of the museum, then housed on the second floor of the Pennsylvania State House (now Independence Hall), places a specialized "Children's Case" in the Quadruped Room. The room also boasted a biblically inspired tableau of the wolf and lamb, conjoining the pursuit of science with biblical prophecy: "The wolf also shall dwell with the lamb, and the leopard shall lie down with the kid; and the calf and the young lion and the fatling together; and a little child shall lead them" (Isaiah 11:6).

This proselytizing sentiment was mirrored in childrearing manuals, textbooks, and children's fiction throughout much of the nineteenth century. Lydia Maria Child, Samuel G. Goodrich, Francis Woodworth, Jacob Abbott, Louisa May Alcott, and others counseled parents to discipline for religious ends their children's curiosity or sense of wonder by inculcating "habits of observation" through the creation of "cabinets" or "museums." Like Peale's Museum, these cabinets were collective endeavors, dependent on the contributions of others. Contents were supplied by family members as well as friends near and far: shells, snakeskins, butterflies and other insects, minerals, leaves, pictures, and other found or (less often) man-made specimens. Little gender differentiation of collecting style or collections is readily discernible in childrearing manuals and textbooks, religious instruction being the goal. But children's fiction reveals in subtle ways the gendered notions of property and possession inherent in the collecting enterprise. Jacob Abbott's *Rollo's Museum* (1855), for example, contains whole chapters of paternal instruction of boys on the legalities of loaning and owning things. Although permitted to contribute to the collection and participate in its society by creating order and rules, an elder sister and baby sister are excluded from the lesson. In another of the Rollo series, Rollo's mother's attempt to instruct her young son and his playmates

on the concept of sharing and the symbolism of things only partially succeeds. Alice, the true Christian of Susan Warner's bestseller *The Wide, Wide World* (1850), has long outgrown her own cabinet of curiosities—and, as the reader learns, is ready to depart this world. Louisa May Alcott's *Little Men* (1871) introduces the natural history cabinet to the prodigal roughneck Dan upon his return to Plumfield because he is confined by a broken foot. Only as a feminized invalid may he grasp the symbolic meanings of the natural history specimens he had gathered and now will order in a museum. Boys in these stories learn the material lessons of the specimens they acquire, whereas girls provide the symbolic, spiritual meanings of God's hand in nature.

Girls' (and boys') collecting habits were influenced and abetted by the spread of market capitalism and technology. By the Civil War girls in particular participated in autograph and photograph collecting, whether those objects represent a celebrity or a dear friend or relative. The printing revolution and high literacy rates resulted in a golden age of children's books and periodicals—*Merry's Museum,* Francis Woodworth's *Youth's Cabinet,* and, of course, in 1873 the successful *St. Nicholas,* under the editorship of Mary Mapes Dodge. The nonfiction contents of these periodicals rehearsed the same lessons of children's collections: natural history and science, history, and travel and geography. Several journals offered pins and awards to be collected and won, and especially after the Civil War objects themselves were topics of essays. Editors of these children's periodicals consistently advised girls to keep and bind issues of a journal into an annual for further use. Like their mothers, girls were charged with reproducing the culture, a responsibility traditionally symbolized perhaps in the keeping of a dowry or marriage chest, later known as a hope chest. Now girls also cared for and preserved objects of sentimental value in albums, folios, and boxes, all of which—like the hope chest—could be purchased for the purpose of collecting.

In the twentieth century the rise of mass consumerism, evidenced in advertising, department stores, and mail order catalogues, ineluctably linked consumption and collecting. Although the Girl Scouts, Camp Fire Girls, and the Boy Scouts encouraged finding, making, and collecting things, these organizations quickly succumbed to consumerism and provided their young charges with craft kits. Indeed, over the course of the century girls and boys would increasingly purchase rather than find objects to augment their collections. Progressive educational professionals were the first to explore this link through several studies of children's collecting. In 1900, Caroline Frear Burk surveyed fifth-grade classes in Santa Barbara and Santa Rosa, California. She collected questionnaires from 607 boys and 607 girls and found that the typical number of collections for each child was three or four. The children in Burk's sample had begun to collect before the age of six. This activity peaked between the ages of eight and eleven, likely due to the desire to imitate others (Burk had been motivated by one class's "spontaneous" interest). Similar results were reported by G. Stanley Hall in his survey of 1,200 California children in 1907. Hall listed more than 300 items collected, with boys reporting (in rank order) cigar bands, stamps, birds' eggs, marbles, seashells, buttons, rocks, and advertising cards. Girls favored (in rank order) stamps, seashells, advertising cards, cigar bands, buttons, marbles, pieces of cloth, paper dolls, and dolls.

A later study, recognizing that collecting was "intimately" associated with the "growing self," sought to divine possible sex differences in collecting. This study by Paul A. Witty and Harvey C. Lehman (1931) revealed that girls more often than boys collected objects of personal adornment or of affection and sentiment, schoolroom souvenirs, and dolls. Boys preferred items evincing outdoor activities and commercially viable goods. Unlike their nineteenth-century predecessors, these children did not employ classification and discernment in their acquisitions. Like their predecessors, girls and boys preferred things that mirrored adults' gender affiliations—with girls curating artifacts of social value that were given to them and boys acquiring (and trading) things that possessed market value. Studies in the late 1920s and early 1930s found that boys' and girls' interest increased with time, as did the age at which that interest peaked and that rural children tended to foster more collections than those in towns and cities.

Care must be taken in utilizing these studies. The results of each study vary, which may be due in great part to the methods of data collection. *Collection* is only loosely defined, and it is not clear at times that the researcher differentiated between a collection that is acquired, classified, studied, and exhibited and a mere assemblage of objects that are possessed. For example, Witty and Lehman state that the children in their study were told that a collection was "assembled voluntarily in order to extend the kind or number" (1930). This definition applies equally to everyday consumption of, say, clothing. In addition, these Progressive educators evince a clear nostalgia for rural life and its supposed connection to the earlier form of cooperative collecting within a shared belief system. Hall and his peers suggested that nature cabinets be installed in schools—and, much like earlier cabinets of curiosities, that these be the product of cooperative, not individualistic, activity on the part of schoolchildren.

Collecting, however, is in practice an individualistic—and now, secularized—endeavor, one that throughout the twentieth century has been colonized and rationalized by toy manufacturers (among others) who seek to create instant collectibles to be purchased rather than found. The Ty Company's Beanie Babies and Pleasant Company's American Girl Collection are but two examples of how consumption has itself been rationalized by the selection, classification, labeling, organization, and presentation skills long required of collectors.

Shirley Teresa Wajda

See also Advice Books; American Girls Collection; Comic Books; Consumer Culture; Dollhouses; Dolls; Girls' Culture; Girls' Fiction; Girls' Magazines; Girls' Rooms; Nancy Drew Mysteries

References and Further Reading
Belk, Russell W. 1995. *Collecting in a Consumer Society*. London and New York: Routledge.
Burk, Caroline Frear. 1900. "The Collecting Instinct." *Pedagogical Seminary* 7: 179–207.
Durost, Walter Nelson. 1932. *Children's Collecting Activity Related to Social Factors*. New York: Bureau of Publications, Teachers College, Columbia University.
Hall, G. Stanley. 1907. *Aspects of Child Life and Education*. Boston: Ginn.
McGreevy, Ann. 1990. "Treasures of Children: Collections Then and Now, or Treasures of Children Revisited." *Early Child Development and Care* 63: 33–36.
Mechling, Jay. 1989. "The Collecting Self and American Youth Movements." Pp. 255–285 in *Consuming Visions: Accumulation and Display of Goods in America, 1889–1920*. Edited by Simon J. Bronner. New York: W. W. Norton.
Whitley, Mary T. 1929. "Children's Interest in Collecting." *Journal of Educational Psychology* 20: 249–261.
Witty, Paul A., and Harvey C. Lehman. 1930. "Further Studies of Children's Interest in Collecting." *Journal of Educational Psychology* 21: 112–127.
———. 1931. "Sex Differences: Collecting Interests." *Journal of Educational Psychology* 22: 221–228.
———. 1933. "The Collecting Interests of Town Children and Country Children." *Journal of Educational Psychology* 24: 170–184.

College Girls

For many American girls, college life is the last transition period from being a "girl" to becoming a "woman." College girls in the United States have had a long and varied history. From the struggles of young women in the colonial and antebellum periods to obtain quality educations to the dorm and sorority life of the twentieth century, American girls have insisted upon educational opportunities equal to those offered to their brothers that at the same time served the unique needs and interests of women. Women's colleges and coeducational schools have sought to meet these needs in both the curriculum and lifestyles offered at these institutions, giving American college girls a chance to mature into college women. Although great efforts have been made to diversify the population of American college women, the majority remain white, middle-class, and in their late teens or early twenties.

Most colonial women were not encouraged or permitted to pursue education beyond basic abilities in reading and writing, and most blacks were prohibited from obtaining even a rudimentary education. Education for white girls and young women in colonial America was largely limited to domestic skills and decorative arts, although dame schools and venture schools operated to teach girls as well as boys reading and writing, along with a small amount of music, art, and a foreign language. A few colonial American women stand out for their educational achievements. These include the poet Phillis Wheatley, a slave whose master taught her to read and write; Eliza Lucas, a South Carolina woman well tutored in the arts and sciences; and Jane Colden, who studied Latin and botany. However, both Lucas and Colden ceased their studies after their marriages, and in general, only about half of American colonial women could read or write at the turn of the eighteenth century.

By the early national period (1770–1820), several women of note, including Abigail Adams and Mercy Otis Warren, advocated the education of young women. Women were expected to use their education not in careers but for the betterment of their families. The concept of "republican motherhood" held that women could use their domestic influence over their husbands and children to produce better citizens, and in this way, women could increase their very limited role in the new country. Because of this recognized role of white women and their different educational needs and expectations, educational institutions for young women were created.

Although dame schools and venture schools had provided some opportunities for young white women, these schools offered extremely limited curricula, very basic or ornamental in nature. More institutionalized schools, or academies, offered subjects such as arithmetic, grammar, history, and literature in addition to the ornamental arts of music, painting, and needlework. Often the young women who attended these academies went on to teach at other academies or to open their own schools; other students used their education to fulfill the prescribed role of republican motherhood.

During the antebellum period (1820–1860), the concept of republican motherhood and the emergence of female academies evolved into the notion of "separate spheres" for women, apart from the urbanized and industrialized world of men. Women were expected to be pure, pious, submissive, and domestic; "true women" emerged as the moral leaders of their families and communities. This moral leadership provided opportunities for women as teachers as well as in the home. This larger sphere of influence required broader, more sophisticated forms of education for young women who were entering the public sphere as professional teachers. The desire of women to teach was matched by demand, especially in the North and West, where public education for children had begun in earnest.

Accordingly, seminaries evolved from academies and provided more rigorous academic training, although ornamental education was still offered. For the most part, seminaries provided a high school–level education for teenage girls and young women. The seminaries, like the academies, were not considered true colleges, although in some cases the academic standards were comparable to men's colleges, and several women's seminaries, like Mount Holyoke, evolved into the first women's colleges.

Women's colleges date from the mid-nineteenth century. Several societal trends contributed to the rise of women's colleges, including the earlier desire for an educated motherhood and the desire of women to teach. The rise of public schools also created a generation of young women who had become accustomed to education and who desired further opportunities. Reading for pleasure also became more popular, especially among the middle class and upper class, and literature specifically designed for women gained in popularity as their leisure time increased. New inventions and industrial innovations enabled women and girls to spend less time in household chores (e.g., soap making, hand sewing, and spinning).

Several colleges lay claim to being the first institutions of higher education for women. Salem Academy, now Salem College, was founded in North Carolina in 1772. Georgia Female College, now Wesleyan College, was chartered as a college in 1836, and Mount Holyoke opened as a seminary in 1837. Mary Sharp College opened in 1851 in Tennessee, and awarded its first bachelor's degrees in 1855. With Latin, Greek, and other degree requirements, Mary Sharp College was widely acknowledged as the first true college for women granting degrees equivalent to those at men's colleges. Mary Sharp College closed in the 1890s after educating more than 4,000 girls and young women at all educational levels. The most important of the early women's colleges, collectively known as the Seven Sisters, are Mount Holyoke, Vassar, Wellesley, Smith, Radcliffe, Bryn Mawr, and Barnard. These colleges served as the models for many other women's schools where the curriculum and lifestyle by late nineteenth century were very similar. Other institutions of higher education opened for women as well, including religious schools, both single-sex and coeducational; coordinate colleges that educated both women and men, although separately; and vocational schools. By the 1870s, approximately 11,000 young women were enrolled in college, and although higher education for women was not yet considered fashionable or popular, it was certainly an option.

This first generation of women students considered college education a privilege and took their academic pursuits seriously. Planning to use their degrees in careers, these young women studied hard and found very little time for recreation, entertainment, or dating. The majority of young women attending college during this time were white, middle-class, and from eighteen to twenty-four years old, but many women college students during this time would today be classified as "nontraditional students," who worked before, during, and after their attendance at college. Most young women who attended college between 1870 and 1900 did not consider marriage as a life choice but attended college to prepare for a career in teaching and medicine primarily, although a few women entered the ministry or became lawyers.

After the turn of the century, there was a slight shift in the population of women college students. Although college girls remained overwhelmingly white, native-born, middle-class, and in their late teens and early twenties, this second generation did not see education and marriage as mutually exclusive. College girls at the turn of the century were much more interested in recreational activities, and their demand that the college life include more extracurricular activities changed the experiences of girls entering college forever.

College also became an option for a variety of other American girls. More African American, foreign-born, and lower-class girls began viewing college as an attractive option in order to better support themselves and their families as educated professionals. According to historian Barbara Miller Solomon, "by World War I college was a very important option to provide a daughter within some circles, and outside these circles, it was something to aspire to" (Solomon 1985, 77).

As the number of college women increased in the late nineteenth and early twentieth centuries, a particularly strong type of female friendship emerged, called the "smash" or "crush." For the most part the "smash" was an intense, platonic friendship characterized by ritualized courting, including the sending of flowers and the writing of love poems. Often the "smash" involved a freshman or sophomore "falling in love" with an upper-class junior or senior. These relationships were viewed as a mentorship wherein older girls taught younger ones the accepted ways of college life. Other women found their "crush" within their own class and created friendships that lasted a lifetime. For most students, "smashing" was just another part of college life, and although women created enduring friendships, they often later fell in love with men, married, and had children. For others, "smashing" led to romantic friendships and life-long companionships.

"Smashing," along with other facets of college life, figured in turn-of-the-century literature written for girls. In her 1995 work, *Intimate Communities*, Sherrie A. Inness discusses the attention given to "smashing," athletics, and stereotyping in girls' fiction. Although the characters discussed in these novels are fictional, many are thinly veiled versions of the authors themselves during their college careers and, as such, are indicators of what college must have been like for many girls between 1870 and 1920.

Athletics was an important extracurricular activity for college girls. In the early years of women's schools, individualized gymnastic exercises made up the bulk of the physical education curriculum for young women. However, basketball and other team sports dominated the interests of women by the turn of the century, although physical education instructors continued to insist that gymnastics was the best course for young, developing women. By 1901, an article in *Cosmopolitan* magazine stated that "college girls are enthusiastic athletes. Basketball is the universal favorite sport" (quoted in Inness 1995, 74).

Girls entering college in the decades around the turn of the century quickly found themselves classified or stereotyped as "digs," "freaks," "grinds," "swells," or "all-around girls." Digs and freaks were at the bottom of the college social ladder, considered outsiders because of their social inabilities or inequities, including class, race, or disability. Grinds, or studious girls, chose their studies above an active social life and were usually liked well enough, but were generally passive in the larger campus life. Swells loved excitement to the exclusion of everything else and had the money to host room parties featuring spreads of "lobster salad on crisp, curly lettuce, delicious thin, little bread-and-butter sandwiches with the crusts off, devilled eggs, stuffed olives, almonds and ginger" (quoted in Inness 1995, 40–41). All-around girls had struck a happy balance of study and fun and gained the respect, admiration, and friendship of their peers. Although swells remained popular and fashionable, it was the all-around girl who was elected class president or became an officer in other school clubs and activities.

School clubs, like drama, debating, and literary societies, were formed as soon as girls were allowed to enter college, and were outlets for students interested in drama, literature, and the like. However, by 1900, many student organizations became socially exclusive sororities, with membership only by invitation, either with or without the characteristic Greek letters. As one historian has argued, "however pleasant for their members, the exclusive societies intensified [class] distinctions among students" (Horowitz 1984, 153). Because of the divisive effect, some colleges banned sororities on their campuses in the early twentieth century. Yet women's student organizations and sororities often provided active participation in self-government, an opportunity that was not offered to most American women in the world outside college.

As the numbers of girls enrolled in college increased, so did their social acceptance, and in turn even more women pursued higher education. The makeup of the college population began to more closely reflect that of the larger society, although most college students, both male and female, were still largely white and middle- or upper-middle-class. Following the passage of the woman's suffrage amendment in 1920, young women began to insist upon a larger place in society. Young women as well as young men began asserting their independence, both from parents as well as from college administrations. Smoking, drinking, and unchaperoned dating prevailed on college campuses, where a more conservative lifestyle had been the norm. In order to attract and retain students, colleges began to relax regulations, although dress codes and curfews were still enforced on most campuses.

College girls of the mid-twentieth century followed the pattern set by the generation of girls who attended college in the 1920s. Books such as Mabelle Babcock Blake's *The Education of the Modern Girl* (1929), Gulielma Fell Alsop and Mary McBride's *She's Off to College: A Girl's Guide to College Life* (1940), and Suzanne Gould Emerson's *Off to College* (1949) aimed to prepare girls for college "life," with chapters on clothes, etiquette, dating, and sororities in addition to studying. Although printed over a period of twenty-plus years, these books' content changed very little, and Blake's *Education of the Modern Girl* was reprinted as late as 1967.

The advent of the women's movement in the 1960s drastically changed college campuses and experiences of women students. College girls and women began to seek more educational opportunities specifically tailored to their needs as women while at the same time branching out into traditionally male academic subjects, such as mathematics, medicine, business, engineering, and the sciences. In many universities in the 1970s and 1980s, women's studies departments emerged, providing a multidisciplinary educational opportunity for the study of women's roles in history, literature, law, the sciences, and other disciplines. At the same time, campuses established women's centers that provided health, self-defense, mentoring, education, and career programs for women. The passage of Title IX in 1972 also encouraged the growth of academic and athletic opportunities for college women and paved the way for a more equitable college climate for girls and women in the twenty-first century.

Tara Mitchell Mielnik

See also Education of Girls; Jewish Education of Girls; Mathematics and Science; Radical Feminism; Sororities

References and Further Reading
Alsop, Gulielma Fell, and Mary F. McBride. 1940. *She's Off to College: A Girl's Guide to College Life.* New York: Vanguard Press.
Blake, Mabelle Babcock, et al. 1929, 1967. *The Education of the Modern Girl.* Freeport, NY: Books for Libraries Press.
Eisenmann, Linda, ed. 1998. *Historical Dictionary of Women's Education in the United States.* Westport, CT: Greenwood Press.
Emerson, Suzanne Gould. 1949. *Off to College.* Philadelphia: John C. Winston Company.
Faragher, John Mack, and Florence Howe, eds. 1988. *Women and Higher Education in American History.* New York: W. W. Norton.
Farnham, Christie Anne. 1994. *The Education of the Southern Belle: Higher Education and Student Socialization in the Antebellum South.* New York: New York University Press.
Gordon, Lynn D. 1990. *Gender and Higher Education in the Progressive Era.* New Haven, CT: Yale University Press.
Horowitz, Helen Lefkowitz. 1984. *Alma Mater: Design and Experience in the Women's Colleges from Their Nineteenth Century Beginnings to the 1930s.* New York: Alfred A. Knopf.
———. 1987. *Campus Life: Undergraduate Cultures from the End of the Eighteenth Century to the Present.* New York: Alfred A. Knopf.
Inness, Sherrie A. 1995. *Intimate Communities: Representation and Social Transformation in Women's College Fiction, 1895–1910.* Bowling Green, OH: Bowling Green State University Popular Press.
Newcomer, Mabel. 1959. *A Century of Higher Education for American Women.* New York: Harper and Brothers.
Solomon, Barbara Miller. 1985. *In the Company of Educated Women: A History of Women and Higher Education in America.* New Haven, CT: Yale University Press.

Comic Books

Newspaper comics have existed since the turn of the century, and comic books have been popular items since the late 1930s. Thought of as a boy's craze, comics have been just as popular with girls, particularly in contemporary times.

Newspaper comic strips became popular at the turn of the twentieth century. Newspapers, anxious to show off new colored ink capabilities, experimented with comics sections. Comics' popularity, especially among young boys, led manufacturers to the mass production of comics in a cheap marketable book form. The first comic book, made in 1932 as a means of advertisement, did nothing more than provide newspaper strips in a small tabloid style. Once the appeal of the books was known, many comic book publishers followed suit. Some books were used as premium giveaways to endorse products; others were sold for minimal fees, usually a dime a book. A real boom began in 1936, when six publishers produced seventy-six different books (Benton 1989, 17). The number of books expanded, as did the variety of stories. Competing companies developed a number of superhero characters who possessed supernatural powers and served humanity by protecting justice, and this expanded variety of superhero stories created a wider range of readers. Believed to be just for young male readers during the early 1940s, comics changed once World War II soldiers clamored for them overseas. Comics became more complex, with elaborate stories told via colorful illustrations and simple text.

As a popular base expanded, publishers offered the public a variety of comic genres: crime, educational, funny animals, horror, jungle, kid, movie and television, mystery and detective, newspaper-comic characters, romance, satire, science fiction, superhero, teen, underground, war, and western. These did not emerge all at once but were created throughout the 1940s and 1950s to serve an ever-growing demand for new comic book material. According to Mike Benton, writing in *The Comic Book in America*, "At the beginning of 1942, there were over 143 comic-book titles on the newsstands being read by over fifty million people each month. The comic book was no longer a passing publishing fad. It had become an established part of Americana, finding its way into the bedrooms and bivouacs of children and service-men everywhere" (Benton 1989, 35).

One of these widely read comics detailed the adventures of a young woman with superpowers. The character Wonder Woman was introduced in 1942, marking the first time that girl readers were spoken to directly. Wonder Woman was spawned from an amalgamation of mythical characters, including Hippolyta and the Amazons. Born Diana of The-

myscira, she left the haven to become ambassador to the world, spreading the message of peace. Diana had amazing abilities that allowed her to thwart evil villains. These included super strength, speed, and the ability to glide through the air. Special bracelets enabled the deflection of bullets, and when villains were caught in her golden lasso, they had no choice but to tell the truth. Six months after her creation, sales of Wonder Woman were strong enough that publishers considered her an established character among the cast of comic book heroes (Wonderland website).

Wonder Woman was created by William Moulton Marston, a psychologist interested in providing young female readers with a positive role model. Marston believed that women had a "fundamentally healthier emotional balance than men." When creating Wonder Woman, he used feminine characteristics he believed would be beneficial to solving problems. Similarly, Marston's comic stories encouraged women to become financially independent and advocated that men and women work together to solve problems ("The Comic Strip and Popular Culture" 1975, 84). These feminist sentiments had never before been available to such a large group of impressionable readers. The incredible attributes possessed by Wonder Woman and her success fighting evil went far to encourage readers, who have adopted her as a super role model since her inception in the 1940s.

From 1947 to 1954, other comic books targeted more mature readers. Books focusing on cowboys and crime stories became quite popular, even surpassing superhero comics. These comics, though intended for adult readers, were easily accessible to children. The comics graph-

The popular Wonder Woman cartoons led to a TV series starring Lynda Carter. (Kobal Collection/ABC-TV)

ically depicted violent acts, suggested rape, and represented women in highly sexually suggestive manners. A crusade against such comics was led by psychologist Frederic Wertham, whose 1954 book *Seduction of the Innocent* blamed comic book content for expanding juvenile delinquency. Wertham complained about books that contained sadism, violence, rape, graphic sexuality, and racism. But Wertham was neither a liberal nor a feminist thinker. He opposed changing mores and challenged new roles for women. Wertham wrote that Wonder Woman was a "horror type" because she "is physically very powerful, tortures men, has her own female following, [and] is the cruel phallic woman. While she is frightening for boys, she is an undesirable ideal for girls, being the exact opposite of what girls are supposed to be" (Wertham 1954, 34). Wertham's efforts led to a U.S. Senate Subcommittee to Investigate Juvenile Delinquency concerning the influence of comic books on children. In addition, the Comics Code Authority was established by comics publishers in 1954 as a means of self-regulation. This action averted strict government interference.

Not all comics designed for girls encouraged them to challenge societal norms. In 1948 twenty-seven out of forty-nine comic books were targeted at young female readers (Robbins 1999, 36). Almost all represented girls in traditional roles. "Funny animal comics" that told the stories of familiar cartoon animals from the Walt Disney Company and Warner Brothers Studios encouraged girls to be nurturers and represented female characters in typical domestic situations. Similar in style, "kid comics" were also popular. Drawn in an unrealis-

tic fashion, these cartoons told tales about the joys and pratfalls of childhood, generally with precocious leading characters. Little Lulu was one such character designed for girl readers. She had been a regular newspaper strip character until 1944, when she made the switch to comic books. Lulu Moppet was a young girl who enjoyed various activities with her friends. She and her girlfriends played with dolls and had tea parties. Lulu had a love-hate relationship with the neighborhood boys, who belonged to the Boys Only Gang. Many stories centered on Lulu's attempts to join the misogynistic club, which never proved fruitful. In her tenacious attempts, however, Lulu generally proved herself more clever than the boys. In part because of popularity derived from an early subtle feminist stance, Little Lulu stayed in print from 1945 to 1984 (Don Markstein's Cartoonpedia website).

Perhaps most successful with girls were "teen comics." These comics told humorous stories about groups of teenage friends who exemplified typical teens who never challenged the status quo. "Archie" comics, established in 1941, focused on Archie, his friends, and the girls romantically interested in him, Betty and Veronica. According to Trina Robbins's study on girls and comics, "the majority of *Archie* readers were girls, age six to thirteen" (Robbins 1999, 12). Because of this, Betty and Veronica played vital roles. Both vied for Archie's attention. Betty was a good-girl-next-door type, whereas Veronica was slightly more vixenish, possessing money, glamour, and the ambition to get what she wanted. Neither Betty nor Veronica had any more personality than necessary in the role of comic girlfriend.

More teen comics followed after the success of "Archie." Character Katy Keene of the "Wilbur" comics, known to her readers as the "Queen of Fashion," was slightly more complex than her "Archie" predecessors. Katy was a career girl, a beautiful fashion model who did worldwide runway work and print advertisements. The first of the supermodels, Katy did not let her success go to her head. She maintained friendships and did all she could to help others in need, including her sis, who was prone to stomachaches from too much sugar. Especially appealing to readers were Katy paper dolls. Publishers encouraged readers to design clothes for the dolls to wear, which would be included in subsequent issues. Girls loved seeing their artwork in print, and collecting Katy's dolls and outfits was a popular hobby among young girls from 1949 to 1961 (Archie Comics website).

Another trend in girls' comics was the combination comics and advice magazine. Publications, like *Miss America, Calling All Girls, Junior Miss, Keen Teens, Sweet Sixteen,* and *Polly Pigtails,* all aimed at entertaining young readers with stories about growing up, fashion tips, and celebrity gossip (Robbins 1999, 45).

In the late 1940s romance comics emerged for female readers. These comics targeted older readers than those who enjoyed teen comics. "Love comics," as they were also known, were designed for young women, older teens, and new housewives. At a time of domestic containment, love comics served to keep women in their place as subservient wives to hardworking men. The basic formula for love comics involved a heroine who became unhappy with her current situation, went on an adventure, and discovered in the end that all she ever really wanted had been at home the entire time (Sadler 1964, 487). Readers were taught that happiness came from the simple things in life and was acquired through hard work. Love comics served as lessons in morality. They also supported the status quo and the ultimate goal of a successful marriage. These lessons taught that beauty was in the eye of the beholder, offering hope for less-than-ideal beauties. Even more important, love comics emphasized a need for concessions in exchange for romance. The most important sacrifice was the desire for a career (Perebinossoff 1974, 825).

With the emergence of television, the popularity of comics waned. Comic books were no longer the easiest mode of quick entertainment. Regular comic books still existed, but a new type of comic was introduced. "Comix," or underground newspaper comics supporting counterculture beliefs, emerged as an alternative to regular reading material in the 1960s. Comix also provided satirical viewpoints that challenged the consensus culture that had prevailed in regularly published comic books. These underground comix were particularly important to feminist writers and cartoonists looking for a new medium in which to express themselves. Unhappy with the males in charge of the establishment, female creators opted to remove the word "men" from "women." After a number of variations ("wimmen" and "wimmin" among them), "womyn" became the preferable spelling for a word that would now designate more radical feminists. Womyn's comix served to oppose girl comics, which had come before and "taught that goodness meant goodey-two-shoeism: Rather than a strong left hook, girls' heroes got by on politeness, obedience, and proper grooming" (Kennedy 1990, 386). A number of underground comix dealt with realistic female issues. Another new trend was the use of an autobiographical style. Comix issues ranged from single parenthood to lesbianism and abortion rights.

The 1990s have seen a large interest in comic books for girls and by girls. Referred to as "grrrls' comix," these stories are written by women for adolescent readers. Inspired by third-wave feminism, these comic books address feminist issues rather than offer advice on how to catch a husband, like girls' magazines of the 1940s and 1950s. Grrrls' comix have continued trends started by earlier underground comix, especially in response to the backlash against second-wave feminists of the 1960s and 1970s (Robbins 1999, 125).

Today, girls have access to a great variety of comics. Newspaper strips, superhero comic books, and teen comics still exist but in updated forms. Most characters have taken on feminist attributes, especially superheroines who refuse to be treated differently in a world that no longer belongs exclusively to men. An alternative to regularly published comics is the underground comix, published in zine form or through independent publishing houses.

Cherie Kelly

See also Collecting; Girls' Fiction; Girls' Magazines; Television; Zines

References and Further Reading
Archie Comics, "Katy's Korner," http://www.archiecomics.com/katy/allabout.html.
Benton, Mike. 1989. *The Comic Book in America.* Dallas: Taylor Publishing.
"The Comic Strip and Popular Culture." 1975. *Intellect* 104: 84–85.
Don Markestein's Cartoonpedia, "Little Lulu," http://www.stormloader.com/markstein/cartoonpedia/lulu.html.
Friends of Lulu, http://www. friends-lulu. org/.
Kennedy, Pagan. 1990. "P.C. Comics." *The Nation* 250 (March 19): 386.
Perebinossoff, Phillipe. 1974. "What Does a Kiss Mean? The Love Comic Formula and the Creation of the Ideal Teen-Age Girl." *Journal of Popular Culture* 8, no. 4: 825–835.
Robbins, Trina. 1993. *A Century of Women Cartoonists.* Northampton, MA: Kitchen Sink Press.
———. 1996. *The Great Women Superheroes.* Northampton, MA: Kitchen Sink Press.
———. 1999. *From Girls to Grrlz.* San Francisco: Chronicle Books.
Sadler, A. W. 1964. "The Love Comics and American Popular Culture." *American Quarterly* 16, no. 3: 486–490.
Wertham, Frederic. 1954. *Seduction of the Innocent.* New York: Rinehart.
Wonderland—the Ultimate Wonder Woman Site, http://www.lacosa.sion.com/ww.

Communication

From the early nineteenth century to the present, girls have used various kinds of communication methods to create their own culture, learn their roles as girls, or subvert adult authority. Communication devices have also facilitated the construction of an underground culture that girls have built in response to their unequal status, both at school and in the larger culture. The actual forms of communication (as well as to whom girls have corresponded) have changed over time, beginning with letters, continuing with telephones, and evolving most recently to include pagers, chat rooms, cell phones, and e-mail.

In the early republic, girls began to systematically use letter writing to communicate with each other. Colonial children did not learn how to write a letter as second graders do today, but their nineteenth-century peers learned that letter writing was an essential part of female socialization. According to *The Young Lady's Friend*, "A letter, written in a fair, legible hand, without any blots or erasures, and properly folded, sealed, and directed, is one very good index of a lady's character" (1837, 281). It was primarily the job of mothers to teach their daughters the "art" of letter writing, in which graceful penmanship was as important as the content. "Madame de Sevigné praises her daughter for attention to dates, which, she says, shows an interest in the correspondence" (280). Drafts of letters were corrected by plantation mistresses who supervised their daughters' socialization. Mothers read not only the letters their daughters wrote but also those they received: "Young ladies under age," *The Young Lady's Friend* explained, "should gracefully acknowledge their parent's right of inspection" (281). Indeed, letters were semipublic documents that were routinely read aloud as a form of family entertainment.

Middle-class girls also learned how to write letters that conformed to contemporary standards and expressed appropriate sentiments by using such books as *Mrs. Farrar's the Youth's Letter-Writer*. Etiquette manuals written just for young ladies often provided information and instruction on whom to write and when, what to write, and how to write it. Manuals urged girls to choose a few correspondents among their friends in order to practice the art of letter writing. Because Victorian girls were also expected to

manage the concerns of others, experts advised writing about those things that would be of interest to the reader, not the writer. Not only did letter writing reinforce emotional restraint, but also it provided girls with an excellent opportunity to learn about order. They were encouraged to organize their thoughts before they set pen to paper so that topics of "inferior importance" did not dominate. *The Young Lady's Friend* advised: "The letters of a regular correspondent should be endorsed and filed, as regularly by young ladies as merchants; this facilitates your reference to any one of them, prevents their being lost, or mislaid, or exposed to curious eyes, saves your table from being strewed, and your letter-case from being crowded with them" (1837, 282).

Experts and other adults urged girls to write letters that were neither informal nor intimate. To them, letter writing provided an opportunity to instruct girls in the importance of self-control, not self-expression. Despite the imposition of social conventions, some girls nevertheless used letters to express their emotional anguish, anxiety, and affection. In fact, adolescent girls routinely used letters to convey their deepest feelings and thoughts about each other. For girls, writing letters provided relationships with continuity. While away at boarding school (attended by even those from relatively poor families), girls wrote mothers, sisters, and other family members. Once back home again, girls had few opportunities other than letter writing to maintain communication, unlike adult women who often arranged visits for extended periods of time.

Girls confined their intimate communication with friends to the postal service until their access to formal schooling began to expand in the industrial era (near the turn of the twentieth century). When in school, they found new ways to communicate with their friends. It is unclear when young girls began to pass notes to each other under a teacher's watchful eye, but a famous scene from Laura Ingalls Wilder's book *Little Town on the Prairie,* set in 1880s South Dakota, depicts a teenage Laura passing her seatmate a slate on which her handwritten poem mocked their teacher (Wilder 1941, 173–176).

Girls' circle of intimates began to expand in the interwar era (1918–1945), which also witnessed a relaxation in rules about content of letters. No longer did girls practice emotional restraint or supposedly embrace order when writing letters; their letters became emotional outlets for their burgeoning circle of intimates, which now included movie stars and radio friends.

Primary among the catalysts for this expanding group of intimates was the proliferation of electronic media (movies and radio in the 1920s, television in the 1950s) and an emerging culture of celebrity that showcased new role models such as movie stars Mary Pickford and Clara Bow. Young girls wrote fan letters to celebrities or broadcasters, desiring to acquaint themselves, to establish an intimate, albeit one-sided relationship, or to describe their love of media. Donna Warren, for example, wrote one Chicago radio broadcaster that she was "just crazy for radio" (Warren 1941). Two world wars provided another impetus to letter writing as young girls wrote soldiers stationed on battle fronts. Finally, advice columns such as "Let's Talk Things Over" and "Dear Beth" told girls

that letter writing allowed them to air "problems [that] usually bring comfort and practical suggestions" (Grayson 1944, viii). Young girls wrote desiring advice on subjects ranging from parental relationships to their sexuality, advice they felt their friends or parents could not give. They also began to use a new kind of communication device to contact their circle of intimates: the telephone.

The telephone, which became a common component of everyday social life in the 1910s and 1920s, typically appeared first on rural homesteads and in middle-class urban households. For those women and girls who lived in rural areas, phones seemed to mute their isolation, at least until cars became common. For those who lived in urban communities, AT&T advertisements claimed that telephones nurtured a "close-knit, personalized society" (Fischer 1992, 223). They did not seek out new intimates but used the phone to reinforce existing relationships. One woman remembered that, when a young girl, she walked home from school with a friend, separated at a street corner, and then called the friend when she got home (227). But because Americans associated telephones with young girls and women, they were consistently derided as "female foolishness" (231).

In the postwar era, a transformation occurred in the ways that girls used communication devices for historical and cultural reasons. First, the Cold War caused Americans to promote conformity to social ideals, especially to gender roles embodied in sit-com television characters. In a process called "domestic containment," Americans believed they could defeat the evil Russians by adhering to these new norms, which identified a patriarchal, almost domineering role for men and a subservient, nurturing role for women. Second, a newly identified group of Americans appeared, spurred on by the postwar prosperity and by the expansion of high school attendance (in 1900, 6 percent of Americans had high school degrees; by 1940, a majority of Americans had their diplomas). Marketers identified these "teenagers" by their age, leisure activities, and spending ability, which by 1960 exceeded $10 billion. To exploit that market, new magazines appeared, most notably *Seventeen* magazine (which actually debuted before World War II ended, in 1944), to promote "wholesome bobby-soxer" and future June Cleaver as the primary role for teenage girls and to exploit the pocketbooks of those who wished to don that image (Palladino 1996, 112). If girls meant to rebel against these images, then it had to be done through hidden means, typically through phone calls, letters, and note passing.

Because they were adults in training, girls were taught communication skills to ensure that they would fight the Russians from their kitchens. There was, for example, a surge in interest in girls' letter writing in the post–World War II era. Research journals, parenting magazines, and *Seventeen*'s etiquette books emphasized how letter-writing skills built character. Research journals such as *Elementary School Journal* analyzed schoolchildren's letters and decried the spelling and grammatical mistakes they found. It seemed the United States might lose ground to the Russians if Americans could not inculcate a sense of excellence even in the most mundane acts such as letter writing.

In parental guidance periodicals like *Parents' Magazine*, columnists advised mothers to teach their girls to "enjoy writing letters" by providing the correct equipment: a desk, a box of pencils or fountain pen, notepaper, and pen pals from all over the world (Burris 1953, 53). Start girls writing at an early age, one article said, by teaching them the fine art of "letter telling," in which three- or four-year-old daughters dictated letters sent to distant relatives (Pratt 1961, 54). The emphasis on young girls as letter writers seemed to be a youthful version of some pundits' belief that "letter writing is a private art; and private life is woman's native and triumphant sphere of achievement" (Cecil 1957, 98). *Seventeen*'s etiquette manuals told girls that letter writing would "be a part of your path of etiquettes [sic] all your life" (Haupt 1957, 79). That etiquette included "a very useful feminine accomplishment ... pretty handwriting" (79). Etiquette manuals also warned girls about sharing certain kinds of information warning "your best friend today may not be tomorrow" (102).

Pen pals, or correspondents who lived at a distance and who were not family members, were a part of this postwar world of communication. The United States' debut as a superpower in the 1950s prompted some girls to write the UN seeking pen pals from far-off countries. Letters to pen pals tended to be more formal because these were messages sent to acquaintances met at places such as summer camp or other instances of chance acquaintance. Girls exchanged information on a variety of subjects, from the weather to Christmas gifts to school schedules. Imparting information was certainly an important component of letter writing, but it also allowed girls to create new friendships. With close friends who may have moved away or pen pals with whom a casual relationship had become intimate, girls discussed more personal information such as their current boyfriends or sought advice for personal problems. Girls had pen pals who were boys, and letters exhibited some of the same themes as those between young women. Weather seems to have been a primary subject, as were favorite musical groups.

One form of letter writing, passing notes, was a means by which girls subverted the authority that etiquette manuals, experts, and parents attempted to exert. Girls used ruled notebook paper, paper scraps, and colored ink pens, while folding their notes in ways that escaped the teacher's notice. As they communicated in this subliminal dialogue, note passing seemed to be almost a conversation since girls used the same paper to write each other several times. Simultaneously, passing notes served a therapeutic purpose while reinforcing girls' nurturing skills. Girls poured out their hearts, dreams, and sorrows to confidantes who dreamed along with them or comforted them. They also gossiped about friends, acquaintances, and, especially, boyfriends. Young girls wrote these notes in a secretive language in case they were intercepted.

Certainly, consumerism was a critical component of this new world since specific kinds of stationery, pens, stamps, and stickers were important, if not crucial, to girls' letter writing and note passing. Stationery featured feminine themes such as flowers or cartoon characters. Snoopy and Hello Kitty were popular choices, as were equally feminine colors like pink and pastels. In some cases, girls personalized their stationery by drawing hearts or other female symbols on white paper. Many chose stamps, flower stickers, and colored

pens that matched their stationery and practiced a flowery script when writing pen pals. Interestingly, girls used their matching envelopes to state demands to mail carriers that were anything but "real life," submissive, and deferential. After sealing their envelopes, they regularly wrote: "Postman: Deliver Deletter, Desooner Debetter, Delater Deletter, Demadder Megetter."

Although letter writing seemed to reinforce girls' supposedly "private" natures, communication remained an avenue for girls to explore their personalities and to develop an identity outside the family circle. Moreover, communication served as an emotional catharsis. Letters to "Let's Talk Things Over," for example, allowed girls to complain of family strictures while providing an outlet for emotional turmoil when parents could not or would not help resolve problems. One troubled fourteen-year-old girl wrote, "I wish I could confide in my mother. I tried once but she laughed at what I called a secret" (Grayson 1944, 12). In an era in which girls turned to friends and outside advisers for advice, etiquette manuals also sought to fulfill these needs. *The Seventeen Book of Answers to What Your Parents Don't Talk About and Your Best Friends Can't Tell You*, for example, discussed traditional subjects like boyfriends and dating as well as issues such as homosexuality and drugs after those issues became important topics of conversation in the 1970s.

Telephones mimicked changes in letter writing as usage surged in the postwar era. Indeed, by 1950, 62 percent of Americans owned a phone, a number that exceeded car ownership; by 1980, 93 percent of Americans owned a phone. The telephone's association with girls

Two teenage girls engage in a serious discussion. (Shirley Zeiberg)

appeared in various media venues, including a song in the movie *Bye Bye Birdie* in 1963 and a famous *Brady Bunch* television episode in which arguments between the Brady kids necessitates the installation of a pay phone. Books such as *The Seventeen Book of Young Living* provided phone etiquette lessons for teenagers, guaranteed to improve their popularity. Girls were also urged not to monopolize the phone. Indeed, only six hours of babysitting each month could pay for a girl's own phone line according to *Seventeen* magazine editor Enid Haupt. Nice girls did not phone boys, and they always used the phone in a precise ladylike manner. "Most boys consider

the telephone call their special privilege, and they don't like girls to call them regularly," Haupt warned in 1970 (Haupt 1970, 39). The constant admonitions against monopolizing the phone and calling boys suggest that girls might have been contesting prevailing stamdards of phone etiquette.

The post-1960s generations utilized new ways of communicating with good friends, particularly through instantaneous devices such as beepers, cell phones, and e-mail. But a "circle of friends" might now include unseen "electronic" friends, developed through chat rooms on the World Wide Web. Thus, the wider availability of e-mail technology and beepers, for example, has moved girls' communication from paper to digital and electronic methods. Girls use beepers and e-mail to keep in close contact with family and friends; nurture them with a coded and, in the case of beepers, abbreviated language ("831" on the display screen means "I Love You"); and send messages that subvert the power of authority figures. Cell phones are now part of girls' everyday attire since the character Cher from the movie *Clueless* considered her cell phone part of her wardrobe. It is as necessary now as the latest handbag or shoes. In this world that demands instantaneous connection, the phone connects girls no matter where they are, whether at school, home, or work.

Chat rooms geared toward teenagers are another new means by which girls have developed their circle of intimates and, simultaneously, have subverted the authority of adults. A variety of Web services such as Yahoo! and America Online (AOL) provide specialized rooms for teens, for example, "Interracial Teen," "Asian-American Teens," and "Down South." Exhibiting the constant links between consumerism and girls' culture is a Yahoo! chat room called "The Mall: A Hang-Out for Girls." Girls discuss a wide variety of issues, but chat rooms have proved to be a dangerous place for teenage girls, as a recent book, entitled *Katie.com*, proved. Written by teenager Katherine Tarbox, the book examines her attempt to rebel against her parents by building a relationship with a man in an AOL chat room. (He turned out to be a pedophile and rapist.) Tarbox's case became the first federally prosecuted case involving an Internet pedophile.

Psychologists have noted the development of an underground girls' culture facilitated by these communication devices. Although there is no way of knowing when this underground originally emerged or the specific ways that communication devices such as note passing prompted its growth, Harvard psychologists Carol Gilligan and Lyn Mikel Brown noticed its importance when conducting a study of girls at an Ohio private school. Despite promises to respect the privacy of the psychologists' questionnaires, girls repeatedly breached that promise by telling their friends what to expect from researchers. This underground—built on relationships developed through note passing, phone calls, and informal discussions over lunch or studying—provided girls with a culture that they used to protect and nurture each other in a world that renders them powerless. In short, this underground is a means to power, albeit of their own making, and phones, beepers, chat rooms, and letters have been the means to building this pathway.

Kristine M. McCusker

See also Advice Books; Emotions; Relational Theory

References and Further Reading
Burris, Gladys Tolar. 1953. "Help Your Child Enjoy Writing Letters." *Parents' Magazine* 28 (December): 52–53.
Cecil, Lord David. 1957. "Letter Writing: A Private Talent of Women." *Vogue* 130 (August 1): 98–99.
Cornell, Betty. 1954. *Betty Cornell's Teen-Age Popularity Guide.* New York: Prentice-Hall.
Farrar, Eliza Ware. *The Young Lady's Friend.* 1837. Boston: American Stationers' Co.
Farrar, Mrs. n.d. *Mrs. Farrar's the Youth's Letter-Writer.* New York: Barlett and Raynor.
Fischer, Claude S. 1992. *America Calling: A Social History of the Telephone to 1940.* Berkeley: University of California Press.

Grayson, Alice Barr. 1944. *Do You Know Your Daughter?* New York: D. Appleton-Century Company.

Haupt, Enid A. 1957. *The Seventeen Book of Young Living.* New York: David McKay Company.

———. 1970. *The Seventeen Book of Etiquette and Young Living.* 2d ed. New York: David McKay Company.

Palladino, Grace. 1996. *Teenagers: An American History.* New York: Basic Books.

Pratt, Joanne. 1961. "I'll Tell You a Letter." *Parents' Magazine* 36 (Fall): 54–55.

Tarbox, Katherine. 2000. *Katie.com: My Story.* New York: Dutton.

Warren, Donna, letter to John Lair, November 30, 1941, John Lair Papers, Southern Appalachian Collection, Berea College, Berea, KY.

Wilder, Laura Ingalls. 1941. *Little Town on the Prairie.* New York: Harper and Row.

Wood, Abigail. 1972. *The Seventeen Book of Answers to What Your Parents Don't Talk About and Your Best Friends Can't Tell You.* New York: David McKay Company.

Consumer Culture

Since its emergence in the early 1900s, mass marketing aimed at children has played a key role in the transformation of twentieth-century childhood. Girls' and boys' growing consumer clout as both shoppers and selling agents within the family has at once reflected and propelled the democratization of family life. As girls gained more freedom and autonomy within the family, they acquired greater influence over family spending. Consumerism has also become a vital arena in which many girls explore new identities and embrace or challenge the values of the dominant culture. Over time, children's culture itself has become less ordered by the adult world and increasingly peer-oriented. For American girls in particular, consumerism has had profound yet con-tradictory influences. Through shopping, many girls have discovered a new brand of independence that comes from making their own consumer choices. At the same time, however, consumer culture has also steered girls toward prescribed gender roles and culturally acceptable aspirations. For girls, consumer culture has thus been a realm of freedom and restraint, satisfaction and disappointment.

Mass marketers first began courting the girls along with boys as consumers in the 1890s through advertising trade cards displayed in grocery stores and pictorial advertisements in children's magazines. Though these efforts were modest at first, mostly reaching well-to-do child and adult readers of children's magazines like *St. Nicholas*, they gathered steam during the mid-1920s as advertisers became tantalized by the lucrative potential of selling to children. In the girl, they believed they had discovered an unproblematic consumer: impressionable, loyal, and—perhaps most important—influential. Mass marketers aimed not only to impress brand loyalty upon future generations of consumers but to enlist girls as active selling agents within the home. Selling the child, advertisers believed, was the path of least resistance to mothers and fathers. Whatever girls may have lacked in the power of the purse—and this itself was expanding—advertisers hoped girls could make up for in their power to nag and persuade. Indeed, by advertisers' own reckoning, the growing egalitarianism and child-centeredness of the middle-class companionate family made girls potent lobbyists for the goods advertised in juvenile magazines.

During the 1920s and 1930s, advertisers reached out to girls through a variety of mass magazines. They courted preteen and adolescent girls in magazines like

Children often spur their parents' consumption, as this photo of them looking through a shop window at Christmas shows. (Library of Congress)

American Girl (the official magazine of the Girl Scouts), *Everygirls'* (published by the Campfire Girls), *St. Nicholas, Youth's Companion,* and *Scholastic* and sought out even younger girls through magazines like *Little Folks* and *Child Life,* which mothers typically read to children. Within these magazines, advertisements preached the merits of a wide array of products, ranging from soap and toiletries to breakfast cereal, food, clothing, shoes, cameras, toys, and dolls. The ads placed in magazines for younger girls aimed to sell mothers and imprint lasting impressions on pliable young minds. Those placed in magazines for preteens and adolescents addressed girls both as consumers in their own right and as mother's helpers whose newfound knowledge

of the best brands could inform family shopping.

Advertisers employed a variety of tactics to raise girls' as well as boys' brand consciousness and cement their brand loyalty. To cultivate consumer consciousness in younger girls, they published advertising jingle books and coloring books, typically offered as special premiums to mothers, which incorporated brand names and advertising trademarks into nursery rhymes and Mother Goose stories. Advertisers also appealed to girls' competitive and acquisitive instincts by offering toys, cash prizes, and other special premiums to those who saved up a specified number of cereal box tops or composed the best testimonial letter explaining the merits of their favorite brand of soap or shoes. Another popular scheme was the advertising club, which awarded membership badges, secret passwords, decoding devices, and other tokens of belonging in exchange for proofs of purchase. The club and prize contest formulas became particularly popular during the Depression, when radio supplanted magazines as the primary advertising medium for girls and boys, and membership in clubs like Cocomalt's Little Orphan Annie's Secret Circle and Post Toasties' Junior Detective Corps swelled into the millions.

Eager to reassure prospective advertisers of the profitability of selling to girls and boys, magazine publishers also devised various schemes to transform their readers into brand-conscious shoppers. Some devoted editorial space to discussing the trustworthiness and superior value of advertised goods. Others, like *American Girl*, aligned editorial content with advertising by recommending that Girl Scouts play brand-name identification games at troop meetings and by reminding readers to mention the magazine when writing away for special premiums. Advertisers, in turn, catered their messages to particular juvenile audiences, showing, for example, how an Eastman Kodak camera could help Girl Scouts earn a photography merit badge or a certain brand of dishwashing soap could be used to secure a homemaker merit badge. Because advertisers ultimately wanted their sales message to reach parents as well as girls, advertisements often supplied girls with talking points that appealed to parental concerns about girls' mental and physical development.

Advertisements, of course, did not merely instruct girls how to be brand-conscious shoppers and effective parental lobbyists. They also taught girls about culturally prescribed ideals of femininity and how to achieve them through consumption. Advertisements frequently reinforced traditional gender norms, addressing girls as future wives and homemakers. During the 1920s, for example, advertisements for Hoover vacuum cleaners taught girls to view such household machines as essential to efficient, scientific housekeeping and their future success as homemakers. Though marriage was still years away, numerous advertisements reminded preteen and adolescent girls that maintaining their charm and good looks was a key ingredient in achieving social success—and presumably in enhancing their marital prospects. Echoing the emotional appeals prominent in the advertising pages of women's magazines, such advertisements cautioned that attractiveness and popularity need not be sacrificed to the wrong dishwashing soap, athletic shoe, beverage, or breakfast cereal. In crafting advertising copy that promised girls beauty and social prestige, advertisers were in part drawing upon long-standing cultural assumptions that vanity and other-directedness were decidedly female traits, ones that could be easily exploited. But advertisers also sought to exploit an increasingly central facet of adolescent social life—the quest for acceptance, popularity, and dates—and they did so by anointing themselves friendly shopping advisers to socially striving teens.

Advertisers did propose less tradition-bound cultural scripts for modern girls during the 1920s and 1930s. Shoe advertisers, for example, hailed the freedoms of athletic girls as a measure of women's progress from the encumbrances of long skirts and the days of horse power. When the *Howie Wing* radio show, a children's serial about a boy's aviation adventures, aired in the late 1930s, the show's sponsor, Kellogg's Corn Flakes, actively recruited girls to join its Cadet Aviation Corps, reminding them that women, too, played a key role in modern aviation as stewardesses and daring pilots. Such acknowledgments of the adventuring spirit of modern girls did not fundamentally challenge deeply rooted cultural expectations that girls would ultimately embrace the private realm of domesticity, but they did concede that women had become fuller participants in the public realm of sports and work. Had the advertising industry, then a predominantly male profession with limited market research tools, had more insight into the social milieu of girls, perhaps they might have more routinely invented less orthodox cultural scripts for girls.

The return of economic prosperity after the deprivations of the Depression and World War II accelerated the expansion of juvenile markets and the creation of distinctive consumer cultures for children and adolescents. Thanks to full employment and a booming economy, many families that had scrimped during the lean years could now afford to allocate more of the family budget to their children's spending needs. Indeed, allowances for girls and boys began to rise during the postwar years, and advertisers and cultural commentators took sharper notice of teenagers' rising stock in the marketplace. As baby boomers came of age in the late 1950s, the size of the youth market made it difficult to ignore.

Demographic shifts and rising incomes were only partly responsible for the postwar expansion of juvenile markets. Much like their early-twentieth-century predecessors, the publishers of Seventeen magazine, which debuted to instant success in 1944, had helped to cultivate a buoyant image of the youth market by touting the buying power and progressive influence of teenage girls on family spending. Seventeen helped shape the teenage girl market through its editorial content, devoting columns to personal grooming, diets, fashion, party plans, and the brand-name goods that could help girls achieve their goals. The magazine's promotion staff also worked with clothing and cosmetics manufacturers to design goods and advertisements that catered to teenage girls' tastes, and they convinced department stores to create tie-in displays that featured merchandise advertised in the magazine. The success of these and other teen merchandising schemes during the 1950s in turn convinced mass merchandisers to undertake more systematic market research, in which teenage girls surveyed the tastes and attitudes of their peers.

Television was an even more powerful shaper and creator of juvenile markets, and unlike mass magazines, its reach extended to preschoolers and younger girls who could not yet read. Toy manufacturers learned that bypassing adults and marketing directly to girls in Saturday morning cartoons and child favorites like the Mickey Mouse Club worked merchandising wonders—not only because girls hounded their parents but because toy retailers, preferring surefire sales makers, stocked their shelves with toys that television-tutored girls could readily spot. As a measure of marketers' faith in the new medium, television advertising to children skyrocketed from about $26 million in 1956 to about $750 million in 1987.

During those years, mass marketers perfected a number of selling and merchandising strategies to entice girls as well as boys. Aware that girls influenced the buying patterns of other girls, advertisers increasingly catered their sales message to girls' sensibilities rather than parental concerns about the educational value of toys or the nutritional value of food. Toy commercials thus featured girls and their peer group culture in a utopian world of fun where "kids rule." By using girls and boys as spokespersons, commercials invited them to identify with their peers rather than adults, only on occasion using adult presenters who were well-known children's personalities. Market research studies also took some of the risk out of product development as toy makers geared toys to girls' as well as boys' fantasies and play preferences. Toy licensing agreements, a staple in children's marketing since the 1930s, became even more widespread during the 1970s with the phenomenal megalicensing success of Star Wars toys. By the 1980s, a new generation of toys—Smurfs, Care Bears, and Teenage Mutant Ninja Turtles—had joined Depression-era favorites—Shirley Temple, Charlie McCarthy, Superman, and the still classic Mickey Mouse—in the pantheon of licensed character toy sensations. Much to the dismay of parents and child experts, however, the proliferation of television-based licensed character toys had the effect of transforming programming itself into one long commercial.

As if advertising itself was not a sufficient sales stimulant, toys themselves taught girls in particular powerful lessons about the joys of spending. No toy, after all, was a better tutor in consumption than Barbie. Arriving on the toy scene in 1959, Mattel's new fashion doll required repeated expenditures to outfit her in Mattel's newest fashion coordinates and accessories. Not a mere plaything but a doll with her own personality profile, Barbie reinforced as many feminine stereo-

types as she broke. Unlike the dolls of the past, Barbie was not a mother figure but rather an autonomous teenager whose doings took her outside the confines of domesticity. Barbie did not, however, model unorthodox roles for young women. Instead, she linked teenage liberation with consumption, teaching girls to associate femininity and being grown up with the joys of shopping, going to the beauty parlor, and having a boyfriend (Ken was introduced in 1961).

Toy manufacturers and toy retailers have also perfected an entire aesthetic code for marketing to girls. Toy stores often demarcate the girls' toy aisles with pink and pastel colors, a sharp contrast to the boys' aisles with their bold, primary colors. These visual cues let girls know what section of the store they are supposed to feel at home shopping in. Toy makers are so committed to these distinct gender-coding formulas that they even try to revive sluggish sales of girls' toys by "pinking them up." Although the revival of the feminist movement in the early 1970s has forced mass marketers to create a broader range of consumer options for girls of all ages—pink and frilly, smart and sassy, athletic and androgynous—marketers' enthusiasm for corralling young girls into rigid gender identifications has continued and perhaps even intensified in the wake of the feminist backlash of the 1980s and 1990s.

Yet by promoting consumption as a form of liberation and statement of identity, mass marketers have also sown the seeds of consumer rebellion. In their own quests for self-expression, girls have long appropriated and misappropriated the symbols of consumer culture to suit their own personalities, needs, and values. During the 1960s, when many youths rebelled against the conformist dictates and ecological excesses of their parents' generation, shopping in nonmainstream venues—the thrift store, the Indian import house, the local cooperative—became an affirmation of alternative values. Rejecting what many regarded as the sexist "uniform" of girlhood, rebellious adolescents and young women turned in their high heels, nylons, and tailored outfits for long billowy skirts, ethnic-inspired garb, comfortable shoes, and secondhand clothes. Resistance and youth rebellion soon enough found their own marketing niche, which advertisers eagerly exploited through generational appeals and nods to the hipness of youth. Indeed, by the end of the twentieth century, youth tastes and youth outlooks acquired a much more expansive kind of cultural authority, influencing the style of advertising directed at adults and children alike. And with the advent of Internet zines created by girls themselves and the explosion of teen-oriented fashion magazines geared to varied adolescent markets in the 1990s, peer-say and peer know-how have come to both antagonize and assimilate the dominant culture. Institutions that formerly had great influence on girls' acculturation—the church, school, and family—not surprisingly have struggled to compete with or accommodate the influence of the mass media and mass market in shaping girls' peer culture. As a result, girls' consumerism has often given rise to heated debate about the growing authority of the marketplace and the demise of family values and childhood innocence.

Lisa Jacobson

See also Arts and Crafts; Barbie; Body Image; Clothing; Cosmetics; Domesticity; Girls' Culture; Girls' Fiction; Girls' Magazines; Hair; Play; Television; Zines

References and Further Reading
Cross, Gary. 1997. *Kids' Stuff: Toys and the Changing World of American Childhood.* Cambridge, MA: Harvard University Press.
Jacobson, Lisa. Forthcoming. *Raising Consumers: Children, Childrearing, and the American Mass Market, 1890–1940.* New York: Columbia University Press.
Kline, Stephen. 1993. *Out of the Garden: Toys, TV, and Children's Culture in the Age of Marketing.* New York: Verso.
Palladino, Grace. 1996. *Teenagers: An American History.* New York: Basic Books.
Seiter, Ellen. 1993. *Sold Separately: Children and Parents in Consumer Culture.* New Brunswick, NJ: Rutgers University Press.

Cosmetics

Cosmetic use signals a passage into adulthood in American culture. Understanding the complex historical relationship between adolescent girls and cosmetics is crucial to understanding the explosion of consumerism and changing ideas about femininity and sexuality in the twentieth century.

Cosmetic use became socially acceptable among some adult women as early as the 1920s. Social commentators continued to deride women who wore cosmetics as sexually loose, and women who wore too much makeup were marked as members of the lower class. The use of cosmetics was largely determined by geographic region and economic standing; the Midwest and rural United States continued to see cosmetic use as a sign of big-city life and its values. Well into the 1930s, many American women and their daughters continued the practice of making cosmetic preparations in their own kitchens with egg whites, oatmeal, and buttermilk. The 1940s signaled the emergence of cosmetics as an everyday practice for most American women, and significantly, teenage girls began to use cosmetics to mark themselves as adult. Cosmetic use among teenagers in this period reflected their emergence as a national consumer market, one sought after by advertisers and marketing firms.

The economic and social conditions of the wartime United States in the 1940s allowed teenagers the social and economic space to define themselves as a distinct group. The term *teenager* came into use in the 1940s, with its first published use attributed to a 1941 *Popular Science* magazine article. *Seventeen* magazine, which most teenage girls for the last fifty years have claimed as the publication that speaks to them and reflects their tastes and habits, emerged on the national scene in 1944. Teenagers had access in the 1940s to unprecedented income as the wartime mobilization created better-paying, skilled positions, which left more marginal positions available for teenagers. New sources of income such as babysitting also gave teenagers the disposable income that they had not had access to during the Great Depression. By 1945, according to one writer's estimation, about 3 million young people had full- or part-time work during the school year. The availability of disposable income that teenagers had to spend made them attractive to cosmetic companies. Avon, for example, began advising their representatives to talk to the "daughter in the house" in their weekly household calls. Cosmetic companies like Noxema created lines of cosmetics specifically designed for teenage girls, such as Cover Girl. The success of Cover Girl was

astounding: annual sales climbed from $1 million to $3 million from 1938 to 1944. Clearly, teenage girls were interested in cosmetics that were packaged exclusively with them in mind.

The disruption caused by World War II provided young people with more freedom from adult control and more opportunities for sexual experimentation. During the war, the incidence of premarital pregnancy, illegitimacy, and venereal disease rose sharply (Mintz and Kellogg 1988, 166). The changing sexual norms reflected in more independent sexual behavior as well as the use of cosmetics were the subject of debate in the 1940s. The use or nonuse of cosmetics and their potential to create generational conflict revealed the pressures of family, peers, and consumption on teenage girls.

Seventeen, the self-proclaimed magazine of the American teenager, sought in the mid-1940s to help teenage girls and their mothers negotiate the issue of cosmetics and how to be a "good girl." For teenage girls in the 1940s wearing lipstick or rouge may have signaled their own interest in being grownup or at least in being perceived as adult. However, many Americans, particularly those from immigrant groups, still did not accept the "made-up" look. Despite the increased use of cosmetics in the 1940s, the lingering identification of cosmetics with prostitution remained. As the advice book *Strictly Confidential* warned its teenage readers in 1944, "good judgment in the amount and application of make-up is very important. Many a girl has ruined her chances for popularity and a successful career because she has made her face look like a paint department" (Hustead 1944, 21). "Looking like a paint department" meant looking like a prostitute or looking like a "loose" girl. The practice of wearing cosmetics, as this advice manual made clear, was fraught with peril for teenage girls. They were encouraged to look sexually attractive, and makeup was seen as a tool to help them accomplish this. At the same time, wearing too much makeup or perhaps the wrong color or combination of colors could give others the wrong message. Wearing makeup signaled one of the rites of passage for teenage girls into the consumer world in which their mothers, aunts, and sisters maneuvered. But it was a consumer world in which they needed direction. Experts that stood outside the hierarchy of the family more often than not provided advice and guidance.

In the 1950s, wearing makeup (at least lipstick and pressed powder) was seen as an essential part of being feminine. On television shows like *Father Knows Best*, the youngest daughter Kathy, or "Kitten," sheds her tomboy image on the advice of her sister, who puts makeup on her, urging that "nothing will make a boy sit up and take notice like a little glamour" (Douglas 1994, 37). Actresses Sandra Dee and Debbie Reynolds portrayed adolescent beauty in movies, and the central message of their films was how to secure a boy. The most popular film representative of the 1950s was Marilyn Monroe, whose soft, lisping voice and voluptuous body reflected an image of femininity that was both childlike and sexualized. Monroe's dyed-blonde hair instructed women and teenage girls alike that beauty required time and products. As Monroe's popularity soared, so did sales of hair-coloring products. For adolescent girls, cosmetics were now only one part of the equation—they wanted to be

accepted by their peer groups, and popularity often required a certain look. In addition to the use of makeup, adolescent girls increasingly used over-the-counter preparations that promised them relief from one of the most obvious signs of adolescence—acne. With products such as Clearasil, girls were told they could discreetly hide the manifestation of their hormones through a medicated cover-up. In their advertising campaign, "Clearasil Personality of the Month," girls were introduced in *Seventeen* to others who had triumphed over pimples and, in doing so, achieved popularity. Avon also jumped on the clear skin bandwagon in the 1950s, offering "Clear-It Shampoo" and "Clear-It Stick" as complete care for troubled skin. A visit to the dermatologist became a rite of passage for many teenage girls whose families could afford the medical expertise offered by such doctors. The expense and time that teenagers devoted to making up continued to rise in the 1950s.

The 1960s would challenge many Americans' consciousness about their beliefs, and for many the superficiality associated with cosmetics and fashion was rejected. The criticism of cosmetics came from many directions. African American civil rights activists rejected the white standard of beauty that had been projected onto African Americans for generations and pointed out that they were not represented in fashion and beauty magazines. Many rejected the hair straighteners and skin bleaches that cosmetic companies (both white and African American owned) had promoted. The "black is beautiful" motto implied both a celebration of African American beauty and difference and a dismissal of white beauty culture.

African Americans were not alone in their criticism of cosmetics and the values they embodied. Feminists who had come of age in the 1940s and 1950s attacked symbols of male domination. In the 1968 protest at the Miss America contest, they threw bras, curlers, false eyelashes, and wigs into a "Freedom Trash Can." The protesters argued that women were forced to compete for male approval, that the cult of youth promoted by the pageant discriminated against older women, and that there had never been a Miss America who was not white. Cosmetics represented to many feminists the misogyny of a sexist culture that devalued women's intellect and demanded that women conform to unrealistic standards of manufactured beauty. Adolescent girls of all ages and races were affected by these arguments. The "natural look" was popularized, and many girls gave up wearing makeup entirely. The emergence and incredible popularity of alternative symbols of beauty like folksingers Joan Baez and Mary Travers, who eschewed makeup and curlers, appealed to many adolescents. The cosmetic industry was quick to respond to the larger cultural changes of the 1960s and promoted the natural look, which in advertisers' eyes was still a manufactured look consisting of long straight hair shaped by Vidal Sassoon, eyes lined with liquid eyeliner, and sheer lip gloss. It may have looked natural, but it still took time and money.

By the mid-1970s and 1980s, adolescent girls were exposed to more than one standard of beauty as the civil rights and feminist movements challenged the beauty industry to look beyond the image of the blond, blue-eyed American. Corporate cosmetic companies saw the economic opportunities in further segmentation of the cosmetic market. Lines of cosmetics designed to appeal to specific ethnic groups were introduced. Adolescents were no longer seen as a small segment of the market. Avon claimed in 1971 that there were 15 million teens in the United States spending $510 million on cosmetics and toiletries.

At the turn of the twenty-first-century, American culture offers few rites of passage for teenage girls. But almost every teenage girl, no matter what her ethnic background, remembers her first "makeover," whether it took place at the mall or at a slumber party. Teens still have to make sense of the complex sexual images that wearing makeup suggests. The 1980s and 1990s exposed Americans to teenage models as young as twelve and thirteen years of age, who with makeup looked like they were thirty. The sexual practices of teens have not been unaffected by this emphasis on appearing grownup as quickly as possible. One expert estimates that "nearly half of all young women ages fifteen to nineteen have had sex, nearly double the rates of 1970" (Pipher 1994, 207–208). Often teenage girls' sexual experiences are violent because they are sexualized but not provided with protection or guidance as they negotiate their adolescent years. Meanwhile, teens are inundated with cosmetic advertising. A new line of cosmetics introduced in 1999 and called SkinMarket has sprung up in malls in California. SkinMarket is a beauty shop designed for teens, with music videos playing and hundreds of lipsticks, shadows, creams, and glitter for teens to try. Teens are invited to "hang out," and the atmosphere is low-key. Girls are encouraged to try on products, and salespeople have been instructed to let teens linger, which is frequently not

A young girl watches as her older sister applies makeup. (Shirley Zeiberg)

the experience at major chains' cosmetic counters. The founders, Tony and Patsy Hirsch, themselves the parents of two teenage girls, believe that makeup is more than an accessory for teen girls. "It's really about a lifestyle," Tony Hirsch comments (ApRoberts 2000, G1). The Hirsches are savvy entrepreneurs who recognize that they have tapped into a market that continues to grow at a phenomenal pace. American teenage girls spend an average of $45 a month on cosmetics, more money than they spend on music and entertainment. Historically, the relationship between teenage girls and cosmetics has been complex, as social mores and economic conditions structured their access to cosmetics. Using make-up remains one way in which teens assert their independence and maturity in the twenty-first century.

Samantha Yates Francois

See also Adolescent Health; Body Image; Clothing; Consumer Culture; Domesticity; Female Sexuality; Hair

References and Further Reading
ApRoberts, Allison. 2000. "About Face." *Sacramento Bee* (May 19): G1–G5.
Banner, Lois. 1983. *American Beauty.* Chicago: University of Chicago Press.
Brumberg, Joan Jacobs. 1997. *The Body Project: An Intimate History of American Girls.* New York: Random House.
Douglas, Susan. 1994. *Where the Girls Are: Growing Up Female with the Mass Media.* New York: Times Books.
Hustead, Alice M. 1944. *Strictly Confidential (for Young Girls).* Minneapolis: Augsburg Publishing House.
Inness, Sherrie A. 1998. *Delinquents and Debutantes: Twentieth-Century American Girls' Cultures.* New York: New York University Press.
Mintz, Steven, and Susan Kellogg. 1988. *Domestic Revolutions: A Social History of American Family Life.* New York: The Free Press.
Peiss, Kathy. 1998. *Hope in a Jar: The Making of America's Beauty Culture.* New York: Metropolitan Books.
Pipher, Mary. 1994. *Reviving Ophelia: Saving the Selves of Adolescent Girls.* New York: Ballantine Books.
Ware, Susan. 1989. *Modern American Women: A Documentary History.* Belmont: Wadsworth Publishing Company.

D

Dance Classes

Formal instruction sessions on dance have been available in the United States since colonial times, yet they have been only one of several ways in which girls learned about dancing, took part in these physical practices, and transmitted them to others. Commercial dance classes supplied professional training for many girls who sought careers as performers in theater, opera, ballet, and musical comedy productions. Equally important, from the eighteenth century to the twentieth century, dance classes showed young females ways to be and ways to act in navigating everyday life. The United States has been a land of ongoing immigration, and the different race, class, and ethnic groups to which girls belonged deeply affected the kinds of dancing and dance instruction they could access. With the introduction of film, television, and then digital media in the twentieth century, girls could tap many more resources with which to learn in dancing, or to find instruction in changing movement practices.

Mastering Dances in Colonial Times

In distinctive ways, enslaved African people and European immigrants to the American colonies used dancing to forge senses of themselves as groups. Dancing figured importantly in many different African cultures as a spiritual or religious expression, a way of establishing group identity and difference from others, and an enactment of gender roles. In the New World, slaves and their daughters and sons continued the pattern of learning to dance in community, to music drummed and played by African Americans, marking important events in slave life.

Many of the accounts of slave dancing were written by whites and white owners, so they must be used with care. But it seems clear that circle and line dances continued African patterns, as did challenge dances. The ring shout built toward a state of ecstatic feeling in dancers, and possibly trance possession. Masters sometimes feared that gatherings of slaves would fuel insurrection. In New Orleans, for example, the city sought to contain the potential for rebellion by designating an area called Place Congo as the spot for slaves' dancing. European immigrants also composed a sense of themselves by dancing, using quite different practices. Girls and boys, like their parents, pursued dancing as a formal study in order to gain skill and display their status in social interaction. They practiced the proper ways to enter and exit rooms and to honor others by bowing. They danced formal choreographies for male-female couples, which led two people in symmetrical patterns through defined ballroom spaces. In

How to dance the minuet: "Dance Manual with Instructions in the Southern Colonies."
(Library of Congress)

the ballroom minuet, the most widely performed of all, they showed their skill in offering and withdrawing their hands from each other. Well-to-do planter families in Anglican southern colonies often employed dancing masters to reside for a period and to offer etiquette and dance instruction to their own and children on neighboring plantations. It was much more common in New England for itinerant dancing masters to travel a circuit each season, teaching classes of girls and boys housed in public spaces, sometimes in homes. Dancing masters might accompany classes on pocket violins as they tutored girls in couple dances and country dances, the latter performed socially in sets where parallel lines of boys and girls wove patterns together. Both these types of dancing could be studied in published period instruction books. At the end of the eighteenth century, the dance practices that American girls pursued were remarkably similar to those of boys. Both sexes aimed to step precisely, to hold the torso upright, and to show a keen musicality. Contact between partners was limited to holding hands.

Nineteenth-Century Models and Modes
As the new United States crafted a national identity, European models continued to shape dancing by native-born and white immigrant girls, and by some elite groups of free blacks in New Orleans. The minuet and dances by a single couple gave way to group dance formations called quadrilles or cotillions. Girls and boys in groups of six or eight moved to popular piano and violin music in geometric formations, giving and taking hands with their partners and others in the set. In addition, close contact was now possible between male and female

partners. When a dance called for couples to waltz or polka around the quadrille formation, for example, a boy encircled the girl's waist with one arm and used his other to extend her arm to the side. In this "round dance position," popular through the 1950s, boys set the course and girls followed their lead. Dancing thus reinforced the deepening distinctions between female and male sex roles that the nineteenth-century cult of domesticity dictated.

The cult of domesticity also emphasized the family as an affective unit and it positioned women as guardians of piety, purity, health, and children. Exercise for girls received new attention, and emerging systems of "physical culture," as it was called, incorporated numerous elements of gymnastics and dance. Catharine Beecher, author of an influential 1843 book on domestic economy, devoted a substantial section of her 1856 book *Physiology and Calisthenics for Schools and Families* to physical training exercises that she culled from contemporary systems. Dio Lewis, who lectured on temperance in the 1860s, developed his own gymnastics program for girls, boys, and adults. Lewis's published books on exercise show that while exercising in neat rows, children frequently moved to live music. Lewis introduced exercises with slender wooden wands to increase the flexibility of the torso, and he added wooden dumbbells to the more traditional metal ones used to build body strength.

After the Civil War, Genevieve Stebbins promoted a physical culture system that particularly appealed to elite and middle-class white girls. She extended the earlier voice cultivation and actor-training dimensions of the system by adding breathing techniques to channel the

These girls dance to choreography inspired by Isadora Duncan in this photograph by Francis Benjamin Johnson. (Library of Congress)

body's energy and achieve a state of dynamic yet relaxed poise. Stebbins also offered instruction in the drawing room performance form called statue posing. Here girls and adult women embodied tableaux drawn from well-known paintings, for instance, and "melted" from one pose to another like human kaleidoscopes. By the turn of the twentieth century, Stebbins's teaching reached aspiring performers like Ruthie Dennis (later Ruth St. Denis) and Isadora Duncan. These young women used the system's aesthetic potential to fashion new dance practices for stage performance. Claiming that their work was "art," they challenged the low social status traditionally given to profes-

sional female dancers. They also challenged the sexual division of labor that had long excluded females from taking, and from imagining themselves as taking, creative and directorial roles.

Those indigenous peoples who survived early contact with Europeans and the attendant disease and warfare had to cope with continued European repression of their culture, including dance. In the Southwest, for example, Spanish Catholic missionaries evangelized among the Pueblo beginning in the sixteenth century. Missionary work at the Tewa Pueblo included attempts to suppress public presentation of masked ritual dances. These dances survived as secret dances, performed by males; only some groups among the Pueblo people offer public performances of them today. Tewa Pueblo dances that continued to be seen publicly involved many members of the community as they marked cycles connected to the agriculture and hunting practices that traditionally sustained Tewa living. Young girls learned to dance by following their female relatives in the line of dancing, learning by bodily repetition the values and aesthetics that dancing enacted. Girls and boys, adults and parents, young and old gathered together in a central plaza of the pueblo to move together for long periods of time across one day. They strived to dance in unison, signaling the importance of the community. Over time, Catholic and indigenous religious beliefs came to coexist, and today Tewa Pueblo dances include Spanish-influenced *matachines* dances and those honoring Catholic patron saints. But the Tewa maintained their own dances, too, and these provided bodily means for learning the Tewa way of being in the world, for addressing and mocking outside events and people, and for communing with the ancestors and the gods. In another part of the country, the Ghost Dance religion offered a form of resistance for Native American people in which girls and boys sometimes joined adults.

From the early nineteenth century, the U.S. government removed Native American people from southern and western territories that whites coveted. By the 1870s and 1880s, U.S. military engagement with indigenous people constituted real warfare. Spreading from the Paiutes to the Plains Indians, the Ghost Dance emerged as a new, rehabilitative movement practice in native cultures that traditionally incorporated dance in their rituals. Dancing and singing for long stretches in circular formation surrounding a central tree or pole, falling into trance states to receive dream visions, young and older practitioners thought the Ghost Dance would restore Native American people to a right relationship with their religious beliefs. They thought their dancing would reverse recent bad experiences, even rid them of the white invaders. The U.S. military prohibited the Ghost Dance because Native American people frequently left reservations to dance it, and because whites feared that Ghost Dance gatherings would result in armed uprising. At the pitch of white anxiety and efforts to suppress the Ghost Dance, the massacre of Native American people at Wounded Knee in 1890 killed about 300 girls, boys, women, and warriors.

Sharing the Dance in the Twentieth Century

The settlement house movement in cities like New York, Boston, Chicago, and Philadelphia placed middle-class men and women in residence among new central and eastern European immigrants. Living in dense urban ghettos, settlement workers tried to forge neighborly relations with newcomer children, working girls and boys, mothers of families, and laboring fathers. Each settlement house developed its own curriculum and gave scope to adventurous settlers, many of whom introduced gymnasium work, Delsarte classes, aesthetic gymnastics, folk dance, and historical dance classes. Daily activities scheduled specific instructors to work with different age groups; girls were usually separated from boys. The social dancing classes that settlements offered to adolescents and young adults played a part in the dance hall reform movement, in which settlement workers, with others, tried to remove liquor from public dance venues and endeavored to stave off embodiments introduced with new "animal" dances like the Turkey Trot and Grizzly Bear that the organizers found vulgar.

As they had at settlements, female teachers provided the impetus for a program of after-school folk dancing inaugurated for New York City schoolgirls in 1905. A woman-run voluntary society, the Girls' Branch of the Public Schools Athletics League (PSAL), created and supported the program that by 1913 involved 26,000 schoolgirls from all five boroughs. In contrast with PSAL boys' athletics, girls' folk dancing limited competition to intraschool contests and emphasized group dances rather than individual accomplishment. Most of the dances taught were from western and northern Europe and did not complement the ethnicity of many immigrant girls on the Lower East Side who participated so avidly. Each year's work was celebrated publicly in Central Park and other boroughs. Newspaper photographs circulated widely the images of these "park fetes," making explicit the links between nature, noncompetitive movement, play, and an ideal femininity. In several ways, this huge folk dance enterprise called into question issues of gender, immigration, and ethnicity.

Settlement houses and Girls' Branch dancing classes set themselves against commercial dancing of two kinds: the orientalist fare that Ruth St. Denis's choreography helped popularize and the sensual, spectacular dancing of Broadway revues and nightclub shows. The dancing displayed in these latter contexts proved very attractive indeed to adolescent girls and young women, and their interest fed a new dance instruction industry. Ned Wayburn started a New York City school for ambitious dancers that trained girls in tap and stepping, acrobatics, ballet, musical comedy, and specialty dance styles. Although some Wayburn-trained working girls joined professional chorus lines, the elite and middle-class students of Irene and Vernon Castle aimed to refine their movement skills for ballroom dancing in social settings. Also cultivating middle class consumers, Russian émigré teacher Louis Chalif sold dance routines through a lively mail-order publication business in the early 1900s. Girls and their mothers could study Greek and aesthetic dancing, classical ballet, ballroom dances, and national forms by following instructions and consulting photographs in Chalif's book, or they could purchase classes at his Manhattan studio.

Surging interest in classical ballet and modern dance added vibrant elements to American teaching and performance culture in the 1920s and 1930s. The School of American Ballet has been one of the most long-lived training schools in the country. Launched in 1934, it nurtured dancers for new companies formed by

George Balanchine between his arrival from Europe in 1933 and the 1948 success of the enterprise Ballet Society, which became the New York City Ballet (NYCB). For girls and boys as for adults, ballet classes followed a time-honored sequence: students first exercised holding a wall-mounted barre for balance, warming up arms, legs, and torsos. Then they moved to the center of the floor where they repeated fundamental exercises, without support. Next came sequences for jumping, turning, and leaping. As they entered puberty, girls added classes in toe work. Still other classes in partnering taught the gendered division of labor that had reigned since the 1820s, in which boys physically supported girls in their performance of balances and turns on one leg, and soaring lifts into the air.

The publication of several dance book series oriented to young females reveals the strong attraction ballet has held for girls since the 1940s and 1950s. Thalia Mara's *First Book of Ballet, Second Book of Ballet,* and *Third Book of Ballet* as well as *On Your Toes* provided many illustrations and simply worded instructions for essential exercises. Noel Streatfeild's *Ballet Shoes, Dancing Shoes,* and *Theatre Shoes* novelized the life and training experiences of plucky young British girls entering these professions.

Men still filled most choreographic and directorial roles in ballet, but American women figured prominently in establishing the new genre of modern dance. Doris Humphrey began her dance training as a girl at the Francis Parker School in Chicago and then with Mary Wood Hinman, who taught at the Hull House settlement and also ran a private studio. Humphrey turned to dance teaching (with her mother as pianist) to support the family when her father lost his job.

She jumped at the chance to study at the Denishawn summer school in Los Angeles, run by Ruth St. Denis and her husband Ted Shawn. From a wealthier family, Martha Graham also came to the Denishawn School as a late adolescent. Both she and Humphrey danced as featured performers in the Denishawn company before striking out to form their own modern dance companies. Helen Tamiris studied dancing at the Henry Street settlement in New York City and also had some ballet and public school folk dance instruction. She too formed a modern dance company and, like her peers in the new genre, pursued themes for dancing that spoke to their American cultural experience.

Ballet instruction everywhere taught similar sequences, but modern dancers generated unique movement styles and taught these materials to their students. Floor work, virtually absent from ballet, was fundamental for many modern dance proponents. These teacher-choreographers produced new talents in the 1930s. The children of immigrants, Anna Sokolow and Sophie Maslow studied at settlement houses and at the Neighborhood Playhouse School of Theatre, where Martha Graham taught classes. Sokolow and Maslow went on to make careers as independent choreographers and were especially important in the leftist dance movement between the two world wars. The Neighborhood Playhouse was a leader among commercial schools in teaching dance composition. Whereas studio instruction in ballet and modern dance tended to focus on movement technique, new university dance courses inaugurated choreography as a subject matter for college girls.

Although the choreography for much ballet and modern dance claimed to make universally understood statements, the training and performance practices for these dance styles were generally racially exclusive through the first half of the twentieth century. The leftist New Dance Group in New York City and Lester Horton's West Coast Dance Theater company proved early exceptions, and each offered student dancers a broad range of classes. Prior to the 1950s, several generations of African American girls had to pursue race-segregated training. Arthur Mitchell, who broke a color line by rising to principal dancer status at the NYCB during the 1950s, left that company to form a new training school and a new company for African Americans. He founded Dance Theatre of Harlem (DTH) after the assassination of civil rights leader Martin Luther King. With Karel Shook he inaugurated a ballet school in Harlem that offers classical training to girls and boys alike and continues to feed dancers to DTH. Katherine Dunham brought extensive anthropological study of Caribbean dance to her Hollywood film, Broadway, and concert choreography. She opened a dance school in east St. Louis that still operates today. Alvin Ailey, first a leading dancer with Horton's multiracial company, also created a company and training school that featured African Americans. The company and the school have continued in operation since Ailey's death in 1989, and the school includes dance history classes in its curriculum.

Interestingly, in accounts they gave of their childhood ballet classes in Oklahoma and Kansas, Native Americans Maria and Marjorie Tallchief, Rosella Hightower, and Yvonne Chouteau reported no racial barriers to their instruction. They went on to make careers as ballerinas in NYCB, Ballet Theatre, and post-Diaghilev Ballets Russes Companies,

Young women in a dance class in the 1990s. (Shirley Zeiberg)

among others. Chouteau danced on the powwow circuit as a girl in the 1930s. The intertribal powwow circuit has gained visibility, especially since the 1960s, and offers Native Americans occasions to revitalize traditional dances, perform competition and exhibition dances, and bring girls into the dances at early ages. Founded in the 1970s, American Indian Dance Theatre, a concert company, offers Native Americans formal training.

Hip-hop dancing has come to be a cross-class, cross-race movement style practiced by young girls and boys, teenagers, and professional performers alike. It was influenced in important ways by break dancing, a street style that black and Puerto Rican boys and some girls introduced in New York City in the 1980s. Responding to the break in the music played by rap music deejays, break dance strove to invent new moves, new "freeze" poses, and new ways of competing with others through bodily movement. Other African American movements added rich possibilities; for example, popping, in which one body part moved suddenly while other areas remained still, or locking, where the ends of a dancer's limbs circle and swing, giving the impression that the joints are locked. Combined with break dancing and even moonwalking, they helped form the new hybrid hip-hop, which infuses the choreography for rock shows and music videos. First winning popularity for its improvisational zest, hip-hop dancing is widely taught today by commercial dance studios in teacher-student formats familiar from ballet and modern dance.

At the end of the twentieth century, the touring stage show *Riverdance* has catalyzed phenomenal interest among girls and boys in Irish step dancing. This evening-length entertainment showcased percussive dancing in a range of different cultures, linking them loosely through history and myths, always connecting sections of the show with hard- and soft-shoe Irish step dancing. Through television, videotape sales, and also live performance, the steely footwork, intricate rhythmic play, and unusual restraint of upper body movement for boys and girls alike fired a new interest in dancing in the United States. Today eager girls can take Irish dance classes in commercial dance studios, on college campuses, and in summer dance camps, sites that respond to the changing interests of girls while continuing to sustain plural movement practices in the United States.

Linda J. Tomko

See also Dances and Dancing

References and Further Reading
Aldrich, Elizabeth. 1991. *From the Ballroom to Hell: Grace and Folly in Nineteenth-Century Dance*. Evanston, IL: Northwestern University Press.
Beecher, Catharine E. 1856. *Physiology and Calisthenics for Schools and Families*. New York: Harper and Brothers.
Castle, Mr. and Mrs. Vernon. 1914. *Modern Dancing*. New York: Harper and Brothers.
Dunning, Jennifer. 1985. *"But First a School": The First Fifty Years of the School of American Ballet*. New York: Viking.
Emery, Lynne Fauley. 1980. *Black Dance in the United States from 1619 to 1970*. New York: Dance Horizons.
George, Nelson, Sally Banes, Susan Flinker, and Patty Romanowski. 1985. *Fresh, Hip Hop Don't Stop*. New York: Random House.
Gonzalez, Anita. 1998. "Powwow Dancing and Native Rap: American Indian Dance Patronage and the Politics of Spirituality." Minneapolis, MN: Society of Dance History Scholars Proceedings, 227–233.
Heth, Charlotte, ed. 1992. *Native American Dance: Ceremonies and Social Traditions*. Washington, DC: National Museum of the American Indian, Smithsonian Institution, with Starwood Publishing.
Lewis, Dio. 1862. *The New Gymnastics for Men, Women, and Children*. 3d ed. Boston: Ticknor and Fields.
Livingston, Lili Cockerille. 1997. *American Indian Ballerinas*. Norman: University of Oklahoma Press.
Mara, Thalia. 1955. *First Steps in Ballet*. Garden City, NY: Doubleday.
———. 1956. *Second Steps in Ballet*. Garden City, NY: Doubleday.
———. 1959. *On Your Toes*. Reprint 1972. Brooklyn, NY: Dance Horizons.
———. 1963. *Third Steps in Ballet*. London: Constable.
Mooney, James. 1865; abridged 1976. *The Ghost-Dance Religion and the Sioux Outbreak*. Chicago: University of Chicago Press.
Page, Ruth. 1984. *Class: Notes on Dance Classes around the World 1915–1980*. Princeton: Princeton Book Co.
Rameau, Pierre. 1725. *Le Maître à Danser*. Paris.
Stebbins, Genevieve. 1902. *Delsarte System of Expression*. 6th ed. Reprint, 1997. New York: Dance Horizons.
Stratyner, Barbara. 1996. *Ned Wayburn and the Dance Routine, from Vaudeville to the Ziegfield Follies*. Studies in Dance History no. 13. Minneapolis, MN: Society of Dance History Scholars.
Streatfeild, Noel. 1937. *Ballet Shoes*. New York: Random House.
———. 1945. *Theatre Shoes*. New York: Random House.
———. 1957. *Dancing Shoes*. New York: Random House.

Tomko, Linda J. 1999. *Dancing Class: Gender, Ethnicity, and Social Divides in American Dance, 1890–1920.* Bloomington: Indiana University Press.

White, Julia C. [Meyna Hahn-a'ae]. 1996. *The Pow Wow Trail.* Summertown, TN: Book Publishing Company.

Wilson, James. 1998. *The Earth Shall Weep: A History of Native America.* New York: Grove Press.

Dances and Dancing

Throughout the twentieth century, dancing has been a particularly popular pastime for teenage girls in the United States. Around the turn of the century, dancing typically took place in a neighborhood hall or room attached to a saloon and was traditionally tied to community and family events or to raise money for charity. Over the next several decades, these dance venues would remain popular, but increasingly American youth began to organize their own dances apart from the prying eyes of family, and entrepreneurs began building commercial dance halls to capitalize on the growing popularity of dance. By the 1910s and especially by the 1920s, dance halls could be found in small and large towns alike, and there were a number of different types of dancing sites from which to choose, the most notable of which was the dance palace, a larger and much more elaborate and ornately decorated dance hall than previous establishments. At the same time, dancing was experiencing many significant changes. Beginning in the first half of the century and gaining speed after World War II, freestyle dancing, or solo performances, replaced dancing in which couples held hands or touched hands periodically. Both the commercialization of dance and changes in dance style in part explain the popu-

larity of dancing, the former affording young men and women the opportunity to couple up without their parents' interference and the latter promoting greater individual expression and spontaneity. But for young women in particular, these changes also helped them shape and influence their relations with men on and off the dance floor.

The traditional working-class dance was known as the "affair," a dance sponsored by mutual aid societies, fraternal orders, unions, or political associations, or dancing was linked to community and family events like weddings. In both cases, the dancing reaffirmed community networks and relations: mutual aid and fraternal dances helped raise money for charitable causes, and neighborhood- and community-based dances ensured that certain customs were passed on to the next generation, including the rituals of courtship. Indeed, young women rarely attended these dances alone. Their parents usually accompanied them, or they found an acceptable chaperone, a practice particularly common among emigrants from southern and eastern Europe and Mexico.

By the 1890s, working-class youth began to organize their own dances called "rackets." These "rackets" were generally sponsored by social or pleasure clubs, which typically included anywhere from about a dozen to fifty or more members who were in their mid- to late teens and early twenties. Club members usually met once a week in saloons, settlement houses, rented halls, cigar stores, cafés, or in their own hangouts they set up in the basements of tenement flats to smoke, play cards, gamble, organize athletic contests, and entertain their dates with dances, skits, and other games. Most social clubs also held a semiannual or

Changing styles in the "flapper era," shown on this 1926 cover of Life *magazine, highlighted young women's new sense of freedom. (Library of Congress)*

annual dance in a neighborhood hall or an uptown hotel, using the money they raised through the sale of tickets and hatcheck fees to pay for club activities, buy uniforms, and outfit and decorate their hangouts.

Over the next few decades, dancing would become a veritable craze, and as the demand for dancing increased, so did the number and types of dance halls. By the 1910s, dance palaces joined the neighborhood or saloon halls as entrepreneurs became more ambitious and as the popularity of dancing continued to grow. New York's Grand Central Palace, which was the first dance palace, opened its doors in 1911, and within ten years entrepreneurs had built five more in New York, the most famous being the Roseland and the Savoy. The Trianon and the Aragon led the pack in Chicago, the Raymor in Boston, and the Hollywood Palladium and the Palomar in Los Angeles. Dance palaces were a more elaborate and conspicuous commercialized attraction than the multiple-purpose hall and saloon and were usually much larger, accommodating anywhere from 500 to 3,000 patrons. The dance palace also attracted young men and women from all walks of life and nationalities, although they appealed more to factory and office workers. Young middle-class men and women preferred the city's cabarets, which also made their debut in the 1910s and cost more because they included dinner and a floor show along with the opportunity to dance. By the 1920s, couples were dancing at more than a dozen different establishments, including roadhouses, dancing academies, dime-a-dance restaurants, dance pavilions, and taxi-dance halls where young women worked as hostesses and danced with the young men in attendance for a dime a dance.

The most obvious difference between the commercial dance hall and the traditional "affair" was the absence of parents. The anonymity female adolescents found at dance palaces and similar establishments enabled them to experiment with alcohol and cigarettes and to cultivate intimate relations. Teenage boys and girls were frequently seen closely embracing one another in the balcony or in the chairs and tables surrounding the dance floor. The dance hall had even earned the reputation as the parlor of certain classes because of the numbers of married couples who first met at a dance. Dance hall entrepreneurs and managers even went out of their way to encourage patrons to take advantage of their time away from parents. Dance halls routinely held lucky number contests, raffles, and even special dance nights or dance contests. Dance marathons, although particularly popular during the Depression when large numbers of young men and women had ample free time to attend a contest that might last several months, initially started in the 1920s. Another popular dance was the shadow dance. During the shadow dance, the ceiling lights were turned off, and a spotlight bathed the dancers in colored lights as confetti poured down from above, providing opportunities for more intimate moments in the semidarkness created by the dance. At the same time, dance hall owners were concerned about attracting female clients. Females were often admitted into the dance hall at reduced admission prices, cocktails were available to help make drinking a more acceptable pastime for them, and some dance halls provided what were known as "spielers," males hired to dance with and entertain any females found sitting alone. Indeed, for female adolescents the dance hall provided one of the few opportunities to smoke, drink, and experiment sexually without their parents' close supervision. Although young men had their saloons, gambling dens, poolrooms, and countless other institutions, similar hangouts were generally unavailable for young women.

The new social dances from the period only reinforced the commercial dance hall's appeal. By the late nineteenth and early twentieth centuries, pivoting, spieling, and tough dancing were beginning to replace the traditional waltz and two-step. Pivoting and spieling were simply a fast parody of the waltz in which couples closely embraced one another and engaged in much twisting and twirling. When dancing a waltz, teenage boys and girls did place their hands on each other. But their shoulders were expected to be 3–4 inches apart, and the dancers were not supposed to look directly into their partner's eyes but over their right shoulder, limiting the contact between dancers and the dance's sexual expressiveness. The tough dances, also known as animal and rag dances, were even more out of control. Unlike the waltz, in which partners held each other by the hands or around the waist, tough dances celebrated bodily contact. Couples not only stood close together with the young man's arms around his partner or on her hips, but the dancing had a much more sexually expressive look and feel than previous dances. Unlike the more rigid waltz, tough dances were performed from a crouched position with knees flexed and body bent. Many of these dances, like the turkey trot, bunny hug, and grizzly bear, imitated animal gestures and movements while celebrating improvisation, giving them a swinging motion and a more sensual and sexually expressive look and feel.

In the first decades of the twentieth century, this form of dancing would continue to grow in popularity. The 1920s saw the rise of the shimmy, the black bottom, and the Charleston. In these dances, partners did not face one another or move around the floor to the beat of the music. These new dances required partners to maintain an arm's-length distance from each other, either by touching hands or not touching at all because they were busy swinging their arms, swiveling their hips, or shaking their shoulders. By the 1930s, swing music, which came from larger or big bands and produced an ensemble sound, began to replace the smaller jazz combos. Swing was less restrained and less ornate than its jazzy predecessors and more individualistic, a sound that fit well with the Lindy, a dance also known as the "jitterbug." Like the Charleston and other dances from the 1920s, the Lindy required partners to touch hands or dance apart instead of in an exclusively face-to-face position. In particular, the Lindy featured two innovations: the breakaway or solo, typically reserved for the male, and the "air steps" in which dancers showed off their skill by dancing with their feet off the ground through a number of gymnastic moves. In short, the Lindy was more of a style of dance than an actual dance, characterized by athleticism and acrobatic maneuvers.

The dance hall did have its critics, however. Besides the problem of having to deal with intrusive parents, dance hall patrons faced endless rules and regulations. As early as the late nineteenth century, cities and states across the country began to establish ordinances to regulate dancing. Many of these ordinances dealt with the location and physical condition of the hall and its proper ventilation and sanitation. But reformers were particularly concerned about the dance hall's link to vice and the unsupervised intermingling of the sexes. In city after city they successfully passed ordinances to restrict the use of alcohol, to prohibit certain dance moves, and to prevent the attendance of youth guilty of "unruly" behavior.

The extent to which these ordinances achieved their intended goal varied considerably. But working-class youth generally found ways to circumvent the rules and regulations they faced. Some young women successfully convinced their parents to grant them more control over their personal lives. Others simply resorted to sneaking out of the house after their parents had gone to bed, or they collectively worked with their siblings to conceal their whereabouts. Once inside the dance hall, young men and women frequently made use of "pass out checks" to leave during intermission, either to consume alcohol or to take part in more intimate encounters, or they simply brought alcohol back in with them. Dance hall patrons also took advantage of the dance hall's dark corners and back rooms to drink or even to dance more sensual steps, effectively allowing them to take advantage of the autonomy dance halls offered despite efforts to regulate their behavior.

At the same time, male and female adolescents often had different ideas about leisure and intimacy. A 1910 survey of 1,000 children between the ages of eleven and fourteen found that among girls, nine out of ten knew how to dance, as opposed to only one-third of the boys. As these boys grew older, more of them undoubtedly learned to dance, but many of them either remained ambivalent about dancing or attended dance halls but refused to dance. Part of their

ambivalence reflected young women's greater skill and ability at dancing.

By the second decade of the twentieth century, dance instruction was cheap and accessible. Printed dance lessons were available through the mail, and magazines and newspapers often featured articles on the newest dance fashions. Yet young men recalled that they typically picked up the new steps from a female friend, sister, or sweetheart. In fact, when young men sought out more formal instruction at a dance hall, young women still played an important role as teacher. In some cases, dance halls admitted females free of charge because they needed more female patrons to help teach the males in attendance how to dance. In other cases, dance halls simply hired females who regularly attended to work on certain nights of the week as instructors in exchange for a week's worth of free passes. By working as an instructor or by simply dancing with a male companion, young women found numerous opportunities to show off their expertise and skills, skills that often set them apart from their male counterparts but that young men coveted because of their value in dating and courtship. Adolescent males, of course, retained the traditional prerogatives of asking for dances and leading their female partners. But these prerogatives did not always protect them from the potential problems they faced from a dance partner who possessed greater skill and ability.

The disproportionate numbers of young men in dance halls also helps explain young women's attraction to dance. Throughout the early twentieth century, there were almost always more males than females at dance halls. The greater numbers of males meant that all of them faced the prospect of being passed over for dances. Indeed, competition for dances was so difficult that some claimed that they had to know someone before being assured of getting a dance, or that they avoided dancing on the weekends when there were greater numbers of males in attendance. A young woman could thus pick and choose until she found an appropriate dance partner or companion for the evening. If a suitable male partner was unavailable or if she preferred, she could simply dance with a female friend, further allowing her to define what she considered acceptable behavior on and off the dance floor as well as the opportunity to challenge the idea that her parents should closely supervise her social life.

Working women did, of course, confront a number of problems. Some young men refused to dance, claiming that they might be awkward or that they never took the time to learn. Male youth who had failed to find a dance partner sometimes formed what were known as "stag lines" at the entrance to the dance floor to harass any unescorted women as they left the floor. And paying for commercial leisure was a particularly chronic problem for young women. In the 1920s, women's wages averaged only 57 percent of men's, and parents generally expected them to turn over what little they made, even though their brothers kept up to half or only paid for room and board. To make up for their low wages, young women often made do without many essential items. They often skipped meals, sewed and washed their own clothes, boarded with other single women, and depended upon their male companions to help pay for commercial leisure. In short, since young women often lacked the means to pay for their

nights out, they participated in a system known as treating in which they traded sexual favors that ranged from a simple goodnight kiss to more intimate sexual encounters for access to commercial leisure.

The problem with the system of treating was that it was an exchange that often failed to meet the expectations of both participants. Adolescent males typically expected females to reciprocate for the money they spent or to "come across" and agree to some sort of intimacy. Although some young women, known as "charity girls," embraced this system of treating more thoroughly than others, most young women feared that the system of treating ensured their dependence on men and threatened to taint their reputations. The dilemma compelled some to attend only chaperoned dances or to try and find ways to accept treats without having to "come across." The most common way was to attend the dance hall with a female friend. Attending with a friend guaranteed companionship for the evening and helped protect young women from unwanted sexual advances. Other young women watched the amount of alcohol they consumed, feigned illness, accepted offers to dance from more than one partner, or looked for the appropriate moment to end a date by slipping away unexpectedly. These strategies only seemed to exacerbate the frustration of male youth. But they also challenged the system of treating upon which young men relied to gain sexual favors. Treating allowed young women to balance the demands their male companions made with their attraction to dancing and the dance hall.

Throughout the post–World War II period, social dancing experienced many major changes with the rise of rock and roll dance. Often connected to names like Fats Domino, Bill Haley, and Elvis Presley, rock and roll was a derivation of the blues characterized by a pounding beat, a simplicity of form, and the newly developed electric guitar, which made the beat louder and stronger than ever before. Rock and roll's use of repeated phrases along with hard and grinding percussion and a driving beat gave rise to dances that emphasized swiveling and thrusting hips, especially after Presley took the stage. Rock and roll dances like the jet, the locomotion, and the bop still required partners, but they frequently lost contact. With the rise of the twist in 1960, partners became nearly obsolete. Popularized by Chubby Checker on American Bandstand, the twist was akin to toweling oneself after a bath while grinding out a cigarette with one's toes. Soon to follow were dozens of hip-swiveling dances know as "mimic" dances such as the jerk, which required dancers to snap their body, or the shake, which required the body to shimmy. Like the twist, these dances were performed solo. Dancers independently gyrated across the floor, often without acknowledging other dancers. In fact, dancers did not even need to face their so-called partners or to worry about keeping in step.

By 1967, the last of the more famous rock dances, the funky Broadway, was waning in popularity, and there was little to replace it. Young Americans were beginning to favor a heavier rock and roll sound, with the rise of bands like Led Zeppelin and stars like Jimi Hendrix. It was more difficult to dance to this brand of rock and roll, and dancing was rarely seen at the concerts these bands staged. The male and female youth in attendance typically preferred to "freak out"

or "trip out," often while vibrating their spines or contracting their torsos and generally under the influence of drugs or alcohol—that is, until the rise of disco.

Disco, which is simply music that is reproduced "on disk" and not performed, can be traced to the late 1960s, when disk jockeys in primarily gay and black clubs began splicing together faster soul songs to produce a continuous dance mix that provided a predictable rhythm and an irresistible beat. For about a decade, disco was confined to larger cities until the release of *Saturday Night Fever* (1977). After its release, disco became a national craze, and discotheques began to replace café jukeboxes in popularity. At discotheques across the country, freestyle dance typically dominated the dance scene. But some of the more popular dances like the hustle encouraged having partners, and group or line dances were not uncommon. The bus stop, a line dance with participants dancing singly but facing in the same direction, was particularly popular.

Responses to freestyle and group dances varied considerably. Many critics decried the rise of these new dances and the supremacy of the solo performance. A single dancer was no longer part of a community of couples. Instead, he or she spent time on the floor alone; males and females rarely touched one another; and couples rarely moved from one spot. To make matters worse, critics charged that there was no way to differentiate between the males and the females. They moved around, or danced, in the same monotonous manner, and they even looked the same in dance, dress, and style, often donning the same bracelets, clothes, and hairstyles. Indeed, by the 1960s male youth had abandoned their barbershops and crew cuts for longer locks, or what became known as

Salt-N-Pepa, a hip-hop rap group, performs at Woodstock II. (Neal Preston/Corbis, 1994)

"Jesus hair." At the same time, both males and females found that the rise of freestyle dance offered certain advantages. Both sexes still faced the problem of finding partners, but with freestyle there was no need to synchronize steps and no need even to practice with a partner because there was no planned-out next step or variation. In short, the freestyle rock and roll and disco dances paled by comparison to the pre–World War II Lindy, which required not only skill and timing but also strength. All that the social dances of the post–World War II period required was that dancers keep up with the beat.

In fact, by the late 1960s and 1970s, youth were attracted to nightclubs and discotheques as much for the drugs, alcohol, and sex as they were to the dancing.

Studio 54, a discotheque in Manhattan, became notorious for the conspicuous culture of drugs and sex both on and off the dance floor. In addition, the continued popularity of communal dances or line dances meant that neither female nor male youth had to have a partner, a particularly attractive feature for females. Although males may have always had problems finding partners, female youth have typically been expected to wait patiently for an offer to dance. Moreover, not only did they find that freestyle dancing promoted expressiveness and individuality, but they could show off their dancing skills without the problem of having to deal with a partner of inferior skills and ability.

Throughout the rest of the twentieth century, dancing would remain particularly popular among women, and group and freestyle dances would continue to profoundly shape the dance scene. In the 1980s and 1990s, line dancing led to a renewed popularity for country and western bars because of the ease with which dancers could pick up the steps, and raves featured trance dancing, or what can be described as dancing with an emphasis on spinal vibrations or torso and pelvic contractions reminiscent of the "tripping out" of the late 1960s. But whether young women actually held their partner's hand when they danced meant little if they could not look the part, with fashionable dress and hairstyle, and take part in the culture of consumption surrounding dance, a problem that has plagued young women throughout the twentieth century. Since World War II, women's work opportunities have expanded. Yet during this time, poverty also disproportionately affected women and children. By the 1980s, women constituted two-thirds of the adults who fit into the federal definition of poverty, and even when women earned more significant incomes, they made about 70 cents for every dollar their male counterparts earned doing comparable work (Ehrenreich 1983, 172; Moberg 2001, 24–26).

Throughout the twentieth century, young women have used dance to embrace the physical and sensual, to find potential partners and spouses, and to challenge conventional gender norms. But dancing still remained embedded in the larger world in which women lived, affecting their experiences with dance culture and their access to it.

Randy D. McBee

See also Clothing; Consumer Culture; Dance Classes; Punk Rock

References and Further Reading
Buckman, Peter. 1978. *Let's Dance: Social, Ballroom and Folk Dancing.* New York: Paddington Press.
Ehrenreich, Barbara. 1983. *The Hearts of Men: American Dreams and the Flight from Commitment.* New York: Anchor Press.
Erenberg, Lewis. 1981. *Steppin' Out: New York Nightlife and the Transformation of American Culture.* Chicago: University of Chicago Press.
Martin, Carol. 1994. *Dance Marathons: Performing American Culture of the 1920s and 1930s.* Jackson: University Press of Mississippi.
McBee, Randy D. 2000. *Dance Hall Days: Leisure and Intimacy among Working-Class Immigrants in the United States.* New York: New York University Press.
Moberg, David. 2001. "Bridging the Gap: Why Women Still Don't Get Equal Pay." *In These Times* (January 8): 24–26.
Nasaw, David. 1993. *Going Out: The Rise and Fall of Public Amusements.* New York: Basic Books.
Peiss, Kathy. 1986. *Cheap Amusements: Working Women and Leisure in Turn-of-the-Century New York.* Philadelphia: Temple University Press.
Wagner, Ann. 1997. *Adversaries of Dance: From the Puritans to the Present.* Urbana: University of Illinois Press.

Dating and Courtship

Dating is a ritual of sexual interaction and, unlike courtship, may or may not lead to marriage. Courting in early America implied a commitment between two people and included traditions such as letter writing. Although Victorians preferred the act of courting, dating and petting occurred first in the 1920s with the advent of the automobile. The World War II era introduced the concept of "going steady," and a couple who was thinking of marriage became "pinned." Since the 1970s, the words *courtship* and *dating* have been replaced by *hooking up* and *hanging out*, after college campuses

Popping the Question, *a lithograph showing the old-fashioned tradition of the formal marriage proposal. (Library of Congress, 1846)*

dropped curfews and allowed coed dormitories.

The earliest forms of courtship in America were practiced by Native Americans. For example, courtship practice among the Iroquois was liberal compared to Christian standards, and out-of-wedlock births were numerous and accepted. Young Iroquois women and men experimented freely with physical contact and spent time together without a chaperone. Since Iroquois society was matrilineal and all the family wealth passed through daughters, matrons took full responsibility for approval of marriage unions. Divorce was common, easily attained, and without stigma (Demos 1995).

In stark contrast to the courtship of the Iroquois, seventeenth-century colonists in New England practiced full authority over courting youth. A New England Puritan law gave parents "the care and power . . . for disposing their Children in Marriage" (Rothman 1984, 26). The patriarchal order of New England families determined that fathers chose spouses for their sons and daughters. "Bundling," or sleeping together fully clothed, was nevertheless a common practice during this period but was reserved only for the very serious suitor. This ritual, as Ellen K. Rothman explains, gave daughters a power rarely allowed in the division of the sexes. It was the young woman who permitted or denied a suitor the access to the bundling bed, and it was a favor granted only to special lovers. By the end of the colonial period, youth had already come to expect autonomy from parents in the matters of courtship as the concept of romantic love emerged and Americans replaced communal values with individual values.

Courtship among the new middle class in the nineteenth-century became more rigid as parents took a protective roll in guiding young people in the ways of love. A young suitor presented a "calling card" at the home of a young lady, who would either "receive" him or turn him away. The system of "calling" provided young women numerous opportunities to meet young men without breaking strict Victorian courting rules. Cards could be exchanged between young people of both sexes, although unmarried women often printed their name beneath that of their mother. Sanctioned activities for a Victorian courtship included playing the piano, singing, talking, attending outdoor events, and by the end of the century, biking and hiking.

Socially acceptable Victorian courtship rituals were included in etiquette books and in periodicals such as *Godey's Lady's Book* by the 1890s. Flirting was accepted as a way for a young girl to exhibit her grace and availability to prospective suitors. Sixteen was the recommended age for a young lady to begin to keep company with young men, and young couples attended social functions with young married friends as chaperones. Acceptable leisure activities for couples included sitting alone in the parlor, with other couples, or sitting together and playing piano duets; one important rule was that a lady should never take a man's arm unless he offered it (Green 1983).

Enslaved African Americans in the plantation South courted on Sundays, during church services, and on walks in the woods. On Sunday evenings, courting couples would join family members in singing, dancing, and reciting poetry. Young courting couples at parties played kissing games, including fruit in the basket and fishing. Wilma King explains, "Young slaves' courting manners were ritualistic and stylized" (1997, 61). Girls used coquetry and cosmetics made of dried berries to secure the heart of a suitor. Sometimes masters who sold one partner broke apart courtships and marriages. Slave families nevertheless worked hard to preserve family unity.

At the turn of the twentieth century, working-class girls in urban areas spent nights and weekends indulging in commercial amusement with young men. In *Cheap Amusements: Working Women and Leisure in Turn-of-the-Century New York*, Kathy Peiss demonstrates that Coney Island promoted romance with penny arcade machines that measured the ardor of a couple's kiss. Rides, such as the Canals of Venice and the Tunnel of Love, provided enough privacy to steal a hug or a kiss.

Working-class courting culture shaped middle-class practices in the 1920s. The term *dating* was used first on college campuses, and it differed from courting in that it allowed a paired relationship without a commitment to marriage. With the advent of the automobile, dating moved from long walks and porch swings to the backseats of cars. The automobile also transformed courting into an act of consumption that included spending money on movies, restaurants, and dance halls (Bailey 1988).

In her book *The Damned and the Beautiful: American Youth in the 1920s*, Paula S. Fass explains that young couples isolated from parental supervision invented ways of staying within acceptable sexual boundaries while at the same time expanding horizons: "The young, reared in a moral standard in which all sex was taboo, redefined that standard according to their own needs and laid the basis for change in the standard itself" (Fass 1977, 261). College youth of the 1920s discovered that "love is erotic," laying the foundation for the dating ritual of "petting." "Petting" was the exploratory sexual activity of kissing, hugging, or touching. This activity evoked criticism from youths' elders, who voiced concerns about deteriorating moral standards.

The stock market crash of 1929 sent the United States into calamity and changed the structure of dating once again. Young people waited to marry because of financial insecurity. In this climate, dating became more competitive, but a couple considering marriage could eliminate competition by becoming "pinned." The pin came from the young man's achievements in academics or sports and served to bond the couple in a premarital agreement to date each other exclusively. Girls were expected to "rate" in order to "get a date" on college campuses.

Getting "pinned" moved to a more secure arrangement known as "going steady" in the 1950s. The young man offered his class ring, and the couple attended school proms that imitated the wedding ceremony. For such occasions, the young women wore an expensive gown, accessorized with pearls, gloves, and a bouquet of flowers. At this time, the average girl married at the age of eighteen or nineteen (Bailey 1988).

Shaped by the rise of feminism and the sexual revolution, dating in the 1960s led young middle-class couples to experi-ment with new sexual boundaries. The invention of the birth control pill revolutionized sexual freedom for women, and "free love" became a model for young couples protesting the values of their parents' generation. Marketed to eight and a half million women by 1968, the Pill changed the meaning and experience of sex for middle-class Americans (Bailey 1999). Although marriage was still a goal, dating college students often lived together. The term *dating* was replaced with *hanging together* and *shacking up.* College campuses dropped curfews and allowed coed dormitories, and some campus clinics distributed birth control.

By the 1970s and 1980s, older dating practices became obsolete as women gained economic, political, and social independence. The wide availability of birth control and the legalization of abortion in 1973 enabled women to postpone marriage and openly choose a single lifestyle or a same-sex mate. Young people attended dance clubs known as discos that featured recorded dance music, disc jockeys, alcohol, and drugs. The "courting manners" that governed the earlier "rules of dating" were disregarded as both genders became confident enough to explore new frontiers.

Many Asian immigrants with traditional patriarchal values were ill at ease with American dating practices. Forbidden from dating casually, Vietnamese young women bound to old world ideas of arranged marriages felt obligated to conform to family practices. Iranians and Jordanians often chose to marry someone from the same nationality after a courtship that followed a strict code of conduct reflecting religious and ethnic traditions. Parents reserved the right to interfere in courtships, and at times arrangements were made between supervising fathers.

By the late 1980s, issues of public health would change the face of dating for all young couples in the United States. The rise in sexually transmitted diseases and acquired immunodeficiency syndrome (AIDS) led to a public health campaign for "safe sex" that curtailed "free love." Condoms were passed out on the streets to young people by health departments in a campaign to promote safe sex. Young couples found ways to express their affection for each other in nonsexual ways such as cybersex, the sexually titillating Internet communication on computers. A casual way of developing a paired relationship arose by the 1990s, in which young people met in public places like restaurants, theaters, and parks to get to know a potential partner. Today, urged by experts, cautious baby-boomer parents of teenage girls set strict guidelines for dating, such as age limits and dress codes. Increasingly, couples engage in premarital coitus only after passing a sexually transmitted disease test.

Rita Papini

See also Acquaintance Rape; Birth Control; Domesticity; Female Sexuality; Teen Pregnancy

References and Further Reading
Bailey, Beth L. 1988. *From Front Porch to Back Seat: Courtship in Twentieth-Century America.* Baltimore: Johns Hopkins University Press.
———. 1999. *Sex in the Heartland.* Cambridge, MA: Harvard University Press.
Demos, John. 1995. *The Tried and the True: Native American Women Confronting Colonization.* New York: Oxford University Press.
Fass, Paula S. 1977. *The Damned and the Beautiful: American Youth in the 1920s.* New York: Oxford University Press.
Green, Harvey. 1983. *The Light of the Home: An Intimate View of the Lives of Women in Victorian America.* New York: Pantheon Books.
Jones, Jacqueline. 1986. *Labor of Love, Labor of Sorrow: Black Women, Work, and the Family from Slavery to the Present.* New York: Vintage Books.
King, Wilma. 1995. *Stolen Childhood: Slave Youth in Nineteenth-Century America.* Bloomington: Indiana University Press.
Larkin, Jack. 1988. *The Reshaping of Everyday Life 1790–1840.* New York: Harper and Row.
Peiss, Kathy. 1986. *Cheap Amusements: Working Women and Leisure in Turn-of-the-Century New York.* Philadelphia: Temple University Press.
Rothman, Ellen K. 1984. *Hands and Hearts: A History of Courtship in America.* New York: Basic Books.

Daughters and Fathers

The father-daughter relationship has undergone many transformations since the colonial period and has played a major role in defining the relationship of girls to men and to family life overall in American culture. Of the Ten Commandments, the one that carried the greatest weight among the Puritans, apart from the first, was the fifth: "Honor thy father and thy mother: that thy days may be long upon the land." For Puritan girls, the weight of the fifth commandment was reflected in both the seriousness and subordination that inhered in their relationship with their fathers. For fathers, the command was not only at the center of their family life but of the political, religious, and social organization as it was enacted by men in seventeenth- and early-eighteenth-century New England. A man's authority in the world at large was exercised through his role as the head of a household, and all political power flowed from and through men's responsibility for enforcing sanctified—or at the very least civil—behavior in their own homes. Within such a political and social framework, fatherhood held a kind of significance in the day-to-day lives of men and girls that was quite unlike that of the modern period. Over the course of American history, the social meaning and formal obligations of the father-daughter relationship have reflected and played a role in larger social, economic, and political developments. And as conceptions about the father-daughter relationship have changed over time, they have transformed the emotional landscape in which successive generations of Americans have grown up and raised families.

Puritan fathers were responsible for teaching all their children reading and writing and instructing them in religion, including teaching them their catechism and exposing them to sermons. Their roles as teachers, however, did not override fathers' investment in nurturing their infant children, both boys and girls. Fathers held their daughters at baptism, kept meticulous diaries chronicling their growth and development, and wrote to friends asking them advice about all manner of infant care. Fathers also referred to the care of their daughters in terms that reflected their sense of mutuality with their wives, often making statements such as "today *we* began to wean ye child" (Wilson 1999, 123).

As girls and boys matured, mothers took over their daughters' care in order to teach them household skills, such as spinning, soap making, and cooking, and fathers oversaw sons' work. Sometimes girls would be "put out" to a neighboring household to learn housewifery under the guidance of another family. The widespread practice of putting out children between the ages of eleven and sixteen is not completely understood, but it has been argued that Puritans did so because they felt that they could not trust themselves not to spoil their own children by too great affection and that children learned better manners when brought up in a home other than that of their parents. Puritan fathers were also afraid of bestowing such an immoderate love upon their children that it would displace God in their hearts. Frequently, when children died young, Puritan fathers believed it was because "the Lord doth strike his people in that child they take too much affection in." Though fathers ultimately spent more time with their sons, there is no evidence that they cared more for sons than for daughters, and there is evidence—from letters and diaries—that fathers mourned the loss of a daughter in terms equal to those of a son.

One of the most important forms of economic and social power that Puritan fathers held over their daughters was that of dictating the terms of marriage, but fathers had rather less control in this arena than is popularly believed. The laws of New England provided that no man could court "the affections of any Maid" without the express consent of her parents. However, a daughter could decline to marry any suitor she believed would not make a good match; hence fathers had more control over when girls married than to whom. The most important role they played was in the negotiation of the terms of the marriage. On average, a girl's dowry consisted of about half the amount given to the marriage by the boy's parents, usually in the form of household furnishings and other movable objects. However, this basic formula left a great deal of room for bargaining, and a father often bickered with the boy's parents until he (and his wife) were assured that the settlement would provide for their daughter's needs. When the bargaining was satisfactorily completed, the financial agreement was recorded in a legal contract, and consent to marriage was given. And at this point, under normal circumstances, a father's responsibility for his daughter ended.

Traditionally, one of the important parental responsibilities involving girls has been that of sexual surveillance. Girls were to remain chaste until marriage, and it was the parents' duty to keep a firm eye on their daughters' sexual behavior. An unwanted pregnancy or gossip about a daughter's liaison could ruin the reputation not only of a young woman but of her entire family as well. Officially, fathers (as well as town magistrates) were charged with both protecting their daughters against and ultimately passing judgment on sexual transgressions, including "fornication" and adultery. In practice, however, sexual surveillance was conducted by mothers and older women in the community during the colonial period. When a girl got into some kind of trouble with a man, she usually turned to her mother or an older woman. Moreover, older women took the most interest in such cases and thus acted as advisers, counselors, and even judges, deciding when magistrates should be appealed to and when a husband or father should (or should not) be informed about a situation involving sexual transgressions, harassment, or rape. Until an older woman or mother had made up her mind—that is, until the women of a community had decided to act—neither fathers nor magistrates were typically brought into the picture.

Over the course of the nineteenth century, the requirements of fatherhood, as well as attitudes toward childhood and maturation, underwent a transformation in the northern United States. As an aspect of life increasingly separate from the world of work, the domestic realm became a central preoccupation among the northern middle class: a place where nurturance and love would provide a respite from the competitive values of the marketplace and the anonymity of the industrializing city. Within this context, the center of power in the household within Protestant, native-born families shifted from the authoritative father to the loving mother; the subordination of the entire household—including mothers, children, and domestics—to the rule of fathers declined. Fathers remained the "head" of a family more in title than in practice. As households produced less and men began to move into wage work outside the home, mothers concentrated on raising children and tending to family concerns. Fathers spent less time with their daughters than they once had, religious instruction fell to mothers and education to schools, and as a result the relationships between fathers and daughters became somewhat more distant.

In the antebellum rural South, more traditional patriarchal family settings remained in place, and the institution of fatherhood underwent less change among whites of both the planter elite and the small-time farming community. Enslaved fathers had no legal control over their daughters, and the legacy of this fact for the African American family has been hotly debated by historians and social commentators. However, there is a great deal of evidence supporting the perception that enslaved fathers did the best they could to support their families and that daughters often formed close bonds with their fathers and viewed them as providers and protectors. Louisa Adams of North Carolina recalled her father's efforts with pride: "My old daddy partly raised his chilluns on game. He caught rabbits, coons an possums. He would work all day and hunt at night" (Griswold 1993, 21). In the period just after emancipation in 1863, the proportion of two-parent black households in the antebellum South was never below 65 percent, and in urban areas it was closer to 80 percent.

There is clear evidence that, beginning in the late eighteenth century in both the North and the South, fathers among the middle and upper classes began to exert less and less control over their daughters' marriages, and that by the early 1800s, young women and men courted without the express permission of parents. However, a father's blessing, if not his formal approval, was generally sought upon entering into an engagement. As in the colonial period, fathers, even though they may have been appealed to in the event of an engagement, seem to have been less concerned with their daughters' sexual behavior than their mothers were. Indeed, there is evidence that many fathers remained quite aloof from the unfolding drama of courtship—leaving their girls unchaperoned when it suited them and generally paying little attention to public perceptions or rectitude—much to the frustration of many mothers.

Nonetheless, letters and diaries from the nineteenth century show that many daughters maintained close and loving relationships with their fathers. Daughters sought their fathers' advice, held their opinion in high esteem, and clearly wanted to please them. It is also perhaps worth noting that the two most famous

women's rights activists of the nineteenth century—Elizabeth Cady Stanton and Susan B. Anthony—had very close relationships with their fathers. In Anthony's case, her Quaker father pulled her out of public school because the teacher would not instruct her in long division along with the boys; he eventually found her a private school that would give her the full education she needed to become a schoolteacher and, eventually, a leader in the cause for woman suffrage. Stanton adored her father—however, it was in large part her father's frequently expressed regret that she had not been a boy that inspired her to try to achieve all that a boy could early in life. Indeed, her father's disappointment in her sex helped fuel her lifelong driving desire to give women the chance to live up to their human potential on equal footing with men.

Meanwhile, among many immigrant groups—particularly Jews and Italians—fathers continued to hold a place in the family much more akin to the late-eighteenth- and early-nineteenth-century models. The reasons for this were several. In part, fathers from the old world simply maintained patriarchal customs in the new world that had undergone little change in Europe. But some immigrant fathers also felt threatened by their daughters' superior English and ability to adapt to American culture, while they remained cut off from their own cultural moorings. Some resorted to exaggerated displays of male authority or became authoritarian figures, demanding and harsh in their judgments. Many immigrant daughters deferred to fathers in all matters, delivered all wages to them, and generally followed their strictures in religious and daily life. In some Jewish communities, the old world practice of fathers arranging marriages for their daughters continued well into the twentieth century.

With the elevation of the maternal role among the native-born middle classes and the increasing geographical distance between the workplace and home, the father became "almost entirely a Sunday institution" by the end of the nineteenth century, according to *Harper's Bazaar* (Pleck 1987, 88). Furthermore, as the middle class began to embrace higher expectations about the amenities of home life, the pursuit of leisure activities, and the responsibilities of providing access to higher education for their children, paternal breadwinning became an even more central factor in family life. According to several studies, the responsibility of providing for the family preoccupied men, and day-to-day interaction with daughters, even interest, seems to have waned.

However, just after the turn of the twentieth century, middle-class attitudes toward domesticity underwent yet another transformation. Men began to be encouraged to spend less time at fraternal clubs and all-male enclaves such as saloons and more time with their children. Nevertheless, calls for paternal involvement in childrearing at this time were explicitly geared toward involving fathers in raising boys: psychologists, sociologists, and a whole host of new family experts called for a "retoughening" of American boyhood in the face of the feminizing influence of mothers. Shared activities between fathers and sons—fishing, sports, or building model ships—would ensure the development of boys into "manly" men. At the turn of the century, the relationship between fathers and daughters was perhaps less valued and commented upon than at any other time in U.S. history.

Social interest in the father-daughter relationship reemerged in the late 1920s and 1930s, when sociologists and psychologists began to link fatherly involvement to healthy personality development among girls. Experts claimed that a daughter learned about the "world of men" from her father and that interaction with him led to self-confidence and a better understanding of her own gender identity. Companionship between father and daughter, it was also alleged, would help a girl to pick out the "right kind of man" for a husband. Much like prescriptions for fatherly involvement prevalent at the turn of the century, images of father-daughter companionship in the 1920s and 1930s centered on leisure activities: articles from *Parents Magazine* show fathers and daughters playing tennis together and working on domestic projects.

The notion that fathers should act as sex-role models for their daughters, limited in the 1920s and 1930s to academic studies and parenting magazines, quickly developed into the common wisdom of the postwar period. The popularization of psychoanalysis after World War II, along with a new self-consciousness about proper sex-role identity in the wake of wartime disruptions, helped to produce a new literature and popular culture virtually obsessed with the interactions—both healthy and unhealthy—between father and daughter. Psychoanalysts offered a diagnosis of "Oedipal conflict" to explain the dramatic rise in female juvenile delinquency, and popular culture quickly embraced this perspective. Films like *Rebel without a Cause* (1955) and magazine stories about "wayward girls" explained female juvenile delinquency as a problem stemming from a father's lack of attention to his daughter's "charms."

Home Sweet Home, *an idealized portrait of Victorian family life. (Library of Congress)*

Underlying these narratives was the admonition to fathers that they remain involved in their daughters' lives, lest their daughters find themselves unable to work through the Oedipal stage. When a father did not live up to his daughter's "Oedipal wishes," the results could be disastrous (Devlin 1998, 104).

Cheerful images of father-daughter relationships also abounded, however, particularly in depictions of the wondrous possibilities provided by postwar affluence in the United States. For the most part, compliments and the doling out of cash allowances informed interactions between fathers and daughters in popular culture: fathers were shown gazing in admiration as their daughters donned new prom dresses or displayed their ability to walk gracefully in their first pair of high heels. But paternal authority also took on new forms as girls became an ever-growing segment of the U.S. consumer market. When it came to the final say on whether a girl was old enough to purchase a black dress or brightly colored nail polish, a father's word was usually final. Hence, as older forms of authority—based on moral instruction and strict ideas about subordination—gave way to a more egalitarian and consumer-oriented family structure, paternal authority did not vanish. Rather, it was replaced by new ideas about the psychological needs of daughters and a new form of paternal surveillance of girls' sexual maturation, particularly in terms of public display.

The popular embrace of social-scientific ideas about the father's critical role in his daughter's heterosexual development contributed to a popular understanding of the father-daughter relationship in which a kind of Oedipal eroticism was central. And as the perception of the widespread potential for father-daughter eroticism grew, scientists, fiction writers, and journalists began to speak and write about father-daughter incest—for the first time—in ways that both reflected and helped produce a popular fascination with the topic. In 1953 Alfred Kinsey published the first widely read statistics on father-daughter incest, reporting that approximately 1 out of every 100 girls had had a sexual experience with her father or another male relative in her youth. Yet Kinsey's report provoked little commentary. More telling were the stories of stepfather-stepdaughter incest in the two most sensational and best-selling books of the 1950s, *Lolita* (1955) by Vladimir Nabokov and *Peyton Place* (1956) by Grace Metalious. In these novels, stepfathers were seduced by the very kind of teenage allure that fathers of adolescent girls had been directed to encourage, solicit, and superintend in popular and didactic literature since the end of World War II. In *Lolita* the lusting stepfather, Humbert Humbert, attempts to rationalize his incestuous relationship with his stepdaughter by referring (in his own mind) to social-scientific and didactic literature that taught fathers to recognize their adolescent daughters' Oedipal needs. Humbert Humbert represented a twisted and malevolent version of the father-daughter relationship at midcentury. Nevertheless, as a parody of American family life, the book reflected some of the very real paradoxes inherent in popular prescriptions of the father-daughter relationship during this period.

In the wake of the feminist movement of the late 1960s and 1970s, however, American fatherhood came under new scrutiny. Black women wrote some of the earliest and most powerful narratives about father-daughter incest from the daughter's perspective, bringing the horror and pain of sexual abuse into the public eye for the first time. In the early 1980s, the psychologist Judith Herman published the groundbreaking book *Father-Daughter Incest*, in which she examined the psychological damage caused by early childhood sexual abuse, particularly at the hands of fathers. In the early 1990s writers and activists from all sectors of the political spectrum—including those on the right espousing "family values" and feminists on the left calling for a more equitable distribution of household responsibilities—began to promote the importance of paternal involvement in family life. But a consensus on what the "new fatherhood" should look like has yet to emerge. All comers to the debate agree that American men need to spend more time with their families; the question that divides them is what role fathers should play.

Feminists have attempted to remake fatherhood in a less sexualized and more nurturing, loving, and supportive mold, particularly when it comes to raising daughters. Experts on adolescent girls have stressed the importance of paternal investment in girls' achievements—whether they be in school, sports, or extracurricular activities. Inspired studies show that girls benefit when both fathers and mothers take an interest in their ambitions. The Ms. Foundation has organized the National Take Our Daughters to Work Day, an attempt to institute a historically unprecedented connection between fathers (when, as more often is the case, the father is the one taking his daughter to work) and daughters around the issue of work, providing a one-day apprenticeship of sorts. It also represents an effort to get fathers (as well as moth-

ers) to think of their daughters as people with careers ahead of them other than homemaking.

From the perspective of traditionalists and religious conservatives, the feminist agenda for fathers ignores the reality of biological masculinity. In a simpleminded (and futile) attempt to recast fathers as mothers, men are stripped of roles that, if never as "natural" as motherhood, were once more in line with the innate capacities and God-given responsibilities of men. As a result, men have become confused and the contributions of men to family life have been trivialized, if not rendered obsolete. David Blankhorn, the president of the Institute for American Values, believes that the United States fosters "a culture of fatherlessness"—a fact that represents nothing less than a national social and moral crisis (Blankhorn 1995, 3). Fathers, he claims, need to be reintegrated into the family as men—that is, as "leaders" (202). Taking up his call, an organization called Promise Keepers has instituted regular religious revivals geared toward teaching men to regain their status as "spiritual leaders" in their homes and to provide "love, protection, and biblical values" to their wives and children while respecting the authority of wives within the realm of nurture and the care of infants. It is a vision of fatherhood that harks back to the colonial household while attempting, perhaps, to maintain the emphasis on "the loving mother" that emerged in the nineteenth century.

Parties on both sides of the debate believe that nothing less than the future of modern gender roles is at stake in the way in which fathers raise daughters. How fathers interact with daughters is part of a larger question of how men interact with women—how the interests,

A young girl with her father. (Shirley Zeiberg)

learned behavior, and social responsibilities of men and women are (or are not) brought together. Since the mid-nineteenth century, each successive generation in the United States has redefined the mutual obligations and emotional substance of the father-daughter relationship. Indeed, it is difficult to find a social relationship that has been more malleable than this one, which means that father-daughter relationships will most likely continue to change while individual fathers and daughters attempt to forge bonds in the context of unsettled questions about the nature of gender and the family.

Rachel Devlin

See also Acquaintance Rape; Daughters and Mothers; Female Sexuality

References and Further Reading
Blankhorn, David. 1995. *Fatherless America: Confronting Our Most Urgent Social Problem.* New York: HarperCollins.
Demos, John. 1970. *A Little Common Wealth: Family Life in Plymouth Colony.* New York: Oxford.
Devlin, Rachel. 1998. "Juvenile Delinquency and the Problem of Paternal Authority." Pp. 83–106 in *Delinquents and Debutantes: Twentieth-Century American Girls' Culture.* Edited by Sherrie A. Inness. New York: New York University Press.
Gordon, Michael. 1978. *The American Family in Social-Historical Perspective.* New York: St. Martin's Press.
Griswold, Robert. 1993. *Fatherhood in America.* New York: Basic Books.
Herman, Judith. 1981. *Father-Daughter Incest.* Cambridge: Harvard University Press.
LaRossa, Ralph. 1997. *The Modernization of Fatherhood.* Chicago: University of Chicago Press.
May, Elaine Tyler. 1988. *Homeward Bound: American Families in the Cold War Era.* New York: Basic Books.
Morgan, Edmund. 1944. *The Puritan Family: Religion and Domestic Relations in Seventeenth Century New England.* 1966. Reprint, Westport, CT: Greenwood Press.
Pleck, Joseph. 1987. "American Fathering in Historical Perspective." Pp. 83–97 in *Changing Men: New Directions in Research on Masculinity.* Edited by Michael S. Kimmel. Newbury Park, CA: Sage.
Rothman, Ellen K. 1984. *Hands and Hearts: A History of Courtship in America.* New York: Basic Books.
Ryan, Mary P. 1981. *Cradle of the Middle Class: The Family in Oneida County, New York, 1790–1865.* New York: Cambridge University Press.
Ulrich, Laurel. 1980. *Good Wives: Image and Reality in the Lives of Women in Northern New England, 1650–1750.* New York: Vintage.
Wilson, Lisa. 1999. *Ye Heart of a Man: The Domestic Life of Men in Colonial New England.* New Haven: Yale University Press.
www.Promisekeepers.com.

Daughters and Mothers

Stories of the mother-daughter relationship are as varied as the diverse circumstances and idiosyncratic personality traits of each mother-daughter pair. From the infant daughter's early attachment to and mirroring of her mother to the longing experienced by a motherless daughter, the importance of cultural, social, historical, and personal differences cannot be underestimated. However, no matter what the individual differences may be, the mother-daughter relationship plays a central role in the lives of both daughters and their mothers. This complex relationship engenders intense and conflicted feelings of love, guilt, anger, and fear. It embraces a host of paradoxes: intimacy and distance; harmony and discord; nurturing and neglect; dependence and autonomy; and deep attachment and fierce "matrophobia," the fear "of *becoming one's mother*" (Rich 1976, 235). Above all, this unique relationship gives rise to an unavoidable mixture of love and hate, pleasure and pain.

Contemporary women scholars theorize that the mother-daughter relationship goes through a number of distinct phases in which boundaries are negotiated, tested, and realigned. In broad strokes, these phases encompass infancy and childhood, adolescence, and adulthood. The first phase begins in early infancy, when a shared biology enhances the mother-infant attachment. The adult woman sees her baby girl as an extension of herself. A special relationship starts to take shape as mother and infant daughter mirror each other. Through this process, the daughter develops a sense of relationship as necessary to the development of self and continues to build on this foundation throughout childhood.

The next significant phase begins with puberty, among the more difficult periods for mothers and daughters. During this time, mothers struggle to balance their need to keep their daughters safe in a hostile world with their equally compelling desire to give them the freedom and confidence to function fully as adult women. Daughters attempt to balance their need to develop as autonomous individuals with their equally strong need to retain their mother's love. In adolescence, mother and daughter engage in a more sophisticated version of their early mirroring as the daughter seeks confirmation and validation for her newly emerging self.

During the third important phase in the adult mother-daughter relationship, shared experiences of work, marriage, pregnancy, childbirth, and parenting can function to equalize the relationship and often provide daughters with a deeper understanding of their mother as a woman with her own subjectivity. Daughters may seek out their mothers or look for surrogate mothers to help them negotiate their new roles as mothers or professionals. The same tensions adhere in this phase, as in all the others. Fluid boundaries and conflicting needs continue to play a role throughout the life span of this relationship.

Looking through a historical lens, it is clear that cultural conditions and ideologies of a given time or place have influenced the mother-daughter relationship. In colonial America and the early years of the republic (the late eighteenth and early nineteenth centuries), some historians have reported close and harmonious mother-daughter relationships. During this time, work and family life coexisted in the largely agricultural economy. Husbands and wives and their children often formed economically interdependent family units. Daughters learned household skills from their mothers as they assisted them in a myriad of chores. Although this arrangement offered few alternatives to the traditional female roles of marriage and motherhood, it did foster intimacy, friendship, and companionship between mothers and daughters.

In the antebellum North, as the population became more urban and capitalist industrialization took hold, work and family life became increasingly separated. Not only did this arrangement lend a special intensity to the mother-daughter relationship and promote tightly knit female communities, but the prevailing ideology of domesticity also gave mothers a special power over their children's lives. Middle-class mothers became solely responsible for teaching their children social, moral, and spiritual values. They became the glue that held the family together and provided the intimacy. This model was dependent on the labor of the working-class woman—African American, rural, and immigrant women who worked in factories or were engaged as domestic servants. For them the story was different. Their mother-daughter relationships were influenced by economic hardships and substandard living conditions.

At around this same time, educational opportunities began to emerge for middle-class girls, and the potential for mother-daughter tensions grew. These tensions were most likely to occur when daughters sought to fulfill personal ambitions in the face of strong nineteenth-century expectations for family service. In fact, the Victorian "cult of true womanhood" placed unrealistic expectations on all women. Under this ideology, mothers were required to socialize their daughters to take on roles that demanded high levels of self-sacrifice, submissiveness, and domesticity. Both mothers and daughters suffered individually and relationally in their efforts to live up to these standards.

The turn of the century, roughly 1880–1920, ushered in the era of the "new woman." Tensions arose between those who espoused traditional attitudes and those who favored progressive ones. Some women used their traditional roles as moral guardians of the family to extend their influence into the public sphere by way of maternalistic philanthropic and political organizations. Many young, middle-class women made choices vastly different from those of their mothers. The proliferation of new opportunities for women in education and employment became sites of conflict between traditional mothers and progressive daughters who sought new aspirations and modern lifestyles. No longer self-sacrificing, the "new woman" rejected traditional female constraints. Not only was she generally well educated and psychologically and sometimes economically independent, but she was considered unladylike and even vulgar by traditionalists. Many college-educated women chose not to marry. For some mothers and daughters, these generational differences exacerbated tensions, but other mothers took vicarious pleasure in their daughters' unconventional choices. These mothers adopted the role of mentor and supported their daughters' aspirations.

By the 1920s, women had won the vote. The youthful exuberance of the "roaring twenties" lifestyle opened the way for more widespread acceptance of new behaviors and values. Mothers and daughters revised their attitudes to accommodate modern lifestyles. During this period, the role of mother declined in prestige and power. Daughters developed new outlets—peer groups gained influence, therapists offered alternatives to motherly advice, and fathers provided support. Under these conditions, the special intensity of the nineteenth-century, middle-class mother-daughter bond began to lessen.

Between 1920 and 1960, the stresses of the Great Depression, the impact of two world wars, and the postwar 1950s took their toll on the mother-daughter relationship. During the Depression, forced kinship networks and abandonment due to economic hardships put tremendous strains on family relationships of all kinds. Communication between mothers and daughters became more informal, opening the way for role reversals to occur. In these difficult times, some daughters provided emotional support for their mothers. Under the economic stresses of the Depression, upward mobility for daughters in the form of a rich husband or a profession became an economic necessity and maternal imperative for many.

World War II brought about painful family separations and housing shortages. During the war, women left home in large numbers and worked in the war industries. At the same time, a psychological discourse referred to as "momism" presented mothers as overbearing, smothering, and even malevolent and destructive. However, just as the war had opened the door to broader opportunities for women, it was quickly slammed shut. The postwar economic boom of the 1950s brought a return to the "cult of domesticity," setting the stage for rebellion by daughters.

During the feminist movement of the late 1960s and early 1970s, alienated daughters expressed hostility toward their mothers. Mothers were portrayed as victims and tools of the patriarchy, complicit in their role as socializers. Feminist scholars have identified the male-dominated society as the cause of much mother-daughter conflict during this period. By the 1980s, however, scholars looked upon these sentiments as expressions of a largely white, middle-class feminist movement. Research into the diverse lives of real women showed that matrophobia was not a universal experience. Women of color described different mother-daughter experiences, pointing to strong mother-daughter bonds. Many daughters of color respected their mothers for their ability to survive in a hostile and racist world. Extended families and surrogate mothering provided much-needed and welcomed support for working mothers and stay-at-home mothers alike. This tradition, called "othermothering," involves sisters, aunts, and grandmothers as well as other adult women from the community in the care of children.

Embracing these ideas and others, post-feminist scholars and psychologists in the 1980s and 1990s returned to the idea that strong, positive mother-daughter relationships exist in the lives of real women. Many mothers serve as effective role models for their daughters and adult women function as mentors to young girls. More importantly, the history of mother-daughter relationships since the birth of the nation shows that irrespective of historical changes in American ideology or social conditions, the mother-daughter bond remains as important and complex as ever.

Since the beginning of the twentieth century, psychoanalysts and developmental psychologists have tried to understand and explain the nature of the

A 1950s housewife tends to her daughter. (Urban Archives, Temple University, Philadelphia)

mother-daughter relationship and its role in the development of gender identity. At the turn of the century, Sigmund Freud and his followers advocated a deficiency model of women's psychological development that defined women as inferior to men. The Victorian-era Freud saw women's anatomy as their destiny. He believed that by nature women became wives and mothers. Much of the change in the theoretical landscape of women's psychology and mother-daughter relationships is a reaction to this early deficiency model that blames mothers for the psychological ills of their children.

Feminist psychoanalytic theorists and developmental psychologists challenged and revised many Freudian assumptions by turning to women themselves for

their data. Adrienne Rich's influential book, *Of Woman Born: Motherhood as Experience and Institution* (1976), exposed motherhood as an institution of the patriarchy in which women were required to live up to male expectations of this role. Rich outlined her own feelings and experiences as a daughter and a mother that were markedly different from the prescribed view, not the least of which was her admission of both love and hate for her own children.

In *Reproduction of Mothering* (1978), Nancy Chodorow argued that gender was more than a biological phenomenon. In her view, a girl's destiny was also shaped by social, cultural, and economic influences. Chodorow theorized that differences in gender identity for boys and girls resulted from their early relationship with the mother as primary caretaker. This exclusively female identification caused boys to move toward separation and girls to gain selfhood through affiliation and connection. Chodorow asserted that the power and intensity of this maternal identification with its threat of engulfment were the source of the ubiquitous mother blame and misogyny. As a remedy, she advocated shared parenting.

Many other women have added their voices to this debate. In *Toward a New Psychology of Women* (1976), Jean Baker Miller attempted to redefine and value traits that under Freudian psychology were considered regressive. She rejected the Freudian model of separation as the only road to maturity and individuation and advocated a model of relationship and connection. Carol Gilligan argued that women make moral judgments on the basis of context and care, suggesting that this was not a lesser condition but a "different voice" available to both men and women. Psychologists at the Stone Center

A member of the National Guard hugs her daughter after returning from a two-week tour of duty in Saudi Arabia in 1990. (UPI/Bettman)

at Wellesley College developed a model of women's psychological development that stressed mutuality, a greater capacity for empathy, and reciprocity between mothers and daughters that began with early infant-mother mirroring. In *Meeting at the Crossroads: Women's Psychology and Girls' Development* (1992), Brown and Gilligan exposed the losses girls experience during the adolescent passage from childhood to womanhood, losses of voice and authentic relationship. These works and others led to a redefinition of the mother-daughter relationship.

Since the 1970s, the mother-daughter relationship has experienced an explosion of attention in scholarship and in representation, for example, fiction, drama, motion pictures, television, newspapers, and magazines. Scholars and artists alike have sought out new visions for this important relationship. Some have written about newly discovered archaeological evidence of prepatriarchal goddess cultures. Others have reinterpreted ancient myths of the mother-daughter relationship. Feminist dramatists and folklorists have revised the classic myth of Persephone and her mother Demeter, the goddess of fertility and nature, by placing the focus on the continuity and power of the mother-daughter bond. Feminist writers have created or adapted stories of all kinds to provide strong female role models for their young readers. Storytellers have rewritten fairy tales and folktales to change the witch from a solely evil character to one that is also a source of maternal power and feminine wisdom. Their stories give young female heroines the agency to determine their own destinies.

The patriarchal model for mother-daughter relationships split a woman's identity into two extremes—a pure-loving, nurturing, and entirely self-sacrificing self and a fearful, malevolent self with the power over life and death or with a threatening sexuality. Writers and artists today have attempted to shift representation away from this demonized or idealized maternal woman to a mentoring figure, challenging all manner of stereotypes of both mothers and daughters in the process. Through these mentor figures, artists and writers unify the split mother into a woman comprised of both positive and negative qualities, one grounded in a historical and personal milieu that stresses the lived social experience of real women. With similar objectives and strategies, these women artists have created young, action-oriented female heroines with drive and courage, characters who challenge the "perfect girl" syndrome of past representations. In doing so, they continue to honor the enormous complexity and diversity of the mother-daughter relationship.

Susan R. Applebaum

See also Daughters and Fathers; Depression and Girls; Domesticity

References and Further Reading
Apter, Terri. 1990. *Altered Loves: Mothers and Daughters during Adolescence.* New York: Fawcett Columbine.
Brown, Lyn Mikel, and Carol Gilligan. 1992. *Meeting at the Crossroads: Women's Psychology and Girls' Development.* New York: Ballantine.
Chodorow, Nancy J. 1978. *The Reproduction of Mothering: Psychoanalysis and the Sociology of Gender.* Berkeley: University of California Press.
Collins, Patricia Hill. 1993. "The Meaning of Motherhood in Black Culture and Black Mother-Daughter Relationships." Pp. 42–60 in *Double Stitch: Black Women Write about*

Mothers and Daughters. Edited by Patricia Bell-Scott, Beverly Guy-Sheftall, Jacqueline Jones Royster, Janet Sims-Wood, Miriam DeCosta-Willis, and Lucille P. Fultz. New York: HarperPerennial.

Coontz, Stephanie. 1992. *The Way We Never Were: American Families and the Nostalgia Trap.* New York: Basic Books/HarperCollins.

Debold, Elizabeth, Marie Wilson, and Idelisse Malave. 1993. *Mother Daughter Revolution: From Betrayal to Power.* Reading: Addison-Wesley.

Estés, Clarissa Pinkola. 1992. *Women Who Run with the Wolves: Myths and Stories of the Wild Woman Archetype.* New York: Ballantine.

Gilligan, Carol. 1993. *In a Different Voice: Psychological Theory and Women's Development.* 2d ed. Cambridge: Harvard University Press.

Jordan, Judith V., Alexandra G. Kaplan, Jean Baker Miller, Irene P. Stiver, and Janet L. Surrey. 1991. *Women's Growth in Connection: Writings from the Stone Center.* New York: Guilford Press.

Miller, Jean Baker. 1976. *Toward a New Psychology of Women.* Boston: Beacon.

Rich, Adrienne. 1976. *Of Woman Born: Motherhood as Experience and Institution.* New York: W. W. Norton.

Rosenzweig, Linda W. 1993. *The Anchor of My Life: Middle-Class American Mothers and Daughters, 1880–1920.* New York: New York University Press.

Walters, Suzanna Danuta. 1992. *Lives Together/Worlds Apart: Mothers and Daughters in Popular Culture.* Berkeley: University of California Press.

Depression and Girls

The study of depression can be traced back to the time of Hippocrates, but the interest in the study of child and adolescent depression is relatively recent. Early classic encyclopedic texts did not list "childhood depression" as a category, but since 1985, a growing body of knowledge has emerged. The classic psychoanalytic view held that childhood depression could not exist because the necessary psychic structure, the superego, was not yet sufficiently developed. Another view held that depression in children differed from depression in adults because it was masked or expressed in depressive equivalents, such as hyperactivity, aggressiveness, school failure, and temper tantrums. Still another view held that depressive features in children reflect a developmental phenomenon rather than a clinical syndrome and thus disappear with time. The consensus view at the turn of the twenty-first century is that depression in children can be diagnosed according to the criteria used in the diagnosis of adult depression.

About 10 to 15 percent of all children report moderate to severe signs of depression (Nolen-Hoeksema and Girgus 1994), and depression onset is occurring earlier in life. Before adolescence, equal numbers of boys and girls are depressed. By age thirteen, however, more than twice as many girls as boys are depressed, a proportion that persists into adulthood (Rao, Hammen, and Daley 1999). This two-to-one ratio exists regardless of racial or ethnic background, and the same ratio has been reported in other countries (Weissman et al. 1993).

There are three types of depressive disorders applicable to both genders and to all ages. In major depression, also known as unipolar or clinical depression, individuals have some or all of the symptoms listed below for at least two weeks to as long as several months or even longer. Episodes of the illness can occur once or more in a lifetime. Dysthymia produces the same symptoms in a milder form, but this second type of depression lasts at least two years. People with dysthymia can also experience major depressive episodes. Manic depression, or bipolar ill-

There are many causes of depression in girls and young women; often it takes them well into adulthood to sort out these causes and to heal. (Shirley Zeiberg)

ness, is not nearly as the common as the other two forms of depression. It involves cycles of depressive symptoms that alternate with euphoria, irritable excitement, or mania. Men and women have about the same rate of bipolar disorder, though its course in women typically has more depressive and fewer manic episodes.

Symptoms of depression common in adults as well as children and adolescents include a persistent sad or irritable mood, loss of interest in activities once enjoyed, significant change in appetite or body weight, difficulty sleeping or oversleeping, physical overactivity or lethargy, loss of energy, feelings of worthlessness or inappropriate guilt, difficulty concentrating, and recurrent thoughts of

death or suicide. Five or more of these symptoms must persist for at least two weeks before a diagnosis of depression is indicated. In children and adolescents, the symptoms may be manifested in frequent vague physical complaints (headaches, muscle aches, tiredness); frequent absences from or poor performance in school; talk of or efforts to run away from home; outbursts of shouting, complaints of boredom, or crying; and lack of interest in playing with friends. In addition, adolescents with depression may be socially isolated, communicate poorly, fear death, be sensitive to rejection or failure, abuse alcohol or drugs, or engage in reckless behavior.

A dramatic gender shift occurs in adolescence, when depression occurs twice as often in girls as in boys. A number of explanations have been proposed: the pressure of the increased developmental demands of adolescence and other factors unique to the lives of girls may contribute to their greater risk for depression. It is not likely that the gender difference is due to only one cause. A genetic component to depression is apparent in many girls. Studies have found a higher percentage of depression and other mental disorders in the families of people diagnosed with depression than is found in the general population. With regard to girls, some research suggests that genetic factors in combination with negative life events are associated with depression more strongly among pubescent girls than boys (Silberg et al. 1999).

Since hormone levels increase dramatically during adolescence, it seems obvious to question whether depression is caused by hormonal fluctuations. The specific influence of hormone levels is, however, difficult to determine. Although researchers report that hormones have an effect on the brain chemistry that controls emotions and moods, a specific biological mechanism explaining the role of hormones in depression has not been identified. Furthermore, the effects of hormone levels on depression have been found to be minimal compared to the influence of social factors (Brooks-Gunn and Warren 1989).

Puberty has different meanings for boys and girls, although both experience the impact of simultaneous changes in biological and social context. The onset of puberty is more accurate than chronological age in predicting depression (Angold et al. 1999). Girls who mature physically earlier than their peers are more likely to feel self-conscious and to have depressed moods (Rierdan and Koff 1997). For some girls, behavioral and physical changes are associated with menstrual cycles, and menstruation can be accompanied by feelings of tension, the perception of loss of control over their bodies, and irritability. Boys view body changes, such as increased muscular development, as positive. Girls view body changes, such as increased fat layers, as negative. Girls are more critical of themselves than boys, and their self-esteem depends more on how they perceive their bodies. Concerns about physical appearance start surprisingly early; by the age of nine many girls report that they are dieting to lose weight. This overemphasis on the body diverts many adolescent girls from developing other talents.

It is possible that a traditional upbringing fosters certain traits that may be a factor in the development of depression in girls. Sex roles take on new importance as adolescents' bodies become more sex-differentiated. In early adolescence, girls compare themselves with the standard female stereotypes, and many become dissatisfied with their bodies, which in turn leads to increases in depressed mood, lowering of self-esteem, and disappointment with their physical appearance. During adolescence, the self-esteem of many formerly self-confident and assertive girls gradually becomes eroded. Self-esteem in girls peaks at the age of nine and then begins to plummet (Hancock 1990). In addition to low self-esteem, some adolescent girls develop certain characteristics—pessimistic thinking, a sense of having little control over life events, and proneness to excessive worrying—and are more likely to develop depression than boys. These attributes may exaggerate the effect of stressful life events or interfere with taking action to cope with them. It has also been suggested that higher depression rates among girls occur when they start to interact with boys more frequently.

Intelligence, assertiveness, and competence are seen as liabilities rather than assets by some adolescent girls. Fearing that competition with boys may interfere with their relationships, they may try to please boys and build up a boy's self-esteem rather than their own. These attitudes are subtly encouraged by society and reinforced by the media. Movies, sitcoms, and teen magazines feature articles about techniques of getting and holding a man as the key to a successful life.

Also critical are family factors, such as the quality of the marriage, parenting style, and role modeling. The emotional status of the parents, particularly the mother, is related to depression in girls. It has been found that daughters of parents who have an egalitarian relationship and are supportive, attentive, and receptive to emotions and guidance, rather than prone to assign punishment show lower levels of depression (Obei-dallah, McHale, and Silbereisen 1996).

Girls learn about being female by modeling themselves on their mothers. Female development is based on the importance of attachment and relationships throughout the life span. Closeness and connection, although admirable qualities, can also be interpreted as overdependence or smothering or an excess of emotion. Some experts think that females' tendency to place greater value than males do on interpersonal connection and relationships with other people renders them more vulnerable to losses and depression.

Girls are more likely than boys to experience negative events in the family, and childhood experiences are more highly predisposing for depression in females than in males (Hankin and Abramson 1999). Most parents give their adolescent sons more independence than their daughters, thus easing their separation from the family. For example, boys are more likely than girls to report that they do not need their parents' permission to stay out late, that they were left at home alone, and that their parents expected them to act older. Adolescent girls, more closely bound to their families, may be exposed to family stresses over a longer period of time.

Daughters of depressed mothers are vulnerable to emotional problems because depressed mothers tend to withdraw and are therefore less attuned to their child's emotional needs. They are more likely to command and to criticize rather than to be warm, playful, and encouraging. Early interference or disruption of attachment bonds can lead to enduring problems with depression. A chronically depressed mother may be unable to help her daughter tackle the tasks of growing up—to develop a posi-tive sense of self, form friendships, and learn ways of interacting with peers and adults. Daughters of mothers with a history of depression and who are controlling without showing much affection are more likely than sons to have low self-esteem and depression (Powers and Welsh 1999; Miller et al. 1997).

Stress plays a critical role in the development of depression, and adolescent boys and girls react to stressful life events in different ways. The depressed mood of girls, not boys, which increases after the age of thirteen, correlates with stressful life events. Childhood sexual abuse is an important early stressor, and the rates of sexual abuse in girls increase substantially in early adolescence, with the greatest increase in rates occurring between ages ten and fourteen.

Sexual abuse may result in heightened physiological responses in females, making them more vulnerable than boys to depression (Weiss, Longhurst, and Mazure 1999). Sexual abuse undoubtedly has a major psychological impact on its victims, although not all individuals are traumatized in the same way or for the same length of time. The effects depend on the type of abuse, whether the abuser was a family member or a stranger, whether the abuse was short- or long-term, and the age of the child at the time of abuse. Children's reactions to sexual abuse may be immediate or delayed or both. In general, sexual abuse causes young children to become very anxious, and adolescents often act out. Long-term reactions occur in two-fifths of sexually abused girls. For many victims of sexual abuse, long-term psychological symptoms include depression, substance abuse, and sexual problems.

Cognitive theorists believe that an individual's interpretation of stressful events affects whether or not she will become depressed. If girls feel they cannot anticipate or predict what will happen to them, they are likely to feel helpless and unable to make changes. A girl who feels helpless sees problems as insurmountable; she becomes overwhelmed and gives up, feeling that she is ineffective and unable to influence the events in her life. Then when something bad actually does happen, it provides her with further proof that her efforts are useless. In contrast, when a girl who does not feel helpless meets with difficulty, she does not give up but tries harder and thinks of other ways to tackle the problem.

The pattern of helplessness results in depression only for some. One important factor is how a girl explains the causes of bad events. Girls and boys typically explain their experiences to themselves in different ways. At a young age, boys tend to have a more negative explanatory style than girls. Then in the upper elementary grades, more girls than boys show a helpless cognitive style. A girl who blames herself or expects that times will always be hard is more likely to become depressed than a girl who does not believe bad events are her fault and will always happen to her.

Coping strategies also make a difference in whether a girl becomes depressed when stressed. During early adolescence, boys and girls develop different styles of coping in stressful situations. Rumination (thinking and talking about a problem rather than seeking out a distracting activity or solution) is one of the risk factors associated with higher rates of depression among adolescent girls (Broderick 1998). In contrast, boys use more problem solving and distraction. A number of studies show that individuals who ruminate when distressed show longer and more severe periods of depression and are more likely to develop a depressive disorder (Nolen-Hoeksema, Larson, and Grayson 1999).

The importance of intervention is highlighted by research that shows substantial continuity in depression from adolescence to adulthood. The risk for both a new onset of depression and recurrence is high during late adolescence and continues throughout early adult years (Rao, Hammen, and Daley 1999).

Depression can be treated effectively. Both medication and psychotherapies such as interpersonal therapy and cognitive behavior therapy, either alone or in combination with medication, have been shown to be useful in helping girls develop more effective ways of dealing with life's problems.

Anita Gurian

See also Acquaintance Rape; Body Image; Eating Disorders; Psychotherapy; Substance Abuse; Suicidal Behavior in Girls; Teen Pregnancy

References and Further Reading
American Psychological Association. 1994. *Diagnostic and Statistical Manual of Mental Disorders.* 4th ed. Washington, DC: American Psychological Association.
Angold, Adrian, E. Jane Costello, Alaattin Erkanlli, and C. M. Worthman. 1999. "Pubertal Changes in Hormone Levels and Depression in Girls." *Psychological Medicine* 29, no. 5 (September): 1043–1053.
Broderick, Patricia. 1998. "Early Adolescent Differences in the Use of Ruminative and Distracting Coping Strategies." *Journal of Early Adolescence* 18, no. 2: 173–191.
Brooks-Gunn, Jeanne, and Michelle P. Warren. 1989. "Biological and Social Contributions to Negative Affect in Young Adolescent Girls." *Child Development* 60: 40–55.
Ge Xiaojia, Frederick Lorenz, Rand Conger, and Glen H. Elder. 1994.

"Trajectories of Stressful Life Events and Depressive Symptoms during Adolescence." *Developmental Psychology* 30:467–483.

Hancock, Emily. 1990. *The Girl Within.* New York: Ballantine.

Hankin, Benjamin, and Lynn Abramson. 1999. "Development of Gender Differences in Depression: Description and Possible Explanations." *Annals of Medicine* 31: 372–379.

Jordan, Judith, et al. 1991. *Women's Growth in Connection: Writings from the Stone Center.* New York: Guilford Press.

Miller, Lisa, Virginia Warner, Priya Wickramarane, and Myrna Weissman. 1997. "Self-esteem and Depression: Ten Year Follow-up of Mothers and Offspring." *Archives of General Psychiatry* 54: 932–942.

Nolen-Hoeksema, Susan, and Joan S. Girgus. 1994. "The Emergence of Gender Differences in Depression during Adolescence." *Psychological Bulletin* 115: 424–443.

Nolen-Hoeksema, Susan, Judith Larson, and Carla Grayson. 1999. "Explaining the Gender Difference in Depressive Symptoms." *Journal of Personality and Social Psychology* 77, no. 5: 1061–1072.

Obeidallah, Dawn A., Susan M. McHale, and Rainer K. Silbereisen. 1996. "Gender Role Socialization and Adolescents' Reports of Depression: Why Some Girls and Not Others." *Journal of Youth and Adolescence* 25, no. 6: 775–785.

Powers, Sally, and Deborah P. Welsh. 1999. "Mother-Daughter Interactions and Adolescent Girls' Depression." Pp. 243–281 in *Conflict and Cohesion in Families.* Edited by Martha J. Cox and Jeanne Brooks-Gunn. Mahwah, NJ: Lawrence Erlbaum.

Rao, Uma, Constance Hammen, and Shannon Daley. 1999. "Continuity of Depression during the Transition to Adulthood: A 5-year Longitudinal Study of Young Women." *Journal of the American Academy of Child and Adolescent Psychiatry* 38, no. 7: 908–915.

Rierdan, Jill, and Elissa Koff. 1997. "Weight, Weight-related Aspects of Body Image, and Depression in Early Adolescent Girls." *Adolescence* 32, no. 127: 615–624.

Silberg, Judy L., et al. 1999. "The Influence of Genetic Factors and Life Stress on Depression among Adolescent Girls." *Archives of General Psychiatry* 56, no. 3: 225–232.

Weiss, Erica, James Longhurst, and Carolyn M. Mazure. 1999. "Childhood Sexual Abuse as a Risk Factor for Depression in Women: Psychosocial and Neurobiological Correlates." *American Journal of Psychiatry* 156, no. 6: 816–828.

Weissman, Myrna, Roger Bland, Peter R. Joyce, and Stephen Newman. 1993. "Sex Differences in Rates of Depression: Cross-national Perspectives." *Journal of Affective Disorders* 29, nos. 2–3: 77–84.

Wichstrom, Lars. 1999. "The Emergence of Gender Differences in Depressed Mood during Adolescence: The Role of Intensified Gender Socialization." *Developmental Psychology* 35: 232–245.

Diaries

Diaries are typically pocket-size bound books with blank pages in which girls write thoughts and feelings. The functions of diaries, however, have changed over the past 300 years. Initially serving as spiritual chronicles in the eighteenth century, Victorian diaries charted the path of self-discipline and moral development for middle-class girls. Though their mothers often read what they wrote, Victorian girls nevertheless used diaries in order to nurture an identity separate from family. In the twentieth century, diaries became intensely private testimonies of intimate concerns, fantasies, and activities.

In the seventeenth century, dissenting religious groups (e.g., Puritans, Quakers, Methodists) who privileged rigorous spiritual self-examination and personal belief over external authorities transformed the genre of medieval spiritual autobiography into the spiritual diary as a means by which individuals could regularly examine their conduct and conscience. Largely settled by dissenters, colonial America fostered a rich literary tradition of spiritual diaries that documented religious conversions and the struggles of believers to live piously.

Diary keeping by girls in the early 1800s reflected the emergence of the post-revolutionary notion of republican motherhood, which emphasized the importance of education in the lives of young women. Educated girls would be the future wives and mothers of citizens in the new democratic republic. The rise of private female seminaries and the spread of public schools in the nineteenth century increased literacy rates among middle-class girls. As Enlightenment thought influenced educational reformers, girls were taught how to write expressive narratives at the many public schools as part of a new pedagogy that flourished in the antebellum United States. With industrialization and the employment of servants, girls' leisure time also increased. Though middle-class girls were still expected to do their chores, the more arduous and time-consuming tasks were now undertaken by domestics, leaving girls with more time on their hands.

Parents and advice experts encouraged keeping diaries (which they often gave for birthdays) because they believed that diaries would contain their daughters' selfish desires, nurture their good character, teach regular habits of order, and promote conformity to social expectations (e.g., improvement and refinement). Diaries were also the consequence of the rise of romanticism and the decline of orthodox Calvinism. No longer were diaries to document the route to religious conversion (as had been the case in the eighteenth century); nor were diaries meant to promote introspective romanticism. Instead, Victorian diaries were intended to regulate as well as demonstrate the development of moral character. Entries—written daily, often in the bedroom at night—were intended to build character and improve the self through the discipline of writing.

This work of character development through diary keeping could begin quite early among girls. Sarah Gillespie, a young woman who grew up in eastern Iowa in the 1870s and was a lifelong diarist, began journal keeping at the age of five when she received her first diary, a small (3-inch by 5-inch) copybook hand-sewn by her mother. Sarah's earliest entries include handwriting exercises and short sentences, such as "I am a good girl" and "Learn your lessons well." Later volumes include writing exercises, such as "Be gentle, Ever be kind" and "Sarah is a nice girl in school," that were to serve the functions of character building and self-discipline (quoted in Temple and Bunkers 1995, 202). Similarly, Charlotte Forten, a middle-class black woman who taught freed slaves on the Sea Islands off the Carolina coast during the Civil War, began keeping a diary to monitor her academic progress and intellectual development when she entered a boarding school in Salem, Massachusetts, at the age of sixteen. Forten wrote:

A wish to record the passing events of my life, which even if quite unimportant to others, naturally possesses a great interest to myself, and of which it will be pleasant to have some remembrance, has induced me to commence this journal. . . . Besides this, it will doubtless enable me to judge correctly of the growth and improvement of my mind from year to year. Salem, May, 1854. (quoted in Gannett 1992, 131–132)

Just as girls were exhorted to keep diaries, they were also advised to include topics acceptable for girls on their path to domestic womanhood. In popular magazines, advisers urged them to record the weather, correspondence, any exchange of money, visits made, and books read but not to indulge in fantasy (and certainly not at the expense of others). Resolutions to do "this" and not "that" were widespread attempts to follow a charted path of self-discipline. Girls followed this protocol in part because parents had access to their daughters' diaries. In fact, in order to ensure the proper upbringing, middle-class Victorian mothers vigilantly monitored their daughters. Thus they thumbed through diaries for signs of character development as they had for evidence of spiritual growth in the previous period. That Louisa May Alcott's parents not only read their daughters' diaries but also wrote in them was not unusual. Diaries were partly public documents: sometimes Louisa and her sisters even read them out loud. That diaries were partly public documents can also be seen in the example of the Gillespie family. Sarah Gillespie, a young rural schoolteacher in 1886, wrote in her diary of the isolation and discouragement that were pervading her life during the winter months. Her mother, Emily, responded by writing an encouraging entry in her daughter's journal:

> Sarah, you said last night, "Ma write in my Journal. I can't." I just thought I would write a line as I saw it in the Drawer. I tried to not read a word, but Sarah my eyes do take in so much that the above could not quite escape. I get lonesome every day—only that I think of Henry & you. how you are getting along so well. His letters and

your Sunday visits I should almost give up. I am so thankful that you are both all my heart could wish and can I really appreciate the blessing. You must never get discouraged with the annoyance which some pupils are ever ready to give. do only the best you can and their cutting words and misdemeanor will give them the most inconvenience. (quoted in Temple and Bunkers 1995, 204)

For all these reasons, nineteenth-century diaries are often devoid of intimate details. Girls would have been reluctant to write about subjects such as sex or to explore their ambitions. For example, girls were very reluctant to express their thoughts and feelings about their body, its changes, and their pains and pleasures. They recorded little about their intimate relationships with boys and men. Instead of frank confidences, girls used a variety of codes: vague expressions, asterisks for kisses, or squiggles for squeals. Victorian gender ideology defined what was acceptable (innocence) and what was not (seduction), inhibited thoughts and feelings, and deprived girls of a usable vocabulary to express themselves. Instead, diarists steeped in religious morality acquired at home, at school, and through social organizations often tended to confide their spiritual problems and pleasures more than other personal concerns. Some extant diaries reveal evidence of a more candid exploration of sexual desire.

As historian Jane Hunter has shown, many girls who kept diaries were able both to satisfy their parents and to develop their separate selves by negotiating between obedience and autonomy. Diaries provided "a way of integrating feelings of independence with social expectations for appropriate behavior" (Hunter 1992, 70). Though diaries give testimony to girls' attempts at self discipline, they also reveal a growing understanding of who they were and who they were becoming. According to Hunter, diaries functioned as transitional objects for girls in the process of separating from the family and investing in peers. In fact, though often a solitary activity, diary writing was occasionally social. Together in their bedrooms, at boarding schools, or on New Year's Eve, girls wrote in their own as well as in each other's diaries. Often, they wrote about each other without the stiffness of spoken communication that conveyed civility at the cost of intimacy. According to Carroll Smith-Rosenberg, sharing diaries was a sign of special friendship among girls, and she cites the comments of a young girl growing up along the Ohio frontier who found that sharing her diaries with "Sisters CW and RT . . . [was] a very great privilege indeed as well as very improving, as we lay our hearts open to each other, it heightens our love & and helps to cherish & keep alive that sweet soothing friendship and endears us to each other by that soft attraction" (1986, 240).

In addition to serving as an audience for the diaries of their peers, girls could become the audience for their mothers' diaries. Judy Nolte Temple and Suzanne L. Bunkers have noted that "some diarists kept their books as a form of ongoing communication with a daughter still too young to be a companion" (1995, 199) and that the diary of a deceased mother could serve as a form of communication with her daughter that transcended the grave. In their detailed analysis of the diaries kept by Emily Hawley Gillespie and her daughter Sarah over the course of ninety-four years, Temple and

Bunkers note that the journals of the Gillespie women were "collaborative and interactive" while Emily and Sarah were alive and that after Emily's death, Sarah and her brother reread the diaries that documented their father's abusive behavior toward his spouse. In the margins, the children annotated their mother's writings with comments such as "O, how she suffered" (204).

Even when diaries were not actually shared with friends or family, young female diarists posited the journal itself as a particularly intimate audience for their thoughts and emotions. The young Anne Frank wrote in her diary, "In order to enhance in my mind's eye the picture of a friend for whom I have waited so long, I don't want to set down a series of bald facts in a diary like most people do, but I want this diary itself to be my friend, and I shall call my friend Kitty" (1952, 13). Fourteen-year-old Helen Ward Brandreth, the daughter of a prominent family in Ossining, New York, similarly named her daily journal in honor of her favorite author. She wrote in her 1876 diary: "I have determined to keep a journal. I shall call it Fannie Fern" (quoted in Culley 1985, 149).

Diary entries began to change after around 1900 because of the rise of a heterosocial culture, changing sexual mores, increased high school and college attendance, more egalitarian marital ideals, and the influence of feminism. As peers and the consumer culture became far more important and influential in the lives of American youth by the 1920s than before, high school–age girls (rather than preadolescents) included more intimate entries in their diaries. They included such topics as boys and sex along with franker entries on their bodies and how (through the use of hairstyles, clothing, and cosmetics) they could make themselves more sexually alluring. These changes trickled down to girls in junior high school in the postwar period, who began to use a more clinical vocabulary when they wrote about the anatomy of their bodies. When they wrote about the boys they adored (which they did in great detail), they drew upon the melodramatic language of movie and magazine romances. The sexual revolution and the second wave of feminism influenced girls whose diary entries by the 1980s were far less romantic than those written in the 1950s. Girls' uninhibited entries about sexual encounters with boys and girls became far more graphic.

Preadolescent girls keep diaries because they find it a useful way of exploring and expressing their private thoughts and feelings to an unjudgmental listener. They can write about or "say" whatever about whomever with the assurance that others will not know. Unlike a friend, sibling, or mother, a diary will not feel hurt or get angry at the expression of direct feelings. Girls can express themselves and at their own pace. Diaries do not demand logical thought and do not interrupt. Girls can write about whatever they want, typically siblings, parents, teachers, movies, friends, fantasies, fears, sex, and love.

That diary keeping has become a highly gendered activity is illustrated by an anecdote related by Cinthia Gannett. The teacher of her son's combined fourth- and fifth-grade class described how she had tried to reward well-behaving students with some blank books for their personal use. According to Gannett, when the teacher held up the books, "someone called out that only girls would want them, because the boys would certainly *not* be interested. There

was a chorus of agreement" (1995, 122). Jane DuPree Begos also quotes a young man who tersely noted: "Diaries are sissy things" (1987, 69). Pocket-size diaries of blank pages kept closed with lock and key are widely available and most often marketed to preadolescent girls. They are even included among books that can be ordered by elementary school children through their school. Diaries may be decorated with recognizable characters from American popular culture or printed in pink shades and pastel colors.

In seeking models for diary keeping, girls throughout history have been able to turn to a number of published diaries, both real and fictional, including twenty-year-old Mary McLane's 1902 account of her passionate inner life, which sold more than 80,000 copies in its first month and was variously hailed as obscene, brilliant, and mad (Culley 1985, 187); Marie Baskirtseff's account of her life as a young artist in Russia; Anne Frank's tragic account of her family's attempts to avoid being found by the Nazis; and Joan W. Blos's *A Gathering of Days: A New England Girl's Journal, 1830–32* (Gannett 1995, 121).

Diaries can be enormously useful historical sources that shed light on a wide variety of topics of concern to girls and female adolescents. Joan Jacobs Brumberg researched 200 diaries stored in libraries, archives, and attics in order to explore girls' attitudes about their bodies and menstruation in *The Body Project: An Intimate History of American Girls* (1997). Reading diaries as historical texts enabled historian Jane Hunter to speculate that diary keeping allowed Victorian girls to develop autonomous selves within the context of family relationships. With an enhanced sense of self, many diary keepers pursued higher education and public careers as new women. Girls' diaries can also serve as a fruitful site for posing questions about the construction of private and public voices, the role of language and narrative in constructing identity, and the development of female traditions of writing. As Barbara Crowther has wisely noted, though, those making use of girls' diaries must be cautious. Diary keeping can be a highly performative act for young women as they represent themselves, constructing and censoring how they wish to be viewed. The myth that diaries are bearers of truth and the use of diaries as forensic evidence are highly problematic. Referring to the use of girls' diaries in legal trials and custody cases, Crowther writes, "It would be dangerous if the myth and mystique of a young girl's diary afforded it special status as material evidence, without reference to the range of possible activities besides record-keeping and self expression involved" (1999, 215).

*Jane Greer and
Miriam Forman-Brunell*

See also Daughters and Mothers; Literacy; Reading

References and Further Reading

Begos, Jane DuPree. 1987. "The Diaries of Adolescent Girls." *Women's Studies International Forum* 10: 69–74.

Brumberg, Joan Jacobs. 1997. *The Body Project: An Intimate History of American Girls.* New York: Random House.

———. 1998. "It's Okay to Talk to Yourself." Chapter 17 in *33 Things Every Girl Should Know.* Edited by Tonya Bolden. New York: Crown.

Crowther, Barbara. 1999. "Writing as Performance: Young Girls' Diaries." Pp. 197–220 in *Making Meaning of Narratives in the Narrative Study of Lives.* Edited by Ruthellen Josselson and Amia Lieblich. Thousand Oaks, CA: Sage.

Culley, Margo, ed. 1985. *A Day at a Time: The Diary Literature of American Women from 1764 to the Present.* New York: Feminist Press.

Frank, Anne. 1952. *The Diary of a Young Girl.* Translated by B. M. Mooyart-Doubleday. Garden City, NY: Doubleday.

Gannett, Cinthia. 1992. *Gender and the Journal: Diaries and Academic Discourse.* Albany: State University of New York Press.

———. 1995. "The Stories of Our Lives Become Our Lives: Journals, Diaries, and Academic Discourse." Pp. 109–136 in *Feminine Principles and Women's Experience in American Composition and Rhetoric.* Edited by Louise Wetherbee Phelps and Janet Emig. Pittsburgh: University of Pittsburgh Press.

Hunter, Jane. 1992. "Inscribing the Self in the Heart of the Family: Diaries and Girlhood in Late-Victorian America." *American Quarterly* 44, no. 1 (March): 51–81.

Smith-Rosenberg, Carroll. 1986. "The Female World of Love and Ritual: Relations between Women in Nineteenth-Century America." Pp. 229–249 in *Feminist Frontiers II: Rethinking Sex, Gender, and Society.* Edited by Laurel Richardson and Verta Taylor. New York: Random House.

Temple, Judy Nolte, and Suzanne L. Bunkers. 1995. "Mothers, Daughters, Diaries: Literacy, Relationship, and Cultural Context." In *Nineteenth-Century Women Learn to Write.* Edited by Catherine Hobbs. Charlottesville: University of Virginia Press.

Disabilities

To begin a discussion of girls and disabilities is to take into account the tremendous changes that have occurred in the way Americans have come to think of both disabilities and girls in general. Late in the twentieth century, disability rights activists presented the United States with a challenge: disabilities, formerly a moral or medical problem, needed to be addressed as a social problem, one that could be ameliorated by a concerted effort by civic, social, educational, and individual parties. Once viewed by the majority (including the disabled themselves) as a fixed, static condition, disability has been increasingly described as a social or cultural construction, one that requires not medical intervention but social and institutional modifications.

Further, although disability activists and scholars agree on certain clearly defined disabilities—deafness, blindness, mental retardation, and paraplegia, to name a few obvious categories that American society defines as disabling conditions—a few experts define eating disorders such as anorexia and bulimia, as well as self-destructive behaviors such as scarification, as disabling conditions that prey on American girls in particular. As they have been treated by medical doctors and psychologists as disabling conditions, eating disorders, emotional disorders, and anxiety disorders have become ripe topics for research and in society as a whole. Even as panic attacks and anxiety disorders have become prevalent diagnoses among young people, especially young women, much more attention is needed to understand girls' images of their own bodies, the significance of those bodies, and indeed the cultural meanings and significance of girls and girlhood in the United States in the twenty-first century.

Some research has been done in the history of children with disabilities (see, for instance, Safford and Safford, *A History of Childhood and Disability*, 1996) but none differentiates between girls and boys. Most scholars believe that in ancient times, defective infants were exposed and left to die, but there seems to be no indication that disabled girls were exposed more often than disabled boys. In Roman times, blind girls were often sold into slavery as prostitutes. With the introduction and spread of Christianity, which dictated that everyone born of woman had an immortal soul, the exposure of infants waned throughout the next centuries and the Holy Roman Empire. A similar process occurred more than a millennium later in the Americas after the introduction of Christianity through European settlement. Abandonment, however, did not decrease, as foundling hospitals and asylums grew in number. Many unwanted, defective, and abandoned children were provided some minimal care in large institutions, although infant mortality within this group remained high for centuries.

Rudimentary efforts to educate and understand the disabled child occurred gradually throughout the sixteenth to eighteenth centuries in Europe. The onslaught and aftermath of worldwide epidemics of such diseases as scarlet fever brought about the establishment of institutions that could treat, train, and educate those left deaf or blind by disease. By the sixteenth and seventeenth centuries in Europe, blind and deaf boys were proven educable; the outcome of the successful education of these individuals lead to a more tolerant attitude toward the deaf by the end of the eighteenth century. However, in Europe, public education of blind and deaf girls did not immediately follow because it was thought that boys benefited more from specialized training. In nineteenth-century Europe, for example, deaf daughters were kept at home or sent to convents. In marked contrast, nineteenth-century American hearing-impaired girls, along with their male counterparts, were sent to special schools by concerned parents who advocated education over contain-

Anne Bancroft as Anne Sullivan and Patty Duke as Helen Keller in The Miracle Worker.
*Helen Keller toured the United States raising public awareness about people with disabilities
for much of her adult life. (Photofest, 1962)*

ment. In fact, the Asylum for the Education of Deaf and Dumb Persons, established in 1817 in Connecticut, was founded by three men, one of whom was the fond father of a deaf daughter.

The Perkins Institution and Massachusetts Asylum for the Blind (founded 1832) made both boys and girls welcome. Its success in training Laura Bridgman, a young girl who had contracted scarlet fever in infancy that left her deaf and blind with no sense of smell, proved that girls with multiple disabilities could be educated and made useful to society. Laura Bridgman entered Perkins in 1837 and stayed until her death, learning how to finger-spell, read Braille, and interact with the other children in a limited fashion. Perkins Institution became internationally famous for its education of one Anne Sullivan (1866–1936), who went on to train her even more famous pupil, Helen Keller (1880–1968), also educated at Perkins.

By the mid-nineteenth century, many states, especially along the eastern seaboard, had founded special schools called asylums for the blind and the deaf. Gallaudet College (founded 1864), later Gallaudet University, is the most well known of these asylums. Although scarlet fever and other viral illnesses made the care and education of all children with hearing and visual impairments crucial, there was a recognition of the need for minimal care for children whose disabilities responded less to training than did blindness or deafness. These were so-called feebleminded and insane children. Special schools and asylums for the care of insane and feebleminded children were established, funded, and staffed during the latter part of the nineteenth century, partially in response to eugenic concerns. Scientists and anthropologists were deeply interested in the question of hereditary acquisition and so studied the feebleminded, concentrating their efforts on the study of mentally impaired girls and women of childbearing years.

Henry H. Goddard, author of *The Kallikak Family: A Study in the Heredity of Feeblemindedness*, published in 1912, conducted his research on a family he dubbed the "Kallikaks" at the Training School for Backward and Feeble-Minded Children in Vineland, New Jersey. Deborah "Kallikak" had been admitted to Vineland at eight years of age and classified as a moron. With time, however, Deborah's skills improved. She learned to read a little, play an instrument, sew, garden, and excel in wood carving.

Deborah's condition was thought to be the result of her ancestors' indiscretion in marriage, thus fulfilling prophecies of early-nineteenth-century eugenics. It was thought that one single mistake in marriage would produce feebleminded offspring for decades, with the deformity or affliction increasing in its intensity. Alleged feebleminded ancestors were studied during the early twentieth century by American anthropologists bent on determining the extent of inherited traits. Girls and young women, especially, had to take precautions so that taints would not be passed down from one generation to the next.

Certain physical disabilities responded neither to special education nor to the medical expertise of the times. Hence, children exhibiting deformities or conditions that nineteenth-century American culture considered too freakish or monstrous were often sold to sideshows and circuses. Girls with conditions perceived by their culture as abnormal lived markedly different lives than other girls within similar socioeconomic backgrounds and were exhibited in sideshows or freak shows. Interestingly, they were photographed in such a way to make the most of both their affliction and their natural femininity.

In literature, especially children's fiction, invalid girls abounded in the nineteenth century, one of the best known being Beth March, the epitome of the nineteenth-century dying girl, in Louisa May Alcott's *Little Women* (1868). The nineteenth-century invalid or dying girl bestowed salvation, redemption, and forgiveness on others. Beth March's illness and death were a constant reminder to her family that life was short, forgiveness was essential, and suffering was the way of the world. Similarly, Kate Douglas Wiggin's *The Birds' Christmas Carol* (1886) features Carol Bird, lame since birth, who spends her short life emulating the Christ child, on whose birthday she too was born. She dies at the age of ten, having enriched the lives of her own family as well as those of a poor immigrant family, the Ruggles, in untold ways.

In fiction, tomboys and hoydens who strayed beyond the control of their parents or guardians needed to be reminded of the consequences of unladylike and unwomanly behavior. Hence, in some novels marketed to young female readers of the nineteenth century, wayward, boisterous, and willful girls were crippled by swings or sleds; endured a long, painful recovery; and eventually came to terms with the limitations of nineteenth-century womanhood. Janey Pecq in *Jack and Jill* by Louisa May Alcott (1881) and Katy Carr in *What Katy Did* by Susan Coolidge (pseudonym for Sarah Chauncey Woolsey, 1872) endure the pain of spinal injuries that leave them bedridden for months—in Katy Carr's case, years. In their beds, the little girls learned how to be genteel young ladies: meek, quiet, biddable, patient, and long-suffering. Once they shed their former roughhousing behavior, they experienced a miraculous cure and could walk again.

Literary use of disabled characters was by no means limited to the martyr figure, nor were stereotypical ideas about girls with disabilities confined to the nineteenth century. Then as now, not only was the fictional girl with a disability an object of pity, but also she was saintly and morally superior to the able-bodied around her. If, however, she fought her disability or denied the reality of it, she functioned as her own worst enemy. Katy Carr and Wilmadeene Fenner of Judy Blume's *Deenie* (1973) cope with their spinal injuries with bad grace. Both must learn how to accept their condition cheerfully, the first step on the road to recovery and ladylike behavior.

The embodiment of this cheerfulness in the face of adversity is Pollyanna in Eleanor Porter's eponymous novel (1913), who after being hit by a car, finally wins her aunt's love and receives numerous affidavits from the townspeople attesting to the little girl's near-magical ability to bring optimism and happiness to every-

one around her. Though Pollyanna's use of crutches is understated in the novel, the 1920 film emphasizes the disability, perhaps in deference to Mary Pickford, famous for her portrayals of physically frail, unwanted, unloved, yet resilient waifs.

In the United States, the 1920s to the 1960s saw an increase in the institutionalization of young people for many different medical and nonmedical reasons. Children diagnosed as insane or feeble-minded were routinely committed to various institutions. The 1930s in particular saw a rise in the acceptance of psychiatric treatment, a result of the popularity of Freudian theory. Special clinics were staffed and funded expressly for the "problem child," which included the mentally retarded, incorrigible, and social misfit. Many of these children and young adults were girls from dysfunctional homes, runaways, and prostitutes who were incarcerated in these asylums as a way to control their "antisocial" behavior.

At the same time that vast institutions threatened to swallow up the individual, offering at best only minimal treatment for the disability or disorder, American fiction and cinema offered audiences compassionate images of girls with disabilities. The 1940s saw a host of young heroines in children's and young adult novels who used wheelchairs and crutches as a result of the ravages of polio, tuberculosis, and scoliosis. Postwar films focused on the girl's ability to adjust herself to her disability and to the physical restrictions imposed upon her by her culture. For instance, Jane Wyman's character Belinda in the 1948 film *Johnny Belinda* teaches both the small-minded people of her town and, by extension, the audience that people with hearing disabilities are essentially no different from them. Experiencing the film, American audiences unfamiliar with sign language were exposed to its power and beauty when Belinda signs the Lord's Prayer.

The 1960s witnessed fewer fictional representations of young heroines who used crutches, wheelchairs, canes, and seeing-eye dogs. "Hidden" disabilities or disabilities whose complexities could not be neatly cured, such as learning disabilities, emotional dysfunction, and mental impairments, appeared increasingly in fiction and cinema as a response to an increase in diagnoses of mental and emotional impairments among American teens. Theodore Isaac Rubin's successful novel and film, *David and Lisa* (1962), treats the growing friendship and mutual dependence between two mentally impaired teens in an adult world characterized by indifference and alienation; *I Never Promised You a Rose Garden* by Hannah Green (1964; made into a movie in 1977) details a sensitive girl's experience of the horrifying trauma of institutionalization.

In popular fiction, the novels of Shirley Jackson present frightening excursions into the mental imbalance of teenaged heroines. Her critically acclaimed novels—*The Road through the Wall* (1948), *The Bird's Nest* (1954), and *We Have Always Lived in the Castle* (1962)—struck a chord with teenaged girls who recognized themselves—if not in the full-blown conditions of psychosis and multiple and borderline personalities—then in the anger, rage, and dissociation that produced these disorders.

In general, cinematic representations responded to audience desires, expectations about disabled people and their capabilities, and the knowledge of particular disabilities represented in films and its relative importance to the times. A disabled girl's social position as an adolescent or child made her even more vulnerable than a boy or a grown woman to familial and societal pressures. Abused and ridiculed by others who see only her limitations, the teenage protagonist in *A Patch of Blue* (1965) falls in love with a black man, whom, of course, she cannot see and does not judge on his race alone. Isolated, overprotected, and limited to an existence redundant with needlework and beading, her life before her involvement with the man who liberates her from a living hell is a cinematic echo of the never-ending entrapment of those very real institutions where people with disabilities, living a diminished existence with little love, care, or recognition, learned a trade to be useful to society.

When not functioning as an example of a long-suffering saintly heroine, the girl with a disability could also show what disabled people, especially females, ought not to be. Helen Keller at age seven, incorrigible and willful, met her match in the equally stubborn Anne Sullivan. In the famous 1962 film *The Miracle Worker*, pupil and teacher engage in a form of combat until Helen is forced to recognize the meaning and importance of language. During the "water pump" scene, she abandons her hoyden ways and finally communicates with her teacher. (The real Helen Keller, however, had a much less combative relationship with Anne Sullivan, as evinced by a photograph in Dorothy Herrmann's 1998 biography of Helen Keller.)

In twentieth-century motion pictures, films continued to romanticize disability and offer audiences a heroine who was morally better than others because of her disability. Recently, in the 1990s, *The*

Other Sister (1999) assured audiences that a mentally impaired girl could find happiness in a fulfilling love relationship and marriage, albeit with a mentally impaired young man. The ten-year-old heroine of *Do Not Disturb* (1999) cleverly eludes and outwits professional hired killers despite being mute. Some films, however, explore the pain of having a disability that severely limits a girl's chances of living a normal life. The teen heroine of *Niagara, Niagara* (1997) is tormented by both Tourette's syndrome and the alienation that it brings her. Two recent memoirs, *Girl, Interrupted* by Susanna Kaysen (1993; made into a movie in 1999) and *The Autobiography of a Face* by Lucy Grealy (1994), explore the emotional agony caused not only by disabling conditions, whether mental or physical, but also by medical intervention their conditions warrant. As seen in so many other fictional depictions of asylums, mental institutions, and hospitals, the girls are dehumanized by the very institutions that are in place to help them.

These cinematic representations of girls with disabilities as complex individuals with the right to live their own independent lives and the right to claim their own attractiveness and sexuality owe a debt to the civil rights activism of the 1960s and beyond. Changes in the social and legal perceptions of persons with disabilities were taking place throughout the United States by the 1960s and 1970s. Disabled people were emerging from the shadows of invisibility and demanding their civil rights. Activists fought for equal treatment under the law in terms of physical modifications and access to buildings, elevators, washrooms, and other physical structures. The 1970s were watershed years for the disabled as a number of important acts and amendments made their way through Congress, and the decade was critically important in terms of facilitating equal and increased opportunities for employment and the pursuit of higher education by persons with disabilities. The 1977 Rehabilitation Act, a law that prohibited discrimination on the basis of disability in federally funded or administered programs and in federal employment, set the tone for the elimination of discriminatory practices. Highly significant for federally funded schools was the passage of Section 504 of the Rehabilitation Act. Section 504 and the 1975 Individuals with Disabilities Education Act laid the groundwork for the mainstreaming of children who formerly would have spent their formative years in "special classrooms," or in some drastic cases would have languished at home or in institutions, receiving little or no education and social interaction with other children. In an atmosphere of accommodation and accessibility, unique "alternative" schools were founded. In 1974, Harmony House in Oyster Bay, New York, opened its doors to girls with emotional disorders, learning disabilities, and severe depression. Here, young women could concentrate on their education and emotional well-being without the usual distractions of typical teen life in a public school.

The 1980s saw an increase in attention given to girls and young women with disabilities. In the early 1980s, the National Disabled Women's Education Equity Project conducted regional training programs for young disabled women in various cities throughout the United States. In addition, the Networking Project on Disabled Women and Girls was founded at the Young Women's Christian Association (YWCA) in New York City. Though these organizations addressed the inequities in the treatment of the disabled, particularly women, more inclusive measures needed to be taken. At the end of the decade, in 1990, the Americans with Disabilities Act (ADA) was passed, in which specific modifications in housing, education, accessibility, and telecommunications became federal mandates. Further, since the passage of the ADA, accommodations have become part of the infrastructure of American life. Computers, books on tape, electric wheelchairs, cutouts in sidewalk curbs, elevator buttons with Braille messages, voice-activated answering machines, electronic doors, and handicapped parking spaces are accommodations that many besides those considered disabled have come to enjoy.

Though the study of disabilities has found its way into graduate programs at many universities, and classes introduce undergraduates and graduate students alike to some of the theories of disabilities and their effects on individuals and our culture, few scholars and theorists have researched girls with disabilities. Quite a few scholars have begun to champion "girls' culture" as a legitimate field of study, however. In recent books such as *Delinquents and Debutantes: Twentieth-Century American Girls' Culture* (1998) by Sherrie A. Inness and *The Body Project: An Intimate History of American Girls* (1997) by Joan Jacobs Brumberg, the authors claim that the study of girls and their concerns is crucial not only to American culture's understanding of young women in general but also to the complex role of gender. Sadly, few, if any, scholars have analyzed the complex role disabilities have played in either fictional or cinematic representations of girls with disabilities or in the lives of real American girls. It remains an area ripe for historical and literary study.

Fran O'Connor

See also Body Image; Girls' Fiction; Learning Disabilities, Reading Disorders, and Girls; Sports

References and Further Reading
Baskin, Barbara. 1977. *Notes from a Different Drummer: A Guide to Juvenile Fiction Portraying the Handicapped.* New York: R. R. Bowker.
———. 1984. *More Notes from a Different Drummer: A Guide to Juvenile Fiction Portraying the Disabled.* New York: R. R. Bowker.
Brumberg, Joan Jacobs. 1997. *The Body Project: An Intimate History of American Girls.* New York: Random House.
Davis, Lennard J., ed. 1997. *The Disabilities Studies Reader.* New York: Routledge.
Donley, Carol, and Sheryl Buckley, eds. 1996. *The Tyranny of the Normal: An Anthology.* Kent, OH: Kent State University Press.
Inness, Sherrie A., ed. 1998. *Delinquents and Debutantes: Twentieth-Century American Girls' Culture.* New York: New York University Press.
MacLeod, Anne Scott. 1994. *American Childhood: Essays on Children's Literature of the Nineteenth and Twentieth Centuries.* Athens: University of Georgia Press.
Norden, Martin F. 1994. *The Cinema of Isolation: A History of Physical Disability in the Movies.* New Brunswick, NJ: Rutgers University Press.
Safford, Philip L., and Elizabeth J. Safford. 1996. *A History of Childhood and Disability.* New York: Teachers College Press.
Saxon, Ruth O. 1998. *The Girl: Constructions of the Girl in Contemporary Fiction by Women.* New York: St. Martin's Press.
White, Barbara A. 1985. *Growing Up Female: Adolescent Girlhood in America.* Westport, CT: Greenwood Press.
Zelizer, Viviana. 1985. *Pricing the Priceless Child: The Changing Social Value of Children.* New York: Basic Books.

Dollhouses

When Mary Jane Sweeney of Omaha, Nebraska, saw film star Colleen Moore's dollhouse in the late 1930s, the girl responded with pleasure. "Oh, boy, would I like to have a doll house like that," she enthused, adding that "my playmates at Dundee school and I would have such good times." Like many American girls, she fantasized about a miniature world of opulence. But few such girls have owned anything remotely as elaborate as Moore's Fairy Castle, which came complete with miniature antiques, running water, and electricity. In fact, in the history of girls' toys, dollhouses have been exceptional rather than common acquisitions. Even so, the history of American dollhouses and girls' use of such possessions have much to tell us about the history of consumer culture, toys more particularly, and the conditions of girls' play.

A fascination with the domestic world made small has ancient origins. Indeed, models of rooms and shops date from ancient times and may have served adults' needs—such as funerary rites— more often than those of children. The earliest European dollhouse on record is that of Albrecht V, duke of Bavaria. The duke commissioned a four-story dollhouse for his daughter around 1558, but she was ultimately not its recipient. When the miniature palace was complete, the duke decided to place the finished structure in his art collection. The miniature rooms included a stable, cow barn, office, larder, wine cellar, and coach house on the first floor; bathroom, kitchen, courtyard, and orchard on the second; ballroom and bedroom on the third; and on the top floor, a chapel complete with priest and musicians. During the seventeenth and eighteenth centuries, large and extravagant "baby houses" or "cabinet houses," as they were called, were built for European royalty and the wealthy—not for children but for adults. These miniature houses displayed not only tiny furnishings but also their owners' taste and wealth.

In the United States, children's dollhouses were relative rarities until the latter half of the nineteenth century. Most early dollhouses were constructed by local cabinetmakers or by family members, and relatively few of them have survived to the present day with their furnishings intact, particularly those that were well loved and used by succeeding generations. Examples of such dollhouses include the one that Caspar Morris made and furnished around 1820 for his Philadelphian granddaughters, Sarah and Elizabeth Morris, when the girls were about six or seven years of age. The little house he made for them had hinged doors that opened like a cupboard to reveal four rooms inside. The dollhouse survived intact over the generations, but the furnishings were added to by subsequent generations of descendants who enjoyed the toy and treated it not as a museum piece but as a treasured plaything.

In the United States during the nineteenth century, manufactured dollhouses, as well as miniature shops and kitchens, usually came from Europe, especially Germany, which was the center of the toy industry worldwide until the early twentieth century. Because most ready-made doll furniture and houses were imported, such toys were prohibitively expensive for middle-class families. The rise of dollhouses in the postbellum United States, like the rise of toys more generally, reflected larger social shifts. First, as more Americans experienced increased affluence, more parents could afford special children's

Three Indian girls of the Plains region play with small tipi dollhouses and dolls. (Library of Congress, ca. 1909)

playthings. Second, new consumer outlets, including department stores and mail-order catalogues, allowed the modest but expanding toy sector to find an expanded audience in both urban and rural areas. Third, attitudes about child-rearing were in flux. Middle- and upper-class families were choosing to have fewer children and saw their children as more individually precious *as* children. These parents privileged notions of extended childhood and a special children's culture that included toys, emphasized formalized play, and would allow their children to imitate (and learn from) adult social rituals (including gender-appropriate skills). The rise of dollhouses reflected this new emphasis on children's right (and need) to play.

Dollhouse owners of the late nineteenth century included Juliette Gordon Low, who went on to found the Girl Scouts in the 1910s. "Daisy," as she was then known, shared a dollhouse with her sisters in the early 1870s in Savannah, Georgia. When President Rutherford B. Hayes was in office, his daughter Fanny Hayes was presented with two dollhouses, one in 1877 and the other in 1878. She and her younger brother Scott played with them. Less elite children had fewer, but improving, opportunities to "play house." As early as the 1790s, Maine tin makers had turned out toy tinware, such as miniature kitchens, for children. In its 1868 catalogue, the J. and S. Stevens Company of Cromwell, Connecticut, offered iron toys in dollhouse sizes, including washstands, fruit baskets, and sofas. From the mid-nineteenth century onward, American toy companies began making their own toys in addition to importing European playthings and produced more affordable items for mass consumption. In the late nineteenth century, the first American mass-produced dollhouses, following the German example, were simple wooden structures to which colorful, lithographed paper scenes had been applied. The finished products created detailed effects but were inexpensive to produce. In 1869, *Harper's Bazar* (as the name of the magazine was then spelled) described big tin dollhouses with real glass windows and doors that sold for $40. But by 1895, Americans could also purchase a lithographed two-story house made by the R. Bliss Manufacturing Company, which came complete with ten pieces of furniture, for $1. Similarly, in the 1890s Dunham's Cocoanut, a New York City firm, packed its wares in crates that could be converted into dollhouses complete with lithographed decor. The company also sold miniature furniture in exchange for proofs of purchase of their coconuts. In 1912, the *Ladies' Home Journal* tried a similar sales strategy, exhorting girls to sell three new subscriptions to the magazine in exchange for "Lettie Lane's Doll House: The Wonderful New Bungalow Home of a Delightful Lady," a four-room cardboard dollhouse and furniture, which included a German bisque doll who could live inside it.

Other dollhouse lovers built miniature homes with what was at hand. In the 1910s, for example, dollhouses made out of recycled wooden cigar boxes were common home projects. In the early years of the twentieth century, popular periodicals such as *Ladies' Home Journal* regularly published patterns for dollhouses

made of paper, cardboard, or wood and explained how to make dollhouse furniture as well. Sometimes, these dollhouse patterns were quite ambitious, boasting such technological innovations as running water and electric lights (features that many "full-scale" homes would not have for decades). Homemade dollhouses, like handmade dolls, combined parents' (and girls') skill, creativity, and ingenuity.

During World War I, when German imports were barred from the country, American toy makers dramatically expanded their market share. The growing toy market was one marker of the rising consumer culture of the period, a time when American retailers began to focus on and market more seriously to children. By the 1920s many department stores began to feature toy departments year-round instead of seasonally. Store-bought dollhouses and furnishings were now available in increased numbers. Tootsietoy furniture, inaugurated in 1922, was modeled on real furniture; made of metal and plastic, the line expanded to include, by 1936, an eighteen-piece kit including clock, flower vase, model ship, a parrot on a stand, a violin, and a banjo, all for $1. From the 1920s to the 1950s, Tynietoy produced miniature wood reproductions of real antique furnishings, along with dollhouses and dolls, and from 1925 to 1936, the Arcade Company made iron dollhouse furniture. In the postwar era, starting around 1945, plastic dollhouses and dollhouse furnishings would reflect the preeminence and economical price of this new material. In the second half of the twentieth century, girls (and sometimes boys) have played with Fisher Price dollhouses and Barbie's Dream House, among others.

Despite the expansion of the industry, dollhouses have never been the biggest toy sellers or the most common chil-

A girl playing with her handmade colonial-style dollhouse. (Hulton Getty/Archive Photos, ca. 1955)

dren's toys. *Playthings,* an industry journal, suggested in 1935 that dolls ought to comprise just over a quarter of a store's inventory and that dollhouses and dollhouse furniture ideally represented 1 percent of inventory. Yet if they were not the most popular toys, they remained important icons of childhood wonder and of consumerism. The prevalence of dollhouse displays in store windows, for example, points to the ways that miniatures have incited consumer appetites and fed spectators' imaginations.

Some historians have concluded that dollhouses, like baby dolls, have encouraged girls to focus on domesticity and homemaking and were thus tools of traditional feminine socialization. Certainly, the process of furnishing dollhouses encouraged girls to learn consumer habits and craft skills and to focus energy on the home. It is likely, however, that girls also used dollhouses—as they used dolls—as symbols of their own power and control over their environment (if, admittedly, within a limited and miniature domain). Catherine Dorris Callicott was, as a girl, presented with a sort of dollhouse: an open-front cabinet with three shelves, which she was allowed to paper and partition as she chose. Although she was not authorized to change the exterior of the cabinet in any way, the interior space of the dollhouse provided a venue through which she could control domestic space and rearrange it to her liking.

The appeal of miniature objects has transcended age and gender divides. Dollhouses have been marketed primarily to girls, just as toy trains have been marketed to boys, but boys have occasionally played with dollhouses as well. Both boys and girls have enjoyed miniature Noah's Arks. And it is adults, more often than children, who can best afford to indulge their miniature fantasies, whether for finely wrought train sets or for dollhouses and their furnishings.

Scholars have disagreed about whether miniatures accurately reflect the social life of their period. To some extent, dollhouses have showcased new trends in design and ideologies of the home. For example, the first Tootsietoy home, introduced in 1925, was a brick colonial house, followed by a Spanish mansion in 1930. Both dollhouses emulated popular architectural revivals of their era. Yet both, gesturing as they did to earlier times, suggested nostalgia as much as contemporary ideologies of domestic life. Dollhouses, in other words, tell us more about the domestic fantasies of their creators than the living conditions of particular periods. In their inclusions and absences, they have gestured toward

what was desirable or inappropriate for public display (for example, miniature toilets, which became more common only in the early twentieth century). At the same time, dollhouses have provided small-scale fantasies of grandeur, allowing girls, on a small scale, physical domination of their own environments.

Leslie Paris

See also American Girls Collection; Barbie; Consumer Culture; Dolls; Domesticity; Girls' Culture; Girls' Rooms; Play

References and Further Reading
Callicott, Catherine Dorris, and Lawson Holderness. 1978. *In Praise of Dollhouses: The Story of a Personal Collection.* New York: William Morrow.
Cross, Gary. 1997. *Kids' Stuff: Toys and the Changing World of American Childhood.* Cambridge, MA: Harvard University Press.
Jackson, Valerie C. 1988. *Dolls' Houses and Miniatures.* London: John Murray.
Jacobs, Flora Gill. 1953, 1965. *A History of Dolls' Houses.* New York: Charles Scribner's Sons.
———. 1974. *Dolls' Houses in America: Historic Preservation in Miniature.* New York: Charles Scribner's Sons.
King, Constance Eileen. 1983. *The Collector's History of Dolls' Houses, Doll's House Dolls, and Miniatures.* New York: St. Martin's Press.
Leach, William. 1993. "Child-World in the Promised Land." Pp. 209–238 in *The Mythmaking Frame of Mind: Social Imagination and American Culture.* Edited by James Gilbert, et al. Belmont, CA: Wadsworth Publishing.
Paris, Leslie. 1998. "Small Mercies: Colleen Moore and the National Doll House Tour, 1935–1939." In *Made to Play House: Dolls and the Commercialization of American Girlhood, 1830–1930.* Edited by Miriam Formanek-Brunell. Baltimore: Johns Hopkins University Press.
Rountree, Susan Hight. 1996. *Dollhouses, Miniature Kitchens and Shops.* Williamsburg: Colonial Williamsburg Foundation.

Stewart, Susan. 1993. *On Longing: Narratives of the Miniature, the Gigantic, the Souvenir, the Collection.* Durham, NC: Duke University Press.

Zillner, Dian, and Patty Cooper. 1998. *Antique and Collectible Dollhouses and Their Furnishings.* Atglen, PA: Shiffer Publishing.

Dolls

As objects of girls' ordinary lives, dolls are readable "texts" that shed light upon the intentions, beliefs, and values of producers, parents, and players. Though popularly conceived of as impassive and mute, dolls provide a body of evidence as well as a method of analysis for studying the history of American girlhoods. A reading of dolls as cultural sources reveals that their role in gender-role socialization in early America was limited by the economic exigencies of subsistence and semisubsistence cultures, both indigenous and transplanted. Increasing prosperity, leisure, and perceptions of childhood innocence among Anglo-Americans led to more people buying dolls in the late eighteenth century. The rise of industrial capitalism and the spread of the ideology of domesticity in the nineteenth century further contributed to the increasing availability of dolls, their centrality in girls' lives, and their role in gender-role socialization. European producers competed with American businessmen and businesswomen, with striking differences in regard to doll aesthetics, production, and purpose. But girls who received dolls on birthdays and for Christmas were often indifferent to them, preferring other forms of more active play. Unable to reject dolls entirely, others vented their anger over limited opportunities for girls in widespread funereal scenarios. In the early twentieth century, American businessmen achieved industry dominance after World War I, eliminated their European competition, and marginalized independent women producers. Dolls produced were predominantly white and also embodied an idealized femininity. Representations of submission, domesticity, maternity, and consumption have continued to triumph, despite changing roles for women and girls since the 1960s. Although more dolls of late aim to represent power, sexuality, agency, and education, all continue to reflect cultural ambivalence about girlhood in the postmodern era.

Little is known about dolls made by Native Americans or the role they played in the lives of children of different tribes during the millennia before European contact. Carved wooden Navajo figurines that look like "dolls" were found on the rubble mounds of the prehistoric Anasazi throughout Arizona and New Mexico. But what role—if any—they served in the lives of girls or boys is unknown. Hopi Indian kachina dolls (one of the many Hopi arts and crafts made since the tenth century in the American Southwest) were used for educational or religious purposes until they began to be sold commercially in the 1850s. Girls of the Plains played with toy miniatures, but Chickasaw girls of the Southeast were busy assisting mothers and other females gathering wild food, tending gardens, hauling water, and performing other agricultural tasks. Iroquoian cornhusk dolls were made from materials native to the region, as were the dolls that belonged to Anglo-American children.

Nevertheless, dolls were scarce in seventeenth-century North America, where play was also limited by participation in labor-intensive economies. Believing in the association of "poppets" with the supernatural and fearing that his children would think "diversion to be a better and nobler thing than diligence," Puritan minister Cotton Mather did not encourage his children to play (Mather 1911–1912, 536). Yet over the course of the eighteenth century the doll population grew, especially among daughters of the colonial elite. Increased prosperity, international trade, secularization, and the influence of Enlightenment notions were a number of forces that gave rise to a new ideological construct of girlhood in colonial America. For example, the philosopher Jean-Jacques Rousseau encouraged parents to provide their daughters with dolls so as to nurture their innocence and promote gender-role training. Especially popular between 1750 and 1800 were wooden dolls resembling adults (known to collectors as Queen Anne dolls), with peg joints, high foreheads, glass eyes, and flax or human-hair wigs. The daughters of prosperous sea captains in Salem, Massachusetts, were among girls who received "babies" transported to New England. Well-to-do parents such as George Washington ordered dolls from a London toymaker for his stepdaughter. With greater acceptance of childhood individuality, more colonial parents celebrated their daughters' birthdays with dolls that required a corps of sartorial experts. Milliners sewed the dresses and shifts-petticoats, whalebone men made stays, and hairdressers created wigs or chevelures. The new idealization of American girlhood that developed can be seen in the family portraits painted by eighteenth-century artists such as John Singleton Copley and others. In these representations girls clutch, but do not yet cradle, fine dolls.

Early in the nineteenth century, the developing market economy fueled an international doll economy that connected the "new" middle class in the United States to doll producers abroad. Perfected techniques and improved methods of mass production led to increasing numbers of papier-mâché, porcelain, and wax dolls. Fashionably dressed and wasp-waisted dolls were imported from German manufacturing towns. Customers typically purchased doll heads (often with molded hairstyles) in newly established toy shops and other small stores and attached them to homemade bodies. Antebellum experts railed against these refined European dolls, fearing that they would promote political degeneracy among the nation's young. To instill democratic values and domestic skills instead, experts such as Catharine Beecher promoted doll making in widely available domestic treatises. Thus over the course of the nineteenth century, dolls, doll play, and the functions that dolls served in middle-class girls' lives changed along with notions about girlhood, gender, family relationships, and motherhood. Because daughters were expected to contribute to the household economy, produce what they could, run errands when they must, and attend to younger siblings, the role of dolls was circumscribed. School attendance and Sabbath observance further restricted the amount of time devoted to doll play. Moreover, many girls often preferred to frolic outdoors instead.

Whether they wanted to play with them or not, middle-class girls were not allowed unrestricted access to their imported dolls. Made out of a combination of cloth, wax, kid leather, and wood, these highly fragile dolls were often kept out of the hands of children. Sometimes dolls were locked in cupboards by parents who considered them valuable enough to mention in their wills. Although an inaccessible doll might have been more desirable to some, many girls preferred dolls of their own making. On the frontier, girls made dolls from mattress ticking and other scrap materials. They also played with dolls made from natural materials such as dried cornhusks, corncobs, and pinecones. They used dried leaves and logs as doll beds and hollowed out stumps for stoves. Native American girls on the Plains made dolls out of buckskin and glass beads, and Seminoles used materials native to the South to make palmetto leaf dolls and cotton textiles for colorful patchwork clothing. The plantation South is credited as the origin of the Topsy Turvy doll, named after the slave girl in Harriet Beecher Stowe's classic book, *Uncle Tom's Cabin* (1851). A white doll and a black one typically represented as a "mammy" were united at the waist. "Mammy" dolls were also made out of a wide variety of materials, from nipples to bottles, and were even put into service as doorstops. Racist representations of female African American house servants, sporting colorful bandannas and holding white babies, endured into the twentieth century.

American men also created dolls. In 1844, Charles Goodyear applied his newly patented process of vulcanization to make rubber dolls painted white or dyed black. In 1858, Ludwig Greiner patented his papier-mâché doll heads. In rural New England, manufacturers and machinists also produced dolls. In Springfield, Vermont, Joel Addison Hartley Ellis (1830–1898), an inventor and carriage manufacturer, utilized the region's abundant waterpower, rock maple timber, labor, and local whittling traditions in order to produce flexible and durable wooden dolls with heavy metal hands and feet. Unable to survive the depression of 1873, however, Ellis's venture failed after one year. Thomas Edison was hardly more commercially successful with the screechy phonographic talking doll he produced in his Menlo Park, New Jersey, laboratory.

In response to the conspicuous consumption, ritual, and display of the gilded age, mothers drew upon the simpler toys of their preindustrial girlhoods. Many customers of dry goods stores purchased rag doll prints (produced by Arnold Print Works and Art Fabric Mills) ready to be cut, stitched, and stuffed instead of making them from scratch. But others inspired by a discourse in popular magazines applied the emerging ideology of "scientific motherhood" to create safe, soft, and sanitary dolls for the marketplace. Drawing upon antebellum domestic values, Martha Jenks Wheaton Chase (1851–1925), among other women, produced white and black "stockinet" dolls of girls and boys. At the M. J. Chase Company in Pawtucket, Rhode Island, women workers produced dolls that sold from coast to coast. Though too costly for working-class girls, Chase "hospital dolls" were used in Progressive-era baby clinics and settlement houses to teach immigrant children how to adjust to the new urban and industrial order.

Despite the efforts of American men and women, French and German "composition" doll bodies attached to unglazed porcelain "bisque" heads flooded toy and department stores in the decades after the Civil War. Produced by firms such as Jumeau, Bru, Huret, and Steiner, idealized girl dolls (*bébés*) replaced romanticized representations of Victorian women in the 1870s and 1880s. Many dolls could now be purchased wearing up-to-date continental fashions. Contributing to the Europeans' success abroad were the printing revolution that gave rise to fashion magazines, textile mills, and the invention of the sewing machine. These new machines were operated by an army of dolls' dressmakers, or "out workers," who were paid a pittance for their elaborate handwork.

This golden age of dolls closely correlated with the steadily decreasing size of American middle-class families, the expanding consumer culture, and changing notions of childhood and the role of play. The first child psychologist, G. Stanley Hall, posited that dolls had assumed a more central place in the lives of girls and boys. But memoirs, autobiographies, biographies, oral histories, and the "language" of play suggest that girls challenged their elders' expectations. Some preferred black rag dolls to white bisque ones. Many enacted doll funerals instead of playing house. Increased invention, production, and distribution of new toy technologies and the acceptance of active recreation by the early years of the twentieth century decreased doll desirability. Many girls preferred to bike and skate.

As separate spheres eroded more rapidly after the turn of the century, young, educated, "new women" artists from small towns west of the Mississippi found employment in burgeoning commercial industries. Rose O'Neill, the best-known female commercial artist at the time, also created the Kewpie, the most widely recognized character in popular culture until Mickey Mouse. She infused the cupidlike cartoon character with a maternalist ethos, suffragist politics, and a whimsical sense of humor. When it was made into dolls, figurines, and numerous spin-offs, the Kewpie made Rose O'Neill a millionaire. Images of children like the Kewpie drawn from popular and commercial culture provided businessmen with an unending source of recognizable images. Grace Drayton's advertising illustrations of the Campbell's Soup Kids that first appeared in the *Ladies' Home Journal* in 1905 were also made into dolls. Immigrant girls were less likely to purchase Campbell's dolls than to produce them, however. They snipped and sewed at home along with their mothers and brothers, who were also pressed into service as industrial workers in immigrant families.

New Kid dolls, like the Campbell's Soup characters, were marketed as adventurous, androgynous, optimistic, intelligent, and humorous, whereas European "character dolls" boasted greater realism. Influenced by similar cultural and social transformations, however, the European bent-limbed baby dolls portrayed a greater range of children's emotions. Some were even made in black versions. But when the African American community called for more black dolls, demeaning pickaninnies and mammies produced by American businessmen were probably not what they had in mind. A study of department store catalogues published from the early 1890s through the Depression years reveals that black female dolls were characterized differently than white ones. Throughout this period, black dolls appear to have disseminated racist notions and gender norms about African American women.

Rather than compete over race and realism, however, veteran companies and newcomers who attempted to dominate the doll industry during World War I tried to imitate European bisque with materials such as "biskoline." In an effort to discredit foreign competition, the industry also promoted patriotic advertising, marketing campaigns, anti-German sentiment, and harmful protective tariffs. After the war, trade associations orchestrated campaigns, intimidated striking workers, and marginalized women producers. The success of American toymen was evident by the 1920s, when more women entrepreneurs such as Madame Alexander (creator of high-priced dolls) delegated authority to male relatives, typically husbands. Women designers were forced into unsatisfactory compromises with male manufacturers both in the United States and abroad. Much to the chagrin of Grace Putnam, the Bye-Lo Baby (1923) she modeled after a newborn baby was compromised by commercial considerations and conventional male aesthetics.

Traditional values about women's roles in the 1920s also led American businessmen, who now dominated the industry, to market cute and content baby dolls that promoted materialism, femininity, and domesticity. In order to combat decreased interest in dolls as well as eliminate the tradition of repairing older ones, industry-orchestrated marketing campaigns generated needs and stimulated desires among girls for new dolls and more of them. Though Raggedy Ann dolls and those based on comic strip characters were also popular (especially Little Orphan Annie in the 1930s), instructional booklets such as "How to Play with a Doll" aimed to teach girls how to play house. The steadily declining birth rate made dolls like Patsy into symbolic siblings, and her wardrobe of ready-made clothing promoted girls' participation in the expanding consumer culture.

Despite the proliferation of commercially produced dolls, many continued to be made by girls and grownups, especially among those who were unable to afford store-bought dolls or who wanted an outlet for creativity, more practice in sewing skills, or dolls that featured racial, religious, or ethnic diversity. These factors contributed to the continued popularity of rag dolls (which were occasionally based on commercially produced ones). Raggedy Ann dolls proliferated after the publication of John Gruelle's classic children's book by the same name in 1915. But Amish and Mennonite communities had been producing faceless cloth dolls in keeping with religious customs and beliefs about the sinfulness of representing one's likeness. Two Mennonite sisters named Lizzie and Ellen Carper had played with their rag dolls in the nineteenth century.

Dolls that resembled Asian American children were made in California, Colorado, New York, and other communities where Chinese families settled. Dolls made by the Navajo, Sioux, and other Native American tribes not only reflected indigenous customs, beliefs, and values but also shed light on the nature of cultural exchange and domination. Extant handmade dolls (often made for the tourist trade) combined traditional Native American artifacts with those of the dominant culture. Yuma Indians who lived on the west bank of the Colorado River from 1774 to the 1850s created ceramic dolls, dressed differently before the reservation period than after it. Tourist miniatures produced in the Northeast reflect the shifts not only in European concepts of native peoples but also Native Americans' representations of themselves.

The arts and crafts tradition did not deter the commercial doll industry, which continued to produce dolls that aimed to be more realistic. In 1934 Effanbee advertised its Dy-Dee Baby doll that drank and wet as "almost human." Though based on a real girl, the Shirley Temple doll first produced by the Ideal Novelty and Toy Company in 1934 represented a rather fantastical version of American girlhood. Ideal's enormously popular product enabled girls to identify with the film star's agency, adventure, and achievement. Close cooperation among the film's producers, movie theater owners, and the doll company led to a marketing extravaganza in 1936. Despite constraints on the family budget, the doll still grossed more than $6 million. For those who could not afford the doll, Shirley Temple paper dolls were widely available. Despite the doll's success, however, severe cutbacks in consumer spending forced many doll firms to close. Such was not the case for the Madame Alexander firm, which manufactured dolls based on the Dionne quintuplets and Sonja Henie, the Olympic figure skater.

World War II further disrupted the industry. Some retooled firms produced prosthetic devices for injured soldiers. Others looked to the consumer application of wartime inventions. Some firms continued to experiment with rubber in order to make inexpensive dolls that did not chip, peel, or flake. But it was the invention of hard plastic that revolutionized the doll industry in 1949. Early industry leaders were Betsy Wetsy, who urinated, and Tiny Tears, who cried. Changing the nature of play for millions of postwar baby boomers were dolls made out of plastic or soft vinyl, with synthetic hair, expansive wardrobes, and accessories. Drawing on Gillette's do-it-yourself permanent wave product, the Toni doll enabled girls to wash, set, and curl her "Magic Nylon 'Hair.'" Ginny, a little white girl doll created by Jenny

Grave's Vogue, was one of the most popular of the period.

Although most mainstream companies produced few black dolls, if any, fledgling companies influenced by changing wartime race relations and the emerging civil rights movement of the 1950s and 1960s, which decried the paucity of black dolls, produced realistically featured dolls such as Patti-Jo, Saralee, and Amosandra. In the early 1950s, Sara Lee Creech created the Sara Lee doll, which reflected issues of race, commercialization, and popular culture in the postwar United States. In 1951, Creech successfully convinced the Ideal Toy Company to market the African American doll. The difficulties of creating an "anthropologically correct" prototype, however, led to its commercial failure. It would be another decade and a half before another black doll would be manufactured in the United States. The paucity of black dolls probably contributed to the preferences of black children for white dolls as revealed in Kenneth and Mimi Clark's 1950 study. Their conclusions that black students' low self-esteem could be read in their doll preference played an important role in *Brown v. Board of Education* (1955). In that case, initiated on behalf of an African American girl named Linda Brown, the U.S. Supreme Court ruled the separate, segregated American education system was unconstitutional. The Sara Lee doll and Creech's social activism on behalf of African Americans influenced public attitudes about race in the United States. Studies conducted in the 1960s and the 1970s would suggest that black children now preferred black dolls.

By the early 1960s, Mattel's teenage titanic blonde bombshell, Barbie—the exemplar of postwar gender roles, materi-

A Sears, Roebuck and Co. catalogue page advertising dolls. (Library of Congress)

alism, consumerism, sexuality, and teen culture—emerged as a triumphant industry leader. Unlike the many generations of girl and baby dolls that engendered maternal behaviors, Barbie's world was one of enthusiasm, opportunity, adventure, aspiration, accessories, and an education in consumption (much to the chagrin of parents, experts, and critics, then as now). Based on a European sex symbol but marketed as an autonomous American fashion model always dressed to the nines, Barbie's chic wardrobe and accessories rivaled the French fashion dolls of the opulent gilded age. Although feminists either rejected dolls for their patriarchal messages or promoted their usefulness in raising sons, Barbie's fluid identity over the course of forty years appropriated selective aspects of changing gender roles. Mod Barbie became a freewheeling disco queen in the 1970s. Shaped by a variety of contemporary forces, an even more glamorous Barbie represented women in the workplace in the 1980s. Barbie became especially popular among the daughters of postwar baby boomers, themselves former Barbie owners. African American and Latina Barbies also represented changing demographics and the commercialization of cultural pluralism. It would not be until the early 1990s, however, that toy companies launched by black entrepreneurs would produce ethnically correct black dolls aimed at instilling a positive sense of self in black children.

The postwar market in baby dolls plummeted until the rise of Cabbage Patch dolls in the 1980s. The success of Cabbage Patch dolls can be attributed to a number of factors. First, the cloth-bodied baby doll personified innocence and vulnerability. Scholars who have studied the women consumers who furiously fought toy store crowds argue that women's desire to parent was exploited by the firm's marketing campaign. Social psychologists posited the view that a collective national wish for a symbolic rebirth motivated both parents and children. Despite the market-driven mania that surrounded their sale, Cabbage Patch dolls seemed to embody an appealing anticommercial ethic, coming on the heels of 1970s glitz and in the face of 1980s extravagance.

In the 1990s, dolls continued to promote self-fulfillment through adornment and consumerism. Some could be made up or have their hair combed, curled, crimped, and dyed. Still others embodied masculine messages about female sexuality. For example, Susie Cupcakes's undergarments—eroticized and sanitized—were scented to smell sweet. When manufacturers produced Baby Spice and Ginger Spice as action figures after the pop music group in the 1990s, however, they relied on the Barbie paradigm and merely replaced the pumps with platform shoes. Combining sexuality with power has not been easy for doll manufacturers. In their attempt to respond to consumer demand for more powerful female figures that embodied a "girl power" ethos, Hasbro produced a surprisingly androgynous doll, suggesting that for them power and sexuality were still at odds in the doll world. Such moneymakers as the high-priced American Girl dolls (purchased by Mattel for $700 million in 1998) emphasize girls' self-esteem, education, and agency. More like Cabbage Patch kids than Barbies, these catalogue-only dolls aim to represent innocence and an anticommercial tradition.

But continued anxieties about changing roles for girls and women in the new

Three- and four-year-olds play with a doll at a day care center in New Rochelle, New York. (Shirley Zeiberg)

millennium continue to find expression in dolls. "Barbie for President" was marketed during the 2000 presidential election, when delegates at the Republican convention received Barbies dressed in Nancy Reagan red. While presidential candidates battled for support of the heartland in political campaign ads, Barbie "Dorothy" also appeared in television spots. Wearing a dress that exemplified midwestern girlhood innocence but sporting eye-catching ruby slippers, this doll reminded girls: "There's no place like home."

Miriam Forman-Brunell

See also American Girls Collection; Barbie; Consumer Culture; Dollhouses; Domesticity; Girls' Culture; Girls' Rooms; Play

References and Further Reading
Beisel, David R. 1984. "Thoughts on the Cabbage Patch Kids." *Journal of Psychohistory* 12, no. 1: 133–142.
Cross, Gary. 1997. *Kids' Stuff: Toys and the Changing World of American Childhood.* Cambridge, MA: Harvard University Press.
Formanek-Brunell, Miriam. 1998. *Made to Play House: Dolls and the Commercialization of American Girlhood, 1830–1930.* Baltimore: Johns Hopkins University Press.
Gillespie, Fern. 1991. "Black Dolls: The Christmas Wish of African-American

Children?" *American Visions* 6, no. 5: 27–31.

Jacob, James E., Paul Rodenhauser, and Ronald J. Markert. 1987. "The Benign Exploitation of Human Emotions: Adult Women and the Marketing of Cabbage Patch Kids." *Journal of American Culture* 10, no. 3: 61–71.

Mather, Cotton. 1911–1912. "The Diary of Cotton Mather." Collections of the Massachusetts Historical Society. 7th series, vol. 7. Cited in Pollock, Linda, 1987, *A Lasting Relationship: Parents and Children over Three Centuries.* Hanover: University Press of New England, 148.

Patterson, Gordon. 1994. "Color Matters: The Creation of the Sara Lee Doll." *Florida Historical Quarterly* 73, no. 2: 147–165.

Pollock, Linda. 1987. *A Lasting Relationship: Parents and Children over Three Centuries.* Hanover: University Press of New England.

Wilkinson, Doris Y. 1987. "The Doll Exhibit: A Psycho-Cultural Analysis of Black Female Role Stereotypes." *Journal of Popular Culture* 21, no. 2: 19–29.

Domestic Service

Domestic service was the number one job category open to seventeenth-, eighteenth-, and nineteenth-century American girls of all races. Serving girls of these centuries were given responsibility for cleaning houses, caring for children, and waiting tables, as well as sewing and mending, ironing, and running errands. Few were asked to shoulder the demanding jobs of cook and housekeeper, but all were expected to live with the families they served and be almost constantly "on call." In the nineteenth century, servants in the urban Northeast were called "domestics," whereas those in rural homes of the North and West preferred to be labeled "help." Both domestics and "help" could be wage earners or "bound." The latter were usually paid only in room and board and were legally required to serve until they reached the age of eighteen or twenty-one. Girls of all races were "bound" servants; the criterion was their parents' inability or unwillingness to provide them with a home. In the southern states, domestic service was usually performed by slaves; it was common, though, for slaveholders to refer to their household staff as "servants." In the twentieth century, when fewer American girls went into service work, most were "day servants" who lived somewhere other than their employers' homes. The majority of girls who served in the twentieth-century United States were of African, Asian, and Latina descent.

In all these centuries, relying on a servant who was waged, "bound," or enslaved was a way to insist on one's membership in the middle or upper class. Thus, although most Americans used serving girls to do necessary household labors, those who had enough money also employed servants to display privilege, leisure, and status. One-function servants such as hairdressers and seamstresses were costly but were not often young. Housemaids who were preteens or teenagers earned relatively good money and did not have to pay for room and board, which meant that the thrifty could save. Oral histories of African American women who had been servants, which were collected by Elizabeth Clark-Lewis and Susan Tucker, recall how a servant's wages could help out kin, make marriage possible, or finance education. Similar experiences have been reported by Irish immigrants who served in the nineteenth-century United States and by some native-born white servants, too. It was harder to save money as a children's nurse because this job was poorly paid or as a "bound" servant because

A portrait of the Stevens family servants, Castle Point, Hoboken, New Jersey. (Byron/Museum of the City of New York/Archive Photos, 1895)

these workers usually were not paid. Girls who worked as "help" often were not paid in wages but instead were recompensed by being allowed, for instance, to run a tab at local stores. The hardest job of all, for American serving girls, was to be a "maid-of-all-work." These all-purpose servants were forced to work very hard and were usually paid very little if young or untrained.

Trying to find out how many girls have served, in how many homes, throughout American history is not easy because early census takers did not distinguish between servants and the families who relied on their work. The best estimates about domestic workers in the antebellum United States are Faye E. Dudden's suggestion that 15 to 30 percent of urban households relied on nonkin staff and

Eugene Genovese's proposition that about one-quarter of the slaves in the South worked as cooks, maids, child-nurses, and seamstresses (Dudden 1983, 1–2; Genovese 1969, 328). However, these figures are not age-specific. In addition, they do not include the girls sent off to western states on "orphan trains" to reduce the number of America's urban poor, the rural "hired girls" in nonslave states, and servants who lived with and labored for relatives other than their own nuclear families. Recognition of these domestic workers makes it clear that the number of American girls laboring as domestic servants was at least as high in the eighteenth century as it was in the nineteenth and that the number dropped significantly from about 1900 as a result of new attitudes toward family life and child labor. Social changes such as enhanced job opportunities and compulsory education were influential, too. Finally, the development of "labor-saving" equipment and of service industries such as commercial laundries helped to reduce the number of girls in domestic service posts.

The nineteenth century was the heyday of serving girls and of the so-called servant problem, a social tension that grew out of new expectations for service workers. In this era, employers commonly used the word *girl* to mean "female servant" (as in the complaint "My new girl sweeps dust beneath the rug") though many such "girls" were adult women. A smaller number were juvenile delinquents or teenagers who were thought to be at risk. Indeed, some female reformatories trained inmates as laundresses. The theory behind this kind of service was that it was good for all girls to learn household chores, but it was especially good for girls with criminal tendencies to appreciate cleanliness and purity. An extrapolation of this idea persuaded some philanthropic societies to find service jobs for young women convicted of theft and vagrancy. The hope was that life in a "good" family would rehabilitate the social deviant. It may seem strange that householders were willing to employ juvenile delinquents or even send dirty linen to them. One explanation is that household labor was so unremitting that homemakers were desperate for domestic servants of any kind. Ideologically, though, the key to this practice is the idea that "nice" homes have redemptive powers. The ideal in such cases was that servants from "bad" homes who would otherwise become social problems could be saved by life with a respectable family in a decent home.

This understanding of domestic service has been used to justify the practice of making poor children do other people's unpleasant, difficult, and menial chores. In a sense, it was used as a rationale for slavery, too. On the plus side, some see family-style management as a good way to counter the heartless exploitation of in-house workers. However, the idea that privileged homemakers should act as surrogate parents to their servants could make it difficult for those dependent on servants to see these workers as "real" labor. Carelessness about paying servants and even resistance to paying them arose out of employers' tendency to equate domestic servants with daughters and wives who did not expect to be paid for doing household chores.

Diaries, letters, interviews, and autobiographical statements left by U.S. domestic servants suggest mixed opinions of homemakers' desire for servants who live and serve as "part of the family." Many of these records show resentment of the assumption that servants have no family lives of their own. Others complain of the emotional energy that servants are asked to expend on their employers. A few note that servants are the only members of "a family" who can be laid off or dismissed. However, some records left by domestic servants express gratitude to employers who displayed an interest in their welfare. African American women, in particular, recall domestic service as a stepping-stone to a better life. Reports from white servants are scattered, but David Katzman includes a few in his history of domestic service in the United States.

Early studies of domestic service focused on the "restless" servants who changed jobs frequently. But in recent years, scholars sympathetic to American workers have shown that domestic workers may have had good reasons to leave a post. Unkind treatment was one concern, and employers' demands for ego boosting was another; loneliness was a common complaint, and sexual harassment was rife. Perhaps the most pressing issues for girls in domestic service was that employers did not always respect the contractual agreements they made with teenagers. Matters were even worse for very young children who were "bound" to service in other people's homes, especially if their parents were far away. *"Our Nig,"* an account of "bound" service from 1859, shows how one young servant was virtually tortured by a cruel mistress with little chance for self-defense. Part of Harriet Wilson's problem was that she was of mixed-race parentage, which made her an object of racist spite. Just as important, though, the status of "bound girl" left her open to a mistress's violent whims. Sadly, after Wilson served her term and became legally free to pursue her own goals, she was unable to find work that her weakened body could perform. The loss of health brought on by heavy labor and little recreation was common among domestic servants. In some cases, it led to abrupt dismissal; in others, it made prostitution look like an easier way to make a living.

American girls' move out of domestic service has been gradual and staggered. The most important variables have been the worker's race and place of birth. Though British North American colonists of the seventeenth and eighteenth centuries put five- and six-year-old children of any race—Native American, black, and white—to work in nonkin homes, most boys left domestic service when they were old enough to be apprenticed to a trade. Girls usually served until

they married or died, regardless of their race, up to the 1840s. Then white girls started to find work in factories and mills. White girls' preference for nonservice jobs was based on the perception that domestic service was degrading because it was like slavery. This perception explains why domestic service jobs were and are dominated by Americans of African descent and by recent immigrants. Some of the latter have been able to serve for a few years or even a generation and then move up the social ladder. But not all have been so lucky.

A good source of information on serving girls in U.S. history is memoirs left by women who cooked and cleaned for other people when they were young. In addition to *"Our Nig,"* three important accounts are *Incidents in the Life of a Slave Girl* (1861), *A Lifetime with Mark Twain* (1925), and *Idella* (1991). The first, a narrative of slavery written by Harriet Jacobs after she became free, describes the life of a house slave rather than a wage-earning servant. Yet because house slaves were exposed to some of the same trials that wage-earning servants faced, this chronicle illuminates aspects of all nineteenth-century servants' lives. So does *A Lifetime with Mark Twain*, though as the title indicates, this book was written to chronicle the life of someone other than its narrator, Katy Leary. Idella Parker resisted this skew in her memoir. She wrote *Idella* to counter a former employer's one-sided view of her as "the perfect maid."

After the abolition of slavery, the biggest innovation in U.S. service was "day service." This form of service was the norm from about 1945. More recently, laws intended to put domestic service on a par with other kinds of labor have been passed. Servants do not always cooperate with these laws because they do not see them getting at the root of their concerns. The laws create new complications for employers, which can be to the disadvantage of the employee in finding a position.

Barbara Ryan

See also Captivity; Enslaved Girls of African Descent; Free Girls of African Descent; Indentured Servants; Work

References and Further Reading
Clark-Lewis, Elizabeth. 1994. *Living In, Living Out: African American Domestics in Washington, D.C., 1910–1940.* Washington, DC: Smithsonian Institution Press.
Dudden, Faye E. 1983. *Serving Women: Household Service in Nineteenth-Century America.* Middletown, CT: Wesleyan University Press.
Genovese, Eugene. 1969. *Roll, Jordan, Roll: The World the Slaves Made.* New York: Pantheon Books.
Jacobs, Harriet. 1861. *Incidents in the Life of a Slave Girl.* Edited by Jean Fagin Yellin. 1987. Reprint, Cambridge, MA: Harvard University Press.
Katzman, David M. 1981. *Seven Days a Week: Women and Domestic Service in Industrializing America.* Urbana: University of Illinois Press.
Lawton, Mary, ed. 1925. *A Lifetime with Mark Twain: The Memories of Katy Leary, for Thirty Years His Faithful and Devoted Servant.* New York: Harcourt, Brace.
Parker, Idella. 1991. *Idella: Marjorie Rawlings' "Perfect Maid."* With Mary Keating. Gainesville: University Press of Florida.
Romero, Mary. 1992. *Maid in the U.S.A.* New York: Routledge.
Stansell, Christine. 1986. *City of Women: Sex and Class in New York, 1789–1860.* New York: Alfred A. Knopf.
Tucker, Susan. 1988. *Telling Memories among Southern Women: Domestic Workers and Their Employers in the Segregated South.* Baton Rouge: Louisiana State University Press.
Wilson, Harriet. 1859. *"Our Nig"; or, Sketches from the Life of a Free Black, in a Two-Story White House, North.* *Showing That Slavery's Shadows Fall Even There.* Edited by Henry Louis Gates, Jr. 1983. Reprint, New York: Random House.

Domesticity

Domesticity was a central component of the Victorian ideology of gender in the nineteenth-century United States. The ideology of domesticity established for white, middle-class girls the boundaries between what was considered acceptable female behavior and what was not. Despite the decline of Victorianism, the legacy of domesticity underpins twentieth-century gender-role socialization theory and practice.

Nineteenth-century fiction was one among a wide variety of cultural products that extolled domesticity. Harriet Beecher Stowe's *Uncle Tom's Cabin* promoted domesticity as a force against slavery. Elsewhere in prints, pictures, poems, magazines, and manuals, experts, writers, artists, and others delineated idealized spheres of influence based on sex. In the public sphere men ruled because they were believed to be innately aggressive, assertive, competitive, and protective. In the domestic realm or the sanctuary of woman's sphere, it was women—widely considered to be more tender, nurturing, submissive, emotional, virtuous, pious, and chaste—who reigned. Middle-class housewives were urged by Catharine Beecher (author of the highly influential *Treatise on Domestic Education* [1841]) to apply scientific methods and religious precepts to the domestic realm over which they exercised control.

The ideology of domesticity that took shape between 1780 and 1830 did so within the wider context of major transformations: representative democracy,

Girls are taught at an early age to aspire to domestic roles that serve a patriarchal culture.
(Library of Congress)

the growth of capitalism, industrialization, urbanization, immigration, changing marital ideals, declining family size, and the rise of the "new" middle class. In the face of these unsettling social, economic, political, and cultural changes, the chief task of the efficient middle-class housewife was to use her domestic skills and moral suasion to create a refuge from moral degeneration, spiritual degradation, and political destruction. The newly devised responsibility of middle-class mothers was to raise her pliant children according to the canon of domesticity, which contrasted the safety of the home to the commercial ethos of the individualistic (masculine) world.

Shaping children's characters, instilling piety, teaching them habits of order and self-control—these were to be accomplished by mothers along strict gender lines. Unlike sons, daughters were raised to follow in the footsteps of their exalted Victorian mothers, whose domestic activities set a standard for them to emulate. Qualifying them for their future roles as mothers, daughters sewed, mended, cooked, cleaned, washed, ironed, ran errands, and tutored and cared for younger siblings. While adolescent brothers served as apprentices or, increasingly over the era, attended school for longer periods, housekeeping and child care most often constituted a girl's informal apprenticeship. They learned about the fundamentals of domesticity from female family and kin as well as from a vast didactic literature. Moralistic children's books, housekeeping manuals, and advice books written primarily for adolescent girls, such as *Letters to Young Ladies* (1837), defined proper feminine behavior and domestic management. Lydia Maria Child's *The Girl's Own Book*

(1833) is one such publication that made domesticity relevant to "little women." Though it emphasized the importance of physical fitness and sound health, the intention was to make American girls into "true women."

Under certain circumstances, domesticity could empower women and girls within the family and beyond the household. Within companionate marriage, "true women" could exert moral influence over husbands, control sexual reproduction, and engage in voluntary activities beyond the household. Cultural and literary historians have recently argued that domesticity as a movement sought to reorder American culture from a distinctly female point of view and from the seemingly apolitical place called "home." For example, Harriet Beecher Stowe's *Uncle Tom's Cabin* also explores a variety of households, North and South, free and slave, to argue for the abolition of a system that breaks apart families, both black and white. Many women, with their daughters following in their footsteps, also engaged in a variety of voluntary social reforms precisely by extending the notions of home and family to the world and thus engaging the larger "human family" to be nurtured, adopted, and raised through such antebellum reforms as education, temperance, abolition, and, of course, women's rights. Within the boundaries of acceptable female behavior were resources to expand those boundaries that at one and the same time circumscribed and empowered their inhabitants.

Although aspects of the domestic ideology more relevant to Victorian culture fell away in the twentieth century, the importance of domestic training for girls persisted in institutionalized forms (e.g., home economics), in recreation (e.g., miniaturized household technology and dolls), and as a cohesive philosophy dictating feminine behavioral standards. Although domesticity served utilitarian purposes during periods of economic retrenchment, prosperity also reinforced domestic ideals. For girls growing up after World War II, a modernized version of domesticity shaped recreation and education and was embedded in the material culture of girlhood and female adolescence. In *Young, White and Miserable: Growing Up Female in the Fifties* (1992), however, Wini Breines examines how sites of male cultural resistance—rock and roll and the Beat movement—enabled discontented middle-class girls coming of age to negotiate domesticity's more restrictive influence.

Miriam Forman-Brunell and
Shirley Teresa Wajda

See also Girls' Culture; Little Mothers

References and Further Reading
Boydston, Jeanne. 1991. *Home and Work: Housework, Wages, and the Ideology of Labor in the Early Republic*. New York: Oxford University Press.

Breines, Wini. 1992. *Young, White and Miserable: Growing Up Female in the Fifties*. New York: Beacon Press.

Child, Lydia Maria. 1833. *The Girls' Own Book*. New York: Clark Austin.

Cogan, Frances. 1989. *All-American Girl: The Ideal of Real Womanhood in Mid-Nineteenth-Century America*. Athens: University of Georgia Press.

Cott, Nancy. 1977. *The Bonds of Womanhood: "Women's Sphere" in New England, 1780–1835*. New Haven, CT: Yale University Press, chap. 2.

Green, Harvey. 1983. *The Light of the Home: An Intimate View of the Lives of Women in Victorian America*. New York: Pantheon.

Matthews, Glenda. 1987. *"Just a Housewife": The Rise and Fall of Domesticity in America*. New York: Oxford University Press.

Nelson, Claudia, and Lynne Vallone, eds. 1994. *The Girl's Own: Cultural Histories of the Anglo-American Girl, 1830–1915*. Athens: University of Georgia Press.

Pollock, Linda. 1987. *A Lasting Relationship: Parents and Children over Three Centuries*. Hanover, NH: University of New England Press.

Vallone, Lynn. 1995. *Disciplines of Virtue: Girls' Culture in the Eighteenth and Nineteenth Centuries*. New Haven, CT: Yale University Press.

Welter, Barbara. 1966. "The Cult of True Womanhood, 1820–1860." *American Quarterly* 18: 151–174.

E

Eating Disorders

One of the most troubling aspects of contemporary girls' development is the extent to which their growing exuberance and skills are burdened by worries about weight and body size. Preschoolers have been heard to ask about the "fat" on their tummies and thighs, and by elementary school many girls have put themselves on diets. These concerns intensify at puberty, and by adolescence a majority of girls say they dislike their bodies and make efforts to change them through diet and exercise. For some girls, these efforts lead to serious, sometimes life-threatening, eating disorders.

Four variants of eating disorders are common today. In anorexia, girls restrict their food intake to far below what is needed to sustain growth or a healthy metabolism. This restriction is accompanied by an increasing preoccupation with weight, calories, and the amount and kind of food or liquid consumed. Bizarre rituals around eating may develop. As malnutrition and starvation increase, these behaviors and preoccupations intensify. The girl has no insight into how distorted her body image and eating behavior have become and is likely to complain that she is fat even when she is starving. The medical complications of anorexia include gastrointestinal distress and constipation; cardiac arrhythmia, a slowed heartbeat, cardiac edema, or heart failure; dehydration and electrolyte imbalance; anemia; weakness or hyperactivity; and hypothermia. Menstruation may stop or fail to develop. Dry or yellowing skin, dental problems, thinning hair, and the growth of fine downy hair can also appear.

In bulimia, girls may try to restrict their food intake for hours or days at a time, but this attempt is invariably followed by periods of binge eating in which unusually large amounts are eaten rapidly. These binges are physically and emotionally distressing, so the girl responds by purging in an attempt to get rid of the calories. She will make herself vomit, abuse diuretics or laxatives, drink too much or too little, or exercise too much in an effort to "burn off" the calories. The pattern of bingeing and purging may be repeated many times a day. The medical complications of bulimia include severe gastrointestinal distress, constipation, electrolyte imbalance, and cardiac abnormalities.

In binge eating disorder, or compulsive overeating, girls eat large amounts of food, often in a short time, but do not attempt to purge afterwards. They may overeat throughout the day or binge at particular times of day, usually after school or in the evening. This disorder can lead to obesity, which increases an individual's lifetime risk for cardiovascular disease, diabetes, and certain cancers.

In overactivity disorder, girls do unusually intense or lengthy periods of exercise in an effort to lose weight, build muscle, or lose body fat. The exercising is done compulsively rather than for pleasure, sport, competition, or skill building.

Estimates of the prevalence of eating disorders vary, but the incidence of the illness has increased dramatically since 1980: 90–95 percent of the cases of eating disorders occur in females; 0.5–1 percent of all women, or at least 1 million women, will have anorexia at some time in their lives. Bulimia affects 1–3 percent of adolescents and young women: 1–2 million women have bulimia, and twice as many have bulimic-like symptoms. Although eating disorders were originally identified in girls from affluent, white households, they now affect youngsters from all races and socioeconomic groups.

Anorexia is the most lethal of all psychiatric disorders. From 5 to 10 percent of people with chronic, severe anorexia will die. The medical complications of bulimia can also be fatal.

Eating disorders develop out of a complex interplay of sociocultural, psychological, family, and biological factors. Although many girls struggle with the pressure to be thin, feel too fat, or try to diet, a number will develop eating disorders because of a specific combination of psychological or family vulnerabilities with biological risk factors.

Historical Perspectives
Women's preoccupations with eating and body size have been recorded throughout Western history. Greek women believed that the Cretans had drugs that permitted them to eat without gaining weight. Roman women starved themselves in order to be thin and may have used the vomitorium to purge after eating.

Students of anorexia have pointed out similarities between modern girls' refusal to eat and the asceticism of medieval saints. Between the thirteenth and sixteenth centuries, some young women fasted in penance or to intensify their prayer. Ecstatic or trance states often accompanied their fasts. Some licked or ingested repulsive matter to mortify themselves or to share in Christ's suffering. The obsessiveness often noted in anorexia could be seen in rituals around praying, self-flagellation or mutilation, and silence. The poor insight into these behaviors and resistance to change characteristic of anorexia were apparent in the fasting saints' resistance to direct orders from their superiors in the church to change their behavior. In the seventeenth and eighteenth centuries, stories spread of girls who were able to fast for long periods of time. These girls were not nuns or saints, but their apparent ability to refrain from eating was seen as a sign of purity and, sometimes, miraculous intervention.

With the beginning of the study of psychiatry in western Europe, anorexia was often described as a prominent aspect of the newly diagnosed illness of hysteria. Pierre Janet reported several cases of anorexia. Sigmund Freud's and Charles Breuer's early case histories of hysterical adolescents and young women included descriptions of patients who refused to eat or who ate in odd, ritualized ways, such as eating only certain foods or drinking only from the wrong side of the glass. Charcot described a girl who tied a ribbon around her waist so she would not become heavier than her mother. The modern illness called "anorexia nervosa" was first described in 1874 by William Gull in England, and a similar set of symptoms was described in 1873 by Charles Lasègue in France.

Although the anorexics of the continent were portrayed as hysterics, the anorexia occurring in the midst of dramatic symptoms such as paralysis, inability to speak, and dissociative states, found in the "fasting girls" of Britain and the United States and described by the contemporary historian Joan Jacobs Brumberg, was depicted as less dramatic but caused as great a stir. Throughout the nineteenth century, a number of individual cases emerged in Britain and the United States in which young girls were reported to live for extended periods of time with no food. They became objects of spectacle and were visited by sightseers, religious and medical leaders, and reporters. Fierce controversy emerged over whether their survival was a hoax, and one young woman died of thirst after a watch was kept to guarantee that she neither ate nor drank. Brumberg documents the transition between an earlier view in which fasting was interpreted as miraculous and a later view, shaped by the emergence of spiritualism, in which fasting was seen as proof of the separation of the soul and the body.

As it became accepted that fasting did lead to death by starvation, girls who did not eat came to be seen as ill. Brumberg describes how by the end of the nineteenth century, with the emergence of the middle-class family, increasing numbers of girls refused to eat in response to their families' coddling and encouragement of dependency. By the beginning of the twentieth century, eating very little was associated with the wish to have a slim figure in order to be attractive to potential mates.

Throughout the 1910s and 1920s, women's growing independence, changes in fashion, and increasingly free relationships with men joined with a new "scientific" attitude toward food and health to create an interest in dieting. Plump girls were encouraged by their families to diet, and increasing numbers of adolescents dieted in ways that led to striking changes in the number of reported cases of anorexia.

The increased prevalence of dieting also led to the emergence of bulimia as a recognized eating disorder. Although Brumberg gives anecdotal evidence, derived from diaries and personal letters, that girls shared the "secret" of controlling their weight by making themselves vomit as early as the 1920s, demographic studies show the emergence of bulimia as a significantly frequent psychiatric diagnosis beginning in the 1960s. There was a rapid rise of the incidence of bulimia in the 1970s, and the diagnostic label "bulimia nervosa" was coined by Gerald Russell in 1979.

Sociocultural Perspectives

As this historical survey suggests, eating disorders have developed in a variety of different social and cultural contexts. At the beginning of the twenty-first century, eating disorders are more widespread than they have ever been, and their frequency has been accompanied by a heightened awareness of the impact of social forces on girls' development. Studies of the eating disorders of adult women have emphasized the difficulties contemporary women have in integrating work, sexuality, and mothering, and girls, too, face these challenges.

One important factor in the current epidemic is that girls are raised by mothers who have their own serious concerns about weight and body size. They may have grown up watching their mothers diet or may have been put on diets by their mothers when they were very

Idealized beauty, as in this portrait of "all-American girl" Sandra Dee, encourages girls to diet in order to achieve a certain body image. (Columbia Pictures/Archive Photos, 1959)

decades, but they are also much younger. In the past, girls could tell themselves "that's how beautiful grownup women look," but now they are forced to compare themselves directly to images of girls their own age, and they often end up feeling inadequate. The expectation that contemporary girls will begin having boyfriends and engaging in sexual activity during their teenage years makes the need to match this ideal of beauty especially urgent. Fears of pregnancy and long-term anxieties about achievement and competition may be hidden in concerns about thinness.

The increasing freedom girls have to participate in sports also leads to conflicting feelings about their bodies. They may strive to be lean or to have the bodies of gymnasts, figure skaters, or ballet dancers. Girls who participate in sports and do become strong and muscular experience conflicts about how their athletic bodies differ from the more slender ideal.

As girls try to learn how to eat to achieve the ideal body, they are faced with a conundrum. Food in the United States and the West is more abundant than it has ever been. Seasonal foods are available year-round, and family meals have been replaced by fast food, takeout counters, all-you-can-eat buffets, and restaurants that serve extremely large portions. Gourmet cooking is popular and presented on how-to television shows and in specialized magazines. At the same time, the growing health consciousness of the last few decades has shaped girls' views of eating in a more restrictive way. Because both accurate and faddish information is widely publicized, many girls grow up with the idea that they should not eat fats, sugars, meat, or starches. They may grow up in families in which parents have adopted

young. What the mothers may not have realized was that the developing girl's view of her body was shaped by a culture very different from the one in which she herself grew up.

Girls today grow up in a media-saturated society and are bombarded by images in which thinness signifies female beauty, sexual appeal, and power. Thinness may have an androgynous quality or reach a point of outright emaciation. Not only have models, film stars, and musicians become thinner than in past special diets. As the culture at large has responded to this emphasis on diet, expectations and manners have changed. Although in the past it was considered polite to eat what was served, now it is seen as the host or restaurant's responsibility to accommodate guests' health, religious, or ethical restrictions. The weight loss industry and diet pills add to the dangerous and confusing messages young girls hear every day.

A final and increasingly important cultural influence takes the form of popular media depictions of eating disorders. Beginning in the late 1960s, a number of books written for young adults took anorexia as their theme. In books like Steven Levenkron's *The Best Little Girl in the World*, anorexics were pictured as high achievers out of touch with their emotions and bodies, whose self-starvation was one more effort at perfection. The character of the books and movies that followed changed in the 1980s and the 1990s. Novels and memoirs began to address the topic of bulimia as well. These books tended to present eating disorders as part of a spectrum of impulsive behavior that included drug and alcohol abuse, delinquency, and promiscuity. Marya Hornbacher's book *Wasted* vividly illustrates these themes. By the end of the twentieth century, eating disorders had become "news," and girls had access to both factual information and sensationalized accounts of the illness. With this widespread popularization of the illness, susceptible girls could be heard to say, not "I want to be thin" but "I want to be anorexic."

Emotional and Developmental Perspectives

Unfortunately, most girls in our culture respond to the idealization of thinness by

An anorexic young woman looks at herself in a bathroom mirror. (Shirley Zeiberg)

becoming concerned about their weight and body size. For some more vulnerable girls, this concern can lead to a serious eating disorder. Their vulnerability comes from a combination of emotional and biological factors.

Eating disorders tend to begin around the time a girl enters puberty. The increased emotional instability caused by shifts in hormone levels can make it hard for girls to integrate important changes in their bodies and relationships. As they approach menstruation, experience new genital sensations, and notice that their breasts are developing and their stomachs, hips, and thighs are becoming rounded, their anxiety about becoming sexually mature finds easy expression in a fear of becoming "fat." A girl's sense that she is fat does not come only from seeing her reflection in the mirror or her weight on the scale but also from the diffuse quality of women's body feelings. Premenstrual tensions, sexual sensations, and emotional reactions can all be labeled "fat." Because of this, the longing to be thin may be an attempt to disown all the new, troubling experiences by returning to the more androgynous body of the little girl.

Fears of growing up can also stem from relational issues. Being more independent from her parents, especially if her family is highly enmeshed, can be threatening for a girl who is not yet secure in her peer relationships. Conflicted family loyalties or family secrets can make it especially hard for a girl to become more autonomous. Girls who have experienced their parents' divorce, physical or sexual abuse, or significant losses may find that adolescent development brings up unresolved early conflicts in ways that are still hard to manage. Carol Gilligan's observation that girls try to maintain relationships at the expense of their own voice and knowledge is relevant, as well, to their management of their hungers and body needs.

The development of anorexia or bulimia may reflect the different personal styles with which girls handle these developmental and relational pressures. Girls who become anorexic are more likely to be perfectionist and achievement-oriented, to value self-control, and to be timid or inhibited. Girls who develop bulimia are likely to be more impulsive, more emotionally reactive, and more focused on social relationships. Once an eating disorder becomes established, though, a number of common reactions can be expected. Girls with either anorexia or bulimia become highly invested in self-control and in controlling others. They become secretive and experience intense shame about their behavior. They may also experience secret feelings of superiority. The eating disorder may become their identity or provide the only meaning in their lives.

Biological Perspectives

Physicians and scientists faced with the intractability of serious eating disorders have speculated about the influence of biological factors on the development of the illness. In the seventeenth century, patients were given "aromatic bags" and "stomach plaisters" of mixed herbs and minerals, to little effect. Early in the twentieth century, eating disorders were attributed to a hormonal deficiency, and patients were treated with thyroid and pituitary extracts, again with little success. In the early 1970s, Gerald Russell explored the possibility that disorders of the hypothalamus led to eating disorders.

Contemporary medicine has made two kinds of contributions to the understanding of eating disorders. First, it has been increasingly understood that restricting the intake of food, by itself, creates many of the symptoms of eating disorders. In the landmark Minnesota study of the 1940s, healthy male volunteers who ate a below-subsistence diet began to exhibit cravings and preoccupation with food, bizarre eating habits and rituals, obsessive-compulsive symptoms, significant depression, and a distorted body image. When the experiment was over, their disordered eating continued, and many developed bulimia. Subsequent work on nutrition and weight led to the concept of "set point" and to an understanding of the physiologically based difficulty people have in maintaining a diet or a weight that is too low. Studies of gastric emptying have demonstrated that both anorexics and bulimics tend to keep food in their stomachs much longer than normal. This leads to a distorted perception of hunger and satiety that, in turn, contributes to patients' disturbed eating behavior.

Second, research has demonstrated that both anorexia and bulimia happen more often in girls who have obsessive-compulsive disorder, depression, and anxiety. This suggests that girls who have family histories or early childhood episodes of these problems, especially obsessive thoughts or compulsive rituals (for example, hand washing, counting, or checking rituals) are more likely to develop eating disorders if they become overly concerned about their weight or begin to diet or exercise too much.

Treatment Perspectives
In addition to medical treatments, behavioral interventions have been a mainstay of the treatment of eating disorders. Since treatment must focus on helping the anorexic eat more and helping the bulimic refrain from purging, older treatments have many features in common with contemporary ones. In the late 1800s, physicians spoke of the importance of separating an anorexic girl from her family and recommended that the "moral authority" of the doctor and carefully trained nurses or midwives be used to encourage the girl to eat a nutritious but bland diet. The girl was kept warm and calm and was encouraged not to be active. This was often very effective, but if the girl did not eat, forced feeding was threatened or used. A specialized form of this general treatment was developed in the late 1800s by Silas Weir Mitchell.

Today, in cases that have become life-threatening, girls as well as boys are hospitalized and treated in a group setting that resembles nineteenth-century treatment. Meal plans with increasing calorie levels have replaced the bland milk diet and are prescribed with the goal of helping the patient gain weight at a steady weekly rate. Nutritional supplements are used if the girl will not eat or drink food, and nasogastric tube feeding of these supplements may be necessary if all nutrition is refused. When a girl's health is severely compromised, surgically implanted tubes may allow the infusion of nutrients and fluids directly into the stomach or subclavian artery. Girls are carefully monitored to prevent purging or obsessive-compulsive rituals around eating. Overactivity and exercising are limited until girls reach a healthy weight.

The current epidemic of eating disorders has also led to the development of many forms of outpatient treatment. These treatments generally involve following a meal plan, recording what is eaten throughout the day, and engaging in planned, increasingly strenuous exercise. Cognitive-behavioral therapy helps girls recognize, question, and change destructive automatic thoughts about their bodies. Behavioral techniques aim at desensitizing girls and boys who have become very anxious about eating or at interrupting compulsive rituals. Education about the cultural pressure to be thin, the dangers of dieting, and the need for adequate nutrition can help girls see the illness more objectively. Once the eating behavior is stabilized, individual, group, or family psychotherapy may help patients explore the emotional factors that led to the development of the eating disorder. In addition to professional treatment, there has been a proliferation of support groups and self-help books and programs for women with eating disorders, and girls with this illness may also find these approaches helpful.

The treatment of eating disorders can be very difficult for girls, their families, and their health care providers. The strong emotions evoked by treatment can be painful, but they provide an opportunity to explore and resolve the vulnerabilities and conflicts that led to the development of the problem.

Sharon H. Nathan

See also Body Image; Consumer Culture; Cosmetics; Psychotherapy; Suicidal Behavior in Girls; Substance Abuse

References and Further Reading
Bruch, Hilde. 1978. *The Golden Cage: The Enigma of Anorexia Nervosa.* Cambridge: Harvard University Press.

Brumberg, Joan Jacobs. 1988. *Fasting Girls: The Emergence of Anorexia Nervosa as a Modern Disease.* Cambridge: Harvard University Press.

———. 1997. *The Body Project: An Intimate History of American Girls.* New York: Random House.

Gardner, David M., and Paul E. Garfinkel, eds. 1997. *Handbook of Treatment for Eating Disorders.* 2d ed. New York: Guilford Press.

Hornbacher, Marya. 1998. *Wasted: A Memoir of Anorexia and Bulimia.* New York: HarperCollins.

Levenkron, Steven. 1978. *The Best Little Girl in the World.* New York: Warner Books.

Minuchin, Salvador, Bernice L. Rosman, and Lester Baker. 1978. *Psychosomatic Families: Anorexia Nervosa in Context.* Cambridge: Harvard University Press.

Palazzoli, Mara Selvini. 1978. *Self-Starvation.* New York: Jason Aronson.

Pipher, Mary. 1994. *Reviving Ophelia: Saving the Selves of Adolescent Girls.* New York: Ballantine Books.

Wolf, Naomi. 1991. *The Beauty Myth.* New York: William Morrow.

Zerbe, Kathryn J. 1993. *The Body Betrayed: Women, Eating Disorders, and Treatment.* Washington, DC: American Psychiatric Press.

Education of Girls

Primary and secondary education for young women was initially limited to preparation for the roles of wife and mother; it is now seen as the primary means to social and economic advancement. In the mid-1600s, early settlers were responsible for educating their own children, and educational standards were modest. A girl received just enough instruction to fulfill her duties as wife and mother. For the next two centuries, most communities saw no point in educating women or in paying for their education because until the mid-1800s, most girls were destined to work inside the home. Private and religious groups were the first to see value in educating girls. Dame schools, initiated around 1650 in Massachusetts, offered girls from well-to-do white families education outside the home for the first time. In 1727 Catholic nuns in the Order of Saint Ursuline started the first school for girls in New Orleans. By 1750, a few girls were allowed tutoring in public schools but only while the boys were on summer recess, and the curriculum was limited to subjects that would improve girls for motherhood.

The period between 1787 and 1837 was a time of great educational expansion on behalf of young women. Founded during this time were the earliest private and public high schools, the first school established by a woman, schools for minority girls, and the first private school to subsidize education for poor girls. However, it was not until after the Civil War that girls attended public high schools in large numbers. By the late 1800s, a major shift had taken place across the curriculum. Young women began to go to school to prepare for work outside the home. The focus of their education shifted to new roles open to women in the community, commonly teaching, nursing, and secretarial work. Secondary classrooms were segregated by gender for certain classes. By 1900 many colleges began to accept women and by 1930 women undergraduates outnumbered men.

The 1960s and early 1970s saw positive changes for women. For African American girls in particular, the change in the high school environment was profound. Enforcement of desegregation rulings mandated racial integration in public schools for the first time. In 1972, propelled by civil rights legislation, many gender barriers in education and school sports were lifted. Since the beginning of the women's movement in the 1960s, more attention has been paid to girls' educational achievements, particularly in math and science. By 1990 social gender biases were drawn to teachers' attention, making the classroom more conducive to the way girls learn.

At the beginning of the twenty-first century, teachers are working more diligently to teach and encourage girls more fairly. Career opportunities for women are principally founded on academic achievement and are more diverse than ever. Economic advantage and social expectations still form part of educational opportunities for young women, but society no longer overlooks the importance of promoting the well-being of girls through education.

1600 to 1700: The Early Settlers

In the early years of the European settlement of the Americas, there was no public education system. The idea of a free public system of education for all children in every community was centuries away from full implementation. Families, rather than the state, bore the responsibility for educating children. Unfortunately, many of those who ventured to this country were illiterate and therefore incapable of passing reading skills to their children. The majority of children would not have had any opportunity for basic education during the very earliest days of immigration.

It was mandated in Massachusetts in 1642 that all children should be able to read, understand the law, and be prepared for work. Because of the centrality of religion in the lives of the Puritans, Presbyterians, and Anglicans, the Christian Bible was the book children learned to read. Parents were responsible for completing this task and bore the brunt of criticism if they did not fulfill this social and moral responsibility. The case of orphans raised an interesting issue because there was no parent to fulfill this social obligation. It is perhaps because of these orphans that the initial idea of gathering children together with a single guide, or tutor, emerged. By the mid-seventeenth century, "dame schools" brought together children whose mothers were occupied with work. Dame schools offered what Americans today might call the first day care centers. Both boys and girls memorized passages from the Bible. Some learned to read, along with learning domestic skills. Boys cut wood, carved, and helped with outside chores. Girls learned to cook and sew, help with the little children, and work inside the house. It is probable that the work these children contributed was payment for the teaching that took place.

Gradually, the education of children became a public issue rather than a family one. In villages of fifty families or more, town schools were required by law in Massachusetts. These were open only to boys who already knew their ABCs. Grammar schools were mandated in towns of 100 or more families and had as their stated goal the preparation of boys for studies at Harvard College. Early religious education meant Protestant education, principally under the Puritans or Anglicans. Gradually, other religions began to establish themselves in America, including Lutherans, Quakers, and Catholics. Religious instruction was still primarily learned within the family or in the church. Before long, churches established schools to provide religious and academic instruction.

The first to bring Catholic education to America were the Franciscan missionaries, who founded a school in St. Augustine, Florida, as early as 1606. The Jesuits, who were first established in the Americas in Canada, expanded into Maryland as early as 1634 and began to lay the foundation for Catholic secondary education. However, it would be 200 years before Catholic education was formally organized and widespread. These early schools educated boys only, as was their tradition in Europe.

1700 to 1800: Western Expansion
Early in the eighteenth century, the society of the day determined that boys needed different schooling from girls. Boys needed arithmetic, reading, and writing, the skills necessary for commerce. Buildings were constructed, male teachers prepared, and public education began in support of the formal schooling of boys. Girls, it was thought, needed to learn about household duties and rarely needed to go outside the home for additional training. Many believed that the educa-

tion boys received would be detrimental to females because it was overly rigorous and demanding of the mind. In addition, educating girls would waste the teacher's time.

However, dame schools were spreading west as girls from wealthier families gathered at the teacher's house and were instructed in the tasks of maintaining a home. The teacher, a woman accomplished in certain skills, would not have had any formal education herself. Subjects included reading, memorization, sewing, and ornamental needlework; some girls learned letter writing and etiquette.

Roman Catholic missionary priests were among the very first formal teachers in the new land. Catholic schools were started within parishes to serve the families of congregations. With the rapid western expansion of the United States, the church population quickly grew. Although priests initiated schools, soon Catholic sisters staffed them. The Ursuline nuns came to the United States in 1727 and began a school for young women in New Orleans. Over the next fifty years, the Ursulines, coming from Ireland and France, established academies of learning for young women in numerous southern and eastern cities.

Aware of the deficiencies of the training girls received in comparison to boys, some parents wanted more for their daughters. By the 1750s, a few girls were allowed into public school buildings but only while the boys were on summer recess. There are accounts of girls being smuggled into the boys' schools under disguise. Some families hired teachers to act as tutors for girls, meeting before and after the regular school hours of eight to four. This would mean additional money for teachers and a sacrifice for the girls. But for some, it offered the only chance to learn to read and write.

It was not until after the Revolutionary War that town schools across New England manifested a more liberal spirit toward the education of girls. The ideals of freedom and democracy led to the creation of the new nation and schools. After the war, children were expected to be educated to a higher standard so that they could more fully participate in the new society. This meant that the American mother needed to be educated at least to the standard that would prepare her male children for their duties as citizens, and her female children for marriage and motherhood. There was greater openness to the integration of girls into the public school classroom so that those young women could be better mothers and teachers of their children. It was expensive to build two schools, so typically boys and girls were educated together in primary school.

The second half of the eighteenth century ushered in very important developments in the private education of girls, the female academy and seminary. These institutions trained almost all girls who received formal education up to the Civil War. In 1787, the Young Ladies' Academy was founded in Philadelphia. Radical for its time and unaffiliated with any religion, this academy gave young girls the opportunity to be taught a curriculum almost identical to that for the best-educated boys. Founded by a group of men who believed that women were as intellectually capable as men, this school offered a completely new opportunity for the daughters of wealthy merchants. In 1778, a Quaker grammar school opened

to educate mothers so that they could educate their children properly. The Quakers had never restricted church leadership to males only. Their schools, like other parochial schools, were internally administered and were free of the restrictions of school committees and boards.

1800 to 1900: Immigrants and Industry

This century witnessed the greatest expansion of education for girls. The curriculum for males centered on the classics—Greek, Latin, math, history, science, and writing—but vocational training was often included. Schools were built at a rapid rate, and large numbers of boys attended, even if only for a short while. When they left school, often at a young age, it was because they were headed to work or, in the second half of the century, to war.

Early in the nineteenth century, many cities began to provide secondary educational institutions for white, middle-class girls, which were soon known as high schools. The goal of the curriculum in the early 1800s was to prepare women for motherhood. Later, girls were taught enough skills to enter the job market and often shared the classroom with boys. Around 1855, normal schools were established to train girls as teachers. By 1900, girls dramatically outnumbered boys in secondary schools as boys left to work. Girls were soon to follow, but with the expectation that, once married, middle-class women would remain at home. However, education still was not equally distributed across social and racial lines. Poor and immigrant girls received very little formal education, and even if an education was available, many left in order to earn money for their families. It was against the law to teach slave children to read from about 1830 until after the Civil War, but Angelina and Sarah Grimké are credited as having done so in defiance of these laws.

The 1800s were the age of the academy and the female seminary, which offered middle- and upper-class families an alternative to the public coeducational high school. Young women were taught Latin, French, mathematics, history, geography, and science, as well as manners and morality. Some seminaries offered music and drawing. Although not often owned by congregations, these educational institutions were typically supported by wealthy church members and religious benefactors. In 1821, Emma Willard established the Troy Female Seminary in New York, with a curriculum that initially focused on training for motherhood. Eventually, the school put more emphasis on education and teacher training. Many of the early women teachers in the United States got their start at the Troy Female Seminary. Oberlin College was the first to admit women, black and white, in 1833. The curriculum for women was simpler than the more difficult courses for men, but Oberlin was years ahead of its time by admitting women students from its founding. In 1837 Mary Lyon established Mount Holyoke Seminary, the first to allow poor girls to be educated alongside wealthy ones. Its goal was to prepare women for teaching and for missionary work. In Oklahoma in 1850, the Cherokee Female Seminary, modeled after Mount Holyoke, aimed to give Native American girls a chance to succeed in the predominantly white world by providing education at a high standard. In the 1850s in Washington, D.C., the first seminary was

opened for black women. The Miner Normal School for Colored Girls eventually became Miner Teachers College. Sophia Packard and Harriet Giles started Spelman Female Seminary in Atlanta, Georgia, in 1881. Like other seminaries, Spelman prepared many of the first black teachers in this country. Today this school is known as Spelman College and has a long tradition of educating black women.

These and other early seminaries not only allowed generations of women a chance to move outside the domestic sphere but established the influence of women in the field of education. Prior to this time, men were not only the teachers but also the administrators and textbook writers. Noted early contributors to women's education include Mary Lyon, Catharine Beecher, Prudence Crandall, Harriet Beecher Stowe, and Emma Willard. These women and many others revolutionized instruction by incorporating new teaching methods, writing new textbooks, and improving the learning environment.

Catholic schools for boys began to expand to postsecondary seminaries in the hopes that soon there would be a native clergy. In boy's schools, priests were the teachers. Nuns made up the majority of the primary school teachers and were the only teachers in secondary girls' schools, now frequently referred to as academies for young women. The number of sisters sent from Europe to teach expanded rapidly in the 1800s. Early teaching orders that expanded Catholic education across the Midwest included the Sisters of Loretto, Sisters of Charity, and the Sisters of St. Joseph.

Catholic sisters educated girls according to the expectations of the times. Early in the century, the girls' curriculum was not the same as the boys'. Boys in frontier schools were taught basic education, with a vocational emphasis on the trades and practical arts. Girls were educated for the private realm, emphasizing the skills needed to be a moral wife and mother. By the end of the nineteenth century, the school curriculum had given way to academic and practical studies. Many girls were prepared for secretarial jobs and teaching, and a few went on to college.

1900 to 2000: Suffrage, Wars,
and the Women's Movement
In 1900 large numbers of women were beginning to enjoy access to public education, although it had numerous critics. Some questioned the effect that strenuous thinking had on women's fertility, whereas others disliked the shift to vocational preparation with less emphasis on preparation for motherhood. Two world wars and women's suffrage radically changed the roles of women in American society in the first half of this century.

The public high school was becoming common, and many students attended for at least a year or two. The curriculum was a combination of the classics and job preparation as education for young women in public schools became more standardized. At the beginning of this century, many girls received more years of education than boys because boys were leaving high school to learn a trade or enroll in business school. Commercial and trade schools prepared boys for work, and some began to enroll girls. Subjects included bookkeeping, typing, and shorthand. Some critics suggested that women would take jobs from men.

Enrollment of female students in colleges soared after the Nineteenth Amendment, giving women the constitutional right to vote nationwide, was passed. In 1920, nearly half the U.S. undergraduate population was female. Not for another fifty years would women represent such a large percentage of the college population.

Reflective of the values of society, as education continues to be, girls were not educated in the same manner as boys. After World War II, most high school courses were open to boys and girls, but part of the curriculum remained gender-specific. The boys went to shop to learn woodworking and lamp making, whereas girls went to home economics classes and learned to cook and sew.

During the 1960s, the civil rights movement drastically changed the position minorities and women held in many fields, not the least of which was academia. Desegregation laws granted access to schools, jobs, and positions of leadership for black and minority students. At the same time, the women's movement further expanded the opportunities for women. Education served as a springboard for those who wanted to escape traditional gender roles. In 1972 Title IX of the Education Amendments was passed, which penalized any educational institution receiving federal funds that discriminated based on gender. No longer could admissions, scholarships, equipment, and other resources be allocated unfairly in favor of men. However, getting these ideals into reality in every single classroom was quite another matter from passing laws. Just as in the case of racial discrimination, the school environment has never become free of inequalities.

Another shift that has taken place in public education since 1970 is the role of schools in the lives of students. No longer are they just about the classics and career

A thirteen-year-old student practices her writing skills. (Skjold Photographs)

training. Schools fulfill broader social functions. As more parents work outside the home, the role of the school has expanded to include feeding children breakfast and offering day care, life skills training, and lessons in conflict resolution. Meanwhile, criticism has been levied against the standard of education in public schools. School grounds are no longer free from the social environment of violence (e.g., sexual harassment and school shootings). Many parents have demanded greater accountability in public schools and more involvement on school boards. Some parents have chosen to send their children to private religious and secular schools or to home school them.

Many parents prefer single-sex schools for their daughters, believing these institutions to be superior at educating and acculturating girls to assume fulfilling careers. Private and parochial schools continue to offer an alternative to public education.

Educating students is costly, and no school is free from the concerns of budgeting. In the 1990s some cities have begun to implement a voucher system to allow parents to choose a private education for their children without additional cost. Technological advances in the workplace demand more expensive equipment in the classroom. More and more service economy jobs require a college education, but college placement and job placement have become more competitive.

It is almost impossible to predict what direction the education of girls will take in the twenty-first century. Current debates include the issue of single-sex classrooms and the different learning styles for girls. Recent studies have isolated problems for girls in today's classroom: teacher gender bias, low achievement in science and math, and the decline in girls' self-esteem during adolescence. However these issues turn out, education will continue to be an important part of the lives of girls in American society. At the same time, society will continue its work of determining the best way to educate young women and enabling them to succeed in the world of our times.

Anita Reznicek

See also Advice Books; African American Girls in the Twentieth Century; Asian American Girls; Chicana Girls; Child Guidance; College Girls; Home Economics Education; Hygiene; Jewish Education of Girls; Latina Girls; Literacy; Mathematics and Science; Native American Girls; Reading

References and Further Reading
Berkin, Carol Ruth, and Mary Beth Norton. 1979. *Women of America: A History.* Boston: Houghton Mifflin.
Bernikow, Louise. 1997. *The American Women's Almanac.* New York: Berkley Books.
Bryk, Anthony S., Valerie E. Lee, and Peter B. Holland. 1993. *Catholic Schools and the Common Good.* Cambridge, MA: Harvard University Press.
Goebel, Edmund J., Rev. 1937. *A Study of Catholic Secondary Education during the Colonial Period up to the First Plenary Council of Baltimore, 1852.* New York: Benziger Brothers Press.
Goodsell, Willystine. 1923. *The Education of Women: Its Social Background and Its Problems.* New York: Macmillan.
McNally, William P., Rev. 1942. "The Secondary School." Pp. 118–140 in *Essays on Catholic Education in the United States.* Edited by Roy J.
Deferrari. Washington, DC: Catholic University of America Press.
Riordan, Cornelius. 1990. *Girls and Boys in School: Together or Separate?* New York: Teachers College Press.
Sadker, Myra and David. 1994. *Failing at Fairness: How America's Schools Cheat Girls.* New York: Charles Scribner's Sons.
Shmurak, Carol B. 1998. *Voices of Hope: Adolescent Girls at Single Sex and Coeducational Schools.* New York: Peter Lan Publishing.
Tyack, David, and Elisabeth Hansot. 1990. *Learning Together: A History of Coeducation in American Public Schools.* New Haven: Yale University Press.
Woody, Thomas. 1929. *A History of Women's Education in the United States.* New York: Science Press.

Emotions
Emotional expectations and ensuing emotional training have formed vital aspects of American girlhood from the early nineteenth century onward. Growing concern over gender differentiation, a staple of nineteenth-century middle-class life, seized on emotional criteria as a crucial divide, though prescriptive writers were also eager to make sure that emotions could help prepare girls for connections with men in marriage. From this vivid tradition, twentieth-century standards setters worked to effect reforms that would reduce, without eliminating, specifically girlish emotions. Girls and emotions thus form a dynamic pairing in American history, and key definitions evolved at a number of specific points.

Historians have only recently begun to devote explicit attention to the history of emotions, and there are many facets still to be probed. Best known are the prescriptions urged on the most articulate segments of society. These are important: they help set standards for judging appropriate behavior in oneself and others, and they guide laws and social institutions such as schools. Less is certain about how standards relate to actual experience—a crucial question for girls, often held to demanding rules of emotions management that they may not have fully internalized. And various subcultures undoubtedly articulated different standards for girls because of different expectations of what roles girls should be prepared for.

Colonial American society did not offer detailed emotional rules for girls. Conduct literature, insofar as it applied to women, focused mainly on adults, particularly in marriage. It was doubtless assumed that girls would be urged toward deference and humility joined with piety. This expectation was particularly true for girls in domestic service, including slaves, but again the assumptions ran sufficiently deep, associated with widely accepted age and gender hierarchies, that elaborate concern seemed unnecessary. Certain gender distinctions were assumed. A hierarchical emotion like anger might be permitted to boys in dealing with inferiors but not normally to girls. Girls might more legitimately display emotional turmoil through sadness or even jealousy (though a jealous defense of honor was a male prerogative).

Certain changes in a religiously guided emotional regime began to appear in the early eighteenth century, but they did not explicitly apply to females. Men began to be urged, as part of an increasingly commercial society, to develop new forms of emotional control. Cheerfulness was one of the injunctions now recommended to help men get along with others and animate successful self-presentation. The same changes were not applied directly to girls and women, who had less of a public role and less contact with strangers.

By the 1760s, however, more elaborate redefinitions began to develop as part of the formation of a new middle class no longer confined to traditional patterns of hierarchy and deference. Manners books urged a new level of emotional and bodily control on both genders as part of polite respectability. A genteel person did not let emotions contort the face or lead to unseemly body movements (it was for this reason that etiquette writers argued against the desirability of laughter). Men, increasingly schooled for a competitive world in which any emotional display might suggest vulnerability, were particularly held to a display of calm. But women, in part because they too faced new challenges as arranged courtships and marriages declined in favor of greater public contact and competition, had similar obligations. Anger was bad for them too, though the justifications varied. According to James Forrester, girls should be taught that anger was "a prodigious enemy to beauty": "it ruffles the sweetest features, discolours the finest complexion, and, in a word, gives the air of a fury to the face of an angel.... I never knew an angry woman preserve her beauty long" (Forrester 1848, 106). The new emphasis on emotional obligations associated with appearance formed part of the larger reevaluation of women as particularly responsible for beauty.

Only in a newly explicit emphasis on the need for modesty were respectable girls held to gender-specific standards in the late eighteenth century. Girls must be taught to be delicate and to maintain a modest countenance. The goal was to please men but also, in an increasingly open society, to discourage unwanted male advances. Manners writers strongly recommended that girls blush as a sign of emotional delicacy while keeping careful control over their eyes. Thus when a girl talks with men, "she must look a little downwards, or on one side, not stare in their faces, lest it be interpreted in the worst sense" (Arthur 1848, 22).

The belief in overall similarities in emotional goals for both genders extended into childrearing advice through the first decades of the nineteenth century. Childish innocence rather than distinctions between girls and boys gained primary attention. Children should not be upset by the use of fear in discipline—a new prompting to parents that would be often repeated in decades to come. If they were not exposed to anger, in turn they would learn to avoid anger themselves. Although advice literature increasingly emphasized the primary role of mothers in bringing up children, the standards applied to children themselves remained roughly the same for girls and boys.

This pattern shifted by the 1840s. An increasingly urban and industrial society seemed to require more differentiated roles for men and women—men in public, work-oriented settings and women at home now shorn of most productive functions. Emotional preparation of children varied accordingly. Boys who seemed emotionally effeminate could now be given a new label, "sissy," whereas girls who displayed boys' rough-and-tumble emotions were (slightly less critically) called "tomboys."

Overall, girls were allowed to be more emotionally open than boys. In fearful situations, it was assumed that girls would and should display fright and tears as part of appropriate female modesty and frailty, whereas boys should summon up a dominant courage. Indeed, girls learned that displaying a bit more fear than they felt was a good way to seem feminine. Jealousy, though disapproved, was another outlet. The emotion was labeled female, a sign of a possessive love by the weaker gender. And girls were definitely expected to learn grief, now expressed in abundance on the occasion of loss, with women leading the way. By the 1870s, families could acquire mourning clothes, coffins, and other appurtenances for girls' dolls to help in this aspect of emotional training.

And of course girls were urged to be loving toward parents, friends, and siblings. Love was an emotion both genders should ultimately share, but it was the quintessential female emotional responsibility. And maternal love, for which girls should be prepared, was outside the male repertoire altogether.

Only in anger was female emotionality to be clearly constrained, for here boys had outlets that girls lacked. Anger was unfeminine, and a good girl neither felt nor expressed it. Older ideas about female delicacy shone through clearly, whereas a boy who felt no anger might be a "sissy."

These distinctive emotional standards were endlessly preached to girls (and boys). They showed up in literature directed at parents. They informed stories about good and bad girls. Louisa May Alcott's *Little Women*, for example, vigorously approved of girlish efforts to keep anger in check, and stories of boundless female love and grief were even more common. They underwrote distinctive children's toys, as was mentioned earlier.

And they mattered. Girls wrote enthusiastic letters about their love and their hopes for love. They used their rights to jealousy, even against each other. Thus a jealous sister wrote to her mother: "I suppose Papa told you of how jealous I was when I heard you are going to allow Emily to go to the Phi Psi musical for it did not seem at all like you to let a child like her go to any such things. . . . I am very jealous of Emily for I think she has more than her share of gaiety when I am away" (Stearns 1985). And they dutifully recorded struggles against anger or a bad temper. It is impossible of course to say how many girls thought they lived up to the emotional standards that were supposed to define their sex. The experience of girls in the lower classes or the countryside is particularly elusive, though ongoing work in emotional history will push back some of the current limitations on our understanding. There is no question, though, of a well-defined set of values for girls' emotions by which good girls were praised and bad condemned. Use of angry curses by female convicts thus seemed far more shocking than similar language by male prisoners and at the same time confirmed the justice of labeling these girls and young women deviant. Emotional rules conjoined with sexual standards lay at the center of gender differentiation in the last two-thirds of the nineteenth century.

Then the signals changed again, particularly by the 1920s. Childrearing literature began to reduce gender distinctions in emotions in favor of common problems and common goals. The evolution was not always clear-cut, and the impact certainly had to do battle against older standards, but the movement was definite.

Jealousy is one example. Prescriptive writers greatly intensified the attack on this emotion, considered to be both childish and dangerous. Jealousy was bad for children, who might do harm to siblings in the grip of newly defined sibling rivalries, and bad for prospective adulthood, for children who failed to control jealousy would not have satisfactory relationships as adults. These messages were identical for girls and boys. But 1920s researchers long contended that girls were far more likely to suffer from sibling rivalry than boys, and the female pronoun long predominated in popular commentary on the subject. By the end of the twentieth century most of this research had been discounted because intense sibling jealousy was both less common and less gender-specific than the transitional researchers allowed (Stearns 1985).

Fear and anger suddenly seemed less gendered. Boys were often irrationally afraid, just as girls might be, and fear was dangerous to children in general. Girls should not be encouraged to be artificially skittish, and they might demonstrate courage on occasion. The rules for managing what was seen as a harmful but common emotional issue merged. Boys were no longer given greater leeway for anger, and at the same time the idea that girls were magically anger-free was abandoned as well. Anger was not good, and children of both sexes should be encouraged to identify it and overcome it, but an occasional mild outburst from a girl did not warrant emotional policing.

The merger of gender standards for children resulted from several trends. Increasingly, emotional advice was based on scientific inquiry, which often overturned nineteenth-century beliefs. Role differentiation between middle-class men and women was narrowing, even before the great movement of adult women into the labor force. The prestige associated with motherhood declined, in part because of a steadily falling birth rate; correspondingly, the emotions associated with motherhood, in which girls should be schooled, were downplayed. "Smotherhood," indeed, was a derisive term applied to a dangerous level of maternal affection. Coeducation brought boys and girls together in new ways, and so did a common pattern of work, at least for a few years. Here were additional reasons to seek girlhoods less fully defined by the emotional emphases of the previous century.

But past standards were not easily set aside, and some argued that key differentiations also reflected some differences in standard emotional makeup. Girls continued to be more constrained in anger than boys were. A girl's anger less fully predicted adult personality than did a boy's, which meant that angry males showed their colors earlier. Girls concealed anger lest they seem unfeminine. They were also much more likely to cry when angry than boys were, and this difference extended into adulthood.

Crying, indeed, posed something of a dilemma for twentieth-century emotional participants. Insofar as girls were to think of themselves as emotional equals of boys, ready to join in similar activities and ultimately work, crying seemed distracting, a sign of weakness. But girls did cry more, and at points feminists would argue for the good health of this emotional release and say that boys should be encouraged to cry too, lest they bottle up dangerous frustrations. Late in the twentieth century, as rates of depression among women increased or were more widely reported, concern about sadness in girls gained new attention as well.

Love presented another dilemma. Growing concern about emotional intensity targeted love along with other nineteenth-century staples. Too much love could be risky. The idea of love was increasingly associated with sex more than with intense emotion (the evolution of the word lover indicated this clearly). Even granting great individual variation in each gender, girls reacted to this change of standards less completely than boys did. Girls' culture continued to be filled with stories of love supplemented by Hollywood films. By adolescence, girls frequently wrote of their tension between a quest for intense love with the perfect man and a desire to be modern and nonchalant. It was a difficult negotiation that often led to tensions later, when girls evaluated marriage proposals. Girls also faced tensions concerning friendship. The flowery terms linked to nineteenth-century friendship gradually declined in favor of less vigorous expressions. Concern about homosexuality—reported by many college women by the 1920s—helped qualify female friendship, though young men were more affected. A recent study suggests that, by the 1920s, young women's friendships were indeed loosening, in part because of concern about emotional intensity and in part because social patterns increasingly pointed young women to dating and other activities with men (Rosenzweig 1998).

Changes in girls' recommended emotional standards were real and led to some definable shifts in emotional expressions and experiences. But they did not merge girls and boys, on average, into a common emotional style. Girls as well as observers, including later twentieth-century feminists, debated this result.

A thirteen-year-old African American girl being comforted by a friend. (Skjold Photographs)

The tension between being more similar to boys and displaying a feminine range related to nineteenth-century emphases could be very real. But having these two choices also provided a certain leeway to find a personally appropriate mixture.

As in the nineteenth century, middle-class standards did not touch all girls. In the 1950s, for example, African American leaders began to highlight a more assertive emotional style, which affected boys particularly but girls as well. Even earlier, many African American churches had encouraged girls to display an expressive religious emotionality different from the white, middle-class mainstream. Immigrant groups often struggled between emotional values imported from traditional cultures and the complex values urged in American media and in prescriptive literature. Again, diverse mixtures resulted.

Most groups of girls did participate in a final emotional pattern in the twentieth century: the interplay between emotional spectatorship and their own emotional rules and experience. From infancy onward, American children were increasingly encouraged to attach emotional meaning to purchased goods and experiences. Cribs were filled with stuffed animals. Experts early in the twentieth century briefly debated this pattern, but the consensus was that attachments were emotionally healthy and would aid later control in interpersonal relationships. Movies and, soon, television provided an unprecedented array of represented emotions. The combination of growing consumerism and considerable concern about uncontrolled emotions in real life led to increasing involvement in emotional fantasy worlds. For very young children, these worlds were not particularly gender differentiated, but by school age they were—often, ironically, replicating nineteenth-century distinctions such as military emotions for boys and domestic affections for girls. This gap was subject to intense debate in the later twentieth century, but it was not substantially reduced. Girls poured emotion into different symbols from those that drew boys, even though a basic commitment to surrogates was common to both genders.

Peter N. Stearns

See also Communication; Female Sexuality; Suicidal Behavior in Girls

References and Further Reading
Arthur, T. S. 1848. *Advice to Young Ladies.* Boston: Putnam.

Brumberg, Joan Jacobs. 1988. *Fasting Girls: The Emergence of Anorexia Nervosa as a Modern Disease.* Cambridge, MA: Harvard University Press.

———. 1997. *The Body Project: An Intimate History of American Girls.* New York: Random House.

Cross, Gary. 1997. *Kids' Stuff: Toys and the Changing World of American Childhood.* Cambridge, MA: Harvard University Press.

Forrester, James. 1848. *Practical Morality.* Hartfort, CT: Andrews.

Hemphill, C. Dallett. 1998. "Class, Gender, and the Regulation of Emotional Expression in Revolutionary-Era Conduct Literature." Pp. 33–51 in *Emotional History of the United States.* Edited by Peter N. Stearns and Jan Lewis. New York: New York University Press.

Hiner, N. Ray, and Joseph M. Hawes, eds. 1985a. *Growing Up in America: Children in Historical Perspective.* Urbana: University of Illinois Press.

———. 1985b. *American Childhood: A Research Guide and Historical Handbook.* Westport, CT: Greenwood Press.

MacLeod, David I. 1998. *The Age of the Child: Children in America 1890–1920.* New York: Twayne.

Rosenzweig, Linda W. 1993. *The Anchor of My Life: Middle-Class American Mothers and Daughters, 1880–1920.* New York: New York University Press.

———. 1998. "'Another Self?': Middle-Class American Women and Their Friends, 1900–1960." Pp. 357–373 in *Emotional History of the United States.* Edited by Peter N. Stearns and Jan Lewis. New York: New York University Press.

Stearns, Peter N. 1985. *Jealousy: The Evolution of an Emotion in American History.* New York: New York University Press.

———. 1993. "Girls, Boys and Emotions: Redefinitions and Historical Change." *Journal of American History* 80 (June): 66–89.

———. 1994. *American Cool: Constructing a Twentieth-Century Emotional Style.* New York: New York University Press.

Zelizer, Viviana A. 1985. *Pricing the Priceless Child.* New York: Basic Books.

Enslaved Girls of African Descent

Enslaved girls in the United States belonged to a category with an extraordinarily high infant disease and mortality rate, yet the growth from 20 Africans (3 women and 17 men) in 1619 to nearly 4 million African Americans in 1860 is the most distinctive feature of bondage in North America. The fact that they survived and procreated makes a study of enslaved girls important, since natural increases were primarily responsible for the growth of slavery after 1808, when the United States banned the competitive, brisk business of importing slaves directly from Africa (U.S. Bureau of the Census 1975, 18).

European traders channeled more than 10 million Africans who had been convicted of crimes or were prisoners of war or victims of kidnappings through the Atlantic's middle passage to the new world. Fewer females than males made the journey, and there is no satisfactory explanation for this occurrence. One argument claims that females were less desirable for heavy plantation labor in the Atlantic world. Another theory suggests price differentials along with supply and demand as the determining factors in creating disparities. Finally, historians posit that Africans limited the number of females they offered for sale because of their own interests in the girls and women, who were highly prized as agricultural workers.

A narrative written by the African-born Olaudah Equiano describes the 1756 raid upon his village, when he and his young sister were captured by a woman and two men. The raiders eventually separated the eleven-year-old boy from his sister and sold him into the new world. "Your image," he wrote as he remembered her, "has been always riveted in my heart, from with [sic] neither time nor fortune have been able to remove it; so that, while the thought[s] of your sufferings have damped my prosperity, they have mingled with adversity and increased its bitterness" (Equiano 1995, 51).

Without a comparable narrative by the Equiano girl, her response to the shock of capture, travel overland through the interior of Africa, sale to a slave owner, or detachment from loved ones remains unknown. Neither will anyone know whether she was enslaved in Africa or was sold into the Americas. But it is reasonable to think that the girl whom Equiano described as his dear partner in all childish sports and his companion in joys and sorrows also experienced the traumatic disengagement he chronicled.

What happened to girls remaining in Africa was as important as what lay ahead for those taken away. Upon arrival at the seacoast, Africans remained imprisoned while awaiting the final processing before sailing through the Atlantic's Middle Passage. Without regard for age or modesty, traders examined and separated the able-bodied from those who were less able before branding and loading them on oceangoing vessels.

Trembling and terrified when taken aboard, they were vulnerable to the wanton rudeness of crew members, who silently divided their prey and waited for an opportunity to abuse them sexually. In some instances girls remained in a squatting position throughout the day to hide their nakedness. If offered canvas to cover their persons, they accepted it willingly. But it was no protection against the frequent exploitation that followed during voyages lasting thirty to thirty-five days or longer.

Unfettered females traveled on the quarterdeck, while males were chained

in the ship's hold. Descriptions of the Middle Passage mention crowded hulls, limited supplies of food, stifling odors, filthy living conditions, and contagious diseases. Furthermore, an eyewitness wrote, "The shrieks of the women, and the groans of the dying rendered the whole a scene of horror almost inconceivable" (Equiano 1995, 56).

Protests from slaves aboard ships of horrors sometimes escalated into mutinies. Crews anticipated revolts, since they did not expect slaves to accept their situation calmly. Teme, Kague, and Margru, girls ranging from seven to twelve years of age, survived a mutiny aboard the *Amistad* in 1839. The uprising and death of crew members must have frightened the children. Margru explained that one of her fellow prisoners, whom she later called Charlotte, comforted her and said repeatedly, "One day we shall [again] all see our native land" (Sarah Margru to George Whipple, September 18, 1847, American Missionary Association, Tulane University, Louisiana). Following an 1841 U.S. Supreme Court decision, the girls and other *Amistad* survivors did return to Africa.

By contrast, the majority of African girls neither witnessed a mutiny nor went back to their homelands. Instead, they and their progeny remained on plantations or in public establishments and private homes in the new world. In 1662, the Virginia Assembly declared that children born in the colony were bound or free according to the mother's status. This legislation, which other colonies imitated and which resulted from concern over the legal condition of children born to black and white couples, was contrary to English common law but in keeping with British ideas about property rights. Enslaved mothers reproduced

Selling Females: Negro Slaves by the Pound. *Woodcut in Bourne,* Pictures of Slavery, *1834.*
(Library of Congress)

chattel who belonged to their owners rather than to themselves. In this context, it is understandable that the slave-born Harriet Jacobs concluded that slavery was terrible for men but worse for women in terms of the exploitation of their reproductive rights and the relegation of their offspring to bondage in perpetuity. When told that her newborn infant was a girl, the nineteen-year-old Jacobs said her heart was heavier than ever (Jacobs 1987).

If Jacobs's daughter and other enslaved children survived more than a few days, they received names linking them firmly to their kin network, as in the African tradition. Girls received a grandmother's name more frequently than their own mother's name. Parents also gave their daughters the names of respected "aunts" and "cousins" among their "fictive" kin within the larger slave community.

As mothers returned to work, ordinarily a month after giving birth, they either carried their infants along or left them in the care of slaves who were too old or too young to work elsewhere. Since there were no gender distinctions associated with the earliest tasks performed by enslaved children, girls and boys cared for children younger than themselves. They also fed chickens, gathered eggs, milked cows, churned butter, gathered wood, carried water, and ran errands.

When old enough to follow along and make some contributions to the larger workforce, girls joined pregnant women and "fractional" hands, persons designated as "one-quarter" or "one-half" hands because of their inability to complete full responsibilities, in "trash gangs." These predominantly female labor units provided teaching-learning experiences for girls, who were taught to perform chores satisfactorily along with the value of cooperative labor in a hostile environment. Furthermore, participation in the trash gang raised their consciousness about gender-related concerns, such as family obligations.

Slave owners initially used youngsters to complement less productive workers, but as they both grew older, the girls became experienced substitutes for aging adults and ultimately replaced them. According to Works Progress Administration testimony collected in the 1930s from former slaves, many of whom were children when slavery ended, few gender distinctions existed in the workplace. One interviewee said she split rails "like a man," and another claimed her mother plowed with three horses. "Ain't dat somp'n," she asked rhetorically before adding, "thought women was 'sposed to work 'long wid men, I did" (Perdue, Barden, and Phillips 1980, 292). Many enslaved girls and women did work alongside boys and men. They shared a mean sort of equality: all of them were exploited.

The greatest gender distinctions and absence of labor exploitation existed in the skilled crafts, a male preserve. Girls could have learned these techniques, but they did not have the opportunity. Childbearing prevented access to trades, since the crafts of artisans, unlike domestic or agricultural chores, could not be completed by substitute workers. Skilled females specialized in domestic and housewifery chores, which could be combined with child care responsibilities. Without the skills of artisans, girls had fewer opportunities for selling their own time, living away from owners, and earning extra money to buy necessities, luxury items, or freedom.

Regardless of the jobs performed, entry into the workplace meant additional food for the newest worker's family, but it truncated childhood by increasing responsibilities and making the girl vulnerable to arbitrary punishment, sexual abuse, and sale. Resistance to these facets of bondage were evident among parents who did whatever was possible to delay their children's entry into the workforce. When their efforts failed, youngsters protested by working slowly, haphazardly, or running away. Although fewer girls than boys appeared in runaway advertisements, this does not mean girls had no hopes for and dreams of freedom or were more willing to endure bondage. Females traveling alone attracted more attention than males and were probably caught and returned to owners before advertisements appeared in newspapers.

Until freed from bondage, girls learned lessons necessary for surviving slavery, including how to wear the "mask." This expression camouflaged slaves' true feelings and allowed them to pay deference to whites while maintaining self-respect. At early ages, girls also learned when to speak, what to say, and to whom it could be said. Other survival tactics came from folklore, which was designed to entertain and educate. Animal trickster tales, an integral part of the slave's oral tradition, taught lessons of survival and self-confidence. The objective was not to become tricksters but to avoid victimization by them.

During their leisure time, some enslaved girls learned to read and write, but the general bias against female literacy and the paucity of opportunities ensured that fewer girls than boys became literate. At other times, girls played with dolls fashioned from corn-

Women Whip Girls, *a nineteenth-century woodcut, shows white women's complicity in the institution of slavery. (Library of Congress, 1800s)*

cobs; jumped rope; joined in ring games; or pretended to cook meals, serve food, and wash dishes. They also engaged in unorganized play and spent time rambling through the woods and swimming in streams or gathering nuts and berries.

As girls matured and became attracted to the opposite sex, there were occasions to woo and be wooed after church services, during seasonal celebrations, or at dances. Girls sometimes made themselves more beautiful for the occasions by using blushers made from dried chinaberries and soot for eye shadow. They wore hoops

African American slaves dancing and playing the banjo, 1800s. (Library of Congress)

made from grapevines under their dresses and tied ribbons on their intricately braided hair. Honeysuckle and rose petals provided sweet fragrances for their bodies.

Some parents insisted upon deciding when their daughters could entertain members of the opposite sex. In all probability, they wanted to prevent their daughters from becoming sexually active and giving birth to children destined for a lifetime of bondage. This facet of girls' lives represented contested terrain in that slave owners often encouraged them to find partners and start families. Children were of little financial worth at birth but became more valuable as they matured into productive workers.

When youthful flirtations led to desires for a lifetime together, slaves occasionally married in religious ceremonies or simply "took up" with a partner. In either case, neither churches nor courts sanctioned their unions. Many couples enjoyed long-lasting relationships, but an estimated 10 percent of them united with persons selected by owners whose primary interests were in the procreation of slaves.

North American slaves, unlike those elsewhere in the new world, reproduced naturally under adverse conditions and contributed to a dramatic increase in the population. Greater parity in the ratio of enslaved women to men in the nineteenth century, along with slaveholders' dedication to providing minimal material and medical help, explains this occurrence. These factors were important, but much credit also goes to enslaved girls who matured, became mothers, and assumed the roles that their own mothers had played in teaching their offspring to work satisfactorily, endure bondage, and maintain the hope of freedom.

Wilma King

See also African American Girls in the Twentieth Century; Free Girls of African Descent; Play; Work

References and Further Reading
Curtin, Philip D. 1970. *The Atlantic Slave Trade: A Census.* Madison: University of Wisconsin Press.

Equiano, Olaudah. 1995. *The Interesting Narrative of the Life of Olaudah Equiano: Written by Himself.* Edited by Robert J. Allison. Boston: Bedford Books of St. Martin's Press.

Jacobs, Harriet. 1861. *Incidents in the Life of a Slave Girl: Written by Herself.* Edited by Jean Fagin Yellin. 1987. Cambridge: Harvard University Press.

King, Wilma. 1995. *Stolen Childhood: Slave Youth in Nineteenth-Century America.* Bloomington: Indiana University Press.

———. 1997. "Within the Professional Household: Slave Children in the Antebellum South." *The Historian* 59: 523–540.

Kiple, Kenneth L., and Virginia H. Kiple. 1977. "Slave Child Mortality: Some Nutritional Answers to a Perennial Puzzle." *Journal of Social History* 10: 284–309.

Klein, Herbert S. 1983. "African Women in the Atlantic Slave Trade." Pp. 29–38 in *Women and Slavery in Africa.* Edited by Claire Robinson and Martin C. Klein. Madison: University of Wisconsin Press.

Parish, Peter J. 1989. *Slavery: History and Historians.* New York: Harper and Row.

Perdue, Charles L., Jr., Thomas E. Barden, and Robert K. Phillips. 1980. *Weevils in the Wheat: Interviews with Virginia Ex-Slaves.* Bloomington: Indiana University Press.

Rawick, George P., ed. 1972. *The American Slave: A Composite Autobiography.* 19 vols. Westport, CT: Greenwood Press.

Schafer, Judith Kelleher. 1981. "New Orleans Slavery in 1850 as Seen in Advertisements." *Journal of Southern History* 47: 33–56.

Schwartz, Marie Jenkins. 1996. "One Thing, Then Another: The Work of Slave Children in Alabama." *Labor's Heritage* 7: 22–33, 56–61.

U.S. Bureau of the Census. 1975. *Historical Statistics of the United States, Colonial Times to 1970.* Washington, DC: Government Printing Office.

Wiggins, David K. 1980. "The Play of Slave Children in the Plantation Communities of the Old South, 1820–1960." *Journal of Sport History* 7: 21–39.

F

Fairy Tales

*One afternoon a big wolf waited in a
dark forest for a little girl to come along
carrying a basket of food to her grandmother. Finally, a little girl did come
along and she was carrying a basket of
food. "Are you carrying that basket to
your grandmother?" asked the wolf. The
little girl said yes, she was. So the wolf
asked her where her grandmother lived
and the little girl told him and he disappeared into the wood.*

*When the little girl opened the door
of her grandmother's house she saw that
there was somebody in bed with a
nightcap on. She had approached no
nearer than twenty-five feet from the
bed when she saw that it was not her
grandmother but the wolf, for even in a
nightcap a wolf does not look any more
like your grandmother than the Metro-
Goldwyn lion looks like Calvin
Coolidge. So the little girl took an automatic out of her basket and shot the
wolf dead.*

*Moral: It is not so easy to fool little
girls nowadays as it used to be.*

—James Thurber

What is surprising about this version of
"Little Red Riding Hood," written by
James Thurber in 1939? What makes us
laugh? Perhaps most noticeable is the fact
that Little Red Riding Hood, referred to
only as the "little girl," is not a passive
victim here. Her use of the gun is unex-
pected and too contemporary for our sense
of fairy tales as being set in a misty past.
And her lack of gullibility undercuts the
fantasy. The moral tells us that this is a
thoroughly modern "little girl."

Once upon a time, there was no concept of childhood and hence no literature
produced especially for children. Fairy
tales, which people think of as the quintessential children's literature, were oral
tales, told by adults to adults; the violence
and sexuality so predominant in the original tales would thus not have been objectionable, given the audience. Fairy tales
were not recorded in written form until
the late 1600s, when their popularity in
the French court led to the publication by
Charles Perrault of *Histoires ou contes du
temps passé* (1697), a collection that
includes such familiar tales as "Sleeping
Beauty," "Puss in Boots," "Cinderella,"
and "Little Red Riding Hood." In 1729,
this collection was translated into English
and published in Great Britain, yet it
would be more than a century before fairy
tales entered the canon of acceptable literature for children.

It was, of course, the Brothers Grimm
who helped achieve this acceptance.
Their collection *Household Tales* (volume 1 in 1812 and volume 2 in 1814) has
sold more copies than any other book

except the Bible. Jacob and Wilhelm Grimm set out to collect as many tales as possible from oral sources in a nationalistic effort to identify Teutonic origins of the tales. Scholars now believe that they also took tales from written sources, including Perrault, and it is evident that they revised the tales, softening harsh endings and excluding references to sex and violence.

Controversy about the appropriateness of fairy tales for child audiences existed almost from the outset of their telling; parents saw the tales as potentially harmful to their children, whom they wished to raise in a religious tradition, shunning the superstitions of the peasant class. And, of course, the cultural script for girls in these early fairy tales was, for the most part, a negative one. As Ruth Bottigheimer has noted, girls and women were depicted as passive and as silenced. The value of beauty is emphasized in many tales; girls and women are often victimized or trapped, and the rescuer is usually a man who sometimes performs the rescue only in return for sex. Alternatively, women are depicted as evil stepmothers, viciously jealous, or wicked witches.

In the United States, where the tradition of children's literature began with stern Puritan warnings about evil, fantasy and fairy tales were considered suspect. Literature for children in the eighteenth and early nineteenth centuries was intended for instructional purposes only. Not until the late nineteenth century did collections of fairy tales become widely available in the United States as part of the revival of interest in the imagination that characterized the era often called "the golden age of children's literature." As these collections were based on the continental and British collections

of tales, they continued to carry the stereotypes of women and girls already noted.

The United States' own effort at producing an indigenous fairy tale is epitomized by L. Frank Baum's *The Wonderful Wizard of Oz* (1900), which gained enormous popularity almost immediately and spawned a number of sequels. In the introduction, Baum stated his intention to produce a "modernized fairy tale" without the terrors and the supernatural elements of the original tales. He places a girl, Dorothy, squarely at the center of the story, not unlike the character of Alice in Lewis Carroll's famous fantasy, which most likely influenced Baum. Dorothy, an orphan as is typical for a character on a quest, is undoubtedly intrepid, but her desire to get back home did little to break the mold in the depiction of girls.

And fairy tales continued to be controversial into the 1950s. The sex and violence of the tales were further sanitized by Walt Disney in his cartoon versions. Ironically, this sanitizing frequently had the effect of rendering girls and women even more passive or, alternatively, unrelentingly evil. For example, in the Disney films *Snow White and the Seven Dwarfs* (1937) and *Cinderella* (1950), the figure of the stepmother has become powerfully menacing and the central character seemingly helpless and hapless; no image of an active, vigorous, intelligent, and righteous heroine is to be found.

In the 1970s and 1980s, parents and teachers began to take issue with the sexism of tales, which still portrayed girls and women as passive victims, lying back in beds and glass coffins waiting to be rescued by the handsome prince. Scholars of children's literature have endeavored to create better understanding of the tales, their origins, their evolution, and the potentially negative impact of the tales on girls. Marina Warner, whose 1994 book *From the Beast to the Blonde: On Fairy Tales and Their Tellers* explores the attitudes toward women—such as contempt and disdain—revealed in the tales, reads a number of tales having to do with rivalry between women, romance, and marriage. Cristina Bacchilega brings the theoretical frameworks of postmodernism to bear on traditional tales as well as their retellings for adults in recent decades by such writers as Angela Carter, Robert Coover, and Margaret Atwood and in various media versions.

A close look at "Little Red Riding Hood" will exemplify some of the more recent critical approaches to fairy tales and will help decode the messages being sent implicitly to girl readers and listeners. This tale is not only one of the most widely read and well recognized of all fairy tales, but it particularly deals with girlhood and features the motifs of clothing, parental warnings, a solo journey, a good deed, deception and victimization, and, in some versions, rescue.

Bruno Bettelheim, a psychotherapist and Holocaust survivor, led the reevaluation of fairy tales with *The Uses of Enchantment* (1977), in which he sought to redeem the tales by demonstrating that they can be healing and reassuring to children. His persuasive argument was that the tales allow children to vicariously experience terror and evil and, through the happy ending, learn that they could manage the danger and anxiety. Bettelheim sees the central themes of "Little Red Riding Hood" as the threat of being devoured and the dilemma faced by a young girl of doing what she wants versus what she should, straying off the path versus staying on. Specifically, Bettelheim reads "Little Red Riding Hood" as a story about a girl at a certain stage of development in which she unconsciously wishes to be seduced by her father. He points out that the father is absent in the tale and hence is present in disguise. He claims that both the wolf and the hunter are the father—the wolf is the father as seductive, violent, and destructive; the hunter is the father as protective, unselfish, social, and thoughtful.

Bettelheim further notes that the tale emphasizes red, a color symbolizing violent emotions and sexuality, and that the need to cut Little Red Riding Hood out of the wolf's stomach introduces the idea of pregnancy and birth by Caesarean section. Bettelheim concludes that Little Red Riding Hood loses her innocence as she encounters the dangers in the world and gains wisdom as she is "reborn" to a higher plane of existence in being cut from the wolf's belly (1977, 166–183).

Jack Zipes has perhaps been the most prolific author of both studies and collections of fairy tales. He calls our attention to the historical context of the Middle Ages in which the tales were originally told; if the tales are about kings and peasants, perhaps they are really about class struggle. Zipes is also one of the earliest scholars to provide readings of tales that attend to the images of women and to the economic and contextual aspects of the tales. He claims that Bettelheim fails to take into account the fact that Little Red Riding Hood is *not* an archetype but rather the product of gifted male European writers who projected their needs and values onto actions of fictitious characters within a socially conventionalized drama. The purpose and themes of the tales did not concern harmony but the depiction of changing social structures. Central to most tales is the concept of

Disney films often sanitized traditional fairy tales for twentieth-century audiences. Here, Walt Disney presents Shirley Temple with an honorary Oscar in 1939 for her portrayal of Snow White. (Kobal)

power. Turning again to "Little Red Riding Hood," Zipes sees this as a tale about male power and, specifically, about rape.

Marina Warner notes that Perrault, in his late 1600s version of the tale, ends with these final sentences: "Now there are real wolves, with hairy pelts and enormous teeth; but also wolves who seem perfectly charming, sweet-natured and obliging, who pursue young girls in the street and pay them the most flattering attentions. Unfortunately, these smooth-tongued, smooth-pelted wolves are the most dangerous beasts of all" (1994, 182–183). So the double image of the wolf as simple beast and as seductive predator has existed from the earliest written versions of the tale.

Little Red Riding Hood has been reimagined by several authors and illustrators. In the 1950s Tasha Tudor created

a sunny edition of the tale, showing a benign wolf and a rather bewildered Little Red Riding Hood, all framed in a reassuring and beguiling border of apples, birds, and chipmunks, which marks the world of the tale as tidy and contained. Trina Schart Hyman's 1983 illustrations continue this tradition. By contrast, Sarah Moon's gritty photographs, also for a 1983 edition of the tale, depict a dark, decayed, deserted urban landscape that is profoundly threatening. The rumpled sheets in the final photograph of the book leave little doubt that a rape has occurred. Jack Zipes's assertion that "Little Red Riding Hood" provides a "warning about the possibility of sexual molestation" is made palpable in this version (1993, 81).

Although Bettelheim argues that tales are beneficial from a Freudian point of view, Zipes argues that they can be dan-

Little Red Riding Hood; from a nineteenth-century trading card. (Library of Congress)

gerous to children. Thus, since 1980, fairy tales have been the subject of much serious scrutiny. In a sense, scholars have found many new reasons to consider fairy tales dangerous, subversive, sexist, inauthentic, violent, and in general, inappropriate for use with children.

In an effort to redeem the tales, those beloved staples of childhood for so many decades, contemporary writers have created new versions of old tales or incorporated their motifs into new stories altogether. A review of a few of these new versions is useful in several ways. Not only will it make parents, teachers, librarians, and others who share books with children aware of the availability of these alternatives, but also by studying what has been revised, we come to understand more fully what has been found objectionable. We have already seen one such revision, that by Thurber at the opening of this entry, which uses humor and contemporary props to undercut the depiction of Little Red Riding Hood as helpless.

A laudable collection of extant traditional tales that nonetheless boasts women characters who are plucky, witty, clever, and victorious is *Tatterhood and Other Tales* by Ethel Johnston Phelps (1978). This wonderful volume can be read along with the more familiar tales, enabling children to compare and contrast their perceptions of characters, plot, and outcome. The stories are drawn from many cultures and countries, including South Africa, India, Scotland, Ireland, Pakistan, and Ecuador, and from Jewish and American Indian traditions. Phelps edited a second collection, entitled *The Maid of the North* (1981), and a similar collection was compiled by Rosemary Minard, entitled *Womenfolk and Fairy Tales* (1975).

Other writers have used familiar fairy tale tropes to invent their own fairy tales. One such creation, *The Paper Bag Princess* by Robert Munsch (1980), depicts an apparently stereotypical princess whose betrothed is carried off by a dragon. Elizabeth promptly takes off after the dragon and urges him to demonstrate his prowess at breathing fire and flying. When his powers are completely spent, she rescues Ronald from the dungeon. When he criticizes her garb (a paper bag donned after the dragon burned off her dress) and her tangled hair and tells her to come back when she is "dressed like a real princess," Elizabeth retorts: "Ronald, your clothes are really pretty and your hair is very neat. You look like a real prince, but you are a bum." And the narrator's dry closing line is: "They didn't get married after all," a happy-ever-after ending in this instance. Another creator of new tales with strong heroines is Jane Yolen. Among these are *Sleeping Ugly* (1995) and "The Moon Ribbon," a 1986 feminist retelling of the Cinderella story, which features a mother who helps her orphaned daughter from beyond the grave, teaching her lessons of self-reliance, courage, and assertiveness.

Yet another variation on such revisions is books set in contemporary times and places that use the devices of fairy tales to positive effect. Some very popular examples are the five books by Francesca Lia Block about a character with the improbable name of Weetzie Bat. At first blush, these young adult novels might seem the antithesis of a fairy tale. The initial book in the quintet, *Weetzie Bat* (1989), takes place in steamy, seamy Los Angeles: the novel is full of punks, gay men, "unwed" mothers, and all the cheap, glittering appurtenances of the movie capital of the world. And yet Francesca Block magically makes it perfectly acceptable to believe in genies, cozy cottages, and true love. "Shangri-L.A.," as Weetzie calls both the city she loves and a film in which she stars, is "a remake of 'Lost Horizon.'" The film is about time travel and a Hollywood that is forever young with Marilyn Monroe, Elvis Presley, and Humphrey Bogart, "magic castles and star-paved streets and Christmas lights" (67).

Though Los Angeles can at times become "Hell-A," when Weetzie's father dies of a drug overdose, when her lover leaves her, or when the reality of the acquired immunodeficiency syndrome (AIDS) epidemic bears down on her gay friends, overall this novel affirms the possibility of genuine affection and caring, even in unlikely, very nonnuclear families. "In L. A., we have a fairy tale house," Weetzie declares (73). And she makes it so by growing fairy tale hedges of roses but refusing the glass coffin. Instead, she has a much-wanted baby and adopts another. *Weetzie Bat* has its very own witch, a "happy [sometimes] ever after" ending, and surfing and sushi. Its postmodern eclecticism creates *frisson* by grounding the eternal themes in the sleaze of Hollywood.

Fairy tales have staying power and are also infinitely mutable as demonstrated by this "upgrade" of a traditional tale for girls:

*I really didn't notice that he had a
funny nose.
And he certainly looked better all
dressed up in fancy clothes.
He's not nearly as attractive as he
seemed the other night.
So I think I'll just pretend that this
glass slipper feels too tight.*
—Judith Viorst

Elizabeth Baer

See also Advice Books; Girls' Fiction; Reading

References and Further Reading

Bacchilega, Cristina. 1997. *Postmodern Fairy Tales: Gender and Narrative Strategies.* Philadelphia: University of Pennsylvania Press.

Bettelheim, Bruno. 1977. *The Uses of Enchantment: The Meaning and Importance of Fairy Tales.* New York: Vintage.

Block, Francesca Lia. 1989. *Weetzie Bat.* New York: HarperCollins.

Bottigheimer, Ruth B. 1986. *Fairy Tales and Society: Illusion, Allusion and Paradigm.* Philadelphia: University of Pennsylvania Press.

Hyman, Trina Schart. 1983. *Little Red Riding Hood.* New York: Holiday House.

Minard, Rosemary. 1975. *Womenfolk and Fairy Tales.* Boston: Houghton Mifflin.

Moon, Sarah. 1983. *Little Red Riding Hood.* Mankato: Creative Education.

Munsch, Robert. 1980. *The Paper Bag Princess.* New York: Annick Press.

Phelps, Ethel Johnston. 1978. *Tatterhood and Other Tales.* New York: Feminist Press.

———. 1981. *The Maid of the North: Feminist Folk Tales from around the World.* New York: Holt, Rinehart and Winston.

Tudor. Tasha. 1965. *Tasha Tudor Book of Fairy Tales.* New York: Platt and Munk.

Viorst, Judith. 1986. "And Then the Prince Knelt Down and Tried to Put the Glass Slipper on Cinderella's Foot." P. 73 in *Don't Bet on the Prince: Contemporary Feminist Fairy Tales in North America and England.* Edited by Jack Zipes. New York: Methuen.

Warner, Marina. 1994. *From the Beast to the Blonde: On Fairy Tales and Their Tellers.* New York: Farrar, Straus and Giroux.

Yolen, Jane. 1986. "The Moon Ribbon." In *Don't Bet on the Prince: Contemporary Feminist Fairy Tales in North America and England.* Edited by Jack Zipes. New York: Methuen.

———. 1995. *Sleeping Ugly.* New York: Houghton Mifflin.

Zipes, Jack. 1986. *Don't Bet on the Prince: Contemporary Feminist Fairy*

Tales in North America and England.
New York: Methuen.
——. 1993. *The Trials and Tribulations of Red Riding Hood: Versions of the Tale in a Sociohistorical Context.* 2d ed. New York: Routledge.

Fan Clubs

Fan clubs are both formal and informal associations of enthusiasts who come together around a particular celebrity. Since the early twentieth century, girls have responded to celebrities by joining together in fan clubs. Through their fan activities, girls can assert their preferences and respond critically to particular cultural forms. Girls have most consistently formed clubs to honor motion picture and television stars and musicians.

The term *fan* originally came from the discourse of sports. It referred to those who were aficionados of specific spectator sports in the nineteenth century and was rarely applied to women. The advent of the "stars" created by the new medium of motion pictures changed the nature of fandom. Before 1909, there were no motion picture stars because work in motion pictures was not consistent. Moreover, because of the stigma associated with film work, few actors were willing to be identified to audiences. Some of the larger film companies made a deliberate effort to ensure their actors' anonymity in order to keep their salaries down. Yet by 1909, fans had begun asking for photographs of their favorite stars and writing "Who?" letters to the film companies to inquire about the identity of the performers. The term "movie fan" was coined in about 1910 to refer to men and women who were regular patrons of the nickelodeons. By 1909, Kalem Film Company offered star photographs for display to theater owners, and by 1911 many theaters gave away calendars and postcard pictures of stars.

In 1910, Carl Laemmle, then an independent producer, staged what is generally considered the first publicity stunt. In the process, he supposedly launched the first "movie star" by staging the "death" of Florence Lawrence, an actress Laemmle had hired from a rival company. On a personal appearance tour shortly thereafter, Lawrence was mobbed by admirers. Thus the movie fan was officially born. Most contemporary film historians, however, consider the story apocryphal because Lawrence had been employed by Laemmle a full six months before his publicity stunt. Moreover, in the same month, another actress, Florence Turner, known as the Vitagraph Girl, was called a "motion picture star" in print after making a personal appearance tour in Brooklyn. After the Lawrence stunt, however, the once despised "Who?" letters had to be taken seriously by film companies.

Even after Laemmle's publicity stunt, some producers of the powerful Motion Picture Trust continued to resist publicizing their stars. Independents were not as hesitant, which ultimately caused a defection of some major actors from the larger studios to the independents. By 1911, the Trust studios began to capitulate to audience demand by issuing film posters bearing the names of their actors. Although roughly between 1910 and 1920 movie fans were both male and female, by the 1920s females predominated in the ranks of fans.

Fandom was facilitated by the creation of fan magazines. In 1911 J. Stuart Blackton of Vitagraph began the first fan magazine, *Motion Picture Magazine,* to publicize Vitagraph films and players.

At first the magazine was distributed only to Vitagraph exhibitors, but the demand for the magazine was so great that it was soon sold on newsstands. Other companies followed with their own publications, and all such publications created star personas through anecdotes, legends, and myths. In 1914, James R. Quirk became the editor of *Photoplay*, which encouraged artistry and quality in film by critically reviewing films. By the mid-1920s, Quirk also made his readers conversant in the language of the film industry by offering monthly features that included insider secrets and read more like a trade journal than a fan magazine.

At first, studio administrators were hostile to fan demands because fans were generally considered a nuisance. Fan mail was regarded as a burden by studios because of the costs involved in hiring clerical support and in answering and sending back photos. Although ambitious actors such as Joan Crawford occasionally answered their own fan mail, they were the exception. By the 1920s, fans began banding together to further the careers of particular stars. Fan club organizers were not allowed within the studio gates in the 1920s. However, by the early 1930s, the situation began to change as studios realized that fans constituted useful pressure groups on local theater owners through which to sell their films via block bookings. Fan clubs offered a free form of publicity, and fan clubs and fan mail were used by the studios to evaluate the popularity of stars. By the 1940s all of the major studios had fan mail departments.

Fans and adolescent girls were thought to be identical in the 1920s because girls were a highly visible segment of the fan population. In the 1930s and 1940s, 75–90 percent of all fans were younger than twenty-one years of age, and approximately 80 percent of them were female. Audience researchers found that girls were more likely than boys or adults to single out stars for their attention, and they were also more likely to write fan letters.

Fans could have an enormous influence on a star's career. In 1924, *Movie Weekly* sponsored a contest for its readers to come up with a new name for starlet Lucille LeSeur. One fan's choice of "Joan Crawford" won the enterprising fan $500. In 1925, *Photoplay* asked its fans to decide what kinds of roles they wanted to see thirty-two-year-old Mary Pickford play. Twenty thousand fans clearly called for Pickford to continue to play children. When Pickford cut off her trademark curls, fans were quick to criticize and stayed away from her films.

Fan clubs operated at international, national, and local levels. For example, the Deanna Durbin Devotees, one of the largest international fan clubs of the 1930s and 1940s, had salaried officers who published the club's journal, *Deanna's Diary*, as well as small branch clubs chartered by the devotees. Some fan clubs were simply informal gatherings of friends with an interest in similar stars. There were also national consortiums of different stars' fan clubs, such as the International Fan Club League and the Fan Club Federation, which would converge on Hollywood for annual conventions.

Fan clubs operated as powerful lobby groups on behalf of stars. A typical fan club meeting might consist of detailing a star's activities and upcoming film roles, sharing scrapbooks and other memorabilia, writing poetry or fan letters, and perhaps determining which fan most resem-

Beatles fans scream from the audience during a concert in Seattle, Washington. (Express Newspapers/A313/Archive Photos, 1964)

bled their favorite luminary. By the 1930s, most studios were supportive of such undertakings and funded the publication of certain fan clubs' newsletters or journals. Sometimes stars themselves supported their fans' endeavors. Some studios even gave club officers unlimited access to the stars. Fan mail departments at studios assisted clubs further in securing possible names for membership, fan letters, photographs, and other publicity material.

Fan activity remained an affordable, easily accessible diversion during the Depression and World War II. Being a member of an organized fan club allowed girls a space to create texts for personal consumption outside the official, market economy and thus outside the realm of the dominant ideology regarding gender. Fans often produced their own texts, which circulated among them and helped to define the fan community. Such publications might include contributions from fan club members, fan letters, pen pal services, contributions from the stars themselves, fan poetry or prose, or production information. The content itself was usually generated by fans, allowing adolescents a forum for expressing their cultural tastes publicly. Many clubs required members to produce scrapbooks or other collections of memorabilia, such as autographs. Many fan clubs publicly proclaimed and signaled membership. Members might be given membership cards and official pins, and some branch chapters had jackets with special insignias.

Fan letters sent to stars were quite chatty or full of personal news, the kind of letters that might be exchanged with a friend. Fans also wrote to give advice and could be quite critical, commenting on the star's film roles, hairstyles, or personal life.

With the advent of the big band craze in the late 1930s, many female adolescents also turned their attention to vocalists like Russ Colombo and Frank Sinatra. They would tune in to *Your Hit Parade* to learn the top ten hits of the week or read the fan magazines *Downbeat* and *Metronome*. Fan adulation of musicians would accelerate in the 1950s because of rock and roll stars such as Elvis. By the early 1960s, there were chapters of the Elvis Presley fan club in nearly every major city in the United States. The adoration of the musical star reached its apogee when the Beatles came to the United States as part of the 1960s British invasion.

Today, teenage girls continue to follow the exploits of their favorite musicians through the proliferation of music videos. A derogatory designation of female rock fans is that of "groupie," the fan who is sexually available to the musician. Throughout the century, fans have often been a fickle group, switching allegiance from one celebrity to another. Yet through their fan activities, girls have found cultural authority, agency, and a uniquely creative voice.

Georganne Scheiner

See also Girl Power; Punk Rock; Teenybopper; Zines

References and Further Reading
Fuller, Kathryn. 1996. *At the Picture Show: Small Town Audiences and the Creation of the Movie Fan.* Washington, DC: Smithsonian Institution Press.
Hopkins, Jerry. 1972. "The Fans." Pp. 161–172 in *Things in the Driver's Seat: Readings in Popular Culture.* Edited by Harry Russell Huebel. Chicago: Rand McNally.
Jenkins, Henry. 1989. "Star Trek Rerun, Reread, Rewritten: Fan Writing as Textual Poaching." *Critical Studies in Mass Communication* 5: 85–107.
Lewis, Lisa. 1990. *Gender, Politics and MTV: Voicing the Difference.* Philadelphia: Temple University Press.
———. 1991. *The Adoring Audience.* New York: Routledge.
Scheiner, Georganne. 1998. "The Deanna Durbin Devotees: Fan Clubs and Spectatorship." Pp. 81–94 in *Generations of Youth: Youth Cultures and History in Twentieth Century America.* Edited by Michael Willard and Joe Austin. New York: New York University Press.
Stacey, Jackie. 1995. *Stargazing: Hollywood Cinema and Female Spectatorship.* London: Routledge.
Vermorel, Fred, and Judy Vermorel. 1985. *Starlust: The Secret Life of Fans.* London: Comet Books.

Female Sexuality

Female sexuality includes feelings, desires, or experiences of an erotic nature, including but not limited to genital sensations, which girls encounter between infancy and adulthood. Ideas and practices related to girls' sexuality have changed over time but not always in a progressive fashion. The opposition of old-fashioned and modern sexuality is too simplistic, and it glosses over the range of behaviors at any given time. Sources of information on sexuality, in addition to being relatively rare, require careful evaluation. Female sexuality today is a realm

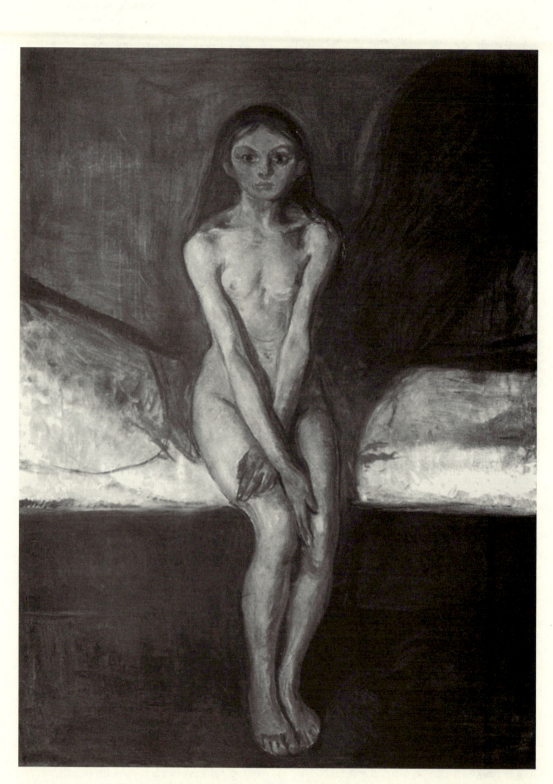

Puberty *by Edvard Munch. (Burnstein Collection/Corbis)*

of conflict, where young people attempt to make sense of contradictory and confusing messages.

Before the turn of the twentieth century, researchers did not collect empirical data about sexuality, much less girls' sexuality. For centuries, women's bodies were presumed to be first the inverse and then inferior versions of male bodies. Until recent decades, nearly all researchers were men, and most research subjects were also men.

Glimpses of girls' sexuality in the past and present appear in personal narratives, works of fiction, and court proceedings. Girls' articulation of their sexuality in judicial proceedings and with casework managers should not be taken at face value; in many cases testimony either complies with authorities' expectations or shocks their middle-class sensibilities. Likewise, clinical data are flawed by bias based on race and class as well as aversion to homosexuality, all prevalent modes of thinking among twentieth-century researchers, and thus produce only a partial and sometimes inaccurate portrait of girls' sexuality. Personal narratives, especially recollections and memoirs composed during adulthood, are necessarily selective, often omitting embarrassing details and forgotten experiences. Most autobiographies avoid sexual explicitness, and the majority of people—whether literate or not—never record their life histories. Survey data may be slightly more reliable and potentially more inclusive, yet forgetfulness and self-censorship are factors. Finally, much of the evidence of sexual activity is based on pregnancy—a poor measure of all heterosexual intercourse, perhaps a better judge of contraceptive practices, and not helpful in attempts to assess a range of sexual behaviors.

Very little information about sexuality remains from the period prior to and during European contact with native inhabitants of the Americas. European observers noted relative freedom to pursue sexual relations in Native American societies, but their descriptions were laden with value judgments and a sense of white superiority. Girls and boys in Hopi society witnessed and participated in rituals of a sexual nature as early as the sixteenth century, and the community valued sex positively (Duberman, Eggan, and Clemmer 1979). Spanish conquerors regarded Pueblo nudity and rituals as promiscuous and punished such behavior (Gutíerrez 1991). Among the Iroquois, adults tolerated children's sexual experimentation. Daughter of Chief Powhatan, eleven-year-old Pocahontas acted as an intermediary between Jamestown settlers and Powhatan natives, eventually marrying John Rolfe at age seventeen to escape captivity (and probably abuse) by the English (Nash 1992). An additional distinctive feature in various Native American societies has been the historical adoption of cross-gender identification and same-sex sexuality (in some areas, such people are called *berdache*) beginning in youth (Roscoe 1998).

Notwithstanding the stereotypes of "Puritan" sexual conservatism, young people engaged in sexual behavior in colonial America. Girls' knowledge about sex stemmed from observation, a consequence of sharing beds and flimsy partitions separating sleeping quarters in homes where young people remained until they married. The tradition of bundling, popular in New England and the middle colonies but abandoned by most communities by the mid-eighteenth century, allowed a courting, unmarried couple to share a bed, either fully clothed or separated by a bundling board, at the girl's home. Parents apparently expected the youth to kiss and fondle one another but did not directly encourage sexual intercourse. The prevalence of premarital pregnancy reveals society's tolerance of unwed sexual relations. As long as the courting couple married, the sex act was a forgivable sin, at least until the mid-1700s.

In plantation society, white slave owners were notorious for consorting with female slaves, and enslaved girls were rarely exempt from white masters' demands for sexual access. In general, white southerners construed black girls and black women as sexually available, as opposed to the allegedly virtuous white girls and women. Sexual freedom for black girls within the slave community was greater than it was for their white counterparts, whose social milieu demanded chastity. Although the state prohibited slaves from marrying, many enslaved young women and men formed meaningful relationships. Defined as chattel, slaves risked being separated from loved ones at the whim of their owners.

Rates of premarital pregnancy rose during the eighteenth century, and as the nation grew, so did opportunities for young couples to engage in courtship with less parental surveillance. The process of urbanization and the movement of work outside the home increased unsupervised opportunities for girls and boys to explore their sexuality. Less frequently conducted under the watchful eyes of a girl's mother, courtship offered a chance for sexual experimentation, usually with a potential marriage partner. In working-class communities, young women—called "girls" by their contemporaries—more openly pursued heterosexual activity in the mid-

to late nineteenth century, with multiple partners over time. Working girls' adoption of fancy dress suggested erotic maturity, and men commonly beckoned them or forced sexual contact. Whereas almost no young women were self-sufficient in the eighteenth century, nineteenth-century working girls lived independent from fathers and husbands. Alarmed by their self-assertion, many Americans associated factory girls with precocity and prostitution.

Sometimes prostitution was a means of survival for working-class girls, although many were only "occasional" prostitutes. Nineteenth-century brothels offered child prostitutes to men, and girls as young as ten were arrested for selling sex in the 1850s. On the West Coast, Chinese girls and women often arrived in the United States to discover that they had been sold into prostitution. Girls in working-class urban environments and bourgeois society were vulnerable to abuse by men, usually perpetrated by family or community members rather than strangers (Odem 1995). Grocers and lodgers gave city girls pennies to keep quiet about sexual contact, and elite southern men took liberties with young nieces as they did slaves, exercising patriarchal prerogative (Faust 1982; Stansell 1986). A sexual double standard tarnished girls' reputations, and although men's honor in some instances may have suffered, never were they considered "ruined."

Intimate relations developed in the nineteenth century between pairs of girls and young women, a phenomenon known as "romantic friendships." Although Victorians understood women as lacking sexual initiative, physically affectionate same-sex relationships flourished in the late nineteenth century, replete with love

letters, kissing, caressing, and bed sharing. Also consensual—but mediated by
an economy known as "treating"—were
sexual relations between urban boys and
girls. Working girls exchanged companionship, affection, sexual favors, and
sometimes sexual intercourse for tickets
to shows, a new dress, or other commodities that their low wages could not
support.

Although urban girls were openly
engaging in flirtation and forming romantic and sexual bonds, reformers sought to
prevent girls' "seduction." Having adopted English common-law statutes that set
the age of consent for girls between ages
ten and twelve, states revised their legal
codes during the Progressive era of the
early twentieth century. Prompted by
women reformers who maintained that
girls past the age of puberty were too
immature to consent to sex and further
fueled by eugenic concerns about public
health and heredity, state legislators
raised the age of consent to sixteen or
eighteen (except in Georgia, where the
age rose to fourteen). Increasing the age of
consent enabled reformers to prosecute
charges of "white slavery," purity activists' term for the abduction of young
women into prostitution or other forms
of sexual exploitation.

By far the most frequent perpetrators of
sexual abuse against girls were older family members and relatives and, especially
for domestic servants, their employers,
yet reformers left male authority in the
household and workplace unchallenged,
instead attacking the lesser incidence of
vice visible on the urban streets. Resistance to lowering the age of consent and
fears that scheming girls of questionable
character (especially African Americans
and poor whites) would use such laws
against "respectable" men were pro-

nounced in the Reconstruction South.
D. W. Griffith's infamous novel and
movie representation of post–Civil War
sexual politics was a sensational depiction of black men's alleged sexual aggression toward white girls and white
women, when in fact white men committed the majority of sexual assaults
and black girls and women were the most
common victims. Another argument in
defense of a lower age of consent for girls
was the fact that girls reached puberty
and maturity before boys; in the late
1800s, menarche (first menstruation) for
black girls occurred around age eleven
and for white girls around age fourteen
(Odem 1995).

In contrast to reformers' assumptions,
working-class young women overwhelmingly chose their unmarried peers of a
similar age and class status as sexual
partners. They entered such relationships
for companionship, enjoyment, and
financial reward, with marriage in mind.
Parents often objected to their daughters'
participation in sexual activity and
nightlife in the early twentieth century,
and the creation of the juvenile court system allowed a mechanism for enforcing
standards of behavior. New York State's
two reformatories for girls in the early
twentieth century could house up to 600
"delinquents" over age sixteen, most of
whom had begun their errant ways earlier in childhood and adolescence. In these
ways working-class parents and middle-
class professionals collaborated to put a
stop to youthful promiscuity.

During the twentieth century, authorities increasingly held girls responsible for
their participation in what was called
"sex delinquency." Crimes linked to sexuality—sneaking out at night, running
away, and committing petty theft, among
others—constituted a "girl problem,"

and middle-class reformers sought to modify girls' behavior by teaching them to be industrious workers and good Christians. Even more disturbing to middle-class sensibility was the spread of illicit behaviors to middle-class youth. Commercialized forms of mixed-sex entertainment swept the nation's cities at the turn of the twentieth century and provided a ripe environment for flirtation and expression of heterosexual desire. Kissing and engaging in heterosexual contact (short of intercourse)—called "necking" and "petting"—were old activities that gained visibility in the world of cheap amusements. At nickelodeons, dance halls, and amusement parks, sexual expression offended an aging generation of reformers and parents. Many girls—city natives or migrants from rural areas and the South—defiantly rejected Victorian mores about chastity.

Sigmund Freud was prominent among twentieth-century thinkers who attempted to understand sexuality, normal heterosexual development, and deviance. He theorized that infants were sexual beings—indeed "polymorphously perverse"—and influenced several generations of thinkers who acknowledged sexual aspects of growing up. Famous for his theories of psychosexual development and penis envy, Freud argued that girls, upon discovery of the male penis during the so-called genital phase, found their own genitals lacking, rejected their mothers, and turned to their fathers as capable of providing them symbolically with the missing male organ. Feminist revisions of Freud have argued that girls envy male power, not male anatomy, and that early influences in girls' sexual development are social in addition to psychological. Less controversial were new theories about adolescence as a period of struggle

and sexual awakening: psychologist G. Stanley Hall acknowledged girls and boys as sexual beings, contributing to the demise of Victorian notions of female passionlessness but also shaping his profession with sexist ideas about girls' health and education.

Patterns of sexual behavior instigated by urban working-class youth spread across the nation during the early decades of the twentieth century, accelerated by the automobile—both a vehicle of escape and a site for sexual activity. By the 1920s, commentators noted that no less than a "revolution of manners and morals" had occurred. During World War I and World War II, girls congregated around military camps, socialized with soldiers, and earned such labels as "khaki wackies" and "victory girls," presumably acting out of patriotic fervor to aid the war effort. The prevalence of "pickups," or casual relations between girls and military men, led San Diego sex educators to warn sixth-grade girls against contact with strangers around military bases. Equally problematic for adults was the trend of "going steady"—studies revealed that girls were more likely to engage in sexual contact with a steady boyfriend than if they dated many boys their age. Teen-oriented magazines advocated group outings and double dating; in order to "rate," one needed to date more than one person. Providing strategies for dating and finding a mate, midcentury advice literature and family life education reinforced conservative notions about female sexuality. Young men were to initiate dates and sexual activity, and girls were to remain passive but enticing.

In contradiction to such advice, biologist Alfred C. Kinsey (1953) discovered that premarital sexual activity, including masturbation and homosexuality, was not unknown among his sample of American women from several generations. Twenty-seven percent of female respondents in his 1953 report recalled sexual response before puberty (103); girls more commonly than boys experienced first orgasm through masturbation (106); 40 percent of girls admitted to having masturbated by age twenty (143); 48 percent remembered preadolescent sex play (both same-sex and with boys) (107); and almost half of women married by age twenty had engaged in premarital coitus (287). In the post–World War II era, unwed pregnant girls received different treatment based on race: social service workers treated black girls as promiscuous "breeders" and white girls as psychologically (but reversibly) disturbed.

In the 1940s and 1950s, a number of girls sought same-sex sexual relationships. Bars in small and large cities provided opportunities for girls to find sexual companions and connect with a growing homosexual community. Although minors were not legally admitted to bars, girls as young as fourteen participated in bar culture. In keeping with Kinsey's findings, a number of lesbians of this generation recalled sexual feelings toward women from before and during puberty, some of which led to sex play. Following the late 1960s and 1970s movements for gay liberation and feminism, more girls and young women talked openly about their feelings and pursued relationships in other venues. Organizations and centers for gay, lesbian, bisexual, and transgender youth emerged in the latter decades of the twentieth century, offering meeting space and support networks.

Over the course of the twentieth century, girls began to reach puberty at an earlier age. Overall, the age of marriage rose, and increasing numbers of young people in the late twentieth century have eschewed marriage altogether. The sexual revolution of the 1960s, associated with college students and heterosexual liberation from conception, courtesy of the birth control pill, had an impact on younger people; however, girls also experienced the backlash against sexual liberalism as parents and schools responded to protect youth. Although one generation may have learned to practice contraception and "safe sex," a subsequent generation was more likely to be taught abstinence as the only way to be safe. Nonetheless, several court victories from the late 1970s protected minors' access to contraceptives and abortion but allowed states to impose restrictions on the latter.

Few people in the early twenty-first century would argue that girls are innately depraved or virtuous, and most recognize that a combination of environmental factors shapes the ways that girls' sexuality finds expression. From an early age, girls receive mixed messages about sexual values. On the one hand, popular culture eroticizes girl bodies, either by presenting girls in a voyeuristic and desirable fashion or by making adult women appear girlish. Taking this eroticism to its extreme is the child pornography industry, with its ubiquitous presence on the Internet. On the other hand, the dominant conception of childhood and especially girlhood consists of a period of innocence during which sexual gratification (or at minimum heterosexual intercourse) should be delayed. Parents and guardians, generally speaking, continue protecting their vulnerable daughters, revealing a perception of girls as defenseless and molestation and abuse as pervasive.

Despite a lack of evidence suggesting its effectiveness, abstinence-only education grew popular in the last two decades of the twentieth century, and in 2000, Republican presidential candidate George W. Bush promised to increase federal funding for education initiatives promoting abstinence. Conservatives have attacked alternative contraceptive education, and schools have replaced former instruction in the use of contraceptives and "safe sex" methods (which increased in the 1970s and 1980s) with an ideal of postponed participation in sexual activity. Critics of abstinence-only education contend that American society still applauds or ignores young men for sexual bravado and stigmatizes young women who engage in similar activity. Opponents of providing youth with contraceptive information (and knowledge about sexual acts) maintain that such instruction sanctions sexual activity among youth. The fact that American society offers young people mixed messages about sexuality, often with severe consequences for girls, is indisputable.

Feminists and scholars who believe that sexuality is socially constructed rather than fixed or innate have shaped discussion of girls' sexuality. Studies have shown that girls are at greater risk for eating disorders and lose self-esteem around the time of puberty, and feminists have argued that such problems result from conflicting cultural messages about female sexuality. Debunking a male-centered biology and definition of sex, late-twentieth-century feminists have clarified the role of the clitoris in sexual arousal, although many girls undoubtedly lack such information. Feminist analysis of rape and sexual harassment has provided clues to unraveling girls' struggles with sexuality, and the late-twentieth-century third wave of feminism includes girls testifying about their own sexual coming-of-age experiences. In addition to being a tool for pornographers, the World Wide Web has become a resource for expert and peer knowledge about sexuality.

Susan K. Freeman

See also Adolescent Health; Body Image; Child Abuse; Clothing; Dating and Courtship; Hair; Menstruation; Teen Pregnancy

References and Further Reading
Alexander, Ruth. 1995. *The "Girl Problem": Female Sexual Delinquency in New York, 1900–1930.* Ithaca, NY: Cornell University Press.
Boston Women's Health Book Collective. 1998. *Our Bodies, Ourselves for the New Century: A Book by and for Women.* Rev. ed. New York: Simon and Schuster.
Brumberg, Joan Jacobs. 1997. *The Body Project: An Intimate History of American Girls.* New York: Random House.
Duberman, Martin, Fred Eggan, and Richard Clemmer. 1979. "Documents in Hopi Indian Sexuality: Imperialism, Culture, and Resistance." *Radical History Review* 20 (Spring–Summer): 99–130.
Faust, Drew Gilpin. 1982. *James Henry Hammond and the Old South: A Design for Mastery.* Baton Rouge: Louisiana State University Press.
Gutíerrez, Ramón A. 1991. *When Jesus Came the Corn Mothers Went Away: Marriage, Sexuality, and Power in New Mexico, 1500–1846.* Palo Alto, CA: Stanford University Press.
Irvine, Janice M., ed. 1994. *Sexual Cultures and the Construction of Adolescent Identities.* Philadelphia: Temple University Press.
Kinsey, Alfred C., Wardell B. Pomeroy, Clyde E. Martin, and Paul H. Gebhard. 1953. *Sexual Behavior in the Human Female.* Philadelphia: W. B. Saunders.
Nash, Gary B. 1992. *Red, White, and Black: The People of Early North America.* 3d ed. Englewood Cliffs, NJ: Prentice-Hall.
Odem, Mary E. 1995. *Delinquent Daughters: Protecting and Policing Adolescent Female Sexuality in the*

United States, 1885–1920. Chapel Hill: University of North Carolina Press.

Pipher, Mary. 1994. *Reviving Ophelia: Saving the Selves of Adolescent Girls.* New York: Ballantine Books.

Planned Parenthood Federation of America. http://www.teenwire.com. Accessed January 11, 2001.

Roscoe, Will. 1998. *Changing Ones: Third and Fourth Genders in Native North America.* New York: St. Martin's Press.

Shandler, Sara, ed. 1999. *Ophelia Speaks: Adolescent Girls Write about Their Search for Self.* New York: Harper-Perennial.

Stansell, Christine. 1986. *City of Women: Sex and Class in New York, 1789–1860.* New York: Alfred A. Knopf.

Tanenbaum, Leora. 1999. *Slut! Growing Up Female with a Bad Reputation.* New York: Seven Stories Press.

Thompson, Sharon. 1995. *Going All the Way: Teenage Girls' Tales of Sex, Romance, and Pregnancy.* New York: Hill and Wang.

4-H

A nationwide system of task-based voluntary organizations for rural youth, 4-H is directed by the United States Department of Agriculture (USDA) Extension Service. This component of USDA rural outreach organized for girls in 1910 was one of several Progressive-era initiatives for encouraging farm families to adopt scientific farming and homemaking practices. Since 1907 legislative mandates, domestic policy priorities, and international events have altered administrative structures, club names and membership criteria, the status of participants, and the projects to which the USDA has assigned top priority. However, active club members have invariably maximized the tangible rewards and educational potential of belonging, constructing meaningful experiences from available opportunities.

Two national reform currents directly supported the formation of girls' clubs in the early 1900s. Progressive rural educational leaders promoted agricultural clubs as a complement to formal schooling for rural youths. Reformers hoped to counteract the growing dominance of urban bias in textbooks and to make rural life attractive to the maturing generation. Many northern and western civic leaders and school districts established state or local rural youth organizations prior to USDA involvement.

Progressive reformers' determination to rationalize agricultural practices provided the second impetus for 4-H work. The boll weevil's attack on southern cotton crops and the USDA's broader interest in increasing yields and combating extreme rural poverty with scientific agricultural practices prompted the USDA to collaborate with private foundations to assist southern farmers and the region's agricultural economy. The General Education Board, distributing Rockefeller Foundation money, provided significant funding for much of the initial USDA Extension Service work with southern youth.

The first girls' clubs for whites were usually named either to signify gender or to identify work with specific crops, animals, or homemaking activities. Girls' canning and tomato clubs, established in Virginia and North Carolina in 1910, spread quickly throughout the South. African American girls enrolled in carefully distinguished homemakers' clubs. The more inclusive "4-H clubs," emphasizing simultaneous training goals (head, heart, hands, and health), served as the common title for USDA Extension Service work with rural girls and boys, ages eleven to eighteen, from the late 1920s until the late 1960s. The current umbrella title for USDA coeducational work with youth ages nine to nineteen, "4-H," also includes new special-interest projects for urban and rural participants.

USDA 4-H clubs, regardless of their name or source of financial support, have consistently been a vehicle for organizing rural young women to accomplish broader domestic and foreign policy goals. Although the clubs have frequently provided opportunities that coincided with girls' interests, girls' self-defined needs have been largely irrelevant to the social, economic, and political goals the clubs were designed to meet. Although the initiative merged contemporary reform currents, the emphasis on national priorities distinguishes tomato and canning clubs from other Progressive-era voluntary youth organizations. Most youth workers designed programs that were explicitly tailored to adolescents' developmental needs.

In fact, the USDA initially involved youth in its programs because of adult reluctance to adopt the scientific farming and homemaking practices that the agency advocated. Extension Service agents hoped to spread new agricultural practices by getting farmers to agree to plant and tend crops according to their specifications. These "demonstration projects" were designed to establish the superiority of scientific farming methods. Administrators and agents expected that the demonstrators' improved yields would be the most persuasive argument for new practices, leading others to adopt them. Farmers' reluctance to try the new methods compelled agents to temporarily work with farmers' sons, who were much more receptive to experimenting with one-acre plots. This improvised strategy produced such impressive results that when the organizers decided to add scientific housekeeping to their agenda, they did not even consider beginning with farm wives.

Ella Agnew and Jane McKimmon, the first USDA home demonstration agents in Virginia and North Carolina, deliberately worked only with girls. Although they ultimately hoped to influence adult women, in 1910 daughters provided the first link between the USDA and farm homes and kitchens. Girls' canning and tomato club members tended one-fourth-acre gardens, kept detailed records of planting and fertilizing activities, learned to preserve tomatoes and other vegetables for their families' winter meals, and submitted report forms describing their activities and yields. Although USDA administrators' priorities were adding variety to menus, improving nutrition, and teaching safe, modern canning methods in order to improve the quality of rural life for farmers, girls benefited and took great pride in their gardens, canned produce, profits, and prizes.

Congress accepted the USDA administrators' contention that rural youth had become integral to efforts to reform rural life and reshaped the program for the first time in 1914. The Smith-Lever Act, which stipulated that 25 percent of each state's Extension Service budget be allocated for boys' and girls' clubs, made the successful work nationwide. By the terms of the legislatively mandated cooperative agreements between the USDA and state land-grant colleges, each state home demonstration agent, the woman responsible for all USDA work with white girls' club members and women within a state, established an office in the home economics department of the land-grant agricultural college or at a nearby women's college.

The Smith-Lever Act expanded the geographic boundaries of the program but altered the conduct of the work in the South. General Education Board funding had been based on need. In 1914 Congress prohibited the use of private money and restricted agents to counties willing and able to allocate matching funds. As a result, as at least one USDA administrator had predicted, some southern girls could no longer participate.

Between 1914 and 1945, legislative mandates and domestic policy priorities exerted the strongest influence on girls' 4-H club membership and activities. There were numerous organizational changes, but with the exception of the official segregation of southern work in 1916, most affected club agents but not the girls who participated. Prior to the 1945 Bankhead-Flannagan Act, which mandated that a portion of increased allocations be used for African American club work in the South, new resources were rarely directed to African American agents and club members. However, within the white programs, the number of 4-H club agents and initiatives for girls grew at rates similar to those for boys.

Domestic policy considerations as articulated by USDA administrators consistently created programs that emphasized traditional gender roles. According to those directing the work from Washington, D.C., an underlying goal of all Extension Service work was to enable the most capable farmers to prosper. A promising farmer, in addition to high yields, needed a happy home. He required a resourceful housekeeper who understood her supportive function and could create an attractive physical setting and prepare good meals. This orientation dictated the staffing and program priorities of the 4-H program for the girls who were to assume the role of farm wife.

Federal administrators wanted scientific housekeeping principles to influence the farm home but expressed skepticism about hiring women who might disrupt the social status quo. State leaders sought female employees with training in home economics but gave priority to applicants likely to have a "rural viewpoint." Thus early girls' canning and tomato club members were not instructed by women who identified themselves to the USDA as feminists.

Beginning with tomato and canning clubs, female home demonstration agents worked directly with girls on projects considered appropriate for females. Agents periodically sought greater flexibility, but USDA administrators in Washington, D.C., issued very clear prescriptions on the gendered boundaries of work for white participants. Tomatoes, kitchen gardens, chickens, yard beautification, and household improvement projects were the most common activities. Individual girls sometimes pursued animal projects that took them into boys' territory, but the only organizational exceptions to the gendered division of labor were poultry clubs, which could be directed by either male or female agents, and the work with African American girls, which typically took place within the context of family- and community-centered initiatives directed by the one local African American agent who might be either male or female.

In addition to initiating projects to preserve traditional gender lines and promote scientific housekeeping among rural girls, USDA administrators kept the program responsive to domestic economic and political priorities. During World War I, girls in 4-H clubs took an active role in food production and conservation efforts. Some northern canning clubs actually produced surplus crops for export. Congress also appropriated funds that enabled the Extension Service to hire agents who would organize urban girls to support the war effort by planting gardens for home use.

Depression-era "live-at-home" campaigns linked 4-H projects to helping rural families survive the economic crisis. Gardens could both conserve and augment the farm income, and organizers stressed the value of the farm family garden. In New York State the average 4-H girl produced $121 worth of vegetables for her family's table. Other projects emphasized renovating clothing and home furnishings, particularly the girls' own bedrooms, as ways to improve the quality of home life with minimal resources.

Girls contributed to World War II in many ways, some of which blurred gender lines as the USDA tried to meet its responsibility for recruiting farmworkers. Urban and rural girls again planted victory gardens, preserved food to improve family health and nutrition, and sold war bonds. In addition, rural girls helped alleviate the farm labor shortage. The 1943 *Annual Report* of the secretary of agriculture specifically mentions girls, not just boys, driving tractors as a patriotic contribution. Girls also learned first aid, child care practices, and home nursing skills. Their work was promoted as good training for participation in community projects, a significant change for white participants. Girls had previously been encouraged to focus exclusively on traditional tasks within their own homes.

After 1945, foreign policy goals affected the focus of 4-H work in new ways. As markets contracted, the USDA deemphasized production. In the context of the Cold War, the traditional American farm family pattern was celebrated as superior to communist agrarian reform efforts around the globe. Thus it is not surprising that career exploration became a major program focus for 4-H boys but not for their sisters. Girls, however, could participate in new nonfarming projects designed to shift the program away from its primarily rural focus. "Buymanship and consumer education" was just one of these initiatives. Cold War foreign policy also motivated an expanded program that emphasized youths' connection to local and national peers. A few 4-H members went overseas to live with farm families, but more hosted foreign youth in their homes under the aegis of the International Farm Youth Exchange, initiated in 1948, and its subsequent expansions.

All members are reminded of global responsibilities when reciting the 4-H pledge, revised in 1973. In addition to retaining the traditional commitment to develop one's head, heart, hands, health, community, and country, the pledge now includes "and my world." Demographic changes, the Civil Rights Act of 1964, urban renewal programs, a recent commitment to include young people with disabilities, and technological innovations ranging from radio to television and the Internet have all altered the contours of 4-H membership for girls. However, regardless of adult priorities, girls since 1910 have consistently made the program serve their individual goals. All who completed projects gained a sense of individual accomplishment, sometimes reinforced by tangible prizes and local, state, or even national recognition. Those who attended state and national camps treasured their contacts with other members and were buoyed by large gatherings, which gave them a sense of participation in an enterprise much broader than their daily experiences might have suggested. The encouragement of adult female agents, who were often significant role models, to pursue education outside their rural communities made 4-H a life-altering experience for many young women.

Kathleen C. Hilton

See also Camp Fire Girls; Education of Girls; Girl Scouts; Home Economics Education; Rural Girls; Summer Camps for Girls; Work

References and Further Reading
Clark, James W., Jr. 1984. *Clover All Over: North Carolina 4-H in Action.* Raleigh: North Carolina State University Press.
Hilton, Kathleen C. 1987. "Growing Up Female: Girlhood Experiences and Social Feminism, 1890–1929." Ph.D. diss., Carnegie Mellon University, chap. 5.
Reck, Franklin M. 1951. *The 4-H Story: A History of 4-H Club Work.* Ames: Iowa State College Press.
True, Alfred Charles. 1969. *A History of Agricultural Extension Work in the United States, 1785–1923.* New York: Arno Press and the *New York Times.*
U.S. Department of Agriculture. *Annual Report of the Secretary of Agriculture.* 1910–1999. Washington, DC: Government Printing Office.
Wessel, Thomas, and Marilyn Wessel. 1982. *4-H: An American Idea, 1900–1980.* Chevy Chase, MD: National 4-H Council.
www.4h-usa.org/4h/4h_history.htm.

Free Girls of African Descent

"To-day school commenced," wrote Philadelphia-born Charlotte Forten, who began keeping a journal May 24, 1854, shortly before her seventeenth birthday. Wednesday, September 12, 1855, signaled the beginning of classes and chances to reestablish the legendary camaraderie that existed among schoolgirls. Rather than rejoicing over the renewal of acquaintances among classmates at the predominately white school that she attended in Salem, Massachusetts, Forten was "most happy . . . to return to the companionship of [her] studies." She considered challenging academic assignments her "ever . . . most valued friends" (Stevenson 1988, 139–140).

What caused the young girl to prize schoolwork more highly than school chums? As a free person of color in the slave era, Charlotte Forten was an anomaly. Neither she nor nearly 500,000 other free blacks in 1860 belonged to the dominant white society or the black society in the United States. In the first instance, northern prejudices based upon color thwarted free interactions with whites. In the second, customs based upon legal status prevented free associations with slaves. Slavery was not compatible with the natural rights ideology of the American Revolution, yet slavery and freedom coexisted paradoxically in the United States, where it was commonly assumed that all whites were free and all blacks were slaves. Contrary to this popular notion, a few black females and males of all ages were among the free population.

In 1790, when the first census of the United States was taken, the number of free persons of African descent in all age groups had increased from several thousand in 1750 to 59,466. The free population constituted 7.9 percent of the 697,624 blacks in the United States at the time. The percentage of free blacks peaked in 1830, when it reached 13.7 percent (319,599) of the total number of blacks in the United States. After 1830, the percentage of free blacks fell to 13.4 percent in 1840, 11.9 percent in 1850, and finally to 11.0 percent in 1860. By that time, the free population had reached 488,070. Of that number, 240,921 were less than twenty years of age, and slightly more than one-half (122,193) of the group were females (U.S. Bureau of the Census 1864, 2).

Free persons who lived in the urban and rural areas of the North and South attributed their status to their being born of a free woman without regard for color, legal suits, private manumissions, and purchases. A study of 176 notarial records in Spanish New Orleans involving the purchase of enslaved children with the intent to emancipate them reveals that free black women paid for 75 percent more children than did the men. Additionally, nearly two-thirds of these children the women liberated were girls. Clearly, the intent was in the interest of posterity: free women gave birth to free children (Ingersoll 1991, 186).

The Revolutionary War was responsible for the largest increase in the free population in the eighteenth century. Afterward, slavery became more firmly entrenched in the South and dissipated elsewhere. States north of Delaware had either manumitted slaves or made provisions for gradual emancipation; therefore, by the end of the 1830s few blacks remained in bondage there. Added to the free black population was an untold number of slaves who "stole themselves." Fewer females than males of all ages were among successful runaways. Those in childbearing years recoiled from fleeing because of the difficulties of carrying children along and their reluctance to leave them behind. Also, females traveling alone attracted more attention than males and were more likely to be stopped and returned to bondage. Nevertheless, the "theft of self" occurred most easily when fugitives escaped into nonslaveholding areas of the North or melded into the general free population in southern cities such as New Orleans, Charleston, and Baltimore.

Regardless of the manner in which they acquired their liberty, free persons were anomalies in North America. Even more of an aberration among them were the "quasi-slaves," persons who were legally enslaved but lived, worked, and behaved as if they had been emancipated. "We were free," declared the biracial North Carolinian Cornelia Smith, who came of age in the home of her paternal grandfather, a white medical doctor and planter, while her mother and young half-brother lived across the yard in the slave quarters. "We were just born in slavery," Smith added, "that's all" (Murray 1987, 49, 162).

Other "virtually free" girls included Suzanne Metoyer, daughter of the French gentleman Claude Thomas Pierre Metoyer and the slave-born Marie Thereze Coincoin; Amanda America Dickson, offspring of the enslaved Julia Frances and slave owner David Dickson, a wealthy entrepreneur and scientific farmer; Imogene and Adeline Johnson, the biracial daughters of the enslaved mulatto Julia Chinn and Richard M. Johnson, attorney, U.S. congressman, and vice president of the United States from 1837 to 1841; and Mary Ann Ellison, daughter of an unnamed slave woman and the wealthy freedman William "April" Ellison, a cotton-gin maker. These girls were hobbled by the absence of legal documents declaring them free—legally. Although they had no papers to prove their status, they suffered little or no interference from their owners, who never threatened them with sales, arduous labor, or corporal punishment. Only legal documents made them chattel. "That's all," according to Cornelia Smith (Murray 1987).

Free blacks enjoyed the most fundamental rights—to their own persons and offspring—along with the right to own property and marry legally. Free persons could also sue and be sued, establish businesses and keep their earnings, pursue an education, and worship in churches of their choice. Despite legal differences between enslaved and emancipated girls, few free persons, including Charlotte Forten, escaped the furies of race-based discrimination in schools, churches, marketplaces, and public accommodations. Given these circumstances, the adolescent Forten remained amazed that African Americans were not misanthropes as a result of living amid racial hostilities and facing routine acts of injustice. "Surely," she wrote, "we have everything to make us hate mankind" (Stevenson 1988, 139–140). Forten based her observation upon the uneven behavior of classmates who were kind and cordial on the school grounds but ignored her when off campus. Forten responded by ignoring the girls and considered the incidents as "trifles" when compared to the great public wrongs her people endured. Yet Forten admitted that the "trifles" were "most wearing and discouraging" to persons who experienced them.

Forten's contemporary Marchita Lyons had firsthand knowledge of such behavior but was not inclined to ignore it. In 1854 the sixteen-year-old girl moved from New York to Providence, Rhode Island, where she attended school after her mother appealed to the governor to ensure her admission. Under the circumstances, "if any girl tried to put 'on airs,'" Lyons wrote, "I simply found a way to inform her of my class record." She flaunted her academic superiority as a way of saying to classmates that she too was entitled to an education and to show that blacks could excel academically if given a chance (Sterling 1984, 188–189).

Forten and Lyons, like many of their northern free black contemporaries, had access to an education. Barriers to literacy similar to those in the South, such as school closings or the enactment of statutes against teaching blacks to read and write following the 1831 rebellion led by literate preacher Nat Turner, did not exist in the North, but educational opportunities were not always ideal. Some school systems prohibited admitting black children altogether, and others maintained segregation.

If protests or direct action did not result in changes, parents and guardians sought alternatives. Frederick Douglass's young daughter Rosetta attended school away from her Rochester, New York, home because its public schools were closed to blacks until 1857. When the wealthy Philadelphia sail maker James Forten objected to the segregated schools in the "City of Brotherly Love," his granddaughter Charlotte received private tutoring and attended school in Salem, Massachusetts, between 1853 and 1856. In Salem, she boarded with John and Nancy Remond, who had relocated from Salem to Newport, Rhode Island, in the mid-1830s so that their daughter Sarah and her brother Charles "might not suffer from the discriminatory practices found in the high schools of Salem" (Sterling 1984, 138).

While Forten was in Salem, the conditions in Pennsylvania hardly changed. In 1856 her cousin Hattie Purvis wrote to a friend that she had been tutoring her younger siblings at home since "there was no school [in Bayberry, Pennsylvania] . . . for them except a Public School" where they had to sit by themselves "because their faces are not as white as the rest of the scholars." The seventeen-year-old Purvis said it made her "blood boil" just to think of the unfair treatment.

When her own private tutoring ended, Hattie attended Eagleswood, a New Jersey boarding school run by abolitionists Theodore D. Weld, his wife Angelina, and her sister Sarah Grimké. At Eagleswood, Purvis mingled with the children and grandchildren of white abolitionists. Although living away from home caused anxiety and feelings of disengagement, Hattie Purvis established meaningful relationships with classmates such as Ellen Wright, who eventually married William Lloyd Garrison (Sterling 1984, 187–188).

The curricular offerings at public and private schools included traditional reading, writing, arithmetic, geography, and spelling courses. At Philadelphia's Institute for Colored Youth, a classical high school founded in 1837 by the Society of Friends, pupils had a greater variety of courses. The freeborn Sarah Mapps Douglass, a stellar teacher in charge of the Girl's Department at the institute, enrolled in medical classes at the Ladies Institute of Pennsylvania Medical University between 1855 and 1858 in order to introduce new subjects, including physiology, into the Institute of Colored Youth's offerings (Lerner 1973, 85–86).

Based upon comments about her final examinations given by H. Amelia Loguen, daughter of J. W. Loguen, an African Methodist Episcopal Zion bishop, she studied an expansive curriculum. On April 10, 1862, Loguen wrote:

Spring has brought with it as usual, the ever dreaded, yearly school examinations, dreaded because they are so very tedious. Monday I thought of nothing but Chloride of Sodium, Nitrate of Silver detection of arsenic, uses of Zinc etc. etc; Tuesday, Parlez-vous francais? Comment-vous

appelez-vouz? And Je me porte tres bien, yesterday oh! Terrible thought Plane Trigonometry; do you wonder then that last night I dreamed of being in France . . . trying to show that Chemistry is one of the most useful and interesting studies imaginable and lastly I was alone in some queer place trying to accertain [sic] the height of a "fort on a distant hill inaccessable [sic] on account of an intervening swamp." O! how refreshing on awaking this morning to know that all such is for a time past and that vacation is close at hand. (Woodson 1969, 541)

Whether it was the end of the academic year or an academic career, many free blacks girls believed it was their social responsibility to acquire an education and use it in the interest of their people. "Knowledge is Power," said Frances Ellen Watkins Harper, a popular freeborn writer and reformer (Still 1872, 757). Moreover, she and Maria W. Stewart, a freeborn lecturer, believed education was vital for the elevation of the black race (Richardson 1987, 30, 46, 47). Both women agreed that it was incumbent upon black females to make a recognizable contribution to that effort. Similarly, Sarah Mapps Douglass penned a pithy reminder in one of her young students' notebooks that reinforced that idea. "Thou hast youth, health, talents," she wrote, "So use these precious gifts that when the Great Householder calls for an account of thou stewardship thou mayest return him his own with usury."

Thoughts of accountability at the bar of God were probably enough to dissuade students from misusing their education or ignoring their social responsibilities to others. Once their formal education ended, the alumnae often entered the teaching profession, one of the few occupations open to young women. In this way, they could help to uplift their race and earn a livelihood at the same time.

A great number of free girls, especially those who were economically deprived, did not attend school regularly. Instead, they entered bound service to whites who agreed to provide food, clothing, and shelter along with domestic and educational training in exchange for their labor. In general, bound free black girls entered service younger, received less educational training, and remained bound longer than their white contemporaries. As a result, the black girls spent most of their formative years performing manual labor outside their own homes.

Skills necessary for preparing food and washing clothes, two of the most exacting domestic tasks, were beyond the knowledge and capabilities of most young girls. Ordinarily, they assisted adults with these demanding chores. The autobiographical writings of Nancy Prince, a Massachusetts-born free African American, reveal the tedious nature of her work as a domestic servant in a family of seven, including a patient suffering from fever and another from consumption. Prince wrote:

Of course, the work must have been very severe, especially the washings. Sabbath evening I had to prepare for the wash; soap the clothes and put them into the steamer, set the kettle of water to boiling, and then close in the steam, and let the pipe from the boiler into the steam box that held the clothes. At two o'clock, on the morning of Monday, the bell was rung for me to get up; but, that was not all, they said I was too slow, and

the washing was not done well; I had to leave the tub to tend the door and wait on the family, and was not spoken kind to, at that.

The fourteen-year-old girl remained on the job only three months before it took a great toll on her health (Prince 1990, 6–7).

The autobiographical fiction *Our Nig* by Harriet E. Wilson, the first novel published in the United States by a black woman, is also illustrative in this regard. *Our Nig*'s well-developed plot focuses on Frado, a six-year-old girl who became an orphan when her African-born father died and her mother, a white woman, abandoned her. The young protagonist worked for an abusive white family in New England before the Civil War.

Wilson clearly shows that racism existed in the North and that Frado's life as a servant girl was not vastly different from that of her enslaved contemporaries in the South. The conditions under which the character Frado and the historical woman Prince worked were more exacting because they lived under the watchful eye of employers. By contrast, when laundresses and other self-employed women, assisted by young girls, worked in their own homes, they experienced some reprieve and did not assume the "humble pose." At early ages, emancipated or enslaved blacks learned how to present a self-effacing posture or pay deference to whites publicly while privately maintaining their self-respect. The much-discussed "mask," a protective device for disguising personal convictions and steeling facial expressions and body language, was a significant facet in maintaining associations with whites whose patronage was critical to their economic survival. Sharon G. Dean attributes the expression "a humble pose" to Frederick Douglass, who was referring to black businessmen who catered solely to a white clientele and displayed deferential behavior or a businesslike facade to woo and maintain white customers (Potter 1991, xlvi).

Given these circumstances, it is not surprising that free persons looked for occupations in which both a source of livelihood and a degree of autonomy were possible. They found such jobs in the needle trade and filled demands for wearing apparel that required more than simple sewing. Because there were no readily accessible and affordable manufactured clothes, dressmakers fashioned garments for black and white clients. Young girls often assisted dressmakers and gained marketable skills as they matured.

Earning a living required a great deal of their time, but it was never so all-consuming that free persons could ignore the daily insults they faced because of their color; nor did they forget their sisters and brothers who remained in bondage. As a result, free women and men often engaged in a dual fight against discrimination and slavery. Girls, especially those who came of age in homes where parents and other influential relatives advocated the abolition of slavery, probably joined in the struggle. Certainly, Susan Paul, Mary Ann Shadd, Charlotte Forten, Sarah Parker Remond, and Frances Ellen Watkins Harper could trace their social consciousness back to childhood experiences in homes where adults recognized ills within the society and attempted to eradicate them.

Reform activities within the James Forten family spanned three generations of activists who assisted in founding, financing, and nurturing six abolitionist societies. More specifically, Charlotte

Forten, along with three of her daughters, was among the founding members of the Philadelphia Female Anti-Slavery Society in 1833. And the youngest member of the household, her granddaughter Charlotte, adopted the family tradition. Her insights about racism among her schoolgirl peers reflect her background within an antislavery household.

It is virtually impossible to find similar data about free girls in the South, but the absence of empirical evidence does not mean that all free southern families supported slavery. Rather, it suggests that they were not at liberty to express their sentiments within an environment in which proslavery whites abhorred the idea of free blacks in their midst. Whites feared that free persons would have an unsettling influence upon slaves and stimulate their desire for freedom. To avoid repercussions, many free persons toed the line, ostensibly. In reality, an untold number of unheralded individuals assisted slaves in gaining their liberty. Without fanfare or membership in antislavery organizations, they helped to destroy slavery whenever the opportunity arose. It was incumbent upon them to do so, since few free persons in the South could not claim a relative or friend who remained in bondage.

During the 1850s, the most politically charged period in the antebellum United States, the subject of slavery moved to the center of national political debates. Free girls in the North and South must have been aware of the shift as the atmosphere became more tense beginning with the more stringent Fugitive Slave Act, an 1850 statute. The law authorized officers of the court to issue arrest warrants for suspected fugitives and certificates for their return to bondage. The fate of an accused runaway depended upon whether or not she or he fit the claimant's description rather than upon prima facie evidence.

Under the 1850 law, authorities received $10 if they deemed an accused person guilty and only $5 if he or she was found innocent. They had a financial incentive to declare any accused person guilty of being a runaway. Since these cases were not subjected to jury trials and accused persons could not testify in their own behalf, the possibilities of kidnapping with the intent to enslave intensified. If free persons lost their free status it was nearly impossible to recover it, yet a limited number succeeded.

Among that number was the freeborn Polly Crocket, who was kidnapped and enslaved as a child and came of age in bondage, which she considered a dismal abyss. Crocket's daughter, Lucy Delaney, published the autobiographical piece, "From the Darkness Cometh the Light, or Struggles for Freedom," which illuminates the family's quest to regain and maintain its freedom. Delaney remembered that her mother "never spared an opportunity" to tell her children to seek liberty "whenever the chance offered" (Delaney 1988, 15–16).

Like many others in bondage, Delaney grew up knowing that slavery was the antithesis of the natural state of being, freedom. Among the earliest published writings of the African-born Phillis Wheatley was a poem that included the lines, "In every Breast God has implanted a Principle, which we call Love of Freedom, it is impatient of oppression and pants for Deliverance." Wheatley's owner emancipated her when she was approximately twenty years old in 1773 (Bruns 1977, 306).

Emancipation for nearly 4 million other enslaved males and females, 56 per-

cent of whom were under twenty years of age, did not come to fruition until the nation endured a bloody civil war. Once the fighting began in 1861, many slaves took advantage of the chaos surrounding them and liberated themselves by running away. Still others flocked to Union lines in hopes of winning their freedom. The fourteen-year-old slave-born Georgian, Susie King Taylor, witnessed the war from within a Union camp where she worked as a cook and laundress. She also helped bandage and nurse wounded soldiers. Moving beyond traditional jobs for women, Taylor said that she "learned to handle a musket" well, take guns apart, and reassemble them. The pressing needs of the war made it possible for her to perform such jobs (Taylor 1968, 26, 32–35).

Susie King Taylor remembered hearing the Emancipation Proclamation read and described January 1, 1863, as a "glorious day." The Emancipation Proclamation proclaimed that slaves within the rebellious areas of the Confederacy were free as of January 1, 1863. In actuality the proclamation did not free any slaves because the Confederacy did not enforce it, but it raised the hopes of blacks who came to believe that it was simply a matter of time before slavery would disappear completely. By the end of December 1865, emancipation became a reality when the Thirteenth Amendment had been ratified by enough states to become law.

Former slave girls could now enjoy the rights similar to those open to free girls before the general emancipation in 1865. Not only were these liberties and guarantees applicable to the former slave girls, but they were extended to their offspring as well. As nearly 4 million blacks made the transition from slavery to freedom, Margaret Nillin, who had worked as a personal servant in Texas before emancipation, reflected upon the changes in her life. "In slavery I owns nothin'," the ninety-year-old Nillin said, who emphasized the futile possibilities of claiming possessions of her own when she added, "[I] *never* owns nothin'." By contrast, Nillin, who was twenty-one years of age at the time of her emancipation, explained the changes over time when she said, "In freedom I's own de home and raise de family." The responsibilities attendant to running a household and guiding children through their formative years into productive adulthood were not without their woes. "All dat cause[d] me worryment," Nillin remembered, who did not have similar frustrations in bondage. But when given a choice between remaining enslaved and being emancipated, Nillin said without hesitation, "I takes freedom." Similarly, Victoria Adams, one of Nillin's contemporaries, after reflecting upon the early years of her life, said: "I like being free more better" (Rawick 1972b, vol. 5, pt. 3, 152–153; Rawick 1972a, vol. 2, pt. 2, 12).

Wilma King

See also African American Girls in the Twentieth Century; Enslaved Girls of African Descent

References and Further Reading

Bruns, Roger, ed. 1977. *Am I Not a Man and a Brother? The Antislavery Crusade of Revolutionary America, 1688–1788.* New York: Chelsea House.

Delaney, Lucy A. 1988. "From the Darkness Cometh the Light, or Struggles for Freedom." In *Six Women's Slave Narratives.* Edited by Henry Louis Gates, Jr. New York: Oxford University Press.

Horton, James Oliver. 1976. "Generations of Protest: Black Families and Social Reform in Ante-Bellum Boston." *New England Quarterly* 49 (June): 51–76.

Ingersoll, Thomas N. 1991. "Free Blacks in a Slave Society: New Orleans, 1718–1812." *William and Mary Quarterly* 48 (April): 173–200.

Lerner, Gerda. 1993. "Sarah Mapps Douglass." In *Black Women in America: An Historical Encyclopedia.* Edited by Darlene Clark Hine, Elsa Barkley Brown, and Rosalyn Terborg-Penn. Brooklyn: Carlson Publishing.

Lerner, Gerda, ed. 1973. *Black Women in White America: A Documentary History.* New York: Vintage Books.

Murray, Pauli. 1987. *Proud Shoes: The Story of an American Family.* New York: Harper and Row.

Potter, Eliza. 1991. *A Hairdresser's Experience in the High Life.* New York: Oxford University Press.

Prince, Nancy. 1990. *A Black Woman's Odyssey Through Russia and Jamaica.* New York: Markus Wiener Publishing.

Rawick, George P., ed. 1972a. *The American Slave: A Composite Autobiography.* 19 vols. Vol. 2, *South Carolina Narratives,* pt. 2. Westport: Greenwood Press.

———. 1972b. *The American Slave: A Composite Autobiography.* 19 vols. Vol. 5, *Texas Narratives,* pt. 3. Westport: Greenwood Press.

Richardson, Marilyn, ed. 1987. *Maria W. Stewart, America's First Black Woman Political Writer: Essays and Speeches.* Bloomington: Indiana University Press.

Sterling, Dorothy. 1984. *We Are Your Sisters: Black Women in the Nineteenth Century.* New York: W. W. Norton.

Stevenson, Brenda, ed. 1988. *The Journals of Charlotte Forten Grimké.* New York: Oxford University Press.

Still, William. 1872. *The Underground Rail Road: A Record of Facts, Authentic Narratives, Letters, &c., Narrating the Hardships, Hairbreadth Escapes and Death Struggles of the Slaves in Their Efforts for Freedom, as Related by Themselves and Others, or the Largest Stockholders, and Most Liberal Aiders and Advisers, of the Road.* Philadelphia: Porter and Coats.

Taylor, Susie King. 1968. *Reminiscences of My Life in Camp.* New York: Arno Press and New York Times.

U.S. Bureau of the Census. 1864. *Population of the United States in 1860: Compiled from Original Returns* of the Eighth Census by Joseph C. G. Kennedy. Washington, DC: Government Printing Office.

Wilson, Harriet E. 1859. "Our Nig": or, Sketches from the Life of a Free Black, in a Two-Story White House, North. Showing That Slavery's Shadows Fall Even There. 1983. Reprint, New York: Random House.

Woodson, Carter G., ed. 1969. The Mind of the Negro as Reflected in Letters Written during the Crisis, 1800–1860. New York: Russell and Russell.

Frontier Girls

Girls played a vital part in the life and labor of the American frontier. They contributed to their families' survival, helped shape society in new settlements, found their own distinctive pleasures and coped in their own ways with the difficulties of pioneering.

The frontier was the edge of European-American settlement pushing into North America. The Anglo-American frontier moved from the region just west of the Appalachian Mountains in the 1770s to the Mississippi Valley in the 1820s, the Pacific coast in the 1840s and 1850s, and the Great Plains in the 1870s and 1880s.

East of the Mississippi River, most frontier families were farmers who labored to clear land of trees and plant it with corn, cotton, tobacco, and other crops. In the far West were mining towns, ranches, lumber camps, and market centers, as well as farms. Many frontier families lived isolated from others and relied heavily on their own resources. Because the continent was filled with well-settled Native American peoples, many frontier girls came into close contact—and sometimes conflict—with people of the tribes who were being dispossessed by the expanding frontier.

In some ways frontier girlhood was out of step with developments elsewhere in the United States. Especially among the urban middle class in more settled parts of the country, girls were contributing less and less to the economies of their families and were increasingly sheltered from the world outside the home. Most frontier families, however, depended heavily on the work of children. They could not afford to hold their daughters apart from the demands of labor inside and outside the home. Girls grew up closely involved with their communities, whether in mining towns, ranching regions, or newly settled farming country.

Girls, in fact, were often essential to a family's survival. They helped their mothers with the extraordinary range of work in the household—from cooking, cleaning, and washing to making and mending clothes, whitewashing walls, and much more. On farms and ranches and often in towns, girls lent their hands to cultivating the gardens that for many families produced much of the food on the dinner table.

During the first year or so of settling in a new area, farmers would have no income from their work until their fields were broken, planted, and harvested. Mothers and daughters often would provide most or all of the cash income from the household by selling not only surpluses from the garden but also eggs, milk, and butter from the chickens and cattle families brought with them.

In mining and market towns, bachelors or married men living on their own frequently boarded with families. The women and girls who cooked for these men and sometimes did their laundry provided income needed for their households' survival. Girls in towns worked at many other jobs—running errands (sometimes for prostitutes and others in the demimonde), peddling pies, and gathering and selling edible wild plants. Everywhere,

Sharpshooter Annie Oakley won a shooting contest at the age of fifteen, competed against champion male shooters, and toured America and Europe with Buffalo Bill's "Wild West Show." (Library of Congress)

girls were vital contributors to the cash incomes all families required to buy what they could not produce for themselves.

Girls did not work directly in some of the heaviest frontier labor, for instance, in underground mining and logging and building fences, but on frontier farms and ranches they shared many tasks with adults. At six or seven years of age, they were in the saddle and herding cattle. They spent hundreds of hours during the summer chopping weeds from the growing crops and keeping birds, cattle, and wild game out of the fields. In the arid West they sometimes hauled water in wagons from miles away for drinking, cooking, and cleaning. They brought in wood and, on the plains, gathered "chips" (the dried dung of cattle and bison) that was sometimes the only available fuel. Many daughters became accomplished hunters, bagging rabbits, deer, and other game for the dinner table. They gathered many kinds of edible wild plants—grapes and plums that grew along the creeks, greens, some nuts, and even some roots.

Frontier daughters (and sons) often engaged in a wider diversity of work than their parents. In this they were continuing the roles children had played throughout American history—and in most societies of the past—even as young Americans in other parts of the changing nation were withdrawing from the working world and living by patterns that would become more common in the twentieth century.

The frontier child's world of play, like that of work, was also somewhat out of step with that of youngsters elsewhere. Middle-class parents in the cities increasingly tried to shape their daughters' and sons' characters by choosing their toys and amusements. For the first time industry was providing significant numbers of playthings. Among the thousands of families moving to the frontier, however, girls mostly were expected to find their own amusements. Play, in fact, was the part of girls' lives most under their own control, and it showed them at their most creative. They sometimes turned part of their work into play. They raced horses while herding cattle, waged mock battles by throwing cow chips and clods of cornfield dirt, and played hide-and-seek during expeditions to gather wild berries.

Other play was a kind of rehearsal for future roles girls saw among adults. With their brothers they practiced branding, using sticks on dogs and cats. They constructed miniature farms and households and the people who inhabited them—matchbox wagons pulled by beetles, houses and fences made of twigs, and tiny corrals, schoolhouses, and chicken coops.

Girls created a variety of toys from the natural world. They skated on wooden floors with melon rinds strapped to their feet and played with balloons made from pigs' bladders. Branches became stick horses and a variety of imagined weapons. The popularity of such items among girls emphasized the frontier's tendency to blur or erase the line between the work and play of female and male. But girls also had more traditional toys. Dolls, the female playthings most common to all cultures, were fashioned from cornhusks and corncobs, pinecones, and other materials found in fields and woodlands, usually graced with bits of cloth and perhaps buttons for eyes. Dolls were placed in cradles and beds imagined from logs and piles of leaves and fed from stumps pictured as stoves.

When parents gave dolls to girls, they were trying to encourage their daughters to imagine maternal roles they would be expected to fill in a few years. As other presents they gave sets of toy dishes and tea sets. A few of the earliest board games that found their way to the frontier promoted dominant values of Victorian America. Such gifts illustrate another theme in frontier life—the determined effort of adults to implant traditional values and patterns of life into the country they were settling. This impulse, expressed in many areas of pioneer life, was especially acute in relations between adults and children. Girls and boys, after all, would be responsible for shaping communities during the first full generation of settlement. Playthings of cultural instruction were one more means of planting a way of life on the frontier.

Children, in their own way, were doing the same. Wherever girls and boys gathered, they played games they themselves imported from elsewhere. Some could be traced back centuries into European history and many had roots in colonial America. Girls preferred some over others—many said fox and geese and red rover were special favorites—but as in work and other kinds of play, the sexes mixed more often than not. These games served another purpose. Girls arrived on the frontier from across the nation and the world, but because they all carried the baggage of organized games with their simple and familiar rules, strangers could come together and form an instant bond. Ring-around-a-rosy, ante-I-over, and other favorites were another part of cultural tradition brought westward. Through them, children did their part in creating frontier communities.

Education was an even more obvious method of transmitting values and culture to frontier girls. Parents were torn between two impulses. Upon settling in a new area, parents typically tried to establish some means of providing educational basics. Yet parents also needed both daughters and sons to help in the prodigious work of making a new life on the frontier. This conflict expressed more broadly the frontier's tension between the patterns of an older America and the tendencies of the new. As they did the work expected of them for generations, girls also were urged toward the educational advantages so strongly promoted by middle-class parents in more settled parts of the nation.

Girls were often educated in the home. Parents took care to bring to the frontier what were considered their society's basic texts—the Bible and a few literary and historical classics—and often added contemporary novels and other writing. Mothers, especially, took time to teach daughters to read with the help of these books, and as William Shakespeare, John Milton, Nathaniel Hawthorne, and other fundamental cultural texts were read, a cultural inheritance was passed on.

Soon after their arrival in a new settlement, parents usually tried to establish public schooling, but doing so could be difficult. Few children lived in mining camps during their first months, and although farms were full of them, early settlement was so widely scattered that a district of 100 or more square miles might have only a handful of students. The frontier consequently often had more schools per 100 children than elsewhere in the country—testimony to the standing of education among adults. Typically, these were one-room schools, some in abandoned sod houses, ramshackle buildings, or even old railcars. Girls attended from the age of five or six through early adulthood.

Education was one area in which the experiences of girls and boys diverged somewhat. Especially as they grew older and were drawn more into the roles of adult women, daughters had relatively more time for schooling, although at peak times of work on farms, at planting and harvest, they were still expected to be in the fields and not in the classroom.

Beginning in the mid-nineteenth century, teaching was one of the few occupations outside the home considered socially acceptable for girls approaching womanhood. This trend, especially true on the frontier with its high demand for adult male labor, led large numbers of girls into teaching. As young as fifteen, they took charge of classrooms. Many would follow this profession throughout their adult lives.

In schooling, girls' domestic and public lives often merged. The same happened elsewhere in frontier society. The frontier's isolation, plus its tendency to throw together strangers from varied backgrounds, left families hungering for such social activities as dances, lectures, school entertainments, and church revivals and dinners. Girls attended them all and often played prominent roles in the entertainment.

Flirtation and courtship were a natural part of these social gatherings. Particularly on the earlier frontiers in the East, girls married at a somewhat earlier age than in more settled regions, but the popular image of pioneer daughters barely into puberty finding husbands is exaggerated. By their late teens, girls were being courted, and most were married in their early twenties.

In those late teen years of courtship, girls were also being drawn increasingly into the traditional working and social world of Victorian women. This could be a jarring change. The demands and opportunities of the frontier required girls to spend much of their time outside the home, learning their own abilities and satisfying their curiosities while playing independently and working with their brothers and fathers in settings usually reserved for men.

Then, as they entered puberty—and coincidentally as the frontier was passing and an area was taking on the traits and social patterns of more settled country—girls were expected to assume roles more traditional for women. Some embraced this life as creative and rewarding, but some resented and resisted the change and kept to lives outside the female norms of the day. The resulting inheritance, as these girls matured and reared daughters of their own, was as mixed as the experience of the frontier itself.

Elliott West

See also Captivity; Education of Girls; Native American Girls; Play; Work

References and Further Reading
Hampsten, Elizabeth. 1991. *Settlers' Children: Growing Up on the Great Plains.* Norman: University of Oklahoma Press.
Peavy, Linda, and Ursula Smith. 1999. *Frontier Children.* Norman: University of Oklahoma Press.
Werner, Emmy. 1995. *Pioneer Children on the Journey West.* Boulder, CO: Westview Press.
West, Elliott. 1989. *Growing Up with the Country: Childhood on the Far Western Frontier.* Albuquerque: University of New Mexico Press.

G

Gifted Girls

The history of education in the United States has been based on the principle of providing education in an egalitarian framework. The concept of providing special education for children identified as gifted and talented has been seen by many educators as creating an elite class. Over the past twenty years, however, there has been a gradual recognition of the need to identify and develop programs for gifts and talents that range from mathematical to musical. Many states have enacted legislation encouraging local school districts to provide special opportunities for high-achieving and talented students. The actual research on the effectiveness of these programs has not been completed.

The school and life experiences of gifted boys and girls differ in a number of respects. In early childhood and through the elementary school years, gifted boys and girls are equal in number. In adolescence, however, a marked turnaround occurs. At around age twelve, gifted boys outnumber gifted girls, and by adulthood there are far more gifted men than gifted women. What happens to those young gifted girls? Many do not capitalize on their giftedness. Their academic achievement and other talents falter, and their gifts may become obscured on the way to womanhood. Research suggests that several factors converge to produce barriers to the achievement of gifted girls, causing the decline in the numbers of identifiable gifted girls as they grow up.

First, gifted girls may not be identified early enough. The identification of gifted children often begins in third grade. This practice, however, penalizes young gifted girls who are often outstanding in early childhood. They talk, read, and count earlier than boys, and in the preschool years they score higher than boys on intelligence quotient (IQ) tests. But by middle school the balance is reversed. Even as early as third grade, many gifted girls have gotten the message, effectively delivered at home and in school, that it is safer not to stand out for academic prowess, that it is more acceptable for girls to be like their peers. Educators, therefore, need to take seriously the signs of developmental advancement in girls during the preschool years.

Second, for gifted girls a gradual loss of self-esteem starts early. Between grades three and eight, most gifted girls' self-concept declines significantly, and by adolescence many gifted girls suffer a marked lack of confidence. Eighth-grade gifted girls report more negative self-regard and lack of self-confidence in behavior, intellectual and school status, and popularity than nongifted girls in the same grade (Kline and Short 1991; Klein and Zehms 1996). Conversely, characteristics such as

A young girl playing the violin. (Francoise Gervais/Corbis)

perfectionism, hopelessness, and discouragement rise with age. Bruce Kline and Elizabeth Short hypothesize that these changes result from conflicts between the psychological needs of gifted girls and society's gender-role expectations, as girls learn from their families, school, and the media which behaviors are approved (Kline and Short 1991).

Third, as they move into adolescence, many gifted girls discover that it is smart not to look too smart. They deny, camouflage, or abandon their talents and see disadvantages in being gifted. Adolescent girls are faced with choosing between the competing goals of popularity and academic achievement, and social relations often take precedence over intellectual interests. Since gifted girls are more socially adept than gifted boys, they pick up social cues and know how to fit in. In order to please others, gifted girls tend to play down their talents. In a study of more than 600 children, Linda Silverman found that girls typically adapt to the ability level of their age-mates (1993). Gifted girls in grades three through nine chose not to leave their friends to join advanced classes.

The middle school years are the most critical period for loss of talent. At this time, gifted girls discover that high achievement may cost them acceptance by their peer group. Girls' groups reward conformity and may ostracize the girl who is a high achiever. In a study of almost 500 students that examined how gifted students are viewed by their peers, gifted boys were found to be the most popular and gifted girls the least. The girls were perceived as generally moody or sad, whereas the boys were described as funny and having a good sense of humor (Luftig and Nichols 1991).

Giftedness and leadership qualities often go hand in hand. Leadership qualities are encouraged in boys, and gifted boys are described as leaders. In gifted girls, however, the same qualities are often described as "bossiness" and are discouraged. The message conveyed to girls is that it is okay for girls not to be assertive and not to assume leadership roles; having friends is far more important.

Adolescent girls make choices that affect their academic careers. They stop enrolling in gifted programs in grades ten, eleven, and twelve (Read 1991) and are at particular risk for academic underachievement in the areas of math and science. The myth in society that task proficiency is gender-related shows up in gifted boys' and girls' attitudes about their abilities and also affects the types of courses they select. Gifted girls do not estimate their abilities as highly as gifted boys; girls' perception of their math abilities is low, whereas boys' perception of their language abilities is low. Thus the message is perpetuated that it is acceptable for girls not to do well in math and science; they can be excellent readers and writers and leave science and math to the boys.

Studies that have examined gender differences in math abilities show mixed results. Although boys appear more active and able in advanced math and science classes, research in basic math and spatial abilities shows no difference. Good math test performance depends on the number of math classes taken, and avoidance of math classes by girls results in lower standardized test scores. However, the gap in math achievement scores between males and females seems to be decreasing, and the number of girls in advanced math and science classes has increased. In 1990 boys made up a higher percentage of precalculus, trigonometry, statistics, and calculus classes, but in 1994 there was an equal or higher percentage of girls in all those classes except calculus (AAUW 1992).

Girls and boys show different test-taking styles. Despite the lessening of the gap between boys and girls on tests such as the Scholastic Aptitude Test (SAT), the results of which determine eligibility for National Merit Scholarships, girls still do less well, according to research by the Educational Testing Service in Princeton, New Jersey. College Board officials point to research showing that boys and girls are treated differently in classrooms as a possible reason for girls' lower scores. Standardized tests that entail short fill-in or multiple-choice responses reward bold, quick answers and a willingness to take risks, characteristics more typical of boys than girls. Researchers such as Carol Gilligan have shown that females process and express knowledge differently and more subtly; they look for nuances and shades of gray.

College and career choices are affected by high school course selection, creating a downward spiral effect (Siegle and Reis 1998). Test results and course selection have important implications for performance on college entrance exams, programs for the gifted, and career choices. It follows that if gifted girls abandon their math and science pursuits for more "socially acceptable" activities, they run the risk of limiting their options for career development as well as their personal satisfaction in the workplace. Despite the catch-up occurring in math and science, there is still a gender gap in technology. For example, in 1996 girls made up only a small percentage of the high school students who took advanced placement computer science exams. Furthermore, the girls who do take computer classes tend to be in data entry, whereas boys are more likely to take advanced computer applications that can lead them to careers in technology.

Programs are being instituted that aim to change attitudes as well as educational practices. Schools and families are tackling the problem in different ways. Some parents choose single-sex schools for their daughters, hoping to encourage independence and the full use of talent. Other parents and schools choose to effect change by encouraging teacher training within coeducational environments and by creating special programs to foster gender equality. Some schools establish single-sex classes in math and science. As changes are implemented, benefits will accrue to society as well as to individual women; their aspirations will be unlimited, and they will benefit in terms of self-esteem, occupational satisfaction, and access to financial resources.

Anita Gurian

See also Education of Girls; Mathematics and Science

References and Further Reading

American Association of University Women (AAUW). 1992. *The AAUW Report: How Schools Shortchange Girls.* Washington, DC: AAUW Educational Foundation.

Callahan, Carolyn M., and Sally M. Reis. 1996. "Gifted Girls, Remarkable Women." In *Remarkable Women: Perspectives on Female Talent Development.* Edited by Karen D. Arnold, Kathleen Diane Noble, and Rena Faye Subotnik. Cresskill, NJ: Hampton Press.

Gilligan, Carol. 1982. *In a Different Voice.* Cambridge, MA: Harvard University Press.

Klein, Ann G., and Debra Zehms. 1996. "Self-concept and Gifted Girls: A Cross- sectional Study of Intellectually Gifted Females in Grades 3, 5, 8." *Roeper Review* 19, no. 1: 30–34.

Kline, Bruce B., and Elizabeth B. Short. 1991. "Changes in Emotional Resilience: Gifted Adolescent Females." *Roeper Review* 13, no. 3: 118–121.

Luftig, Richard L., and Marci L. Nichols. 1991. "An Assessment of the Social Status and Perceived Personality and School Traits of Gifted Students by Non-gifted." *Roeper Review* 13, no. 3: 138–153.

Read, Carolyn R. 1991. "Gender Distribution in Programs for the Gifted." *Roeper Review* 13, no. 3: 188–193.

Siegle, Del, and Sally M. Reis. 1998. "Gender Differences in Teacher and Student Perceptions of Gifted Students' Ability and Effort." *Gifted Child Quarterly* 42, no. 1: 101–110.

Silverman, Linda Kreger. 1993. *Counseling the Gifted and Talented.* Denver, CO: Love.

Girl Gangs

For a small segment of girls in the United States, joining and participating in a gang has become a defining aspect of their adolescence. Historically, the issue of female delinquency and girls' subsequent involvement in gangs has been subsumed by the attention given to boys. When female delinquency was studied, theories were built on sexist assumptions and evolved in starkly different ways than theories of male delinquency. Despite the paucity of theoretical development and research, recent media attention has been given to the idea that a "new," more violent, "masculine" girl has emerged. This type of coverage has popularized the public's notion that society is now confronted with predatory girls in gangs who have assumed the social traits of males. It is difficult to get a clear picture of the prevalence with which girls participate in gangs and the degree to which they may be increasingly violent since studies to answer these questions are lacking. The small amount of research that does exist shows many differences between girls' and boys' gang involvement and delinquency. To understand why girls join and participate in gangs requires an examination of the unique realities of their lives, which are shaped by gender, race, ethnicity, and class. Ultimately, this type of analysis highlights many issues, such as sexual victimization, that lead to a more accurate assessment of girls and gangs.

Historically, gangs emerged as a response to needs for protection and self-

An eighteen-year-old member of the Circle City Piru Bloods gang in Los Angeles, California. (Jim Tynan/Impact Visuals/PictureQuest)

identity. Girls have been a part of gangs since the initial accounts of gangs in the early 1800s, when "criminal" gangs first formed. Girls' gangs were initially described as auxiliary groups to male gangs, and female gangs were only briefly mentioned in reference to their association with existing male gangs (see Thrasher 1927). In the late 1950s girl gangs' strong ties to boy gangs began to form. Unfortunately, early gang activity by girls is not well documented or researched. Current research reveals tremendous variety in girl gangs, from autonomous all-female gangs to mixed-gender gangs. Further, there may be more useful ways to conceptualize and categorize girl gangs by examining differences between gangs regarding their reliance on fighting, drug-selling and use, age, and race (Hagedorn and Devitt 1999).

As criminological theories evolved to explain subcultural delinquent groups, they were almost exclusively applied to boys, ignoring girls. In fact, peer groups have come to be seen as a crucial determinant of male delinquency. Several assumptions have prevented the application of peer group theory to explanations of girls' delinquency. In many ways, theories of girls' delinquency have remained fixed in dated but "classic" studies that noted that their behavior was dictated by biological, hormonal, or genetic attributes unique to females, for example, sexual promiscuity or maladjustment to the "normal" feminine role.

Increased attention is now being given to girls in gangs for several reasons. One of the more negative reasons for this attention is the inaccurate and sensationalized image of girls in gangs created by the media. Rather than providing a holistic picture of girls in gangs, the media tends to spotlight particularly heinous and rare crimes committed by minority girls from the lower class. A comparison with "typical" female delinquency is often made to demonstrate the masculine nature of the gang-related offense and is cited as support for the influence of female liberation and increasing independence on girls (Chesney-Lind 1993). This perspective represents a continuation of theoretical ideas that emerged in the 1970s, which suggested that the women's liberation movement, by promoting female independence and equality, was responsible for increases in female crime and delinquency (see Adler 1975). Although there has never been empirical evidence to support these assertions, the media frequently relies on this explanation when it comes to girls in gangs. Unfortunately, this type of attention results in the portrayal of girl gang members as evil and ultimately leads to ineffective policies to address their problems.

Evaluating studies of girls' involvement in gangs and delinquency challenges public perceptions created in part by the media and reveals many differences that exist between girls and boys. In a recent study by the Office of Juve-nile Justice and Delinquency Prevention (1999), law enforcement officials reported that females accounted for 11 percent of all gang members. This estimate is consistent with the average estimate of 10 percent from existing studies (Pollock 1999). Studies of delinquency relying on self-reported data indicate that for nonserious offenses, girls and boys engage in similar rates of delinquency, but for serious offenses there is a wide gender gap that has remained constant over time. Small increases in arrest rates for girls are often falsely cited as evidence that girls' violence has skyrocketed. It is important to examine these increases closely before such generalizations are accepted. For example, although the proportion of girls arrested for violent crimes rose 5 percent between 1980 and 1995, the entirety of that increase was attributable to an increase in aggravated assaults. Feminist scholars have suggested that this increase may be due to a reclassification of status offenses rather than reflecting an actual change in the behavior of girls (Chesney-Lind and Shelden 1992). Meanwhile, rates of other offenses included in the violent crime index and committed by girls, such as murder, rape, and robbery, have decreased or stayed the same.

Regardless of gender, gang members are more likely to participate in delinquency and to participate with greater frequency than nongang members. However, studies specific to gangs and gang delinquency have found that girls in gangs commit fewer and less serious offenses than boys (Bjerregaard and Smith 1993; Chesney-Lind and Brown 1998; Joe and Chesney-Lind 1995). Girls' violence was found to be less likely to result in death and more likely to be directed at relatives and friends as a result of disagreements when compared to boys' violence. Girls have been more likely than boys to report getting into trouble due to running away or other status offenses in response to a difficult family environment that often included abuse. With the exception of marijuana, boys in gangs also reported more substance abuse than girls in gangs and more involvement in selling drugs than girls.

Fortunately, increased attention is now being given to girls in gangs because of qualitative, feminist research exploring, for example, why girls join gangs. The reasons for gang involvement are currently being sought by highlighting the realities that constitute everyday life for many girls. Initial research in this area pointed to the desire for popularity and the excitement provided by gang involvement. Although this may be part of the answer, girls' involvement in gangs today is theorized to be a natural response to adverse socioeconomic conditions and further powerlessness caused by inequalities regarding gender and race. Studies of girl gangs suggest that gang involvement is seen either as a vehicle to escape the anticipated and often demeaning role of wife and mother or as an alternative to the seemingly unattainable dream of having a successful marriage and family. In addition, a desire for respect and status as well as access to moneymaking opportunities were motivating factors for girls' gang participation.

Another reason girls join gangs may be isolation from and failure in traditional institutions, such as family and schools. Girls join gangs to fulfill needs not met by their families—needs such as acceptance, belonging, and loyalty. Girl gang members are more likely than boys in gangs to have come from abusive homes and from families with serious parental drug use (Hagedorn and Moore 1996). Because of these problematic issues in families, gangs provide an alternative as girls describe their gangs in language mirroring idyllic family life (Quicker 1983).

Educational difficulties provide another motive for girls to join gangs. One study found that having low expectations of completing school increased the chances of gang membership 20 percent for girls but only 1 percent for boys (Bjerregaard and Smith 1993). Another study found that although more than one-half of male gang members had dropped out of school, about 80 percent of female gang members were dropouts (Felkenes and Becker 1995). These difficulties experienced by girls support the idea that exclusion from traditional institutions leads some girls to pursue alternative opportunities that can be provided through gang membership.

Female gang members face unique problems and may suffer more from their gang involvement for longer periods of their lives. Male gang members acknowledge that girls are treated like possessions or sexual objects, with a strong double standard in place determining acceptable behavior for girls and boys. Reports of domestic violence and brutal sexual victimization on the part of girls in gangs reinforce the existence of attitudes and behaviors that devalue females. In-depth qualitative studies with girl gang members emphasize their exposure to violence and the resulting acceptance of pain and brutality as a daily and unavoidable part of life. Additionally, girls in gangs face issues of teen pregnancy, teen motherhood, and the challenges of raising children under difficult socioeconomic circumstances. Unfortunately, rather than attempts to understand and address the problems of girls who choose gangs, the response has been to condemn them, which ultimately leads to ineffective policies.

Kristi Holsinger

See also Graffiti; Juvenile Delinquents; Substance Abuse

References and Further Reading
Adler, Freda. 1975. *Sisters in Crime.* Prospect Heights, IL: Waveland Press.
Bjerregaard, Beth, and Carolyn Smith. 1993. "Gender Differences in Gang Participation, Delinquency, and Substance Use." *Journal of Quantitative Criminology* 9, no. 4: 329–355.
Brotherton, David C. 1996. "'Smartness,' 'Toughness,' and 'Autonomy': Drug Use in the Context of Gang Female Delinquency." *Journal of Drug Issues* 26, no. 1: 261–277.
Chesney-Lind, Meda. 1993. "Girls, Gangs and Violence: Anatomy of a Backlash." *Humanity and Society* 17, no. 3: 321–344.
Chesney-Lind, Meda, and Marilyn Brown. 1998. "Girls and Violence: An Overview." Pp. 171–200 in *Youth Violence: Prevention, Intervention, and Social Policy.* Edited by Daniel J. Flannery and C. Ronald Huff. Washington, DC: American Psychiatric Press.
Chesney-Lind, Meda, and Randall G. Shelden. 1992. *Girls, Delinquency and Juvenile Justice.* Pacific Grove, CA: Brooks/Cole.
Felkenes, George T., and Harold K. Becker. 1995. "Female Gang Members: A Growing Issue for Policy Makers." *Journal of Gang Research* 2, no. 4: 1–10.
Hagedorn, John, and Mary L. Devitt. 1999. "Fighting Female: The Social Construction of Female Gangs." Pp. 256–276 in *Female Gangs in America: Essays on Girls, Gangs, and Gender.* Edited by Meda Chesney-Lind and John M. Hagedorn. Chicago: Lake View Press.
Hagedorn, John, and Joan Moore. 1996. "What Happens to Girls in the Gang?" Pp. 204–218 in *Gangs in America.*
Edited by C. Ronald Huff. Thousand Oaks, CA: Sage.
Harris, Mary G. 1988. *Cholas: Latina Girls and Gangs.* New York: AMS Press.
———. 1994. "Cholas, Chicano Girls and Gangs." *Sex Roles* 30: 289–431.
Joe, Karen A., and Meda Chesney-Lind. 1995. "'Just Every Mother's Angel': An Analysis of Gender and Ethnic Variations in Youth Gang Membership." *Gender and Society* 9, no. 4: 408–432.
Office of Juvenile Justice and Delinquency Prevention. 1999. *1996 National Youth Gang Survey.* Washington, DC: U.S. Department of Justice.
Pollock, Joycelyn M. 1999. *Criminal Women.* Cincinnati, OH: Anderson Publishing.
Quicker, John C. 1983. *Homegirls: Characterizing Chicana Gangs.* San Pedro, CA: International University Press.
Thrasher, Frederic M. 1927. *The Gang: A Study of 1,313 Gangs.* Chicago: University of Chicago Press.

Girl Power

Girl power, a term coined in the mid-1990s by Great Britain's ubiquitous pop stars The Spice Girls, represents a primarily commercial form of popular feminism where girls, for the first time in history, take center stage in the media as political subjects. Through television heroines like Buffy the Vampire Slayer, who fights demons in a miniskirt, girl power promotes the idea that in this new and enlightened era, girls can do anything to which they set their minds. Traditional feminism has little relevance in this discourse because problems of gender inequality are considered largely solved, and girls are no longer hindered in the same ways that their mothers were. As one of The Spice Girls states their mission: "We're freshening up feminism for the nineties. . . . Feminism has become a dirty word. Girl Power is just a nineties

The British band The Spice Girls. (Reuters New Media Inc./Corbis, 1998)

way of saying it" (Douglas 1997, 21). In other words, girl power is firmly aligned with "postfeminism"—the idea born in the 1990s that feminism has outlived its immediate usefulness and, as a result, is incapable of offering anything substantive to young women and girls.

Girl power is the manifestation of a decade-long fascination with teenage girls and girlish things—one that started with the feisty resurrection of the term *girl* in the early 1990s by members of the musical and zine-based movement riot grrrls. Arguably a more radical and overtly political movement than girl power (if girl power can be called a "movement" at all), riot grrrl represents the flipside of girl power in that it is largely outside the commercial and media-saturated realm. Riot grrrl possesses the political muscle

often lacking in girl power; it also has the cohesion of a bona-fide youth culture. As one early manifesto states: "Riot grrrl is . . . BECAUSE we need to accept and support each other as girls; acknowledging our different approaches to life and accepting every one of them as valid. BECAUSE we seek to create revolution in our own lives every single day by envisioning and creating alternatives to the status quo" (Carlip 1995, 32).

Those who identify as riot grrrls, therefore, are aware of the forces against them—of their doubly marginalized position as youth and as women. Girl power, on the other hand, is less a movement than a broad and somewhat nebulous cultural phenomenon. In a sense, girl power represents the tamer, more palatable version of riot grrrl—a version largely created

GUERRILLA GIRLS' POP QUIZ.

Q. If February is Black History Month and March is Women's History Month, what happens the rest of the year?

A. Discrimination.

BOX 1056 Cooper Sta. NY, NY 10276 **GUERRILLAGIRLS** CONSCIENCE OF THE ART WORLD

The Guerrilla Girls are an example of a third-wave feminist group involved in the "girl power" movement. (Courtesy of the Guerrilla Girls)

by the media. The focus for girl power is on "feeling good"—on tapping into individual power as opposed to focusing on the forces curtailing it. As one twelve-year-old girl puts it: "It means equality . . . that girls are strong, each one in her own way" (Lemish 1998, 164).

As with most media-hyped phrases, however, girl power is multivalent. It has absorbed everything from girls' friendships to their fashion sense. In fact, its commercial capital has so defined it that the intersection between philosophy and consumerism is very blurred indeed. In terms of its relationship to actual teenage girls, girl power carries a commercial message, in that it signals the emergence of teenage girls as a powerful economic force. With the immense popularity among teenage girls of films like *Scream* (which grossed $103 million in the box office upon its initial release), bands like The Spice Girls (whose single "Wannabe" sold 1.8 million copies in the United

States alone), and television shows like *Buffy the Vampire Slayer* and *Sabrina the Teenage Witch*, the economic clout of adolescent girls is not so difficult to figure. The number of teenagers in the United States was on the rise in the 1990s for the first time in fifteen years, and their ranks were growing at a faster rate than the overall U.S. population. Moreover, according to one market research firm, teenagers spent an estimated $84 billion of their own money in 1997 alone. Clearly, teenage girls ages thirteen to seventeen—88 percent of whom "love to shop," according to one consumer survey—represent a viable market. And marketers have been quick to capitalize on that. Empowerment through style—in terms of both fashion and attitude—becomes something girls can buy in a Delia's clothing catalogue. Yet, despite its almighty consumerist ethos, girl power nevertheless resonates on an emotional level with today's adolescent girls.

In part, girl power appeals because of its relevance to a teenager's life. As the following quotation indicates, girls are well aware that their concerns are frequently overlooked by older women and in contemporary feminist discourse. As one sixteen-year-old girl reflects on her early adolescence:

> I was stuck in the middle. I was changing. I wasn't a woman, but I wasn't a little girl. I wanted to play with dolls, but then I wanted to go out and meet guys. I wanted all these clothes, but then I wanted toys, too. . . . It was a lot of changes. I was really stuck in the middle, that's how I felt. I don't know if my mother understood that or if she remembers how that feels. (Cassidy 1999, 40)

Not only do some girls today feel that older women typically ignore them as conscious subjects, but also they are quite clear about the ways in which they are different from "older" feminists. The new girl power feminism—as defined by postfeminist websites, in anthologies like *Listen Up! Voices from the Next Feminist Generation* (Findlen 1995), and by The Spice Girls' liner notes—fits more comfortably with the current self-conceptualizations of teenage girls, particularly in terms of pleasure (the old feminists did not approve of makeup), sexuality (the old feminists were puritanical and antisex), and empowerment (the old feminists claimed victim status). Although these representations of earlier feminist positions are myopic or even blatantly inaccurate, it is nevertheless the case that today's girl power feminism looks quite different from the feminism of the 1970s and 1980s. For example, girl power relies on the machinery of the media and less on grassroots organizing or academic production to convey its meaning. And much like the message suggested by Nike's "just do it" advertising, girl power's message is about individual power and achievement.

And yet, girl power also puts a high premium on girl bonding. As The Spice Girls propose in their song "Wannabe": "If you wanna be my lover, you've got to get with my friends. Make it last forever, friendship never ends." These lines are perhaps the most famous in The Spice Girls' canon and were probably largely responsible for their meteoric rise as girl power heroines. The notion that adolescent girls might privilege female friendship over romance created a minirevolution—one that can certainly be felt in various mainstream films like Herbert Ross's *Boys on the Side* (1995) and Annette Haywood-Carter's *Foxfire* (1996).

Although clearly a discourse of empowerment for girls, the question remains as to just how revolutionary girl power actually is. Girl power's ethos can be found everywhere in the popular media—in teen magazines that emphasize issues like "The Power of Positive Thinking" and in films like Andy Tennant's *Ever After* (1998), billed as "the girl power Cinderella story." Girl power suggests an orientation in which, if a girl works hard enough, she can achieve anything she desires. It is a brand of feminism that projects a tough and powerful teen image, but one that is unrealistic and unattainable for all but the most privileged girls. According to the girl power line of reasoning, girls need not worry about structural inequalities based on race or class because they are meaningless in a world dominated by individual achievement. Unfortunately, in most cases, this individual can only be one who possesses the privilege of whiteness and an upwardly mobile class position. In the final analysis, then, girl power cannot guarantee power for all girls—rather, it is primarily for those who have the financial and educational resources to obtain it.

Kimberley Roberts

See also Fan Clubs; Teenybopper; Zines

References and Further Reading

Budgeon, Shelley. 1998. "'I'll Tell You What I Really, Really Want': Girl Power and Self-Identity in Britain." Pp. 115–144 in *Millennium Girls: Today's Girls around the World*. Edited by Sherrie A. Inness. Oxford: Rowman and Littlefield.

Carlip, Hillary. 1995. *Girl Power: Young Women Speak Out*. New York: Warner Books.

Cassidy, Carol. 1999. *Girls in America: Their Stories, Their Words.* New York: TV Books.

Douglas, Susan. 1997. "Girls 'n' Spice: All Things Nice?" *The Nation* (August 25): 21–24.

Findlen, Barbara, ed. 1995. *Listen Up! Voices from the Next Feminist Generation.* Seattle: Seal Press.

Lemish, Dafna. 1998. "Spice Girls' Talk: A Case Study in the Development of Gendered Identity." Pp. 145–168 in *Millennium Girls: Today's Girls Around the World.* Edited by Sherrie A. Inness. Oxford: Rowman and Littlefield.

Munk, Nina. 1997. "Girl Power!" *Fortune* (December 8): 132–140.

Press, Joy. 1997. "Notes on Girl Power: The Selling of Softcore Feminism." *Village Voice* (September 23): 59–61.

Girl Scouts

The Girl Scouts is one of the largest international organizations of girls ages 5 to 17. Currently, there are more than 3.6 million Girl Scouts in the United States, and since its founding in 1912, more than 40 million girls and women have been in the organization. Girl Scouting and Girl Guiding encompass the world and exist in 136 countries. From its inception, Girl Scouting promoted both traditional gender norms of domesticity and new feminist ideals that were illustrated most clearly in outdoor activities, career preparation, and citizenship education (8 years before women had the vote nationally). Girl Scouts are expected to uphold the ideals expressed in "The Promise" and "The Law." The trefoil pin signifies the three parts of the promise, "On my honor, I will try: / To serve God and my country / To help people at all times / And to live by the Girl Scout Law."

The organization was founded by Juliette Gordon Low (nicknamed "Daisy") of Savannah, Georgia. Low was born into an aristocratic, southern family on October 31, 1860. Low became partially deaf because of childhood mastoid infections, and during her wedding in 1886 to William Mackay Low of Great Britain, a piece of rice lodged in her good ear. A doctor punctured her eardrum trying to remove it, leaving her almost completely deaf. For the rest of her life, Low used her deafness to ignore points of view contrary to her own.

The marriage was an unhappy one, but before they could divorce, Willy Low died in 1905. While still living in England in 1911, Low became acquainted with Robert Baden-Powell, the founder of the Boy Scouts. As an ally of Baden-Powell's sister, Agnes, Low became involved in the Girl Guides and founded a troop in Scotland. She returned to Savannah in 1912 to start Girl Guides in the United States. At the behest of the girls in her troop, Low began using the term *Girl Scouts* in 1913, because it seemed more "American" and adventurous. In 1915 the Girl Scouts of the United States of America was organized with Low as president, and a national headquarters was established in New York City.

Low worked tirelessly to promote Girl Scouting "for all the girls in America." She envisioned the organization as including a mixture of play, fun, work, and healthy values that would guide girls to womanhood. Initially, Girl Scouts grew because of Low's network of friends and her intuitive sense of identifying what girls would want to do and what they might find fun. From the beginning, an integral part of Girl Scouts was its focus on outdoor activities for girls. The first ten years of scouting included developing an American program that was distinct from the British program, incorporating diverse types of girls, staffing and training leaders, and laying the foundation for an international organization, the World Association of Girl Guides and Girl Scouts (WAGGS). The organization also began what would become an ambitious publishing venture, producing handbooks, pamphlets, songbooks, and magazines, including what would become *The Leader*, a monthly guide for troop leaders, and *The Rally*, which would shortly be renamed *The American Girl*, at one time the largest magazine for teenage girls in the United States. During World War I, Girl Scouts experienced enormous growth, partially because of the war and the patriotism it inspired. Girl Scouts worked in hospitals, grew victory gardens, and sold war bonds to contribute to the war effort.

The now universal connection between Girl Scouts and cookies also began during World War I. The first "cookie sale" was held on Wall Street at a rally, with Mary Pickford challenging stockbrokers to buy homemade cookies from Girl Scouts to help the war effort. This event spawned the move to cookie sales for many troops, though all the early cookies were homemade in the women's bake sale tradition. In 1934 the Philadelphia Girl Scout Council became the first to sell distinctive commercial cookies, and a national tradition began connecting uniformed girls and entrepreneurial commerce.

After Low's resignation as president in 1920, Girl Scouting began its transformation from a highly personalized form into a stable, bureaucratic, national organization independent of Low under the direction of Jane Deeter Rippin. By 1926, the organization had a training center for leaders in upstate New York, Camp Edith Macy. Still coping with extraordinary growth, Girl Scouting began to develop a program that institutionalized domestic feminism. Girl Scouting saw itself as a conscious promoter of "up-to-date womanhood" but also as a bulwark against flappers and American moral decline.

Both the Depression and World War II caused Girl Scouts to modify their programs and work to include new groups of girls. They began expanding their outreach to girls beyond the middle class. Although Girl Scouting had included minority girls in northern troops as early as 1913 and had set up troops of "handicapped" girls as early as 1917, the movement became much more conscious of including racially diverse groups, sometimes in integrated settings. During the Depression, the Girl Scouts joined with other women's and youth organizations to respond to the needs of girls and the "hard times" of the country, including a project to work with Dust Bowl migrant girls.

Like World War I, World War II had a profound effect on the organization. Girls flocked to Scouting to promote the war effort and to reach the goal of "a million or more in '44." Additionally, the longtime internationalism of Girl Scouting helped members support U.S. entry into the war and aid underground resistance scouting groups in Europe, since scouts and guides were outlawed as European countries fell one by one to the Nazis, who installed new organizations of Hitler Youth.

In the post–World War II period, the Girl Scouts shifted their focus from the "war-ready" scouts to a more traditionally feminine version. Nevertheless, the Girl Scouts remained a place of choice and varied experience for women and girls trying to escape the pervasive feminization of women's roles in the postwar world. The world of Girl Scouting often became an avenue into paid professional work for women, as well as a haven for girls. Between 1945 and 1959, the organization continued to grow, reaching more

A group of Girl Scouts watches a parade in Alexandria, Virginia. (Richard T. Nowitz/Corbis)

than 3 million paid members and becoming both the largest female voluntary organization and the largest single employer of women in management positions in the United States. Girl Scouting continued training girls in patriotism and civil defense while maintaining its strong internationalist stance. Ironically, because of its unwavering support for the United Nations and internationalism, Girl Scouts were accused of subverting young girls into "one-world" proto-communism by the Veterans of Foreign Wars during the McCarthy era.

In 1956, Girl Scouts bought the birthplace of Juliette Low in Savannah to be a national center and also a "safe place" for racial dialogue in the South. Although it did not figure prominently in the change that swept the South, it is one of the few historic houses dedicated to a historic woman, and it remains a destination for scouts and guides of all races from all regions.

In the late 1950s, Girl Scouting became a force for racial change for white and African American girls and women in the South by beginning integrated activities in some southern communities. Yet racial issues remained highly charged, and change was not easy. Noted educator Gloria D. Scott became the Girl Scouts' first African American president in 1975, but the organization still faced challenges of multicultural inclusion.

Further, by the end of the 1960s, Girl Scouts had to respond to the "youth rebellion," which was increasingly affecting women's roles and visions of girlhood. Girl Scouting found itself embattled, having to make decisions about whether or not to make substantial programmatic changes to retain its place as the premier girls' organization in the United States.

Girl Scouting was forced to respond to the growing feminist movement and the changing demographics of women's lives in the 1970s. Claiming to have always been a "feminist organization," in a series of votes Girl Scouts opted to remain an all-girl organization, whereas Camp Fire Girls moved to a completely coeducational program and changed their name to Camp Fire, admitting boys at all levels, and Boy Scouts began admitting girls to senior Explorer troops.

Attempting to stop membership losses, the Girl Scouts made sweeping program changes, and the National Board made its first political endorsement in sixty years when it put Girl Scouts on record as supporting constitutional ratification of the Equal Rights Amendment. There was some fierce resistance within the organization to this identification with feminism, however, which crystallized around the controversy over the "Woman's Badge" in Philadelphia. Because of the information about birth control and abortion included in earning the badge, the Roman Catholic Church in Philadelphia withdrew all its support and affiliation with Girl Scouting. To a lesser degree, these issues generated controversy in other areas. Included in the 1970s program revisions, the Girl Scouts also instituted Eco-Action, an environmental program popular with girls and less controversial with adults and sponsors.

Today the Girl Scouts have renewed their commitment to physical education by instituting a health and fitness national service project in 1994 and a sports initiative in 1996. They have also supported programs that have encouraged girls to study math and science.

The pledge "to be a sister to every scout" that concludes the Girl Scout Law underscores the organization's lifelong commitment to diversity. The new Girl Scout slogan, "Girl Scouting: where girls go strong," continues to reflect the Girl Scouting emphasis on physical fitness, outdoor skills, and "practical" feminism.

Mary Rothschild and
Georganne Scheiner

See also Arts and Crafts; Camp Fire Girls; 4-H; Saturday Evening Girls; Summer Camps for Girls

References and Further Reading
Brown, Fern G. 1996. *Daisy and the Girl Scouts: The Story of Juliette Low.* Morton Grove, IL: Whitman.
Choate, Ann Hyde, and Helen Ferris, eds. 1928. *Juliette Low and the Girl Scouts: The Story of an American Woman.* Garden City: Doubleday for the Girl Scouts.
Girl Scouts of the U.S.A. 1986. *Seventy-Five Years of Girl Scouting.* New York: Girl Scouts of the USA.
———. 1997. *Highlights in Girl Scouting, 1912–1996.* New York: Girl Scouts of the USA.
Inness, Sherrie A. 1993. "Girl Scouts, Campfire Girls and Woodcraft Girls: The Ideology of Girls' Scouting Novels 1910–1935." Pg. 229–240 in *Continuities in Popular Culture: The Present in the Past and the Past in the Present and Future.* Edited by Ray B. Browne and Ronald Ambrosetti. Bowling Green, OH: Bowling Green State University Popular Press.
Jeal, Tim. 1990. *The Boy-Man: The Life of Lord Baden-Powell.* New York: Morrow.
Rosenthal, Michael. 1984. *The Character Factory: Baden-Powell and the Origins of the Boy Scout Movement.* New York: Pantheon.
Shultz, Gladys Denny, and Daisy Gordon Lawrence. 1958. *Lady from Savannah: The Life of Juliette Low.* Philadelphia: Lippincott.

Tedesco, Lauren. 1998. "Making a Girl into a Scout: Americanizing Scouting for Girls." Pp. 19–39 in *Delinquents and Debutantes: Twentieth-Century American Girls' Cultures*. Edited by Sherrie A. Inness. New York: New York University Press.

Girls and Sweets

Before the Mother Goose rhyme that described their constituent ingredients as "sugar and spice and everything nice," girls were in some part synonymous with not only sugar but also all manner of other sweet things made from sugar. This association of girls with sweets and the more abstract corollaries of sweetness—piety, purity, refinement, and femininity—became ever more intensified and naturalized as sugar itself became more democratized in American culture. At the same time, paradoxically, the act of a girl consuming sweets suggested her budding sexuality as well. It was this dual set of cultural connotations that made the connections between girls and candy highly politicized in American culture.

The feminization of sugar in general and confections in particular was part of a larger trend in the United States beginning in the nineteenth century that imbued marketplace commodities with personal characteristics, forging human links with the material world that defined both people and the goods around them. Sugar's shift in monetary value during the nineteenth century caused a concomitant shift in social value: at the beginning of the century, when refined sugar was still an expensive rarity, it was a symbol of male economic prowess. By the end of the century, refined sugar was so prevalent and so affordable—people were eating nearly 80 pounds of it per person per year—that it became socially devalued as well. What had once been a material symbol of wealth and power had transformed, in less than 100 years, into a marker of social weakness connected with women, children, and the sickly. And as sugar became feminized, women and girls became sweeter in the American psyche. Eventually, the consumed and the consumer became conflated, making sweetness and femininity synonymous.

At this time, when refined sugar and the confections made from it became more familiar to Americans as affordable marketplace goods, the popular culture—including medical treatises, domestic manuals, recipe books, and advertising—created links between abstract ideas and physical characteristics. Refined sugar—white, granular, ephemeral, and sweet—was the physical repository for conceptual qualities such as refinement, gentility, purity, and femininity. At the same time, these same sources introduced the idea that confections could embody the more dangerous aspects of girls as nascent sexual beings. Candies were both innocent treats and luxurious and potentially addictive morsels that represented adult female pleasures in girlhood form.

Sweets were pleasing indulgences that held no nutritional value and were therefore worthless from a practical dietary standpoint. Medical advisers recognized this and warned against the sin of, for example, bonbon eating by girls and women, defining it as a self-indulgent act that they linked to masturbation. Prolific health advocate John Kellogg, for one, wrote in 1884 that "self abuse" and sexual precocity in girls was caused by, among other things, eating "exciting and irritating food," which in his mind included candy (Kellogg 1884, 330). At

"*Dangerous habit-forming drugs are sold freely to women and children.*"

Death Serves Soda. *Even in the early twentieth century, as this picture shows, people were concerned about the dietary dangers of sugar.* (The Soda Fountain, *June 1909, p. 27)*

the same time, however, other domestic advisers continued to emphasize the purer aspects of sugar and candy by using the same language to describe them that they used for females, linking the nature of the commodity directly to the nature of the consumers themselves. (Eventually these were analogized to such a degree that a recognizable icon like the wedding cake served as a sweet and edible surrogate of the bride, the role that most little girls dreamed about during their entire childhood.) Indeed, popular advisers were instrumental in forging such cultural definitions. Women like Sarah Tyson Rorer warned against the harmful effects of eating too much candy—especially adulterated penny candies—at the same time that her articles in *Ladies' Home Journal* and her cookbooks featured numerous saccharine recipes aimed at the mouths of children.

Other material connections reinforced the links between girls and sweets. Like all children, girls had a strong appetite for sweets; children comprised the main consumers of hard candies and accounted for the success of most candy manufacturers during the nineteenth and twentieth centuries. In addition, many girls and young women at the turn of the century made candies in their own kitchens and sold them at local stores in order to earn an income. Still others worked in candy factories as chocolate dippers, candy wrappers, and box packers. Although working conditions there were typical of most turn-of-the-century factories (dark, crowded, and poorly ventilated), the owners of these factories used their young female workforce as a collective symbol of their products' unadulterated properties: virginal girls made pure candies.

The business world presented the most clear-cut cultural meanings through advertising, especially for products such as bonbons and prepackaged desserts. In these texts, the images of particular girls functioned as popular and recognizable icons that stood for the supposedly pure and upstanding reputations of the companies and their products. These images were also meant to reassure the grownup women using novel products that they could do so with ease and success; after all, even a little girl could master such a process. One of the most recognizable of these corporate images, the Jell-O girl, was originally modeled on the company's advertising illustrator's own four-year-old daughter, named Elizabeth King. She faithfully reappeared throughout the first decades of Jell-O's advertising, from 1904 on, and was later redesigned by Rose O'Neil, artist of the kewpie dolls. With blonde locks and ruffled dress, the Jell-O girl, a future housewife who could easily prepare impressive desserts, symbolized the purity of the granulated gelatin product itself and also represented the company image as a whole. Other dessert companies used the same kind of visual rhetoric to sell their goods, including the Junket "dainty Junket girl" and the Knox gelatin cherubs. These companies' recipe booklets, printed by the thousands and given away free with the products, helped to sell both the idea of sugar as a worthwhile consumable and the idea of girls as sweet.

Private individuals at the turn of the century also capitalized on the cheapness and abundance of refined sugar by publishing their own books on home candy making. These, too, sparked culinary fads: fudge-making and taffy-pulling parties were all the rage with girls of the time. Girls not only ate sweets but also incorporated them into their lives through domestic activities like making them. Mother Goose was right: by eating so much candy, girls *were* made out of sugar and spice, and in turn they made other things out of sugar and spice. By the twentieth century people saw sweets as trivial, sensual indulgences eaten with little forethought and for little worthwhile purpose. They were the consummate products consumed by females, young and old, who could not control their own desires and were easily satisfied by life's trifling things.

To many minds, confections were dangerous in the hands (and mouths) of girls and women. Boys ate candy, certainly, but this was often seen as a purposeful endeavor: they often bought licorice sticks or chocolate cigars and spit pretend tobacco juice or smoked pretend cigarettes in imitation of their fathers. For girls, imitating their mothers was seen as a less than worthy occupation. Developing an early taste for sweets meant that they were doomed as adults to the luxurious dissipation provided by the sensational novel and box of bonbons. But candy was one of the few things on which girls spent their own money, and unlike needlework supplies and clothes, candy did not last—it was ephemeral, and it disappeared, deliciously, at the moment of consumption. Eating sweets was a way for girls, at least in small part, to sate their own appetites.

This idea manifested itself not just with candies but with other confections as well. Ever since the 1870s, the soda fountain was a highly feminized social space. Middle- and upper-class women often took their daughters there to sample the frozen treats and to partake in a social atmosphere whose focal point was the consumption of sweet things, much like the tea party of a century before. Women who were taking breaks from their urban shopping excursions often met up with friends at a nearby fountain; in this way, they also trained their daughters in the art of socialization and habituated them to the important role of sweets in such ceremonies. These daughters, then, grew up to be young women who met up with their own friends and beaus at the local fountain. A verse written in a 1909 trade journal, entitled "Phoebe at the Fount," encapsulated the connection between sweets and romantic affection but made the soda a surrogate for romantic interest: "I don't care much for boys, / For only twelve am I, / In my fresh youth, a sweeter tooth, / Would other pleasures try; / So Mister Druggist-man / Fill up a cup for me / Of icy cream, a perfect dream, / And chocolate spread free" (Dennis 1909, 32). The popularity of the soda fountain for young women continued through the 1950s, by which time it had become a familiar institution for courtship rituals: meeting a boy at the soda fountain and sharing a soda with him was both a safe and socially acceptable form of consorting with the opposite sex.

By the mid-twentieth century the candy industry also used other, more directed ways to deliver sugar to the mouths of girls. Penny candies, popular from the 1840s on, appealed to children's sensibilities on all levels. They were affordable, enabling children to spend their money on their own choices. What is more, these treats often mimicked familiar objects like locomotives, flowers, and horses or were static depictions of allegorical scenes and, seen behind the merchant's windows or in glass jars, were

A young girl eyes candy in a store. (Shirley Zeiberg)

very enticing to the young mind and appetite. During the next 100 years the candy industry became much more sophisticated at marketing their products to their young consumer base by manufacturing sweets that were gender-specific. For girls in particular, candy jewelry was popular and appealing. Candy necklaces—"beads" of pastel-colored confections strung on elastic cords—were worn and eaten at the same time. These were accompanied by candy rings—pieces of plastic set with candy imitating gemstones—and later by candy lipstick—sugary cylinders that could be applied, like makeup, to one's lips and then licked off.

As with items like the lipstick, candy marketed toward girls was highly suggestive, melding innocent childhood pleasures with the more adult sexual pleasures of their mothers. The ambiguous rela-

tionship of girls to sweets was highlighted (and used as savvy marketing in some cases) once again. Sweets were also signifiers of seduction itself and of illicit sex. Historically, children and especially girls were warned about strangers who enticed with sweets but were interested in their own kind of gratification. This connection was also capitalized on by late-twentieth-century marketing far removed from the candy industry in which, for example, the music group the Archies sang the lyrics, "Sugar, ah honey honey / You are my candy girl / and you've got me wanting you," in their hit song "Sugar Sugar." In another instance, the movie poster for the re-release of Stanley Kubrick's 1962 film adaptation of Vladimir Nabokov's *Lolita* showed the eponymous figure wearing red heart-shaped sunglasses and sucking suggestively on a red heart-shaped lollipop, which served as a surrogate penis. The image juxtaposed a young girl's supposed innocence with her awakening sexuality: an appetite for candy signified an appetite for sex as well. And shoes with extremely high stiletto heels, called Candies, were popular with the junior high and high school girls of the 1970s, many themselves called Candy outright or as a shortened form of Candice.

The complete success of these disparate connections between sweets, purity, sexuality, and femininity—suggested since the late eighteenth century—was revealed in the vernacular language of the late twentieth century. Common appellations such as "sweetie pie," "sugar," and "honeybunch" were endearments that also tended to infantilize. But "popping her cherry," a commonly used phrase in the late twentieth century, perhaps best expressed the conflation of young women and sweets because it meant the action of breaking a girl's hymen and her subsequent loss of virginity.

Wendy A. Woloson

See also Body Image; Consumer Culture; Eating Disorders; Girls' Culture

References and Further Reading
Belden, Louise. 1983. *The Festive Tradition: Table Decoration and Desserts in America, 1650–1900.* New York: W. W. Norton.
Campbell, Helen. 1888. *The American Girl's Home Book of Work and Play.* New York: G. P. Putnam's Sons.
Chapman, Robert L., ed. 1997. *Dictionary of American Slang.* New York: HarperCollins.
Charsley, Simon. 1992. *Wedding Cakes and Cultural History.* London: Routledge.
Dennis, Charles. 1909. "Phoebe at the Fount." *The Soda Fountain* (May): 32.
Kellogg, John. 1884. *Plain Facts for Old and Young.* Burlington, IA: I. F. Segner.
Levenstein, Harvey. 1988. *Revolution at the Table.* New York: Oxford University Press.
Macleod, David I. 1998. *The Age of the Child: Children in America, 1890–1920.* New York: Twayne Publishers.
Mintz, Sidney. 1985. *Sweetness and Power: The Place of Sugar in Modern History.* New York: Viking.
Nasaw, David. 1985. *Children of the City at Work and at Play.* Garden City, NY: Anchor Press/Doubleday.
Shapiro, Laura. 1986. *Perfection Salad: Women and Cooking at the Turn of the Century.* New York: Farrar, Straus and Giroux.
Woloson, Wendy. Forthcoming. *Refined Tastes: Sugar, Confections, and the Cultural Use of an American Commodity in the Nineteenth Century.* Baltimore: Johns Hopkins University Press.

Girls' Culture

Girls' culture encompasses the commercial market of mass-produced commodities—books, dolls, clothing—created by adults for young female consumers, as well as girls' varied responses to those products. Although these cultural forms attempt to instill in girls socially acceptable notions of gender and desirable feminine behavior, girls do not always respond accordingly. Thus girls' culture also refers to the rebellious culture that girls make themselves through innovation and imagination, as well as by transforming the commodities and contexts of commercialized girls' culture.

The recognition of the role that girls' culture has played in the shaping of girls' gendered identity (and women's lives later on) is a product of recent scholarship. Until recently, girls' activities, associations, and actions were widely regarded as trivial aspects of their upbringing unworthy of scholarly inquiry, especially when compared to the magnitude of the issues adult women faced. Aside from the pioneering work in the 1970s by Angela McRobbie, who focused on British girls' cultures, American girls and their cultures remained relatively unexamined until the early 1990s. In part because of the political origins of women's studies scholarship in second-wave feminism, scholars tended to focus on adults to explain gender relations. A second factor that inhibited serious inquiry on girlhood was the dominant scholarly perspective that popular culture was uniformly repressive.

When a more innovative scholarship on youth and children's culture did emerge, it unfortunately privileged the experiences of boys over girls through the use of such gender-neutral terms as "childhood" and "youth." But some anthologies, such as *Small Worlds,* began to include essays that focused on previously unexamined aspects of girls' lives (West and Petrik 1992). Within a few years, pathbreaking

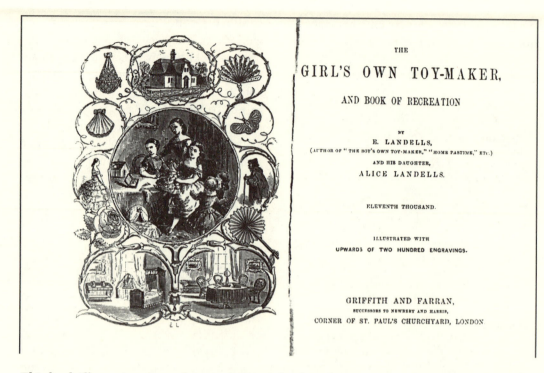

This book illustration shows the construction of girls' culture as one of domesticity. (Library of Congress)

book-length studies were published that examined the gendered meanings encoded in dolls, movies, fiction, magazines, advertisements, and other cultural products that aim to shape girls into women.

Informed by the literature on women, youth, and childhood and influenced by cultural studies and gender history, scholars since the 1990s have engaged in a lively debate about girls' culture. Are its origins in the early twentieth century, the antebellum period (i.e., before the Civil War), or earlier? Another debate concerns the very nature of girls' culture. Is it repressive or transformative? Lynne Vallone (1995) argues that eighteenth- and nineteenth-century literary and nonliterary sources aimed to "conquer" the Anglo-American girl; contain her "desire, hunger, anger, ignorance, and aggression"; and inculcate Christian morality. But other scholars, such as Mary Celeste Kearney (1998), have shown how girls also subvert the conservative aims of adults to socialize them into idealized women. Whether reading books or playing with dolls, girls have expressed their independence from adult expectations by defiantly transforming cultural products into sources of liberation. For example, the girls' culture that slaves made through "ring games" served as an expression of feelings and a source of comfort. These girls were able to express their resistance to adults who sought to instill traditional roles based on race and sex.

Miriam Forman-Brunell
and Kimberley Roberts

See also Collecting; Consumer Culture; Domesticity; Girls' Fiction; Girls' Magazines; Reading; Zines

References and Further Reading

Formanek-Brunell, Miriam. 1998. *Made to Play House: Dolls and the Commercialization of American Girlhood.* Baltimore: Johns Hopkins University Press.

Inness, Sherrie A. 1998. *Delinquents and Debutantes: Twentieth-Century American Girls' Cultures.* New York: New York University Press, intro., chap. 13.

Kearney, Mary Celeste. 1998. "'Don't Need You': Rethinking Identity Politics and Separatism from a Riot Grrrl Perspective." Pp. 148–188 in *Youth Culture: Identity in a Postmodern World.* Edited by Jonathan Epstein. Oxford: Blackwell.

Leadbetter, Bonnie J. Ross, and Niobe Way, eds. 1996. *Urban Girls: Resisting Stereotypes, Creating Identities.* New York: New York University Press.

McRobbie, Angela. 2000. *Feminism and Youth Culture.* 2d ed. New York: Routledge.

Mitchell, Sally. 1995. *The New Girl: Girls' Culture in England, 1880–1915.* New York: Columbia University Press.

Nelson, Claudia, and Lynne Vallone, eds. 1994. *The Girls' Own: Cultural Histories of the Anglo-American Girl, 1830–1915.* Athens: University of Georgia Press.

Vallone, Lynne. 1995. *Disciplines of Virtue: Girls' Culture in the Eighteenth and Nineteenth Centuries.* New Haven, CT: Yale University Press.

West, Elliott, and Paula Petrik, eds. 1992. *Small Worlds: Children and Adolescents in America, 1850–1950.* Lawrence: University of Kansas Press.

Girls' Fiction

Historically, American fiction for girls has reflected adult efforts both to shape and to please its readers. Consequently the fiction of any given period reveals less about what girls were really like than it does about what adults believed or wanted them to be like—itself an enormously important clue for the understanding of girls' lives in the United States. Because most fiction aimed at girls addresses a girl protagonist's role within her family or peer community, girls' novels typically share a fascination with the nature of feminine strength, a focus on girls' conflicting desires for independence and for dependence, and an emphasis on the home as a source of both turmoil and power. Domesticity, indeed, is an overarching theme for the genre, which explores and models—sometimes conservatively, sometimes subversively—girls' aspirations within or away from the private sphere.

American girls' fiction is considerably more recent than America itself. Colonial children of both sexes read imported books, often religious works such as the Bible; John Bunyan's *Pilgrim's Progress* (1678); or James Janeway's *A Token for Children, Being an Exact Account of the Conversion, Holy and Exemplary Lives and Joyful Deaths of Several Young Children* (1671–1672). Homegrown texts were few, and those there were, notably the long-lived *New England Primer* (ca. 1680), likewise tended to prefer a puritanical, antifiction approach. After the American Revolution, British publications remained popular, although by the 1820s nationalist sentiment increasingly dictated that American children should read American books. But the most successful of the new self-consciously *American* writers for the young, among them Jacob Abbott and "Peter Parley" (Samuel Goodrich), usually preached to children in general rather than to girls in particular, so that researchers seeking American fiction that specifically targets young females will find the post-1850 period richer than its predecessor.

A landmark work in this context is Susan Warner's *The Wide, Wide World*

(1850), which outsold every earlier American novel and succeeded brilliantly in Britain also. Warner's saga, variously preoccupied with rural housekeeping, adults' emotional cruelty toward children, the satisfactions of hymn singing and Bible reading, and the nature and difficulties of good behavior, exemplifies what is often disparagingly termed "sentimental" writing—that is, writing that seeks to elicit tears. In thus manipulating her readers, Warner's primary goal is clearly to bring her audience of adolescents and adults to an understanding of the Christian life as one of soul searching, self-abnegation, and devotion to duty. But simultaneously, Warner's well-nigh exclusive focus on the emotions and gradual perfecting of young Ellen Montgomery may allow the reader to confuse soul searching with self-absorption, and the narrative's contention that housework builds character coexists with an awareness that for bright girls, domestic labor is as stultifying as it is arduous.

If Warner holds that duty requires girls to stay where others put them, she nonetheless recognizes that they may long to run away; the remarkably mobile Ellen travels from city to country and from the United States to Scotland, belonging to no fewer than four families over the course of the story. Similarly, Warner harps on the commandment to honor father and mother but exposes at length the sins of Ellen's insensitive father and two subsequent guardians: her rigid, grasping aunt and her worldly, domineering uncle. If the narrative affects to trace Ellen's progress in controlling her own nature, stigmatized as faulty and passionate, the reader is nonetheless permitted to conclude that Ellen is innately superior to almost everyone. Thus even

as nineteenth-century adults seeking improving fiction for their offspring could consider *The Wide, Wide World* uplifting and Christian, many girls ignored its didacticism and focused instead on the gratifying Cinderella story at its heart, in which Ellen gains wealth, status, and the love of the novel's worthies.

The Wide, Wide World set the pattern for much that followed. The passionate heroine struggling to coexist with society's strictures, the possibility—so dear to the Victorian mind—of wielding a peculiarly feminine power by influencing others for good, and even the conflation of romance and the father-daughter tie (an unpublished conclusion clarifies that Ellen marries the clergyman who has dominated her training) recur in the works of authors from Louisa May Alcott to Martha Finley to Jean Webster. Alcott's semiautobiographical *Little Women* (1868–1869), the quintessential American girls' novel, follows sisters Meg, Jo, Amy, and Beth March but focuses particularly upon strong-willed Jo, who over the course of four books develops—some would say "deteriorates"—from hobbledehoy into wife, mother, headmistress, and successful author. Less insistently Christian than Warner's tale, *Little Women* nonetheless invokes the same religious models (Bunyan and the Bible) and draws on many of the same character types, including the saintly mother wrapped up in her daughters' well-being, the spirited protagonist who has trouble curbing her temper and tongue, and the domestic paragon who achieves an exemplary death. The ambiguities surrounding the role of women that are latent in *The Wide, Wide World* are more overt in *Little Women*, a quality that has fascinated feminist critics in recent decades.

A scene from the MGM 1949 movie version of Little Women, *based on Louisa May Alcott's' famous book series. (Bettmann/Corbis)*

Most readers consider the teenage Jo Alcott's most fully realized character, although this prolific writer produced many other popular girls' novels. As much as Ellen Montgomery, Jo has been an ongoing influence upon American domestic fiction for girls. Although today's Alcott fans often resonate to Jo's impatience at constraint, however, late-nineteenth-century writers appreciated the moral didacticism that Alcott inherited from her own models. Alcott imitators such as Susan Coolidge (pseudonym for Sarah Chauncey Woolsey) emphasized not only their heroines' tomboy vitality,

playfulness, and talent with words but also the girls' taming as they are forced into femininity. In *What Katy Did* (1872) and its two sequels, for instance, Coolidge's Katy Carr reaps the moral benefits of a serious injury caused by her own disobedience. Although Katy arises from her invalid's sofa before the end of the first book, she never loses the hard-won maturity, virtue, and importance to others that invalidism has conferred upon her; she unites Jo's energy with Beth's halo.

But by the nineteenth century's end, the "taming" imposed upon Jo's heirs sometimes meant only that they would outgrow their initial immaturity. The increasing romanticization of late Victorian childhood infected even such strongly religious works as Finley's *Elsie Dinsmore* (1868), close kin to *The Wide, Wide World*. As Anne Scott MacLeod observes, the key difference between the two novels is that whereas Ellen Montgomery must struggle to accept Christ as a living presence, eight-year-old Elsie is always presented as the narrative's spiritual authority. This view of the child as savior was to become increasingly important from the 1880s through the 1910s, culminating in Eleanor Porter's best-seller *Pollyanna* (1913), the tale of an orphan whose determination to find something to rejoice at in the darkest situation reforms the adult community. The argument that adults suffer from a spiritual malaise that only childish innocence can cure is common in girls' fiction but rare in stories aimed at or written by American males, a discrepancy reflecting the gendered dichotomy between action and affect in Victorian America. The heroes of boys' books *do*; the protagonists of domestic novels for girls *are*. Readers of Kate Douglas Wiggin's *Rebecca of Sunnybrook Farm* (1903), Frances Hodgson Burnett's *A Little Princess* (1905), and many other narratives learn that certain girls wield a formidable power manifested not through adventure and accomplishment but through their ability to attract love. For such heroines, femininity itself is the ultimate career.

The 1920s and 1930s, however, witnessed important changes in female gender roles as women increasingly began working outside the home. Girls' fiction responded in multiple ways. Most obvious, perhaps, is the rise of narratives in which girls aspire to glamorous jobs. (One might argue that such novels are the heirs of the many turn-of-the-century fictions depicting life at women's colleges; the earlier stories do not usually reveal whether the newly minted graduates embark upon professions, but they put a premium upon the activity and energy needed for financial independence.) Typical is Elizabeth Enright's Melendy family series, beginning with *The Saturdays* (1941), in which sisters Mona and Randy dream of becoming, respectively, an actress and a ballerina-cum-painter. That such ambitions are both legitimate and realistic is made clear in *The Four-Story Mistake* (1942), when fourteen-year-old Mona stars in a radio soap opera. Much mass-market series fiction also relies upon the romance of the public sphere. Girl detectives such as Nancy Drew (who debuted in 1930), Hollywood phenomena such as screenwriter/director/actress/producer Ruth Fielding (1913–1934), and nurses such as Sue Barton (1936–1952) all helped to construct an image of the young American woman as energetic, competent, independent, and successful, dominating her environment and often her menfolk.

But the years after World War I also saw a boom in historical fiction for girls and especially in novels emphasizing the strength demanded of American women through the centuries. Caroline Dale Snedeker, known for her tales of ancient Greece and Rome, produced *Downright Dencey* (1927), set in Nantucket in the 1810s. Snedeker dwells on the demands and rewards of Quaker austerity for women; imaginative and undisciplined Dencey civilizes a waif into a desirable fiancé and matures into a young woman worthy of respect by heeding her New England conscience. Rachel Field's *Calico Bush* (1931) traces the travails of a French "bound-out girl" whose life in sparsely settled Maine in the eighteenth century consists of much more privation than pleasure. Another frontier child is the eleven-year-old protagonist of Carol Ryrie Brink's *Caddie Woodlawn* (1935), daughter of an English aristocrat who has moved his family to Civil War–era Wisconsin. As the family tomboy, Caddie responds warmly to farm life and to interactions with Indians, but the narrative explains that more conventionally feminine women, Caddie's mother included, find such an existence agonizingly hard.

Still, many of these tales emphasize the ongoing theme that rigor has its own attractions. Take Ruth Sawyer's novels about Lucinda Wyman, *Roller Skates* (1936) and *The Year of Jubilo* (1940), both set in the 1890s. Born into a wealthy Manhattan family, Lucinda has spent her early childhood hedged about by rules. When her mother's health requires her parents to make an extended stay in Italy, she is overjoyed to be separated from her family and thus enabled to lead a less structured existence. This break in routine is vacation rather than privation, but the sequel starts on a darker note by killing off Lucinda's father and impoverishing the family, who must leave their New York mansion for their erstwhile summer cottage in Maine. Facing the harshness of winter, her older brothers' contempt for her as girl and child, and the depression and anxieties of all the Wymans at their changed circumstances, Lucinda finds herself happy to meet the challenges of her new life. In part, of course, the attractiveness of this life is that she may shed some of the constraints of aristocratic femininity and lead a more "natural" existence, an ideal popular in girls' fiction since the days of Alcott and Warner.

The volumes that today's readers most readily associate with frontier values and reverence for the hardscrabble American past are surely Laura Ingalls Wilder's nine Little House books (1932–1971), which describe her own early life and that of her husband-to-be in the 1870s and 1880s. As the Ingalls family moves from Wisconsin to Oklahoma to Minnesota to the Dakotas, they must cope with wild animals, plagues of locusts, illness, solitude, and blizzards. There are social challenges, too; as a teenager, Laura has to leave home to work as a teacher in order to assist with her blind sister's college tuition. Always restless and ungovernable, Laura refuses to include the word *obey* in her wedding vows, a moment that underscores her kinship to countless other girl protagonists in a body of literature that has historically placed a high value on feistiness.

Critics have complained that girls' fiction of the era immediately following World War II lacks the emphasis on grit present in many earlier tales and that the 1950s renaissance of domesticity (as many women left the workplace) fed adolescent novels that preached that fulfillment lay only in romance. But if the "junior novel"—precursor of today's "young adult novel"—typically features heroines who lack Jo March's independence of mind, it may nonetheless suggest that standing out from the herd is no bad thing. Thus, for example, in Beverly Cleary's *Jean and Johnny* (1959), Jean learns to reject handsome, popular, and selfish Johnny for a less conventionally attractive rival. Although the novel posits that teenage girls should find their happy endings in relationships with boys, it teaches also that girls have the right or the responsibility to question the crowd's definition of satisfying romance and to seek a more egalitarian partnership. Similarly, Madeleine L'Engle's early heroines Philippa Hunter (*And Both Were Young*, 1949), Camilla Dickinson (*Camilla*, 1951), and Vicky Austin (introduced in *Meet the Austins*, 1960) consider themselves losers until they find validation in boys' eyes, but L'Engle makes clear that the boys in question are no Prince Charmings—they have serious problems of their own. Girls and boys must help each other mature, as neither can expect to be in control.

If the didactic urges in nineteenth-century girls' fiction often concern religion, those of the later twentieth century often concern sexuality. The anxieties about dating addressed in "junior novels" by Cleary, Betty Cavanna, Mary Stolz, and other popular authors gave way to a sometimes ostentatious frankness by the mid-1960s, as such authors as Judy Blume (*Are You There, God? It's Me, Margaret*, 1970) and Louise Fitzhugh (*The Long Secret*, 1965) broached hitherto taboo subjects such as menstruation. Teen pregnancy became a staple of the young adult "problem novel," as in Ann Head's *Mr. and Mrs. Bo Jo Jones* (1967). And increasingly, girls' fiction began to focus on sexuality outside the mainstream. L'Engle's Polly O'Keefe (*A House Like a Lotus*, 1984), an avowed but untried heterosexual, develops a mentor-disciple bond with a middle-aged lesbian; Nancy Garden's Liza Winthrop (*Annie on My Mind*, 1982), a high school senior, discovers her own lesbianism and has a passionate and loving sexual relationship with a girl her own age; and the characters in Francesca Lia Block's *Weetzie Bat* (1989) and its sequels inhabit a world of polymorphous perversity in which sexuality is to be accepted in any of its manifestations. At least superficially, the trend has been to cele-

brate sexual freedom, tolerance, and the "progressive," although some texts (*A House Like a Lotus* is one) seem conflicted on this issue.

Race and ethnicity are another locus for late-twentieth-century didacticism, as the American "melting pot" ideal increasingly gave way to one of heterogeneous multiculturalism. Minority protagonists, once rare to the point of nonexistence, became commonplace after the 1960s civil rights movement, whose spirit continued to inform multicultural texts of the 1990s. The dominant message is that of taking pride in one's heritage, but readers are also asked to be aware of prejudice and injustice, past and present. Historical novels on these themes are common, and some settings are especially prevalent: the slaveholding era and the racially tense 1920s, the late-nineteenth-century Jewish diaspora and the Holocaust. Fantasies and domestic tales address ethnicity as well, and sometimes realism and fantasy combine in time-travel books in which contemporary American girls inclined to reject their heritage are forced to experience what they have despised, as happens in Belinda Hurmence's *A Girl Called Boy* (1982) and Jane Yolen's *The Devil's Arithmetic* (1988). With the interesting exception of the novel on Native American themes, which not infrequently subordinates family to larger cultural concerns and suggests that family weakness is offset by individual and/or ethnic power, multicultural fiction is prone to validate the family as the great source of strength and hope, although other agendas are also discernible—consider the American Girls Collection (1986–), in which books coexist with elaborate merchandise, so that multiculturalism and an interest in American history are inextricable from consumerism.

Late-twentieth-century pro-domestic novels diverged from the overall direction of American girls' fiction, which even in its infancy never unilaterally assumed the family's benevolence. *The Wide, Wide World*, among many other nineteenth-century examples, directly criticizes fathers in multiple ways. And if Victorian mothers were usually beyond reproach, mid-twentieth-century texts such as *Caddie Woodlawn* sometimes exalted the father at the mother's expense. Girl readers have long been encouraged to observe fictional parents' flaws: fathers, mothers, or both are skewered for being domineering, detached, irresponsible, weak, selfish, insensitive, or simply unpleasant. Novels thus often exalt the peer group or urge the discovery of more satisfactory surrogate parents, although some narrators observe that the protagonists' culpable turbulence prevents them from bonding with biological families that may be entirely acceptable. This phenomenon is apparent in many "social problem" novels of the 1960s and 1970s, for example, John Neufeld's *Lisa, Bright and Dark* (1968), in which the schizophrenic title character turns to her friends for amateur group therapy because her parents, worshipping normalcy and respectability, ignore her cries for help; or Lee Kingman's *The Peter Pan Bag* (1970), in which Wendy flees her pleasant family in order to "find herself" in Boston hippiedom under the watchful eye of a friend's older brother. Similar attitudes toward family crop up in domestic novels—for example, Fitzhugh's *Harriet the Spy* (1964), in which wealth has barred Harriet's parents from participating in her life—and in historical fiction by authors such as Elizabeth George Speare and Sally Watson, whose strong-minded heroines usually escape home early in the narrative to combat domestic stability by joining pirate crews or helping to start the American Revolution. More recently, Karen Hesse's *Out of the Dust* (1997), set in Oklahoma in 1934–1935, continues the tradition of dissecting parental flaws, even as it also focuses on the need to forgive the serious errors of one's parents and oneself. That Hesse's sequence of free-verse poems won the Newbery Medal and the Scott O'Dell Award suggests the willingness of the children's literature establishment to reward girls' books that question domesticity. As this overview has suggested, such willingness is by no means new.

Claudia Nelson

See also Advice Books; American Girls Collection; Chicana Girls; Comic Books; Domesticity; Fairy Tales; Girls' Magazines; Literacy; Nancy Drew Mysteries; Reading; Zines

References and Further Reading
Avery, Gillian. 1994. *Behold the Child: American Children and Their Books 1621–1922.* Baltimore: Johns Hopkins University Press.

Foster, Shirley, and Judy Simons. 1995. *What Katy Read: Feminist Re-Readings of "Classic" Stories for Girls.* Iowa City: University of Iowa Press.

Keyser, Elizabeth Lennox. 1999. *Little Women: A Family Romance.* New York: Twayne Publishers.

MacLeod, Anne Scott. 1994. *American Childhood: Essays on Children's Fiction of the Nineteenth and Twentieth Centuries.* Athens: University of Georgia Press.

Nelson, Claudia, and Lynne Vallone, eds. 1994. *The Girl's Own: Cultural Histories of the Anglo-American Girl, 1830–1915.* Athens: University of Georgia Press.

Tompkins, Jane. 1987. "Afterword." Pp. 584–608 in *The Wide, Wide World.* By Susan Warner. New York: Feminist Press.

Girls' Magazines

In the late 1990s, girls could choose from a multitude of girls' magazines that covered the latest teen fashions, beauty, music, movie stars, new ways to meet boys or friends in the never-ending quest for "popularity," and advice on parents, school trouble, or dating dilemmas. By the turn of the twenty-first century, girls were a well-established magazine audience, but this was not always the case. In the early twentieth century, most girls read family, women's, and romance magazines and, later, movie magazines. By the late 1920s, however, some women's magazines began to recognize their younger readers and offer monthly columns like "Sub-Deb" and "Teens of Our Times." These columns addressed teenage girls directly and spread information about teen social life but remained only a section in adult magazines. By the early 1940s, magazines had been developed specifically for girls and addressed young fashions, dating, friends, school, movies, and music. Their success paved the way for an abundance of girls' magazines and led to the newest forms of teen-centered publications, grrrl zines, and Internet sites.

The first publications to speak to girls directly were *American Girl* and *Everygirls' Magazine,* the official magazines of the Girl Scouts and the Camp Fire Girls, respectively. These magazines catered specifically to organization members, though, and few outsiders subscribed. In the late 1920s, editors at the *Ladies' Home Journal* discovered that girls were sharing their mothers' copies or even buying their own. They established a column entitled "The Sub-Deb, a Page for Girls," and led the way for mass-circulation magazines to address their younger readers. The first "Sub-Deb" editor wrote as though her readers were wealthy debutantes-to-be with an endless supply of friends and funds. The column advised girls on how to plan and host elaborate parties, grow out their bobbed hair, dress elegantly, and develop homemaking skills such as decorating, cooking, and knitting.

When Elizabeth Woodward took over the column in 1931, the tone shifted to that of a big sister. Woodward added an emphasis on boys and relationships. She strongly advised girls to attract dates, rather than pursue them, by cultivating looks, listening skills, and a fun personality. The cardinal rule was to play games well, but not too well. These traits were also recommended for making friends and gaining approval from teachers. Throughout the 1930s, advice on relationships expanded to include debates on going steady, petting, responsibility, and avoiding the dangers of peer pressure—issues that appealed to an audience beyond the glamorous subdebutantes.

As the column grew in popularity, articles and advertisements for girls appeared more frequently in the *Ladies' Home Journal.* Short stories praised virtuous teenage heroines who did not neck, drink, or smoke yet always won the boy. Other characters had aspirations beyond marriage until they met the right man, that is. The advice, party ideas, and fashions were still designed to cultivate responsible, glamorous young adults. One article advised girls to pause and revel in the swish of their party dresses before rushing off to dates or dances. But by February 1938, the subdebutante column "Shaggin' on Down" marked a new attempt to follow as well as lead by imitating teen slang to teach the latest dance steps. In October 1942, *Ladies' Home*

Journal published *The Scoop*, a newspaper with features, fiction, fashions, and club news produced just for girls.

The word about teens was starting to spread. *Parents' Magazine* launched a "Teen-Age Problems" column in the mid-1930s, but it served primarily as a forum for parents. In February 1941, however, *Parents' Magazine* introduced "Tricks for Teens," which featured high school fashion ideas. The column, which originated in a department store contest on teen fashions, invited teenage girls and their mothers to send descriptions and pictures of high school fads. The initial column was written to mothers and sympathized with their struggles to understand high school "fad-shions." Due to the enthusiastic response from teenage girls, however, the column soon spoke to girls directly: "TEEN-AGE high-schoolers, this is *your* feature. Urge mother to read it, too" (*Parents' Magazine*, April 1941, 108). And *Parents' Magazine*, a magazine intended for adults, began to carry articles and advertising targeted specifically at teenage girls. *Parents* sponsored fashion design contests for teenage girls, created a "Hi-School Board Fashion" label to promote teen fashions, and devoted several pages in each issue to teen fashion spreads.

This interest led the Parents' Institute to create *Calling All Girls* in July 1941, the first general magazine designed exclusively for "girls and subdebs." Primarily filled with comics, *Calling All Girls* also contained short stories and advice on fashion, manners, and beauty. Advertisements for the new magazine assured mothers that its content would be entertaining and wholesome. In March 1944, "Tricks for Teens" was moved to *Calling All Girls*, and *Parents'*

again focused on its original adult audience. *Calling All Girls*, almost titled *Susan, a Magazine for Girls*, started as a quarterly magazine but quickly became a monthly due to high circulation and reader response.

Calling All Girls was not destined for long-term success, however, because the publishers never quite understood the audience or advertising base. Circulation initially reached 250,000 and by 1945 had grown to a respectable 500,000. The emphasis on comics kept the average age of the reader around 13, and the magazine never gained readership among the more fashion-conscious high school girls. In addition, the format of the magazine did not attract the highly profitable fashion advertisers, and the publishers did not actively seek more appropriate advertising.

Seventeen magazine debuted in September 1944 and had much greater teen appeal. The first issue sold out quickly—400,000 copies in six days. Circulation exceeded 1 million copies by February 1947 and 2.5 million by July 1949. *Seventeen* declared that it reached more than half of the 6 million teenage girls in the United States through copies shared with friends and family. Readers were mostly from white middle-class and upper-middle-class families, but *Seventeen* reached across broader age and class boundaries than *Calling All Girls* and previous girls' columns.

Seventeen was created from the similar recipe of young fashions, beauty, movies, music, dating, boys, friendships, parents, careers, and education. But girls liked it because it tried to make them better teenagers rather than good little girls or elegant adults. Helen Valentine, *Seventeen*'s first editor in chief, envisioned a magazine that would treat teenage girls seriously and respect their emotional and intellectual needs in addition to helping them choose their first lipstick. To achieve this goal, the magazine included occasional articles on World War II, international issues, and postwar inflation. *Seventeen* also acquired substantial advertising revenue and worked to translate its editorial message and the buying power of this age group to businesses and the advertising industry.

Boys were also active magazine readers. The "Sub-Deb" column in the *Ladies' Home Journal*, *Seventeen*, and other girls' magazines claimed that boys were reading and writing in for advice on girls. By 1935, the "Sub-Deb" column was occasionally titled "For Men Only," and *Parents' Magazine* received so many unsolicited responses from teenage boys for "Tricks for Teens" that they began including boys' fads. Most boys, however, were primarily reading picture magazines such as *Life;* general-interest magazines such as *Reader's Digest* and the *Saturday Evening Post;* or science, mechanical, and sports magazines. By the early 1950s, automobile magazines such as *Hot Rod* had a strong hold on the magazine market for boys.

No magazine for boys, however, enjoyed *Seventeen*'s enormous success with both readers and advertisers. Although *Seventeen* drew from the experience of its predecessors, it quickly surpassed them. *Calling All Girls* attempted to mimic *Seventeen*'s success by dropping its comics and investing additional money in art, writers, and production. Parents' Institute also tried to redirect its efforts to attract preteens, ages nine to twelve, to a new publication, *Polly Pigtails.* Despite these efforts and competitors such as the glamour magazine *Junior Bazaar,* which covered fashion almost exclusively, *Seventeen* remained the leader for decades and firmly established the market for girls' magazines.

In the 1950s, an explosion of gossip magazines for teenagers, such as *Modern Teen, Teen Time, Teen Parade,* and *Hep Cats,* sought a working-class market with advice columns and fan clubs. *Seventeen,* while retaining its hold on the middle-class market, changed in the 1950s as well. The original staff was replaced, and the magazine entered a period of transition by forging closer ties with advertisers. The attention to responsible citizenship was almost entirely overshadowed by an emphasis on fashion, dating, and marriage.

In the 1960s and 1970s, *Seventeen* and other girls' magazines responded to the feminist movement with a shift toward personal growth and independence. *Seventeen*'s thirtieth anniversary edition in September 1974 heralded the new opportunities available to teenage girls since the 1940s and claimed that workplace discrimination based on sex no longer existed. Girls could be anything they wanted to be and could successfully combine careers with family life. The conservative 1980s, however, marked a return to more domestic and traditionally feminine content and a decline in articles encouraging self-development.

Sassy entered the market in the 1980s and created the first serious competition for *Seventeen. Sassy* was more outrageous and tried harder to imitate teen slang. Magazines like *Young Miss* also began to place more emphasis on boys and sex. Although *Seventeen* responded in kind, it tried to retain a balance of fashion, beauty, relationships, school, and entertainment, as well as boys.

A teenager sitting on the couch reading magazines. (Hulton Getty/Archive Photos, ca. 1955)

Girls' magazines emerged as teenagers began to rely more heavily on their peers and on the commercial popular culture for guidance and entertainment. This balance shifted again in the late 1990s, as teenagers' patience with adult-driven information, guidance, and taste waned. The proliferation of noncommercial girls' magazines and Internet sites has ensured that a multitude of voices speak to and for teenage girls. These zines and virtual magazines have created a new and very different kind of competition.

Girls' zines started in the mid-1980s as noncommercial, low-budget magazines produced by teenage girls themselves to challenge mainstream society and media. *Riot Grrrl*, for example, brings together young women in the punk music scene, provides an alternative to mass media and consumer culture images of girls, and offers readers a forum for self-expression. By the late 1990s, teenage girls were one of the fastest-growing populations of Internet users. Building on the explosion of grrrl music and styles, websites such as "echick," "chickclick," "teenmag," and "teengrrrl" offer articles, fashion advice, and a forum for discussions on topics relevant to girls today. These sites are created and run by girls themselves and devote much of their space to readers' input.

They provide a safe community where girls can share their experiences and discuss tough issues.

Kelly Schrum

See also Advice Books; Clothing; Comic Books; Girls' Fiction; Latina Girls; Literacy; Reading; Zines

References and Further Reading
Budgeon, Shelley, and Dawn H. Currie. 1995. "From Feminism to Post-feminism: Women's Liberation in Fashion Magazines." *Women's Studies International Forum* 18, no. 2: 173–186.

Duncombe, Stephen. 1998. "Let's All Be Alienated Together: Zines and the Making of Underground Community." Pp. 427–451 in *Generations of Youth: Youth Cultures and History in Twentieth-Century America*. Edited by Joe Austin and Michael Nevin Willard. New York: New York University Press.

Lyness, Paul I. 1951. "Patterns in the Mass Communications Tastes of the Young Audience." *The Journal of Educational Psychology* 42, no. 8 (December): 449–467.

Palladino, Grace. 1996. *Teenagers: An American History.* New York: Basic Books.

Schrum, Kelly. 1998. "'Teena Means Business': Teenage Girls' Culture and *Seventeen* Magazine, 1944–1950." Pp. 134–163 in *Delinquents and Debutantes: Twentieth-Century American Girls' Cultures.* Edited by Sherrie A. Inness. New York: New York University Press.

"Tricks for Teens: Fashion Fads That Hit High School Fancies." 1941. *Parents' Magazine* (April): 108.

Girls' Rooms

Since the creation of separate sleeping quarters, girls' rooms (also referred to as bedrooms or sleeping rooms) have been decorated with an eye toward reinforcing prevailing gender ideals by adults (chiefly mothers) and redecorated by girls to express their individuality, often in adolescence.

In seventeenth-century America, girls did not have rooms of their own; no one did. Colonial families were large (with eight to ten children), and houses were not. As a demonstration of rank among family members, parents slept on the first floor in the most valued social zones of colonial houses. Infants slept in cradles in a central room that accommodated many productive activities, but as they got older, children shared trundle beds or straw pallets. Along with siblings and servants, children slept in upstairs attics and outbuildings of houses with undifferentiated space that afforded little privacy or comfort. Nor were these sleeping arrangements ever permanent; children were frequently moved from one bed to another depending on changing circumstances. In her 1992 study of colonial children, historian Karin Calvert found only one reference to a children's room in early America. A prosperous colonel was at the forefront of cultural change in eighteenth-century Maryland when he designated the closet between the hall and the parlor as the "children's room."

Increased affluence, the influence of eighteenth-century Enlightenment notions about childrearing on Victorian family life, the increasing size of houses, and room specialization were factors that led to the emergence of upstairs "chambers" designated for sleeping in more prosperous middle-class households. Cradles were now placed in parents' rooms or in a nursery (a room mother and infant shared following childbirth). The choice of a nursery, located farthest from the locus of family activity, was determined by its location (often at the back of the house or third floor) and for its utility. Because the sparsely furnished nursery was not as yet a site on display for admiring guests, parents invested little in its decoration. But believing that children were better off if supervised by an adult meant that most siblings also slept with servants, as they had in the seventeenth century. The four daughters of a wealthy Virginian, for example, shared a sleeping chamber with female domestic servants. In Philadelphia, Harriet Manigault slept in her mother's room for the first eighteen years of her life, whereas her two younger sisters shared a room on the third floor with a maid (Calvert 1992).

Infant daughters and sons—along with older children—often slept in the beds or bedrooms of their parents or grandparents well into the middle of the nineteenth century. But antebellum doctors' and health reformers' concerns about the safety of small children smothered or smashed by slumbering parents contributed to the overall trend toward single bedsteads and separate rooms. The healthy development of girls could only occur without such injurious agents as grandmothers, siblings, dogs, and cats living in their bedrooms. Health concerns, increased prosperity, a domestic ideology, and decreasing family size (fewer siblings) were all factors that contributed to the diversification of household interiors over the course of the nineteenth century. New notions about the importance of education and cultivation also contributed to providing children with a room separate from adults. Though by the 1830s children's rooms separated children from adults, sisters and brothers shared "nurseries" that were gender-neutral.

It was not until preadolescence that sisters were likely to have a room of their own, but only in families where circumstances permitted. Middle-class parents expected daughters to write and often rewrite their diary entries because of the importance placed on self-cultivation and self-control. But behind the closed doors of their bedrooms—and beyond the watch of others—girls could indulge their imaginations. In the protected space of the bedroom, girls could chart "a middle way between the fiery rebel and the good daughter of advice books and fiction" (Hunter 1992, 59). In fact, in order to preserve girls' privacy, domestic advisers devised a code of etiquette, advising: "If you make a point of never going, uninvited, into the sleeping-rooms of your young companions, you can keep your own sacred from intruders" (Farrar 1937, 276). In later years, experts would recommend including a cozy seat for socializing, inviting confidences, or for just sitting and reading a book. But such advice was largely irrelevant to working-class and immigrant daughters who lived in cramped tenement apartments. For them, privacy could only be found on crowded, busy city streets.

Although girls in the nineteenth-century United States slept in their own rooms, it was not until shortly after the turn of the twentieth century that articles about girls' rooms began to appear regularly in popular magazines. It is no coincidence that *Peter Pan* takes place during Wendy's last night in the nursery she shares with her younger siblings. Although it was considered acceptable for younger sisters to share a room, with the "discovery" of adolescence and its turbulence at the end of the nineteenth century, adults began to take more seriously the needs of adolescent girls. They would "need" their own room when they "reached that longed-for period in life when her needs are worthy of consideration, when a quiet, retired spot is deemed a necessity for [her] study and work . . . Her sense of individual possession is coupled with a delightful sense of importance and newfound dignity, which renders her association with 'the children' unworthy to her seriousness" (quoted in Cromley 1992, 126).

To Progressive-era parents (and most since), girls' rooms were designed to reflect and reinforce their daughters' feminine identity. For example, the room with that "girlish charm" included a dressing table, "that important feature of feminine existence," which was best when draped with a flounce of muslin (Shrimpton 1912). Other items included a tea table, sewing screen, sewing table, and writing desk. In keeping with prevailing notions of femininity, experts recommended pink or blue chambray wallpaper with cutout borders. Girls' rooms were to reflect such feminine virtues as beauty, good taste, and sincerity. The rose, considered the "favorite" flower of girls, could be embroidered, painted, or appliquéd onto curtains, bedspreads, and walls. Fresh air and sunlight were important considerations to Progressive-era adults worried about the dangers of cities. Bare floors and no upholstery were essential in the germ-free rooms of young, delicate girls.

At the turn of the twentieth century, contemporaries asserted that girls' socialization as future homemakers made them experts at decorating their rooms: "Since earliest childhood she has manifested the homemaking spirit, expressing her ideas in her doll houses, and fitting up corners of the nursery to realize her ideas of interior decoration. Indeed, she is by right of heritage the prospective home-maker" (Tachau 1915, 10). The value placed on homemaking coincided with other turn-of-the-century developments. The influence of Sigmund Freud's psychological theories and the "discovery" of adolescence by the first

American child psychologist, G. Stanley Hall, both contributed to the wider acceptance of a separate domain for developing daughters: "The most exacting household tasks are invested with new dignity when they become part of the daily routine of keeping her own apartment neat; and perhaps nothing can have so fine a psychological effect as this feeling of responsibility for her own possessions" (Tachau 1915, 10). Feminism also contributed to the reallocation of household space. Virginia Woolf would soon explain the importance of having "a room of one's own."

But in the twentieth century, having one's own room was often determined by larger economic forces that affected both family size and household space. The prosperity of the 1920s was followed by two decades of austerity. Having separate rooms for all family members was a lesser priority among families forced to tighten their belts during the Great Depression. Unemployment compelled numerous families to move to living quarters that were both less expensive and less expansive. For some families, there were only one-room shanties in makeshift Hoovervilles. Thousands of teenage girls who slept on park benches in New York City abandoned pretenses of family life altogether. Despite increased opportunities for employment during the World War II, the scarcity of housing forced several generations of families to crowd into small apartments. A room of one's own was a luxury few could afford. A shortage of space, especially in urban apartments or in big families, often meant that children, usually of the same sex, shared bedrooms. Twin beds and matching furniture divided rooms and, occasionally, roommates.

A teenager gets dressed in her bedroom. (Shirley Zeiberg, 1970s)

Girls in the postwar United States were far more likely to have their own room or share one with a sister. Child-centered suburban houses were designed to accommodate the baby boom generation. Since the 1950s, mothers have decorated their daughters' bedrooms following the suggestions of interior decorators, furniture makers, and toy companies. With bold primary colors designated for sons, pink or lavender rooms have come to be associated with femininity, passivity, innocence, fantasy, daintiness, and love.

Inevitably, girls come to feel that they have "outgrown" their rooms: the decor no longer matches who they think they have become. Girls also feel the need to separate themselves from their parents, whose hopes and expectations are encoded in their daughters' bedrooms. Bedrooms can become a contested terrain as girls assert their individuality and autonomy and even punctuate their anger with a slammed door! "Keep Out" signs designate claims to privacy and autonomy.

In the highly personal arena of the bedroom, developmental issues are expressed in visual ways and material terms. Expressing personality and identity—by giving a soul to things in their rooms—

provides girls with opportunities to experiment and adjust without public scrutiny. Walls become screens upon which girls project their fantasies with pictures of pets and posters of people. But the bedroom is not only a representation of the mind; it can also be an extension of the body. Girls decorate their rooms as they adorn their bodies. Contemporary advice books even encourage girls to think this way. Using the language of fashion design, they recommend that girls give their rooms "makeovers" and use "accessories" (e.g., pillows, lamps, curtains) in order to "choose a look that fits you" (Roehm 1997, 41).

Perhaps girls invest more time in decorating their rooms because they spend more of their waking time in them than in centuries past. Once designed for sleeping only, bedrooms containing computers, telephones, televisions, and other technology provide girls with a wide range of new opportunities to transport themselves beyond their bedrooms. Although in *Sound Effects* Simon Frith argued that "girl culture . . . starts and finishes in the bedroom," he neglected to consider the other possibilities that also take place there (cited in Kearney 1998, 285).

Miriam Forman-Brunell

See also Consumer Culture; Domesticity; Girls' Culture

References and Further Reading
Calvert, Karin. 1992. *Children in the House: The Material Culture of Early Childhood, 1600–1900.* Boston: Northeastern University Press.
Cromley, Elizabeth Collins. 1992. "A History of American Beds and Bedrooms, 1890–1930." Pp. 120–144 in *American Home Life, 1880–1930: A Social History of Spaces and Services.* Edited by Jessica H. Foy and Thomas J. Schlereth. Knoxville: University of Tennessee Press.
Cutler, Martha. 1906. "Girls' Rooms." *Harper's Bazarre* 40 (October): 935–940.
Farrar, Eliza Ware. 1837. *The Young Lady's Friend.* Boston: American Stationers' Co.
Hunter, Jane. 1992. "Inscribing the Self in the Heart of the Family: Diaries and Girlhood in Late Victorian America." *American Quarterly* 44, no. 1 (March): 51–81.
Kearney, Mary Celeste. 1998. "Producing Girls: Rethinking the Study of Female Youth Culture." Pp. 285–310 in *Delinquents and Debutantes: Twentieth Century American Girls' Cultures.* New York: New York University Press.
Kellogg, Alice M. 1910. "Decorations and Furnishings for the Home, IX—Furnishing a Young Girl's Room." *American Homes and Gardens* 7 (November): 420–423.
McMurry, Sally. 1987. *Farmhouses and Families.* New York: Oxford University Press, 178–185.
Perrett, Antoinette R. 1910. "Girls' Rooms." *St. Nicholas* 37 (May): 595–596.
Roehm, Michelle, comp. 1997. *Girls Know Best: Advice for Girls from Girls on Just about Everything.* Hillsboro, OR: Beyond Words Publishing.
Shrimpton, Louise. 1912. "Furnishing the Girl's Own Room." *Woman's Home Companion* (May).
Tachau, Nina. 1915. "The Girl's Room." *House Beautiful* 38 (June): 10–12.

Graffiti

The word *graffiti* is derived from the Italian word *graffiare,* meaning "to scratch," and was probably first used to refer to the writings and drawings ("little scratches") found on ruins. In the contemporary United States, *graffiti* refers to unauthorized or illegal writings, drawings, and art in public spaces and on highly visible private property. Often done in aerosol paint, graffiti is not to be confused with art in that medium that is painted legally and with permission.

Humans have written and drawn on walls since at least the Paleolithic period of human history, but these markings are usually thought to have been sacred or in some way unique and collectively sanctioned. Among the oldest graffiti are those found in Turkey dating from about 1000 B.C.E., but graffiti have also been found on ancient architecture around the globe, including the ruins of the Mayans, Greeks, and Romans and the Great Wall of China. Since the eighteenth century, all expressive and creative works, including graffiti, have been understood as at least partly reflecting the culture and society in which they were created.

Graffiti in its contemporary meaning is commonplace and requires reasonably widespread literacy, a readily available means to make a recognizable mark without too much effort, and public or accessible private spaces that are unobserved at least part of the time. In the early nineteenth century, larger and increasingly diverse populations moved into tightly packed cities. Mass production made the means of writing more accessible, and mass education spread a shared literacy to more people, particularly young people. Amassed into schools and organized around its schedules, young people developed a shared age-based culture of their own, which included graffiti as one means of public expression.

By the mid-nineteenth century, graffiti was a well-established object of scholarly study as well as a popular source for ribald and humorous writings. Young people's graffiti continued to be collected and photographed throughout the twentieth century, and examples ranged from carvings in tree bark and school desks; to chalk writings on freight trains, walls, and sidewalks; to writings in public toilets; to radical slogans on public walls; to the contemporary mural-like works of graffiti artists, many of whom continue to create art as adults. A new kind of graffiti emerged in Philadelphia in the mid-1960s and blossomed in the New York City subways a few years later. This elaborate, artistic, and usually illegal public script has sometimes been called "graffiti art," but its originators called it "writing."

Writing became the first of several new artistic forms, such as rapping and break dancing, created by urban youth in the 1970s and 1980s and now collectively known as hip-hop. Writing transforms language into a direct social challenge for public space, art, and social recognition and fame. At the same time, its illegal placement in urban space questions many of the established cultural values surrounding private property, organized aesthetics, social status, and identity. Today, most of the writing has been removed from the New York City subways, but this art-without-permission has not simply vanished; instead, the art has adapted itself to public and private walls while simultaneously moving outside its original locations in East Coast U.S. cities. The early 1970s writing culture of New York City was made up primarily of working-class African American, Puerto Rican, and immigrant youths between the ages of twelve and seventeen. But writing, like hip-hop in general, is now an international cultural movement, a controversial art form around the globe that exists between galleries and street corners, between authorized murals and illegal masterpieces.

Setting aside issues of law, order, and ownership, writing is a well-organized artistic and literary urban movement with an established social structure and a set of cultural traditions. Writers rarely write their birth names. Instead, they choose a name and meticulously design a "tag," or moniker, with striking visually rhythmic lettering in order to catch the eyes of passersby who see their work. Most writers are part of one or more "crews," a group involved in writing that can be identified by their initials written near the work of its members. A new writer enters the culture as a "toy" and builds a reputation as her or his skills and quantity of work increase. At the top of this hierarchy are "kings" whose names are well known within the local and sometimes the national and international graffiti scene. Although there is fierce competition between writers for recognition and fame, rules of reciprocity, support, respect, and communication are the central cohesive forces within writing culture.

Because of graffiti's ephemeral nature and illegal status, documenting its history has proven to be very difficult for scholars. Ascertaining the role of girls and women in writing culture is even more elusive. Graffiti have been widely used by females involved in social movements since 1960, including the women's rights and feminist movements. More recently, latrinalia—graffiti in public toilets—was used by college women to publicize the identities of date-rapists on some U.S. university campuses. However, contemporary studies indicate that females participate less frequently in writing than males, a difference usually explained by the ways in which the two genders are socialized to behave in public space.

All available evidence points toward a small but important number of young women who helped to shape the practice of writing at its inception in New York City. David Schmidlapp and Phase 2 (1996) mention Barbara 62, Eva 62, Michelle 62, Barmaid 36, S.Pat 169, Big Bird 107, Irene 159, Line 149, Tash 2, T. T. Smokin 182, Charmin 65, Stoney II, and Grape 1 as "pioneering female writers." In the early 1970s the number of female writers appears to have diminished. After the mid-1970s, famous female writers were very rare. Jack Stewart (1989) documents only 122 names by female writers from 1970 to 1978 in New York City, when tens of thousands of individuals wrote on the subways. Since 1994 there have been only a handful of young women who considered themselves dedicated writers and even fewer who were considered to be so by their peers.

Very few women have gained widespread reputation for their aerosol art (any work produced in aerosol paint, primarily on canvas for sale in art galleries or as commissioned murals), much less as writers producing illegal works. Only Lady Pink gained national and international recognition as an accomplished aerosol artist and writer during the "art boom" period of the early 1980s in New York.

There was what, ten, fifteen thousand graffiti writers in New York City at the time [late 1970s and early 1980s] and I was the female. There had been girls before me in the 1970s and some girls that did things on their own, not because of a boyfriend, like Charmin and Z73 and Eva 62 and Barbara 62. They were girls that wrote for a few years and got their kicks but then life takes over. You have to find a job, you end up getting married, having kids, and you no longer have that time to go recklessly running off and getting arrested for the weekend. You end up growing up. When I started in 1979, 1980 I was the only girl, so I immediately became famous all over town because I was the only girl and my boys that were hanging with me became famous too. Right along side my name they said their names too. Yeah, she hangs out with Seen and Doze. (Lady Pink 1998)

There is evidence to suggest why there is a disproportionately smaller number of female writers than male writers. A few of the recognized female writers, like Stoney, were more or less "uninvited" to join some of the early writing crews. Although some widely respected male writers stood up for young women in these groups, most males did not seem to have been willing to do so, which reflects a lack of importance placed on gender diversity. In fact, actions by male writers may have served as a deterrent to potential female writers. Males tend to write the names of their girlfriends as a public sign of the male's devotion. Although there is certainly no restrictive intent in such gifting, it may indicate that young women are not expected to write themselves. Moreover, women's art is often crossed out with words such as "girle," "bitch," "slut," or "whore," whereas male graffiti art is defaced by other writers who cross it out with their own tags. The demeaning "crossings" insinuate that it is the female artist's gender and sexuality that are lacking the desirable qualities and not necessarily her artistic skills. Still, Stoney felt as if most male writers of her time treated her as an equal in all respects.

In most respects, writing is a form of communication dominated by young men. Males tend to be dismissive of female action and young women's active (rather than reactive) role in writing. As several female writers have stated, the greatest deterrent to their participation

in this art form has been the damage to their reputation during their early years as a toy traveling in the company of male writers.

I personally feel that, even though some of the male writers are my friends, I feel a little bit intimidated. Intimidated by their skill and by them being male. Because I'm female, I feel like I have to work three times as hard to prove myself. With another female to bomb [paint] with, you don't feel that uneasiness and you can just let go and have fun. Yet, when you try to write, as a female, even though they might not be overtly sayin' anything negative to you, the female feels this pressure. And that makes it all that much harder. I think that's why a lot of females don't write. Because they are intimidated as hell. Actually to tell you the truth, I think some guys are intimidated by female writers. They either totally think it's cool or they just don't like it. (Girle 1997)

However, there are numerous stories of male and female writers working together successfully. In an interview with *Siren* magazine, Lady Pink explained that "Very early on, I gathered very strong friends. I was down with a lot of important painting crews. I had a lot of back [support], so guys wouldn't mess with me." Girle's and Lady Pink's experiences with writing hint that there are other reasons for low rates of female participation.

Apprentice relationships are the primary means by which painting skills, the necessary knowledge of the local graffiti scene's history, and writers' ethical codes are handed down. When females are not welcomed as peers among male writers, the pool of potential teachers is narrowed. This is not to say that males have not acted as teachers for female writers, because they have. In the early age range when most writers are initiated, however, females are more likely to learn from males when they are involved romantically. Some then choose to take on writing as an extension of their relationship; in other cases, young women have ceased writing altogether when their relationship ended. As Lady Pink's remarks above show, most young women who stuck to writing got started in graffiti with the help of writers not romantically involved with them.

Moreover, female writers work within traditional and culturally determined limitations that are set outside the graffiti culture; thus gender standards in the wider society inevitably influence the decisions of young women to become writers. Women's involvement in writing is affected by some key cultural meanings associated with property relations. Property is central to the Western cultural concept of self. One is defined by what one owns and controls. Within this framework, property is an icon of power. Writing on another's property is a way in which those without power can symbolically appropriate it. At the same time, women and girls have historically been objectified, purchased, traded, and owned by males. Within this Western cultural framework, males tend to expect a space of their own within the massive urban landscape (even if they must acquire it illegally and symbolically), whereas females have not been raised with this same expectation.

Another reason for low female participation involves the conditions under which graffiti art is produced. Stewart argues that young women involved in this illegal art form were deterred from writing by their boyfriends, who were concerned about their being hurt or arrested. But male prejudice cannot solely account for young women's apathy toward graffiti. In the 1970s and early 1980s, subway trains became the preferred site for writing. Since the train yards at night were the prime place and time for painting subway cars, some young women who would have otherwise joined in might have considered this "illegal" space too dangerous. However, fears of being in the subway yards at night cannot be explained solely by the possibility of being captured and beaten by authorities or by the more rugged terrain of the yards, since female writers had already demonstrated a fearlessness toward these conditions at par with males. Most likely, concerns about being targets of sexual violence in the yards created enough apprehension to keep novice females away from the practice. Many potential female writers could not count on the kind of support given to Lady Pink, whose peers prevented "guys" from "mess[ing]" with her.

Apprehensions of painting in the yards aside, it is undoubtedly more difficult for most young women to escape from their parents' homes at night. In many family households, daughters are much more likely to be assigned domestic chores, like housecleaning or child care, which obligate them to stay home at night when most writing is done. In contrast, young men are seldom expected to perform these tasks, thus allowing them the space and time to engage in writing. Because of the division of labor among the genders, young women cannot participate in graffiti or, if they do, transcend the toy stage as easily as males.

The struggle for recognition and fame is also harder for young women once established as writers. Their work tends to be compared with other women's graffiti art rather than writers in general.

It's funny when guys say to you, "you are way better than that person" or "you and this girl are the best," as if I would only be compared to other girls. But I mean it's so many things, like boys expect so little of you being a girl writer. Cuz' if I do two fill-ins [a relatively simple form of writing] somewhere I'll get like six times more props [fame] than a boy would just because I'm a girl. Because of that I get stuck in these little ruts where I won't want to do more than that. So that's kinda hard. Like if you walk in to a room with a bunch of boy writers who don't know you write they won't even look at you. But that's true of everything, not just writing. They won't acknowledge that you have anything to offer other than a good time. (Eskimo 1999)

Statements like this suggest that young women writers are considered as either oddities or novelties in the graffiti culture. This view, along with overtly sexual references of disrespect made by young men in graffiti art, serves to place young women in an inferior class of writers. Inevitably, these actions create greater competition among female writers, encouraging them to battle for the minor status allotted to women.

Despite all the hazards and although their numbers are small, women play an integral role in graffiti art. In each city, there tends to be at least one girl writing next to hundreds of boys. But it is the scarcity of female writers that creates the conditions for them to become key figures in the development of graffiti as an art form and a social movement. The relatively small number of works by female writers have a greater impact than those by males. They have been essential to the migration and evolution of regional graffiti styles. Since the early 1970s, female writers have acted as bridges between the art styles created in different cities. Because of the lack of local or regional female role models, female writers in smaller U.S. cities look outside their locality for influence, style, technique, and compatible mentors. Of necessity, they made allies with and role models of female writers across the United States and beyond. In doing so, their work has rapidly influenced regional styles, more so than male writers' work. Male toys look up to and attempt to emulate the style of local male artists, whereas female toys turn to both local writers and female writers in other cities and countries. Thus young women tend to make a greater impact in the evolution of a city's graffiti art style, specifically because fewer of them are writing.

Writing and aerosol art have changed mainstream art, advertisements, urban images, youth culture, and public art. The historical role of young women is integral to the future role of writing as this art form takes off in many different and sporadic directions across the globe. From the art galleries to the streets, writing continues to expand and include girls as both significant aerosol artists and important graffiti writers. Yet the central role of young women in the development of graffiti as an art form has received

Graffiti in hip-hop spray-painted letters, Seattle, Washington. (Joel W. Rogers/Corbis)

minimal attention and recognition by scholars and fellow writers.

In the available records, which include popular culture productions, female participation in any aspect of hip-hop culture, including writing, has remained relatively subordinate and hidden behind secondary or stereotypical images of women as girlfriends of more important male artists. Since the 1970s, the development and subsequent commercialization of hip-hop culture have encouraged a fantasy image of male artists scratching records, rapping, break dancing, and writing in an aggressive display of youthful exuberance and an explicit resistance to the mainstream values of white, middle-class society. In this environment, young women (as girlfriends) serve as a familiar and reassuring social "bridge" between hip-hop subculture and its potential mainstream audiences, but their status as important artists and writers in their own right is overlooked.

Dramatic action and a commanding presence (like illegally writing a large and striking name) within the public arena tend to be culturally associated with males, whereas the feminine self has been more often culturally associated with passivity, quietude, and privacy, particularly at a young age. The exclusion of females in most historical documentation of graffiti art and the persistent representation of women in secondary roles such as bystanders, art objects, or recipients of dedications (girlfriends/mothers) reinforce the perception that the female role in graffiti is secondary and subordinate to that of male writers. All this has made it very difficult to understand a feminine role within writing, other than in relation to men.

A handful of women ethnographers are trying to deconstruct the perception that young women's participation in graffiti is limited to subordinate and secondary roles. Nancy Guevara (1985a) and Rivière have found that young women have developed styles unique to them. Female writers are more likely to include images in their work or to be identified solely by images instead of names and letters, as is the most common style. Women are more likely to use bright mixes of colors, including pastels, and tend to place greater attention on the accepted conformity of letter shapes in the names they write. Although no color scheme is ever exclusively gender-bound, the images, use of colors, and aesthetic patterns most often produced by female writers constitute a feminine voice breaking with the male standard of language, just as that (writing) language has already broken from dominant proscriptions.

Young women also have particular ways of identifying themselves in graffiti. Names, assumed to precisely disclose gender identities in most other areas of everyday life, are likewise assumed to reveal the gender of female writers in most instances, as the tag-names of Girle, Lady Pink, and Ms. Maggs illustrate. Names can be further manipulated to construct a gendered tag-name with phonetic and symbolic interpretations such as Ms. Red or Ms. Taken, which read as "misread" or "mistaken." But names can also function as a way to mask gender identity, since the illegal nature of writing demands that the name be exhibited without the body, the art without the artist. Some young women have chosen to remain androgynous in graffiti writing or have intentionally manipulated graffiti names to make their gender more elusive. Androgynous monikers such as Rukus, Snear, Phant, Ropas, Kaos, and

Since have allowed young women to hide their gender. This tendency would seem to provide writing with the opportunity for a nongendered art.

Since 1990, there has been a resurgence of female participation in writing culture, surpassing the levels of participation that Stewart (1989), Schmidlapp and Phase 2 (1996), and Craig Castleman (1982) documented in the early 1970s. No doubt, more women will be recognized nationally and internationally as accomplished aerosol and graffiti artists, capturing the title of "queens" and thereby challenging the patriarchal language and structure of this writing culture.

Melisa Rivière and Joe Austin

See also Communication; Girl Gangs; Juvenile Delinquents; Substance Abuse

References and Further Reading
Austin, Joe. 2001. *Taking the Train: Youth, Urban Crisis, and Graffiti.* New York: Columbia University Press.
Castleman, Craig. 1982. *Getting Up: Subway Graffiti in New York.* Boston: MIT Press.
Chalfant, Henry, and Martha Cooper. 1984. *Subway Art.* New York: Henry Holt.
Eskimo. 1999. Interview with Melisa Rivière, July 13.
Girle. 1997. Interview with Melisa Rivière, March 1.
Guevara, Nancy. 1985a. "Graffiti Talk: Words, Walls, Women." *Tabloid,* no. 9: 20–31.
———. 1985b. "Women Writin', Rappin', Breakin'." *Year Left* (London) 2, no. 2: 160–175.
Lady Pink. 1998. Interview with Melisa Rivière, August 11.
Mediati, Ellen. 1997. "Hot Pink: An Interview with Lady Pink." *Siren* 2: 21.
Miller, Ivor Lynn. 1993. "Aerosol Kingdom: The Indigenous Culture of the New York Subway." UMI 1349354 Master's thesis, Yale University.

Ortner, Sherry. 1996. "Is Female to Male as Nature Is to Culture?" In *Anthropological Theory*. Edited by R. Jon McGee and Richard L. Warms. Mountain View, CA: Mayfield Publishing.

Reisner, Robert. 1971. *Graffiti: Two Thousand Years of Wall Writing*. New York: Cowles Book Company.

Schmidlapp, David, and Phase 2. 1996. *Style: Writing from the Underground, (R)evolution of Aerosol Linguistics*. Viterbo, Italy: Stampa Alternativa/Nuovi Equilibri.

Stewart, Jack. 1989. *Subway Graffiti: An Aesthetic Study of Graffiti on the Subway System of New York City 1970–1978*. Ph.D. diss., New York University, UMI 9004328.

Stoney. 1999. Interview with Joe Austin, August 11.

H

Hair

Going blonde changed my life. It was the summer of 1966. I was fifteen. I was at the cottage and I felt overweight and really unattractive. To make matters worse, my sister was older than me and extremely popular. So one night I got a bottle of peroxide and bleached my hair. I thought I looked glamorous. The boys did too.

     —*Anonymous interviewee (quoted in McCracken 1995, 116)*

Like the millions of American women and girls who frequent beauty salons in search of the perfect cut and color, countless teens understand the potent symbolism of hair. Fashion experts ponder the meaning of clothing styles, underwear, and millinery items but overlook hairstyling despite its obvious importance as a fashion statement. Shape, color, texture, and style all lend themselves to the visual analysis of hair, much as they create a language of design in the world of fashion or fine arts. Hair is transformative, a type of self-invention through which a woman can change her appearance to coincide with varying visions of herself. It is a public statement of how she wishes to be viewed. In this way, analysis of hairstyle and color offers rich insights into the lives of women and girls and the culture in which they live.

Hairstyling has a long and complicated past, from the fancy perfumed wigs of ancient Egypt to the elaborate headpieces of eighteenth-century France to Sinead O'Connor's bald minimalism. But the story of styling is more than an examination of simple fashion whimsy; it has to do with technological advances, notions of privacy, theories of childhood development, and concepts of personal hygiene. These components not only interact with each other but also define what is feasible. For example, in eighteenth-century France when bathing and shampooing were not common occurrences in women's daily hygiene routines, hair was fashioned elaborately. As long as women kept their hairdos dry and slept upright in bed or in chairs, their labyrinthine styles could last for weeks. Large doses of perfume and powder were used to disguise the rancid smell of lard-based mousses. However, when daily or even weekly baths and shampooing became the norm in the twentieth century, this process was too time-consuming to be tackled as an everyday occurrence; hair had to become easier to maintain in order to accommodate a daily bathing regimen.

Technology is also an important aspect of hairstyling. Invented in 1897, the Marcel waving iron permitted a number of straight-haired young women to sport fashionable ringlets. But the waving iron was expensive and took six to twelve hours to work, effectively excluding most girls who could not afford the fee or time to undergo the procedure. It was not until Charles Nestle invented the permanent wave in 1915 that a sizable number of girls and young women could have trend-setting curls. Throughout the twentieth century, advances in technology continued to influence and democratize the hairstyling industry. When the first hand-held hair dryers were invented in the 1920s, hairstyling became quicker and easier for a vast number of American women. By the 1950s, Clairol introduced a one-step home hair-coloring kit that revolutionized hair care. For the first time, almost any teen could afford a bottle of "tint" and, in the privacy of her own home, transform herself into a blonde beauty before first-period study hall.

Besides personal hygiene and technology, society's view of public and private functions played another important role in fashioning women's hair. This phenomenon is exemplified by three American paintings. *Anne Pollard* (1721) was 100 years old at the time of her portrait. Despite her age, she is portrayed with her hair appropriately covered. In colonial times, it was said that the sight of women's hair would make the angels sin. Social mores dictated that even as a century-old matron and liberated tavern owner, Anne Pollard's hair had to be wrapped.

Accompanied by her mother, Mrs. Freake, little baby Mary suffered the same fate in 1671. Viewed not as a child but as a little adult, Mary's hair is tastefully covered just as that of her mother and centenarian successor. Although these hair coverings were discarded well before the nineteenth century, hair in the Victorian era continued to be fashioned and patterned in the privacy of the home. As Joan Jacobs Brumberg notes, with the "growing focus on appearance . . . girls spent more time in front of mirrors arranging their hair. In many families, mothers, daughters, and sisters spent considerable time brushing each other's hair" (1997, fig. 10). But because of the traditional notion of the erotic nature of tresses, only the immediate family saw mother or sister with her hair down.

Hairstyling emerged from the private sphere when the first public salons were established in the late nineteenth century. John Sloan's painting *Hairdresser's Window* (1905) portrays a youthful woman having her hair fashioned in one of these public salons before the eyes of a lively metropolitan crowd. By the turn of the century, as single women left the home to work in offices and factories, hair became a more public spectacle in the high-pressured and impersonal atmosphere of urban life.

Theories of childhood psychology also added to the complexity of hairstyling. As Karin Calvert notes in *Children in the House* (1992), by the mid-nineteenth century, childhood and adolescence came to be viewed as distinct developmental stages. By the twentieth century, childhood was seen as a distinct phase of life, one fundamentally different from adulthood and requiring special nurturing and protection. As if to visually reflect these various stages of life, little girls, adolescents, and women sport different hairdos. Little girls' hair is styled in a more unregulated, ungendered, and practical fashion, often hanging freely down the back or tied in pigtails. When girls' figures begin to change, they are encouraged to don more mature hairstyles. With the

Girls' and young women's hair was often covered when they went out in public in the nineteenth century, as this 1846 portrait by James Baillie shows. (Library of Congress)

onset of adolescence and the transition to adult responsibility and privilege, girls' hair is arranged in styles that mediate between the simplicity and practicality of children's styles and the more sophisticated ones of adults. The ponytail—a popular style of the late 1940s and 1950s—is a good example of this phenomenon. Although grown women sometimes wore it in an attempt to look young, the ponytail was popular mostly with teens. The ponytail's name harkened back to horses, animals considered to be erotic fixations among young girls. In this style, the hair is pulled back to reveal a maturing face. At the same time, the hair is playfully coltlike in the back, wiggling and bouncing as a girl walked. Revealing yet sprightly, innocent yet erotic, this look reflected the cultural position of the teenage girl in the postwar United States.

Social mores and technological advances played a significant part in hairstyling in the twentieth century but so, too, did the cultural role of women. When girls begin to assume the position of an adult, their hairstyles often reflect the role that mature women will play in society. Predominant trends in styles often parallel significant events in gender relations; they mirror a fluctuation in the social order. For a more nuanced glimpse into the position of young women in the late nineteenth and twentieth centuries, hairstyles offer significant clues.

For example, as mistress of her home, an ideal Victorian woman oversaw her children's upbringing and provided a sanctuary for her weary husband from the cruel demands of the working world. The *public* sphere was dominated, however, by men. A proper woman remained in the home: her lack of autonomy in civic life were reflected in the heavy corsets, bustles, and long skirts that limited her physical freedom. Most little girls grew their hair long in anticipation of the time when they could pin it up as their mothers and older sisters did. Little girls could look forward to the time when they too would rule the domestic realm as wives and mothers. When they became adults, their hair would be kept long but primly pinned up on their heads. Privacy was of the utmost importance. A Victorian lady would never let her hair down in public. In that respect, her well-contained hair matched her cloistered life in the home.

This straitlaced style continued well into the twentieth century. The big change in women's hair occurred in the 1910s and early 1920s, with the introduction of the bob. At the time, this short, over-the-ear cut was seen as a major act of liberation because it seemed to defy the social order of Victorian propriety. Short and breezy, it was worn by teens and flappers and reflected a busier and more liberated lifestyle. The bob was considered outrageous by many and was believed by critics to have been worn by French prostitutes during the early part of the century. Despite its naughty reputation, many young women—including the popular dancer Irene Castle—embraced this trend. It was easy and free, much like the reputation of the flappers themselves. Whether riding in a new convertible with the top down, dancing the black bottom in public dance halls, earning a living as a working "girl" in the city, or voting in national elections after the successful passage of the Nineteenth Amendment in 1920, women seemed to have more freedom in the 1920s. The short bob cut and the accompanying slimmer silhouette mirrored these liberated times.

During the 1930s and early 1940s, hairstyles were notably lacking in innovation, although variations on the bob and curl abounded. Examples included feathercuts, pageboy bobs, and the "over the eye look" popularized by such movie stars as Greta Garbo and Veronica Lake. During the Depression and World War II, attention to hairstyles waned. In these troubled times, people focused more on financial security and winning the war. Fashion houses from France—the inspiration for many of these chic new haircuts—closed during the occupation. In the United States, female defense plant workers were encouraged to keep their hair short or pulled back in a bandanna to prevent accidents. With a Depression to conquer and a war to win, fancy hairstyles were relegated to the back burner. Although young girls dreamed of looking like their favorite movie star, the times dictated a more discreet look.

With the return of prosperity in the 1950s, however, hair reentered the fashion arena. The next dramatic change in hairstyles began with the advent of home hair coloring and the introduction of the bouffant hairdo, an elaborate style in which large quantities of hair were back-combed or teased and frozen into place with aerosol spray. Unlike their counterparts from earlier centuries, 1950s teens bathed and washed their hair regularly. As a result, much sacrifice was required in order to maintain the bouffant. Not only did girls wear curlers to bed, but frequent trips to the hair salon were crucial. The complexity of the bouffant dictated that young women depend on their stylists to sculpt their hair and keep it in place. Much like the earlier hairstylists in eighteenth-century France, a 1950s hairdresser was all-important to customers, for it was his or her vision of a particular style that was imposed on their faces. A girl conformed to the bouffant; the style did not conform to her features.

Because the bouffant was frozen in place with hairspray, the aesthetic of this style was one of control. In that respect, it mirrored the inflexible and rule-driven atmosphere of the United States during the Cold War. A strong nuclear family and adherence to stringent gender roles were considered imperative for the United States to beat the godless red menace. As anthropologist Grant McCracken notes, the bouffant was "controlled, it was everything women were supposed to become: meek, unthreatening, compli-

Annette Funicello in "Beach Party" demonstrates the ideal hairstyle of the late 1950s and early 1960s. (Photofest, 1963)

ant, and disciplined" (McCracken 1995, 36). The bouffant and spray kept older women's curls in place much like the nylon brassiere and girdle restrained their bodies. Armed with their AAA training bras, white lipstick, and cans of hairspray, young girls were inculcated early into 1950s gender ideology.

Mouseketeer Annette Funicello epitomized this look. On an album cover for the soundtrack for her movie *Beach Party* (1963), Annette stands next to her personalized surfboard, apparently ready to hit the waves when the surf comes up.

This photograph did not reflect a scene from the film because Annette rarely surfed or even entered the water in her beach movies. Her hair, eye makeup, and figure had to keep their shape under all circumstances, never shifting, smearing, or wiggling despite water, wind, and sand. At the same time that her body was controlled, it was also highly sexualized—cinched at the waist with her breasts artificially uplifted. She was erotically enticing in her snug suits and nylon supports, and she embodied the romantic and passionate promise of a perfect 1950s wife.

On the occasion of the release of her movie *Back to the Beach* (1987), Annette Funicello recalled her original role as Dee Dee in *Beach Blanket Bingo* (1965). She noted: "Oh my God. When I look at those movies now and see my hair. . . . It never moved. The wind would blow and every hair stayed in place. Even when I'd go into the water, my hair never got wet. We're not talking real life here" (Sherman 1987, 50). If in her movies she ventured into the water, she emerged looking as if she had not left the shore. As Funicello's quote testifies, a girl's place was not in the water but on the beach, looking pretty and preparing lunch. Her fixed appearance signaled to the public that her role on the domestic front was secure. She had found the perfect balance; her controlled hairstyle and artificially uplifted figure suggested that she was enticing and seductive and at the same time morally chaste and untouchable until the day of commitment. She embodied postwar domestic ideology from head to toe.

Besides the bouffant hairdo, the 1950s also marked the popularization of home coloring aids. In a May 1961 issue of *Harper's Bazaar*, a picture appeared of a young brunette bending over a bassinet, looking down at her baby and smiling proudly. The text read: "She's happy, confident—just as a new mother should be—and she looks as wonderful as she feels"; no tired eyes from those 2 A.M. feedings, no weight gain, no postpartum depression. Clairol provided the reader with an intimate closeup of a mother and child. The advertisement asked the viewer, "Does she or doesn't she?"—then offered a coy hint: "Hair color so natural only her hairdresser knows for sure."

The "Does she or doesn't she?" pitch—an advertising slogan associated with the Bristol-Meyers Miss Clairol product line—was one of many hair-coloring campaigns originating in the 1950s. Before the 1950s, using peroxide, dying, or tinting hair not only was tedious and expensive but was considered trashy and inappropriate for well-bred girls. Platinum blondes had an especially bad reputation since they conjured up images of the bleached-blonde sexpot of 1930s films. Described as the "bad girl with the heart of gold," movie star Jean Harlow, for example, was the "smart slut who cracked gum and one liners" (*Time* 1935, 26; Haskell 1973, 11). Mae West had a similarly tainted reputation, often portraying prostitutes in motion pictures and reciting off-color jokes. Although Harlow and West were frequently described as plucky, good-humored, and good-natured, they were still wanton women, lovable but tarnished. Photographs of Clairol's happy mothers and contented children counteracted this bad-girl image of the woman who dyed her hair. In the age of domesticity, when the family unit was so important, what could be more sacred than the intimate bond between mother and child? If a *mother* could change her hair color, why not any decent young girl? Clairol made coloring "as much a part of a woman's beauty routine as lipstick and powder" ("No Question" 1963, 8). But more importantly, the company made it a respectable and *private* affair. A teenage girl could do the deed in the privacy of her own bathroom, and technological developments allowed her to do it in one simple twenty-minute procedure.

During the 1960s, a new trend in styling emerged. This milestone in hair care occurred when Vidal Sassoon entered the hairdressing scene. Unlike 1950s stylists such as Ernest Adler and Mr. Antoine who sculpted elaborate bouffants on the platformed heads of their clients, Sassoon believed that hair should follow the natural dictates of the shape of the head. Dispensing with chemicals, rollers, and hairspray, Sassoon was, according to McCracken, a modernist who believed in the adage that "form followed function." No more would the customer have to endure the rigid rules of the bouffant. With a swish of the head, a Sassoon cut fell neatly in place on the head of his client. In the 1960s, hair could be a unique form of self-expression in which the design followed the dictates of each individual. Young women's hair symbolized the new social freedoms of the sexual revolution and the women's liberation movement. It was during this period that unisex salons entered the scene and wigs allowed a girl the freedom to change her hairstyle like a hat. No more was one hairstyle the defining trend of the period. With improved portable hair dryers, home permanents, and styling gels, hair was easier to manipulate. As the rock musical *Hair: The American Tribal Love-Rock Musical* intimated, anything seemed permissible in the age of Aquarius.

A young woman with dyed hair in the 1990s. (Skjold Photographs)

From the 1970s to the 1990s, hairstyles continued this liberatory trend. In the postmodern era, no particular cut dominated for any length of time. Various fads came and went. In the 1970s, Farrah Fawcett's big hair was all the rage. For feminist critics, this fad reflected a step backward in the fight for women's rights. They claimed that Fawcett's cut was a return to the 1950s with its emphasis on height, sculpted shapes, and hairspray. But for many teenage girls, Farrah's big hair symbolized a sense of authority without a loss of sexiness. Fawcett popularized the style while playing in the successful television series *Charlie's Angels*, which featured female detectives who packed pistols, beat up bad guys, and solved dangerous crimes. It was one of the first programs to feature women engaging in physical feats of daring. For girls growing up in the 1970s, *Charlie's Angels* and Farrah Fawcett were their first active female role models; copying Fawcett's hair or purchasing a Farrah Fawcett doll was a way of pledging allegiance to their favorite star.

In the 1980s, as more women entered the ranks of the corporate world, a plethora of "blunt cut" styles reflected women's new professional positions. As McCracken notes, the blunt cut "was symbolically everything the 'dress for success' look was. It had the same standardized severe, disciplined character to it" (McCracken 1995, 169). With its emphasis on a sleek and sharp aesthetic, this efficient style signaled women's ability to "bring home the bacon."

Although conservative blunt cuts were popular among women, the 1980s also produced the antistyles of bald stars like Sinead O'Connor and Sigourney Weaver and the magenta mohawks of the punk rockers. With Madonna and her postmodern performances that emphasized constructed personae, Americans girls became intrigued and aware of the rhetoric of personal style. Much of this awareness began in the 1960s, but by the 1980s, it seemed even more obvious that choices of clothing and haircuts revealed the ideological bent of the person who wore them. Mohawks and baldness were recognized by many as rebellious statements criticizing the conventional view of women's beauty. As contradictory styles proliferated in the 1980s, people developed more of an understanding of the position that hair played in personal and public lives. Although there is still no agreement as to

what constitutes the perfect cut, more people appreciate hair as a vehicle for self-expression and transformation in an increasingly impersonal world.

Barbara J. Coleman

See also Body Image; Clothing; Consumer Culture; Girls' Culture; Surfer Girls

References and Further Reading
Brumberg, Joan Jacobs. 1997. *The Body Project: An Intimate History of American Girls.* New York: Random House.
Calvert, Karin. 1992. *Children in the House: The Material Culture of Early Childhood, 1600–1900.* Boston: Northeastern University Press.
"Fine Feathers Make Fine Fans." 1935. *Time* (August 19): 26.
Frasko, Mary. 1994. *Daring Do: A History of Extraordinary Hair.* New York: Flammarion.
Haskell, Molly. 1973. *From Reverence to Rape.* New York: Holt, Rinehart and Winston.
McCracken, Grant. 1995. *Big Hair: A Journey into the Transformation of Self.* New York: Overlook Press.
"No Question Now That Many Do—But with Whose Color?" 1963. *Printers' Ink* (August 16): 8.
Sherman, Eric. 1987. "Frankie and Annette: Back to the Beach." *Ladies Home Journal* (July): 50.

Handbags

Bags have a long and rich history in the life of American girls and women. More than purely utilitarian objects, bags have been decorative accessories to clothing as well as expressions of artistic talents. They have also served as markers of the status and occupation of those who carry them. Although men and boys have also carried certain types of bags, in the United States purses and handbags are associated with females and their gender socialization. In games of dress-up and in children's books, purses and handbags are symbols of womanhood. The use of backpacks, the most popular type of bag among students, has recently raised concerns about health and safety. They have been banned at some schools due to concerns over students carrying weapons or drugs to school. At other schools, students are carrying such heavily loaded backpacks that parents and pediatricians worry about shoulder and back strain. Among the solutions to these problems are clear vinyl or mesh see-through backpacks and bags on wheels. The latest styles of bags conform to the shape of the body and distribute weight more comfortably. Some are worn around the waist, hips, arms, or torso and enable the wearer to exercise greater freedom of movement.

In the eighteenth century girls and women carried personal essentials in pockets suspended from a waistband under their long, full skirts. The often flat, pear-shaped pocket bags with vertical slit openings were worn singly or in pairs. Slit openings in skirts and underskirts allowed access to the pockets. It is this type of pocket that "Lucy Locket" lost in the famous nursery rhyme. Although not visible to others, pocket bags were often decoratively embroidered by girls and women.

The influence of the Enlightenment on clothing styles near the end of the eighteenth century led to softer, more slender silhouettes based on classical styles. As a result, bulky pockets were replaced by drawstring bags called "reticules" that young women suspended from hand or wrist.

Needlework skills were considered important accomplishments and condoned activities for girls and women in the eighteenth and nineteenth centuries.

Portrait of Miss Harriet Leavens by folk artist Amy Phillips. (Fogg Art Museum, Harvard University, gift of the estate of Harriet Anna Niel, ca. 1815)

Embroidery, knitting, crocheting, tatting, and sewing were regular activities, and the materials and equipment for those endeavors were organized and contained in workbaskets and workbags. Girls and women used these baskets and bags in their homes and sometimes carried them along on visits to friends. Bags and purses were among the many items made or embellished by girls and women using their needlework skills. *Godey's Lady's Book,* a popular women's magazine published in the nineteenth century, included a "Juvenile Department" that occasionally featured patterns for purses that children could make for fairs or for gifts. The intricacy of these patterns attests to the high level of skill attributed to the children who would make them. Patterns for making bags and purses appeared also in other magazines and in commercial pattern books, although commercially manufactured bags were available as well.

As garment styles and silhouettes changed throughout the nineteenth century, attached pockets were incorporated in or on women's and girls' clothing, but bags and purses continued to be carried as well. These bags held scarcely more than a handkerchief, calling cards, and money. The personal items women carried with them in the nineteenth century were fewer than most women would feel comfortable with today. Popular bag styles included narrow knitted tubes called "long purses," chatelaine bags that hung from belts, and a variety of crocheted and beaded bags that were carried by hand or on the wrist. Advertisements in mail-order catalogs show diminutive versions of some of these bags for children.

Throughout the twentieth century, women's roles in society broadened, and the items that women carried in public proliferated. The variety of sizes, shapes, and materials used in women's purses and handbags increased. At various times bags have been hung from belts or around the neck or have been carried in hand, dangled from wrist straps or finger rings, clutched under the arm, hung from the crook of the arm, or slung over one shoulder or both. They have been made of leather, suede, silk, velvet, wool, metal, beading, mesh, plastic, nylon, rubber, and more. They have been closed with drawstrings, flaps, folds, buttons, snaps, zippers, and a variety of frames and clasps. Bags and purses have increasingly been manufactured for and marketed to girls. Often they have been small versions of the bags sold to women. Sometimes they have included a variety of juvenile decorative motifs such as popular cartoon characters.

Handbags and purses have become so closely associated with women in the United States that their use may be seen to have gender role associations. Purses and handbags can be used as tools of feminine socialization; one example can be found in the activity of dress-up that is so popular among young children. This type of imaginative play helps children try out different roles and practice social skills. Handbags or purses are often seen in such play as elements contributing to the image of an adult woman. This idea is reinforced by illustrations in some children's books in which characters play dress-up and purses and handbags are among the objects associated with women. In some other board books and easy readers written for young children, purses and handbags are associated with girls striving to act grownup or like their mothers.

Near the end of the twentieth century, girls of all ages could be seen carrying a wide variety of bags. Purses, backpacks, athletic bags, dance bags, book bags, tote bags, and others help girls organize the personal belongings that they find necessary for daily life and the equipment for particular activities. Each type of bag can be found in an array of sizes, shapes, materials, and colors. They range from toys for young children to sophisticated, functional bags either resembling or identical to bags carried by adult women. Very young children may carry small toys, books, dolls, or other amusements. In their bags older girls store personal hygiene and grooming products, writing materials, books, snack foods, cellular phones, pagers, water bottles, keys, money, identification, and more. In specialty bags they may carry athletic equipment, dance supplies, and clothing for after-school activities. Some girls carry a purse as well as a backpack or book bag to school.

Despite their usefulness, bags have become part of certain health and safety issues. Safety experts advise girls and women that the way they carry purses or handbags can make them more or less vulnerable to attack by purse-snatchers. For example, purses dangling from a shoulder, wrist, or hand can easily be grabbed away. Bags with straps slung across the chest are more securely anchored to the body, but if they are grabbed, personal injury to the wearer may result. Personal injury may result as well from attempting to hold on to any bag if it is being stolen.

The backpack has become the most popular type of bag among students for carrying books and other school supplies. As such, it has become one of the complex problems facing school administrators, teachers, parents, and students in the effort to achieve and maintain a high level of safety and security in the educational environment. In response to the dangers presented by some students bringing weapons and drugs to school,

some schools have banned the carrying of backpacks to classes. Some others have attempted to eliminate contraband by requiring students who carry backpacks to use a type of see-through pack made of mesh or transparent vinyl.

Conversely, some schools have eliminated lockers for reasons of space and economy. As a result students carry heavy backpacks full of the day's necessities, which has prompted concern among parents and pediatricians over back and shoulder strain among students of all ages. Some parents have provided wheeled backpacks for their children, and pediatricians advise children to distribute weight throughout the backpack and to carry it by both shoulder straps.

The newest styles of bags being marketed to girls and women at the beginning of the twenty-first century are designed variously to be worn around the waist, hips, arms, or torso. Some resemble vests, others holsters. They conform to the shape of the body and empower the wearer with a freedom of movement that is not possible when clutching, dangling, or otherwise holding on to a bag or strap.

Marsha Propst Carothers

See also Arts and Crafts; Clothing; Consumer Culture

References and Further Reading

American Academy of Pediatrics. 1998. "Carrying Backpacks a Weighty Issue for Students." *AAP News* 14, no. 9: 31.

Chaiet, Donna. 1995. *Staying Safe while Shopping.* New York: Rose Publishing Group.

Foster, Vanda. 1982. *Bags and Purses.* Costume Accessories Series. Edited by Aileen Ribeiro. London: B. T. Batsford.

Haertig, Evelyn. 1983. *Antique Combs and Purses.* Carmel, CA: Gallery Graphics Press.

———. 1990. *More Beautiful Purses.* Carmel, CA: Gallery Graphics Press.

Home Economics Education

Home economics education, a curriculum historically aimed at girls, focuses on improving the health and strength of girls, their families, and their communities. The scope and emphasis of home economics education have evolved since 1850. Historically, girls and women gained access to education through the home economics movement under the guise of learning to be better homemakers, mothers, and wives. For most of its history, home economics education at the secondary school level has differed from the home economics education offered at the postsecondary level. At the junior high school and high school levels, home economics has focused on the household—cooking, sewing, financial home management, and parenting and relationship skills. At the college level, the curriculum has been more scientifically rigorous, offering classes such as food chemistry and child psychology and also providing female graduates entry into academia when appointments in traditional departments were closed to them. For most of its history, the paradox of home economics education has been its twofold existence: the general population perceived that home economics education taught girls to be better wives and mothers, whereas colleges (notably the land-grant institutions) taught female students to be home economics teachers—in effect providing them with a profession.

Reacting to the popular but inaccurate stereotype that home economics "is just cooking and sewing," home economics education programs at the secondary level more recently have tried to break out of the gendered mold by recruiting boys and expanding offerings to vocational training in subjects such as institutional or commercial food preparation and child care. At the postsecondary level, home economics programs have changed their names to the College of Human Ecology or School of Family and Consumer Resources, for example. The professional organization of home economists, the American Home Economics Association (AHEA), voted to change its name to the American Association of Family and Consumer Sciences to provide a more accurate picture of its purpose and rid itself of demeaning stereotypes. In this era of lamenting the increase in teen pregnancy, poor consumer skills, and increased violence, it is surprising that the subject matter taught in home economics classrooms is still devalued and derided. The home economics education movement provided a lasting and irrevocable contribution to our society by providing education for girls and women from 1850 onward and continues to highlight the positions of women and families in American society today.

The home economics movement in the United States started in the mid-1800s. Catharine Beecher, sister of Harriet Beecher Stowe, is credited as the founder of the home economics movement. Her 1841 *Treatise on Domestic Economy for Use of Young Ladies at Home and at School*, was considered to be the first home economics text suitable for use in public schools and by American women who needed to manage their homes. Between 1820 and 1865, Beecher wrote frequently on home, children, health, and the body and promoted the idea of teaching women to be better mothers and housekeepers, thus designating the management of a home as a scientific discipline. Beecher discussed qualitative motherhood rather than quantitative motherhood at a time when the United

States was in the middle of the greatest drop in fertility in its history, from 7.04 children for the average white woman in 1800 to 5.92 in 1850 to 3.56 in 1900 (Woloch 1996). This decrease in family size meant that women could spend more time rearing and nurturing their children, rather than just spending time bearing them. The enduring quality of Beecher's manuals was the promotion of domesticity—the belief in female power in the home. This ideology put women in charge of the home sphere. Women could assert themselves within the family as much as their husbands attempted to assert themselves outside the home. This ideology advocated the moral authority of women, whose scientific methods of management could help stop the decay of family life.

Leaders of the Progressive movement promoted the professionalization of homemakers for the betterment of families and society. Ellen Swallow Richards, an instructor in sanitary chemistry at the Massachusetts Institute of Technology, believed that teaching women to think critically would not just help individual families but also give women the skills to help cure society's ills. Her passion led to the Lake Placid Home Economics Conferences, held from 1899 to 1907, and ultimately the founding of the American Home Economics Association (AHEA). The conferences that started with eleven people in 1899 had hundreds of attendees by 1907.

To promote the importance of the domestic sphere, home economics had become an appropriate and acceptable course of academic study for young women. Land-grant institutions created by the Morill Land-Grant Act of 1862 provided college-level vocational education (as opposed to liberal arts education) to rural Americans. As young men learned about farming at these colleges, rural young women took up home economics, learning to assume the roles of efficient farm wives or small-town housekeepers. The first home economics curriculum was offered at Iowa State in 1871. Kansas State began its domestic economy curriculum two years later, and in 1874 Illinois Industrial University followed suit.

Teaching practical subjects also influenced curricula at the historically black colleges, although home economics usually began as skills development for newly freed blacks at the precollege level to help them obtain employment. In Louisiana, Southern University's high school offered domestic science classes to girls starting in 1880. At the college level, Alabama A&M University began offering home economics classes in 1881, and its Department of Domestic Science was established in 1891. But for colleges aimed at both black and white American young women, the curriculum evolved over the years into teacher training, as well as more scientific subjects such as child psychology, household engineering, and chemistry.

At the same time these college women were studying home economics as a way to better themselves and society as a whole, home economics curriculum entered secondary schools. Domestic science was introduced into the public schools in Boston in the late 1800s, and Emma Willard, another pioneer in home economics, included domestic instruction at Troy Seminary in New York State. "Home economic courses would train girls for both their roles in the community and at home. Through such education girls would become responsible consumers and citizens, establish and run healthy households, be productive and confident homemakers" (Apple 1997,

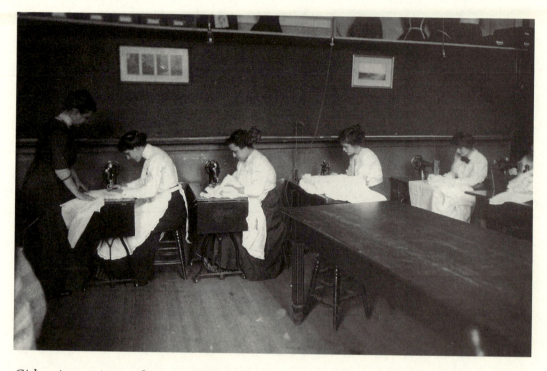

Girls using sewing machines to make "dollar dresses" at Washington Irving High School, New York City, New York. (Library of Congress, 1911)

81). In 1910, the National Education Association (NEA) endorsed home economics as an effective way for girls to ameliorate the problems of an urban industrial society.

At the time, many thought that instruction should start at age five or six. However, the majority of girls then, just as they do today, usually had their main experience with a home economics class in junior high school. In the early part of the twentieth century, many girls would drop out of school by the eighth grade, and the contingent of people who wanted to teach girls the proper way to run a house urged that the curriculum be offered in junior high school to make sure as many girls as possible got the training. In addition, historian Jane Bernard Powers provides evidence that

girls who shouldered the expense of time and money to go to high school wanted training for employment, not housekeeping: "For the majority of young women who went to high school, homemaking was something to be learned in junior high school, or learned at home; it was not relevant to high school goals" (Powers 1992, 96).

The twofold nature of home economics education continued with the training of college women. The Smith-Hughes Act of 1917 provided funds for training home economics teachers who would then teach in the primary and secondary schools. They were given this professional training so as to teach their younger sisters not to aspire to be professionals but to be better wives and housekeepers. Thus their students had unusual role models: working women who instructed them to assume the role of homemakers.

As the twentieth century progressed, the idea that home economics education provided girls with the knowledge necessary to run households became widespread, outweighing the Progressive-era notion that homemakers could be moral saviors and ignoring the fact that many women had no choice but to work. In the 1920s and 1930s classes at the secondary level focused more exclusively on skill development for the individual homemaker. Homemaking was women's work, as is evidenced by the fact that "in 1938–1939 barely 1 percent of boys enrolled in home economics courses" (Apple 1997, 92). The main funding for home economics education continued to come from legislation interested in supporting rural life. In 1936, the George-Deen Act called for equal appropriations for home economics education and agricultural education, the outcome of which continued to give home economics legitimacy as a course of study. Although it was passed into law, the funds were not appropriated because of the Great Depression.

Although the postwar era could be seen as the golden age of the homemaker (having the largest percentage of stay-at-home mothers the United States has ever seen), home economics education was actually threatened. In 1958, the National Defense Education Act, prompted by Sputnik, promoted funding for high school science, math, and foreign languages instead of home economics. Home economics programs at the postsecondary level were going through a crisis as well; just like the high school programs, the curriculum was not seen as academically rigorous enough. According to historian Margaret Rossiter (1997), many prominent programs, including those at Cornell University, Iowa State University, and Michigan State University, were downsized. Home economics departments at the University of Chicago, Teacher's College at Columbia University, and University of California at Berkeley were eliminated outright.

The pressure continued to increase in the 1960s as the women's movement joined in criticizing home economics education. Second-wave feminists, possibly remembering their own experiences sewing aprons and preparing unappetizing food, argued that the coursework fostered restrictive roles for women and girls and saw home economics education at the junior high and high school levels as problematic. (They did not consider that home economics also provided employment for women.) In response to the changing awareness of women's place in society in the 1960s, the role of home economics education in providing vocational training for employment purposes began to be critically examined. The 1963 Vocational Education Act required that a certain percentage of funds earmarked for home economics education be used for home economics–related occupational training. This is the first time that the public demanded more vocational education from home economics classes to aid students in getting a job in the paid labor force, not just to be better mothers and housewives. Of course, the irony is that training girls and women for a profession was what the college-level home economics departments had been doing since their inception, but they had failed to influence public perceptions that home economics went beyond cooking and sewing. The act did, however, strengthen the position of home economics education at the secondary level.

The Vocational Education Act has been renewed and modified over the last three

Students with teacher in a home economics cooking class, Prairie Farms, Alabama. (Library of Congress, 1939)

decades of the twentieth century. In the 1970s, in an attempt to "de-gender" home economics, boys became an appropriate audience for home economics education curriculum in the secondary schools; courses were renamed and reengineered to attract more males. The 1970s was also the first decade in which colleges changed their official names from home economics to human ecology or family resources and consumer sciences. The Carl D. Perkins Vocational Act of 1984 continued the tradition of providing money for home economics education.

Home economics education has now come full circle. In the 1990s, home economics courses focused on decisionmak-

ing and problem solving, the cornerstone of the home economics discipline posited by Ellen Richards at the end of the nineteenth century. In 1994, the AHEA Delegate Assembly voted to change its name to the American Association of Family and Consumer Sciences and, the same year, the American Vocational Association (AVA) Division of Home Economics Education voted to change its name to the Family and Consumer Sciences Education Division of AVA. The underlying cause of both name changes emerged from a 1993 conference titled "Positioning the Profession for the 21st Century," which was attended by representatives of several home economics professional associations. As one home economics education teacher put it: "If only cooking and sewing were the pressing issues at hand. Instead, we have teen pregnancy, theft, alcohol and drug abuse, domestic violence, violence in the streets and pressure to join gangs" (Weate 1995, 25).

But even as the profession works to break free of stereotypical images of home economics, it is nearly impossible to "de-gender" the nature of home economics. Even though many home economics classes today have been renamed "Life Skills" and few college programs named "home economics" remain, the fact that at the beginning of the 1990s an overwhelming 98.5 percent of secondary school home economics teachers were women indicates the continuing gendered nature of the field. But instead of trying to ignore its past, home economics education should celebrate its heritage and the strong force the home economics movement has been in educating and providing career opportunities for American girls.

Deborah B. Smith

See also Domesticity; Education of Girls; Mathematics and Science

References and Further Reading

Apple, Rima D. 1997. "Liberal Education or Vocational Training? Home Economics Education for Girls." Pp. 79–95 in *Rethinking Home Economics: Women and the History of a Profession.* Edited by Sarah Stage and Virginia Vincenti. Ithaca, NY: Cornell University Press.

Data File. 1992. *Vocational Education Journal* 67 (September): 37–39.

Fahm, Esther Glover. 1990. "Home Economics: Our Roots, Our Present, Our Future." Pp. 190–252 in *Historically Black Land-Grant Institutions and the Development of Agriculture and Home Economics, 1890–1990.* By Leedell W. Neyland, with Esther Glover Fahm. Tallahassee: Florida A&M University Foundation.

Powers, Jane Bernard. 1992. *The "Girl Question" in Education: Vocational Education for Young Women in the Progressive Era.* London: Falmer Press.

Rossiter, Margaret W. 1997. "The Men Move In: Home Economics in Higher Education, 1950–1970." Pp. 96–117 in *Rethinking Home Economics: Women and the History of a Profession.* Edited by Sarah Stage and Virginia Vincenti. Ithaca, NY: Cornell University Press.

Schultz, Jerelyn. 1990. "Middle Schoolers Dig into Voc Ed If It's about Real Stuff: Home Economics Programs." *Vocational Education Journal* 65 (November–December): 42.

Stage, Sarah, and Vincenti, Virginia, eds. 1997. *Rethinking Home Economics: Women and the History of a Profession.* Ithaca, NY: Cornell University Press.

Vincenti, Virginia. 1997. "Chronology of Events and Movements Which Have Defined and Shaped Home Economics." Pp. 321–330 in *Rethinking Home Economics: Women and the History of a Profession.* Edited by Sarah Stage and Virginia Vincenti. Ithaca, NY: Cornell University Press.

Weate, Gwen M. 1995. "Suffer the Children." *Vocational Education Journal* 70 (April): 24–25, 45.

Woloch, Nancy. 1996. *Women and the American Experience: A Concise History.* New York: McGraw-Hill.

Hygiene

Although the meaning of the term has varied widely, hygiene has played an important role in girls' self-image and social interactions throughout American history. Hygienic beliefs and practices among girls have never been entirely private. Over time, however, American girls have developed a particularly public, commercial connection with hygiene. For all its variation, girls' hygiene now has the common feature of putting girls in the spotlight as consumers.

In colonial days, girls had as casual an approach to hygiene as their brothers and parents. Few colonists saw any reason to bathe even once a week, other than the customary daily rinse of face, hands, and perhaps neck and feet. Clothes were laundered rarely and with difficulty. Parents expected girls to help with the constant chores, which included keeping self and home tidy, but adults did not focus special attention on female cleanliness. Once girls got their periods—an event that usually occurred at age fifteen or sixteen rather than today's average of twelve—their mothers or older sisters showed them how to soak, boil, and discreetly store the reusable monthly cloths. The subject provoked little discussion yet also little shame: a girl's entry into puberty was quietly publicized by her adoption of longer adult dresses and pinned-up hair.

Hygiene took on new meaning with the onset of industrialization. Baths became easier to procure with the new wood-burning stoves and galvanized tin tubs, and public bath facilities served the rapidly expanding cities. Repeated cholera epidemics gradually yielded to improved public sanitation. For individuals, too, medical thinking emphasized that clean skin could prevent or cure many illnesses. Beginning in the 1820s, cultural ideas about women's special moral purity found a parallel in physical cleanliness. Female grooming thus took on an extra importance, part of the process of gender separation made famous in the Victorian era. As girls gained access to academic opportunity over the next several decades, forward-thinking educators used exercise to balance sustained study, and a debate raged over the merits and risks of tight corsets. A number of girls' schools even taught anatomy, physiology, and hygiene; by 1850 the latter term denoted knowledge of the body's functions and informed self-care, including exercise, temperate diet, looser dress, and frequent bathing. Middle-class women in particular saw hygiene as a female domain, since mothers would care for the bodies of their families, and girls were expected not only to keep cleaner than boys but also to study hygienic living. Meanwhile, girls from very poor backgrounds, those who lived in less settled regions, or those stuck in slavery had little opportunity to take up or even know about the new higher hygiene expectations.

Only with the germ theory of disease, developed and popularized in the late nineteenth century, did the notion of hygiene become equated with freedom from germs. In the same years, immigrants poured into the United States from more distant, different lands and humbler backgrounds than ever before. Urban areas increasingly invested in public health campaigns, including those based at schools and in settlement houses. Many foreign-born girls would have their first encounter with American-style hygiene at the immigration office or required nurse's examination at school. Americanization included adopting the new antiseptic version of hygiene for home and body. Immigrant girls often led their families to this goal, stimulating intergenerational conflict. At the same time, national advertising campaigns in magazines began to picture female models in advertising for many personal care products such as soaps, strengthening the link between female attractiveness and cleanliness. In many families, a girl's purity remained a key value; mothers frequently chose to tell their daughters nothing about physical maturation, believing that the information threatened female innocence.

Wherever Ivory Soap goes, it carries with it the Spirit of Cleanliness. The white floating cake suggests cleanliness. Its bubbling, copious lather feels clean. Its purity and quality have come to mean cleanliness at its best.

IVORY SOAP................... $99\frac{44}{100}\%$ PURE

Advertisement for Ivory Soap showing the Spirit of Cleanliness standing on a bar of soap which is floating on a body of water, 1913. (Library of Congress)

By the 1920s, hygiene was fast becoming an American obsession, with girls and women leading the way. Economic prosperity, ever-increasing advertising budgets in magazines and radio, and more national brands stood behind the explosive success of such new products as disposable sanitary napkins, shaving supplies, and deodorants. As women shortened their skirts and sleeves, cut their hair, wore skimpy bathing suits, and tanned their skin, they also began shaving their legs and underarms, washing their hair more often, and using more makeup. Well-appointed homes now had electrically lit bathrooms with mirrors over the sink. Able to see themselves in brighter light, middle-class girls sought medical treatment for acne. Poor families, immigrants, and African Americans often had different hygienic values or lacked the new amenities, but the power of national advertising enticed young girls to strive for the middle-class white ideal. This era's intergenerational clashes included the use of tampons starting in the 1930s, which many mothers considered a breach of virginity. Mothers could no longer hope for their daughters to remain in the dark about such matters because sanitary product companies sent representatives to schools armed with instructional films, pamphlets, and samples. Girls often knew more than their mothers had at the same age and talked more openly about hygiene.

By the 1950s, Americans had an international reputation for clean personal habits, and girls led the charge. Teenage girls outspent their male peers almost threefold on grooming items and clothes. Deodorant sales soared as advertising in magazines, on the radio, and on television pitched a widening array of hygiene products. Training bras and girdles offered girls "junior figure control" for the first time. School training films and health classes hammered away at the necessity of good grooming for everyone, but standards of female cleanliness continued to signify attractiveness, far more than for men and boys. Even poorer Americans often had private bathroom facilities, allowing most girls to spend time preening and cleaning as the media, advertising, and their peer group expected.

In the 1960s and 1970s, girls' relationship to hygiene changed again. With the backlash against 1950s culture and the greater availability of birth control and changing sexual behavior, some girls embraced the "natural" state of their bodies. Shaving, daily bathing, and the wearing of perfume, makeup, bras, and girdles declined among girls who, along with many adults, questioned whether control of the body really equaled attractiveness and success. In quest of greater control over bodily needs, tampons were redesigned in the 1980s for greater absorbency. But the superabsorbent tampons caused dozens of women to sicken and die from toxic shock syndrome. Tampons were reformulated as a result, but some girls and women still opted for pads, including a new breed of reusable pads made from organic cotton.

One constant about girls' hygiene has been its changing meaning over time and among different subsets of American girls. Though less widespread now than in the 1970s, the naturalistic alternative to the American hygienic ideal has persisted. Today about 10 percent of young women decline to shave their legs and underarms for cultural reasons. Douching is widespread among some ethnic and racial groups yet almost unknown in others. However, the commercial and public aspects of hygiene have steadily increased plies are marketed to satisfy the wide range of different hygienic practices. Most mothers now tell their daughters about menstruation; but if they do not, television, store displays, school hygiene classes, or peers surely will. Girls remain vulnerable to suggestions that their bodies are unclean and therefore unworthy, making them still lucrative targets for companies selling personal care products. The relationship between girls' identities—both private and social—and hygienic care of their bodies remains a powerful aspect of girlhood today.

Rebecca R. Noel

Thirteen-year-old girl washes her face in the bathroom sink. (Skjold Photographs)

See also Adolescent Health; Advice Books; Body Image; Child Guidance; Menstruation

References and Further Reading
Banner, Lois W. 1983. *American Beauty.* Chicago: University of Chicago Press.
Brumberg, Joan Jacobs. 1997. *The Body Project: An Intimate History of American Girls.* New York: Random House.
Hoy, Suellen. 1995. *Chasing Dirt: The American Pursuit of Cleanliness.* New York: Oxford University Press.
www.cybergrrl.com.
www.mum.org.

over time and across cultures. Cosmetics, hair and skin products, and sanitary sup-

I

Immigration

To date there have been no historical studies of immigration as it affected girls. Although historians of immigration have become increasingly sensitive to issues of age and gender in the immigration and adaptation process, no body of literature has specifically focused on the ways in which immigration shaped and was shaped by dependent children of either sex. To understand what it meant to be an immigrant girl must be cobbled together from studies on other aspects of immigration.

This necessity is due in part to the fact that there is no singular history of immigration. How girls participated in the emigration process, how they went through the actual move from one place to another, and the ways in which they adjusted to a new home, new language, and new set of social and cultural options varied from group to group and time to time.

Since the history of immigration is a thread that runs through all American history, beginning in earnest in the 1820s and continuing into the twenty-first century, the history of girls within it has been shaped by vastly changing circumstances. This reality complicates and defies the possibility of writing an integrated history of immigrant girlhood.

For example, young girls migrating with families in the 1820s from Wales or Scotland to American farms did not have to contend with issues of extended compulsory education or the impact of public schooling in heterogeneous urban settings. If they received an education, it was brief and probably seasonal. It most likely took place with few nongroup members present, and their parents relied heavily upon these girls' labors on farms, in workshops, and in family stores. The changes in their expectations and options probably proceeded more slowly and with less outside influence than that which confronted young girls migrating in the 1990s, for example, from Korea to Los Angeles or from Pakistan to New York.

In these latter cases, education extending into the late teenage years and the powerful impact of popular culture have most likely complicated the process by which the cultural norms and social practices of the sending society and those of the receiving one interacted with each other. Therefore, differences in time, place, and the level to which state policies limited parental authority mattered a great deal in the shaping of the many histories of immigrant girlhood.

Among the 45 million immigrants who came to the United States between 1820 and 1924, no one model can be employed to describe conditions on any matter, this one included. Just as the history of each immigrant group differs in

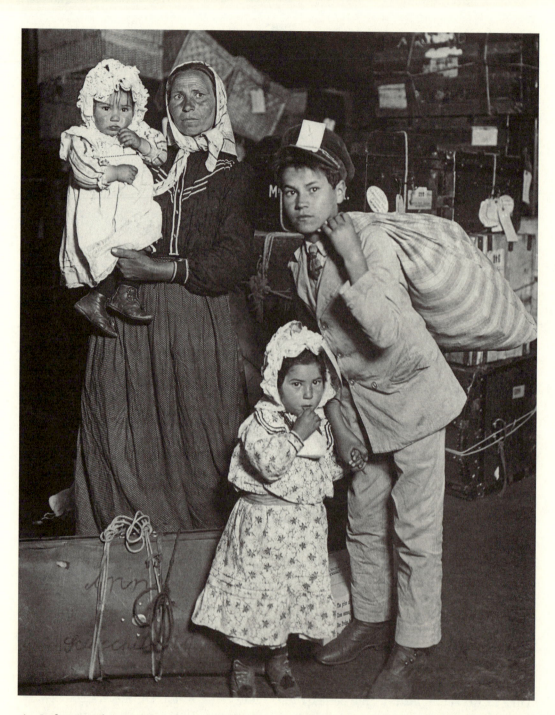

An Italian mother with her three children arrives at Ellis Island in this photograph by Lewis Hine. (Bettmann/Corbis)

terms of causation, timing, structure of the migratory pool, and modes of adaptation, so too the ways in which girls participated in these vast human movements must be seen as many individual histories. No single narrative can trace this dynamic, and no single paradigm can be employed to illustrate the particular history of girlhood among "immigrants." It is too large and amorphous a category of analysis.

Despite both the absence of any previous historical inquiry into this matter and the many variations on the theme, a number of patterns can be discerned in the experiences of different groups. In order, however, for any case studies and the differences between them to make sense, certain overarching concerns must be presented. Most emigrations have been shaped by economic concerns. Men and women left homes because changed economic circumstances made it impossible for them to continue living as they had. Many also hoped that emigration to the United States would better the conditions of their lives. Therefore, most decisions about who within a family—men, women, adults, children—should move, and when, grew out of a complex economic calculus.

Most immigration to the United States involved the movements of able-bodied workers who could labor, underconsume, and save money. Decisions about migration were made in part by assessments as to who could work best and underconsume the most while suffering the least harm. This consideration helps explain why children were not present in large numbers, at least in the earlier stages of most migrations.

A great difference can be seen between those groups who emigrated to the United States directly into agriculture and those who migrated for jobs in industry. Immigrant families bound for farming had a history shaped by the fact that full families migrated together. Many immigrants from Sweden, Norway, Denmark, parts of Germany, Bohemia, the Netherlands, and various places in central Europe, as well as Japan, hoped to become independent farmers. Such migrations required the labor of full families, and wives and children, boys and girls, provided the labor necessary for the kind of intensive small-scale farming with which immigrants began.

Girls within these families tended to replicate, in age-appropriate ways, their mothers' chores and roles. Their lives were structured around the performance of tasks deemed natural for women, particularly the myriad details involved in cooking, cleaning, and tending smaller children. They also had specific farm chores, including gardening, churning butter, collecting eggs and taking them to market, and putting up preserves, some of which were sold and others of which were kept for family consumption. Farm daughters also helped their mothers tend to the needs of the hired hands and seasonal crews of workers brought in for harvesting. At peak moments of the agricultural year, gender and age barriers broke down, and girls labored briefly in the fields with their brothers. Additionally, immigrants in agriculture tended to settle in ethnic clusters, creating relatively isolated homogeneous communities. What schooling immigrant girls got in these farm settings therefore tended to take place within an ethnic framework, and little mixing with outsiders took place.

Most immigrants came to the United States for work in industry, however, and they settled in cities. In most migrations, some family members arrived first. Those who spearheaded family migrations struggled to amass enough money to facilitate the subsequent emigration of other family members, those defined as most dependent and least able to earn money. As such, particularly during the period of the European immigration from the 1880s through the 1920s, men far outnumbered women as immigrants. In some cases, this tendency was extreme. Among Italians, men outnumbered women until the second decade of the twentieth century three to one, among Greeks about eight to one, and among the Chinese about twenty to one (Nee and de Bavy 1972). When married men migrated, they generally brought their sons and other young male relatives—nephews, brothers, and cousins—who could work and contribute to the family fund. They seemed to have known that women of all ages earned less than men and that children consumed more than they produced.

The histories of girls in immigrant communities were shaped in large measure by this issue of the age and gender balance of the group. The more male-heavy the group, the fewer girls lived within the immigrant enclaves. The more equal or even female-heavy the group in terms of the representation of women among the immigrants, the more girls were present. This reality in turn shaped the options and expectations of immigrant girls in the United States in terms of education, work, leisure, position in the family, and ultimately decisions about marriage that took them out of the ranks of girlhood.

Two cases studies, of Italians and eastern European Jews, can be used to demonstrate the impact of the structure of migration on girls. They may provide templates from which historians interested in pursuing the subject further can proceed.

The majority of the Italian migration to the United States began in the late nineteenth century, taking off as a transformative phenomenon in the 1890s and flowing heavily from Sicily and the south. Until the short period between the end of World War I and the passage of restrictive immigration legislation in 1924, most Italian immigrants were men. It was rare for full families, with parents, sons, and daughters, to immigrate together. Many of the men actually hoped that they could return to Italy and live well there on their savings from labor in the United States. When married men decided that they were going to stay in the United States, they brought over their families. Single men who decided to stay went about the process of finding a wife and starting families in their new country. Not surprisingly, as more men decided to remain in the United States after the war and throughout the 1920s, women and children began to make up the bulk of the migrants from Italy.

In the Italian enclaves that developed in most large American cities in the late nineteenth century, women were decidedly outnumbered by men. As a result of men's motivations and women's minority status within the communities, Italian women who were the daughters of immigrants tended to marry relatively young. Only a short period of time came between the end of compulsory education, as mandated by the state, and marriage.

From the scattered secondary studies as well as the memoir and social reform literature of the immigration era, it becomes clear that among Italian immigrants, girlhood was relatively brief. Few sources chart an elaborate leisure culture of Italian girls in the immigrant generation or the development of any sense of entitlement on their part for consideration within the family as individuals.

Parents tended to worry a great deal about the honor and supervision of their daughters, and girls had relatively little freedom to partake of recreational activities. They had as little formal schooling as possible, since parents in the immigrant generation saw no need for girls to extend their education beyond literacy and formal state requirements. Girls had thrust upon them a substantial amount of domestic responsibility, including cooking, cleaning, and taking care of smaller siblings. Daughters accompanied mothers gleaning empty lots and parks for mushrooms, dandelions, and other wild edibles, which were used to supplement the family diet.

The work lives of Italian immigrant girls also took place within the relatively protected environment of family supervision. Italian mothers contributed to the family economy by taking piecework into their homes. They shelled nuts, made artificial flowers, put the finishing stitches on garments, and performed a myriad of other manufacturing tasks at homes. Daughters and young sons worked along with their mothers. In warm weather, Italian mothers and daughters hired themselves out as families in cranberry bogs, canning plants, and many other regional enterprises that blurred the line between industry and agriculture. Even when Italian immigrant girls in their mid- to late teens worked outside the home, they were likely to labor for townspeople and relatives. They worked primarily with other young Italian girls rather than with women and men of mixed backgrounds.

The girls of the immigrant Italian communities tended to replicate their moth-

ers' lives. Although the physical setting in which they found themselves was different, girls' lives were lived in order to support a collective family effort. They did so in the context of roles and responsibilities defined as female-appropriate, and girls had little chance to experience the immigrant enclave and the large city as individuals.

Like Italians, eastern European Jews began to move to the United States in massive numbers in the 1880s, and that migration continued apace into the 1920s. But unlike that of their co-immigrants, Jewish migration to the United States was defined as permanent and involved full families. Certainly, unmarried young people did make the move by themselves or accompanied by peers. This was true of single young women, many still girls, and men. But primarily this was a family migration. Of those Jews who migrated, 25 percent were either under age fourteen or over age forty-five, indicating that children were well represented as well as older, less productive adults (Kuznets 1975, ix). The presence of children meant that girls and boys made up a substantial part of the immigrant communities.

The typical pattern of eastern European Jewish immigration to the United States involved husbands coming first with their older children. The sex of the children was irrelevant, and fathers took daughters as well as sons with them to earn money to pay for the fare for the rest of the family. This meant that some teenage Jewish girls came to the United States in the vanguard of their families and without their mothers. The absence of mothers may have given them a somewhat free hand in exploring the city and learning about American culture and its gender expectations. It also meant that the labor of these girls was highly valued and that they took their work seriously.

Jewish girls worked in the same kinds of sweatshops and factories as Jewish boys and men. Married Jewish women were less likely than any other group of immigrant women to be employed outside the home, but unmarried Jewish women not only had high rates of employment but exercised a high level of control over where they worked. They "shopped around" for better-paying factories. The high rates of unionization of Jewish women, particularly after the "uprising of the 20,000" female shirtwaist workers in New York in 1909, ushered in an era in which young Jewish women helped influence communal politics. That strike was actually declared by a sixteen-year-old girl, Clara Lemlich, who spontaneously got up at a meeting at Cooper Union and called upon the shirtwaist operatives to go out on strike.

Jewish immigrant girls took advantage of the educational opportunities in the United States in numbers similar to their brothers. In the immigrant generation in most American cities, Jewish girls stayed in school just as long as Jewish boys, although schools pushed girls into vocational tracks. The key factor in immigrant families as to which child received the most extensive education, including high school and even college, was age, not sex. Younger children, those either born in the United States or who came there as very small children, were the ones who got to stay in school. This held true for girls as much as for boys and may help to explain why, in New York in particular, the daughters of immigrants made such a dramatic leap by the 1920s into the ranks of public school teaching.

Memoir literature points to an immigrant Jewish culture in the United States in which young girls did not function with high levels of parental supervision, despite the fact that they maintained a high level of responsibility toward their families. Older girls were expected to clean and mind younger children. If their families owned a small shop, which up to half of them did, they were expected to work in the store.

But despite these chores, Jewish immigrant girls participated in a street culture of games and friendships and eagerly went to the libraries, parks, and other kinds of public amusements. Those girls who worked were less likely to be able to hold on to as much of their earnings as their brothers for pocket money, although what they kept from the family's coffers they used to buy clothes, snacks, and leisure-time activities. This consumption took place in an emerging American Jewish culture that gave girls a relatively well-developed sense of their own individual tastes and predilections. This sense of individuation may not have been as solid as their brothers', but then, the gap between their lives and that of boys in the United States was probably greater.

These two case studies—out of potentially hundreds—indicate that there was no single history of immigrant girlhood. Rather, each group dealt with the dichotomy between "old world" expectations for girls and American realities differently. Each one of those historical narratives deserves to be explored.

Hasia R. Diner

See also Asian American Girls; Chicana Girls; Domestic Service; Enslaved Girls of African Descent; Free Girls of African Descent; Indentured Servants; Latina Girls; Little Mothers; Mill Girls; Saturday Evening Girls; Work

References and Further Reading
Cohen, Miriam. 1993. *Workshop to Office: Two Generations of Italian Women in New York City, 1900–1950.* Ithaca, NY: Cornell University Press.
Ewen, Elizabeth. 1985. *Immigrant Women in the Land of Dollars: Life and Culture on the Lower East Side, 1890–1925.* New York: Monthly Review Press.
Kuznets, Simon. 1975. "Immigration of Russian Jews to the United States: Background and Structure." *Perspectives in American History* 9: 35–124.
Lamphere, Louise. 1987. *From Working Daughters to Working Mothers: Immigrant Women in a New England Industrial Community.* Ithaca, NY: Cornell University Press.
Nee, Victor G., and Brett de Bavy. 1972. *Longtime, California: A Documentary Study of an American Chinatown.* New York: Random House.
Peiss, Kathy. 1986. *Cheap Amusements: Working Women and Leisure in Turn-of-the-Century New York.* Philadelphia: Temple University Press.
Weinberg, Sydney Stahl. 1988. *World of Our Mothers: Lives of Jewish Immigrant Women.* Chapel Hill: University of North Carolina Press.
Weiner, Lynn. 1985. *From Working Girl to Working Mother: The Female Labor Force in the United States, 1820–1980.* Chapel Hill: University of North Carolina Press.
Yans-McLaughlin, Virginia. 1977. *Family and Community: Italian Immigrants in Buffalo, 1880–1930.* Ithaca, NY: Cornell University Press.

Indentured Servants

In the seventeenth century, girls and young women were among the first settlers of the Chesapeake, a region that encompasses Virginia, Delaware, and Maryland, where they worked as contract laborers to planters. Their enthusiasm for taking a job across the ocean was shaped by the lack of opportunities at home as well as dishonest advertising circulars. The harsh conditions of life and their servitude precluded marriage; out-of-wedlock pregnancy was punishable by the addition of a year or two to their tenure.

The Chesapeake region was the first area settled by the English. In 1606 a group of London merchants received permission from King James I to establish a joint-stock company for the purpose of digging for silver, gold, and copper in the new world. Their interest in quick profits led to an expedition to establish a trading post, not a colonial settlement. In 1607, 104 ill-equipped men with rarefied skills and inexperienced young boys landed in Jamestown (named after the king). Within six months, most had died of salt poisoning or infectious diseases (e.g., dysentery and malaria) caused by inadequate food rations and brutal living conditions. In 1619, the Virginia Company of London abandoned its original goal and encouraged settlement instead.

Three times as many young (between ages fifteen and twenty-four), single men as women immigrated to the Chesapeake. Many were displaced farmers and unemployed laborers who were attracted by false promises of upward mobility. In order to promote family life and settlement stability, the Virginia Company recruited young, single women such as nineteen-year-old Alice Pindon to migrate to the New World by distributing pamphlets advertising for "maids." Because the vast majority could not afford the journey across the Atlantic, however, they promised to work for five to seven years as an indentured servant to a Chesapeake planter.

Although in the long run the future looked bright, in the short run it was bleak. Conditions of servitude on tobacco farms were harsh. Colonists lived in less than comfortable circumstances in crude, cramped one-room shacks with few material possessions. Serving girls were likely to share a loft where all bedded down together. Girls in their late teens and those in their early twenties worked ten to fourteen hours a day, six days a week. They grew food, which they also prepared and preserved. If indentured to a poor planter, a servant would have spent much of his time in the fields, planting crops, enriching seedbeds, transplanting seedlings, stripping cured tobacco leaves, and packing them into barrels. Hoeing, weeding, stripping, curing, harvesting, and packing tobacco were repetitious and time-consuming.

The quality of life for nearly everyone was poor, but especially so for indentured servants. Because everyone lived on isolated farms along river banks, sociability was limited. There was little organized religious worship and no small towns (as in rural England) because Chesapeake subsistence farmers did not rely on trade. As a result, the diet was monotonous and not nutritious. Meals were limited to pork and corn, and vegetables were scarce. Many felt hungry much of the time. The generally poor diet increased susceptibility to diseases (e.g., typhoid, smallpox, pellagra) from which they had no immunities. Many newcomers did not make it through a year, unable to survive their "seasoning" as they succumbed to "agues and fevers." Mortality rates were much higher in the Chesapeake than in New England.

Indentured servants were legally entitled to shelter, food, and clothing but little else. Instead, they faced numerous onerous restrictions. They could be sold or disciplined (though the courts protected them from excessive beatings from abusive masters). They faced penalties for running away or for sexual transgressions. Adolescent girls raised in this land unsupervised by protective patriarchal fathers experienced greater sexual freedom, but as a result, the risks of bearing a child out of wedlock were high. At least 20 percent of all young women in the seventeenth-century Chesapeake gave birth outside marriage. (One-third of those who did marry were already pregnant before the ceremony.) But pregnant servants were not permitted to marry unless the father was willing to pay her master for the rest of her contracted term. Because pregnancies deprived masters of able-bodied workers, pregnant servants could be fined and whipped and made to serve an additional twelve to twenty-four months to repay their masters for their trouble and expense. The burden also befell their daughters or sons, who were inevitably bound out for service.

Young women who survived their indenture became planters' wives. But because they did not begin their childbearing until their mid-twenties, most young women had only two to three children before they died in childbirth or from disease. Still, mothers were more than twice as likely to survive their husbands, who collectively left behind thousands of orphaned girls and boys. As a result of high mortality rates, seventeenth-century Chesapeake families were typically made up of stepparents and step-siblings. Widows were likely to remarry because men still outnumbered women. Moreover, no one person, male or female, could run a plantation alone.

Some fathers made provisions in their wills supporting their children or authorizing overseers to remove children from households with abusive or wasteful stepfathers (of which there were many), but most did not. Mary Empson was four years old when her father died. Because her mother was too poor to provide for her, Mary was traded for four cows. Girls who had no fathers to provide for them were often bound out. Until their mother remarried, they could learn useful housekeeping skills. Even girls over the age of three were expected to work. But the experiences of girls and boys differed. Fathers expected sons to learn how to read and write, but daughters were taught to sew. Some girls were taught to read the Bible. In his will, one planter, John Lawson, requested that his two daughters "receive learning and sewing instruction" so as to be "brought up to huswifery [sic]" (Walsh 1979). In general, girls assumed their place in the gendered world of the Chesapeake household with fewer problems than their brothers.

Miriam Forman-Brunell

See also Domestic Service; Enslaved Girls of African Descent; Free Girls of African Descent; Immigration; Work

References and Further Reading
Berkin, Carol. 1997. *First Generations: Women in Colonial America.* New York: Hill and Wang, chap. 1.
Walsh, Lorena. 1979. "Till Death Do Us Part: Marriage and Family in Seventeenth Century Maryland." In *The Chesapeake in the Seventeenth Century: Essays in Anglo-American Society.* Edited by Thad W. Tate and David L. Ammerman. Chapel Hill: University of North Carolina Press.
Walsh, Lorena, and Lois G. Carr. 1977. "The Planter's Wife: The Experience of White Women in 17th Century Maryland." *William and Mary Quarterly* 34, 3d series.